"I'd like to have a book like this written about me. Absolutely!"
—Bette Davis

"I wish I could have met Groucho, and
now I have. In *Hello, I Must Be Going*,
Groucho never disappoints."
—Tennessee Williams

"The definitive book on Groucho
Marx." —Irv Kupcinet,
Chicago Sun-Times

"Knowing Groucho was fascinating,
but this book knows Groucho better
than I did." —Mike Nichols

"*Hello, I Must Be Going* is as funny,
even funnier than Groucho has ever
been." —Otto Preminger

"Charlotte Chandler's book is the real
thing. Absolutely authentic, beautifully researched, a joy to read."
—Billy Wilder

"*Hello, I Must Be Going* is
fabulous. The best book
of its kind."
—Elliott Gould

Praise for *Hello, I Must Be Going*

"I am so grateful to Charlotte Chandler's *Hello, I Must Be Going* for
helping me to understand why I always laughed so hard at Groucho
Marx before I could even understand what he was saying."
—Mstislav Rostropovich

"The person I most wanted to meet in my life was Groucho Marx, and
reading *Hello, I Must Be Going*, I have."
—Federico Fellini

"Here at last is the book we have all been waiting for, the real inside
story of the legendary Groucho. Witty, provocative, highly readable."
—Sidney Sheldon

"Charlotte Chandler writes about Groucho Marx with great humor and
love. Sei molto brava! Grazie e buona fortuna, *Hello, I Must Be Going*!"
—Luciano Pavarotti

"If Groucho Marx amused you, Charlotte Chandler's extraordinary
book, *Hello, I Must Be Going*, will delight you."
—George Cukor

"*Hello, I Must Be Going* makes me feel the love I felt in Groucho's
house."
—Marvin Hamlisch

"Charlotte Chandler's *Hello, I Must Be Going* is a must-read."
—Liz Smith

"Charlotte Chandler's book, *Hello, I Must Be Going*, brings back to us
one of our favorite people."
—Betty Comden and Adolph Green

"Why aren't you doing a book like this about me?"
—Fritz Lang

"An exceptional book about the most odious man we adore."

—René Clair

"This book made me laugh all over, all over again."

—King Vidor

"I'm glad for Groucho that he 'never kissed an ugly girl,' but this book should be read by more than just beauties."

—Jacques Tati

"It was lovely to be able to say hello again to my dear old friend Groucho in Charlotte Chandler's enchanting *Hello, I Must Be Going*. She brings him back into our lives so vividly that when Groucho finally says 'I must be going,' I was sorry to have to close the book."

—Maureen O'Sullivan

"Charlotte Chandler has plunged into her subject as deeply as any biographer could."

—*The New York Times*

Hello, I Must Be Going

Groucho and His Friends

Charlotte Chandler

Introduction by Bill Cosby

Simon & Schuster Paperbacks

New York London Toronto Sydney

Simon & Schuster Paperbacks
1230 Avenue of the Americas
New York, NY 10020

First Simon & Schuster trade paperback edition August 2007

SIMON & SCHUSTER PAPERBACKS and colophon are registered trademarks of Simon & Schuster, Inc.

For information about special discounts for bulk purchases, please contact Simon & Schuster Special Sales at 1-800-456-6798 or business@simonandschuster.com

Manufactured in the United States of America

10 9 8 7 6 5 4 3 2 1

The Library of Congress has cataloged the hardcover edition as follows:
Chandler, Charlotte.
    Hello, I must be going: Groucho and his friends: with a new introduction by Bill Cosby/ by Charlotte Chandler.
        p. cm.
            Originally published: Garden City, N.Y.: Doubleday, 1978.
    1. Marx, Groucho, 1891–1977. 2. Comedians—United States—Biography. I. Title.
    PN2287.M53C5
      792.6'028'092—dc20
      [B]   92–18030

ISBN-13: 978-1-4165-4422-7
ISBN-10:   1-4165-4422-4

Acknowledgments

With Special Appreciation
Woody Allen, Bob Bender, Bill Cosby, Elliott Gould, Zeppo Marx, Ken McCormick, David Rosenthal, and Sidney Sheldon.

With Appreciation
Michael Accordino, Lauren Bacall, Jack Benny, Marcella Berger, George Burns, Charles William Bush, Betty Comden, Wyatt Cooper, Bud Cort, George Cukor, Ron Delsener, Nelson Doubleday, Jane Elias, Julius Epstein, Érté, Erin Fleming, Joe Franklin, Steve Friedeman, Max Gordon, Bert Granet, Adolph Green, Marvin Hamlisch, Karolina Harris, George Jessel, Nunnally Johnson, Grace Kahn, Bronislaw Kaper, Ted Kheel, Norman Krasna, Ted Landry, Jack Lemmon, Johanna Li, Goddard Lieberson, Andy Marx, Eden Marx, Gummo Marx, Walter Matthau, Mike Nichols, Jack Nicholson, Nat Perrin, Robert Pirosh, Morrie Ryskind, John Sargent, George Seaton, Mary Sheldon, King Vidor, Herman G. Weinberg, Arthur Whitelaw, Billy Wilder, and Tom Wilhite.

The Theatre Collection of the New York Public Library at Lincoln Center.

To Groucho

Contents

June 21, 2007

Dear Reader,

Hello, I Must Be Going began when someone gave me the home telephone number of Groucho Marx. When I was in Beverly Hills, I called the number.

Groucho answered the phone. I only found out later how lucky I was. After I knew him, I learned that he never answered his own telephone. He always had someone there who could answer it for him. He didn't like to speak on the phone because he couldn't see the reaction of the other person. This went back to his days in vaudeville when he and his brothers tried out their material and watched the reactions on the faces of their audiences. His philosophy was, "If it gets a laugh, leave it in."

I had called Groucho because I wanted to do an interview with him. When I told him why I was calling, he said, "*Life* magazine just offered me $25,000 to do an interview, and I told them I wouldn't do it with them for $35,000, and I wouldn't do it with *you* for $50,000! Where are you calling from?"

I told him that I was using a phone at the Beverly Wilshire Hotel, which wasn't far from Groucho's house.

He said, "Why don't you come over, and I'll tell you *No* in person."

I went right over0..

Groucho showed me his collection of Marxabilia. That's what he called all of his Marx Brothers souvenirs of a lifetime in show business— photographs, programs, scripts, letters, and a number of embroidered pillows sent to him by fans.

He asked me to stay *to* dinner, not *for* dinner.

After dinner, he said to me, "Why aren't you writing?"

That's when I knew I was doing the interview that would become *Hello, I Must Be Going*.

When Groucho asked me if I would like to write a book about him, I hesitated—about five seconds. *Hello, I Must Be Going* was my first book, and Groucho said it would change my life. He was right.

All best wishes,

Charlotte

Introduction by Bill Cosby

Charlotte has asked me to say something for this new edition of *Hello, I Must Be Going,* and if I were Groucho Marx, I could say, "Something," and let it go at that. But I'm not Groucho, so I have to be less explicit. Therefore, let me tell you several "somethings" about Groucho which are not already included in this fat, erudite book.

The first television encounter Groucho and I had was when he hosted *The Tonight Show.* I was a hot new comedian, and he asked for me on the show when he was substituting for Johnny. The night I did the show, before going on, he called me into Johnny's office. This was in New York. He was changing clothes, and he just had his shorts on. I stood there thinking, "I'm looking at the great Groucho Marx in his underwear."

We went on. It wasn't a great meeting of the minds, because at that time I was really interested in telling my stories, and I didn't want to trade quips with him. But after the show, I regrouped. I told myself, "If I work with him again, I will not serve as the funny person. I will serve as the catalyst for his punch lines." And it worked, each and every time after that, because he was the boss.

In 1974, when I had my own show, I asked for Groucho, who was then well into his eighties. Of course, the thought of the producers was, "Isn't he too old and will he be able to read or remember his lines?" There was a very negative feeling about bringing someone on who had, in fact, slipped that far chronologically—and maybe mentally. All of the questions of whether he could do it or not came out, and I kept saying, "But this is television, and we have plenty of tape, and you guys have the scissors. I'm sure that with a man like this, if we do nothing more than sit and talk, Groucho cannot help but throw a line here and there, and I feel that

I can feed him enough. If anything goes badly, I can always get back to pretty girls, which will wake him up and light him up."

Groucho went out, according to his rest schedule, and we did the show.

Now, there are certain priorities that people have. Let's say if a big, big star wanted to do my show, people would get excited, but here's what he or she wants: They want food flown in from Mexico, and they have to be out by ten-thirty. Everyone would say, "Yeah, fine. We'll get food from Mexico, and we'll get them out by ten-thirty." Then they're coming back at one-thirty, and can give you ten minutes, so you'll have everything ready for the ten minutes. The star's manager comes ahead and the next thing is, Can you get a private dressing room for him, too? You give the manager a TV set along with the star's TV set, and all these things you go out of your way to do.

Now here's Groucho, and all that's asked is that when he gets tired, let him rest. People are going, "You know, it's a lot of time, and we don't know, and . . ."

"Let's do it, please."

And we did it—and had a ball! He wanted to go and go and go. What that show did for him—you could see the juices, you could see it exciting him. Now, when you're in that condition, physically, to get excited burns as much energy as to be totally depressed. So, he would perform for a while, and then he *would* get physically tired, and he'd have to go off and rest. Well, that was all right for me, because that's exactly what he was supposed to do. That's what you're supposed to do at that age. Whatever your body dictates, that's what you have to do. I spent an awful lot of time with my grandfather, and for some reason, I have a feeling for and a respect for elderly people.

For the television show, we played it until he got tired. We did some of the lines over. We had a lot of fun, which for some reason is not part of the performance, because they cut it out. It's strange how people want to make comedy so slick. That's the part that ruins everything. Because, you see, his moment of waiting and realizing what's happening is just as much skill within comic timing as if he had said it quickly. The impatience of the people around me was just not welcomed by me at all.

Television has a great fear of silence. Silence means there's no money being made. Just because you're not speaking doesn't mean you're not thinking. Maybe you should bring along some kerosene and a match.

"What's that for?"

"It's just in case I become dreadfully boring, I can always set myself on fire."

So, we came off of it with a lovely, lovely show. His lines were funny. Sometimes I'd say something, and you'd see him think, and you'd see him still thinking, still thinking. Then, boom! the line would come, and the people would laugh, and love it. No, it wasn't as fast as Buddy Hackett or Don Rickles. But you could see in his eyes that they were working, the IBM cards were being flipped around, and they may not have been in the condition that they once were in. Maybe a little dog-eared, and some of them may even have been in the wrong alphabetical order. But you could see him flipping through those cards, and then that line would come.

If you gave him time to think about it and get it rolling, those lines would come out. You had to have patience, but it wasn't overbearing. There's nothing that put you in the ranks of Job. It was a matter of knowing that you were going to get it and taking your time.

Groucho and I ad-libbed a lot. I feel ad-libbing is relying on everything that you can think of in order to come up with humor, on your feet, not knowing when or where. That to me is ad-libbing. That's working without a net. You know, the role of the catcher is not an easy one, because you have to look and see what you can catch. But to stand there and think it up, and then put it out, is the most difficult part.

Groucho thought funny, and ad-libbing is thinking funny. It doesn't make any difference whether you've had this particular line and you've used it before. When and if the line comes, you don't know when it's coming, and then you use it, you are ad-libbing. You have to be on top of it. You have to play the moment. And that's what Groucho was absolutely brilliant with when we did the show together. I purposely switched things around for him so that he would *have* to think in a fresh way.

I always felt that it was my role, whenever we were together, in a way to be the most effective straight man ever. If I could feed something ridiculous or give him something he could think five or six punch lines on, I was perfectly happy to do it. Because it's absolutely true that's what happens when you do that. He continued to think, and it was mental exercise.

When he appeared on my show, I was just very, very proud of what he had done, although Charlotte tells me Groucho wasn't happy with his performance. But, you see, what happens is, with a show like that, producers have their own idea of what they want to do. I think that what might have set him back was not necessarily his performance, but the other things around him that made it look like window dressing.

I think that what Grouch may not have been tickled about was the way he sounded. That's something that anybody who's human feels—the older we get, the more we don't particularly like the way we sound. Especially when the voice begins to sound weak. We really don't like that. Time does have a way of taking a peak period away from you, a peak look, and you really know time has done its job. There is a bit of sadness there, about what time does. It does take away, and it happens with everyone. But if it were the other way around, and things just got better and better, I don't know if that would be good, either. Because, then, some people might just become a pain in the ass.

As far as I'm concerned, when you have someone like Groucho Marx come out and perform, that's really all you need. The greatest show would have been just Groucho and me. But a producer can't really see that far, and they're afraid of something like that. There are so many sketches that could have been done with just the two of us sitting, and run the tape forever—and then splice it together. Many times a great line comes out of a few minutes of very serious talk.

It was during that period when Groucho could still come out, and he would come out for friends of his, or he'd come out for an event—any of the two that'd get his juices going. Once he came to the house I was renting from Martin Landau. My mother was there; my wife, Camille, was there; Eubie Blake was there with a Mr. Browning; and Erin Fleming, of course. Browning was at the time eighty-three, Eubie was something like ninety-two, and Groucho was eighty-four.

We all had dinner, and the table chit-chat was fair. There was no trading of lines, no trading of stories, or anything. I carried the table as far as the conversation was concerned, and Grouch threw in a few lines here and there, and Eubie might have told one or two stories, and Browning would say something. But I don't think anybody was really paying attention to anybody in particular. And it wasn't because the food was that good. I think it might have been just that there were three strangers there.

We moved into the living room. There was a piano there. Eubie sat at the piano, and Groucho took a seat on the sofa, with Erin. Browning, who was a tenor, got up and sang some of Eubie's Broadway songs. Well, after a while, they got into these "hot" numbers, you know, like "I'm Just Wild About Harry." Everybody's smiling and enjoying, and I can't describe the sound Groucho was giving off, but to him, it was singing.

Everybody started to look around at Groucho. So he got up, unsteady, of course, and once he got up, he was up. He went over to Browning and Eubie, and he started to sing, of course in this terrible, almost dog-like sound. You know—wolfing—and what he was doing, he was trying to harmonize with Browning. But the range Browning was singing in was so far above Groucho's, all Groucho could do was try and harmonize in that key, and what came out was this dog-like wail. We all started to laugh, and Groucho started to smile, and Mr. Browning broke up laughing.

Eubie, he was just playing, because he was concentrating on the song. I don't know if Eubie even heard what was going on. Well, they got near the end of the song, and Groucho decided that he wants to high-kick. And he starts to cross one leg in front of the other, kicking. He starts to dance, and Erin stands up, and her face is flushed, and she's excited about the whole thing. But he's really dancing!

They continued on. I don't know whether there were three or four more songs, but I do know that the evening was important enough fun for Groucho that he missed *You Bet Your Life* that night. That was the biggest compliment Groucho could give to a party. He *never* missed reruns of *You Bet Your Life*. Erin said, "Groucho, do you want to go and see your show?" and he said, "No, I want to sing."

"But you look tired."

"No! I want to sing."

For him, it was absolutely the biggest thing. My mother still talks about it. And laughs! She laughs so hard whenever we talk about it, because it was a great tribute. He was there, high-kicking, and just doing this dog's wail, trying to harmonize. Then, he'd do "Lydia," and Eubie didn't know it, but he faked it. They all sang that together, faking it, and they tried to find *his* key. But he had a ball. He left that evening before Eubie, and afterwards, Eubie, who was the oldest of that group, said, "You know, he's in pretty good shape."

I said, "Yeah, and tonight he's in *better* shape than he's *ever* been in." You know, there's no medicine for that. A pharmacist can't just put that in a bottle.

Erin called back the next day and said, "When he woke up, his spirits were just great, just lovely." Because of that evening.

I was fortunate enough to be able to meet three of the four comedians I most admire. Besides Groucho, there were Buster Keaton and Charlie Chaplin. I never met W. C. Fields, of course. But Groucho was the only one I ever really knew. I talked with Buster, but at that time it wasn't good at all, because Buster was ready to go. I met Chaplin once. The funniest thing about it was his granddaughter told him who I was. She was really excited about it.

It was my pleasure to meet Groucho and to get to know him. I think, other than that, it probably would have been even better to have known him when he was at his prime. If we could have worked together, both at our prime, that would have been extraordinary. To me, Groucho will always, always be appreciated and respected as a human being who thought funny.

Now, more than his movies, I appreciated *You Bet Your Life*. I broke my neck to get in there and watch that, and that's where I really knew Groucho from. Woody Allen speaks highly of the films, but to me, Groucho Marx is *You Bet Your Life* and coming up with the lines off of which the people said what they said. That I appreciated more than anything. As a matter of fact, I appreciated him so much in it, that I wanted to do a show like that, the kind of thing that really made for good viewing. The people on *You Bet Your Life* became human beings instead of the blithering idiots you usually see on these television quiz shows. As you'll notice in *Hello, I Must Be Going*, Groucho considered the audience the straight man. That's important. And you weren't really giving anything away. No big bucks.

I always wanted to do *You Bet Your Life*. We even went into meetings with the old producers of the show. I felt very confident I could deal with the people on the show the way Groucho did. Not slick, natural. I've been waiting a long time to do it.

The audience I'd most like to have for the show is Groucho. I hope he's watching. I'd like for him to smile that funny little smile of his that meant more than other people's out-loud laughs. I'm tickled that I'm getting the chance to do *You Bet Your Life* while I'm still crisp.

Titles page

(Other titles suggested for this book)

Groucho Marx and Other Short Stories — suggested by Groucho Marx

Groucho Marx and Other Short Stories, and Tall Tales — suggested addition by Marvin Hamlisch

Crouch — suggested by Bill Cosby

The Other Side of Groucho — suggested by Sidney Sheldon, author of *The Other Side of Midnight*

Tell 'Em Groucho Sent You — suggested by Erin Fleming

Sitting Duck — also suggested by Erin Fleming

Groucho the Great — suggested by Jack Benny

One of a Kind — suggested by Bert Granet

Andy's Grandfather — suggested by Andy Marx

Nothing Sacred — suggested by Julius Epstein, writer of *Casablanca*, knowing that this title has already been used but feeling that no other title so perfectly described Groucho, or:

No Relation to Karl

Here Comes Captain Groucho — suggested by King Vidor

Art Ducko — suggested by Erté

Beware the Ids of Marx — suggested by Goddard Lieberson

"I'm as young as the day is long, and this has been a very short day."

GROUCHO MARX

"Hello, I must be going"

Groucho did not grow old gracefully, because there is no such thing. It was an indignity with which he lived, with the greatest dignity possible. "Growing old is what you do if you are lucky," he said, and though any decline was a constant offense to his pride, Groucho mustered all his strength for what in the end had to be a losing battle.

The Groucho legend, however, didn't age; it was frozen in time. The *Duck Soup* Groucho was expected by some; others expected to find the *You Bet Your Life* Groucho. After one of his jokes you could hear echoes of "He's the same, he's the same as ever!" People didn't want to see their idol fall. If Groucho was aging, so were they—someone else's old age is a threat to one's own immortality. Time may pass for them as it does for other mortals, but they are shocked to find that it also passes for an immortal of the silver screen and the video tube. Captain Jeffrey T. Spaulding, Professor Quincy Adams Wagstaff, Impresario Otis B. Driftwood, and Dr. Hugo Z. Hackenbush are ageless, but Groucho was in his eighties.

In his daily life, the most difficult competition Groucho had to face was competition from his younger self. His professional appearances, though happening until shortly before his death, were constantly diminishing in number—to avoid growing old in technicolor close-ups, and because growing old isn't funny.

Groucho had a perspective different from those of most of his friends, since virtually none of them had ever been that close to a century old. Health and survival became what was important. He gave the highest priority to remaining able-minded. "I want to go on as long as I can, as long as I'm in good shape, especially mentally." But he did not find the rigors of growing old or the supposed secrets of longevity to be a diverting topic of discussion.

"Age isn't very interesting to talk about. Anyone can get old. Everybody gets older, if you live long enough."

In answer to Jack Nicholson's "How old are you, Grouch?" he raised his eyebrows and said, "It's not how old I am, it's *how* I'm old."

During Groucho's last visit to New York City, Betty Comden, Adolph Green, and Penelope Gilliatt joined Groucho and me for lunch in his suite at the Sherry Netherland Hotel. We gathered in a football huddle in the living room, glasses in hand. Groucho raised his glass of tomato juice in a toast and said, "To health. That's all there is." Mystified, Betty pondered the toast. "Is that *all* there is?" she asked. Groucho shrugged and said, "*Vay iz mir.*" Adolph translated: "That means 'Woe is me.' What kind of a toast is *that?*" Groucho didn't even try to explain that for him the greatest luxury in life was being able to take good health for granted.

While we were having dinner before going to see *Juno and the Paycock*, Billy Marx, Harpo's adopted son, asked Groucho what was the most exciting thing that ever happened to him.

"The most exciting thing that ever happened to me was when my doctor said I was good and healthy."

"I mean in show business, Groucho," Billy persisted.

"I was in show business when the doctor said that."

He also tried to explain his feelings to virile young friend Jack Nicholson, who couldn't really put himself in Groucho's house slippers:

JACK NICHOLSON
We ought to be goin' around the town together, Grouch. We'd have *some* time!

GROUCHO
You reach a certain age, and you don't care about sex anymore. You just care about health.

JACK NICHOLSON
There *has* to be more than *that*. You can still always do *something*. You can just lay around and . . .

This conversation was interrupted by the entrance of nurse "Happy," whom Groucho always described as "the only woman who can put me to sleep." He was referring to her tickling of his feet, a minor passion of his, "one of the few I can still satisfy." He added wistfully, "That wasn't the way it always was. But when a guy is eighty-three, he should forget the whole thing. I know if I do it, it's going to be lousy, so why cheapen myself? It doesn't depress me. I know I can't do it properly anymore; if I could, I'd still be doing it. I've talked to a lot of guys who are seventy-eight, seventy-nine, and they all say it's hopeless. When you can't get it up anymore, you should quit. When a guy is eighty years old or thereabouts, he should read a book."

I
Is there anything in your life you would do differently?
GROUCHO
I wish I were young enough to make the same mistakes all over again.
I
But isn't there something you would do if you had your life to live all over again?
GROUCHO
I'd try more positions.

Animal Crackers had not been shown in theatres for more than twenty years when Groucho obtained a print and screened it at home for us. Mike Nichols and Jack Nicholson were invited for the event, and they clearly thought the film was great. Jack was particularly impressed by Groucho's dance. "I'd sure like to be able to do that," he told Groucho. "It must be really difficult to get it just the way you did it." Groucho said, "I'll give you lessons."

The next day, Jack appeared for his lesson. Groucho got up and did the dance, but it was a pale reflection of his 1930 performance. Jack looked momentarily stunned, and Groucho was angry at himself for not being the man he had been. Then the moment passed and the conversation turned to other topics.

Jack Nicholson, who was born almost a decade after Groucho danced that dance—perhaps even after Groucho had already *forgotten* it—had not fully appreciated the interval of time that had elapsed between the 1930 performance and the 1973 performance—and neither had Groucho. On the screen the performers remain unchanged over the decades. The motion picture can be rather frightening for the performer who is able to watch his own wide-screen wrinkles appear. When Jack had left, Groucho told me, "I hope I look that good when I'm his age."

In 1974 Groucho returned to New York for the opening of *Animal Crackers*, and Doubleday Editor Ken McCormick asked him, "What do you find most changed, Groucho?" He replied, "Me, I'm eighty-three." At his Carnegie Hall appearance in New York, Groucho summed it up: "I come from a world that doesn't exist anymore, and hardly do I."

Groucho was fortunate that his character was never extreme youth. Who's ever heard of a youthful lecher? He never had to face the trauma that confronts the motion picture ingenue. The Groucho character was middle-aged in his earliest films and remained so for a very long time. He was, in fact, still readily recognizable in his middle eighties, as one learned on even the shortest saunter down any street with him. Harpo's innocence was like that of a child who was never supposed to grow up, let alone grow old, while Groucho, who wooed dowager Margaret Dumont or soubrette Thelma Todd, didn't have to contend with losing his youth. He could still joke about it. "My youth is slipping," he said. "Someone should tell him to be more careful."

There were those who felt that any public appearances by Groucho in his eighties should be curtailed or better yet, curtained. They felt that his forays into the world of show business were destroying the myth of a Groucho Marx who should not grow old in the glare of the klieg lights. It is part of the limitation of the human condition that the mystique of glamour and the mistake of excessive accessibility have enough difficulty coexisting without the complication of aging.

For Groucho, the important day of his life was today, and he loved playing himself. As the years ahead grew shorter, the tributes grew longer, but he was not ready to be enshrined. "I don't want to be put in a case in a museum like Harpo's harp." As for his fans, some of them young enough to be his great-grandchildren, the thrill of Groucho in his eighties was still a thrill, even if—especially if—the name he mischievously signed in the autograph book was "Mary Pickford," which he did on occasion.

As one grows older, one is constantly losing illusions, learning that the "real" Santa Claus is working for the Salvation Army and Macy's at the same time, and that romantic, true, and perfect love rarely ages as well as cognac. But Groucho managed to remain at least somewhat illusioned in the face of disillusioning realities. Life itself, after a certain point, operates under a law of diminishing returns, and eighty-five-year-old optimism is rarer than twenty-one-year-old optimism or even seventy-five-year-old optimism.

I

Was it a hard life in the early days when the Marx Brothers didn't get much money, had to travel all the time living in rooming houses, eating chili every day?

GROUCHO

Well, I was young. And there's no hard life when you're young. Everything is easy.

I

Yes, but unfortunately, when you're young, you may not realize that.

GROUCHO

Yeah. You don't know it, so it seems hard. But when you're young, you're not afraid. You don't know any better.

Then Groucho put his finger on what was different for him about being old: "Everything comes harder. You have to concentrate to do what you didn't have to think about before. You can't take things for granted. You can't even take salt for granted."

Having dinner with Jack Nicholson, Groucho suggested to him, "Maybe you should stop using salt while you're still young, so you won't miss it when you have to give it up. I don't use salt, I don't drink now, and I don't smoke.

"I used to be crazy about Somerset Maugham. He lived to be about ninety years old. He still smoked cigarettes. The doctor said, 'You ought to quit. You'll die if you don't quit smoking.' And Maugham said, 'What can you give me to replace it?' The doctor went home in a huff. He was driving a blue Huff at the time."

Happiness consists largely in the ability to live each day without too great an awareness of the passing of time. The ability to be oblivious to the passing of time is one of the greatest luxuries of youth, but Groucho in his eighties still had that casualness about time which allowed him to waste it in nonconstructive pursuits without feelings of pressure or guilt. "I take one day at a time. And I won't put it back."

Another aspect of happiness is the ability to reconcile one's hopes-and-dreams world with the real world. Groucho had made his peace with what he was and what he had. "Getting old is what hurts. After you get there, you're glad to wake up in the morning." He was a realist, if a romantic realist. He accepted the natural law of diminishing returns not as a situation tragedy but as his due "for having too many birthdays." He had the satisfaction of being able to answer "Groucho Marx" to the question "Who would you like to have been?"

Groucho was the first to recognize that he was not the man he used to be:

"I called my tailor, and a girl answered. I said, 'This is Groucho Marx,' and she said, 'You're foolin' me. He's dead.' And she was right."

When I asked Groucho, "What do you want to be when you grow up?" he responded soberly, "I'm growing down."

Nothing made Groucho unhappier than when a young woman held a door open for him, unless it was when an old woman held a door open for him.

Groucho was well aware that old age is not the ideal state, only the best of all possible choices. He read to me the words Vincente Minnelli had written in the front of a book he had given Groucho:

" 'To the greatest comedian alive,' " then Groucho paused and added, "Only he was wrong. I'm not alive."

Groucho sometimes told a story about a baseball game between two vaudeville teams. He and Will Rogers were on opposing sides. When Groucho tried to steal second base, the catcher threw to second-baseman Will Rogers, who yelled, "You're out!"

"But you're ten feet off second base," Groucho protested.

"Groucho, at my age wherever you stand is second base," Will Rogers explained.

Old age can be like the tortures of Tantalus. The fruit is still there, but not only is it out of one's grasp, one may no longer care about grasping it. Groucho still cared.

Although it is common for older people to begin liquidating their estates in advance, Groucho eagerly continued to acquire possessions and enjoy them. His inanimate world as well as his animated world was not in a state of diminution. Going through several books every week, he remained an avid reader, able to be alone without being lonely. He practiced his guitar, still taking frivolity seriously. He continued trying to improve himself, even while all the forces of nature were at work against him. True old age commences with the feeling there is nothing to look forward to; Groucho was still looking forward.

His detailed accounts of long ago never ceased to amaze friends like Elliott Gould, George Segal, Jack Lemmon, and Dinah Shore. Inability to remember is sometimes associated with aging. Those who think that way fail to take into consideration how much there is to remember when you're past eighty-five. Young people just don't have as much to remember. Groucho would be asked by a fan, "How did you feel before the battle scene in *Duck Soup*?" He answered, "Geez, that was a thousand years ago." Or, "That was 1933. It's almost fifty years ago. I don't remember everything."

It's true that most people aren't expected to remember their lives in infinite detail, as was Groucho. But the advantages of being Groucho Marx outweighed any disadvantages. At least people *did* want to know about his life, and most people never have that kind of experience. Memory is capricious rather than pragmatic. We don't choose what we remember, it chooses us.

GROUCHO
You remember the damnedest things.
I
You've lived such a long life, does that boy Julius Marx on Ninety-third Street ever seem like another person, a stranger to you now?
GROUCHO
You've seen the pictures. Don't you think I've changed?
I
I mean on the inside.
GROUCHO
I don't know. No, I guess I'm the same, only older.

Everyone has problems, and how people deal with their problems reveals a great deal about their personalities. There may even be a basic human need for problems, since anyone so fortunate as to be temporarily without any will probably hurriedly create some. One is fortunate when the little things seem very big—Groucho was still worrying about little things.

There are problems you can solve and problems you cannot solve. Groucho recognized the importance of cutting his losses and not throwing good time after bad. Even though old age is a condition that is difficult to accept as well as being a disability from which one cannot look forward to a recovery, he didn't consume his energies, efforts, and time in useless pondering, complaints, and regrets.

In old age, the questions often become more important than the answers. One learns more than one might wish to know of problems about which one would rather remain in total ignorance, and one is constantly reminded of one's own vulnerability. Groucho told me, "When you're eighty-five, you've learned how to live with things you don't want and how to shut the door." He had learned to sweep those problems that have no solution under a wall-to-wall carpet. Old age was for him that kind of problem.

Goddard Lieberson, whose friendship with Groucho went back thirty years, remembered a younger Groucho who was so healthy that he would notice any insignificant ache and complain about it. "But now," Goddard noted, "when I say, 'How are you, Groucho?' he says, 'Fine,' and never complains about anything."

Old age is like taking out one consolidated loan to pay off all of your debts. The debts don't disappear, but all of the problems are wrapped up in one not so neat package. Old age is a problem so complete, so all-encompassing, so totally pervasive, so insurmountable in any desirable way, that it distracts from all others.

Perhaps the single quality that Groucho most valued and respected in a man was strength. In his middle eighties, he was leaned on by a great many people, but he didn't like to lean himself. Norman Krasna said of his longtime friend, "Groucho is not a complainer. He had so many years of terrible family problems, but he always went onstage funny." The Groucho I knew always went on funny, and his stage was his daily life.

When a person reaches a certain age, he is expected to assume the role of an old person. He is beseeched to rest, almost as if in rehearsal for that final inevitable rest. "Act your age," a young world admonishes, when there's no fun in that. Groucho chose to put up a fight.

Early in life he learned that life is a battlefield, and that for every winner there are lots of losers. Thus he was careful never to go forth into the arena or the one-liner's den with his suit of armor askew. And always emblazoned on the breastplate was "Tell 'em Groucho sent you."

On the theory that the best defense is a good offense, Groucho got in the first blow, and he could on occasion be somewhat offensive. Most people, however, would rather have received an insult from Groucho than a compliment from anybody else. He was considered by those who didn't like him (and even Groucho had a few of those—one may measure one's success by appraising one's enemies) to be selfish. What he did have was a highly developed sense of self, which is not to be confused with selfishness.

People are born with an undamaged self-esteem which is constantly under assault from that first jarring slap on the back. We are born liking ourselves; Groucho continued to do so. Headstrong, headlong, he loped through life, his self-confidence unshaken, through turbulence and turmoil unperturbed. He didn't break the rules: he ignored their existence. He remained never self-conscious, but calmly conscious of self.

Groucho avoided ruts, accepting routine but not acting from force of habit, remaining predictably unpredictable.

Well into his eighties, Groucho still eschewed conformity:

"It's a good idea not to live your life just to please others. You don't please yourself, and you end up not pleasing anyone else. But if you please yourself, maybe you'll please someone else."

A waiter at Hillcrest Country Club in Beverly Hills greeted Groucho with, "How do you feel, Mr. Marx? You look younger." Groucho responded, "I'm getting younger. Next year I'll be eighty-three. And the next year I'll be eighty-two."

One day, having lunch at Hillcrest with Groucho, we were joined by George Jessel. Their conversation stopped in midsentence as Adolph Zukor, then well past one hundred, was wheeled by.

GEORGE JESSEL
It's good to be alive.

GROUCHO
I don't want to live that long. I took her (*Indicating me*) to see Durante the other day. I sang for him and he liked it. I asked him, "How's Mrs. Calabash?"

GEORGE JESSEL
I hear he's not so good.

GROUCHO
He'll never work again.

Once I asked Groucho, "In your many years of experience, what have you learned that you would like to share? Do you have any advice to offer?" He shared with me the benefit of his wisdom: "Never sit down at a party because you may have somebody sitting next to you that you don't like."

Groucho didn't like to have anyone he cared about say goodbye to him. "Never say goodbye," he admonished friends.

Though in attendance at Jack Benny's funeral, Groucho assiduously avoided funerals. He just had been to too many. Looking through his address book and seeing all of the people who, though he didn't cross them out, could no longer be reached was a traumatic experience. He said about George S. Kaufman, "I still never get used to his being gone." The death of friend Harry Ruby deeply saddened Groucho, as did the hospital visits to Arthur Sheekman—visits which he continued to make regularly.

Groucho told me, "I'm still alive. That's about it."

He was less than impressed by one well-meaning fan's admonition "Don't die—just keep on living." Dismissing it peremptorily, Groucho said, "Some line."

He once discussed life and death with Woody Allen:

GROUCHO
I'm still alive.
WOODY ALLEN
How do we know that?
GROUCHO
I can tell when I get up in the morning. If I don't get up, that means I'm dead.

Groucho liked to quote Woody's line which was one of his favorites: "I don't mind dying. I just don't want to be there when it happens."

One day grandson Andy rushed in and told us that he'd been to a hilarious film. Laughing at the very memory of it, Andy said, "I died laughing."

"If you've gotta go, that's the way to go," Groucho commented soberly. "You know, I have a friend who works for an organization that tries to prevent people from committing suicide. If you want to kill yourself, you call this man up. He'll do it for you."

As Groucho left Chasen's after dinner with *Minnie's Boys'* producer, Arthur Whitelaw, a solicitous captain rushed anxiously after us, mother-hen-like cautioning Groucho, "Careful, Mr. Marx! Careful!" His tone implied that Groucho was not just less than agile, but as helpless as a very small child. The patronizing manner was not lost on Groucho. Stooping over and putting his hand on his back, he began walking in a bent-over posture that would have been appropriate to the oldest man in the world. As he creaked along, he made low groaning sounds and cackled like one of Macbeth's witches, repeating, "I'm an old man, I'm an old man."

The captain, failing to take the hint, added, "Watch the step, Mr. Marx!" Groucho instantly froze, his stare fastened on the steps. The parking attendant arrived with his Mercedes and announced, "Your car, Mr. Marx."

Groucho responded without unriveting his gaze, "I'm watching the step."

Once when Groucho talked with me about being old, he said, "I don't mind it if I can work." As for his total retirement from show business, Groucho said when he was eighty-four, "I'm not gonna retire, I'd like to die right onstage. That would be the way to go, right onstage." He added to that sober thought, "But I don't plan on dying at all."

In *Animal Crackers*, Mrs. Rittenhouse pleads with Captain Spaulding to stay, and Groucho answers:

CAPTAIN SPAULDING
Hello, I must be going. I cannot stay, I came to say I must be going. I'm glad I came, but just the same, I must be going.
MRS. RITTENHOUSE
For my sake you must stay. If you should go away, you'd spoil this party I am throwing.
CAPTAIN SPAULDING
I'll stay a week or two, I'll stay the summer through, but I am telling you, I must be going.

And without Groucho, the party never can be the same.

"I'm too rich to eat bread"

Dinner was served at the Marx residence, but everything was wrong for Groucho. Some of the food was burned. The fake salt was missing. There weren't any sliced tomatoes. Vegetables and potatoes crowded the entree on the same plate. The dessert grapefruit, having been frozen, was full of ice splinters.

During the meal Groucho didn't complain. He ate as he always ate—slowly, with the abundant but meticulously controlled pleasure of one who really liked to eat but who didn't like to gain weight. After the meal, he rose from the table and announced:

"Some meal. They can't treat me like that. I used to be Groucho Marx."

The celebrated irreverence for established institutions remained as strong as ever, even when the institution happened to be Groucho himself.

He did much the same thing when, in a restaurant or at home, the bread basket was offered, and he responded disdainfully:

"I'm too rich to eat bread."

Groucho was proud of his self-made success and of the financial independence it had provided for him and those he cared about. In spite of this, he maintained his irreverent perspective, even toward himself.

"I'm not really that rich," he explained. "In fact, the way the market's been acting lately, I may soon be saying, I'm too *poor* to eat bread."

The stock market rarely interfered with Groucho's appetite, though it accounted for numerous sleepless nights after 1929, when his life savings were wiped out. Of his insomnia, he said, "I'm trying to sleep it off. I subtract sheep."

"I remember when a day-old loaf of pumpernickel cost four cents, which probably dates my childhood somewhere between Marie Antoinette and the invention of the guillotine, the ultimate slicing machine. I have nothing at all against bread, except butter.

"When I say I'm too rich to eat bread, I mean the opposite of what I say, or vice versa. Or better yet, weiss wurst."

Groucho took his bread very seriously, especially when it was pumpernickel, a constant on his table at home and often in the restaurants he frequented. This pumpernickel was always accompanied by sweet butter, a staple at Groucho's, "Or heads will roll—I'm master in my house!" Favorite restaurants Chasen's and the Beverly Hills Hotel kept a private stock of sweet butter for him.

I had brought Groucho a loaf of Zabar's raisin pumpernickel from New York. "I'd like to be raisin' pumpernickel," he commented at dinner. "Want some more?" he asked me. "I don't think there's anymore left." I promised to bring two loaves next time. He shrugged. "It runs into money."

Groucho's commitment to pumpernickel and sweet butter went all the way back to the 1890s, when he was a small boy growing up in Yorkville, New York City's German neighborhood. In Groucho's family, his father, Sam, wore the *toque blanche*, while his mother, Minnie, preferred eating to cooking. "Minnie couldn't make anything except my father," he recalled.

"She could make bean soup and smoked tongue. She cooked badly. It was good enough to eat. My father was the good cook. He made pies— apple and lemon. It was through his cooking that my mother got plenty of jobs for us."

Born in Alsace, Sam Marx was known to everyone, even his young sons, as "Frenchie." As Groucho told it, "My mother spoke German and my father spoke French, but they had six boys anyway." Frenchie was renowned in Yorkville circles for his culinary triumphs. As an amateur chef of prodigious talent, he whipped up Lucullan feasts to woo recalcitrant theatrical agents, bookers, and anyone else Minnie thought could help "the boys." If agents or theatre owners didn't fancy the boys' act, Minnie fed their fancies, and Frenchie fed them fancily, until they succumbed.

Living with the Marx family in Yorkville was Aunt Hannah. One of Groucho's earliest, most vivid and most cherished childhood memories was of Aunt Hannah's clam chowder, which was so memorable that, into his eighties, he could still almost taste it. "Aunt Hannah used the same pot for making clam chowder that she used for doing the laundry," he recalled. "I think it improved both—both the clam chowder and the pot."

The taste of a food is a sensory impression so ephemeral that with the passage of time it becomes impossible to recall perfectly. Reminiscing with me about his mother's bean soup, Groucho said, "I wish I could remember just how it tasted."

Although Groucho and his brothers were far from rich, they didn't know it. Heroic portions of beans and chowder were cooked in that huge pot that doubled for washing clothes. Both the food and their shirts were heavy on starch. Sam Marx, whom Groucho described as "the world's worst tailor," may not have had much to work with, but he could convert leftovers into what Groucho remembered as "something fit for the gods, assuming there are any left."

Eating well was a Marx value, and there was an importance placed on enjoying good food. Enthusiastic eaters, the brothers often ate their egg sandwiches on the way to school, then for lunch they had to return home for replacements. After school they were regulars at any neighbors' apartments from which the aroma of freshly baked cookies wafted forth. Groucho remembered it as a world of iceboxes ("We used to suck on pieces of ice we stole from the ice wagon"), *pfeffernüss* and cheesecake with raisins, and his father's apple pies and lemon pies—as well as a world of hiding when the landlord came around to collect the rent.

When Groucho and I went in search of pfeffernüss at Benes, a Los Angeles Czech bakery, the experience brought back memories:

"Where are the samples?" he asked on entering. "In New York when I was young, we used to get cheesecake with raisins or huckleberry pie for only ten cents. An ice-cream soda—a *chocolate* ice-cream soda—was only a nickel. And you could buy pumpernickel for a nickel, too. But we ate day-old bread that cost four cents. That was how I saved up the seventy cents to take Annie Berger to the movies. But I have no regrets. I loved her madly. I'd do it again."

"Look! Pfeffernüss! When I was a child we used to have those for Christmas."

Groucho spoke to the German saleslady, giving his order in surprisingly fluent German. Recognizing him, she said, "I didn't know you understood German, Mr. Marx."

"I don't. But I speak it fluently," he informed her.

As we were leaving the bakery, he noticed a young blond woman seated at one of the tables with a very young baby. *"Wie alt?"* Groucho asked, and the woman responded, *"Drei Wochen."* "Oh," Groucho said, and left eating his pfeffernüss.

Like pfeffernüss, chocolate was always one of his minor passions. As we passed Mrs. See's candy store, he confided, "Mrs. See is a wily old girl." Being a man of will power (which he called "won't power") and discipline, he limited himself to only two pieces of chocolate a day. After we had each eaten our two chocolates, he announced, "Well, now I've had my two chocolates. There's nothing to do but wait for tomorrow."

The temptation of chocolate went back a long time in Groucho's life: "When I was five years old and I had blond curls down to here, I went to Germany with my mother. My mother had borrowed money from Sarah Wolfenstein, and then got the three boys together and said, 'You can either get an express wagon or go to Germany.' So Harpo took the express wagon, and Chico and I went to Germany. On the boat there was a man who took care of the horses—it was sort of a cattle boat—and they had horses belowdecks, too. He was stuck on my mother, but she wasn't stuck on him. You can imagine how he smelled!

"On the last night of the voyage, they had a party, but my mother wouldn't go to the party with this man. So he decided to get revenge. He came up to us with two bars of chocolate, one for Chico and one for me, and he said, 'Your mother wants to see you at the party. She wants you to go up there naked.' We would have done *anything* for a bar of chocolate, so we two kids went up to the party naked. But the man didn't get what he wanted, because my mother just thought it was funny."

Groucho would probably still have done almost anything for the right chocolate bar, except get fat. Even though he was quite slim, when his weight went up a couple of pounds, he became displeased with himself. One of the things he liked was to stop during his morning walk for an ice-cream cone. But if he was gaining weight, he didn't do that, and our walk would then assiduously avoid the sites of temptation. We walked on the other side of the street.

Apart from pleasure and sustenance, food was always an important measure of the quality of life for Groucho, and meals offered a prime occasion for social contacts. He liked to eat well, and he liked to share the experience with his friends, who often joined him as mealtime guests. What was really important to him were people, and meals offered some of the best social opportunities.

"The best food in the world isn't worth eating unless you have someone you like to eat it with you, and someone to complain to if the toast is burnt. But it's got to be the right someone.

"I remember in New York when I was young, eating at Horn & Hardart. You'd sit at a table with six strangers. I didn't like that particularly."

Groucho's interest in eating well was also a reaction against the ptomaine-touring days of his early career in vaudeville. Nevertheless, he preferred relatively simple food and was far from preoccupied with eating per se. One of his great favorites was ice cream and saltines, together. "Cuisine," he would say to me when we ate in an elaborate restaurant, "we used to call it grub."

At Groucho's home everything was served on a separate dish. As a result of those vaudeville boardinghouses where the food was all thrown together on one plate, Groucho insisted on the preservation of the separate identity of each thing eaten. "I'm very rich, and I can afford to eat everything on a separate dish," he announced. Gravies and sauces were served apart. The vegetable was on one plate, the salad on another. Generally, Groucho didn't even like one-pot cooking, although for clam chowder he made an exception.

Groucho still remembered "as if it was today" the day he and his brothers had fish for Thanksgiving dinner at a New Jersey boardinghouse because they were behind in their rent. Undaunted (Groucho would say "undented"), the Marx Brothers waited until the proprietress was asleep. Then they wended their way to the kitchen and consumed all that was left of the turkey. At his home on Thanksgiving, Groucho served turkey with all of the trimmings imaginable, but *never* fish for Thanksgiving.

He remembered those days when he spelled heartburn with a capital H "as if it was only a hundred years ago, which it was."

GROUCHO

I want to tell you about Max's Busy Bee, where I worked. A sandwich was three cents. They used to take it and dip it in some kind of greasy sauce or gravy. Coulda killed ya.

I

Did you eat any of the sandwiches, or did you just serve them?

GROUCHO

I used to eat 'em. I was hungry. I used to have fifteen cents every day for lunch. It was ten cents carfare, and fifteen cents for lunch. That was a quarter. I used to buy cream puffs. They were six for a quarter. One day I ate six of 'em. They weren't cream puffs, they were charlotte russes. I don't know if you know them. I don't see 'em anymore. I don't think they make 'em. Shaped like this, got cardboard on the outside. On the inside, some kind of dough, and then whipped cream. I ate six of them, and I vomited that day. I used to vomit from Max's Busy Bee sandwich. I did a lot of vomiting in those days.

Although Groucho never ate alone, he was particular about who sat at his table. If you were there, it was because Groucho *meant* for you to be there. He didn't like to be "stuck" for such a long period at a meal, or to be put in the position of having to perform for strangers who might have expected one-liners for the appetizer, one-liners for the entree, and one-liners for dessert.

After almost seventy years as a performer—most of these as a highly visible public person—Groucho still felt the tension of being "on" for any kind of performance or public appearance, ranging from a major television appearance to lunch with a few relative strangers.

I
Is it only my imagination? I know you don't like eating with strangers but I can actually feel the tension. And what we're going to do today isn't really very important . . .
GROUCHO
Lunch is a performance. I don't like eating with strangers. You can't ever let up, except with a few people.

Groucho regularly had guests at his house for lunch and for dinner, or else he was a guest at someone's house. Often he went out to a restaurant, usually with a guest or two. In restaurants the party frequently consisted not only of those Groucho had brought, but also included the captains, waiters, and busboys as well. On occasion, the diners at neighboring tables also joined the entourage, though peripheral involvements were only for brief intervals. His appearances in restaurants were as likely to disorder the established protocol and leave everyone amused and confused as in *A Night at the Opera*.

Sidney Sheldon, George Seaton, and other friends of Groucho's recalled his asking waiters and waitresses, "Do you have frogs' legs?" George Seaton remembered a tearful waitress who broke down over the question. When I was with Groucho at "21," he asked owners Jerry Berns and Sheldon Tannen that question. They responded by raising their trouser legs. I asked Groucho what he would do if it turned out that someone he asked really *had* frogs' legs. Unhesitatingly he answered, "I'd go to another restaurant."

Once as we entered the Beverly Hills Hotel restaurant, he handed his coat to the checkroom girl and said, "Have this cleaned and ready by Thursday."

The maître d' approached, and Groucho said, "I'd like a cheap table for two."

Indicating the best table in the house, the maître d' asked, "Will that table be satisfactory?"

"It's a lousy table," Groucho answered.

"But, Mr. Marx, it's the table you always request."

"Is that table big enough for four?" Groucho asked.

"Yes, Mr. Marx."

"Good. We'll be two."

"The fish is very good today, Mr. Marx."

"We won't have time to eat. Just bring the check."

On another occasion, as we passed through the Polo Lounge of the Beverly Hills Hotel, Groucho ambled along, picking up a thin slice of pumpernickel from the first table he passed, much to the amusement of the table's occupants. At the next table he stopped to butter his bread amid surprised and delighted giggles. Farther along he pilfered a radish from another table. At the next table, he buttered his radish. By the time he was seated, the whole mood of the room was one of merriment following his impromptu floor show.

After we were seated, the waiter asked Groucho if he would like an aperitif.

"Vitriol," Groucho answered.

"I'm sorry, we don't have any vitriol, Mr. Marx."

"You don't have any vitriol? What kind of a restaurant is this?"

After a glass of tomato juice, the clam chowder arrived. One of Groucho's all-time favorites was clam chowder, which the Beverly Hills Hotel chef would make for him even on days other than Friday, and without salt.

The restaurant was very crowded when Groucho finished and was ready for the main course. He said loudly:

"If I'm not waited on right away, I'll leave in a huff. Will someone please call me a huff?"

"Look, I only have two hands," the overwrought waiter said.

"Do you know anybody who has three?" was Groucho's reply.

"That's like 'laughing your head off,' " he explained to me afterward. "What does 'laugh your head off' mean? You can't laugh your head off."

Following our clam chowder, Groucho ordered a big German-style apple pancake with sour cream. As we finished, the captain returned and asked us what we would like for dessert.

"Do you have any fruit in the kitchen besides the chef?" Groucho said.

Before the nonplussed captain could respond, Groucho continued:

"Have you got any stewed prunes?"

"Yes, Mr. Marx."

"Well, let 'em go home and sleep it off."

Knowing that Groucho was a member of "Nescafé society," having given up coffee, the waiter asked:

"Sanka, Mr. Marx?"

"You're welcome," Groucho responded.

After the meal, the captain asked how everything was.

"Everything was all right," Groucho said, "but tell the chef the food was lousy."

Then Groucho exited singing "Singin' in the Rain."

When leaving restaurants, Groucho frequently stopped and talked to people at the other tables, even if he didn't know them—*especially* if he didn't know them. He understood that he was part of their lives even if they weren't part of his, and he usually treated each person with courtesy even when he was insulting them. Most of them cherished being insulted by Groucho.

It was rare that Groucho was on the receiving end of an insult. People were reverently respectful toward him. Everywhere, even in Beverly Hills, where he lived and was a familiar figure, he was treated as a super-celebrity, a living myth, the cynosure of all eyes. Wherever he went, there was the ubiquitous "Hi, Groucho!" The room echoed with appreciative recognition; there were whispers of "That's Groucho Marx."

"We saw *You Bet Your Life* last night," Groucho was told, but he didn't look overly impressed. "They say it as if they were the only ones who saw me."

Wherever he was, people came up to him. Groucho was annoyed when they didn't tell him their names. If he had met them before but only briefly, he preferred that they say "I'm So-and-So, and we met in such-and-such a place." "I can't remember everyone," he explained. Frequently, they introduced themselves and anyone who might be with them.

"I'm Emil Sloop from Danksville, and this is my wife, Gilda. I have a pet shop, and she's a dental assistant. [He takes out his wallet and shows Groucho a photograph.] This is our son, Rupert. He was only eight when this picture was taken, but he's fourteen now, and second in his class. When Gilda—that's Gilda, my wife, here—and I were first married, we used to watch you . . ." And so on. Needless to say, Groucho could not take just a short walk, because people not only wanted to recognize *him*, but to be recognized *by* him.

Everyone knew Groucho but he knew relatively few people. Occasionally, he was approached by someone from the past whom he really did remember, or someone who was associated with one of his films or with *You Bet Your Life*, who did stir a pleasant memory. And he was always pleased to see an old face—especially if she was a young one.

There was no anonymity and very little privacy for Groucho, but he enjoyed his supercelebrity status. "The time to start worrying is when they stop recognizing you." He was, therefore, always in character, never disappointing his fans. In one of his more frivolous moods, we strolled through Beverly Hills with Groucho wearing a Harpo wig.

Asked, "How was your day?" Groucho would frequently respond, "I had a good walk." His feeling was that most of life is "a lot of little things." The big things you can't do much about anyway.

"At my age you can't expect things to get better. You hope they'll stay the same."

Groucho's pace was slower than it once was, his daily walk through Beverly Hills less jaunty, but no less prized. His appreciation of physical well-being had been enhanced by the negative blow of seeing about him so many of his friends becoming much less physically fit than he was.

Groucho's walk was a social experience, and almost a professional appearance, during which he greeted and was greeted by his public. This produced a constant reaffirmation of the recognition which had been his reward for being Groucho Marx. "I can't walk as fast as you can," he told me, "but you can't walk as slow as I can."

I told Groucho that I was impressed by the response of construction workers calling down to him from their lofty steel precipice, by teenage girls rushing up to him, by the garbage truck that screeched to a stop so the driver could salute Groucho, and by the waitress who spilled the soup (fortunately not on us) in her glee at serving him. Just as I was speaking, a gardener who was watering the lawn we were passing hosed our feet. Groucho looked down at our soaked shoes and the immense puddle we suddenly found ourselves standing in, and said, "Yeah." Meanwhile the gardener had fled.

Talking later that day with Goddard Lieberson about the incidents of our walk, Groucho referred to the Southern California emphasis on the automobile: "Anyone who *walks* in Beverly Hills is a celebrity."

When he went to places like Chasen's and the Beverly Hills Hotel, Groucho was treated with restrained affection and somewhat shielded from mass adulation. Sometimes, though, his food did get cold while he signed autographs or greeted those who came over to say, "Hi, Groucho. Stay well!" After they had passed he would say, "Yeah, I'll try."

There was one kind of autograph hunter who would present a little scrap of paper for a signature. Groucho wouldn't really feel like stopping, but he would be prevailed upon to sign it. He would start to write "Groucho." Then the person would say, "To Billy. Could you please make that 'To Billy.' " So he would start to write "To Billy." "No, with an *ie*," the person would say. Groucho would make an *ie* over the *y*. "To Billie Jo. Could you please make that 'To Billie Jo.' That's 'Jo' without an *e*." He would start to write again, and the person would say, "Kempner. 'To Billie Jo Kempner.' That's spelled K-E-M-P-N-E-R." And so on. They usually would have some other ideas about what they wanted on the little scrap of paper, but by this time they would be lucky if they even got Groucho to sign his name. When the next person said, "Would you please write 'To Harold,' " Groucho would sign his name and say, "*You* write 'To Harold.' " After several such encounters, Groucho told me, "It's no wonder they usually say the autograph is for someone else."

Groucho drew the line at signing Kleenex when it was occasionally presented, especially if it was used.

At Nate 'n' Al's Delicatessen a man came up to our table with a big smile and said, "Hi, Groucho. You remember me?"

Groucho didn't, so the man introduced himself.

"Don't you remember, Groucho, I was in the audience of *You Bet Your Life* the second year that you did it? I wasn't on your show, but I raised my hand, and I was almost on the show. I just wanted to come over and say hello. I'm here with my wife and couple of people. I wanted to say hello."

There was still no response.

"I wanted to say how good it is to see you, Groucho, and stay well,

Groucho, and we're all pulling for you. It's really good to see you again, Groucho. And . . . I'm glad to see you, Groucho . . . and, well, uh . . . see you, Groucho . . ."

He backed away, as though from a royal audience.

"Nice conversation," Groucho commented after the man had left.

At Chasen's one night, Groucho had just been served his favorite banana shortcake, when a captain hesitantly approached to tell him that a lady at a nearby table was celebrating a birthday and desperately wanted his autograph. The banana shortcake was the *pièce de résistance* of the meal for Groucho, who was just about to devour it impetuously. Nonetheless, he left it, staking out his claim first: "Forks will be crossed if this shortcake is any shorter when I get back!" Then, going to the woman's table, he sang "Happy Birthday." The birthday lady responded ecstatically, and Groucho returned to his banana shortcake.

When Groucho entered Chasen's, he would come face-to-face with a picture of himself on the wall inside the entrance. There was also a picture of the late Dave Chasen, himself a former vaudeville performer.

Groucho greeted Maude Chasen with, "Is the food good here?" after which he was led to the best table in the house.

"Would you prefer a larger table?" she asked.

"A larger table and smaller food," Groucho answered.

After we were seated Groucho looked up from the menu and said, "I remember when I started coming here. I used to look first at the prices.

"Did I ever tell you when we had just started to be successful, Harpo and I went to a fancy restaurant in Oklahoma City? They gave a long menu to Harpo, and he looked at it and said, 'Yes, and a cup of coffee.' So we had everything on the menu. And a cup of coffee."

Most of the people who came to Groucho's house were in show business because these were the people toward whom he felt the greatest affinity and with whom he was happiest, most comfortable, and best entertained. The bond between them was comparable to the bond that exists between circus performers. A community of interest exists between the bareback rider, the clown, the lion tamer, and the high-wire artist, even though they all ostensibly do quite different things. There is that same bond between the fat lady, the smallest man in the world, and the snakeskin girl. At Groucho's, the fame of the show business guests varied greatly, but that wasn't important; what mattered was that one and all they understood the drive of the sword swallower who stands up there alone, literally and figuratively prepared to cut his throat for that moment of applause.

Marvin Hamlisch, who was Groucho's pianist in concert appearances before he won his own three Oscars, summed it up one night at Groucho's:

"Listen, the minute you get me onstage, it's like I want to *stay* there! Forever! I'd like to do a telethon where you don't get paid or anything — you just go on forever and forever saying 'Thank you' and performing."

Morgan Ames, who also played the piano for Groucho, told this story:

"We did this benefit one time, and I was playing for Groucho. It was at the house of a Beverly Hills lady. Very hoity-toity. Much of 'How do you do, Mr. Marx, this is my husband who used to work for . . .' etc., etc. We were sitting there, and at one point Groucho got a twinkle in his eye. I could sense a minor outrage coming. He leaned over and said to me, quite audibly, 'You know, in my whole life I've never been comfortable with anybody who wasn't in show business.' End of remark. And I think that's quite true of him."

When performers like George Burns, Bill Cosby, Milton Berle, or George Jessel gathered at Groucho's table, there was certain to be amusing (and competitive) conversation. While Groucho would contribute an occasional pithy *bon mot*, he was quite content to let his guests carry the conversation. He didn't particularly like to have to talk a lot while eating. And he didn't like to be asked questions that required long answers from him during meals. If asked a question requiring a lengthy answer, he usually said, "I'm eating."

Sometimes at meals, Groucho was in a pensive mood or just a quiet one. His silences could be very silent indeed. He was not afraid of long pauses in the conversation, and he had no need to fill in those pauses, though others may have felt uneasy.

Always a generous host, Groucho had two giant refrigerators that were always crammed with delicacies from Jurgensen's, his favorite Beverly Hills food store. While not one to dismiss a modern convenience, Groucho did lament the disappearance of the icebox, which long ago had provided him with some of his best material, jokewise, if not necessarily foodwise. "Refrigerators aren't funny," he advised me.

"We used to get big laughs on icebox stories," he said, remembering vaudeville days. "But who would understand now about the tray you had to use to catch the dripping water? When I was young, which was about a hundred years ago, there were no refrigerators. There were no airplanes, no automobiles, no radio, and no television. There was practically nothing.

"Well, anyhow, they used to sell ice on the street in those days. The ice wagon would come around, and for twenty-five cents you would get so much ice. When the iceman went up to deliver to somebody, we boys would jump on the ice wagon and eat the ice in the summer. So, one day he was delivering ice, and this woman who lived on the fourth floor called down to the iceman that she wanted twenty-five cents' worth of ice. He called back to her, 'I don't know what floor you're on. Tell me your floor and I will deliver the ice.' She says, 'Four Q,' and he says, 'Fork you, too, madam.'

"That's not a made-up story," Groucho added.

Groucho, who always preferred to pick up the check, recalled a friend who did not:

"Al Boasberg was very stingy. We used to eat lunch every day at M-G-M. It'd be Kaufman, Morrie Ryskind and the boys, and Boasberg. Then we'd toss for the check. Boasberg lost one day and had to pay the check, and he never showed up for lunch again at the studio restaurant. He would get hamburgers and hot dogs at the lunch wagon.

"But he wasn't stingy on Christmas. Then, he would get all the actors who were out of work, and invite them to his house, and buy them dinner, and give them shirts and ties and things like that. He was great. I miss him.

"I was on the bill with another fellow on the Orpheum Circuit, and he would never eat in a good restaurant. He'd always go to a place where he could eat a whole dinner for seventy-five cents. Eventually he died from eating in those joints because the food was so terrible."

Although Groucho gave a glittering party on the occasion of winning his Oscar, he told me that he didn't like to go to big parties anymore.

"I don't drink. I don't smoke. I just stand around sober."

On doctor's orders Groucho had given up the cigars that were his trademark, as well as all alcoholic beverages. He never did drink very much. "I only got drunk once in my life," he recalled, "and that was in Jamaica drinking those sweet rum drinks." The occasional Cinzano which he used to drink before dinner was replaced by salt-free tomato juice. One evening while drinking a second tomato juice aperitif, Groucho observed, "I'm drinking this like there's no yesterday." He was reminded of his father's wine. "You never tasted anything like the wine my father used to make. In New York my father used to make wine in the cellar. It was during Prohibition, and he decided that since he was a Frenchman, he'd make some wine. We lived across the street from where there was a sewer, and the rats used to come out of the sewer and go into the cellar. And that was where my father was making the wine. It was a real rathskeller. One night there was a tremendous explosion. It was like an earthquake. The wine had exploded in the cellar and killed all the rats! We never had any rats after that. And we never had any wine, either."

About smoking Groucho was like a reformed alcoholic who has given up drinking and joined the Woman's Christian Temperance Union. "One day my doctor said, 'Stop smoking,' and I did." Jack Nicholson, cigarette in hand, knew the lecture by heart.

GROUCHO
Why don't you give up smoking?
JACK NICHOLSON
I did. I gave it up ten years ago.
GROUCHO
You don't look like you gave it up. (*Jack was chain-smoking*)
JACK NICHOLSON
I started again two years ago. I'm going to be on a boat for ten days, on Sam Spiegel's yacht. Maybe I can do it then.
GROUCHO
You mean (*Raising his eyebrows*) S. P. Eagle? (*Mention of producer Sam Spiegel often elicited this response from Groucho*)

Groucho told me about T. S. Eliot requesting a photograph and then sending it back because it didn't show Groucho smoking a cigar. Groucho sent the cigar-smoking photo, and they became good friends. Winston Churchill's daughter once gave him some cigars, and Groucho asked her, "What do you know about cigars?"

"I smoke them," she said. "I smoke them with my father. We used to have competitions to see who could have the longest ash."

Groucho's barroom, filled with Marx Brothers memorabilia, was just off the dining room, and was where guests used to congregate in the half hour before meals. After Groucho began abstaining from both alcohol and tobacco, they usually went directly to the dining-room table.

Cook-watching became a popular sport at Groucho's soirées when Robin Heaney joined the Marx ménage to become, as Groucho described her, "the only cook I ever kissed." Groucho told me that on seeing Robin in the kitchen, Jack Nicholson had asked him, "Where do you get one of those things?" Tall, slim, young, and blond, she was not scullery typecast, and guests always asked in disbelief, "Is she *really* your cook?!" Robin was mistress of what Groucho referred to as "la Belle Kitchen." Sometimes when Groucho was invited out to lunch in a restaurant, he took Robin along with him, introducing her as his cook. This was usually received as a joke.

A college graduate, Robin always wanted to cook, preferably elaborate specialties for large numbers of people, but she found her career hampered by her appearance. Few wives were willing to install her in their kitchens. Groucho rarely went into his kitchen, but he was concerned with what came out, and he assiduously clipped recipes from the Sunday *New York Times*. Although Groucho didn't think of himself as a gourmet and "salt-free" is hardly an Escoffier-like admonition, Robin found working for him a challenge—a purely culinary challenge, since he had announced his retirement where girls were concerned. "Now I only look," he told me.

Robin decorated his kitchen with her presence and his table with repasts like curry sauce and vegetables, cream cheese balls, rolled veal stuffed with dried fruit, broccoli, tomato stuffed with spinach soufflé, mushrooms stuffed with sausage, vegetable-fruit-nut salad, and fresh papaya halves with strawberries and cream for dessert. Frequently, Robin walked around barefoot, and sometimes even served that way. When Groucho went to New York, he brought her along to cook in his Sherry Netherland Hotel suite. Her dress was informal. She wore a T-shirt with a large open mouth across the front of it. As she breathed, the heaving of her bust made it look as if the mouth were laughing.

Before Robin, Groucho had two black cooks. Martha, who was with him for many years, had as a specialty a fruitcake that she baked and aged for Christmas. Another specialty was "Sidney Sheldon Soup," a meal in itself, consisting of boiled beef and vegetables, and named for a frequent dinner guest. When Martha was cooking for Groucho, a typical meal would have been carrot salad, ground meat and peas with mashed potatoes, and raspberries with a creamy topping.

Before Martha there was Sarah, about whom Groucho told this story: "Sarah was a very attractive colored woman who never married. One day I said to her, 'Why didn't you ever get married? You're a good-looking dame. You must have had a lot of men after you.' And she said, 'I would say, in Dallas I was very well known.' "

He paused after telling this story, as if to enjoy the imagery evoked.

Groucho always ate so slowly that those who ate with him for the first time were often dismayed when they realized that they had finished virtually everything on their plates while Groucho's plate was still nearly full. To cover their embarrassment at seeming to have ravenously gulped their meals, they nervously nibbled as slowly as possible on whatever crumbs they had left. They accepted with alacrity second helpings, even thirds, not wishing to leave Groucho the lone eater.

Eventually, however, they conceded defeat, laying down their forks and just waiting for Groucho to finish. The whole procedure was often lengthened by Robin's extra-crunchy salad, which Groucho devoured down to the last nut and seed even though health food per se didn't interest him. During one of our first dinners together, I finished eating after he did. This wasn't missed by Groucho, who commented, "She can stay. I may keep her here permanently."

Groucho lived alone until after a serious illness at eighty-three, a round-the-clock shift of nurses joined the cast at Groucho's. Young and attractive, they often seemed more like starlets cast to play nurses. While bemoaning that he couldn't make a vice out of necessity, he came to enjoy their companionship and the role he played in their lives. He enjoyed the obvious pride and pleasure they took from the job with Groucho Marx. Donna, one of these young nurses, described her mornings with him:

"Groucho has everything timed out so cute. He gets up in the morning at seven o'clock and takes a shower. Then he gets back into bed and reads his paper until eight-thirty. At eight-thirty he gets his messages, and at nine o'clock he eats breakfast. Then, after breakfast, he gets up and brushes his teeth and shaves, and if he doesn't have to do anything, he gets back in bed and finishes reading the paper. He has a set time for everything."

Breakfast for Groucho consisted of freshly squeezed orange juice, soft-boiled eggs, and decaffeinated coffee. This was all prepared by the Guatemalan maid, Ora, who would arrive just before nine o'clock.

Occasionally an early-rising friend would drop by to join him for breakfast. Elliott Gould, who sometimes rose with the sun, might come by when he wasn't working on a film, but it was strictly for Groucho's company, since Elliott's favorite kind of breakfast wasn't on the menu—an egg salad sandwich with a milk shake.

Elliott told Groucho that he had met Zeppo for the first time at Groucho's Oscar-warming party.

"He let me get in front of him at the buffet," Elliott said.

"Zeppo always was very polite, unless he was hungry," Groucho confirmed.

Lunch was always at one o'clock even when Groucho went out for lunch. He used to go to Hillcrest, his club, for lunch with George Jessel, George Burns, Jack Benny, writer Irving Brecher, or banker Al Hart. The regulars referred to their group as "the Roundtable." In later years, however, Groucho usually had lunch at home, often with a guest.

Hillcrest Country Club undoubtedly missed Groucho's daily visits, but on the occasions he did show up for lunch, he usually made up for lost pandemonium. Erin Fleming, his secretary–business manager–companion, and I were with him on one such occasion:

ERIN

What are you going to order, Groucho?

GROUCHO

I would like to have sockeyed salmon.

ERIN

I thought you said popeyed salmon?

GROUCHO

I did. I was cockeyed when I said it. (*To waiter*) You say there's no salt in that cockeyed salmon?

WAITER

Yes, Mr. Marx.

GROUCHO

I'll have that and cold borscht. But no salt. I'd have a breast of turkey, but it sounds so sexual. (*Reading*) "Sales tax will be added to retail price on all taxable items." So, remember that, girls. Don't go overboard. 'Cause I'm not *made* of money. (*To waiter*) I still want the borscht and I will have cottage cheese, sour cream, fruit, and buttermilk. And see what the boys in the back room'll have. (*To Erin*) Don't you like borscht?

ERIN

No, and I don't like buttermilk, either.

GROUCHO

What else can a cow give but her milk?

ERIN

Groucho, do you want apple or strawberry pie for dessert?

GROUCHO

"Apple pie for me. Because I'm an American. Strawberry is for fags." (*He was referring to the line of the comic homosexual in the Marx Brothers' Fun in Hi Skule vaudeville act who always insisted on strawberry pie*)

Sunday brunch at Hillcrest Country Club was a special event for members, an effective antidote for Sunday terminal boredom. The buffet usually included *matzo brie*, lox, cream cheese and bagels, as well as the conventional items.

After lunch at home, Groucho sometimes adjourned to the living room to crack nuts from a big wooden bowl. But he didn't use the cradle of the telephone to crack them as he did in *Horse Feathers*, settling instead for a more conventional nutcracker.

Dinner was *de rigueur* at seven o'clock, and usually with guests. Even if Groucho went out to a supper after a film premiere or to a late buffet party, he always had his dinner at home at seven o'clock, not gambling on the late fare, especially after salt-free fare became mandatory.

On being asked, "Are you having Billy Wilder for dinner?" Groucho wore an expression of mock shock. "I'm surprised at you," he admonished any grammatical offender. "Are we going to eat him?" Groucho always had people *to* dinner.

GROUCHO
You know about the oysters who were invited *for* dinner?

I
I believe it was for a picnic. But it's too sad. I try not to think about it.

CROUCHO
You seem like an *Alice in Wonderland* person . . .

I
Of course. So do you.

CROUCHO
I'm gonna tell you something else he [Lewis Carroll] wrote: "He thought he saw an elephant that practiced on a fife. He looked again and found it was a letter from his wife." That's good.

A dinner party at Groucho's, on any given night, might have included Sidney Sheldon, Mae West, Dinah Shore, Mike Nichols (who sometimes brought his baby, Max), George Jessel, Elliott Gould, Jack Lemmon, Walter Matthau, Edgar Bergen, George Burns, George Seaton, Buddy Hackett, Dick Cavett, or Goddard Lieberson. Groucho expected everyone to be on time.

Besides the usual impromptu entertainment by the guests, Groucho sometimes showed a film, such as *Animal Crackers*, or the Jack Benny parody of *You Bet Your Life*, or *The Mikado*, with Groucho as Ko-Ko, the Lord High Executioner.

While I was staying at Groucho's house, he asked me to call Edgar Bergen and invite him to dinner. I asked if I could invite Charlie McCarthy and Mortimer Snerd, too. Groucho said, "No, maybe he won't like it. That's how he makes his living. He might think he has to come over here to work. Tell him we'll serve him a hock-hock and a roll. That's a frankfurter. I used to pay three cents for one."

Parties at Groucho's house started early enough to end before eleven o'clock, especially when *You Bet Your Life* was on, because Groucho didn't want to miss it. If the party lasted longer than expected, just before the program came on, he would announce, "The pâté is over," and retire to his bedroom, where he watched it with only his closest friends. Groucho played the game along with the contestants, and was pleased when he guessed all of the answers correctly. He would call out "Richard Lovelace" in answer to what seventeenth-century poet wrote, "Stone walls do not a prison make." He knew or remembered the answer to virtually every question. Enormously fond of *You Bet Your Life*, he told me, "It was some of the best stuff I ever did. I really had to think. I never worked so hard."

During the reruns of *You Bet Your Life* Groucho received a lot of fan mail from viewers. Each day Groucho, with the help of Steve Stoliar, who had organized the CRAC Committee at UCLA that helped bring about the rerelease of *Animal Crackers*, went through the piles of mail that came in, checking the return addresses for known names. One of these was an Italian lady named Bettina Consolo, who appeared three times on the show. Groucho, very pleased, showed me her card. "She always writes, 'God Bless You.' Only that."

After *You Bet Your Life*, Groucho often enjoyed his favorite indulgence, one that his mother had also enjoyed: nurse Happy tickled his feet.

At Eric Ross's men's clothing store in Beverly Hills, some people from Kansas came up to Groucho to tell him how much they enjoyed watching *You Bet Your Life*. They had just seen a show with a contestant they said was "so dumb" they couldn't believe it.

"They're all dumb," Groucho told them. "That's why they're on the show. Why do you think *I'm* on the show?"

Groucho usually watched *You Bet Your Life* from bed in pajamas. During his show he rarely smiled, watched raptly, seriously. A discriminating viewer, he carefully studied *TV Guide* beforehand to make his selections. Early arrival at the TV set was a must, for he insisted on seeing programs from the beginning to the end. Then the set was switched off. He never just left it on after a program was over.

His attitude toward TV was far from being casual. It was actually closer to the respect many people feel for the legitimate theatre. Groucho sincerely believed that all the entertainment media of the past—theatre, radio, and the movies—were summed up in television, "right in that box." He appreciated that "being entertaining is hard work."

The choice of topics discussed at Groucho's during mealtimes was unpredictable. One day, at lunch with nurse Donna, the conversation turned to hamsters in general, and Donna's in particular:

GROUCHO
What do you hear from your hamsters?

NURSE DONNA
Just chewing all night long. I haven't slept for nights, ever since they got loose in the house. I've put out food to catch them, but they eat the food and get away.

GROUCHO
Hamsters can be pretty wily, like the Six Flying Hamsters.

I
Were the Six Flying Hamsters like Swayne's Rats and Cats?

GROUCHO
Nothing was like Swayne's Rats and Cats.

I
Are you going to tell us about the Six Flying Hamsters?

GROUCHO
Yeah. The Six Flying Hamsters was one of the most famous acts in show business. They did a flying act. They played all over the world. In Paris they were a great hit, and ate the cheese—the soft cheese, not the hard cheese—and wine. In China they learned to eat with chopsticks, and did their act in Chinese. In New York they played the Palace, and *Variety* said they were "socko." They were the biggest, and they were impossible to follow. Nobody could follow them. They were next to last on the bill, and there were some acrobats after them, but they couldn't follow the Six Flying Hamsters. They used to do three shows a day. At the end of their act, they'd fly out, but they were always back for the next show. The act lasted about forty minutes.

I
What could they do for an encore?

GROUCHO
For an encore one of them sang. She sang "Josephine in Her Flying

Machine." Just that one song. The act died when the female committed suicide. She was hopelessly in love with one of the males, Irving Hamster. You see, he was the only Jew of all the Hamsters. The female Hamster was the one who smoked the cigar. She always smoked it. It ruined her throat, but she smoked it anyway. The Six Flying Hamsters was a very important act. They were the headliners. E. F. Albee, the head of the United Booking Office, said it was one of the greatest acts he'd ever seen. And he hadn't seen many acts. They don't have acts like that anymore. Too expensive. They got paid in zlotys. They'd be around yet, but the price of oil got so high they couldn't afford to travel anymore. They had very few contract problems because they had a very good agent. He was a beaver. Before that their agent was S. P. Eagle.

I

I never heard of an act like that before.

GROUCHO

(*With a twinkle in his eye*) There isn't that kind of talent around anymore.

When Richard Adams came to the United States in 1974 on a tour to promote his best-selling book, *Watership Down*, he had one request to make of his publishers: He wanted to meet Groucho Marx. Groucho was approached, and one afternoon he, Erin, and I had lunch with Richard Adams, his wife, and their daughter at the Beverly Wilshire Hotel. Richard Adams was there waiting, and he was totally prepared for the visit. He was more familiar with the specifics of Groucho's films than Groucho, having seen some of them more recently than Groucho had, and perhaps more times. His approach was also more analytical and more detailed than Groucho's, whose approach was always more intuitive and more pragmatic. Asked about some specific bit, Groucho would say, "I never analyzed it." Adams was highly articulate in his discussion of the films, especially the first five Paramount films, and Groucho was clearly pleased by the respect of this intelligent and successful fan. Groucho, however, failed to appreciate Adams's criticism of *Room Service*. Richard Adams also unwittingly produced copies of *The Marx Brothers Scrapbook*. At that very moment, Groucho was embroiled in a costly legal action over that book. Richard Adams's daughter was sent next door to Brentano's in quest of something else to autograph. She returned with a copy of *Groucho and Me*, and Groucho wrote in the book, "To a very Bunny Man." Adams had brought a copy of his own book, which he gave Groucho.

As we were finishing the appetizer course, we were greeted by French Consul General Jacques Roux, who had arrived to eat lunch and who had been a visitor with his wife and Henri Langlois of the Cinémathèque Française at Groucho's house. Groucho said, "Hi, General." Sometime later, after a leisurely European-style lunch, Monsieur Roux nodded to us as he departed. Groucho was just finishing his entree, carefully working on the last forkful, meticulously dissecting it into two forkfuls under the nervous gaze of the waiter. Disbelievingly, he had been trying to seize Groucho's plate for more than half an hour, laboring under the delusion that he had finished, simply because no one could possibly eat that slowly. But Groucho defended his plate, and may indeed have increased his slowness. It was a long, long lunch.

At the end of the day Groucho was still mulling over what Richard Adams had said:

GROUCHO
He said he didn't like *Room Service.* Did you hear what he said?
I
Of course, but I also heard him say how much he admired just about everything you did, and it was certainly clear how much he respects you. Besides, you told me that you weren't *that* enchanted yourself by *Room Service.*
GROUCHO
I can say it. (*Raising his eyebrows for me*) I wasn't going to let him say it.

One of Groucho's virtues was that he usually recognized when he was being unreasonable—even though that insight didn't make him any more reasonable.

A year after the fact, Richard Adams, discussing the event with *Newsweek,* told them how furious his publishers were with him when he refused to terminate a long lunch with Groucho Marx in order to plug his own book at a previously scheduled appearance on a television show.

". . . It would have been dishonorable and ungentlemanly to leave the hotel before Groucho, the greatest comedian of the century. If I'd walked out on Groucho Marx to go on some moneymaking affair of my own, I wouldn't have had any self-respect left."

Groucho made his own brand of fun. At a tea party with a group of socially prominent and proper ladies to plan his appearance for charity at an affair called "A Day at the Races," the conversation remained on an elevated plane. The ladies conversed in well-modulated tones until Groucho interrupted with: "I've got to take a leak. There's one thing that's true: no matter how rich you are, sometimes you have to take a leak."

"The ladies really broke up over this," Erin commented. "The whole atmosphere relaxed, and a great deal more was accomplished."

There were frequent visits to charitable groups that were planning to raise money through Groucho. I once asked him if he minded being so exploited by everyone for something, and if it ever made him feel the way a beautiful girl feels. He answered, "No—to both questions."

Groucho admitted to me that "big parties were never exactly my glass of tea," but he continued to turn out for a few anyway. His appearance at any Hollywood party was often the scene-stealing event. Irwin Allen, who produced some of Groucho's pictures, rediscovered this when he gave a party for the Hollywood premiere of his *Towering Inferno* at the Beverly Hilton Hotel. Many celebrities were there, including William Holden, Henry Fonda, Fred Astaire, and Jennifer Jones, but the picture in the papers the next day was of Groucho dancing with Red Buttons.

Groucho had first asked Fred Astaire, who declined to dance with him. Next, he asked Red Buttons, who was sitting nearby, and who leaped to his feet. Strobe lights started flashing as reporters gathered around Groucho and Red Buttons, who made the most striking couple on the floor.

When the photographers were satisfied, Groucho relinquished Red, who danced with his wife, Alicia, while Groucho danced with me. I was surprised to find that the same person whose walk at eighty-four was no longer always steady was still a graceful and professional dancer who not only looked good on the dance floor, but who could make his partner look good.

Groucho liked to dine out with friends, but because of his salt-free diet, he found it a bit complicated. This didn't stop him, though, so when Elliott Gould and George Segal suggested a Beverly Hills Chinese restaurant called Mr. Chow, Groucho accepted in a Chinese accent. The group consisted of Groucho, Erin, Elliott and his wife Jennifer, George and his wife Marion, and me.

At the restaurant the first blow was struck when Groucho announced he couldn't eat anything with salt in it. Next, George and Marion Segal declined anything with monosodium glutamate in it because they suspected that they had been poisoned elsewhere a few nights earlier by this chemical additive. Elliott Gould told the waiter, "No food, just seven glasses of water."

Eventually they compromised by ordering everything on the menu, just as Harpo had done many years earlier. The meal included such varied delicacies as fried seaweed, Peking duck, and assorted Chinese entrees. Groucho had never eaten with chopsticks, but when he saw mine, he couldn't resist trying them himself. Even in his eighties he was ready to experiment. Being a quick study, he used his chopsticks with considerable dexterity throughout the whole long meal.

When actress Michelle Phillips invited Groucho to a dinner in his honor, all of the other guests would be beautiful young women, she promised—a promise kept. A few nights later, he and I arrived at the Summit Ridge site of the party. We were a little early, and the door was slightly ajar. Groucho pushed the door the rest of the way. Just inside, deep in concentration arranging the table, was a young lady unclad only in a towel. Seeing Groucho, she screamed, which he didn't take personally. Then she dashed for the stairs, covering her confusion as she fled. A little later she reappeared coiffed and composed and fully dressed, wearing a perfectly see-through top.

Michelle appeared with her daughter, Chynna, and Michelle played the piano and sang for Groucho, who was sharing some avocado dip with actress Helena Kallianiotes. Groucho enjoyed his unique position with "these lovely young things" until photographer Harry Benson arrived with his camera to be the only other man present and to immortalize the moment for *People* magazine.

Despite the inevitable insults Groucho was a desirable guest. Jorja Sheldon (who had been actress Jorja Curtright) had been at the receiving end of Grouchoesque humor since her marriage more than twenty years ago to writer Sidney Sheldon, one of Groucho's closest friends. But Groucho never joked about Jorja's talent as an actress. "She was a good actress," he always said, an accolade he took very seriously.

When Jorja first entertained Groucho, she was anxious to make a good impression as a hostess, and she offered him a drink from their well-stocked bar. He asked for Bushmill, the only thing they didn't have. Only mildly shattered, she was prepared for his next visit:

JORJA SHELDON
Will you have some Bushmill, Grouch?
    GROUCHO
I never drink Bushmill. I'll have a Campari.

When Groucho next visited them, Jorja was ready.

JORJA SHELDON
I'll fix a Campari for you, Grouch.
GROUCHO
No, thanks. I'll have some aquavit.

And so it went through the years, and the Sheldons built up their bar with assorted liquors no one ever drank, especially Groucho.

"But now," Jorja said, "Groucho has mellowed; he's even sweet. When Groucho gave up drinking, I offered him a glass of tomato juice, and I waited . . . for him to ask for orange juice, but it didn't happen. Groucho has mellowed."

Sidney and Jorja once took Groucho to a restaurant they liked, Jack's at the Beach. Sidney told me about their entrance:

"Jack was still alive then, and he was really thrilled to have Groucho there, making a tremendous fuss over him. Jack went on like that, and after a while Groucho said, 'Jack, stop groveling!' "

The Sheldons' collective heart sank; they knew Groucho really meant it. Sidney understood the extent to which Groucho's humor is based on telling the truth. They had visions of never being able to return to the place. But everybody laughed, including Jack. Groucho's voice accompanying an insult was like Picasso's signature on a drawing. Sidney observed, "Even when Groucho *wanted* to insult someone, he couldn't, because no one would take the insult seriously."

At one Sunday brunch, Jorja had spent the morning on a *matzo brie*, an omelet with lox, and toasted bagels. She and daughter Mary, Groucho's goddaughter, carefully arranged the food on lovely china. The silver was shimmering, the linen was crisp, and Groucho had arrived about twenty minutes before. Groucho, Sidney, Marty and Frenchy Allen, Erin, and I were sitting in the living room when Jorja announced triumphantly, "Brunch is served."

Groucho looked up and said, "It's about time."

Dorris Bowdon Johnson, the wife of Nunnally Johnson, a former actress who played in *The Grapes of Wrath*, also learned to accept Groucho without taking exception. Groucho often visited Nunnally, whose friendship went back to when he worked in New York and lived in Great Neck, as did Nunnally. We were at the Johnsons' home when Groucho asked Dorris for some milk, so she brought him a glass of milk. He drank it and asked for another glass of milk. He drank that glass as well. Then, as he was leaving, he turned to Dorris and said, "That's the lousiest milk I ever had."

One afternoon we found Lauren Bacall having tea at the Johnsons'. Groucho invited her to come over to his house.

GROUCHO
Why don't you come over to dinner, Betty?
LAUREN BACALL
Are you entertaining?
GROUCHO
Not very.

Groucho ate dinner only once at director George Cukor's home, but it was a memorable occasion—for George Cukor:

"Olivia de Havilland came from Paris on one of her frequent trips here—she lived in Paris—and I asked her for dinner. She said, 'May I bring someone?' I said, 'Yes, of course, Olivia,' and she said, 'I'd like to bring Groucho Marx.' 'Well,' I said, 'I never knew he was a beau of yours!'

"Then they came, and he was very, very funny and very charming. But during dinner I had a tablecloth that was rather grand on the table, and little unshaded candles in little open holders. We had dinner, and Groucho was very funny throughout. Then we left the dining room, and Groucho remained. He was dazzling some girl, and he was talking and talking, and they remained after the rest of us had left. Then he came and joined us in the other room.

"Theodore, the temporary butler who serves at all these parties, came in a few minutes later, rather pale and shaken. 'There's been a little fire in the dining room.' He said that when Groucho got up, being absolutely gallant, you know, he just tossed his napkin on the table, as we all do. But he didn't reckon that it would catch fire, and it caught fire, and there was nobody in the dining room.

"By the time they came to undo the table, the whole table was blazing. Fortunately there was a very heavy mat under the tablecloth, so that was that. There was no damage except the cloth, which was ruined. Nothing else happened, but if they hadn't come in, it would have taken off. I never used that kind of candleholder again.

"That happened years ago, and I never told Groucho. You said you told him, and he was unmindful that he had committed any arson or anything like that, because it was a very lighthearted evening."

On those rare occasions that Groucho went to a nightclub, he often became the featured attraction. One night out on the town with Elliott

Gould, George Segal, and their wives, Groucho was persuaded to visit a place called The Speakeasy on Sunset Strip.

The place was packed when we arrived, and there didn't seem to be room enough left for "even one more sardine." Groucho suggested, "This is the kind of nightclub you should go to during the day." When the young people there saw who was trying to get in, they were respectfully ecstatic. "Hi, Groucho!" "Look, it's Groucho!" resounded throughout the neo-Twenties atmosphere.

Immediately some people got up from their tables and offered them to Groucho. The crowd of young people parted to form a path through which we could pass. They found room where there was no room. Groucho took it all in stride, smiling and wondering what he was doing there.

"It's like being in a hookshop," he observed.

Groucho used to go to Palm Springs to see Gummo and Zeppo, and occasionally Gummo or Zeppo would drive to Beverly Hills to have dinner with him. Just before Christmas, a year before Gummo's death, Groucho decided that we would go to have dinner with his brothers, a trip involving more than five hours of driving back and forth, but he took that right in stride. As Martha, then his cook, put it, "He doesn't worry about it, he just does it."

Nurse Donna accompanied us. The driver of the limousine Groucho hired turned out to be a young man from England named Leonard, a good start, as far as Groucho was concerned. ("I had a brother named Leonard.") During the trip there, Groucho said that he didn't think he would be happy living in Palm Springs.

"I don't play golf or tennis or swim, so what would I do? I lived in Palm Springs for eleven years, but I didn't know any better. I brought Ben Hecht to Palm Springs once, and he looked around and said, 'There's nothing here but a lot of fat, old, sunburned Jews.' "

The trip to Palm Springs took three hours, and when we arrived, right on schedule, Zeppo, Gummo, and Gummo's wife, Helen, were waiting to meet us. Gummo was still married to his first and only wife, something which Groucho greatly respected. When Gummo started to give our chauffeur some money to go and have his dinner, Groucho insisted that Leonard come with us and join the party.

Zeppo, on seeing me (I'd been to Palm Springs before to visit with Zeppo and Gummo at Tamarisk Country Club), exclaimed to Gummo, "Look, here's the good writer again." But he told me, "I'm all played out. You won't get much from me, honey. I'm tired of all this. That's why I got out."

Although Zeppo was then in his seventies, he looked much younger. He had fair hair, and his voice sounded as it did in the Paramount comedies. He told me that he was always "a very shy person," but I didn't know if I should completely believe him, because he had his hand on my knee at the time.

Zeppo went on to say that he had been "nervous, usually very uneasy" when he had to perform. He said he wasn't as fortunate as Groucho, who he believed never experienced that kind of pressure. "He was always confident. Groucho could get up and tell something that was supposed to be funny and have it fall flat, and he didn't care."

Groucho's superabundant charisma was showing as blatantly in Palm Springs as everywhere else he ventured. Heads turned constantly. The only difference between one setting and another was people's obviousness about staring. Zeppo and Gummo were totally aware of their recogniza ble brother's recognition. Gummo even got a few autographs for friends.

In the chic restaurants you can judge your celebrity status by how noisy and uncomfortable your table is. When your chair is the one every person in the restaurant has to bump into in passing and you can't hear what you are saying, let alone what anyone else is saying, then you know your rank is high.

We were awarded "the best table in the house," a calamity as far as conversation was concerned. We got the table next to the piano. The piano player looked at Groucho, gasped, and was overwhelmed. Groucho was underwhelmed. The piano player proceeded to give his all. Each person at our table could only hear, and that barely, what he himself was saying. The piano player did occasionally go out, and during those brief moments the conversation flourished. It always turned to the old days, to East Ninety-third Street, to Chicago, to Minnie and Frenchie, and to Chico's escapades. They talked about Uncle Julius, after whom Groucho was named, who had lived with them for a while on Ninety-third Street, and about "Opie," their German grandfather, who was incorrigible and encourageable in his flirtations well into his eighties.

In the Ninety-third Street reminiscing, Zeppo was relegated to second-class-citizen status as a much younger brother ("you're too young to remember that"), for though the Marx Brothers of East Ninety-third Street no longer existed for anyone else, for each other they were still little boys and young men: Julius, Milton, and Herbert, the children of Minnie and Sam.

Groucho called his brothers "Zep" and "Gum." Gummo, during the conversation, referred to George S. Kaufman as "only a play doctor," voicing an opinion that could not have been more exactly opposite to Groucho's. Groucho seemed annoyed. Helen looked at Gummo as if to indicate that this was not the first time that subject had been raised.

Zeppo glanced at his watch, as he did frequently, because he knew that somewhere there was a card game being played without him.

Groucho and Zeppo discussed their mutual overweight problems. Groucho was disturbed because he had added two or three pounds. Zeppo was somewhat less disturbed, having gained fifteen pounds. Groucho ordered half a grapefruit for dessert, and Zeppo demolished a *Schwarzwälder Kirschtorte* with whipped cream, down to the last cherry and crumb of chocolate cake.

On the way back to Beverly Hills, I told Groucho that I'd forgotten to take a menu for my collection. He consoled me. "That's all right. Ask Zeppo and Gummo. They'll steal one for you. Then they'll sell it to you." He chuckled. He rarely laughed at anything he said, the exceptions being comments about his own family, which evoked for him unusually rich imagery.

A pivotal person in Groucho's life was the piano player who accompanied him and other guests at his parties. When a party was being planned, no guest was selected with greater consideration and forethought than the piano player, and he or she was often the first guest invited.

For Groucho, a party without a piano player would have been like Lydia without her tattoos, and his standards for piano playing were indeed high. The songs he liked to sing at parties, like "Lydia, the Tattooed Lady," were obscure and stylistically difficult. They required someone who knew Groucho's repertory and had a secure knowledge of many popular music styles, such as classically trained Marvin Hamlisch. Marvin also played at Groucho's special concert appearances at Iowa State University and Carnegie Hall, and he provided the accompaniment for *An Evening with Groucho*, Groucho's successful record album.

While playing for him, Marvin was busily writing music for *The Way We Were* and *The Sting*, films that ultimately won for him three Oscars—on the same night that Groucho won his special Oscar. Then he left Hollywood to do *A Chorus Line*. Although he returned to Groucho's from time to time, Marvin's piano bench was frequently vacant. Arthur

Whitelaw was often called upon to play, which he did with skill and elan.

When composer Boris "Lalo" Schifrin moved into one of Groucho's ex-houses, Groucho went over to check out the new occupants. Lalo was immediately invited to take his turn on the Marx piano stool, accompanying Groucho in such classics as "Peasie Weasie" and "Show Me a Rose." Morgan Ames also dropped by to play "There's a Girl in Maryland with a Watch That Belongs to Me," "Father's Day," or "Stay Down Here Where You Belong."

Sometimes Groucho kept it in the family, in which case Billy Marx was invited to play musical piano benches at Groucho's. He was quite proficient at playing the Groucho repertory, including a parody on "Tiptoe Through the Tulips" called "Slipshod Through the Cowslips." Groucho sang this version, proclaiming, " 'Tiptoe Through the Tulips' is too good for this crummy crowd."

Another familial stand-in (or, rather, sit-in) as piano player was Groucho's grandson, Andy Marx. Andy's maternal grandparents, Gus and Grace Kahn, were composers of, among other songs, "Oh, How That Woman Could Cook!" one of Groucho's standards.

Others who also played piano socially at Groucho's included George Gershwin, Bronislaw Kaper, Oscar Levant, and Goddard Lieberson. George Gershwin was a friend and a great fan of the Marx Brothers, as they were fans of his. "He'd drop by, sit down at my piano, and stay there playing all night," Groucho told me.

In London, actress Luise Rainer talked with me about George Gershwin and his great admiration for the Marx Brothers:

"One of my very first experiences in America was with George Gershwin. My mother was immensely musical but not permitted to become a pianist because it wasn't done. George Gershwin told me that I inspired him. It wasn't an affair; he just felt that he wanted to write some music for me, but he died before he could do it. He told me the *first* thing I had to do in America was to go to see the Marx Brothers in a film. So, he took me to the theatre to see a Marx Brothers film. Everyone in the theatre was laughing the entire time, but I wasn't able to understand all of it. I spoke British English."

One Sunday afternoon, Elliott Gould invited Barbra Streisand to Groucho's house. Elliott wanted his two friends to be friends, and Barbra's feelings had been hurt at an earlier meeting when Groucho got a laugh at her expense. Arriving at a big Hollywood party, Groucho had encountered Barbra, who had arrived a moment before, in the hall near the door. Taking off his coat, he handed it to her and said, "Here, check this, have it cleaned, and see that it's back by Thursday."

Barbra started the visit off on a flat note by disregarding Groucho's penchant for punctuality. Due at 3 P.M., at 3:45 she was nowhere in sight, nor had she called. Groucho sat in his living room and declared, "If she doesn't get here by five o'clock, I'm going home."

He didn't have to make good his word, because a moment later, the entourage appeared. With Barbra and Elliott were Elliott's wife, Jenny, and Barbra's friend, Jon Peters, and Jason, who is Elliott's and Barbra's son, and Sam and Molly, Elliott's and Jenny's children, and Jon Peters' son.

Erin and I were there, as well as nurse Donna, and David Hixon, a young actor who had been doing some odd jobs for Groucho while waiting to be cast for a better part. Barbra wore a semi-sheer blouse and faded jeans. Elliott was attired in a plaid blanket coat worn over blue painter's coveralls and a short-sleeved pink sweater. Barbra was given the seat next to Groucho, and she assumed a dueling position. Groucho, ready to make peace, or pieces, made the first move, a usual one for him: "Kiss me," he said.

Barbra looked a bit taken aback. Unruffled, Groucho said, "Aren't you going to kiss me?" Barbra answered as simply and directly as Groucho himself might answer, "No."

Groucho never got discouraged easily on or off screen. "Jenny will kiss me." Jenny untangled one-and-a-half-year-old Molly, who was wrapped around her legs, and murmured, "Oh, oh! Confrontation!" But détente was maintained when Erin, grudgingly, gave Groucho the kiss.

Groucho decided to honor Barbra's visit by singing a song for her. "There are so many songs about mothers," he told us, "but hardly any about fathers. There's no Whistler's father." Groucho sang "Father's Day" for her. Barbra was visibly moved—toward the front door. "It's funny," she said, "that you want to be recognized as a singer, too, when you're already recognized as a great comedian."

Groucho told Barbra that a long time ago Irving Berlin offered to give him a dollar for every time he did not sing "Stay Down Here Where You Belong." Barbra nodded approvingly, indicating that she thought Irving Berlin had shown pretty good sense and suggesting that the amount could be adjusted upward to allow for inflation.

"I love to sing," Groucho volunteered. "I'm going to sing another song for you." He hesitated momentarily while he pondered his choice. The momentary respite was enough for Barbra, who dove for her purse, luck-lessly failing to come up with a dollar. She found a twenty-dollar bill but apparently wasn't quite ready yet to go that high for the privilege of being spared one of Groucho's musical offerings. She looked to Elliott in her moment of need. Elliott dug deep into his painter's coveralls but came up with only sixty-seven cents, and Groucho was already clearing his throat, menacingly, threatening to burst forth into song. Barbra groped for the twenty-dollar bill. Groucho offered to lend her a dollar.

Then Barbra found enough change to pool her money with Elliott's, and she gave Groucho a dollar in change, which she called "hush money."

"You have real audacity, Groucho, just to insult people and make a ca-reer out of it. It's wonderful when a person finds out what he can do, and does it, and makes a whole career out of it." Groucho accepted the "com-pliment" and asked her if she had seen any of their films. Barbra said she had and that she particularly liked the roller-skating bit, but she didn't re-member the title of the film. (It was *The Big Store*.)

GROUCHO

Harpo was a good roller skater. He was a good roller skater and a lousy harp player. Did you know that Harpo taught himself how to play the harp? My grandmother played the harp in Germany.

BARBRA STREISAND

You were lucky to work with your brothers, to have people to work with all the time with whom you had rapport, and not to have to go out there alone . . .

GROUCHO

Do you want me to sing?

BARBRA STREISAND

Did you know Mae West?

GROUCHO

I knew her before she was famous, in vaudeville, when she just had a piano and three dirty songs. The police were always after her for those dirty songs.

BARBRA STREISAND

She never married, did she?

GROUCHO

She used to live with a middleweight fighter. I saw her when she had the act with the muscle men. I said, "Are you getting any, Mae?" She said, "No, what a waste of manpower!" Do you want me to sing?

BARBRA STREISAND

It's interesting the way people liked your nonsense songs.

GROUCHO

We have more fans now than we did then.

BARBRA STREISAND

Did the people understand and accept the nonsense then?

GROUCHO

Of course.

BARBRA STREISAND

And they seem to like it especially now. There's nothing exactly like it.

GROUCHO

I'm going to sing "Show Me a Rose."

Elliott suggested bringing the party to an end, saying, "I guess I'll be going shortly."

"How can you go shortly when you're six feet six?" Groucho said, adding the aside, "He's tall for his height."

As the group departed Groucho gave Barbra back her dollar.

Playboy West in Holmby Hills is more than just a home or a house. It's a headquarters for *Playboy* in California, and the reflection of its owner, the creator of *Playboy*, Hugh Hefner. Built in 1927, the English Tudor–style mansion is stone with a slate roof and leaded windows. The grounds are elaborately landscaped with exotic and indigenous trees and flowers. There is a tennis court and a very special swimming pool with its own waterfall. A grotto with Jacuzzi baths to which you must swim through a waterfall is reminiscent of the social area beyond the pool in the Chicago Playboy House, which could only be entered by swimming underwater to it. There are exotic birds and animals flitting and roaming about, not to mention rare fish in the pond. Monkeys swing in the trees, flamingos pose, and male peacocks fan their tails to make an impression on the dowdy female peacocks. Parrots sit about, needing no cages, because they have no thoughts about flying away, for surely they couldn't hope to better their lot.

At the gate we were carefully checked. After a phone call to the house, Groucho was authenticated as the genuine "Groucho Marx with one guest," and we passed through up the driveway. At the house, there were the ubiquitous young men to park the cars, and we entered the balconied reception hall, with its impressive hand-carved oak stairway. Sugar Ray

Robinson was standing there admiring the stairway as we entered. He commented to us, "Pretty nifty." Groucho nodded. "Yeah, some joint."

What had brought Groucho and me there was the live closed-circuit relay of the 1974 Foreman-Norton fight. Groucho loved the fights. "I don't usually go with a girl," he informed me. "I'll take that as a compliment," I said. Security was tight, and so was the fit into the screening room. Squeezed in around us were Sugar Ray Robinson, Jack Nicholson, Bill Cosby, Dick Rosenzweig, and Mick Jagger. The audience was almost entirely men, but Bunnies and gatefold girls decorated the periphery. As the fight began, Groucho called out, "I remember when there were white fighters."

Foreman knocked out Norton in the second round. "Foreman had an early date," Groucho said. Then he offered the opinion, "He's better than Dempsey." Groucho was the only one there who had seen Jack Dempsey fight.

The opulent buffet-style dinner was served early. For Groucho only, there was a special done-to-order, salt-free sirloin steak.

Returning from the men's room, Groucho confided to me that it was "all mirrors." I never found out if he was joking. He also mentioned that "a girl with the world's biggest knockers came over and offered me a feel."

During a visit to New York City, in 1974, Groucho, Erin, *New York Times* writer Mel Gussow, and I went to "21" for dinner. Among New York City restaurants, "21" and La Côte Basque remained among the last bastions of jacket and tie tradition. In the history of "21" no one had entered or departed its portals tieless until that fateful night when Groucho darkened its doorstep. (He told me later, "I also darkened their towels.")

When we entered, he was conventionally garbed, but somewhere between the soft-shell crabs and the decaffeinated coffee, Groucho, accustomed to Southern California informality, removed his tie. "I haven't worn a tie in years," he announced. In response to Erin's "Groucho, you can't do that *here*," he rose from our table and walked over to a rather formally attired group at the next table. Showing them his tie in hand, he suggested that they follow suit. Clearly, they would have preferred not to do so, but when it came to risking the loss of their place and face at the revered "21" or saying no to Groucho, the men removed their ties.

He moved on to the next table with the same results, and on to the next, creating no small stir. The captains and maître d' gathered for a conference of war, and the owners, who quickly arrived on the scene, huddled. Meanwhile, Groucho continued making his round of the tables, and ties kept coming off, although not with enthusiasm. To make sure his ends were accomplished, Groucho stayed at each table until every man had removed his tie.

The owners hesitated and finally decided not to pit themselves against a living legend, who was obviously the sentimental favorite and who would certainly become more so if they opposed him. But the owners did not smile as the tieless began to outnumber the tied.

Groucho met his match only once. At the last table he approached two men who were speaking an Arabic language and who failed to understand him. They also didn't seem to recognize him. When Groucho had completed his rounds, the owners, the captains, and the two Arab patrons were the only ones on the second floor of "21" who were wearing ties.

Ice cream and Sanka consumed, we headed for the stairway with Groucho boldly twirling his tie as he passed Pete Kriendler and Jerry Berns. On the stairway, Groucho flaunted the tie with a smug "I've won" look. The maître d' smiled a small smile for what he knew was a small victory.

As Groucho had passed each table on his way out, behind him the men were hastily donning their ties. By the time Groucho had begun his descent, every man in "21" was once again wearing his tie.

The next day the story appeared in all of the newspapers and on radio and television. A few nights later, arriving at the elegant La Côte Basque restaurant, Groucho was greeted warmly but warily at the door by Madame Henriette and Albert. Groucho hesitated for one brief instant, then said:

"Okay. Give me a tie."

There was a round of applause from patrons, and the story appeared in Earl Wilson's column the next day.

Reminiscing with me months later about the "21" incident, Groucho showed no remorse. "I was driving the headwaiter crazy. I think it's silly to wear a necktie. I can eat without a tie. You don't need a tie to eat. They're lucky I didn't take off my pants."

Talking with Jerry Berns, one of the owners of "21," about Groucho's visit, he summed it up for me: "Groucho is a law unto himself. He's a king. He could do no wrong. He's above convention."

During a 1973 visit to New York, Groucho had dinner at Lutèce after the theatre with Goddard Lieberson, Ron and Ellie Delsener, Erin, and me. Just before the theatre, Groucho became very upset when he noticed that his Standing Room Only lighter, his gift from producer Ron Delsener on the occasion of Groucho's "hot ticket" Carnegie Hall concert, was missing. His suite at the Pierre Hotel was searched meticulously but to no avail. Groucho was visibly distraught, a rare occurrence.

There was a small overtone of panic as Groucho, Erin, and I retraced his steps of that day. In Goddard's limousine on the way to the theatre, we continued to search unsuccessfully. Goddard had the chauffeur stop at Sardi's, and we waited while Erin rushed in to look for the lighter. Having checked futilely for it, she returned.

GROUCHO
Did you see the way she looked for the lighter? See how she loves me?
ERIN
You mean how I love the lighter.

Groucho was too distracted to enjoy the play. By the time we met Ron and Ellie at Lutèce, it was all too apparent that Groucho was not himself, though he insisted on going on with dinner. Ron commented later that if he had not known better he would have thought Groucho was "inebriated."

Seated downstairs on the platform at the number one table at Lutèce, Groucho summoned his reserves and carried on. Chef-owner André Soltner greeted Groucho.

GROUCHO
(*Indicating me*) She tells me you're from Alsace. My father came from Strasbourg, so I'm half from Alsace, once removed. It's pretty crowded here tonight. Are they (*Indicating all the filled tables*) all Alsatians?
ANDRÉ SOLTNER
No, but we did have Charles Münch coming here. He always came when he was in New York, and he always started with *tarte à l'oignon*.
GROUCHO
I used to know a tart, but her name wasn't Onion.

Coincidentally, when Henri, the maître d', came over to take our orders, the first thing he offered Groucho was a *tarte à l'oignon:*

GROUCHO
That's a real tearjerker.

HENRI

We have an excellent *soupe de poisson* . . .

GROUCHO

First base, second base, and bouillabaisse. How about some blueprint oysters?

HENRI

Perhaps you would like *poulet en croûte*, Mr. Marx? It's a whole baby chicken in a pastry shell with black truffles.

GROUCHO

All right, but I'll not be truffled with. The truffle, the whole truffle, and nothing but the truffle.

HENRI

Or perhaps the *canard à l'orange*.

GROUCHO

Is that the Duck of Wellington? For dessert do you have any Barbarian Cream Pie in the house?

All through dinner, diners at neighboring tables stole discreet and sometimes indiscreet glances at Groucho. During the entree, Ron Delsener put on his Groucho nose, glasses, and fake mustache and wore this through the rest of dinner, which amused and bemused the usually serious waiters, as well as everyone else. When Groucho got up to go to the men's room, he exited to a round of applause. On his return from the men's room, there was an even grander round of applause, and he was only just spared a standing ovation. He rarely, if ever, had the luxury of doing anything inconspicuously.

Groucho was obviously not feeling well, however, and the next time he said, "I'm going to retire to the can," Goddard went with him. When they came back, Goddard said that Groucho was shaky and had difficulty zipping up his fly, so Goddard assisted him. Just at that moment, two men entered the washroom, took one look at Goddard zipping up Groucho's fly, and turned to rush out. "It's all right," Groucho called after the retreating figures. "We only just met."

Ron Delsener, who wasn't told at dinner about the loss of the lighter, was horrified to learn about its effect on Groucho. "I would have bought him another lighter. I could have bought him a couple of them." But for Groucho only that one SRO lighter was the real one.

The next day, the lighter was found in a drawer at the hotel, overlooked during the panicky search. But the damage had been done. Groucho had suffered another stroke.

Back in California, Groucho and I were having lunch. The pumpernickel bread that I had again brought from New York was prominently placed on the table in front of us. He looked wistfully at it and then at me.

GROUCHO
I don't eat pumpernickel anymore.
I
Is that because you're "too rich to eat bread"?
GROUCHO
(*Nodding*) People wouldn't eat caviar if it were cheap.
I
I would. But why are you giving up pumpernickel?
GROUCHO
When I was a young man and I went into a restaurant, I used to look first at the prices. (*Slicing the bread*) Now I'm an old man, and I look first at how fattening it is. (*Buttering the bread*) But one swallow does not a supper make.

"He never kissed an ugly girl"

Talking with Jack Nicholson about Jack Benny, Groucho said, "He was a nice man and a great comedian. You can't have a better epitaph than that." He added, "I've got a good one for myself. Do you want to know my epitaph?" Without waiting for Jack Nicholson's reply, Groucho proclaimed:

"Here lies Groucho Marx and lies and lies and lies. He never kissed an ugly girl."

Women were extremely important in his life, and he was extremely important in the lives of a number of women. "Man does not control his own fate," Groucho said. "The women in his life do that for him." Summing up his eighty-five years of experience with women, Groucho admitted, "I haven't learned anything." I asked him if he felt women understood him. "Yeah, they do. But I don't."

Groucho came into the world on October 2, 1890, and wasn't at all embarrassed to find himself in bed with a woman. Minnie Marx was the first woman in his life, chronologically speaking, and in importance she has never been surpassed. Groucho affirmed, "Without her, we wouldn't have been anything."

Although Minnie died before the boys became Hollywood stars, she did live to see them become stars on Broadway, and to see their first film shortly before her death in 1929. The review Groucho prized most was the four words his mother said to him after the opening of the film version of *The Cocoanuts*.

"My mother saw *Cocoanuts*, and I said, 'Mom, how was the picture?' And she said, 'They laughed a lot!' "

When Groucho received the Oscar from the Academy of Motion Picture Arts and Sciences in 1974, in his acceptance speech he paid special tribute to his mother. Without Minnie's dedicated managing and constant guidance, the natural talent of her zany sons might well otherwise have been dissipated by their often conflicting pursuits of survival and pleasure.

"My mother came from Germany, my father came from France," Groucho recalled. "When he first met my mother, neither one could understand a word the other was saying, so they got married. And my father learned German. My father wasn't formally educated. Neither was my mother, but she was the stronger."

Groucho's parents were far ahead of their time in role-sharing. Initially, Minnie tried to keep house and to cook, but her heart just wasn't in it. Sam, who had decided to become a tailor since assuming his new role as head of a household, didn't have enough money to rent a shop, so he opened shop in their flat. This meant that Sam was around all day to supplement his wife's halfhearted housekeeping efforts and to do the cooking, which he loved to do as much as she disliked it.

Freed, Minnie applied her talents and energies to launching her younger brother and sons on show business careers. She herself came from a show business family—her mother and father had toured Germany in a wagon, drumming up a show "wherever the peasants outnumbered the pheasants." The feature attraction was Minnie's father, Lafe Schoenberg, who was a magician and a ventriloquist. His wife, Fannie, yodeled and played the harp for dancing. Minnie, who was then Minna, was born in 1864 in Dornum, Germany, where the family recuperated between tours. Life in Dornum was no bowl of cherries. "It wasn't even a barrel of pickles," Groucho said. The family members took those odd jobs for which strolling players could qualify while repairing and preparing for their next arduous tour. It was a hard life even for the hardy. Minnie had some vivid recollections of this precarious existence, but after the success of her younger brother, Al Shean, she recognized the opportunities offered by show business in the New World. As she told her sons, "Where else can people who don't know anything make so much money?"

Minnie came to America in 1880, when she was fifteen years old. Since the demand for German-speaking ventriloquists and yodelers was limited in New York City, she and her brothers and sisters became the family breadwinners, although as Groucho observed, it was "pretty crummy breadwinning." While working as a submenial in a straw-hat factory, Minnie met Sam Marx, a dapper young Alsatian who taught dancing in a Lower East Side dancing school. Sam (then Simon) had arrived from Alsace-Lorraine in 1878 at the age of seventeen, and in a very short time firmly established himself as an impecunious immigrant. Naturally, they got together or, as Groucho put it, "They got together naturally."

There is some disagreement about where Sam and Minnie actually met. Groucho claimed that his mother and father met in the dancing school, while Groucho's son, Arthur, heard the story that they met on a Sunday ferryboat excursion. To this Groucho responded, "There are no ferries in the Marx family." Whichever account is true, they did meet in 1882 and were married in 1884, when Sam was twenty-three and Minnie nineteen. Although it didn't turn out to be the conventional idyll, this marriage seemed truly to have been made in heaven.

Minnie's constant companion on East Ninety-third Street was her sister, Hannah Schickler, who for a time appeared in the act with the boys. Her picture, a gift from Zeppo, hung in Groucho's dining room. It showed her with Zeppo, whose golden curls rivaled the later ones of Shirley Temple. Groucho remembered his aunt with affection:

"When my Aunt Hannah wanted to smoke a cigarette, she had to go to the toilet. Now women smoke pipes and cigars. And marijuana."

"The two sisters were inseparable," East Ninety-third Street neighbor Ethel Wise recalled.

"They were so lovely. They always wore big hats, and they were poor, but they always looked so attractive in those hats and pretty dresses. Minnie Marx was a fascinating woman—good-looking and always jolly. That woman was really something. Those boys owed everything to Minnie Marx. Except Groucho. He would have made it on his own.

"I can remember when Mrs. Marx learned that she was going to have another baby. They didn't know I was there, but I heard her talking with my mother. They didn't have much money. She said, 'What am I going to do?' And my mother said, 'You'll have another baby.' And she did. That was Herbert [Zeppo]."

Of all her children, Harpo perhaps most resembled her, especially with his curly blond wig. "My mother had blond hair like Harpo and like you," Groucho told me. Above all, Minnie Marx was a strong woman who, once having set a goal, never wavered in her march toward it. In this respect, Groucho was much like her. When I asked him what he thought his mother's feelings on women's lib would have been, he answered without hesitation, "My mother would have been *for* women's lib," adding reverently, "She was a great woman." (He always considered the use of the word "woman" a much greater compliment than "lady.")

Fortunately for her boys, Minnie set as her goal their success in show business. To achieve this, she not only drove herself hard, but she drove her sons hard. Morrie Ryskind reminisced about Minnie with Groucho and me:

"I'll never forget the time she came up and smacked Chico. We were in Philadelphia, and I'm not sure which show it was—I think it was *Animal Crackers*—and if you knew Chico like I knew Chico! He was fooling around and coming in late and missing cues and everything else, but they loved the show, thank God.

"When the curtain came down, we were backstage. Minnie Marx came out and smacked Chico right across the jaw, right there in front of everybody. She said, 'How dare you give a performance like that! Those people out there paid for that. You have no right to do this!' Boy, she bawled the hell out of him that night. She had a determination!"

Harpo had described Minnie as having "the stamina of a brewery horse, the drive of a salmon fighting his way up a waterfall, the cunning of a fox, and a devotion to her brood as fierce as any she-lion's."

In Palm Springs, Gummo told me about his mother's determination:

"My mother and I were driving in from La Grange, Illinois, to Chicago—we had a farm in La Grange during the First World War—and my mother spoke to me. She said, 'Gummo, I must talk to you. There are five Marx Brothers, but Zeppo is too young to be drafted, and Chico is married. If Groucho or Harpo had to go into the service, it would break up the act.' I said, 'What do you suggest?' She said, 'I want to go to the draft board, and if you are willing to go into the service, I can get the others out,' which she could do, because she was very strong. I said I'd be glad to go into the service. So she went to the draft board, and they agreed that if one of the five went in the service that would be sufficient. So I went. But I never told the other boys—not to this day—what my mother said to me driving into Chicago, that I was expendable. And I was!"

To this Zeppo added:

"Honey, let me tell you, her whole life was wrapped up in us. Most of what she did was before I joined the act. When Gummo had to go into the Army, she called me and said, 'Go to Rockford!' It was exciting at the time. I had to learn the straight man's part and to dance.

"My mother was a very kind woman, a very good person. She'd take anybody in and did . . .

"You want to know about my mother, honey? Well, one night a robber came into the house and went into my mother and father's bedroom and took all the money out of my father's pants. My mother woke up, but the robber said, 'Shhhh!' and she didn't say anything. After the robber was gone, she woke up my father and said, 'Sam, you've been robbed. He took the money right out of your pants.' At first he didn't believe it, but it was true."

I asked Zeppo if his mother was afraid the robber might injure his father, or was she so kind she didn't want the robber to be caught. Zeppo answered me with a cryptic "No" and wouldn't elaborate further. I asked Groucho to explain Zeppo's relatively unclear answer. He unexplained:

"It was because she didn't want my father to get caught."

On the night that Groucho received his Oscar, he told me:

"My mother was a great woman. She collected us, got us together. She gathered us together like you gather flowers. Can you imagine with all her struggles, she finally saw us become stars? Without her we would have been nothing."

Getting the Marx Brothers together was no easy task. The boys were as madcap in real life as they were onstage and in films, but the family shared a rare *esprit de corps* that held them together through thick and thicker. "We were the only act that never argued among themselves," Groucho said proudly. But they weren't always as sure as Minnie was that their destiny lay in the theatre.

Hattie Darling, who starred with the Marx Brothers in *On the Mezzanine Floor* (later shortened to *On the Mezzanine*) in 1921, recalled that the boys didn't call their mother "Mother," but "Minnie." They treated her as if she were one of the boys herself—at times even as if she were one of the pretty young chorus girls. "Mrs. Marx loved that. But they all had a lot of respect for their mother."

Widow and collaborator of songwriter Gus Kahn, Grace Kahn, who was for a time related to Groucho through the marriage of his son and her daughter, told me about the Minnie she remembered:

"Minnie was determined that those boys were going to be a hit, and she made them a hit. She was, I suppose, what you would call an agent. Not only the agent, but she was the boss of everything. It's funny how well I remember her, because I didn't know her very well."

Whatever was needed to further the boys' careers in show business Minnie provided or found somebody else who could. Occasionally, she even took part in the act herself, until she and Hannah accidentally sat

down on the same frail stage chair during a performance of the Six Mascots act in Atlantic City. This got a lot of laughs and Minnie briefly considered making their fall a permanent part of the act.

Minnie, who was short and loved to eat Sam's culinary *chefs d'oeuvre*,
eventually resorted to a whalebone corset to turn the clock back to the
days of her hourglass figure. She felt that she had to look as youthful as
possible in order to convert an intractable male broker's or theatre owner's
"No" into a "Yes."

"She used to book us herself," Groucho told me. "She thought she
ought to look young, so she wore a corset and a blond wig when she went
to see agents. She was probably around fifty then, and everybody knew it
was a wig."

Since the corset was uncomfortable, whenever Minnie stopped feeling
the necessity of wearing it, "she would take it off—wherever she was."
Groucho remembered this happening at friends' houses where Sam and
Minnie had gone to play cards:

"My mother used to be crazy about playing poker. They played what
they called two-cent poker. And she wore a corset. My father used to put
his foot up on the rear end of my mother, and tighten the squeeze of the
corset. Then when she got to the place where they were playing cards,
she'd get tired of wearing the corset and wrap it up in a newspaper with
the strings always hanging out."

Minnie led her boys through years of tortuous one-night stands in
small-time vaudeville before *Home Again* brought them to the attention
of the major circuits. Sensing that they needed a more ambitious theatrical vehicle to impress the booking agents, Minnie asked her younger
brother, Al Shean, to write them an extended comic skit that would uti-
lize some grandiose staging effects she had in mind, as well as salvaging
some of the scenery they had left over from a fiasco called *The Cinderella
Girl.* The set Groucho remembered best was a flimsy steamship cutout
that rolled away on wobbly wheels from a shaky pier. Whenever the
wheels jammed, which was often, Harpo had to tow the ship out of the
harbor in full view of the audience.

Home Again was the turning point in the collective careers of the Marx
Brothers, and Minnie's role as their manager and agent became less demanding. When the Marx Brothers made the big time, Minnie and Sam
moved into a comfortable house in Great Neck where they were driven
everywhere by an elaborately liveried chauffeur. Sam adjusted better to
the limousine life than Minnie, who was still stagestruck and so full of her

old energy that, far from accepting her backseat, she tried to promote a theatrical career for the chauffeur! In 1929 Minnie died of a heart attack after a family party at which she played pinochle and Ping-Pong for several hours. Her obituary was carried in Alexander Woollcott's column.

Although Groucho knew many women in his long lifetime, none ever took her place. Indeed, he and his brothers always talked about her almost as if she were still alive, still an important part of their lives. Her German-bisque-doll countenance looked at Groucho every day from the omnipresent photographs of her on the walls of his front hall and bedroom.

As a tribute to her, all of the daughters of the Marx Brothers were given names beginning with M for Minnie. Groucho's oldest daughter is Miriam, and his youngest daughter, Melinda. Harpo's adopted daughter is Minnie, and Chico's daughter, Maxine.

One of Groucho's earliest recollections of his awareness of the opposite sex was an experience with an aunt who had "red hair, high heels, and had been to Chicago, St. Louis, and once had even spent the night in Denver." She was glamorous and exciting, with a scent more provocative than that of the kerosene stove which usually pervaded the atmosphere of their home. Groucho said later that he recognized it as "the standard odor of a bordello."

He was totally devastated as she bestowed her admiring smile upon him and spoke the magic words to Minnie: "Julius has the loveliest big brown eyes I've ever seen." He felt transported to ecstasy. For one who had never before received a feminine accolade from anyone but his mother, Groucho's appetite grew with the eating, and he hungered for more attention. Suddenly he was overwhelmingly conscious of his eyes, which he had never before realized were so beautiful. He paraded incessantly before his aunt, lifting his eyebrows as high as they would go, but her fickle attentions wandered, and the glory was fleeting. Even exhausting efforts at feigned consumptive coughing proved to be of no avail. Finally he gave up.

Much later, a certain retrospective examination in a mirror revealed to Groucho that "my eyes are gray."

"When I was thirteen," Groucho told me, "I thought I loved a girl who was rich. She was eleven. Her name was Rosie, so I sent her a rose every day. Her family took her for a trip to Europe and when she came back, she didn't look at me. Some romance."

Groucho had his first meaningful encounter with the fair sex with precociously beautiful Annie Berger. He has told the story many times, but at Marvin Hamlisch's request he retold it to Mike Nichols and me:

MARVIN HAMLISCH

Would you please tell me that story again about Annie Berger? I love that story.

GROUCHO

When I was fifteen years old, I lived in the same apartment house with Annie Berger. And she lived a floor above us. And I used to watch when she came home from school, and I would sit on the stairs and look up her clothes. I was crazy about her.

MARVIN HAMLISCH

So romantic!

GROUCHO

I loved to look at her legs. She had a great pair of legs. And she had two of them. It was very seldom you could see a girl with two legs. So anyhow, I used to buy bread for my mother, and fresh bread was a nickel a loaf. I used to buy one-day-old bread which was four cents. So I saved seventy cents and I called Annie Berger and I said, "I want to take you to the theatre."

It was twenty-five cents each for the theatre tickets. That's fifty cents. And ten cents carfare each way. So as we were going into the theatre, she sees this guy selling taffy, and she says, "Gee, I'd love to have some of this taffy." I only had ten cents left. That was the fare home. I bought her the taffy, and now I only had a nickel. And she ate the candy and didn't offer me any. So when we left the theater, I said, "Look. You had the candy and you didn't give me any of it. And I want to be fair with you. I'll match you to see who walks home from Forty-second Street." That was from Hammerstein's Victoria to Ninety-third Street. And she had to walk home.

MIKE NICHOLS

Was she a good sport?

GROUCHO

I don't know. I left her standing in the snow. It was a winter's day.

Sometime later, at his house. Marvin recalled the Annie Berger story: " 'And she didn't even offer me any taffy,' it's a killer line! Here she is, up there in the second balcony watching this thing, and they're gonna be walking home in the snow, and the thing that's bothering him all the time is she never shared the taffy."

But Groucho's romance with Annie Berger didn't end at Hammerstein's Victoria. He continued the story for Marvin, Mike, and me: "I met Annie Berger ten years later when I was playing the Palace Theatre. A pretty girl in a box waved to me. She was a chorus girl then at the Winter Garden, and she had gotten over walking home. We had two wonderful weeks together . . . in her apartment." Groucho sighed.

"Then, when I did the Merv Griffin show I told the story about Annie Berger, and her older sister saw me on the show, and she called me up and said, 'I'm Annie Berger's sister.' And we had her over here."

Ethel Berger Wise told me about the dinner at Groucho's:

"I called him and he invited me to have dinner at his house. We hadn't met in seventy years, and he was old the way I am. But he was still lively and telling jokes and making quips. It was one of the most memorable nights of my life. Sidney Sheldon, the nice writer, was there. Groucho was like he was as a boy, always saying funny things.

"Groucho and my sister were in love. It was only puppy love. He was about fourteen, and she was about twelve. She was already a *very* beautiful girl, but he was going to be an actor, and we all thought that was very shocking. We all knew, or thought we did, the way actors lived. We looked down on them because they were actors, but Annie thought she wanted that life too.

"I remember when Groucho opened at the Star Theatre in New York on Lexington Avenue. Is it still there? We all went to see him, my whole family, and everybody in the neighborhood. It was advertised in all the groceries in the neighborhood, and in return for the advertising, the stores each got some free tickets. That was how we went. Everyone turned out to see Julie become a star.

"We went out to California then, and Julie and his family went to Chicago for years, and it was a long time before Groucho and Annie saw each other again. Annie loved good times and the theatre. She loved to go out. I know that Annie saw him in New York, and my sister was very intimate with Groucho. I looked down on them because they fooled around. I was a serious girl."

Ethel Wise revealed the denouement of the Annie Berger story:

"Annie loved to play poker, and Minnie Marx loved to play poker. When the Marx family moved out to California, Annie and Minnie used to play poker together along with some other women. They would talk about Julie and what might have been. Annie told Minnie, 'You look back and you wonder why do you do things.' I think that Annie regretted that it didn't go on with Julie, and maybe that they didn't get married.

"Annie was married twice. She went onstage, not the Follies, but the other one. She met a stage door Johnny, an Englishman. He waited for her at the door, and she went out with him, and married him.

"Annie was *so* beautiful, and she was very conscious of beauty. One day we were walking along Beverly Drive and saw Groucho coming toward us. Annie turned her head away, and started talking to me, and rushed across the street. I said, 'Look, that's Julie. Don't you want to see him?' But she didn't. She was still very good-looking, but she was middle-aged, and she wasn't beautiful the way she'd been as a girl. She didn't want him to see her that way.

"I thought that it was foolish, because I said to her, 'Think of the fun you and Julie could have had talking about old times.' But she didn't see it that way at all. People think different ways. Annie died a few years ago. We were very close. We lived together for the last fifteen years."

Groucho's early life was far from a succession of romantic triumphs.

"The whole first part of my life was spent sleeping with colored girls. They were chambermaids in the hotels we used to stay in. In those days, all hotels had black chambermaids. You'd give her a couple of bucks and take her in your room and lay her. That was very common. They were no different from a white girl. No, that's not true; some of 'em were even better. We couldn't get a white girl when we were in small-time vaudeville. They were afraid of actors. A lot of girls had been raped by actors. So we took what we could get, which was black chambermaids. But I remember doing a big act once with W. C. Fields, and we had twenty girls in the show. They were all white and they were all friendly. I knew them by number rather than by name. There was really some humping."

He got more than he bargained for, as he revealed in a conversation with Erin and me:

ERIN
What was your first physical relationship with a woman?
GROUCHO
To go to bed, of course.
ERIN
No, I mean who was the girl?

GROUCHO
Geez . . . I can't remember. It's been almost a thousand years.
ERIN
Where did you lose your virginity?
GROUCHO
In a hookshop in Montreal. I was sixteen years old—I didn't know any-thing about girls. And before I left town I had gonorrhea.

Talking with Groucho, Jack Nicholson happened to mention that he was from New Jersey. This stirred an old memory for Groucho:

GROUCHO
Where are you from in New Jersey?
JACK NICHOLSON
Around Asbury.
GROUCHO
Asbury Park? Gee, I'll never forget, I was fifteen years old and I kissed a girl, and she put her tongue in my mouth.
JACK NICHOLSON
In Asbury?
GROUCHO
In Asbury Park.
JACK NICHOLSON
Aw, they'll do anything there.
GROUCHO
I was so excited I couldn't sleep for a week after that.

As Groucho's show business career accelerated, his sex life also picked up.
"I didn't have girls when we first started traveling in small-time vaude-ville. We really weren't in towns long enough to meet anybody. We'd go to hookshops. We were the floor show. Harpo and Chico played the piano and I sang. The girls used to come to watch us at the theatre—the madam and the girls—and if they liked us, they'd send a note backstage. 'If you're not doing anything tonight after the show, why don't you come over and see us?' Sometimes we stayed all night. We were always after girls. We'd get into a town, and there was a hotel, and they had a piano on the mez-zanine floor. Chico would start playing and there would be twenty dames there. Chico would pick out girls for us, too."
In those days actors weren't considered fit companions for "nice" girls,

so the Marx Brothers took whatever girls were available. Groucho told me what happened when Gummo met a "nice" girl in New Orleans:

"Her father came up to him after the show and said, 'You took my daughter out tonight. If you take her out again, you'll go back to New York in a box.' Actors weren't very popular in those days. Except in hookshops. There was no place for an actor to go in most towns, except if you were lucky maybe you'd pick up a girl. But as a rule, you'd have to go to a hookshop."

When Groucho was in New York, we were approaching the Flatiron Building and he had the limousine slow down. "There's the Flatiron Building," he said pensively. "That's a nice building. The Marx Brothers used to stand on that corner and watch the girls go by. But then," he added, "we used to stand on a lot of corners and watch the girls go by.

"When I was young, I was crazy about girls. Especially if they wore silk stockings. In those days they had rumble seats in cars. Some philosopher said, 'You can tell more about a girl watching her climb into a rumble seat than you can being married to her twenty years.' "

Groucho reached the two-decade mark in marriage only with his first wife, Ruth. The next two wives came along years after the demise of the rumble seat, and neither marriage lasted that long; but even if there had been rumble seats when he married Kay and Eden, he felt "I still would have been as much in the dark after twenty years as I was on the first date." He often said that women baffled him.

"I don't understand women. They're a different breed entirely than the male. There are a lot of things I don't understand about women, like why do girls always stand with one hand on their hip? Men don't do that. But I think a woman can be a wonderful companion. After all, my mother was one. I didn't find that out until a couple of years ago."

Although he may not have understood women, this never stopped women from liking him. Hattie Darling remembered him in those days as "a very sweet man":

"Groucho has a lot of humanity in him, and he has a lot of charm. He always had a lot of charm, and he was very good-looking, even though he had that mustache. I think Groucho was the better-looking of all the brothers, even Zeppo. Zeppo, of course, was so young, but he didn't have the character in his face like Groucho had. Groucho had something in his face that was strong. That's what I thought he was. I've always had a warm spot for Groucho, more than anyone in the act."

Groucho himself was aware of the special appeal he had for a number of women:

"Girls liked me. I don't mean like Clark Gable or Valentino, but when I was younger, women found me attractive. They found me funny. Certain kinds of women like a funny man."

George Jessel talked with me about the sex appeal of the comedian in general and Groucho and the Marx Brothers in particular:

"To be really big, you've got to have a staying quality, and a part of that staying quality is sex. This isn't saying that women in the audience will get up and say, 'Groucho, I want to go to bed with you.' But the Marx Brothers had a feeling of sex."

Charlotte and Bert Granet, longtime friends of Groucho, discussed his sex appeal as a man and as a performer:

CHARLOTTE GRANET
Groucho was always attractive to me as a man.

BERT GRANET
I hadn't realized that. Do you think it was the man or the image created by the writers and the fame?

CHARLOTTE GRANET
The man. Well, I guess it couldn't be separated.

I asked Groucho about his "reputation" with women:

I
You once said that you had quite a reputation for lechery. Do you feel that you've earned this reputation?

GROUCHO
Not anymore. But certainly fifteen years ago, maybe a little longer.

I
How did you earn it?

GROUCHO
I tried to get women into my bed.

I
How did you do that?

GROUCHO
Charm. Witty, fascinating talker. I'm seething with charm.

I
What was your batting average?

GROUCHO
With the dames? About fifty-fifty.

I

That's a .500 batting average!

The fifteen years ago he was talking about were his late sixties. On another occasion, however, when he was talking with interior decorator Peter Shore, Groucho was not so optimistic:

PETER SHORE
I'm designing a house for a fifty-year-old bachelor whose whole image is a swingin' bachelor. Very *macho.*
GROUCHO
It's not so easy to swing when you're over fifty.
PETER SHORE
Oh, you can put on a good show.
GROUCHO
It's better to swing when you're twenty-five.

Chico's incredible prowess with women was often mentioned by Groucho. George Jessel told me, "Chico didn't button his fly until he was over seventy." Without envy, Groucho pondered the Chico mystique—something he was never able to explain:

GROUCHO
The girls were crazy about him. I never saw a man who could attract as many girls as he could. We all had girls, but Chico was the one who really had something for the girls.
I
What do you think was the secret of Chico's great charm for women?
GROUCHO
A certain look in his eyes. I never quite knew what it was. The secret died with him. Only a woman who knew him could tell you. But he had enough to go around. He used to get girls for all of us. He was a great ladies' man and crazy about women. But he had no respect for women at all. Chico said that in California the flowers don't smell but the women do.
I
You couldn't say Chico was a romantic.
GROUCHO
No. He was a practical lover. He'd lay them and leave them, but they were crazy about him. He had charm.

I
And men liked him too.

GROUCHO
Yes, everybody liked him, except the people he owed money to.

"I was the only girl in the act Chico didn't make," Hattie Darling told me. "I was a nice little Jewish girl. Someone always traveled with me."

Bobbe Brox, who appeared with her sisters in the stage version of *The Cocoanuts*, confirmed Hattie Darling's appraisal of Chico and added:

"Chico was the kind of man that would chase us into the dressing rooms. He didn't have the class that Groucho has. Harpo I didn't know too well. Because Harpo generally in the show would pick one girl, and that would be it, you know, for the run of the show. I don't remember him bothering anybody.

"The one we knew the best and loved was Groucho. The other boys we were not close to. But we were very friendly with Groucho, because he wanted to sing harmony all the time. He loved being with us and singing with us. The friendship continued long after, out here in California, when we all lived here."

Maureen O'Sullivan, who worked with the Marx Brothers in *A Day at the Races*, was more impressed by Groucho than by Chico:

MAUREEN O'SULLIVAN
I was very fond of Chico. He was a very quiet, serious person.

I
Groucho always thinks of Chico as having had an extraordinary appeal for women, and he suggested I ask women who knew him what it was.

MAUREEN O'SULLIVAN
Groucho was the one I noticed. He was much easier to know.

Groucho took his marital vows seriously, according to Hattie Darling, who described him as being "very much in love" with his young wife, Ruth. But Groucho didn't deny that before his marriage he too had sown a few wild oats in his heyday:

GROUCHO
Once at the Adolphus Hotel in Dallas I did it eight times in one night. I was nineteen.

I
If you could, would you trade all of the awards and rewards of being

Groucho Marx—the Oscar, the Legion of Honor, the thousands of letters—to be a virile young man again?

GROUCHO
They could give me the awards next year.

Even though Groucho always found the romantic vision of lasting marriage illusory and elusive for himself, he still believed it was possible.

I
Do you think that there is such a thing as ideal marriage, a really good marriage?

GROUCHO
Gummo is an example. Harpo didn't need a divorce. It's only suckers like me. If two people really love each other, they don't cheat. My grandmother and grandfather celebrated their golden wedding. It's true. But when he was more than eighty years old, we had a colored maid in the kitchen, and we couldn't keep him away from her.

Although Groucho didn't believe that the male is naturally a monogamous creature, he was uncertain about the female. He and Erin discussed the double standard.

ERIN
You say that man is not a monogamous creature, and it's natural for a man to look at other women and be interested in other women. Do you think it's natural for a woman to be interested in other men? What do you think about women having affairs while they are married?

GROUCHO
Having an *affair* with another guy? It's not gonna be much of a marriage.

ERIN
But you think it's all right for a man?

GROUCHO
A man is the chaser of the two. It's nature. The woman is subconsciously the chaser, but the man is—a man is a man. And if there's an attractive girl, he'll make a play for her. I think that's wonderful.

ERIN
Even if he's married?

GROUCHO
Well, not if he's going to be a jerk about it. Let's say he's been married for twenty years. How exciting do you think that woman is to him?

ERIN

But you don't think it's a good marriage if she cheats on him?

GROUCHO

I don't think it comes out that way. I think the average woman, if she has a man, and she's married to him, and she likes him, I don't think she'll necessarily cheat.

ERIN

But if they did?

GROUCHO

They get a divorce, and the man pays alimony.

ERIN

Why couldn't they keep the relationship going and have extramarital affairs as well? Both of them, not only the man.

GROUCHO

Then they shouldn't get married.

ERIN

Why not?

GROUCHO

If they're both cheating, why should they get married?

ERIN

Why not, if they like each other?

GROUCHO

How can he like her if he's after another dame, and she's after another fellow?

ERIN

You don't think women are naturally promiscuous?

GROUCHO

Not like men, no.

ERIN

Women just don't tell.

GROUCHO

(*Annoyed*) That's a subject I'm not an expert on. If she's after another fellow, that's a hell of a marriage. That's why I believe it would be much better for two people to live together, and not get married.

ERIN

So you believe in trial marriage?

GROUCHO

It's better than trial parenthood.

Because Groucho lived so long and never closed his mind to new ideas, sometimes he expressed personal views that appeared to be incompatible—because they were. At first glance, the foregoing exchange may seem that way, but it was logical for Groucho because he was a paradox. Always on the prowl for the not so elusive female, the reputed chaser was in reality a staunch believer in the sanctity of marriage. Groucho was married a total of forty-seven years—albeit to three women. We talked about his youthful ideas of courtship and marriage:

GROUCHO
When I was young, I read all those stories about Horatio Alger, about how he married a rich man's daughter.

I
How did they influence you?

GROUCHO
The boys in those stories were so honest and courageous. The story would be about a rich man's daughter who was driving in a carriage with two horses, and the horses ran away, and the young boy grabbed ahold of the horses and stopped them. Later he married the rich man's daughter. These were stories about work and win. (*Laughs*)

I
It worked for you.

GROUCHO
It certainly did. I married three women, and between them they didn't have two cents.

Ruth Johnson, Groucho's first wife and mother of two of his three children, was born in 1901, the daughter of Swedish immigrants. Her father was a sea captain. She joined the *Home Again* company as Zeppo's adagio dance partner in 1919 when his regular partner quit in the middle of a tour. Gummo told me how Ruth came into Groucho's life:

"Zeppo's partner in the act quit. Groucho called me and said that I could find the new girl over at Doyle's Billiard Parlor, on Fiftieth Street and Broadway. Her father, who was a Swede, was there all the time. Groucho said, 'See if you can get her and teach her the dance so that she could come out to the act and know the dance in advance.' So I hired a rehearsal hall, and I got hold of this girl through her father, and I taught her the dance, step for step, that I did before and that Zeppo did after I left. Well, eventually Groucho married this girl. She was his first wife. She couldn't dance too well, and neither could I. But, after all, dancing was only a minor part of the act. It was the comedy that counted."

Once again Zeppo lost a dancing partner—and this time gained a sister-in-law. After courting Ruth for a year while on tour, Groucho married her in 1920, when the company passed through Chicago. "I spent my honeymoon in an upper berth going through Iowa," Groucho remembered. "Ruth was up there with me." Groucho was thirty and Ruth nineteen. The next year their first child, Arthur, was born—the same year that Kay, who was to be Groucho's second wife, was born. Groucho's third wife, Eden, would not be born until 1934, seven years after the birth of his second child, Miriam.

Grace Kahn, who knew Groucho for over half a century and was related to him through the marriage and divorce of her daughter and his son, remembered Ruth as "a beautiful, beautiful girl, and a nice one. She was a very sweet person and, I would say, a negative person, in that she sort of lived in Groucho's shadow. I first met Ruth in Grand Rapids when she was part of the show, before she and Groucho were married."

Morrie Ryskind's wife, Mary, described Ruth in the same way:

"I thought she was a very dear, loving, sweet person. But she never grew up with Groucho. She was a thoroughly nice person, but she never had any of the kind of interests that he had."

Bobbe Brox remained a good friend of the Marxes' years after she and her sisters appeared in *The Cocoanuts*. She talked with me about the Ruth and Groucho she knew:

"Ruth was, you know, the frustrated dancer. She always wanted to be the dancer. That was her problem. One time my husband, William Perlberg, and I went to Honolulu with Groucho and Ruth, and they were such fun. So, she got the teacher right away to learn the hula, and it was dead serious with Groucho. He's lying on the bed with the guitar, playing this crazy Hawaiian music, and Ruth trying to wiggle around the room with a Hawaiian teacher. Groucho was so amusing, because the ad libs were terrific while this is all going on."

Groucho talked with Erin and me about his first marriage and his first divorce:

GROUCHO
I got rid of my first wife with Gilbert and Sullivan.
ERIN
With Gilbert and Sullivan?
GROUCHO
Yeah. She didn't quite understand it, and I kept playing it.

ERIN
It drove her crazy.

GROUCHO
No, it didn't drive her crazy, but she wasn't very happy to have to listen to Gilbert and Sullivan because she wasn't educated. Until I married her, I don't think she'd ever heard of Gilbert and Sullivan.

The marriage lasted until 1942, when, after twenty-one years, they were divorced. Like all three of his wives, Ruth left him. Groucho lived in the present and didn't talk much about his former wives. On occasion, however, he did speak about Ruth, with sadness:

"I was working very hard, and I was single. And I had a wife who was drinking. We were married twenty-one years. She was so beautiful when I married her. She weighed 109 then. The last time I saw her she'd gained so much weight I could hardly recognize her."

In 1944, Norman Krasna's hit play *Dear Ruth* was produced on Broadway. He told me that the model for the family in *Dear Ruth* was the Marx family, to which he was very close. The judge was based on Groucho, and the title character was based on "beautiful, vivacious" Ruth Johnson Marx.

After the divorce, Groucho saw Ruth occasionally. Ruth had become a friend of daughter-in-law Irene, and remained so even after Irene and Arthur were divorced. The last time Groucho saw Ruth was briefly in 1961 at Chico's funeral. Ruth died eleven years later, never having remarried. At the time of her death, Groucho not only had divorced his third wife, but had met Erin Fleming.

Groucho married his second wife, Kay, in 1945. The ex-wife of erstwhile dead-end kid Leo Gorcey, she was twenty-four, and Groucho was fifty-five. In spite of Groucho's assertion that after fifty-five a man's sex life becomes drastically curtailed, Melinda was born in 1946, when Groucho was fifty-six. This marriage lasted only until 1951. Again he had chosen a pretty face that couldn't keep pace. In the evening when Groucho would retreat to his literary pursuits, Kay read the dictionary in an effort to keep up with Groucho and the people who populated his world. Kay loved to sing and dance, and during World War II entertained with Groucho at bond rallies.

Besides Melinda and support payments, Groucho retained a frequently used coffeepot that Kay had "borrowed" from the Dorset Hotel to remind him of her. We would have coffee together (in his pre-coffee substitute days), and he would read from the pot, " 'Hotel Dorset, 30 W. 54th Street,

New York City' — that was more than twenty-five years ago." Groucho and Kay continued to speak on the phone.

Mary Ryskind remembered Kay as ". . . sweet and dear. She was a very friendly girl. I think Kay was someone he was sorry for. Gummo's wife, Helen, was just wonderful to her. She beat Kay over the head and said, 'Look! Go out and get some clothes! Groucho can afford it!' But Kay didn't care. Groucho was just as dear with her as he could be, but it was just one of those things you couldn't do much about."

In 1954, at the height of the popularity of *You Bet Your Life*, Groucho married Eden Hartford.

"You said Eden looked just like Ava Gardner," Erin reminded Groucho. "Don't you remember telling me how much you liked Ava Gardner? You told me you met Ava Gardner at Nunnally's house in London. She peeled off her long white gloves, and you said, 'Wowee!' I think Eden also looked like Bianca Jagger."

Groucho was given to summarizing a person in one simple sentence. About Eden, he would always say, "She was a beautiful girl." The line so regularly followed his mention of her that it seemed like her last name.

Like Ruth thirty-six years earlier, Eden was nineteen, but Groucho was nearing an age when many men retire. His first gift to Eden was a round bathtub like the one she had admired at Zeppo's house in Palm Springs — in fact, he built her a house around her round bathtub. Groucho continued to live in the house, but Eden moved out in 1969, leaving behind her round bathtub, and Groucho. The round bathtub lasted until some years later, when Erin had the room redecorated.

For a while after she left him, Eden still traveled with Groucho when he made trips to New York or Europe. Never one to be out of touch with modern trends, Groucho admitted on the Dick Cavett Show that being with Eden under these circumstances was even better than being married. Groucho was willing to try trial divorce, not believing divorce is something that necessarily lasts forever. One evening after their divorce, Groucho brought Eden over to Bert Granet's house for a dinner party, explaining, "I wanted to be near my money." Groucho could never be accused of being overly sentimental in public.

Of his last marriage Groucho said, "I'm sorry it broke up. I guess it was partly my fault. I did everything I could. I even stopped smoking. I like her, and she likes me. She sent me a bathrobe last year for Christmas."

Just before Christmas of 1974, Eden dropped by for dinner at Groucho's. Goddard Lieberson also came to dinner, and I was there, staying as a guest at Groucho's house during a visit to California. Eden brought him her Christmas gift—a sweater that didn't fit. He was all dressed down for the occasion. He wore his bathrobe, "my dressing gown without gravy," and a big black bow tie to make the outfit "formal." Eden reminisced about happy times in their marriage, especially in London.

She also told about being taken, along with sister Dee Hartford (a well-known model) to visit George S. Kaufman in New York. Kaufman and Groucho would converse intently, and after a long period of time would remember the presence of Eden and Dee and acknowledge their presence by directing some conversation toward these young, beautiful girls, who would answer, "Yes, oh yes." Then Kaufman and Groucho would go back into their world and become oblivious of the respectful girls until, remembering them, another "Oh yes" was called for. They spent a few hours saying very little "in the presence of the great men." As they were leaving in the elevator, Dee commented to Eden, "We're just the Greek chorus."

Groucho complained about having to continue paying out alimony (once married to Groucho, women didn't seem to remarry), sometimes saying, "Paying alimony is like feeding hay to a dead horse." He, however, went on paying, and still continued to like women, even ex-wives, as Arthur Whitelaw found out:

ARTHUR WHITELAW
Richard Rodgers is working on a new show. He's doing a show about Henry the Eighth.
GROUCHO
Nobody ever does a picture about Henry the Ninth.
I
That was Henry the Eighth's problem. He wasn't able to manage a Henry the Ninth.
GROUCHO
He couldn't manage his wives. In those days, if they didn't like their wives, they had their heads chopped off. Sounds like a good idea, instead of paying alimony.
ARTHUR WHITELAW
Chop off their heads?
GROUCHO
Yeah.
I
Do you think you could bring yourself to do it?

GROUCHO
No. I'd want to kiss them.

Groucho's wives were all pretty, but none was prepared or equipped to play straight woman to Groucho's barbs as did Margaret Dumont with such forbearance onstage and in the films. Friends remembered how distraught his young wives sometimes became after enduring long evenings at the mercy of Groucho's sharp wit, and how they had tried to adjust. Ruth learned to play excellent tennis, Kay read her dictionary, and Eden learned to paint well enough to have one-woman shows. All of them learned to drink. None of them ever stood up to Groucho the way Erin did.

Bert Granet speculated on the problems of Groucho's pretty young wives:

"Of course his wives were well taken care of materially, but they were abandoned intellectually, and perhaps emotionally. Often they were ignored by a world of people who were only interested in knowing Groucho. Groucho's friends were always very important to him and Groucho loved to be in the company of writers. This might have left his wives feeling lonesome and left out sometimes."

Groucho avoided verbalized sentiment and didn't like to articulate emotions. No one ever accused him of wearing his heart on the sleeve of his frock coat.

If he and I ever had tickets for seats that weren't together, he always gave me his seat, which was certain to be the best one in the house. I wasn't allowed to decline, even on the grounds that his supercelebrity was expected to occupy the seat. The public comedian scoffed at chivalry and sentimentality, but with Groucho I always had the feeling that if there had been a muddy puddle to cross, and he'd had a cloak, he would have spread it out for me to walk on.

At the premiere of *Towering Inferno*, Groucho pushed me into the center row seat next to William Holden.

GROUCHO
(*To William Holden*) Take good care of her. I want her back after the show.
I
But the other seat is in the last row on the side . . .
GROUCHO
It's better for taking a leak.

Once when I mentioned to Groucho that I found him a very private person, he looked at me quite seriously and responded, "Better a privateer than a buccaneer."

A reserved, private individual, he showed little emotion. This could be and was frustrating for wives, who wanted to hear him say, "I love you," and who couldn't even provoke him to sufficient anger. Groucho's extreme control and self-discipline were not due to a lack of feeling or caring. He was only superficially superficial. But a hug might have been more effective than a shrug with wives who felt unable to hold their own with his supercelebrity.

Groucho said that even though each of his marriages had some good years, he was generally pessimistic about the possibilities of romance enduring permanently. He told me that he had felt this way as far back as 1929, when he wrote his first book:

"I wrote in *Beds* that when a man first gets married, he's always the first one in bed. Because he wants to warm the bed for his bride. And after five years, he's still in bed first. But for different reasons. He wants to get out of winding the clock, turning off the lights, and seeing to it that the maid is covered."

Almost half a century later Groucho admitted, "I don't believe in being in love for a long marriage. I believe two people can like each other, and I think that's more important than love. I was 'in love' every time—or I thought I was. So I paid three alimonies. I had good times with all of my wives while it lasted. I was happy with each of them for a while." Then he added somewhat wistfully, "A few good years isn't so bad—maybe that's all you can ask for."

GROUCHO
What do *you* think is a good marriage?
I
I would say it's one in which both participants *think* it's a good marriage.
GROUCHO
Good line.

Speaking of the marriage where romance has vanished, Groucho told me:

"I always think of a place like Chasen's, and there's a married couple sitting at a table, and somebody comes along who knows the husband. They will grab a hold of this guy and keep him there as long as they can so the married couple won't have to talk to each other. Because they have nothing to say to each other if they're married any length of time. They're so happy if somebody that they know comes along and sits down there with them for a few minutes and talks. They're bored with each other. Marriage is a very boring thing after a while. The average couple, after they've been married a few years, unless there are the children to talk about, have very little to say to each other."

I asked Groucho if he believed that a marriage, or any significant relationship between a man and a woman, could be successful if the two people weren't of similar intelligence. "I could love a stupid woman," he answered. "But I wouldn't like her. It's in the head, not the bed. I married women because they were pretty, and that's not the reason to marry a woman. You get fooled by their looks. They weren't stupid, but they weren't Einsteins, either. It's better to choose brains. Beauty fades. I don't think most men are satisfied with their wives. I think most of them are looking around for another piece of tail. *Cherchez la femme.* It's the story of man's life. It's very difficult for a man to be true to only one woman for a whole lifetime."

Asked what he thought of that *cherchez la femme* male propensity, Groucho said:

"I think it's great! I think it's wonderful! If I was twenty years younger, no dame could get out of this house alive."

But he tended to be true to one woman at a time, anyway. He may not have always been the perfectly faithful husband that Harpo was, but he was never a philanderer like Chico. "Chico would be on the phone with his wife," Groucho said, "while he was in bed having his hat blown by another woman. But Harpo was steady. That's what I respect."

Groucho lamented that while Chico could charm any woman into his bed, "I had to marry them." Though undoubtedly an exaggeration, Groucho never took man-woman relations casually, his Mangy Lover image notwithstanding. There was more of Werther in Groucho than there was of Don Juan. Sidney Sheldon noted that love and marriage went together for Groucho, who was always encouraging him to marry Jorja because, as Groucho put it, "I like to see people married."

Sidney Sheldon remembered Groucho as "always a supporter of the institution of marriage":

"Groucho and I had just seen *Minnie's Boys* when it opened in New York, and we were at the airport boarding a plane back to Los Angeles. Groucho had wanted to postpone the flight a day or two because the ground controllers were on strike, but I'd talked him out of it because I thought it might get worse.

"So we get on this plane, and the pilot says, 'There'll be a delay of fifteen minutes!' That's not bad. We start taxiing, then over the loudspeaker, 'There'll be a delay of thirty minutes!' We were on the ground for five hours! They started slowing it down to one plane every twenty minutes, and for five hours we were taxiing.

"After the third hour, the pilot said, 'The hell with the laws of New York, we're gonna serve drinks on the ground!' It was incredible to be locked up on the ground for five hours. Nobody could get out. At the end of four hours, Groucho pressed the button for the stewardess. She came over and said, 'Yes, Mr. Marx, what is it?'

" 'Is there a minister on board?' he said.

" 'I don't know, Mr. Marx. What's wrong?'

" 'Some of the men are getting horny.' "

Groucho never married a Jewish girl, nor did he even go out much with Jewish girls. He attributed this, not to chance, but to choice. Groucho's answer as to why he was never married to, and scarcely ever romantically involved with, a Jewish girl was, "It just always seemed to me that making love to a Jewish girl would be like making love to your sister."

If people succeed, there is a tendency for them to feel that they did it all themselves, and, if they fail, to feel they were pushed. But Groucho neither took all the credit himself for his show business successes nor placed all the blame on his wives for his marital failures. He told me that his exaltation of physical beauty in a woman was a mistake. "If I had it to do all over again, I'd marry someone smart—like Erin. It's true what you said, that while a man marries a wife, a woman marries the man's way of life." I had suggested to him that his three marriages were like that.

When I asked Groucho if anyone had ever left him speechless, he answered, "My wives." But he added, "They didn't leave me speechless, they told me what they thought of me."

Groucho pretty much gave up on marriage or as he said, "It's given up on me. Three strikes and you're out! Who the hell wants an eighty-five-year-old man? There's nothing funny about that." He readily admitted that an active sex life is not one of the joys of old age. "I'm not interested in sex anymore," he said frankly. "I like to see a good-looking woman—that's about as far as it goes. Sex is a goddamn nuisance when you get older. Women still accost me, mostly elderly ones. Younger ones know there's nothing going on."

Groucho was in many ways a young man forced to go around in an old man's body—a body that incessantly admonished, "You can't, you can't." But just because you can't run around the block as fast as you used to doesn't mean that you're still not the same person. Just after his eighty-fifth birthday, a young man interviewing him for television asked him if he still liked to look at pretty women. Groucho responded with a look of disgust.

"No. I close my eyes."

Groucho was a competitive person. Success did not come and find him. In each of his marriages, as in his career, he sought the gold ring—he chose someone who seemed at the time to be a prize. He was the first to question the value he placed on physical beauty, although he was also the first to admit that his appreciation of it had scarcely diminished. "There's nothing lovelier than a pretty girl." He also said, "Man is the only rat who's always looking for cheesecake instead of cheese."

We enjoy being with people who see us the way we want to be seen. One of the problems in marriage is that sometime after the honeymoon, the view of one or both of the partners often comes to include an ever-increasing number of imperfections. Groucho felt that part of the problem was that "a wedding ring protects only one finger."

Groucho's own image of himself was of the utmost importance to him. He saw himself as a person of responsibility and a good provider. An aspect of his image in which he took special pride was as the family father. Even his cats, Blackie and later Frankie and Johnny, became part of the family. He was the authority in his home and in his relationships with those close to him. As he expressed it frequently, "I'm master of my house."

Not being a person with 20-20 hindsight, Groucho was not one to indulge in much crying over spilled buttermilk. In the School of Experience, he said he would rather have had a "girlship" than a fellowship. He felt he had learned a lot from his mistakes, and could repeat them. "If I were to go back, I'd probably make the same mistakes over again," he stated confidently.

Groucho was a romantic. Trusting in intuition, with romantic hopes and dreams, he married three times in search of an ideal. "I was in love each time," he told me. Norman Krasna felt Groucho had difficulty in reconciling his conception of the feminine ideal with reality. "Groucho was always a sap about women. He's a romantic—he expects so much."

During the time that he was satisfied with his marriages, the satisfaction was based on limited expectations. He didn't ask too much of the women in his life, little more than that they be beautiful objects, but the objects objected. One of the things they minded most was that he didn't expect *enough* from them. He always had a tendency to put the women in his life on a pedestal, but they kept leaping off.

"Women are a different breed entirely than the male," he repeatedly told me. I asked him in what ways he found women so different, and he explained:

"In every way. Their thinking is different. They can be a big help to a man because they think completely differently from men. Walk down the shopping district with a woman. The average man isn't going to stand and look in window after window where there are clothes. A woman'll do that, because it's her business to look attractive. That's how she captures the male. If a woman looks like a sludge or something, she won't get anybody.

"Women are brighter than men. If a woman is married to a guy, and she likes him and she loves him and he's given her two or three kids, it's most unlikely that she's going to stray away from him. I think generally women are morally far superior to men. Man is a beast. He wants to get laid. Women maybe would *like* to be promiscuous. But don't forget, if she's a mother with children, she's gonna defend those children. She wants those children. In those cases they are satisfied with what they have—the children and the husband.

"Women are miles ahead of a man. They can outfox him from the time they're born. From the moment a girl meets a man, she's casing his bankroll, arranging the furniture, and picking out names for the children.

"Men are fooled by women. I told you one of my favorite stories is about a married woman who picks up a fella, takes him to her apartment, and they get into the sack. After a couple of hours the man says, 'I've never had a woman like you. You're the most extraordinary woman in bed that I've ever heard of. You know, I'm not a religious man, but when I die, if there is such a thing as a hereafter, I'm going to come back and find you, no matter where you are in the whole world.' And she says to him, 'Well, if you do come back, try to come in the afternoon.' "

If Groucho was with understanding friends (or what he termed his "overstanding friends"), he might have added with a gleam in his eye, "That's true. It's a true story. It happened to me."

At lunch at the Beverly Wilshire Hotel, the British writer Richard Adams mentioned an attractive woman photographer who'd come to take his picture and whom Groucho also knew. Adams commented, "She's a formidable woman."

"They all are," Groucho said, adding, "Women, I'm nuts about them."

Talking with Walter Matthau backstage after a performance of *Juno and the Paycock,* Groucho spoke admiringly about the decorative attributes of a certain young actress Matthau had introduced him to that evening:

WALTER MATTHAU
Sure she's good-looking, but she's boring.
GROUCHO
All young girls are boring. You shouldn't expect more.

Groucho felt that most men are easily "fooled" by women, and he explained that by "fooled" he meant "being more concerned with the wrapping than with what was inside the package."

Discussing the poet T. S. Eliot with goddaughter Mary Sheldon, who was doing a school term paper about Eliot, Groucho told about his own visit to T. S. Eliot's home:

MARY SHELDON
And what was T. S. Eliot's wife like? Was she brilliant and complex?
GROUCHO
No.
MARY SHELDON
Then why do you think he married her?
GROUCHO
'Cause she had blond hair. Men are easily fooled by women. And *he* served dinner for us that night.
MARY SHELDON
He served the dinner?
GROUCHO
Yeah.

A popular turn-of-the-century couplet (Groucho's definition of a couplet was "a little man and a little woman") described the masculine ideal "a lady in the drawing room, a cook in the kitchen, and a whore in the bedroom." But Groucho never held his wives to either Escoffier or La Belle Otéro standards. In fact, he avoided women who knew too much or were too practiced in the bedroom, as well as in the kitchen. Although he might jest, "You can have more fun with a woman than a lady," when it came down to brass bedposts, his ardor was dampened by anything in a woman that he felt was vulgar. Asked what he *didn't* like in a woman, he answered without hesitation, "Vulgarity. I don't like vulgarity."

I asked him what he meant by vulgarity.

"Before I was married, I had a girl whose father was very rich in Portland. I could have married her, but I didn't like her behavior in bed. She did *everything*. She was too sophisticated in bed. She knew too many tricks, and I didn't want a girl like that. I wanted a girl that was more feminine. Oh, she liked me, but she always wanted to go to bed."

"Wouldn't some men like that?" I asked.

"A nymphomaniac? No. They want a nice feminine girl who they can go to bed with and who they can talk to."

Groucho discussed with Elliott Gould what a man finds attractive in a woman:

ELLIOTT GOULD
(*Talking about his former wife, Barbra Streisand*) It was fun eating with Barbra. She really appreciates food. The first real money we ever got together we bought this really great antique bed we'd been looking at, and that took all our money. We had just enough left to buy a bag of knishes, so we did, and we went home and sat in this great antique bed, eating knishes. Barbra was so vulnerable. I wanted to take care of her.
GROUCHO
A man wants a nice girl he can take care of.

The rigors of three divorces did not dim Groucho's romantic vision of matrimony or his enthusiasm for feminine charms. "I think everyone should get married," he continued to say, "even if they get a divorce." One night at dinner, Sidney Sheldon reminded Groucho that before he married Jorja, Groucho was always importuning him to get married.

SIDNEY SHELDON
Why was that, Grouch?
GROUCHO
I had no interest in either of you. I just wanted to get you married. Who was that other girl before Jorja, the one with the big knockers?
SIDNEY SHELDON
It was either Helen Twelvetrees or Zasu Pitts. So then, Grouch, if you had no interest in us, why were you so anxious to have us get married?
GROUCHO
Because I was married, and I thought everybody should get married — even if they get a divorce. Hook the schnook.

This is certainly not to say that Groucho believed in divorce. He merely accepted it as a possible negative side effect of marriage, which he believed in wholeheartedly. He was a responsible person who always took family ties seriously. Privately, he cared a great deal about the little children in his life: grandchildren Miles and Jade. Publicly he was more likely to fashion a semishocking unsentimental rejoinder, especially for a feminine audience. Composer Bronislaw Kaper remembered such a moment:

"We were at La Scala Boutique restaurant, and there was a group of women with some very little children. They were all looking at Groucho, and Groucho waved back and made some gestures. They were all very thrilled and impressed. One of the women said, 'Oh, you like children.' And Groucho responded, 'No, I like to make them.' "

Whatever jokes Groucho made about parenthood, marriage, and divorce, what he respected most was the lasting marriage. Along with the marriage of his mother and father, the marriage that he most admired was that of brother Harpo and Susan Fleming Marx.

Groucho's wives pleased him by catering to his penchant for punctuality, order, and discipline. He liked to eat his lunch at one o'clock and his dinner at seven o'clock exactly. In marriage, the dining room was important to him, if not as important as the bedroom. Once when Charlotte Granet met him, she happened to mention some mutual friends who were getting a divorce. He commented, "Nobody knows what goes on in people's bedrooms." Talking with me about this, he added, "A man's love life is his own affair. It isn't politics that makes strange bedfellows; it's matrimony."

Groucho generally preferred innocence to worldy-wise sophistication in women. At dinner with Arthur Whitelaw and me, he greatly enjoyed introducing his nurse, Linda, to her first vichyssoise, Malpeque oysters, and steak tartare. The private Groucho was frequently guilty of the chivalry the public Groucho character scorned. Taking Erin and me to a party or to the theatre, he would say:

"I always take out two women. I hate to see a girl walk home alone."

Once at Chasen's I happened to order something relatively inexpensive. He observed, "You're inexpensive. That's dangerous." But Groucho, who never liked to leave an unused light burning, later approved my behavior: "You're a careful eater. Waste isn't luxury."

Bert Granet revealed a Groucho faux pas which Groucho said was "more of a 'fox's paw' ":

"It was during the time when Groucho wasn't married, and we thought he seemed lonely. We suggested that he might like to take out a very attractive lady we all knew whose husband had died. And Groucho said, 'That old bag,' and then he stopped because suddenly he realized that all of the women at the table, all of his friends' wives, were older than the one he had just scorned. Groucho did some pretty fancy ad libbing which he could be great at, but he didn't quite get his foot out of his mouth for the rest of the evening."

Terry Hamlisch, as Marvin's sister and as a pretty young girl, had a special place in Groucho's affections.

"He always kisses me on the lips. Very European. Big, wet kisses. As we gave each other a big wet kiss, my opening line would be, 'Have you been true to me?' and he would say, 'No, but at least I'm telling you about it.' "

Marvin Hamlisch, who saw him in action, was not unimpressed by Groucho's propensity for inspiring and commanding lip service. "I love the way he goes up to a girl and says, 'Kiss me, honey,' and practically has her over his shoulder. He'll say, 'Kiss me, you fool,' raising his eyebrows. I love watching him do that. I love the way he can get away with anything and he loves getting away with it. It's fantastic. Terrific!"

Groucho made a vice of necessity, his advancing years providing a haven for his advances. "When I was young, they would have slapped my face for that, and so would I."

He learned to capitalize on his age, at least with pretty young girls, and the rebuff was rare. Most were flattered and pleased by his attentions. Groucho Marx was a sacred bull, and you couldn't slap an institution. He was also quick to suggest that a young girl couldn't take an old man too seriously. Hearing about an old man who had married a young girl, Groucho observed, "It can't work out, and it can't work in. It can't last." I said, "You mean a fool and his honey are soon parted?" Groucho looked at me only slightly askance and corrected my statement: "A fool and his honey are soon potted."

Not many women rejected him, but when it happened, he was not disconsolate. In vaudeville he learned that you can't expect a laugh every time, and he didn't expect a kiss every time, either. I asked him if, in the battle of the sexes, he had ever been defeated, and he answered, "Even Napoleon was defeated by Josephine."

"And you?" I asked.

"No," he answered, "dismayed, not defeated."

Just before Christmas 1974, Groucho and I went with Billy Marx to the

Mark Taper Forum Theatre in Los Angeles to see *Juno and the Paycock*, which was being directed by George Seaton, and which starred Jack Lemmon and Walter Matthau. He was offered a program by the trim young usherette.

USHERETTE
(*Wide-eyed*) I'm glad to see you, Mr. Marx.
GROUCHO
I'm glad to see you. (*He kisses her*)

Giggling, she fled to report, "Groucho kissed me! Groucho kissed me!" to her cohorts. Several of the other usherettes rushed over to help show him to his seat, hoping for similar treatment. Meanwhile, the other patrons, many of whom were celebrities, groped and fumbled their ways to their seats unattended.

Groucho, of course, understood that they were kissing the legend, and not necessarily the man, but the man enjoyed it no less.

One day, after Christmas shopping, he and I walked to the parking lot in back of the Beverly Hills Saks Fifth Avenue. We were carrying bottles of perfume that were his nurses' Christmas gifts. Suddenly he handed me his packages, went up to a pretty blonde who was standing by her car, and kissed her. "I had to," he explained. "Look at her license plate. It says, 'BIG EYS.' "

Groucho would have been the last to deny that he always enjoyed the admiring attention of a pretty young girl, although it didn't always live up to his hopes. Sidney Sheldon told of one disappointing encounter:

"Many years ago, he went to some nightclub with us, and a cute little dancer who was in the show came up afterwards and asked if she could sit with him, and he said, 'Of course.' I think Grouch tried to make every pretty girl he could get his hands on, at least verbally. Anyway, this pretty girl sat down, and they started talking, and she said, 'I've only done this once before in my life, but could I have your autograph?' Grouch said he was very flattered, and he gave her his autograph. Then he said, 'By the way—you said you've done this only once before. What other autograph did you get?' She said, 'Fifi D'Orsay,' and Grouch nearly threw her out."

Terry Hamlisch told me, "He's always kidding me about men. He always wants to know why I'm not with a man. Then, when I am, he doesn't like them. I love his smile. It's not a wide smile, it's all in his eyes. You know what he did for my birthday? He gave me a negligee—a white lacy thing, really right for *Playboy*. The card said, 'To Terry. I wish I could do to you what some lucky man is going to do to you in this. Wowee! Love, Grouch.' And then it said, 'And soon.' "

Terry said that even in his eighties, "When the lights go out at Groucho's house, it's every girl for herself." She found this out the easy way:

"New Year's Eve last year, we were watching *Duck Soup*, which Groucho always calls the 'war picture,' and kinda necking in the dark, and Groucho really enjoyed the film. He really thought it was terrific. The lyrics, the songs, the numbers and everything, he remembered how each thing was shot. He got so excited, he almost broke my knee in the dark, which was a big thrill."

Terry described Groucho as someone for whom life was too important to be taken seriously.

"He walked over to his own picture on the chest on the day he got the Academy Award, and he slowly smiled and said, 'Who is that jerk?' He really endeared himself to me, because he really knows that the thing I think people sometimes forget is the question, 'So what?' We all try hard, we all struggle and strive, yet he's in a place where he sees the ups and downs, and he can keep his perspective on life and laugh at himself."

I went with Groucho to the Zandra Rhodes fashion show in Beverly Hills, where the girls modeled see-through fashions that left little to the imagination. He commented, "This is a nice undress rehearsal," and as the bevy of sheer-topped models in "gownless evening straps" paraded by, he announced vociferously, "It's a gala day." Then he added with mock modesty, "I never could handle more than a gal a day." He was happily distracted from his next comment by Michelle Phillips, who, modeling a wispy creation, stopped by to kiss him.

Groucho's nurses enjoyed a certain reflected celebrity, and each one became, for her own friends, something of a celebrity herself. They traveled with Groucho, visited his friends with him, ate meals with him, and shared his life for a shift. Around him work often became a diversion, and even his captive audience was captivated as his nurses confided in him and frequently solicited his counsel on all manner of subjects:

NURSE DONNA
Oh, Groucho, I'm afraid I'm gonna wind up an old maid.
GROUCHO
Well, bring her in and we'll wind her up together.

NURSE DONNA
Do you believe in computer dating?
GROUCHO
Only if the computers really love each other.

Groucho, nurse Linda, and I went to a film that he and I were ready to leave after a few minutes. But we stayed until the end because Linda was obviously deeply engrossed and much amused. Observing that, he settled back into his seat, advising me, "We can't leave."

For Groucho's entertainment Robin, his cook, sometimes did her "Rapunzel act," letting down her long blond hair at the end of the meal at his request.

GROUCHO
How did you decide to become a cook?
ROBIN
Because I did it well, and then I decided that I liked to do it, and I might as well try and make some money while I was doing something I liked to do.
GROUCHO
Strange profession for a young woman . . . who is pretty. A lot of cooks look lousy. They ought to be ashamed of themselves.

Miriam Marx was always a mysterious, enigmatic figure in Groucho's family. Her half sister, Melinda, was known to millions through appearances on *You Bet Your Life,* and her brother, Arthur, was a well-known tennis player before he became a writer. But Miriam rarely shared the spotlight with her father. He told me this story about Miriam:

"One day Miriam came home late from school, and I said, 'Where have you been?' She said, 'I've been to the movies, and I saw the Ritz Brothers, and they're *really* funny.' "

Everyone who remembered Miriam described her as an extremely sensitive girl who adored and worshiped her father. She was indirectly responsible for the birth of her half sister, Melinda. It was Miriam who introduced her friend Kay to Groucho, who married Kay, and Melinda was their daughter. Miriam and Kay remained good friends. Very briefly, Miriam herself was married.

When Miriam attended a party at Groucho's, she would introduce herself to guests, saying, "I'm Miriam. I'm the one no one talks about."

Groucho remembered without bitterness that Melinda never watched him on television: "When Melinda was ten years old, she didn't watch my quiz show. She used to look at Westerns or wrestling instead."

He never made a secret of his special affection for Melinda, believing that she would be the Marx to carry on the show business tradition in the family, but Melinda disappointed him in that. She could sing and dance, and he never tired of watching the film of a twelve-year-old Melinda dancing with Gene Nelson. Years after all the appearances on *You Bet Your Life*, she told him that she had disliked having to perform as his daughter. Melinda grew up, married, and had two children of her own, but Groucho still continued to have vivid memories of her as a little girl.

ROBIN

Did you ever play Santa Claus for Melinda?

GROUCHO

No, I didn't dress up like Santa Claus.

ROBIN

Did she believe in Santa Claus when she was a little girl?

GROUCHO

Until she was three years old. The truth came out in kindergarten. She heard it from the other kids. One day she came home from school, and I said, "Melinda, what'd you do all day?" She said, "Nothing." I said, "You're there every day from nine to twelve. You must do something." She says, "All we do is paint and go to the toilet."

The youngest woman in Groucho's late years was one without much past. With only a few years behind her, he said of her, "She's not as young as she used to be. She's been around." The youngest of his grandchildren, Jade was his only granddaughter, although son Arthur had a daughter many years ago who died in infancy. Irene Atkins, Arthur Marx's former wife, told me this story:

"I have one story about Groucho I'd like to tell. I've never seen it published anywhere, and I don't think very many people know about it. It certainly hasn't been in any of the books about Groucho, and I'm not even sure it's the sort of thing you're interested in. It's slightly maudlin, and it's not typical Groucho.

"In 1947 my older son, Steve Marx, was born. As this was my first child, and Groucho's first grandchild, I was very excited, and I presumed everyone else was. Everyone came to the hospital to visit and to get a look at this new baby. Everyone, that is, except Groucho, and I was beginning to feel a little bit hurt. You know, like new mothers do, and I said to Arthur, my husband at that time and Steve's father, 'Everyone's been to see the baby except your father, and I'm a little bit insulted.'

"Finally, after several days, Arthur said to me, 'I have to tell you that my father's father died at the Cedars of Lebanon Hospital, and he swore never to set foot in a hospital again. That's why he hasn't come to see the baby. It's just a phobia about hospitals.' So I said, 'You know, you should have told me immediately. I would have understood.' When I came home from the hospital, Groucho came immediately to see the baby.

"Now, as I said, this is a little bit maudlin, but exactly two years after that, we had another baby, and she only lived a short time. Well, I think the next morning Groucho was at the hospital to see me to kind of pay a condolence call. I felt shattered, but it was so nice of him coming to console me. And I felt, 'Gee, what a trauma, to have not only to come to the hospital for this reason, but also after he'd sworn he'd never come to a hospital.' I thought it was really a nice gesture on his part, and it isn't really the kind of thing that you hear about.

"Well, two years after that, Andy was born, and by this time the whole thing about his father was put aside or he had broken the barrier. He rushed down to see the baby, and not only saw Andy, but put on kind of a show for the nurses. He did all his eyebrow-raising, and practically danced in the hall. He signed autographs and did just about everything, and it was the talk of the hospital. But I always remember not so much the visit when Andy was born, but the condolence call. He was trying to cheer me up, and it ended up that I was cheering him up because he was much more depressed, I think, than I was.

"He was terribly apprehensive the whole time I was pregnant with Andy. I think this happens with people who have lost a baby—they are just so anxious the next time that same person gets pregnant. I think that's why he was so relieved when Andy was born. He was so elated to see Andy, who, incidentally, weighed eleven pounds at birth—a huge, monstrous baby."

Although Groucho was considered by some to have scant sympathy, and he wasn't given credit for much empathy, there were those who found him both sympathetic and empathetic. His goddaughter, Mary Sheldon, was a girl in his life who brought out these feelings. Sidney Sheldon described an instance of Groucho's consideration for his goddaughter:

"A number of years ago, Mary did a play at a boys' school, and she was the only girl in the play. Grouch went to see it, and afterwards he went backstage, and the boys were very excited about having Groucho there. So Jorja suggested having a party over at the house, and I walked into a rather large den that we had, and I saw Groucho sitting in an armchair, and on the floor all over the room at his feet were these high school boys, drinking in every word that he was saying. He was just charming to them. It was a wonderful evening."

There were a number of women for whom Groucho had affection and admiration.

"I was in love with the girl who played the lead in *Day at the Races*, the mother of Mia Farrow. I'd like to see her again. She was an Irish beauty. But she was married."

Maureen O'Sullivan remembered Groucho too:

MAUREEN O'SULLIVAN
Groucho was great fun all day. He was always putting himself out to make it more fun for everyone. It was a real pleasure to work with him. The one word that comes to mind when I remember working with him is "fun."

I
Groucho remembers you well—as an ideal dream girl.

MAUREEN O'SULLIVAN
Well, I'm glad I was a dream rather than a nightmare.

I
He told me you didn't seem to notice how much he liked you because you were married at the time.

MAUREEN O'SULLIVAN
Well, he was married too!

I
Did you ever see Groucho after *Day at the Races*?

MAUREEN O'SULLIVAN
We used to meet on the lot, but we only spoke a few words each time.

Budd Schulberg's ex-wife, Virginia, was another woman Groucho sometimes talked about with nostalgic affection:

"I was also in love with Virginia Schulberg. She was beautiful. When I went to a party with Virginia—I went with her for a while, you know— well, ten minutes after we were at somebody's house, there were eight men around her, because she was so pretty and she was so bright. Oh, she was bright! I'd have married her, too."

Groucho was also fond of Carole Lombard, whom he admired, though in a totally different way. He told me about meeting her on the street just after she married Clark Gable:

"I loved Lombard. She was a great dame. I did a whole series of shows with her, you know. I met her on the street one day, and I said, 'How are you and Gable getting along?' And she said, 'He's the worst lay I ever had in all my life.' That's the way she talked. Very sexy dame. She spoke the way a lot of men speak."

When I said, "Maybe she was just angry at him that day," Groucho disagreed:

"You don't know very much about life. Just because a guy's tall and good-looking and his ears stick out doesn't mean he's a good lay. She said he was lousy, and she oughta know. She talked like a man, words men use with other men. She used everything. She was a gutsy dame. She was a real show business girl."

Groucho also liked Carmen Miranda. In addition to his respect for her talent, he respected her family values. "She always sent all her money home to her family. She had a big family back in Brazil. She was *very* small, and she wore special shoes."

I told him that I had seen the collection of her tiny, high-platformed shoes in a museum in Brazil, as well as some of her costumes that were there.

GROUCHO
She had talent, and she was a nice person. I told you Harpo's harp is in a museum. I'm gonna be in a museum myself pretty soon.

I
Your *Animal Crackers* jodhpurs and safari pith helmet . . . ?
GROUCHO
No. Me.

Groucho liked Zeppo's former wife, Barbara Sinatra, too. "She wasn't only a beautiful blonde, but Zeppo's ex took care of him while he was sick."

Groucho told me of his interest in what he called "The Monroe Doctrine":

"First job Marilyn Monroe ever got was with me. Tell you what happened: the producer had me over to his home, and he says, 'I got three girls. I want each one to walk up and down, and you tell me which one you like best.' First one walked up and down, then the second one, then the third one was Marilyn Monroe. He says, 'Which one do you pick?' I says, 'You're kidding. How could you take anybody but *that* one?' It was for a bit in *Love Happy*. She wore a dress so low, I couldn't remember my lines.

"I tried her. I mean, I tried, but I didn't get anywhere. She was so beautiful, *everybody* was stuck on her.

"While she was married to DiMaggio, she went over to the Far East and did some shows over there. When she came back, DiMaggio said, 'How did you do?' She says, 'You never heard such applause!' He says, 'Yes, I have.' Because he'd been a star outfielder with the Yankees. Many were crazy about her."

One of the ladies in his life whom Groucho remembered most fondly was the only one who never laughed at his jokes. When he was awarded the special Oscar of the Academy of Motion Picture Arts and Sciences in 1974, he acknowledged his gratitude to this *grande dame*—or, as Groucho said, "great dame"—of the straight line by specifically mentioning her along with his mother and Erin Fleming as the most important women in his life. For Groucho, this was no offhand encomium, but a reflection of carefully considered enduring respect and admiration.

Born Daisy Baker in 1889 in Atlanta, Georgia, Margaret Dumont was brought up in the home of her godfather, Joel Chandler Harris, creator of Uncle Remus, Brer Rabbit, and Brer Fox. Groucho talked about her at dinner with Arthur Whitelaw and me:

ARTHUR WHITELAW
How did you discover Margaret Dumont, Groucho?
GROUCHO
Sam Harris. She had worked in some show of his.
ARTHUR WHITELAW
She was really that lady offstage as well, wasn't she?
GROUCHO
That was why she was great. But she never understood any of the jokes.
ARTHUR WHITELAW
The first time she appeared in a film with you, was she supposed to appear in just one film and then you continued on?

GROUCHO

In one film. She was so great that we used her in a lot of pictures.

ARTHUR WHITELAW

Was she really a wealthy woman?

GROUCHO

No. She didn't have any money.

ARTHUR WHITELAW

She certainly played a lady with a lot of money.

GROUCHO

She wouldn't go on my quiz show unless we gave her a thousand dollars. She wanted to get paid. Nobody got paid on that show. If they won money, that was all right. Peter Blatty went on one night and won $10,000. Then he wrote *The Exorcist*. She would have been great on my quiz show.

Margaret Dumont was the widow of John Moller, Jr., son of a wealthy businessman and a member of New York's 400. Her husband's family "didn't entirely approve of my return to the stage," she used to say. She had been known as Daisy Dumont and was playing "Trixie Fluff" in a musical, *The Summer Widowers*, when she married Moller in 1910. Earlier she had appeared in Lew Fields's *The Girl Behind the Counter*, in which a reviewer described Daisy Dumont as "tall, statuesque and beautiful," in her role of "a forelady in a London department store." Her big number was "I Want to Be Loved Like a Leading Lady." Opera-trained, she had served her apprenticeship for two years as a showgirl in the music halls of England and France. She made her debut at the Casino de Paris, later playing with George M. Cohan on Broadway before joining the Marx Brothers in the stage version of *The Cocoanuts*.

"She'd been a social lady, and her husband died, so she needed a job," Morrie Ryskind told me. It was while she was playing the part of a social climber in *The Four Flushers* that Sam Harris, who was producing *The Cocoanuts*, cast her as Mrs. Potter, the first of her many comic trysts with Groucho.

Lorayne Brox, one of the three Brox sisters who appeared in *The Cocoanuts*, also remembered Margaret Dumont as the same character off-stage as she was on. "She was the perfect foil for Groucho," she told me. "She was a wonderful elegant lady. *That's who she was*. She was always indignant. She was always dignified."

Margaret Dumont once expressed her own conception of her inner and outer dignity:

"It isn't the gown or its fine material that makes a woman stylish or otherwise nowadays, but her carriage and the amount of clothing she has on beneath the gown."

As the straight woman in the Marx Brothers' act, Margaret Dumont could expect no better than the wrong end of the slapstick, but offstage she did expect some respite from the onstage indignities she suffered. The Marx Brothers, however, never needed a proscenium arch to justify an impractical joke.

"We took her clothes off once," Groucho tells. The occasion was a trip in a Pullman car late at night during the *Night at the Opera* tour. The boys had wearied of cards and chorus girls, and were looking for a novel *divertissement*. "And we took off all her clothes. She screamed so loud you couldn't hear the train whistle."

"After that first week with the Marx Brothers," Morrie Ryskind recalled, "she was never the same. In fact none of us were ever the same."

MORRIE RYSKIND
She hadn't quite been used to this sort of thing. At most of the big dinners she'd gone to, they didn't do that, you know. But she got used to them.

GROUCHO
She never understood any of the jokes.

ERIN
Did she really not understand?

GROUCHO
No.

MORRIE RYSKIND
She came to me one day, and I forget, but it was some scene about Rembrandt, but anyway, she got it mixed up, and so she said, "What're they laughing at?" And I explained it to her. And she said, "Oh." So the next night she said, in front center stage, "That was Rembrandt, and nobody gave a *damn!*" It was like an important announcement—here was the greatest joke of the ages, and she came back crying. She said, "What did I do?" I said, "You tried to punch it. Let it alone. You were doing all right."

GROUCHO
She was a comedian but didn't know it. We bounced laughs off her, like the bridge game where Harpo kicks her, hitting her in the stomach.

One of Margaret Dumont's most famous parts was as Mrs. Claypool in *A Night at the Opera*. Groucho described a scene between them that brought down the house during one of the live tryout performances:

"We were sitting in a box, supposedly a box in an opera house, and the opening line was, 'Well, toots, how do you like the show?' I was nervous, and I said, 'Well, tits, how do you like the show?' The audience laughed for five minutes." I asked Groucho if that was really an accidental ad lib. His only answer to me was an enigmatic raise of his eyebrows.

Margaret Dumont herself was far from naïve about her contribution:

"I'm a straight lady, the best in Hollywood. There is an art to playing the straight role. You must build up your man but never top him, never steal the laughs from him."

George Seaton, talking with Groucho and me over brunch at Hillcrest, remembered that the instance in which the Marx Brothers undressed Margaret Dumont was not unique, nor even a rare occurrence:

"Harpo was just the dearest, sweetest man. I don't think you can find anyone who has a bad word to say about Harpo. But he was a leprechaun, an elf. He used to do silly, wonderful things, like stealing Maggie Dumont's wig. She was as bald as a billiard ball and always wore a wig. He'd take great delight in stealing her wig before we got off the train. In Chicago or someplace, here would come Maggie with a towel wrapped around her head, and on it it said 'Pullman.' "

To this Groucho added:

"I enjoyed all my romantic scenes with Margaret Dumont. She was a wonderful woman. She was the same offstage as she was on it—always the stuffy, dignified matron. She took everything seriously. She would say to me, 'Julie, why are they laughing?'

"At first I'd try to explain, like the line when Chico and Harpo were stealing a painting in *Animal Crackers*. She and I came into the room, which was pitch dark. She said, 'My, it's so dark in here you can't see your hand in front of your face.' And I came back with, 'Well, you wouldn't get much enjoyment out of that.' The audience laughed like hell, but she couldn't understand why. She said, 'Julie, what was funny about that? It was dark and I couldn't see my hand.'

"In *A Night at the Opera*, I'm having a rendezvous with Mrs. Claypool, and when she arrives at my room, fourteen people come out. But she never understood what was funny. At the end of *Duck Soup*, we're alone in a small cottage and there's a war going on outside and Margaret says to me, 'What are you doing, Rufus?' And I say, 'I'm fighting for your honor, which is more than you ever did.' Later she asked me what I meant by that.

"You know, people used to ask if we were married. A lot of people thought we were married."

Maureen O'Sullivan told me that Margaret Dumont actually believed that *A Day at the Races* was a serious picture:

"I used to get a lot of fun out of Margaret Dumont. She had no idea why *A Day at the Races* was funny or even that it *was* funny. When we started, she told me, 'It's not going to be one of *those* things. I'm having a very *serious* part this time.'"

The writer J. B. Priestley said of Margaret Dumont, "She could maintain her social presence and style while being fired out of a gun." The Marx Brothers used her in seven of their thirteen films. Whenever she was absent from a Marx Brothers movie, the studio always received an avalanche of letters demanding her return. She worked in other pictures as well, but sometimes there were lean years even for a dowager. George Seaton remembered such a year:

"I was doing a film—as a matter of fact, it was my first directorial effort. Zanuck wanted me to start with a small picture, and I said, 'No.'

"I wanted to do something very big, because I knew if I made a successful small picture, I'd be known as a good small picture director. So I chose a Betty Grable musical, and in it was a dream sequence. The character that Betty Grable played always wanted a mink coat, so she dreams that here she is in this beautiful mink coat. She's going up this tremendous flight of stairs, and at the top is Mrs. Rich-Bitch, and all she had to say was, 'Good evening, my dear. So good of you to come.'

"So I was thinking, and I said to myself, 'Maggie Dumont would just be perfect!' I called Maggie, who lived at the Knickerbocker Hotel, and I had tea with her. She used to hold court there, and she would serve tea in the afternoon. I called her and I said, 'I just hate to offer you this, Maggie, but if you would do it, it would be a great favor for me, because nobody could do it the way you do.' She said, 'Well, send me a script and let me read the character and see if I'm right for it.'

"I sent her the script, and she called and said, 'Yes, that's quite an interesting small part. I'd be very pleased to do it. Who will design my clothes?' Well, Charlie Le Maire, the great designer, who was at that time head of the Fox wardrobe department, had worked with Maggie back in New York. So I said, 'Charlie, she hasn't worked in a long while. Let's do something for her.' And he said, 'Oh, wonderful!' So he found three outfits in the wardrobe department. They were all there already, but he made sketches, new sketches.

"We went to tea at the Knickerbocker Hotel and laid out the sketches for Maggie to pick the one she wanted, and she chose one. She said 'How long will it take to have this made?' 'Well,' he said, 'I'll put on an extra crew. Don't worry, it'll be ready on time.' Of course, he just took it off the rack.

"My partner, Bill Perlberg, went right along with it. He said, 'Let's get the biggest trailer we've got, and we'll put a star on the door—"Margaret Dumont"—and we'll fill the place with roses,' which we did. Now came the day. I tipped Betty Grable off, and Betty was just thrilled by it. She rushed in with flowers for Miss Dumont and said, 'Miss Dumont, I've admired your work so much over the years. Please, if there's anything you can do to help me with my performance, I would be only too happy to have you tell me.' Maggie said, 'It's quite all right, girl. Let's do it.'

"Well, we came to shoot it, and Betty came up the stairs. Margaret Dumont said, 'Do you mind if you step back just a little bit. Not quite so close, my dear child.' So Betty said, 'Yes ma'am.' Then we did three takes, and Maggie said, 'Now which take are you going to use?' I said, 'Well, I have to see the dailies first, but I'll call you immediately after seeing them,' which I did.

"I said, 'I thought Take 2 was the best, Maggie.' She said, 'Well, isn't that strange? I thought Take 3 was better.' So I said, 'Well, I tell you, why don't you come to the studio? We'll run the three takes for you, and *you* select the one that you think is best.' She saw all three of them, and she said, 'No, I must agree with you. Take 2 is better.' So she left in a blaze of glory. She was queen for a day.

"At a party a couple of weeks later, I was sitting at a table with Groucho, and I told him this whole story. He said, 'George, that's the most wonderful thing anyone could do for that dame. You know, she hasn't worked since the last Marx Brothers picture.' Then he paused, and he said, 'What am I talking about? *I* haven't worked since the last Marx Brothers picture!' "

Although she will always be remembered as the archetypal dowager of the Marx Brothers films, Margaret Dumont was a versatile actress. She herself was happily resigned to being typecast: "I'm always the Newport dowager, whether I'm reclining on a chaise longue or hanging from the top of a tent in my drawers." In addition to seven of the Marx Brothers films, Margaret Dumont also appeared in sixteen other films, including *Never Give a Sucker an Even Break*, with W. C. Fields. In her last film, *What a Way to Go!*, she played Shirley MacLaine's shrewish mother so convincingly that few recognized her as Mesdames Potter, Rittenhouse, and Claypool.

Groucho told me about the last time he saw Margaret Dumont:

"She was a tall, good-looking woman. She looked like she came from high society. I was in the last show that she ever did—on *The Hollywood Palace.*

"I'll never forget. After the show she stood by the stage door with a bouquet of roses, which she probably sent to herself. Some guy came along in a crummy car and took her away. A couple of weeks later she died. She was always a lady, a wonderful person. Died without any money."

Groucho and I entered the Beverly Hills Hotel one afternoon on the way to the Polo Lounge to have lunch with Jack Nicholson and Mike Nichols. In the lobby there were about twenty girls in long pink tulle dresses trimmed with rhinestones, with an equal number of young men in dinner jackets. Standing with the group of teenagers was a mature blond woman, also wearing a long pink tulle dress. She wore her straight blond hair pulled back tight from her face in a 1940s upsweep.

The group observed Groucho's entrance, and he observed them. Heading in their direction, he asked, "Who's getting married?" The woman, who later explained that she was their chorus leader, answered, "I hope no one."

GROUCHO
Why? What do you have against marriage? You must have been married.
LADY
I was, but not now.
GROUCHO
Oh, it didn't work out? Or, it didn't work in?

Not a bit flustered by the giggles of the students, she continued in the same serious vein, announcing, "This is the Pasadena High School chorus." Whirling back to the chorus, she began to direct them in a song. As the chorus of about fifty sang, everyone in the lobby of the glamorous Beverly Hills Hotel gathered about to witness a show that promised to rival the best moments in any Marx Brothers film. Behind us a woman was saying to her little girl, "This is a day you'll remember all your life." Groucho soon joined in, singing out "Drink to Me Only with Thine Eyes" loud and clear.

After the chorus ran through a brief repertory, Groucho explained to the teacher that he used to sing with a church choir in New York City, and that they used to pay him a dollar. "That wasn't very much," the teacher said.

"It was quite a bit then," Groucho said. "I could buy a pumpernickel for a nickel."

Then he raised his eyebrows, rolled his eyes, and thrilled the assemblage by doing the Groucho look. "Well, I must be going. But before I do . . . ," and his gaze focused hard on the prim and proper blond chorus leader, ". . . I'd like to kiss you. Is that all right?" Completely unruffled, she nodded affirmatively. Groucho swooped in and grabbed her, bending her way back and kissing her hard and long on the lips.

As we went into the restaurant he explained to me, "She was a good straight woman. She reminded me of Margaret Dumont."

When Hugh Hefner invited Groucho to present *Playboy*'s Playmate-of-the-Year award, Groucho needed little urging. Of the event, he recalled:

"It was some sight. The winners were beautiful and the losers were beautiful. They asked me to give the *Playboy* award to the most beautiful girl of the year, and they had these twelve beautiful girls, and they pointed to one and said to me, 'You give the award to her.' I got up and said, 'You're beautiful, but you aren't *more* beautiful. All of the girls are beautiful girls. You're just luckier.' "

When I asked Groucho, "What were your hobbies?" he answered unhesitatingly, "Women." "And, generally, what do you think of women, Groucho?" He answered with the utmost sincerity, "Always. I was girl crazy. There's nothing more wonderful than a beautiful young woman."

I

Alfred Hitchcock once told me a woman should be like a suspense movie, not revealing everything at once. The questions should be answered gradually. But you say that for you the questions never got answered at all.

GROUCHO

The more you think you know, the less you know. I'm old enough to know I don't know anything. They get harder to understand, but I don't care.

I

Then, considering all the problems and cost, monetary and otherwise, were girls worth it?

GROUCHO

Yeah.

I

Do you think women are very different now than they were when you were a young man?

GROUCHO

They're allowed to talk dirty now, same as men do. And smoke cigarettes. When I was young, no women wore pants. They all wore dresses. Now, in America, they all wear pants. I was young so long ago that when my wife, Ruth, went to the beach, she had to leave her silk stockings on. It was more shocking then to take off your stockings than it is now to take off everything. Now they've got Women's Lib, and I'm all for it. I think if there's a war, for example, and a man has enlisted, I think his wife should take a job, not necessarily in the front lines shooting at the enemy, but there are so many things that a woman can do in an army. Since the man is risking his life, why shouldn't the woman do something? I don't know if that's a good explanation. I think they should have all the salary advantages and everything. I think there'll be a woman president. I expect to see it someday in America. No reason why it shouldn't be.

I

You like the idea.

GROUCHO

I think it's a great idea.

I

Do you think women should have to pay alimony?

GROUCHO

Depends on the amount of money. If the woman's rich, and she marries a man and it breaks up, I don't see any reason why she shouldn't give her husband some so *he* could get married again if he wants to. There are a lot of men that would like to get married and can't because they don't have any money after paying alimony to a woman.

I

Besides enlisting in the Army and paying alimony, what else do you think women ought to be free to do?

GROUCHO

Everything. They do it anyhow.

I

What do you like most in a woman?

GROUCHO

A woman who likes me.

I

But what are the characteristics or qualities or features that have always most attracted you in a woman?

GROUCHO

You can't put everything into words.

I

Isn't there *something* you can single out?

GROUCHO

Femininity.

He added, "You can't answer questions like what makes one woman attractive and another not. It's like trying to say what's a winning personality and what isn't."

Groucho, having skipped merrily over several generation gaps, was confident enough of his own modernity to unabashedly espouse an occasional old-fashioned value. He told me, "When I heard you were coming to see me for *Playboy*, I thought they'd send a jerk, but you're shy and diffident and everything a woman should be."

When it came to women, the living legend was very much a living man. Groucho's lifelong philosophy toward women was perhaps best summed up in the last two words of one of his favorite stories:

"I once knew a girl who wore an anklet that said 'Heaven's above.' "

"If I didn't have Erin, I'd have old furniture"

For Groucho-watchers, Erin Fleming needs no introduction. A young Canadian with New York acting credits, she came into Groucho's life to answer his fan mail and, as Groucho said, "to answer my prayers." Although she continued her acting career with appearances in Woody Allen's *Everything You Always Wanted to Know About Sex*, a Los Angeles stage play, and some television dramatic shows, her most recent acting was in real life, playing Margaret Dumont, Thelma Todd, or even Erin Fleming in everyday scenes with Groucho.

Energetic and high-spirited, she made powerful men quake in their Gucci shoes. Groucho paid tribute to her importance in his life in his acceptance speech at the Oscar ceremonies, along with his mother and Margaret Dumont, as one of the most important women in his life. Erin commemorated the occasion by wearing around her neck a tiny gold Oscar made for her by a Beverly Hills jeweler.

Following the 1974 Academy Awards, Erin received an avalanche of mail from secretaries who identified with her and were gratified by Groucho's heartfelt tribute. "Letters came from all over the country," she reported, "saying they've never felt that their bosses have appreciated them, and that at last a boss appreciated a secretary."

When she was very young, Erin was married to a successful New York lawyer. This marriage ended amicably in divorce, which was at least partially brought about by Erin's avid pursuit of a career on the stage. Her friend and agent Harvey Orkin suggested that she visit California to further her career. There he introduced her to producer Jerry Davis.

While she was sitting in his office, the whole course of her life was changed by a telephone call from Groucho that came through coincidentally at that moment. Jerry Davis, who didn't have a part for her, was glad to place the insistent Miss Fleming in something, even if only lunch. Erin relived that moment with Groucho and me while we were having lunch at Hillcrest Country Club:

ERIN

I was in Jerry Davis's office at Paramount looking at the pilot script for *The Odd Couple* when Groucho called him. Jerry said, "I'm sitting here with a pretty girl named Erin Fleming." "Erin Fleming!" Groucho said. "Is her name really Fleming?" Jerry asked me, "Is your name really Fleming?" I said yes, and Groucho said, "Send her over. Harpo had three girls named Fleming. I'd like to meet her." He had had a secretary for years, the one who saved up the Groucho letters. But she had caught a husband and moved to Portugal, so Groucho needed a secretary. He was complaining about this to Jerry on the phone. After Groucho hung up, Jerry said to me, "That would be a good job for you, Erin. You'd only have to work a couple of hours a day answering the mail and writing Groucho's letters. You'd have the rest of the time to look for acting work." But I said, "I don't want to be a secretary!" Anyway, at this time I had just moved to the Chateau Marmont to a writer's apartment who was out of town for a month, and I didn't know whether I was going to stay or what I was doing. When I got home, there was a message that Groucho called. So with trembling fingers I dialed Groucho, and he answered, "This is Groucho Marx, I would like you to come to dinner." He said his cook was off, and we could go out and have a bite to eat. We went to Dupar's and had buttermilk hotcakes. That's true, and Groucho flipped me . . .

GROUCHO

A five-dollar bill.

ERIN

No, you flipped me to see who paid, and I had to pay. It was about $3.25.

GROUCHO

We matched for the check?

ERIN

We matched for the check. I know when it was. It was around the first of August. Groucho asked me how old I was. I said he'd never get that kind of information out of me, but that my birthday was August the thirteenth, which was a couple of weeks away. So he called me several times. But at that time I was running around meeting all these producers and everything. Groucho called me and said, "Your birthday is next week. Would you like to come to my house to dinner?" So I went to Groucho's place for dinner on my birthday, and he had the Granets there and Arthur Jacobs, the producer of *Planet of the Apes*. Groucho had gone to Saks and bought me a bottle of perfume, which I still have. When he was at Saks, he ran into Anne Jackson and invited her to dinner the next night. He told me that she was coming to dinner the next night and could I come to dinner the night after my birthday. By then he had me around his little finger. He had a birthday cake, my favorite kind—a special carrot cake Martha made. And Arthur gave me a part in one of the *Apes* pictures.

GROUCHO

She was the leading ape.

ERIN

I wanted to be an ape, but I couldn't wear the contact lenses. My eyes hurt too much. So they just gave me a little part as one of the humans in it. I worked a couple of days, and made a lot of money. Then I became Groucho's secretary. You should have seen the mail he had. Boxes full! And he said, "I have a little mail to be answered."

GROUCHO

The little male was me.

ERIN

Yeah, that's true. You were the little male that needed answering.

Asked what was his first impression of Erin, Groucho answered, "I thought she was just a fleeting girl from New York." This attitude changed very quickly, to: "If she ever quit me, I'd quit show business."

Erin brought *future* into his life, both professionally and privately. With her, Groucho looked forward. Before she appeared, offers had been coming in all the time because he was still in big demand, but no one had paid any attention. Erin provided someone to do things *with* and someone to do things *for*. His late show-business years were linked to Erin, who was his personal manager without the official title for his triumphant trip to Ames, Iowa, and for his return to New York and the SRO Carnegie Hall performance. She also played an important role in planning the television appearances, the opening of *Animal Crackers* in New York, at which Groucho's attendance precipitated a riot (a good-natured riot), and the concerts in Los Angeles and San Francisco. With Erin, he felt he had turned over a new leaf.

Groucho had great respect for Erin's ability as a business manager, and talking about her business acumen, he frequently said, "She's much smarter than I am." He didn't like to concern himself much with the business of show business. He also took pride in Erin's talent as an actress who had done Shaw and Shakespeare. He felt, however, that she didn't *have* to take her clothes off, as she did in a Los Angeles stage production.

"You don't need to do that," he told her. "I've never taken off my clothes in a movie, and I don't see why you should, either. I don't belong in this world of nudity. What's sexy is what you don't see. Women are sexy if they have clothes on and you take them off. Then, you've triumphed. Once Boasberg wanted me to take off my pants. I wouldn't do it. I said I didn't need to take my pants off—on the stage, that is."

Erin regarded his attitude as outdated. Still, he did manage to see everything she did. He never tried to stop her from acting, even if he didn't deem the vehicle worthy of her talents. It was imperative to their relationship and rapport that Erin was *not* a "civilian," but a working member of the theatrical profession.

Groucho trusted Erin's judgment in most matters artistic, in all business matters, and he relished her accolades. Her influence was especially evident in his increased sartorial splendor. Her taste, and that of Bernie Schwartz and Peter Jarem, oracles of chic at the Eric Ross men's clothing store, was reflected in Groucho's English woolens, blazers, Marx Brothers print shirts, and colorful turtlenecks. "They have a vested interest in me," Groucho said.

But Groucho did have veto power, as he did in everything. While he joked about the ordeal and wiggled through fittings as if he were trying to extricate himself from the most excruciating discomfiture, there was deep down a bit of the male peacock whose prideful strut on catching a glimpse of himself in a full-length mirror indicated that the veto would not be exercised.

Groucho told Erin and me that too great an interest in shopping is feminine. "If you watch people walking down the street, the ones whose heads turn to look in all the store windows are women. Of course," he added, raising his eyebrows, "there are other ways to tell, too." He frowned on *nouveau riche* excesses, and ostentatious baubles were his verbal targets, although he was pleased by banker Al Hart's gift of a vicuña coat. Sometimes if something was too gaudy, he would tell Erin, "This is for people outside of show business who want to look like they're in show business."

Erin encouraged him to wear his beret, feeling that it kept him more readily identifiable as the Groucho character. As he put it, "She always berates me when I don't wear my beret." Sometimes he would add, "She redresses me."

Groucho liked order and didn't care for change where his house was concerned. When he said to Erin, "I'm the master of my house, girlie," his tone was light, but his meaning was serious.

His feeling for Erin was demonstrated when, at her instigation, he permitted interior decorator Peter Shore to, as Groucho put it, "tar and feather my nest." Erin said, "Grouch, your nest needs refurbishing." He countered, "Then I'll get new furbs." He added, muttering, "I think it's all a chip in the dale." Secretly, he liked the finished result, "especially that it's finished," and Peter Shore became a regular visitor at meals and to hang pictures. Groucho called me to announce the completion of the decorating: "Everything's new but me."

He summed it up in something less than gushing sentiment:

"If I didn't have Erin, I'd have old furniture."

Erin said, "If anyone writes a book about me, there is one thing they should say: the thing I can be remembered by is that whenever I arrive in a hotel room, the first thing I do is move the furniture around. I rearrange the furniture. I always do. You can quote me."

She meticulously arranged the furniture at Groucho's house or in his hotel rooms to be certain that his choice place was protected in any grouping for conversational chairs. But more important than arranging furniture, Erin was always going around looking for that unnoticed lamp or TV cord that might cause Groucho to trip.

Erin had her own separate residence, first an apartment, and later her own house. The house, which used to belong to Dorothy Parker, is located unfashionably just out of Beverly Hills.

Gossip usually had Erin living with Groucho. This was true only after her return from a hospital stay, during which time she recuperated at his house for a few weeks. Gossip also had Groucho buying her house for her, a story which displeased her because she felt it intruded on her privacy and distorted the facts. She felt it was *part* of a house, and the house was less than the mansion gossip built. Rumor reconstructed the modest residence into something more nearly resembling the palatial Harold Lloyd manor. Originally, Groucho wanted to pay cash for the whole house and give it to her, because owning one's own home free and clear was a kind of security he respected. He often repeated proudly, "I have the key to my front door." Erin refused this offer and spent a great deal of time deliberating about how many rooms of the house she should permit Groucho to give her before he prevailed.

On Valentine's Day, Groucho surprised her by sending her a gift of an oriental rug. Happily surprised, she asked him, "How did my rug get laid on Valentine's Day? I came home, and there it was. Did you lay my rug, Groucho?"

Groucho answered, "I'm not in the habit of laying rugs."

Erin's domesticity did not extend to the kitchen. Like Minnie, she would rather eat than cook. She did so with a ravenous abandon that astounded all who witnessed her devouring an entire sauceboat of Chasen's hot chocolate, butterscotch sundaes galore, or a good part of one of Dorris Johnson's chocolate cakes, while retaining a slim figure. All that brought her into the kitchen was some menu-planning or the fixing of tea that she drank with true British enthusiasm. Before the death of her beloved white Persian cat, however, Erin did cook Gabrielle's meal.

Having had her choice of a litter of pedigreed kittens, Erin chose Gaby, who was born crippled, because she felt that if *she* didn't take her no one else would.

Not liking to leave Gaby alone, Erin would sometimes drop her off with Groucho so he could "sit her." There was always someone cooking or working in Groucho's house. Gaby, however, objected to the strange surroundings and the presence of Groucho's own big black tomcat, Blackie.

One afternoon Groucho and I returned to find Gaby apparently having a fit. "That cat's gone mad," David Hixon told us as he let us in. "She's hysterical!" The cat was trying to climb the wall, flinging herself against furniture and making grotesque faces.

I phoned Erin, who said she was on her way. In the meantime, she said, "Tell David he should catch her so she doesn't hurt herself."

During the next ten minutes, there was intermittent bloodshed as a scratched and bleeding David tried to take hold of what had turned into a ferocious beast. "She's imitating Erin," someone suggested. Groucho said we should call the police. Just then, Erin arrived.

"Where's my poor baby?" she said. "What have you done to her?"

Rushing straight to Gaby, she scooped her up. Erin cradled the cat, who was purring loudly and had gone completely limp in her arms.

Erin likes things, but she doesn't take out much time for them. Occasionally, she enjoys shopping, remembering her mother's frustration at having to order from catalogues in the small town in Canada where they lived. She is an aficionado of garage sales and auctions. She likes clothes, but doesn't buy very many, wearing mostly pants and sweaters, with a small repertory of long dresses and a boa for the many formal affairs she and Groucho attended. Always busy and in motion, with the grace and agility of a professional dancer, extroverted, and energetic, Erin doesn't allot much time for vanity. Her hair, dark with a reddish cast, is worn loose, shoulder length or shorter. She is fair with high cheekbones, and a turned-up nose.

She could usually be found not far from Groucho's telephone, which was where the action was, or where she made it happen. She was as totally enchanted by Alexander Graham Bell's invention as Groucho was totally disenchanted by it, but Groucho didn't try to change her (knowing it was impossible) and she didn't try to change him (knowing it was impossible).

I asked Groucho how *he* saw Erin, and he answered, "Every day."

When her name was mentioned, he would sometimes say, "She's a cute girl, and I'm crazy about her" or "She's cute—for a girl."

Groucho said that she was an example of a "liberated" woman. Asked to explain what he meant by a liberated woman, he said, "She does as she damn well pleases."

He added, "I don't care what she does, as long as she doesn't tell me about it."

While Groucho sometimes encouraged her to go out with other men, there were few indeed who could measure up to his standard for her. Groucho referred to one potential suitor, "He's a wolf in cheap clothing." On another occasion, Erin mentioned someone with whom she had a dinner date:

GROUCHO
He's too old.
ERIN
He doesn't think so.
GROUCHO
They never do, until they're in bed.

During the years that Erin knew Groucho, several men showed interest in her, but none came to stay. Even in his eighties, there was only one Groucho Marx.

Occasionally, Groucho and Erin playacted commedia dell'arte style just for their own amusement. For a while Groucho would act as if he were Disraeli, whom he greatly admired, and Erin would act as if she were Queen Victoria.

Or Erin played frivolous conversation games with the master of uncommon nonsense. Groucho would say, "Pfeffermint," and Erin in mock exasperation said, "Oh, Grouch, you know it's *peppermint*. Say it, say *peppermint*." And Groucho knowingly responded, "Pfeffermint. There, I've said it."

Erin encouraged him to tell her about the old days with the Marx Brothers. One day he had been telling us about some actors he had known in vaudeville, and she commented:

ERIN
That must have been a long time ago.
GROUCHO
Everything I did was a long time ago.
ERIN
Not me!
GROUCHO
Except you.

He relished Erin's "Eye-talian" impression of actress Gina Lollobrigida. To encourage Erin, he would go to great lengths ("Great Lengths, Montana, that is"), even threatening *not* to sing "Omaha, Nebraska." Erin was always persuaded.

"When we were in Cannes there was a huge press conference after they gave Groucho his medal. And for some mysterious reason, they did not allow the American press in. And there were huge screams and hollers from Chuck Champlin and Hollis Alpert. And so Margaret Varga, who handled the press, decided to have a huge private luncheon in a very beautiful restaurant that's a house in the middle of the countryside. It was very elegant. And right down the whole center of the dining room, they had a huge table with all of the American press, perhaps seventy people. And the president of the Cannes Film Festival was Robert Favre Le Bret, who was very fond of Gina Lollobrigida, only we did not know this. And everyone sat where they were supposed to sit, and next to Groucho was Rex Reed, and Rex and Groucho were carving up the world together, and they were having a high old time. Opposite Groucho there was an empty space at the table. And it didn't dawn on me that somebody important would be sitting there.

"All of a sudden, Robert Favre Le Bret ushered in Gina Lollobrigida. Well, there was no way that I could tip him off, because it was all press, and Groucho was geared for press. And I was thinking, 'Oh, my God! What will he say, what can I do about it?' All of a sudden, she begins to talk, and he looked up from his lunch, and he said—and there was a great hush, because everyone wanted to hear every word that he said—'Hey, aren't you that Eye-talian broad who was on Perry Como with me about thirty years ago, the worst dog he ever produced?' And she said, 'I was just a child at ze time!' And he said, 'Oh, I see. Now you're all grown up, and you shave three times a day, huh?' By this time, Rex Reed is under the table, Chuck Champlin is in his soup, and I said, 'Oh, Miss Lollobrigida, he means you have a very lovely complexion,' and he said, 'Yeah, but you can't see it under all that paint and paste.' Silence. Everyone is dying. No one knows what to do. All of a sudden, in this void, Groucho says, 'Hey, Gina! What do you hear from the Pope?' And she said, 'Ze Pope, he iss a very beeg star. And I, Gina Lollobrigida, I am a very beeg star. And two very beeg stars together, zat iss very boring.' And at that point, Groucho went over and took her hand and took her out to all the photographers, and they had a lot of pictures taken together."

Groucho was so pleased by Erin's recital that he failed to keep his threat and sang "Omaha, Nebraska" twice.

The man who had the talent to amuse so many people was highly apprecia-tive of those who had the talent to amuse him. Erin had the knack of amus-ing Groucho, and she worked at it. A performer herself, one of her more shining moments was at the end of Groucho's party for his Oscar at Hill-crest. There was a relatively impromptu amateur hour by the guests who were celebrities, and the stars rose spontaneously to perform and to pay trib-ute to their host. The evening's repast had been converted into bones, shells, crumbs, and dirty plates, and the orchestra members were about to pack up, when Erin took the stage and began a dance that would have put a whirling dervish to shame. The orchestra managed with effort to follow her as she built from wild to wilder. Her professional skill, combined with her zeal, produced a few minutes which were memorable for the last linger-ing guests, the Hillcrest Club waiters and busboys, and especially for Grou-cho, whose eyes never left her. It was her gift to him, and he knew it.

Groucho was never confused about Erin's identity, but some of his old friends occasionally slipped and called her "Eden." At such moments, Erin was definitely not amused, and there were spirited reverberations. In-dividual and flamboyant, more odd than even, she never bored Groucho. She was his last leading lady and first fan.

Certainly Erin was the fan Groucho cared most about pleasing.

Actress Anna Strasberg told me of meeting Groucho at Tana's Restaurant in Beverly Hills. Burgess Meredith, who was with her and her husband, Lee Strasberg, introduced them. Anna was pleased to meet Groucho for the first time, and he was thrilled to meet Lee Strasberg. "Wait till I tell Erin," Groucho said with gleeful jubilance.

On another occasion, Groucho returned from his daily Beverly Hills peregrination to find Erin at his house for lunch. He reported, "I met a woman I used to go out with thirty years ago, and now she's a big, fat woman." Erin pointed out, "You mean she got older and you didn't get any older." He immediately got her message and came back with, "No, I'm as young as the day is long, and this has been a very short day."

The world looked somewhat askance at their relationship, emphasizing the half century of age difference, but Groucho and Erin shared a relationship that had more *quid pro quo* than is customarily assumed. They saw their relationship as complementary and complimentary.

At a charity dinner we attended in honor of Jack Benny, Jack greeted Groucho and Erin saying, "I'm glad you're here." Groucho responded, "If not for her, I wouldn't be here, but then she wouldn't be here if it weren't for me."

Erin was Groucho's secretary and personal manager, confidante and companion, and girl Friday-through-Thursday. Their age difference, while fraught with serious problems, did have its lighter aspect. Erin told Groucho and me about one perceptive observation made by Bill Cosby:

"When we were in Reno last weekend, Bill told me that he went into the casino, and a girl there said to him, 'I saw Groucho Marx, I saw Groucho Marx coming into the hotel, and he was with a very young girl.' When Bill saw me he told me about it, and Bill said, 'That's what *he* does for you. If you walked into this hotel with me or a man my age, they wouldn't say that. But you walk in with Groucho and they say, "There's a *very* young girl." ' "

Asked to explain their relationship by a Canadian newspaperman who was interviewing her, Erin sought Groucho's advice in answering some of the questions:

ERIN
Can you explain our relationship?
GROUCHO
Yes. I'm madly in love with you, and you're my secretary.

ERIN

They ask, "Why is it that you've never married me, Groucho?" What's the answer to that?

GROUCHO

I'm too old. I wouldn't marry you, because I can't give you what you need sexually.

Later Groucho told me, "It's a strange thing. You can still love somebody even if you're not going to bed with them." Erin told me many times her reason for not marrying him:

"I love Groucho, but I want to have a child."

Sometimes, however, he treated their relationship lightly, with a flippant irreverence. When the three of us had lunch with British writer Richard Adams, Groucho and I arrived first, then Erin dashed in for a moment and dashed right away. Adams asked, "Who was that?" Groucho answered, "That's Erin. She's just a simple, foolish girl. I can't do anything for her, except physically."

Groucho explained to me how he managed Erin: "I let her think she's having her own way. Then . . . I let her have it."

While Groucho's own Jewishness was not something he gave much thought to, it was something to which Erin gave a great deal of thought. She attributed much of his superior adjustment to life to a security and stability which grew out of his ethnocentric, if not theological, orientation. She hoped that conversion to Judaism would bring her a contentment and feeling of peace in a troubled universe that no religion had yet successfully given her. Her respect for Judaism was enhanced not only by her relationship with Groucho but by that with others of his friends who were born Jewish. She liked the family values and the group cohesiveness as well as the mystical nature, and the precepts seemed suitable to her own needs.

Deciding to convert to Judaism, to commemorate the event, Erin wrote a song entitled "Jewish in June" and set forth to be not only Jewish but more Jewish than Groucho ever was. She adhered not only to the cultural traditions which he and his Jewish friends took for granted, but she strove for the more formalized procedures. Her attendance at temple with Groucho, who hadn't gone to a temple for many years, was a regular Friday night occurrence. She studied Hebrew and the religious tenets. On Friday nights she lit the candles in the silver menorah, following a tradition that had not been practiced in a home of Groucho's for more than half a century, saying, *"Bo-ruch at-taw a-do-noy elo-hay-nu meh . . ."* She was sponsored by an adopted Jewish mother, Eve Lazarus, and supported by the ten Jewish men who formed the requisite minyan, among them Elliott Gould and George Segal. Erin wore a long white suit and described the experience as "like being a bride." Her Jewish name became "Chayah."

Erin told me about her experience:

"They were preparing me all winter. Elliott and I went through the Talmud together.

"At my mitzvah, it was like a spaceship. The designs were brought from Israel, and they're all spaceship, outer space. It was incredible, like a five-thousand-year-old mosaic design. It's a tiny round chapel. It was as if we were floating in space, quite a sensation. Elliott Gould organized the minyan, ten men all dressed in white suits. Eve Lazarus arranged for a song that the choir girl sang. I knew what I had to do, but I didn't know what the service would be like. There were two cantors and the rabbi. In the middle of the service, there were all the tears. He grabbed both my hands, and everybody in the audience cried."

Groucho took the whole experience less reverently than Erin. He called me to tell me that Erin had become Jewish, and he added, "Now I'm converting. I'm becoming a Catholic, and I'm changing my name to O'Hoolihan. Pat O'Hoolihan." He added, "The Reverend Patrick O'Hoolihan."

In relationships of any consequence between a man and a woman, from time to time there may be some variation in roles. Regardless of age, the man may at times be the woman's father, and at times her child, as well as her brother and her friend. "If I adopt Erin, she'll be my only Jewish daughter," Groucho noted, Miriam and Melinda each being only half Jewish. (Erin's own father had died when she was quite young, and her mother died a number of years ago after a long illness.) But Groucho felt he always had to encourage Erin to find a young husband for "love, marriage, and baby carriage."

Erin was sometimes criticized for leading a superannuated Groucho back to stage center. It was Groucho, however, who did the leading. He was never pushed except in the direction he wanted to go. Erin was accused of overexposing the legendary Groucho Marx through too much enthusiasm and too little discretion, but Groucho was not among those critics. His love of performing had not diminished with the years. If anything, it had increased.

This was most evident in his social life. Any party at his or anyone else's home where he didn't sing about Lydia the Tattooed Lady or Peasie Weasie was not a party in Groucho's book. "I leave early, even if I'm at home." Erin, understanding Groucho's love of performing, often joined him in the song and dance for "Peasie Weasie" and always made certain that a capable piano player was high on the list of guests invited to every party at Groucho's house. Erin was the girl in Groucho's act, whether on-stage at Carnegie Hall, or in Elliott Gould's living room. And the audiences, paying or invitation only, were still SRO.

Sometimes Erin envisioned some exceedingly ambitious plans for a future that would have required decades. Once, as she enthusiastically reeled off a dizzying array of future possibilities, Groucho commented dryly, "In the meantime I plan on dying."

Groucho had absolute faith in Erin's business sense, but she was less than perfectly confident. She felt the necessity to present a façade of total competence in order not to be patronized as a woman.

At one office meeting between several sets of lawyers and agents, Erin tried to represent the personification of sophisticated composure. She looked intensely absorbed while Groucho, leaving it all to her, flipped casually through a magazine.

Voices were raised in a climax of dissension. Everyone turned toward Groucho, who wasn't paying any attention. Then they turned to Erin. With aloof disdain, she rose and excused herself to go to the ladies' room. She excused me, too.

Just outside in the hall, Erin turned to me and said, "How'd I do? Was I good?" Then she asked, "What was that last part all about?" Groucho joined us at that moment and filled in the answer:

"About forty minutes."

As Groucho's business manager, Erin made a brief foray into product licensing. There were Groucho watches, which did a land office business. (Groucho said they should have opened a land office instead.) Although there was a tremendous demand for the long-awaited wristwatches, only a small number of the fans who would have liked them ever had the chance to buy them, since Groucho decided he wanted to give them to his friends—and he had a great many friends. At Groucho's Oscar party at Hillcrest Country Club, a watch was put at each guest's place. The temptation was too great for some culprit, who made off with half the watches. As Groucho put it, "Those watches weren't even going, and now they're gone." He made good on the watches, which was more than the manufac-

turer had. As Groucho said, "The second hands often came in third."
Groucho bought more watches than anyone else, and the whole project
proved less than a profitable venture. The last Groucho watch was worn
by him to the New York re-premiere of *Animal Crackers*, where he took it
off his wrist and gave it to me with the admonition, "It's half-past Groucho."

"Tell 'em Groucho sent you" sweatshirts were also part of the same
business. Groucho gave the last one to Dick Cavett, who immediately
stripped (to the waist, that is) and put on his gift. "How do you like it?"
Groucho inquired. Dick Cavett replied with wavering enthusiasm, "I
don't know if I feel good about wearing you on my stomach."

The profits of the licensing operation were destined for a company that
combined "Groucho" and "Erin" to make "GRIN" but which, at times,
seemed more "CHAGRIN."

The business of licensing Groucho products lost out to more interesting competing projects before the "Stateroom Jam" could be spread on
bread and before "Tell 'em Groucho sent you" jockstraps, facetiously suggested by Goddard Ueberson, could be marketed.

In November 1974, Groucho called me long distance and said, "Erin's
going to Paris to do a film. You *have* to come right now and stay with me
at my house." Later Erin called, saying, "You've got to come. You're the
only one I could trust."

Just before leaving, Erin counseled me, "Now you handle Groucho
just the way I do." She might as well not have spoken.

Groucho liked to spend the morning clad in pajamas while he read
until it was time for us to walk. One day we had a lunch appointment
with Jack Nicholson and Mike Nichols at the Beverly Hills Hotel. As the
time drew near, Groucho made no move to get ready. Gently, I reminded
him that we would be late unless he started right away, *even* if he started
right away.

Nothing happened.

After a decent interval, I forced myself to mention lunch again. Still
nothing happened.

I
Do you plan to go to lunch in your pajamas?
GROUCHO
I shot an elephant in my pajamas once.

I
I know.
GROUCHO
You know everything.
I
Not really.
GROUCHO
You're too young to know that.
I
No one is too young to know *that*. And I know you don't like to be late for an appointment, even less than I do.
GROUCHO
You're the only person besides me who goes early not to be late.
I
But today I think we're going to keep Jack and Mike waiting.
GROUCHO
Hello, I must be going.

We did go to lunch but were quite late. Groucho didn't mention it, though, and neither did anyone else.

When Erin returned from Europe, history repeated itself. The three of us were due to have lunch at the Beverly Hills Hotel with Jack Nicholson and Mike Nichols, who was bringing along his baby, Max.

"That baby's going to grow up if we wait for you, Grouch," Erin announced loudly enough so that even if the batteries in Groucho's hearing aid had run down, he couldn't have missed a syllable. She pulled off his pajama top, which he seemed to enjoy, and she threatened to pull off the bottom part too if he didn't get ready.

"There's nothing there," he said softly.

"We'll see about that if you don't step on it," she shrieked, reaching for the drawstring, and Groucho retreated to the bathroom.

We were the first to arrive at lunch.

Because Groucho's and Erin's relationship defied routine categorizing and didn't fit the so-called normal niche, they, and especially she, offered a highly visible target at which many took aim. Wounded by innuendo and pained by the gold-digger gossip, Erin, who is naturally an extremely extroverted person, tended to retire from an arena where she had seen too many thumbs turned down. In her 1975 "Santa Claws" list, columnist Joyce Haber suggested as a Christmas present to Erin and Groucho "a pre-reading of the will." Erin said emphatically, "I never want to see my name in the newspaper again."

At lunch at New York's Sherry Netherland Hotel with Betty Comden, Adolph Green, Groucho, and myself, Erin explained why she no longer cared about being an actress, if it meant being typecast: "I never wanted to see my name in print again. I just couldn't stand all that pain. I'm not a hooker, and there I was being fitted for black garters again. I was in Paris, and it was the same old thing. I asked Woody [Woody Allen, for the film *Love and Death*] if I could be the one to have a little red-haired baby at the end of the film. Instead, I got fittings in black garters. If I played that part, with the publicity, well, I just couldn't take that kind of punishment. I don't want to play the hooker. I'm tired of being cast in that part."

While Groucho would have treated a light subject seriously, he would rarely have treated a serious subject any way but lightly. On receiving Erin's telephone call to say that she was back from Paris, Groucho remarked, "It's a gala day," adding, "I can't handle more than a gal a day." When Erin arrived at Groucho's house, he greeted her:

GROUCHO
I'm glad you're back, if only temporarily.
ERIN
Temporarily glad?
GROUCHO
I'm not completely glad.
ERIN
(*Laughs*) Why not?
GROUCHO
I love you.
ERIN
So?
GROUCHO
That's why I'm glad.
ERIN
So why not completely?
GROUCHO
Modesty.

Since Erin was a permanent member of Groucho's audience while the other constituents of it were constantly changing, she had occasion to hear a favored story more than once. When Groucho told a story she had heard a few times before, she would get up and stalk out, saying, "I'm leaving the room," or she would say to him, "I've heard that one before," to which he would respond softly, "So have I."

Groucho and Erin were both compatible and combatable. Some people objected to the forceful way she pushed him verbally and, at moments, even physically. They speculated on her screaming at him, which some considered "cruel" but which Groucho found exhilarating. Buoyed by the tension, he liked being the object of passionate feelings.

Whenever Groucho and Erin would have a quarrel, as she had more to say, he would have less to say. As her voice grew louder, his became softer until sometimes he was just barely moving his lips. Shortly after I met Groucho, I was in his bedroom with them when a grand-scale quarrel broke out. I could find no place to hide. The three of us were just about to go out to dinner at Chasen's, but the raging battle didn't promise a festive meal ahead or good digestion.

ERIN
(*Screaming at Groucho*) I'm not *going* to dinner with you!
GROUCHO
(*Softly*) Good. (*Turning to me and taking my arm*) We're going to dinner.
ERIN
She's having dinner with *me*.
GROUCHO
(*To me in a tone that indicated it wasn't a question*) Are you ready.
ERIN
She's not going with you either.

Groucho turned and walked slowly toward the front door. As he disappeared from sight, Erin pushed me out the bedroom door, saying, "Hurry, go with him!"

At Chasen's, Groucho was quiet and petulant during dinner. He spent a lot of time studying his plate intently. At intervals he would look up at me and announce, "I don't need her."

We were interrupted by the approach of the maître d':

MAÎTRE D'
Mr. Marx, there's a call for you from Miss Fleming.

GROUCHO
(*Studying his plate intently*) I'm not here.
    I
(*To Groucho*) Would you like me to tell her?
    GROUCHO
Yeah.

I went to the phone and spoke with Erin, who told me that she would call back in half an hour. The next call came in the middle of the banana cream pie. Usually a highlight of Groucho's dinner, he was eating it as if it were a cardboard model.

    MAÎTRE D'
Mr. Marx, it's Miss Fleming calling.
    GROUCHO
I'm not here.
    I
Should I tell her that?
    GROUCHO
Yeah.

I took the call, informing Erin that Groucho still wasn't ready to come to the phone. "I'll be waiting at the house for you," she told me.

When I got back to the table, Groucho was still toying with the same forkful of banana cream pie. He wouldn't have asked me what Erin had said if we'd sat there for a million years, so I volunteered the information.

"I don't need her," Groucho replied.

Arriving at his house, Groucho proceeded directly back to his bedroom, where all of the lights were on and the door was slightly ajar. I stopped in the living room.

After several minutes, Erin called out for me to come to the bedroom, where Groucho was now smiling and she was plotting the next day's schedule, exuberantly persuading him to do exactly what he wanted to do anyway.

Although others might have been horrified, the *Sturm und Drang* that Erin provided was the slice of strife Groucho relished. His happy life as a performer was filled with exciting stress. If there was a need for stability, there was also a need for instability, because one way to die is of boredom.

With Erin around, he was never bored. If he was perpetual motion, she was perpetual emotion.

Groucho was speaking very intensely to Erin about what they had together and what they didn't have. Erin, discomforted by so much seriousness and having no easy answer, tossed her hair, and said coyly in a playful tone to Groucho, "Oh, Grouch, you say that, but a more beautiful girl will come along, and you'll forget all about me." A straight line like that one immediately brought Groucho to his nonsenses: "No, I won't. I'll write twice a week."

If Groucho's and Erin's relationship were to be summed up in one word, that word would have been *"Steckrueben,"* which Groucho explained means "turnips" in German. It was their private communication. Whenever Erin felt that he was not reacting to someone in an appropriate manner, she simply said *"Steckrueben"* and he managed an extremely pasted-on smile. "It means, 'Be in a good mood because you're being an old, crabby grouch,' " Erin explained. "I am not," Groucho grumbled.

Erin took Marvin Hamlisch and Mike Nichols into their confidence, explaining the need for "a code" between her and Groucho:

"We have signals for various occasions because we've been through some disasters. We have things that nobody can possibly catch on to. *Steckrueben!*"

At the sound of *Steckrueben,* Groucho immediately assumed a forced-looking sugar-coated grin, much to the amusement of Mike and Marvin. "Pretty subtle," remarked Mike Nichols. "We'd never have guessed," seconded Marvin Hamlisch.

Erin continued the demonstration:

"Would you like to see some more? Okay, Groucho."

Erin coughed.

"What does that mean, Erin?" asked Mike.

"It isn't the cough that carries you off, it's the coffin they carry you off in," answered Groucho.

"Oh, Groucho," scolded Erin, "you know that's not it!"

"I don't remember," he said quite honestly.

"That's right!" she said. "That means you say you don't remember." Then she cleared her throat quite obviously.

"That means I'm not supposed to talk too much. I'm supposed to be Harpo," Groucho said, "and keep my mouth shut."

"We decided we *had* to do this," Erin explained, "because sometimes he'll get to talking, and I'll catch on that they're nasty and they're gonna zing us!"

Erin might have said *Steckrueben* in any situation from a charity dinner to a legal session with lawyers and depositions, or just on a walk along the street when they passed someone she thought Groucho *ought* to have remembered. Perhaps *Steckrueben* reminded him of "Greenbaum"—Minnie's whispered warning from the wings to her boys when they started clowning around too much onstage. Greenbaum was the name of the banker who held the mortgage on their house in Chicago. Minnie was admonishing, "Don't fool around so much that you get fired and we can't pay off the mortgage."

Just after his eighty-fifth birthday, Groucho, Erin, and I were at lunch at Groucho's with writer Jon Nordheimer from the *New York Times*, who had come to do a feature on Groucho. Groucho was expounding on a frequent and favorite subject, the importance of Erin in his life. He was extolling her virtues when she interjected:

"Grouch, don't you remember when you were angry at me? You said you were New York, and I was Newark."

Groucho, with a look of utter sobriety (and nobody could look more sober than he could), answered, "I'm Los Angeles, and you're Paris."

"The Lord Alps those that Alps themselves"

"Beyond the Alps lies more Alps, and the Lord Alps those that Alps themselves."

GROUCHO, as Napoleon in *I'll Say She Is*

Groucho's ethnocentricity manifested itself in certain residual attachments to food and a few of the customs, but even where his religion was concerned, his eccentricity exceeded his ethnocentricity. He had the traditional Jewish, as well as German, extreme respect for education and for writing. He was an avid, inveterate, incessant reader in the tradition of the *yeshivah bucher*, the pure Hebrew scholar. Reading several hours a day, especially nonfiction, he could always find satisfaction and escape in the pages of books. In the afternoons we would sit together in his bedroom and read. Books were the gifts most often given to him by his friends whose only problem was, as Goddard Lieberson pointed out, "to find something he hasn't already read." Groucho took greater pride in his works as a writer than he did in his talent as a performer.

If there *was* any regret he had in life, it was in not having had more formal education and in not having gone to college. He joked, "That's why I don't care about football, because I didn't go to college." But, as usual, he was speaking lightly of what he took most seriously. He valued tremendously the friendship of writers, and he was proud of having had as friends George S. Kaufman, Ring Lardner, T. S. Eliot, James Thurber, S. J. Perelman, Morrie Ryskind, Goodman Ace, Adolph Green, Betty Comden, Nunnally Johnson, George Seaton, Sidney Sheldon, Goddard Lieberson, and Woody Allen.

Groucho's German and Jewish heritage also manifested itself in his desire for precision, punctuality, and perfection. Always giving the best he had, he was intolerant of those who gave less than one hundred per cent. The work ethic was an integral part of him, and he was still in motion, if indeed slower motion, still maintaining a partial work schedule into his middle eighties.

He had a strong belief in family life. The Marxes no longer here—Grandfather Opie, Frenchie, Chico, Harpo, Aunt Hannah, and especially Minnie—all lived on with Groucho, for whom blood was thicker than celery tonic. As one who greatly respected marriage, Groucho three times pursued his childhood ideal of marriage. His children, as well as his grandchildren, were important to him.

Groucho faced life with a kind of stoicism that well may have stemmed from the influence of the endurance of the immigrant. His grandparents and parents came to a new world, not of *pâté de foie gras* but of liverwurst; not of roast goose but of chicken soup; not of caviar but of wilted cabbage and ham hocks. The opportunity was here, but the streets were not exactly paved with gold, nor were they always even paved. It is quite probable that the daily immigrant struggle of his parents helped to teach him how to exist from day to day, living life in the present, twenty-four hours at a time.

Occasionally Groucho reminisced about his own bar mitzvah. On our way to dinner, he talked about it with Arthur Whitelaw and me:

"I remember my bar mitzvah speech. It was a great speech. My father bought it for five dollars, and all five boys used it. Each of us boys used the same speech. A dollar a man."

Groucho still remembered how it began:

" 'My dear parents: For thirteen long years you have toiled and labored for my happiness. From the moment I saw the light of day you have watched over me . . .' Or 'washed over me'—I forget which."

Arthur Whitelaw asked where we were going to have dinner.

"You're *treif,* and you're *treif.* But I'm kosher, so we're going to a kosher restaurant," Groucho informed us.

He took us to Chasen's, which he advised us "is as kosher as pork chops."

Ethel Wise, whose family lived above the Marxes in New York's Yorkville section, remembered Groucho's grandfather's ties to Jewish tradition:

"I can still see Grandfather Marx sitting in the front room on Ninety-third Street reading the Torah. He sat on the stoop and told all of us children stories from the Haggadah in German. He also did magic tricks, which we liked even more."

Minnie, however, was more occupied with building her brother's and her boys' careers, and Sam was more interested in gastronomy than in Deuteronomy. Groucho was proud of Frenchie's Gallic apron-string ties to France. "He didn't know about blintzes; he made crêpes."

Groucho sometimes referred to "my Italian brother, Chico." He said, "People always asked me, 'Is Chico really Italian?' " The two of them had visited Germany as children to see Minnie's birthplace, choosing the trip instead of proffered express wagons. Groucho's world was never purely chicken soup but always a melting pot.

The Marx family was always ready to celebrate a holiday—*anyone's* holiday: Christmas, Chanukah, Thanksgiving, St. Patrick's Day—as long as there were good things to eat. Groucho's cook, Robin, whom he called "the first cook of spring," once asked Groucho about Christmas:

ROBIN

Are you looking forward to a Merry Christmas, Groucho?

GROUCHO

Is that a girl?

ROBIN

Seriously, are you sick of it at this point in life? You can remember more than eighty Christmases. After all these years isn't it just too commercial and the same old thing?

GROUCHO

No.

ROBIN

Did your family celebrate Christmas when you were a little boy?

GROUCHO

They celebrated it, but we didn't get anything. I got a pair of black stockings and half an orange.

I

Did you believe in Santa Claus?

GROUCHO

Yeah, my father.

ROBIN

What else did you do at Christmas when you were a child?

GROUCHO

Well, we used to build forts out of snow in New York.

ROBIN

Did you sing Christmas carols?

GROUCHO

I didn't know any.

ROBIN

Did you have a Christmas tree as a child?

GROUCHO

No, I had a branch.

Groucho was innately but not blatantly Jewish. He felt that he was not "a professional Jew." On a walk in New York along Park Avenue with actor Bud Cort and me, Groucho used that phrase to describe someone he knew.

"What's a professional Jew?" Bud Cort asked.

"Someone who sees everything from a Jewish point of view," Groucho explained.

Groucho did not follow religious orthodoxy, but then he was not an orthodox person. Religious and personal unorthodoxy characterized Groucho, who was always questioning. His old friend Julius Epstein, who co-wrote the screenplay for *Casablanca*, said that if it had not already been used and if he were writing a book about Groucho, he would call it *Nothing Sacred*.

Groucho, however, had an abiding respect for ethical tradition in all religions. This did not mean that his religion, as well as any other, might not at one moment or another be at the receiving end of one of his barbed comments:

"There used to be an old joke at an Irish wake. The body is laying there, and some woman says to the widow, 'The body is still warm!' And the widow says, 'Hot or cold, it goes out in the morning.' "

On Chanukah, Groucho would greet friends, Jewish or Gentile, with "Happy Harmonica."

Generally, Groucho didn't like ethnic humor. At lunch with Goodman Ace, he stopped "Goody" during a foreign accent joke. "The Marx Brothers didn't depend on ethnic humor," Groucho said. "Either a joke is funny or it isn't. Making the person Polish or Italian or Jewish doesn't make it funny if it isn't." Privately, however, Groucho sometimes did share a small ethnic joke with a friend. "Would you like some Jewish ice cream?" he asked me as we walked along Rodeo in Beverly Hills. "An ice cream Cohn?" He added, "It's not much of a joke." Inside the ice-cream parlor, I was a bit short-scooped. When he saw my meager portion, he said, "It's not much of a cone, either."

In his eighties Groucho started going to temple on Friday nights—Temple Emanuel on Burton Way in Beverly Hills. This is a Reform temple, modern in an affluent community. The rabbi was articulate and interested not only in theology but in community affairs. Groucho was invited to be the guest of honor. Erin talked with him about the invitation:

ERIN
The rabbi wants you on the pulpit, Groucho.
GROUCHO
On the what?
ERIN
On the stage. How about it, Groucho?
GROUCHO
When is it?
ERIN
Next Friday night.
GROUCHO
I'll let you know.
ERIN
When?
GROUCHO
Next month.

I went with Groucho and Erin to the temple, where we were joined by Eve Lazarus, Erin's "adopted Jewish mother." As guest of honor, Groucho was seated on the dais. It was children's night at the temple, and Groucho was called upon by Rabbi Meyer Heller to say something to the assemblage.

"Can I tell a story? A married woman with two children killed her husband with a bow and arrow. They asked her, 'Why a bow and arrow?' She said, 'I didn't want to wake the children.' "

The children (of all ages) were quite amused. As we got into the car while Groucho was signing some autographs after the service, Erin commented to me, "Children really love him, because he has the same kind of innocence they have and is as open to life as they are."

Afterward she asked Groucho, "Weren't the children cute?"

"All children are cute," he answered. "It's only after they grow up that the trouble starts."

Groucho had apparent immunity from having to worry about what other people thought. The Marx Brothers were never bound by anyone else's rules, Groucho even less than his brothers. The inhibition barrier that stopped others was nonexistent for Groucho Marx. He did what others wanted to do, wading in where ordinary mortals feared to tread, and he was usually rewarded where anyone else would be punished.

He brought Marxamania even to temple. At the beginning of the service the rabbi said, "Please be seated," and Groucho got up. Later he asked the congregation to rise, and Groucho sat down. The rabbi then asked the question traditionally asked on the first night of the seder:

"*Mah nishtanaw ha-lahy-lah ha-zeh mi-cawl ha-lay-los . . .*" ("Why is this night different from all the others?")

Groucho answered, "Because *I'm* here."

Afterward the rabbi announced, "And now I'm going to deliver the blessing."

"Whoopee!" Groucho exclaimed.

On another night as he was leaving another temple, he said to that rabbi, who was surrounded by people and who happened to be bearded, "Rabbi, your whiskers are on fire."

Even for a rabbi in a temple in Beverly Hills, following a Marx Brother wasn't easy. Groucho didn't hesitate to take aim at the establishment, even when it was his own religion. But when he was involved, everyone turned out the better for wear. The next Friday night, word had spread that Groucho Marx might be on the bill, and the house was filled. Even when the performance was unscheduled, and even in temple, Groucho was a "hot ticket" personality.

One night Erin brought the car to a stop in front of the temple, and Groucho tried to open the door. The night before when he had found it difficult to open the door on his side, Erin had shot around to open it for him. "You don't *ever* open the door for me, girlie!" he had said then, about as sharply as I'd ever heard him speak to her. He grumbled and muttered the rest of the evening. When he again experienced difficulty in pushing open the car door, Erin just sat back in the driver's seat while Groucho looked out of the corner of his eye at her.

"Don't you look at me, Grouch. We'll just sit here all evening." For some very long minutes it appeared that we were going to do exactly that. Meanwhile a crowd of the temple-goers had gathered by the car, eagerly awaiting the temple's most celebrated member.

Making a great effort, Groucho heaved with all the strength he had, the door swung open, and he pitched forward. He would have fallen on his face except for Eve Lazarus, who had been waiting for him, her arms outstretched. As he fell on top of her, she cushioned his fall.

"This doesn't mean anything," he said from a prone position on top of the supine Mrs. Lazarus.

Neither of them was injured, and he recovered his aplomb and, with our help, his balance.

Once when Groucho went to temple on Friday night, the rabbi's subject for discussion was "mixed marriages." The rabbi posed two questions: 1) Should a Jew and gentile marry? 2) What are the consequences of such a mixed marriage? An audience discussion followed which was very serious and rather heated.

Groucho let everyone have his say, and then he spoke:

"I think it's all right for a Jew to marry a gentile girl, as long as she's rich."

Everyone laughed, including the rabbi. Although Groucho had been married to three gentile women, he certainly wasn't speaking from personal experience. He never had a Jewish wife or a Jewish child. When his son was rejected by an exclusive pool club, Groucho wrote back asking if young Arthur could go into the water up to his waist, "since he's only half Jewish."

Hoping to steep daughter Melinda in tradition, Groucho sent her to Israel, but she departed precipitously, disappointing her concerned father.

At a Christmas holiday dinner at Groucho's, he and Goddard Lieberson talked about the phenomenon of the Yiddish theatre in its historical perspective, mentioning names like Tonieschevsky and *The Dybbuk*. Goddard discussed "its display of virtuosity comparable to that of Italian opera." But the Yiddish theatre was a subject Groucho admitted he never knew much about. "It was important in its time," he commented. "Paul Muni was great. Fred Allen used to go. George Jessel used to go. I didn't talk Yiddish. But I looked Jewish, and oddly enough I still do." Groucho learned German in his home, but he never knew Yiddish.

World War II was a rude shock to Groucho, who was an American first, but who also felt very strongly his German-Jewish heritage. He told Arthur Whitelaw and me how, after the war, he made a special trip to Germany. "I wanted to dance on Hitler's grave."

An event which upset him as much as anything during the time I knew him was the murder of the Israeli athletes at the Munich Olympics. Groucho felt sports intensely, as he did Jewish things, and as he did wrongdoing. The horror of the crime was something he felt as deeply as if a member of his own family had been a victim. "When they shot those Jewish boys over there," he told me, "I took eight sleeping pills that night, and the next day I was in the hospital. That was one of the most shocking things in my whole life."

Two people in the world for whom Groucho felt great admiration were Golda Meir and Henry Kissinger. They are Jewish. Nevertheless, Groucho felt that if their names were O'Meir and Von Kissinger, it wouldn't have made any difference.

Usually Groucho answered the question "Who would you like to have been?" with "Groucho Marx." But one night on the way to temple, Erin asked him this question, and he answered, "Disraeli."

Groucho's friend director George Seaton, of Swedish descent, baptized a Roman Catholic, grew up in a Detroit Jewish neighborhood, and described himself as a "Shabbas goy." On Saturday the Orthodox Jewish boys all wanted to go to the movies, but they couldn't buy the tickets on Saturday afternoon. George Seaton was elected to carry all of the money and stand at the box office and buy all of the tickets. One day when it was raining and he was waiting outside on the temple steps for his friends, the rabbi came out and invited him in. So he went on to learn Hebrew and was even bar mitzvahed. He still has the fountain pen he received as a gift.

When he settled in Hollywood, George Seaton decided to join a country club, but not a restricted country club that excluded Jews, so he turned to Hillcrest. At a Hillcrest luncheon, he talked with Groucho and me about the difficulties he had encountered:

GEORGE SEATON
Did I ever tell you the story about how I got into Hillcrest? I'm not Jewish, you know.

GROUCHO
Just what we need. More gentiles.

GEORGE SEATON
When I decided to play golf, I was invited to Bel Air, and I said, "Are you restricted?" And they said, "Oh yes." And I said, "Thank you very much. I don't believe in that kind of nonsense." And I left. I went to Lakeside — the same thing. So, finally I said to my partner, Bill Perlberg, "Is there any chance that I can get into Hillcrest?" And he said, "Sure, come on." So I put in my application and I was turned down because they didn't take gentiles.

GROUCHO
We had a big meeting right after that.

GEORGE SEATON
So they said that they couldn't take me, and I asked why. I appeared before the committee, and they said, "Look, we'll give you all the privileges, which will be the same thing that Skouras had. You can sign bills and you can

play, but you cannot be a member." So I said, "I don't want to be tolerated. I'm either in or I'm out." I had to go before the admissions committee and they said, "You must understand our point of view. If you let one in, then you let two in, and pretty soon they'll take over the club." I fell through the floor, it was so funny. Well, Dore Senary heard about this, and he went before the committee and said, "I resign unless Seaton gets in." So they said, "All right, resign." He cashed in his membership for $4,000, which is what it was at the time. Then Groucho and my partner, Bill Perlberg, and Harpo and Chico had a big meeting, and they had about eighty signatures . . .

GROUCHO
Jack Benny.

GEORGE SEATON
Jack Benny, Al Jolson, and they said if I didn't get in, they were all going to resign. Well, the club couldn't withstand that, so I was the first gentile member of the club. Dore Schary had won his battle. I was in. Now he comes back and says, "All right, he's in. I'll come back." And they said, "We're sorry, but there's a waiting list." Well, when his turn came around . . .

GROUCHO
Good joke on him.

GEORGE SEATON
. . . it was $8,500 to get in. He said it was the most expensive principle that he ever adhered to. Now we have Jack Lemmon as a member, and quite a few others.

When Groucho received his Oscar, he said he wished that Harpo and Chico could have been there to share it with him. Afterward he and Sidney Sheldon were talking about the Academy Awards, and Groucho added that it was too bad that they hadn't given the Oscar sooner when Harpo and Chico were alive.

"Maybe they know," Sidney Sheldon said.

"I don't believe that," Groucho said. "When you're dead, you're dead."

He told us that he and his brothers had once agreed to try to make contact from the afterlife when one of them died. "But I haven't heard a goddamn word."

But behind the flippant façade he was a serious person.

"Do you know what I say when I go to bed every night? 'Unborn yesterday and dead tomorrow. Why fret about them if life be sweet?' Right now is the only moment there is."

"And you're really able to live that way?" I asked.

"It's the only way to live," Groucho responded soberly.

In the Jewish religion, the seder is the religious service celebrated on the first night of Passover, which includes a festive meal. There is a specific order of services that accompany the meal. Arthur Whitelaw told about going to a seder at Groucho's house:

"I hadn't been to a seder for years. If Louis B. Mayer and Irving Thalberg were still alive, it might have been called A *Night at the Seder.* Over there was a dais. Besides me, Elliott Gould, George Segal, actor Warren Berlinger, Groucho's lawyer Ed Pearlstein, and a Mr. Schubert were there. I asked, 'J.J. or Lee?' and Erin said that Groucho had asked the same thing. Andy Marx and Ahmet Ertegun were there too. Ahmet Ertegun was the token gentile for the evening. Mr. Schubert was officiating, and after each prayer, Groucho said, 'Is this when we drink the wine? When do we drink the wine?' Then there's another prayer, and Groucho says again, 'When do we drink the wine?'

"Then, Mr. Schubert asked, 'Can anyone play the piano? We need someone to play the hymns.' And Groucho said, 'Arthur and Andy, get to the piano!' I looked at the music, and I said to Andy, 'I can't read this. Let's play Joplin.' Well, Groucho's having the best time, and this poor man is still trying to officiate. He reads a prayer. Meanwhile, we're playing Scott Joplin, and Groucho's saying, 'When do we drink the wine?'

"Mr. Schubert says, '*Now* we drink the wine.'

"And Groucho says, 'Do we *have* to drink the wine?'

"Mr. Schubert says, 'We have one more prayer.' And Groucho says, 'No, we don't. I'm gonna sing.' And with that, he goes to the piano.

"It was the most irreverent religious service I have ever been to in my life.

"Ed Pearlstein looked at me and he said, 'I don't believe what's going on here.' I said, 'This is supposed to be a pretty religious kind of day. It's the parting of the Red Sea, a very meaningful holiday in the Jewish religion,' and Groucho was carrying on like it's A *Night at the Opera*, and he was going to say, 'I wouldn't pay this bill if I were you.' "

Groucho himself didn't exactly define what it is to be Jewish. He said, "I haven't ever seen a Jew." But being Jewish did remain a part of him. "It's not something you can lose." He told this story:

"A Jew and a hunchback were passing a temple, and the Jew said, 'I used to be a Jew.' And the hunchback said, 'I used to be a hunchback.' "

Groucho thought about making a trip to Israel. "I want to visit Harpo's harp." (Harpo willed his harp to Israel.)

Groucho always read the Bible; but he read it more as a great work of literature, and he didn't look for all of the answers in it.

Perhaps his own reverent disbelief or irreverent belief in luck and a mystical unknown, in ethical tradition, as well as in himself, could be summed up in the *I'll Say She Is* and *Horse Feathers* quote which *Time* featured on its Marx Brothers cover:

"The Lord Alps those that Alps themselves."

"We're four of the three musketeers"

Reminiscing about his relationship with his brothers, Groucho told me, "For years we played five shows a day and split weekends, but we never argued." The madcap, steadfast relationship of the Marx Brothers was best summed up in these lines from "The Musketeers," a song in *Animal Crackers* that Groucho sang for me almost half a century after he had sung it in the original Broadway production:

> It's one for all and two for five.
> We're four of the three musketeers.

This song expressed a zany, loyal camaraderie where 2+2=22, especially when the two plus two equaled Groucho and Harpo, Chico and Zeppo. Actually, there were five musketeers. Groucho, Harpo, and Chico were the most famous, probably in that order, but Gummo and Zeppo had their moments too. Zeppo explained his junior-straight-romantic lead position in the act to me:

"I came along late, and three comedians were enough."

Gummo had played Zeppo's roles during the vaudeville days but was never well known because he retired from the act before films gave the Marx Brothers permanence.

There was a sixth Marx Brother. Manfred Marx was born in 1885 and died in 1888 just before he was three years old.

GROUCHO
Manfred died about ninety years ago. I never knew him.

I
Did your mother talk much about him?

GROUCHO

No. He died when he was three years old.

I

What happened to him?

GROUCHO

It was a lousy accident. My mother told me about him. I wonder what would have become of Mannie . . . ?

The year before Manfred died, Chico was born. A year later, in 1888, Harpo was born, and two years later, in 1890, Groucho. Gummo and Zeppo were born in 1897 and 1901 respectively.

Shortly after Groucho was born, the family moved to East Ninety-third Street on New York's Upper East Side, to the German community of Yorkville. When Groucho was born, the Marx family had lived on East Seventy-eighth Street between Lexington and Third avenues. As the Marx Brothers grew up, they were conscious of "other-streeters" all around them—the Irish, Italian, and German immigrants who shared Yorkville.

When the Marx family first moved to Ninety-third Street, there were Sam, Minnie, and the three boys, Minnie's parents, Lafe and Fannie (who were called "Opie" and "Omie") Schoenberg, and Cousin Polly. Fannie died in 1898, shortly after celebrating her golden wedding anniversary, leaving as her only legacy the battered, stringless old harp that she had played for dancing after Lafe's ventriloquist act and magic show during their German show business days. The harp was an endless source of wonder and fascination for Adolph, sometimes known as Arthur, later to be Harpo, who eventually took from it a name and a way of life. When the Schoenbergs immigrated to the United States, they found so little demand for their specialized talents that they retired while their children got "civilian" jobs in New York City.

Grandpa Schoenberg shared a world that at the beginning included Napoleon and at the end John Kennedy. He was born in 1818, three years before the death of Napoleon, and he died in 1919, two years after the birth of John F. Kennedy. Up until his death from double pneumonia at the age of 101, he remained physically active. His favorite diversions were skating, movies, girls, and eating, not necessarily in that order.

GROUCHO

He was a big eater. He'd get up in the middle of the night, and he'd eat a couple of pumpernickel sandwiches with Limburger cheese at four in the morning and go right back to sleep. Every once in a while he had to go down to the ghetto around Grand Street and Canal—all the way down-town—and he'd buy a lot of tobacco. A bag of tobacco in those days cost about fifteen cents. He'd bring it home and go to his room—he was the only one in the house that had his own room—and then he would take this tobacco and make cigars.

I

You told me he never learned English.

GROUCHO

Not much, no. Sometimes he'd sit through the same movie two or three times. He'd make up his own stories to go with the pictures. He used to go skating in Central Park in the winter. He was in his eighties then. A very powerful, strong man.

Annie Berger's sister, Ethel Wise, had fond recollections of "Grandfather Marx":

"I especially remember Groucho's grandfather. He was a beautiful man, a real magician. He was tall and stately."

The last years of Lafe Schoenberg's long life were spent traveling in the family troupe, just as he had done so many decades before in pre-Bismarck Germany. Groucho remembered his grandfather's insistence on giving up his lower berth on the train to the boys, saying that they needed the rest between performances. After forty years in the United States, Grandfather Opie spoke only very limited English, but he could name all of the makes of automobiles. Of his family, Groucho said, "They came over on the *Augustflower,* having missed the *Mayflower.*"

Why Sam Marx chose to support his family as a tailor was never clear, especially to those who ordered what were his usually unsuitable suits. He billed himself as "Samuel Marx, Custom Tailor to the Men's Trade." Minnie was supposed to make the measurements for him, but since she was always out trying to get theatrical bookings, Sam would size up his customers without resorting to a tape measure. According to Groucho, these calculations were "about as accurate as Chamberlain's predictions about Hitler."

Ethel Wise recalled the way it was:

"Their father had a little shop on Lexington Avenue. He was a nice man. But the boys were wild, and he couldn't control them. For a while, he had Leonard [Chico] help him, but he took the trousers he was supposed to deliver and pawned them. He went to play craps, and didn't show up all night.

"I can still remember their father when he did come home. 'Var vuz you?' I can remember very often hearing him say, 'Var vuz you?' to the oldest boy. He was such a bad boy. The next one, Adolph [Harpo], was mischievous too. Those boys were really wild. They couldn't be controlled."

Nevertheless, Ethel Wise remembered a happy Marx family:

"There was always good food at the Marx house. Their father could really cook. We used to go there after school for cookies. It was always a lot of fun at their house. They were wild youngsters with a talent for having fun. The place would be a shambles, especially if Mrs. Marx left them alone. They would tear down the draperies. There was a woman across the way, a doctor's wife, who used to send over notes that she was going to call the police, which probably made them do it even more.

"The whole family was always kidding. They used to have a lot of fun and make good times, though they all had respect for their mother. Groucho was the most serious, and he was the most ambitious. He wanted to be somebody and make something of himself. He wanted to make it better for his whole family, like Mrs. Marx did. He was the most like her."

Groucho never completed the seventh grade in school. Harpo never even got through the second grade. Although Groucho always had intellectual interests, he admitted that he was something less than a standout student:

GROUCHO
We had a teacher who always had a bunch of keys in his hand, and he'd twirl 'em like that. If you did something bad, he'd throw the keys at you.
I
You value education so much now. At the time, did you like school?
GROUCHO
I wasn't very good at it. Grammar mystified me.
I
But you write grammatically.
GROUCHO
I taught myself. I read everything. My education is self-inflicted.

In spite of his limited formal education, Groucho was justifiably proud of his literary accomplishments. When I first met Groucho, he told me, "I didn't get past 7B and I wrote five books."

Harpo dropped out of school after a year and a half in the second grade because he got tired of being dropped out of the classroom window by two burly Irish classmates. Gummo was a sickly child whose attendance at school was sporadic. With his phenomenal memory and genius for figures, Chico could have been an outstanding student, except that all he bothered to remember were betting odds, and the figures that interested him wore skirts. Zeppo didn't do much better in school, not applying himself until later when he was successful as a manufacturer of precision instruments. His chief scholastic accomplishment was having beaten up every other kid in school.

It was at home and in the tough Yorkville streets that the boys received their real education. Harpo developed the resourcefulness to carry something of value, like a dead tennis ball or an empty thread spool to ransom his way to freedom if cornered by a rival street gang. Chico prepared for life by becoming a master of dialects to avoid being the wrong "streeter."

Groucho's earliest memory was his impression of riding on the back of a moving van:

"Gummo and I were back there. We must have been pretty young, because we didn't have our piano yet. And I remember playing stickball. We were surrounded by three breweries where we lived. When I went to school I could smell the malt. We used to go over to Park Avenue, where old man Ruppert lived in a big house with a fruit orchard, and we'd steal his apples and pears. There was a spiked fence about eight feet high, and dogs. We might have been dog meat, but we were very young, and we sure liked those apples and pears.

"I also remember the iceman delivering ice. You'd holler out the window to tell him how much you wanted. We had no icebox; we were very poor.

"We were so poor that when somebody knocked on the door, we all hid. We were paying twenty-seven dollars a month, and there were ten of us. The five brothers, my father and mother, my grandmother and grandfather, and an adopted sister. There were ten of us and one toilet. And no toilet paper.

"Chico worked for a firm called Klauber-Horn and Company in Brooklyn. They were wholesale distributors of paper. They had a crap game going in the cellar, and Chico was getting three dollars a week. Every week he lost his salary. Finally my father said, 'You come home one week again without your salary, I'll kill you!' Next week Chico was paid and immediately got into a crap game. Naturally he lost all his money, and he was afraid to come home. They had big bales, like cotton, except it was toilet paper. So he took that whole thing, and got on the elevated train, and came home with it. That was the first time we had toilet paper. Before that we always used *The Morning World*."

Groucho took me to visit the East Ninety-third Street apartment. According to him, surprisingly little change had taken place, but he added, "Everything looks smaller . . . or I'm bigger." Some people who lived in the building told us, "The Marx Brothers used to live here, right there." Groucho looked blank and said, "Who are they?" Then he was recognized.

Ethel Wise described what the apartments were like:

"Our apartment was directly above theirs, about eight rooms all in a row, with what was called an air shaft in the center to let in light and air."

The East Ninety-third Street neighborhood they lived in was not especially affluent, and the Marxes were not the neighborhood's most prosperous inhabitants. "Everyone else's garbage was richer than ours," Groucho remembered. During his childhood, a room of his own was beyond his wildest dreams. A bed of his own was all he could hope for. "We slept four in a bed, two at each end."

Minnie spent her days making the rounds of theatrical booking agents while Sam cooked. An invitation to the Marx home for one of Sam's culinary miracles often softened an otherwise obdurate agent, and a booking was thus obtained. Before the Marx brothers had embarked on show business careers, Minnie had concentrated her efforts on promoting her younger brother Al Shean. He was a pants presser who couldn't keep a crease or a job, so he went into vaudeville.

"I don't think he was a very good pants presser," recalled Groucho, "because as soon as he got a job as a presser, he formed a singing quartet, and the fellow who ran the factory threw all four of 'em out. He was always forming quartets and getting fired."

Groucho claimed that as a child he didn't think about being an actor. "When I was very young, I thought about being a doctor, but then I really wanted to be a writer. I became an actor because I had an uncle in show business who was making $200 a week, and I wasn't making anything, not even an occasional girl. My first job was sitting on a beer keg in Coney Island and singing. I got a dollar for it. That was my start in show business. Later I got a job in a Protestant church singing in a choir, until they found out what was the matter with me. That was my second job."

As the eldest son, Chico got the piano lessons. All of the boys were supposed to have received lessons in turn, but there was never enough money. Chico was a quick-study, no-practice artist who, as soon as he could play a few songs, turned his newly acquired skills to profit. Piano players were in great demand at nickelodeons, saloons, and bordellos, so Chico quickly found employment, often accepting more jobs than he could simultaneously hold. He solved this problem after a few days by substituting Harpo. Harpo had learned a couple of tunes of his own, and at that time looked enough like Chico to be his twin brother. Harpo's even more limited repertory soon got both of them fired, but not until after he had collected a few days' salary and was ready again to double as Chico on another job.

Although they were quite different in temperament, Harpo and Chico were very close as children growing up. Harpo, being out of school all day, was either idle, getting in or out of mischief, or job hunting, so he naturally looked up to older brother Leonard, who, it seemed to him, was good at everything. Billy Marx told me, "They looked so much alike, and they really complemented each other." Chico, as he would be named years later for his prowess with the "chicks," has remained to this day an enigma. Much has been written about and by Groucho and about Harpo, but scarcely anything about Chico. "He was by far the most fantastic character that I have ever known," Gummo told me.

Maxine Marx, Chico's daughter, told me that she had tried for years to write a book about her father, but had found him "too ephemeral, and impossible to capture on paper." Descriptions of Chico, including Harpo's, portray him as someone who always liked the hunt better than the kill. "I always had the feeling that nobody could ever say anything really bad about Chico," said Billy Marx, who had toured the British music halls with his father and his Uncle Chico. Billy also pointed out that Chico, though seemingly an extrovert, was really a loner. Groucho agreed:

"He always was. Even when we were kids. He never played with us. He went over to the next block, Ninety-fourth Street, and had a crap game."

Hattie Darling described Chico as "nice and very bright. He was also always getting advances on his salary to pay gambling debts and trying to outmaneuver his wife, Betty, who was extremely jealous." Groucho affirmed that Chico's wife's suspicions were not unfounded.

With Al Shean's success in vaudeville, Minnie became convinced that at least one of her sons could make it in show business too. The son selected was Groucho. Not only was he serious and intelligent, but he could also sing—a talent highly prized in the Marx family. Groucho was the possessor of an excellent boy-soprano voice. "Unfortunately, I grew up," he said. Even in his eighties, Groucho still loved to sing and would do so "at the drop of a pimp."

Groucho's first real job in show business was as a female impersonator in a small-time vaudeville group billed as "The Leroy Trio." This was in 1905, a year after the Protestant choir had disowned him. A few months later, Mr. Leroy ran off with the other boy in the trio and Groucho's salary, leaving him stranded in Cripple Greek, Colorado, where he managed to get a job as a wagon driver until Minnie could send him his train fare home. "I'd never even seen a horse before, and the horses knew it."

The same thing happened again when he was hired as a singer by an Englishwoman named Lily Saville. In Waco, Texas, she ran off with a married lion tamer who shared the bill, leaving Groucho with a return ticket to New York, but without his "grouch bag"—the small chamois bag actors wore around their necks to hold their savings. His next job was a distinct improvement: he got stranded in Chicago.

"It was my first dramatic part, in *The Man of My Choice*. I was the boy hero. In the second act, the man tries to steal the important papers from the ingenue, who had them in her pillow in the hospital. I came onstage with a gun, and I said, 'Stop! Move one step and I'll blow you to smithereens!' And the curtain came down." When Groucho once told this story on television, he ended with, "Does anybody know what a 'smithereen' is?" He received hundreds of letters defining "smithereen."

When the show unexpectedly closed in Chicago, Groucho was again left penniless. He had sent home to his family half of his weekly salary of twenty-five dollars and had spent the rest on room and board. In the meantime, Harpo was working at whatever menial jobs a first-grade graduate could qualify for in those days, and Chico had become a professional pool hustler, and then a lifeguard until he had to be rescued by another lifeguard, and finally a song plugger. Eventually he went to work in that capacity for Shapiro-Bernstein in Pittsburgh, where he almost settled permanently. For a time, Groucho was also a song plugger for Jerome Remick, getting twenty-five dollars a week for singing one of their songs.

Groucho knew that he wanted to stay in show business, but sometimes the closest he could come to it was cleaning actors' wigs, a job he described as "a hair-raising experience." In 1906, however, he did get to sing at the Metropolitan Opera House in New York. He talked about it with Erin, Ted Mann, who is director of the Circle in the Square Theatre in New York City, and me:

GROUCHO

It was after the San Francisco earthquake. Thousands of people were killed. We volunteered to go on at the Metropolitan Opera House to raise money for the people who were injured. And I sang "Somebody's Sweetheart." I was in the Gus Edwards vaudeville act, where I played a German comedian, and I was fifteen years old.

TED MANN

You fellows were certainly not known at that time. So why did they let you on the Metropolitan stage?

GROUCHO

Because it was a whole group of us. Gus Edwards had an act, with about eight people in it, and Jessel was one of them. And we all entertained. At least, we thought we did. We didn't get any money. I remember chasing Gus Edwards once to get our salary.

Groucho's experience with the famous Gus Edwards school act undoubtedly influenced the Marx Brothers' later *Fun in Hi Skule* act, but for the moment Groucho remained a boy soprano and an actor, giving little thought to continuing as a comedian. "We tried comedy, but I wasn't exactly hilarious," Groucho told me. He and Harpo put on makeup and what they thought were funny costumes, and presented themselves at a Coney Island theatre one night. The manager took one look at them and told them, "Wash your dirty faces and get the hell out of here." On another occasion, they actually did get a chance to do their comedy act down on Fourteenth Street. But the manager got them off the stage almost instantly because he considered their begged and borrowed material too risqué, though Groucho told me, "We always worked clean." This is how some of it went:

HARPO

Yonder in the distance an island lays.

GROUCHO

Lays what? Eggs?

HARPO

No. Lays on the bosom of the ocean.

GROUCHO

Oh, what a fresh island!

More successful was a vocal duet featuring Groucho and Gummo that

Minnie organized in 1909. Gummo was thirteen and by the standards of that day more than old enough to go to work. Having a fair singing voice, he was paired with Groucho in an act which soon became The Three Nightingales when a cross-eyed girl named Mabel O'Donnell was recruited by Minnie. The girl was selected for her voice, looks, and dress size, which had to be the same as the costume Minnie had already bought on sale at Bloomingdale's. She also had to be willing to work for practically nothing. Mabel O'Donnell filled the dress and the bill perfectly, except for the crossed eyes and the unfortunate tendency of her voice to crack on a certain note. The crossed eyes were remedied by a wig that covered one eye, and the crack in her voice was almost remedied by very loud singing on the part of Groucho and Gummo whenever that certain note was approached. She also had another fault, which Gummo described for me: "Mabel had a beautiful voice, but would start in one key and end in another." Minnie soon joined the act herself and easily lured Harpo away from an unpromising career as bellboy at the Seville Hotel, where he had contracted the measles and crabs simultaneously.

Earlier Gummo had had a fling at show business that left him less than stagestruck. A certain Uncle Heimie, wishing to become a ventriloquist but having no aptitude for it, built a dummy that was hollow so that a midget or a small boy might be concealed inside. Gummo was pressed into service. To remove any doubts that he was working with a real dummy, Uncle Heimie planned to close his act by sticking a pin into one of its legs. To accomplish this with Gummo really inside, the dummy was constructed so that both of Gummo's legs fit into one of the dummy's legs, while the other leg was only dummy. During their debut in York, Pennsylvania, Uncle Heimie pierced the wrong leg, prematurely ending what promised to become "the second worst act in vaudeville next to the Whangdoodle Four."

That dubious accolade might have been awarded Minnie's Nightingales, except that competition at the bottom was fierce. George Jessel recalled for Groucho and me an act called *Osterman's Oysters,* and there actually were acts called *Van Camp's Goats and Pigs* and *The Musical Farm,* featuring a farmer and his wife singing "The Blue Bells of Scotland" while they milked a real cow. It was that milieu into which Minnie waded with alacrity.

One of the first lessons that Minnie learned was that in small-time vaudeville an act was paid according to the number of performers—the more participants, the higher the booking rate. Evidently, managers took comfort in a stage full of actors, even when the actors outnumbered the audience, as they not infrequently did. For that reason, The Three Nightingales soon hatched a fourth Nightingale—Harpo. Then, The Four Nightingales became The Six Mascots when Minnie and Aunt Hannah joined the act. The Marx Brothers were still not playing it completely for laughs, although Groucho donned a butcher boy's smock and carried a basket with sausage dangling out while he sang in a comic German accent. Remembering this routine, Groucho said softly, "I went from bad to wurst." He explained to me that in the days before World War I "This was considered a classy act." After the sinking of the *Lusitania*, he switched to a safer Jewish accent. He recalled the moment:

GROUCHO
Then I put on a derby and became a Jew comedian. And I sang "There I Was Waiting in My Shirt," which was a parody on "There I Was Waiting in the Church."
ERIN
You just got up during intermission and sang the songs?
GROUCHO
Three songs.
ERIN
What were the other two?
GROUCHO
I don't remember.
ERIN
Did you get any laughs?
GROUCHO
Not that I remember.
ERIN
Didn't they think that was funny, "There I Was Waiting in My Shirt"?
GROUCHO
I thought it was, but the audience didn't agree with me.
ERIN
How did you get the idea to sing during intermission?
GROUCHO
I always sing. I may sing right now.
ERIN
But that was the habit of the day, to have someone entertain during intermission?

GROUCHO

Sure. When I was playing the Howard Theatre in Boston—that was a burlesque house—they had acts during the intermission, and we were one of the acts, between the first and second act. We were The Four Nightingales. Are you familiar with Boston? Well, the Howard was down in a very tough neighborhood, and the theatre was full of sailors. We were singing "How'd You Like to Be My Little Sweetheart?" and a sailor leaned over the box and spit in Harpo's eye with tobacco juice.

In 1910, Minnie decided to try Chicago. Al Shean swore that any act could make it in the Midwest, and that even included nightingales and mascots. Selling their furniture and giving up their Ninety-third Street flat, the Marxes set out for Chicago by way of the South. The idea was to work their way there by playing circuits that were so desperate that they would book anything, and in those days few Yankee acts cared to tour the South. As insurance, while Minnie, the boys, and Aunt Hannah were playing in southern theaters, Sam and Uncle Julius (after whom Groucho was named) planned to sell cloth to local tailors. As it turned out, the sideline became the main line that financed the expedition. The Marxes finally reached Chicago, where conditions were better—for a while.

At first Minnie was able to get plenty of bookings for the act, perhaps not in the best theatres, but they were working. Then she ran out of small-time vaudeville houses in Chicago, and the act went on the road again, this time in what seemed like the final curtain.

Another swing through the South left them stranded in New Orleans during the summer of 1912. Without money to get back to Chicago, they accepted the only bookings offered, in Oklahoma and Texas. This was in the days before air-conditioning and insecticides. Any act willing to brave the mosquitoes of the open airdromes and the steam bath conditions of the theatres would have been welcome—even Osterman's Oysters or The Musical Farm. In Nacogdoches, Texas, they even emptied a theatre during their act in what seemed like the ultimate blow. But according to Groucho, it was actually the turning point for them.

"We were playing a small town in Texas, a farming town. The farmers came in and tied their horses up beside the Pantages Theatre. We were doing a singing act, The Six Mascots. None of us could sing. While we're doing the act, a mule runs away, and the whole audience left to catch the mule. Then they came back. By this time we were so angry we started making sarcastic remarks. Like, 'Nacogdoches is full of roaches,' and 'The jackass is the finest flower of Texass." Instead of getting mad, the audience laughs. This is the first time we ever did comedy like that."

After this unexpected triumph, they attempted comedy whenever it seemed appropriate, but with mixed results. Sometimes audiences laughed, sometimes they didn't. "It was like being in an old Western shoot-out with pistols that were loaded for Russian roulette," Gummo recalled.

Word got around fast that a funny singing act was on the way, so in Denison, Texas, The Six Mascots were received enthusiastically. The theatre manager invited them to stay over with a guarantee, provided that they could offer his audiences, which included a teachers' conference, a comedy sketch. Wishing to please the audience of visiting teachers, Groucho wrote an act influenced by the Gus Edwards school act. Groucho became Herr Teacher; Harpo, Patsy Brannigan or the stupid boy; Paul Yale (who was the bass singer), the "nance" or comic homosexual; Aunt Hannah, the bright girl; Minnie, the stupid girl. This act was called *Fun in Hi Skule*. Much of what the Marx Brothers did afterward was influenced by *Fun in Hi Skule*. Most notable of all, Harpo donned his famous red wig and became himself. Groucho assumed a stern countenance and an air of unqualified authority. Gummo played the juvenile straight man character, which Zeppo later inherited. (Chico later joined the school-days act and fitted in perfectly as the confidently ignorant "Eye-talian"). The Marx Brothers shows that followed *Fun in Hi Skule*, including the films and even Groucho's TV program, owed something to it. *You Bet Your Life* is to some extent *Fun in Hi Skule* in modern dress, with Groucho still playing Herr Teacher. *Horse Feathers* is *Fun in Hi Skule* graduated to college and Hollywood. As the great white hunter in *Animal Crackers*, the prime minister in *Duck Soup*, or the bogus doctor in *A Day at the Races*, Groucho is still in many respects Herr Teacher, although when World War I began he had to make some changes in the character:

"I was a German comedian, but like I told you, I lost my accent in one day when they sank the *Lusitania*. That night I just took off the chin piece I used to wear, and I became a Jew comedian. It was at the Chase Theatre in Toronto. I went into a cafeteria there and said, 'I'd like some German fried potatoes.' And the woman behind the counter said, 'We don't have German fried potatoes. We have home fried potatoes.' I said, 'Well, give me some sauerkraut,' and she said, 'We don't have sauerkraut. We have cut cabbage.' "

Fun in Hi Skule was successful in the Southwest, but it received a less warm reception in the Midwest as the act headed back toward Chicago.

About 1913 Chico quit his job with Shapiro-Bernstein, where he had been promoted to salesman, and started to travel the vaudeville circuits himself with a fellow song plugger. Billing themselves as Marx and Gordini, Chico played the piano and his partner sang. When Gordini quit the act in Cleveland, Cousin Lou Shean joined Chico, and for some unexplained reason they called themselves Van and Schenck. This partnership lasted until Milwaukee.

In Milwaukee, Chico saw his first musical tabloid and became convinced that this was the wave of the future. Rejoining the family in Chicago, he persuaded Minnie that they ought to mount a "tab," using the school-days act as its nucleus. The result eventually was *Mr. Green's Reception*, which included more elaborate musical numbers and stage effects, as well as a second comedy sketch. This was simply a continuation of the school-days situation, with the grown students returning to their class reunion. Chico joined the act, contributing his dialect and "shooting the keys" piano technique, as well as his buoyant optimism.

About this time, Harpo received a package in the mail from Minnie while they were playing downstate Illinois. It was a secondhand harp that was limited to one key. Blissfully ignorant of all harp technique, Harpo tuned the instrument by ear, fortunately tuning it flat, or the battered harp would have collapsed. Through trial and error, he patiently taught himself how to play, acquiring an unorthodox technique that has since astounded other professional harpists. Throughout his life, according to Gummo, Harpo continued to tune the instrument incorrectly, even after he was able to afford an expensive new chromatic harp.

Visiting with Mildred Dilling, Harpo's harp teacher, at a private recital she gave in her New York apartment in 1976, I was told about her first meeting with Harpo and their subsequent relationship.

"I met Harpo at Lyon & Healy at the Charles Ditson Company opposite Altman's. The Woollcott article had just appeared in *The New Yorker*, so it must have been the late twenties. They were on the stage. (I don't remember if it was *Cocoanuts* or *Animal Crackers*.) I was trying out a new harp for a pupil. I noticed a solemn-looking young man staring intently at me while I was playing. He listened till I finished, and then he came up to me and said, 'Lady, learn me that.'

"He told me his name, and I'd read about him in *The New Yorker*.

"I said that I would, and he asked me when. I said anytime. And he asked, 'Now?' I said yes, and he said, 'My place or yours?' I said mine. We took a taxi, and that's how it started.

"He tuned his harp in the key of B flat instead of G flat, and he always kept his second finger there, keeping his place. He only worked with three fingers. His harp should have been tuned in C flat, but he had it tuned in B flat. It made everything sound very peculiar. Three flats in the key of E flat is normal. He'd started on a single action harp, a kind of harp made before 1810.

"He always had a lesson every day whenever we were in the same town at the same time—in New York, or in California, or in Paris, or in Étretat on the Normandy coast. I introduced Harpo to my harp teacher, Henriette Renié, who was the greatest harp teacher, and Harpo had lessons from her. She lived in Paris, but in the summer she lived in Étretat, which was the most beautiful seashore in the world. There was a great cultural artistic movement there about 1850. It was a center for the arts. De Maupassant and Offenbach lived there.

"Harpo was dead serious about music. Classical music filled his life. Music was an overwhelming passion which enriched his life.

"I was in my teens. He was older than I was, but he had great reverence for my knowledge. Harpo never changed. I don't know how old he was when I first met him.

"After the lesson he'd stretch out on the sofa and say, 'Now, Dilling, you play for me. And if I should fall asleep, that's the greatest compliment I could pay you.'

"Sometimes we would use my apartment for the lesson, and sometimes we would use Woollcott's apartment on Fifty-second Street by the river. I lived in a very well-built building with good walls, and we worked very late, but no one ever complained.

"I always had a box at the theatre during the days when they were playing in New York, and I did all my entertaining there. Only, we went through backstage, and if there were any men in the group, it was hard to get them past the girls. I used to take a lot of famous people there, and they always enjoyed it. I remember taking Andrés Segovia and his first wife, and he really enjoyed it. Harpo would crawl into the box on his hands and knees so no one could see him.

"I was a little shy of the others. I felt they thought I was making him too 'regular.' The family thought I'd spoil him. But it didn't hurt him.

"The way he is on the screen, the way everyone knows him, is the way he played after I began teaching him. We met before they made any of the movies. Harpo had individuality. I never could make him learn to read music.

"He was full of tricks. He had a rubber bass string, although I never saw it. He would do things like sit at his harp and twist his nose with his left hand and pluck the string with his right hand. He would hide part of what he was doing with his body, and it would seem as if his nose made a sound.

"Harpo wasn't really an intellectual. He wasn't the intellectual Groucho was. He had a lot of intellectual friends, but Groucho was really the intellectual in the family. Harpo was brilliant, though.

"Harpo had this lovely swimming pool, and when he and Susan adopted the children they had the pool filled in. That's the kind of people they were.

"I remember once when I was appearing in California in the San Fernando Valley. It was after Harpo had stopped making movies. He said to me, 'Billing, you're going to be tired tonight, so I'll help you out. I'll do the encores for you.' I said, 'With the wig?' and he said, 'Yes.' And he did. After the performance he pushed his harp onstage and played, and I joined him."

Mildred Dilling recalled Harpo finishing a number, then rushing off the stage in the middle of the applause. Even though the ovation grew and there were cries from the rear of the auditorium for an encore, Harpo didn't reappear. He couldn't. He was the person yelling, "Encore!"

"The last time I saw him was at a recital I gave in California. He came and brought the family.

"It was an unromantic friendship based on music, which is a great bond. I believe that Harpo, Renié, and I were the three people who cared more about the harp than any other people in the world."

Talking with me about Harpo and his harp, Groucho summed up his view.

"The harp wasn't my favorite instrument, but Harpo was very serious about it. And there weren't many harpists in vaudeville."

As for Chico, Groucho said:

"Chico's idea of practicing was to dip his hands in a basin of hot water. He may have been a piano player, but he was more interested in fiddling around."

George Seaton talked about the appeal of Chico's piano playing:

"We were in San Francisco, and this was *Day at the Races* on the tryout, when we took those comedy scenes and played in the public houses and worked them out. Chico was on the stage playing his piano and shooting the keys, and I was standing in the wings with Groucho. Groucho just never could understand why an audience would appreciate

Chico's playing the piano the way they did. The audience was applauding Chico, who was doing an encore. Groucho walked right out on the stage and said jokingly, 'If you come near a tune, play it.'

"He thought he would get a big laugh, but the audience hissed him instead. He came back into the wings and just couldn't understand how an audience could possibly enjoy Chico's piano playing so much that when he ad-libbed, they hissed instead of laughing."

It was in Rockford, Illinois, in 1914 that the Marx Brothers were rechristened, "assuming that four Jewish boys can be christened in the first place." They had become acquainted with Art Fisher, a monologist on the same bill with them who had a penchant for giving nicknames to his friends. At the time there was a popular comic strip called "Sherlocko the Monk" (later "Hawkshaw the Detective"), which was supposed to have inspired Fisher to change Julius, Adolph, Leonard, and Milton to Groucho, Harpo, Chico, and Gummo. There actually was a character in this strip named "Groucho."

Julius became Groucho because of his serious demeanor. Adolph became Harpo for obvious reasons. Leonard became Chico because of his passion for the chicks; thus his name is correctly pronounced "Chicko." Milton became Gummo because he wore rubber overshoes, rain or shine. "I always had holes in my shoes," he explained, "so I'd always wear rubbers, or gumshoes, over them even when it wasn't raining, and I got called Gummo." Herbert was only thirteen and at home in Chicago when Fisher was renaming the boys, so he became Zeppo later. No one, especially Zeppo, was certain why. The names stuck, but they continued to use their real names until *I'll Say She Is* in 1924.

Minnie had remained in Chicago, where she established the Minnie Palmer Agency, which handled the Marx Brothers and other smalltime vaudeville acts. Realizing that her sons could languish forever in cheap boardinghouses and crumbling small-town theatres, she resolved to book them into the more prestigious circuits. By 1914, however, school acts were in decline. Minnie turned to her brother Al Shean, who was by now an established and respected figure in big-time vaudeville.

Al Shean looked at *Mr. Green's Reception* and noticed that, instead of exiting with a flourish, they simply ended the act whenever the laughter and applause died out. To remedy this, Uncle Al gave Minnie $25 to have vaudevillian Charley Van write "Peasie Weasie," which turned out to be a big hit. "Peasie Weasie" was a genre of patter song designed to be sung at the end of a vaudeville act until the audience became surfeited with its endless doggerel verses. "It was doggerel," Groucho admitted, "but doggerel is man's best friend—even in a cathouse." He loved to sing it and would do so at just about any party occasion.

Uncle Al decided that the way to improve their act was to write a new one, so one night he sat down at the Marxes' kitchen table and wrote *Home Again.* This sketch was an elaboration of the second half of *Mr. Green's Reception,* with the school-days routine omitted. Adoring elaborate theatrical effects, Minnie was especially pleased with the possibilities offered by *Home Again.* Groucho remembered vividly one of her miracles of *mise-en-scène:*

"In *Home Again* we had a boat. We're all standing in the boat, and Harpo would give it a fast shake with a rope, and the people would fall down on the boat. It wasn't a real boat, it was just a flat piece with wheels on it. It was a fine piece of scenery!" Groucho chuckled at the memory.

Home Again also brought the Marx Brothers another step closer to their mature comic characters. Uncle Al gave Groucho most of the lines, relegating Chico to dialect straight man, and Harpo to pantomimist. Both felt slighted and said so. Chico demanded some laugh lines. "So Uncle Al had to make the straight man's part funny too," Groucho recalled.

He said that prior to *Home Again,* Harpo was far from silent:

"He talked a lot in the school act. He played a boy called Patsy Brannigan. In those days, if you did a school act, you usually had a Patsy Brannigan in the act. Patsy Brannigan was a kid with red hair and a funny nose. That's where Harpo got the idea for his wig. A fella had taught him a lot of big words, and sometimes Harpo would dumbfound the audience by making this speech with all those big words. He didn't understand most of them, but he loved the speech."

Groucho explained that Al Shean felt that Harpo's voice did not match his whimsical appearance. Harpo was disappointed, but he accepted Uncle Al's admonition, and thereafter Harpo talked only once again during his entire professional career. A quarter of a century later, he spoke at the end of the stage tryouts for *Go West,* reeling off the same kind of uncharacteristic erudition that had convulsed *Fun in Hi Skule* audiences. The brothers decided that his speech, while comically effective, departed from the innocent Harpo character, and it was therefore omitted from the shooting script of the movie. "Character is everything," Groucho frequently told me. Over the years, Harpo was besieged with attractive offers to speak publicly, but he turned them all down, even when they were from his good friend Jack Benny. Jack talked about his disappointment with Groucho and me:

"Harpo was probably the sweetest man you would ever want to meet, but I couldn't get him to talk on my TV show. He never would do it. He had this idea that once he talked he would ruin his character. I never believed that. I felt that when he did someone else's show, he could be another character who talked. But he didn't think my way, so that was it, and he didn't talk."

Groucho told me that the question most often asked him was: "Could Harpo talk?" Groucho always answered, "No."

Home Again gave Minnie what she needed: a showcase for the Marx Brothers, and she was able to book them into the better houses. Encouraged by *Home Again*'s moderate success, she tried to put them into an original musical comedy, in hopes of attracting the attention of a visiting Broadway producer. The result was *The Cinderella Girl*, with book by Jo Swerling and music by Gus Kahn. An ill-prepared tryout company opened and closed in Battle Creek, Michigan, during the Spanish influenza epidemic of 1918. Even if the show had been good (which Groucho admitted it wasn't), there was no chance whatever of merely breaking even at the box office, since local health regulations allowed them to sell only every other seat and every other row. At the beginning of the second act, Groucho stepped forward and said:

"Folks, that first act wasn't so good. We're gonna ad-lib from now on."

Back in Chicago, they tried to salvage what they could from *The Cinderella Girl*, recycling the expensive scenery and costumes into a more sumptuous production of *Home Again*. This was during World War I, when good vaudeville acts were scarce. Minnie had no trouble at all booking the improved production into the Wilson Avenue Theatre, a house controlled by E. F. Albee, ruler of the Orpheum Circuit.

At the beginning of the entry of the United States into the war, the Marxes had bought a farm in La Grange, Illinois, a northwestern suburb of Chicago. As might be expected, the Marx Brothers on the farm were funny but not agriculturally fruitful. "After a while we had to buy eggs for our chickens to sit on, so as not to be embarrassed in front of visitors." Groucho explained the problem with their farm: "We spent most of our time at Wrigley Field watching the Cubs." He talked with me about those days:

GROUCHO
Did I tell you about the farm we had in La Grange, Illinois?

I

When you were farmers?

GROUCHO

We weren't farmers. We had a farm. It was during the war.

I

The First World War?

GROUCHO

Yeah. My eyes were bad. They wouldn't take me. Took Gummo. So we bought the farm.

I

You said that you started out with a lot of enthusiasm, getting up very early in the morning. And it got later and later, and finally you just got up and went straight to the baseball game without going to the farm.

GROUCHO

We finally wound up in Wrigley Field in Chicago. We had guinea pigs in the cellar, and we were all afraid to go down there. That was the way we used to get our water, out of a pump in the cellar.

I

How did guinea pigs get into your cellar?

GROUCHO

We thought if we raised guinea pigs, we could sell 'em to somebody like they sell rats. We had so many of them. We must have had three or four hundred guinea pigs. The chickens all died. We made some money because there was a golf course across the street from our farm, and if anybody lost a golf ball, we'd find it and they'd give us a quarter. There was a girl in that town that I used to be madly in love with. She worked in a bakery. If you wanted doughnuts or coffeecake or anything, she waited on you. She wouldn't have anything to do with me. She was crazy about Chico.

When it finally became evident that at least one of the boys would have to go into the service, Gummo went into the Army. After World War I, he returned to show business, not as a performer but eventually as a theatrical agent. Even during his show business days, Gummo had liked helping Sam make ends meet during summer lulls by selling paraffin boxes to butchers in towns around Chicago.

The Marx Brothers returned to the stage with *Home Again*, and Zeppo, who was then seventeen, took Gummo's place as dancer, singer, and straight man in the act. When it was possible to persuade Zeppo to talk about his show business days, which wasn't often, he was far from nostalgic. Except for the chorus girls, being a straight man in the Marx Brothers act wasn't fun for him. He wanted to be a comedian too, but there just wasn't room for another funny Marx Brother, especially the youngest brother, who came in after the act had already taken form. Zeppo always knew he could be funny, and once he got his chance when Groucho had an emergency appendectomy in Chicago. Following the shows, Groucho's friends would go backstage, fully confident that they were going to be able to talk with Groucho in his dressing room.

Recalling the incident, Groucho said, "Zeppo was so good, I got better faster."

Groucho remembered Zeppo as a nervous actor and a confident fighter:

"He didn't want to be an actor. The first chance he got, he quit and became an agent. But offstage he was the funniest one of us. He always tried to get Norman Krasna as a client, but Krasna was handled through another agency. So one night we're at the Clover Club in Hollywood, and some drunk comes after Krasna and makes all kinds of remarks, and Zeppo's a good fighter. He leaned over and hit this guy on the chin. And knocked him under the table, then turned to Krasna and asked, 'Does Mike Levy give you this kind of service?' Zeppo was a good fighter. He used to fight anybody."

On the strength of *Home Again*'s successful reception at the Wilson Avenue Theatre, the Marx Brothers were signed to a thirty-week contract on the big-time Orpheum Circuit. On the bill with them on the Western swing was a young monologist named Ben K. Benny, later Jack Benny.

The Orpheum Circuit's New York Palace Theatre truthfully billed itself as "the topmost rung" and boasted "Here Genius not Birth your Rank insures." Naturally, it was the ambition of the Marx Brothers to play the Palace. Success at the Palace would truly mean "Home Again" for the expatriate New Yorkers. Once her boys began to do well on the Orpheum Circuit, Minnie started pushing for a Palace Theatre booking.

The honey-snacking prime minister of E. F. Albee's powerful stage empire, J. J. Murdock, famed for the ever-present jar of honey on his desk, agreed to let the Marx Brothers try out at the Boston Palace. If they were successful there, they would be booked into New York's Royal and Palace theatres. The last time the Marxes played Boston, it had been far from a triumphant appearance.

Home Again was a much better act than *The Four Nightingales*, and the

Boston Palace's audience more appreciative (and genteel) than the old Howard's. The run was successful beyond even Minnie's wildest expectations. But at the Royal in New York, "We fell flatter than yesterday's soufflé." The New York audience was cool toward what had convulsed the audience in New England. So was J. J. Murdock, who immediately canceled the Palace engagement. But Minnie wasn't going to let one bad showing under adverse conditions keep them from their destiny. In the face of Minnie's intrepid persistence, Murdock agreed to let them play the Palace but only if they went on first—the toughest spot on the bill. In spite of latecomers and a traditional apathy toward first acts, the Marx Brothers soon won the audiences and became a mainstay at the Palace, where, Groucho said, "We became known as 'The Palace Stock Company.'"

By 1919 the Marx Brothers were at the apogee of vaudevillian success. There was apparently no place to go from there, so Minnie retired and Chico more or less took over management of the act. Chico, who never made enough money to finance his gambling losses, couldn't afford to believe that they had reached the peak of their potential. Even when they were down and out, Groucho remembered Chico saying, "We won't always be playing these dumps." From then until the Thalberg years, Chico's influence offstage was important in catapulting them from vaudeville to Broadway to Hollywood and to world fame.

During the successful run of *Home Again*, Groucho married Zeppo's dancing partner, nineteen-year-old Ruth Johnson. This indirectly led to Groucho's famous greasepaint mustache. Since it was concurrent with another important event in his life, Groucho remembered the circumstances well:

"We were playing at Keith's Flushing. My wife was having a baby at the time, and I used to spend a lot of time in the hospital with her. One night I stayed too long, and by the time I got to the theatre, it was too late to paste on my mustache, so I just smeared on some greasepaint. The audience didn't seem to mind, so I stuck with it."

Many of Groucho's celebrated performing characteristics were acquired in a similar fashion:

"I would try a line. If it didn't get a laugh, I'd take it out and write another line. Pretty soon I had a character."

The inimitable Groucho walk evolved that way:

"I was just kidding around one day, and I started to walk funny. The audience liked it, so I kept it in." Oscar Levant, who sometimes played the piano at Groucho's house, said about the walk, "I wouldn't stoop so high."

In the early twenties the Marx Brothers decided that they would like to be in the movies. They had observed friend Charlie Chaplin's success. So they arranged to shoot a film themselves. Groucho told me about *Humorisk*:

"I never saw it. Jo Swerling wrote it. We were playing at the Palace Theatre, but we used to run over to Weehawken. We made two reels which didn't make any sense at all. But it wasn't trying to make sense, it was just trying to be funny. Nobody directed it. There was nothing to direct. We put up the money ourselves. We wanted to be movie actors."

Tiring of *Home Again*, the Marx Brothers opened in a new act called *On the Mezzanine Floor* in 1921. The backer for this show was world lightweight boxing champion Benny Leonard, who was also an ardent Marx Brothers fan. Since Benny Leonard also wanted to be an actor, he bought a vehicle in which he could appear as himself with his idols, the Marx Brothers. The result was *On the Mezzanine Floor*, which was important in the Marx Brothers' professional climb because some of the material from this show was incorporated into *I'll Say She Is*, the big turning point in their careers. Hattie Darling, who starred in the show, reminisced with me:

"Benny Leonard was in love with me, and he wanted me to marry him. My brother, Herman Timberg, was a great writer, and he wrote *On the Mezzanine*, and Benny Leonard put up the money for the show. I managed the act and collected the salary at the box office, which Chico couldn't stand. The four Marx Brothers were only getting a thousand dollars a week, and Chico was quite a gambler. He loved to gamble and was always losing, so he had to come to me for advances, and this would irk him so much. Groucho loved it because he didn't want Chico to gamble.

"The Marx Brothers were wonderful to me. Of course, I was the kind of girl who never ran around, and they knew it and they took me out for dinner. They took me all over. The best notice I ever received was with the Marx Brothers in *On the Mezzanine*.

"I had about four or five changes in the act, but the Marx Brothers were the stars, so they had the star dressing room. I went up to them once and said, 'Look, I make all the changes and you four boys don't even make any changes at all. Why can't I get the star dressing room?' They said, 'All right.' But when we played in, I think, Brooklyn, they put the star on a dressing room way upstairs, so I could barely make it onstage in time. They were such pranksters! So I took Harpo's red wig, and I wiped the whole floor with it. But they were wonderful to me. And Groucho had a sense of humor I have never seen in anybody else."

One evening Groucho talked with Erin and me about *On the Mezzanine Floor*:

ERIN
What was *On the Mezzanine* about?
GROUCHO
It was about forty minutes.
ERIN
And what happened?
GROUCHO
Well, there were supposed to be two sets, an upstairs and a downstairs. I remember the last line. "This is the last time I cross the ocean. Next time I'll take the train."
ERIN
Then there's another one right away. "The garbage man is here."
GROUCHO
"Tell him we don't want any."
ERIN
And then what happened?
GROUCHO
And then Chico says, "I'd like to say goodbye to your wife." And I said, "Who wouldn't?"
ERIN
And there were a lot of doors on the upstairs and downstairs of the set.
GROUCHO
I used to dance up those steps.

When *On the Mezzanine Floor* was finishing its tour in Cleveland, Chico got "a notion to cross the ocean," so their agent arranged an English tour starting at the Coliseum in London. There, audiences didn't understand the Marx Brothers' American humor, and responded by throwing pennies onto the stage. "In those days it was the custom when audiences didn't like an act—a pretty dangerous custom, too, since the English penny was as large as a silver dollar." Groucho waded into the shower of coppers and addressed the unfriendly British audience:

"We came all the way from America to entertain you, so you might at least throw some shillings."

Groucho's ad-lib almost helped to make the London audience more receptive, but the boys decided to play it safe on their tour of the provinces, and resurrected the less sophisticated *Home Again*, which was received enthusiastically even on their return to the London Coliseum. Such was not the case when the Marx Brothers returned to New York.

Because they had played abroad without the approval of Keith-Albee, they were put on the performers' blacklist and banished to second-rate bookings. Even though it had been the end of the season, the Marx Brothers had been expected to remain on call in Cleveland after *On the Mezzanine Floor* closed. At the time, Albee's United Booking Office controlled vaudeville.

The Shubert Brothers, who had successfully fought a similar monopoly in the legitimate theater, decided to take on United Booking. Signing up as many disaffected acts as they could coax away from the Orpheum Circuit, the Shuberts strung together their own vaudeville circuit, often having to accept inferior facilities in Keith-Albee strongholds. Now feeling that they had nothing to lose, the Marx Brothers left the Orpheum Circuit and joined the Shuberts, becoming one of their top attractions.

Despite an auspicious opening at the Winter Garden in New York, the Marx Brothers soon found out that the Shuberts were up against a formidable foe. Not only were Shubert theatres often substandard, but too few headline acts had been lured away from Keith-Albee, and many of these were now contritely returning to the fold. The boys, however, could not go back, so they stuck it out with the Shubert Brothers until their vaudeville circuit collapsed. At that point, they were on everyone's blacklist, and the only way to go was up.

After some unsuccessful negotiations with Charles Dillingham and Flo Ziegfeld (Al Shean was now a big star in the Ziegfeld Follies), Chico chanced to meet another independent, if less illustrious, producer by the name of Joseph M. Gaites, who was looking for talent to put in front of some expensive scenery left over from several flops. His backer was James P. Beury, a millionaire Pennsylvania coal dealer who had just bought the Walnut Street Theatre in Philadelphia and needed something to play there during the summer of 1923.

The Marx Brothers hastily put together what amounted to a gigantic musical tabloid. It was based nominally on an unsuccessful musical comedy by Will and Tom Johnstone called variously *Love for Sale* and *Gimme a Thrill*. Some of the songs and the basic idea, that of a millionairess looking for thrills, were kept, while mostly new material, suitable for the Marx Brothers, was added. Some of it, like the audition scene later filmed by Paramount in 1931, came from *On the Mezzanine Floor*, while a lot of it was written by Groucho and Will B. Johnstone, who was more famous as a cartoonist for the *New York World-Telegram*. The celebrated Napoleon scene was such a collaboration.

Tryouts in Brooklyn and Allentown, Pennsylvania, gave no indication that a Broadway hit was gestating. Then, on June 1, 1923, *I'll Say She Is* opened at the Walnut Street Theatre as "Philadelphia's first annual summer revue." Although the critics immediately recognized it as an elaboration of *Gimme a Thrill*, which had already played itself out over the Shubert circuit, they were impressed. So were audiences.

Groucho continued to be proud of the unexpectedly successful Philadelphia run of *I'll Say She Is*. "We played the whole summer through Labor Day. No show had ever done that before. It was the most important thing that ever happened to me."

At Erin's urging, Groucho described the show for me:

GROUCHO
J. P. Beury was in the coal business. And he was laying one of the chorus girls. So was Harpo, but he didn't know that. He put up the money. We had scenery that was from all the different shows in Kane's warehouse. We didn't have one piece of scenery that really belonged to us.

ERIN
They had to make up the play to match the scenery. It starred Lotta Miles, and Groucho played Napoleon. He had a costume that had a string in the back, and his epaulettes went up and down. Tell Charlotte what you said when you came onstage.

GROUCHO
"My name is Sammy Brown . . ."

ERIN
That's it! Then what happens?

GROUCHO
Metcalf is onstage, and Zeppo comes in and sings, "My name is Sammy Brown, and I just came into town." And the straight man says, "What's your act?" "You can make a mint on me." "What do you do?" "I dance and sing. I do imitations." "Do a Joe Frisco imitation." And he does it. The second one comes in, Chico, and he does the same thing. In the meantime, Harpo is sitting on Metcalf's head.

ERIN

They used to do it in vaudeville all the time. You did Al Shean for a while. Each one would come in and do an imitation to start off. And it changed through the years. At this time it was Joe Frisco, then it was Maurice Chevalier in *Monkey Business.*

GROUCHO

The idea of the show was there were eight men . . .

ERIN

The butcher, the baker, the candlestick maker, the lawyer, the doctor, the Indian chief . . .

GROUCHO

The butler says, "Isn't she a beauty?" And we all say, "I'll say she is!" And that was the title of the play.

ERIN

Then what happened?

GROUCHO

We left the theatre.

ERIN

No!

GROUCHO

The audience left.

ERIN

No, tell about the dancers and what they did. I wish Zeppo was here. He tells it great.

GROUCHO

They did "The Thrill of Wall Street." Then after that, we came out . . .

ERIN

Who were the dancers?

GROUCHO

I don't remember who they were. It was a man and a woman, both lesbians. Then we came out as tramps, and we did a ballet.

ERIN

They did the same dance as the very, very accomplished dancers had done . . .

GROUCHO

Dressed as tramps. And we danced better than they did.

With the Philadelphia success of *I'll Say She Is*, the Marx Brothers started to feel more secure about their future in show business. The show, which cost only $5,000 to produce, was now grossing $4,000 a week. Groucho celebrated by buying a car:

"I had just bought a new car, first new car I ever had. It was a Studebaker. Paid a thousand dollars. So the guy brought the car around. He was a Frenchman, he called it "Stu-da-bak-*care*." I was dying to take a ride in it. So, during intermission, I got the car, and there was one lane of cars in front of me, and one lane of cars in back of me. I was trapped in there and had to go on the stage in five minutes. So I started running toward the Walnut Street Theatre. Here I am dressed as Napoleon, running down the street. And a cop starts to chase me. He thought I was crazy. I got to the theatre just in time. I left the car in the single lane. The streets are very narrow. There's room for a streetcar and an automobile. The traffic jam is probably still there."

When *I'll Say She Is* ended its Philadelphia run the day after Thanksgiving, the show was taken on the road, where it played the rest of the year and into 1924. Gaites had wanted to open immediately on Broadway, but he was discouraged by New York producers, like Lee Shubert, who were unimpressed by the Philadelphia production. The reception accorded them outside Philadelphia almost convinced the Marx Brothers that they really weren't ready for Broadway. Boston, where they opened the road tour, was cold, and Toronto was colder. "When we got to Toronto, it was ten below, and the audience was forty below," Groucho recalled.

Fortunately, Chicago received *I'll Say She Is* warmly. After three SRO months there, they set out on the road again, ending their tour where they had begun it, in Boston. The show must have improved with age, for this time, Groucho said, "The audience was staid, but at least they stayed." Now the Marx Brothers knew they were ready for Broadway. So, on May 19, 1924, *I'll Say She Is* opened at the Shuberts' Casino Theatre in New York.

There's an old stage superstition that forbids anyone to wish an actor good luck before an opening. Instead, one is supposed to say, "Break a leg." It actually happened to Minnie just before the New York opening of *I'll Say She Is*. While standing on a chair during a fitting for her gown, she fell and fractured her ankle, and had to be carried to her box in the Casino Theatre on opening night. Minnie was always a person with a strong sense of theatre, and her entrance on this memorable night was befittingly dramatic.

Generally, the first-string critics would not have covered the opening of a show like *I'll Say She Is*. Even the producers must have had doubts that it was of Broadway caliber, because "We were warned not to put our trunks into storage," Groucho recounted. But another show that was supposed to open on the same night had been postponed, so critics like Alexander Woollcott and Franklin P. Adams, having no place better to go, appeared at the Casino Theatre. Woollcott is supposed to have been forced to attend because he forgot to tell his replacement to cover the opening until it was too late. Led by Woollcott, the critics raved unanimously.

I'll Say She Is ran for almost two years on Broadway. "We were the toast of the town," Groucho said, "which is a lot better than being in a breadline." Harpo spent most of his time outside the theatre at the famous Algonquin Hotel Round Table, where he judiciously maintained his silent role in the presence of some of the most celebrated wits of the time. It didn't take Chico and Zeppo long to find out where the action was, and they went straight to it.

Groucho, more of a homebody, spent most of his spare time at his new house in Great Neck with his wife and children. (Daughter Miriam was born in 1927.) From there, he wrote articles that were published in *The New Yorker* magazine under the name of Julius H. Marx, "As unlikely a pen name as I've ever heard," Groucho told me, "unless it's Charlotte Chandler." Gradually Groucho became the spokesman, onstage and off, for the Marx Brothers. He explained to me how this happened:

"I talked, and Harpo didn't. He played the harp and stood on his head, and Chico played the piano. Zeppo was funny offstage, but onstage he was the straight man and didn't have that much to say. I had some dialogue with Chico which he never remembered because he was always off chasing some dame. So I became the leader of this group of gypsies."

Toward the end of the two-year run of *I'll Say She Is*, the Marx Brothers became acquainted with Sam Harris, a universally respected Broadway producer. Harris wanted to produce the next Marx Brothers show, engaging George S. Kaufman to write the book. This was a most appropriate choice, since the critics had already deemed the Marx Brothers' comedy "worthy of George S. Kaufman," which became a self-fulfilling prophecy. As collaborator, Kaufman chose young Morrie Ryskind. Irving Berlin did the musical score. The result was *The Cocoanuts*, the Marx Brothers' next Broadway show.

Sometimes, working with the Marx Brothers was too much even for so seasoned a man of the theatre as George S. Kaufman. Morrie Ryskind talked with Groucho and me about a time when Kaufman thought he could endure no more.

"George Kaufman wanted to leave once. It was during *The Cocoanuts*. We'd been up all night working on a scene, and George had called a rehearsal at ten, and there wasn't a Marx Brother in sight. And I swear to you, George wanted to leave me. At that time he was the big guy in the theatre, and he said, 'I'm not going to put up with that stuff.' I virtually had to grab him. I said, 'Look, it's all right for you to go, but what happens to *me*, George!' "

The Cocoanuts opened at the Lyric Theatre on December 8, 1925. Opposite Groucho was an actress named Margaret Dumont—a Sam Harris discovery. Again the critics raved, although Percy Hammond found it "not so laughable as its predecessor, *I'll Say She Is*." (This was the same Percy Hammond who in Chicago several years earlier had described *Home Again* as "an elaborate disorder of amateur antics said to have been a riot in lesser vaudeville.")

There is a saying in the theatre that plays are rewritten, not written. As might be expected, the Marx Brothers carried this maxim to its maximum, rewriting the dialogue every performance, even after it was out of rehearsal. For Groucho, especially, ad-libbing was as essential as breathing. During its three-year run, so many changes were made that hardly anything remained of the original dialogue. Groucho remembered how George S. Kaufman became resigned to the Marx Brothers' use of his and Morrie Ryskind's lines as springboards for their zany extemporizations:

"Kaufman was standing in the wings one night talking with Heywood Broun. Broun was in the middle of telling a story when Kaufman said, 'Just a minute,' and left him. In a moment George returned to Broun, who was annoyed, and said, 'Sorry I interrupted your story, but I thought I heard one of the original lines.' "

Groucho's penchant for adding new material as the inspiration struck him sometimes bewildered his fellow performers. The Brox Sisters—Lorayne, Patricia, and Bobbe—shared with me their reminiscences of Groucho's extemporizing, on and off the stage, in *The Cocoanuts*:

LORAYNE BROX

On our exit, Groucho would love to join in. All of a sudden we would find the audience laughing at us when they weren't supposed to be. It was because Groucho was trailing after us, and he'd start to sing a chorus. We never minded. We never had more fun than working with the Marx Brothers, especially Groucho. Groucho was particularly fun. Groucho used to sing, and he loved to play his guitar.

PATRICIA BROX

We would travel by train, and Groucho would bring his guitar. We'd sing all the way wherever we were going. In the trains we'd sing all the songs we knew, and that was quite a repertory. And then we'd find we'd arrived at our destination.

BOBBE BROX

We always had a lot of fun with him. I think he's the most fabulous ad-libber in the whole world. He's a naturally funny man. I always loved being with him because it was such a ball.

I

Has Groucho changed over the years?

BOBBE BROX

No. Not a bit. He was always like that.

I

Do you remember your first meeting with the Marx Brothers?

BOBBE BROX

I remember only that we were very young, and Irving Berlin, who was our sponsor and guardian, told us one thing: "Now, stay out of the way of those fellows." But they couldn't have been nicer to us! They were wonderful, 'cause we were kids, and they were really good to us. But that was our first meeting, so we were a little timid and shy. Finally one of the boys went to Berlin and said, "What's the matter with those girls? They don't speak to us, and they run when we come around." And Berlin told them, "Well, I told them to." It's very funny, because they couldn't have been nicer to us. But he frightened us by telling us that we'd better stay out of their way. Years later, I used to see Zeppo when he was married to Barbara. I'd see him at Sinatra's, because we were at Sinatra's house every night. Once Milton Berle said, "You know, the Brox Sisters were in every show that Berlin put on." And Zeppo spoke up and said, "Yes, he *made* us take 'em!" I don't know if that's true or not. (*Laughs*)

King Vidor told me about a night when the Marx Brothers threw away the script entirely at a Los Angeles performance when *The Cocoanuts* was touring:

"Greta Garbo and John Gilbert and Eleanor Boardman and I went to see the Marx Brothers in *Cocoanuts* at the Biltmore in 1928. That afternoon I went to the makeup department and got four black beards and other funny things, and we took the things to the show. It was the closing night, and when the curtain went up for the second act, we all had our beards on, as well as funny hats. We thought we would break them up, but we didn't. Groucho just started ad-libbing a lot of jokes about us. He looked down at us and said, 'I thought that was Greta Garbo in the audience, but it was General Grant.' We threw our black beards up onstage, and they started throwing costumes and props down at us."

Kaufman and Ryskind agreed to write the next Marx Brothers vehicle, which turned out to be *Animal Crackers*. Bert Kalmar and Harry Ruby wrote the lyrics and music, notably the famous "Captain Spaulding," which became Groucho's theme song. None of the songs in *The Cocoanuts* had become hits, although Morrie Ryskind explained that it wasn't Irving Berlin's fault:

"Berlin wrote some excellent music for our show, but nobody paid any attention, because these guys could ruin anything. They run around for fifteen minutes, and then the young lovers do a song. Nobody gives a damn if the boy loves the girl or not."

By the time *Animal Crackers* opened at the Forty-fourth Street Theatre on October 23, 1928, the Marx Brothers were becoming famous enough to interest Hollywood. Paramount signed them to a contract, and in the spring of 1929 they shot *The Cocoanuts* on newly built soundstages in Astoria, Long Island. Robert Florey was the director.

When I was staying at Groucho's house, he, Morrie Ryskind, and I were talking about *The Cocoanuts* and Robert Florey's name was mentioned. I suggested that we invite him to lunch, and Groucho said, "Fine." I called him, but, though he seemed pleased by the invitation, he declined, pleading ill health. Later I learned that Robert Florey had long been displeased, to say the least, by Groucho's version of the filming of *The Cocoanuts*, which depicted him as a non-English-speaking director.

In spite of a distinguished Hollywood career spanning five decades, Robert Florey is frequently best remembered as the director who brought the Marx Brothers' stage play *The Cocoanuts* to the screen. Groucho often mentioned him when talking about the Broadway days and the early films he made at Paramount's Astoria studios. These comments seemed pejorative to Robert Florey. In a 1976 letter to writer–film historian Herman G. Weinberg he told his side:

Dear Herman:
Thanks for the Groucho interview, by Joe Adamson. Just received it and cannot understand the reason for which, for the past forty-six years,

Groucho keeps on telling that at the time Paramount produced *Co-coanuts*, I was a foreigner who didn't understand English.

In the first place, I had become an American citizen during the '20s and was no longer a "foreigner." Before *Cocoanuts*, I worked for years in Hollywood. I had been a gagman with the Sunshine comedies, an assistant director to Al Santell, Louis Gasnier, and Bill Beaudine. I even was a first assistant director on important productions for Samuel Goldwyn and Joseph M. Schenck (motion pictures with such stars as Norma Talmadge, Ronald Colman, Vilma Banky, etc.), positions in which it was indispensable not only to understand but also to speak English. For two years at MGM, I worked with King Vidor, Robert Z. Leonard, John Stahl, Edmund Goulding, Phil Rosen, Von Sternberg, and others. I had to speak English when I directed silent features for Harry Cohn (Columbia), Phil Goldstone (Tiffany), Joe Rock, or second units. I had also worked with Mary Pickford and Douglas Fairbanks for almost two years, and before meeting the Frères Marx, had directed at the Paramount Astoria studio three films and a dozen sound shorts during a year's time. I had not just arrived from Paris as Groucho always implies.

Once while I was directing a TV show for Four Star, Harpo came on the set and told me: "I always understood you clearly while making *Cocoanuts*. I do not know what is the matter with Groucho, persisting in saying that you spoke only French, and that Santley was your interpreter. Santley didn't speak French, so how could he have translated what you were saying?"

During the first year I directed at Astoria, Edward G. Robinson, Raymond Hitchcock, Fanny Brice, and dear Eddie Cantor didn't complain about my English, nor even about my French accent. Later when I occasionally met him at Arrowhead, Palm Springs, or Musso-Franks, Groucho was always cordial, and I do not know what he has against me.

I do not know Mr. Joe Adamson, author of the interview. If you are acquainted with Mr. Adamson, please do tell him that back in 1928 I did understand English, as we often spoke together. And, by the way, I did not choose to "direct" *Cocoanuts*. My understanding with Monta Bell was that I would mostly work on dramas, and I had been assigned to *The Letter* when this story was switched to Jean de Limur.

Bell and Wanger were, as they said, "gambling" on the Marx Brothers. They wanted to shoot *Cocoanuts* quickly and inexpensively, if possible within three weeks, discounting the matinees, the boys then being on a show. Monta Bell suggested photographing *Cocoanuts* with four cameras as it was presented on the stage. My idea was to get some second unit stuff in

Florida and more action and movement. This was rejected. I then told Monta Bell that he should let the Marx Brothers do *Cocoanuts* some morning on a theatre stage in New York, and have four or five cameras photograph the complete performance—like a live show—in ten-minute sections, just the time to reload the magazines, and he could have a finished product in one day. Bell answered that the quality so obtained wouldn't be good enough. He wanted me to photograph some "interesting angles"(?), particularly the musical numbers, dances, etc., and to let the boys do their routines as they had done them 1,000 times previously on the stage.

In his memoirs [*Harpo Speaks*] Harpo wrote that during the takes I laughed so much at what they were doing that I spoiled them. Groucho says not only that I didn't smile at his jokes, but I didn't understand them. The chalk marks limiting his walking space, the position of the cumbersome microphones were a constant source of Groucho's irritability. He would step over the chalk mark, his head going out of the shot, and I would stop the cameras, asking him to remain within the camera range and to speak directly into one of the mikes. It would make him angry.

He didn't understand photography and insisted on painting his mustache with a shiny black varnish. After having seen the first rushes, Monta Bell tried to explain to Groucho that it might be better to use some crepe instead of paint, as his closeups looked pretty bad with the light reflecting between his nose and his mouth, and Groucho got extremely offended and insulted. He was so angry that he wanted Bell to be fired. Bell called me, asking me to try to "do something about the varnished moustache." Bell added, "As far as I am concerned, I am giving up, and I don't care if the SOB wears a monkey suit in the picture or what he does . . ."

In any case, I enjoyed the company of Zeppo, Harpo, Chico, and Mary Eaton. I often had dinner in New York with Harpo and Chico. But to work—or to be—with Groucho was no bed of roses. I did my best with the film, finished it in time, within the budget or less, got a few good angles, mostly while shooting the musical numbers, added a few gags for Harpo and Chico, and still hope to find out someday the reason for Groucho's antagonism.

Votre ami,
Bob

The Marx Brothers commuted between Astoria and Manhattan daily, shooting scenes for *The Cocoanuts* in the day and performing *Animal*

Crackers onstage at night. They were, in fact, unable to attend the motion picture premiere of *The Cocoanuts* at Broadway's Rialto Theatre because they were doing *Animal Crackers* onstage simultaneously at the Forty-fourth Street Theatre only two blocks away. Minnie attended for them.

Two weeks later she died at sixty-four. When Groucho received his special Oscar in 1974, he said, "I'd like to thank my mother, without whom we would have been a failure." Frenchie outlived her by four years, reaching the age of seventy-two before he, too, died in Hollywood in 1933.

By 1929 the Marx Brothers were a huge success, both onstage and on the screen, but the ensuing stock market crash hit them hard. "I was wiped out," Groucho told me. "I had $250,000, which I'd saved up over a period of many years playing small-time vaudeville, and I lost it in two days when the market crashed." Harpo managed to meet his margin calls and sell before he was wiped out, while Chico had already lost everything he had ever earned gambling. Zeppo, being only a salaried member of the cast, had little to lose. The Marx Brothers were, however, in great demand, so the market crash and the Depression did not stop them from earning good livings. Even after the crash, *Animal Crackers* was sold out every performance, and tickets were selling then for ten dollars a seat.

After a tour of *Animal Crackers*, they returned to New York in 1930 to film it on Long Island, beginning the zoological tetralogy that was completed in 1933 with *Duck Soup*.

The director for the *Animal Crackers* film was Victor Heerman, a veteran of silent films. Apparently, he feared the worst, for he immediately assigned assistant directors to watch over each brother, and even had four small cubicles built to contain them between takes. But he still couldn't get them to the studio on time. Lillian Roth, who played the ingenue in the film, described how Zeppo might arrive at nine-thirty, then someone would have to give Groucho a wake-up call at ten. Later, Chico would stroll in, while Harpo was getting so bored by the delay that he would go off somewhere else where he couldn't be found. After a whole morning of this, Chico would bound back in, cheerfully asking, "Anybody for lunch?" She characterized it as "one step removed from a circus."

To complete their Paramount contract, the Marx Brothers and their families moved to California in 1931, where *Monkey Business* was shot that year, followed by *Horse Feathers* in 1932 and *Duck Soup* in 1933. Groucho fell in love at first sight with Southern California. Gummo, having turned to the garment business when he was discharged from the Army, remained in New York. Later, he joined his brothers in Hollywood as a successful agent; but first he established a branch of Zeppo's theatrical agency in New York after Zeppo himself had left the team upon completion of the Paramount contract. Harpo, meanwhile, was touring Russian music halls between films.

Although devoted fans revere the Marx Brothers' Paramount pictures as classics, Groucho, on occasion, irreverently referred to them as "those five turkeys." But whenever he was asked which of his films he liked best, it was always the "the war picture" (*Duck Soup*) and "the college picture" (*Horse Feathers*) right after the Thalberg pictures.

During the time that Groucho was getting established in films, he was also writing. In 1930 his first book, *Beds,* was published after having been serialized in *College Humor* magazine a year earlier. He had been published before, but never as the author of a book, even if he later described *Beds* as "a thin book."

Groucho was always especially proud of his early writings for *The New Yorker* magazine. As Julius H. Marx, Groucho appeared in *The New Yorker* as early as 1925. His writing ranged from dialogues between Vaude and Vill (Vaude: "Didn't you have a wife the last I saw you?" Vill: "Yes, but her husband asked me to give her up.") to satirical comments on Boston, Chicago, and press agents. In 1929, he wrote a letter "To the Editors of *The New Yorker*" very much along the lines of his later published correspondence. He complained:

> Three-fourths of my brothers called my attention to the fact that the last issue of your esteemed gazette stated that Governor Alfred E. Smith had seen but four shows to date, namely, "Whoopee," "Scandals," "Three Cheers," and "Street Scene." I'll give you just twenty-four hours to retract that statement before I call on you and horse-whip you within four or five inches of your life.
>
> Stack your Bibles, bring on your notary public! I can prove that Governor Smith attended a performance of "Animal Crackers." I know because I saw him smile at Zeppo, snicker at Chico, chuckle at Harpo, and roar at me. When he wasn't roaring at me, he was guffawing; when he wasn't guffawing, he was helpless with mirth; when he wasn't—I could keep this up for hours, but I won't.

Twelve years later his next book, *Many Happy Returns,* appeared, and then in 1959, *Groucho and Me,* followed in 1965 and 1967 by *Memoirs of a Mangy Lover* and *The Groucho Letters.* Always having aspired to be a writer, even before he wanted to become an actor, he was prouder of his literary output than of anything else he ever did.

In 1934 he and Chico went on radio with a program called *Flywheel, Shyster and Flywheel*, a modest beginning that many years later would culminate in the enormously popular *You Bet Your Life* on both radio and television. Until *You Bet Your Life* in 1947, the kind of success that Groucho, the great talker, seemed to deserve on radio always eluded him. He told me more than once with obvious pride, "Chaplin said to me, 'I wish I could talk like you.'" But Groucho's appeal seems to have been as much visual as aural, as the pantomime mirror sequence in *Duck Soup* reveals.

This scene was the inspiration of Leo McCarey, director of *Duck Soup* and, according to Groucho, "the only great director we ever worked with. Working with him was a lot of fun." Groucho told me that the three directors with whom the Marx Brothers would have most liked to work were René Clair, Ernst Lubitsch, and Rouben Mamoulian. All three also admired the Marx Brothers.

Often Groucho said how much he wished the Marx Brothers could have had René Clair as a director: "There was nobody better than him."

At lunch in Paris at Grand Véfour restaurant, René Clair talked with me about the Marx Brothers:

"I knew Harpo much better than Groucho. There was a great difference between their humor. Groucho's humor was aggressive; Harpo's was sentimental. Harpo would have been the easier character for me to direct because I find it easier to write for characters who are sympathetic for me.

"An unrealized dream of mine would have been to do a Marx Brothers film. That was something I wanted to do when I went to Hollywood. Then, much later, I met Groucho, and he said that was just what he wanted, to do a picture with me. He said to be directed by René Clair was exactly what the Marx Brothers had wanted. It was a case of *par hazard*, just like the title of my book."

I asked him which films of the Marx Brothers would he have liked to direct.

"All of the great ones. I liked the early ones. Leo McCarey was a fine director. But the important thing would have been the writing. I think of myself as a writer. Being a director doesn't mean much. You don't have to go out and create with a studio of people. You can do it on paper. Anyone of some intelligence can get a picture from a detailed, good script."

Groucho told me about Ernst Lubitsch's enthusiasm for writing and directing a Marx Brothers film:

"Lubitsch was one of the best directors, I guess, in this country. He wanted to do a movie with us, but we were tied up with Paramount. I remember Lubitsch had an opening line that he tried out on me one day. It went like this: 'Ya haf a girl in her betroom, and she iss married. And her husband comes home unexpectedly just as a streetcar iss going through the betroom.' And I said, 'What's the joke?' My next line, he said, was, 'Believe it or not, I was waiting for a streetcar.' That was an expression then. And I was supposed to step out of the closet and onto the streetcar. He was a genius."

One night in Beverly Hills, talking with Rouben Mamoulian at dinner at the Beverly Wilshire's El Padrino restaurant about the Marx Brothers, I asked him whether he would have liked to direct them.

"No, I don't think I would have liked doing a Marx Brothers picture. I admired them greatly, but I thought what they did was just right. I wouldn't have wanted to change them, so it would not have been a creative experience for me. It would have been like doing a quarter of a play."

He remembered going backstage to the Marx Brothers' dressing room between acts of *The Cocoanuts:*

"Sam Harris was there, and the Marx Brothers started putting on a show for us, ad-libbing. They were very funny, and when people came into the dressing room to tell them to go onstage, they made those people part of the act, and then they put the people out and continued doing the show just for us. Of course, eventually they got back onstage to finish the performance."

The Marx Brothers enjoyed performing for the audience of Sam Harris and Rouben Mamoulian, which, though small, so commanded their respect. Also, the Marx Brothers were entertaining themselves. Their extemporizing provided the essential spontaneity without which they themselves became bored. As Groucho told me, "First I had to entertain myself."

Not everyone enjoyed Groucho's predilection for having fun with their names. Rouben Mamoulian was one who did.

"Groucho and I were at Paramount at the same time. I'd walk into the commissary, and the four of them would be there together, and I'd hear them singing, 'I'd walk a Mamoulian miles for one of your smiles . . .' every time I came in."

He also appreciated Groucho's ability to enjoy occasionally being on the receiving end of a well-turned insult.

"There was a period of time, not too long ago, when I would run into Groucho wherever I was, and he would say to me, 'Do I have to meet *you* wherever I go?' Then, one day I saw Groucho sitting with some people at Nate 'n' Al's, and I walked up to him and said, 'Do I have to meet *you* wherever I go?' He smiled and didn't say anything."

Salvador Dalí told me that he had wanted to work with the Marx Brothers. He told me that he once did a complete script "with full pictures" for the Marx Brothers, a script which apparently has been lost. In the bar of New York City's St. Regis Hotel, Dalí told me about his friendship with Harpo:

"Dalí wanted to meet Harpo. Dalí called Harpo. Harpo wanted to meet Dalí. Dalí went to Harpo and presented Harpo with a harp, a harp which had chords of barbed wire. Harpo went to the harp and played and his hands became covered with blood. After that day, Dalí and Harpo were always friends, and Dalí painted a picture of Harpo with a lobster on his head."

In Dalí's own words, the script he did for the Marx Brothers was "very surrealistic," and the whole idea of the film was symbolized by his painting which showed "gondolas riding on a sea of bicycles."

Groucho's comment to me was, "It would've been a great combination. Dalí didn't speak much English, and neither did Harpo."

During one of Groucho's visits to New York, we met Salvador Dalí at the Russian Tea Room, and Groucho was warmly greeted with "Butterfly-eeee!" When Dalí had departed, Groucho, who was usually the one who did the perplexing, turned to me and said, "What did he say? You speak Spanish and French. It sounded like "Butterfly-eeee!" I was unable to translate. But at a later date, when I had tea with Dalí, he translated for me:

"When Dalí first meets Harpo, we see a butterfly, and Dalí says, 'Butterfly-eeee,' the Spanish pronunciation of the word, not understanding how to say the *y*. Harpo explains, and it is our private word. I thought Groucho would understand it."

Although *Duck Soup* has since become a classic, in 1933 Paramount was hesitant about renewing the Marx Brothers' contract. Groucho, as usual, was worried, Harpo was abroad, Zeppo was out of the act, and Chico was heavily in debt. Fortunately for Groucho and Harpo, Chico was in debt to Irving Thalberg, the executive producer in charge of production at M-G-M.

Thalberg was the youngest man ever to hold such an important post in

Hollywood, and had in fact been appointed while he was still in his twenties. When he wasn't working, his favorite recreation was playing bridge. It was inevitable that he would meet Chico at a card table, and it was equally inevitable that Chico would soon owe him money.

In his inimitable fashion, Chico managed to convince Thalberg that the Marx Brothers were still a valuable property. Since Paramount had expressed no interest in retaining their services, they had talked with Sam Goldwyn, who was mildly interested. Thalberg, who wasn't getting along with M-G-M head Louis B. Mayer, wanted to start his own production company, featuring stars like the Marx Brothers. He didn't care much for what they had done for Paramount, but thought that under his guidance they could make pictures that would have wider audience appeal. Happy to have found such a man, the Marx Brothers signed with M-G-M and made two films, A *Night at the Opera* and A *Day at the Races*, for Thalberg before he died at the age of thirty-seven during the shooting of the latter film. Groucho greatly respected Thalberg, and considered A *Night at the Opera* his best movie. Whenever we talked about Thalberg, Groucho said, "He was a genius. He was the greatest producer. They named a building after him. Thalberg would come every day and look at the rushes. If he didn't like it, [Sam] Wood would shoot the scenes over again. He [Thalberg] was really the director."

Thalberg was certainly one of Hollywood's most esteemed producers, and he was willing to spend a great deal of extra time, effort, and money to achieve the results that he thought the Marx Brothers' talents merited. At Groucho's suggestion, he brought in Kaufman and Ryskind, and he allowed the Marx Brothers to tour a tabloid presentation of both scripts so that audience reaction could be gauged before the films were actually shot. He also understood mass taste, and introduced production elements into the films that gave them a much wider appeal than before. Today, film buffs may not care that much about some of the musical numbers and the plots that Thalberg considered so important, but Groucho felt that at that point Thalberg was vital to the Marx Brothers' careers.

Thalberg left his mark on the Marx Brothers' films that followed. Groucho quoted him as saying, "The first five pictures weren't real pictures because they weren't about anything. Sure, they were funny, but you don't need that many laughs in a movie. I'll make a picture with you fellows with half as many laughs, but I'll put a legitimate story in it, and I'll bet it will gross twice as much as *Duck Soup*." A *Night at the Opera* actually did double *Duck Soup*'s gross.

Thalberg also had great personal charm, Groucho felt. George S. Kaufman, who had sworn he would never work in Hollywood, came to work for Thalberg and described him as "another Sam Harris." George Seaton told me how Thalberg, who was always known as "Mr. Thalberg" to everyone at M-G-M, asked Kaufman to call him by his first name. "I'll call you Irving if you call me Mr. Kaufman," he answered.

Goldie Arthur, Irving Thalberg's personal secretary, shared with me her impressions of what it was like working with the Marx Brothers at M-G-M in the thirties.

"I always enjoyed their comedy, and I really enjoyed working on *A Night at the Opera*, which I thought was a very funny picture. Apparently a lot of people thought so too, because it did a tremendous business—and this was at a time when their pictures did very poorly and they were thought to be washed up. I look on this as another proof of the talent of Mr. Thalberg, who produced the picture.

"When I was told they were going to be doing a picture for Mr. Thalberg, I was personally very pleased, because I did think they were very funny men. They came on the lot and were assigned offices, and we had a few amusing phone calls from them. Chico called shortly after they moved in and said they had found some black widow spiders in the office and 'somebody better send over some flies before they start eating us Jews.'

"When they came in to see Mr. Thalberg they usually arrived with some gag or other—none of them were really very funny or I'd remember them—but it was never dull when they were around. I do remember one time they had to wait because Mr. Thalberg was not finished with a conference—and I think it was Chico who tried to blow some smoke under the door into Mr. Thalberg's office, but it didn't work because the door was insulated.

"When they were shooting the scene where Groucho rides to his stateroom on top of his trunk, I remember that he didn't want to do it because he thought it was 'out of character'—but apparently Mr. Thalberg didn't agree with him, and he did it, and it was a funny scene.

"Chico was apparently a very good bridge player and played fairly frequently with Mr. Thalberg and some of his friends, and Mr. Thalberg was always after him to learn a new song. It seems he would rather play bridge than work up a new number on the piano—but he eventually did have one ready in time.

"I remember Harpo as a very sweet, gentle man who really loved to play the harp. I was told that he would play—just for his own pleasure—until his fingertips were raw. He was self-taught, and a number of talented harpists who watched him play told him that it was not possible to play the harp with that technique (or lack of it)—but play he did and beautifully, too. It was always interesting to me to watch his face during his harp solo in the movies—you could always tell it was something he put his whole being into.

"As far as I remember, the picture went along quite smoothly. The director, Sam Wood, was thoroughly experienced in comedy, and the Marx Brothers were professionals who were very much interested in helping to turn out a good picture. They were terribly pleased when it did turn out so well, and were grateful to Mr. Thalberg for resurrecting their careers."

Although the Marx Brothers' films were always big, important Hollywood productions, not every actor was thrilled at the prospect of appearing in them. Lillian Roth considered her assignment to *Animal Crackers* a form of banishment, and Maureen O'Sullivan was initially unenthusiastic about *A Day at the Races*:

"I hadn't particularly wanted to do it," she told me. "I was into more serious things—*The Barretts of Wimpole Street* and *David Copperfield*. It was such a long time ago, and I didn't expect that I was ever going to be asked about it. We never know what posterity is going to remember and judge us for.

"Doing it was a real pleasure. There was a lot of fun and nonsense every day, but it didn't slow down getting the job done. I remember stepping on a boat, and my skirt blew up—that sort of thing. I've always been glad I did it. When I've seen it recently, I've been pleased."

After Thalberg died, the Marx Brothers did three more pictures for M-G-M, *At the Circus* (1939), *Go West* (1940), and *The Big Store* (1941), as well as *Room Service* (1938) for RKO, a special deal engineered by Zeppo. The Thalberg formula without Thalberg continued to serve them, but there was less magic. Louis B. Mayer was reputed to have personally disliked the Marx Brothers, and Groucho confirmed that any animosity was reciprocated. One day Mayer came up to Groucho on the set and asked him how everything was going. "I don't think that's any of your business," Groucho snapped. By 1942 it wasn't any of the Marx Brothers' business, either, for they were finished with M-G-M. At that time they announced their first "retirement," and Groucho added, "in anticipation of popular demand."

Groucho's domestic life changed during these years, too. His marriage to Ruth had been failing and "her solution was alcohol." His was to get a divorce, which he did in 1942. Three years later he married his daughter Miriam's best friend, 24-year-old Catherine Marvis Gorcey, who had been the wife of former Deadend Kid Leo Gorcey. In 1946 Melinda was born.

After a long-confirmed bachelorhood, Harpo had married actress Susan Fleming in 1936. They adopted four children. Of the five brothers, only Harpo and Gummo avoided divorces. Gummo married his wife, Helen, shortly after leaving the act, and they had a son. "I remember when Bobby was a little boy," Groucho told me. "I'd give him a nickel for shining my shoes. Now he's forty or fifty years old."

Faced with the responsibilities of a new family, Groucho quickly unretired. But, then, *he* never really had retired, only the brothers as an act. During World War II he remained active on radio and toured military bases as well as joining nationwide Hollywood war bond rallies. By 1946, however, Groucho's new status as a papa-to-be at fifty-five and Chico's old status as a pauper-to-be at fifty-eight brought the team back together again for *A Night in Casablanca*. Groucho supplemented this with solo appearances in *Copacabana* (1947), *Mr. Music* (1950), *Double Dynamite* (1951), and *A Girl in Every Port* (1952).

In *Double Dynamite*, Groucho worked with Frank Sinatra. Groucho was fastidiously punctual, usually arriving on the set early. Frank Sinatra was more casual about time, so Groucho, who said, "I don't even wait for myself," found himself waiting around for Sinatra's arrival. It reminded him of the days "before we made it big, when we used to have to wait for everybody." His answer was to come *later* than Sinatra, causing Sinatra to come even later and Groucho to come still later, and so on. Finally a détente was reached.

"Sinatra talked with me about it, and I said, 'You come on time, and I'll be there.' He did and I did." Later, Frank Sinatra became almost a member of the Marx family when he married Barbara Marx, Zeppo's former wife.

Although they would appear together again a decade later, the last true Marx Brothers' film was *Love Happy* (1949). *Love Happy* was an unhappy affair that Harpo had been persuaded to do alone, then he was joined by his brothers. The film was Marilyn Monroe's first and the Marx Brothers' last.

During the middle 1930s, Groucho had met a young writer with few credits whom he immediately liked. He and Norman Krasna started collaborating, and the first result was Warner Brothers' *The King and the*

Chorus Girl in 1937. After Norman Krasna had firmly established himself as one of Broadway's best playwrights, Groucho and he again joined farces to write *Time for Elizabeth*. The play opened and closed after seven performances on Broadway in 1948, but ten years later enjoyed a modest success in summer stock when Groucho played the lead himself.

At mid-century, when Groucho reached sixty, nationwide television became a reality, and Groucho a part of it. *You Bet Your Life* was a success on radio (it had won a Peabody Award in 1949), so it was natural that the show would move over to the new medium, which it did in 1950. *You Bet Your Life* was more of a Marx family show than most people realized. Both Gummo and Chico participated behind the scenes. Gummo was Groucho's agent, and Chico was the family's "lost soul," as Groucho described him. Chico made no material contributions to the show, but he was put on salary, and the salary was doled out whenever he needed to pay gambling debts, which was most of the time. Gummo told me that if Chico called him and started the conversation with "Gummy," he knew what was coming and as a reflex pulled out his checkbook. This was, however, not Chico's sole income. He was also appearing in nightclubs, usually in Las Vegas, where his income was always more of an outgo.

Sometimes Harpo would join him in a nightclub act. Harpo was also doing harp concerts. By now, Zeppo had sold his rights in the agency that he and Gummo had built up from a few clients to one of the largest in Hollywood, and was a successful manufacturer.

At least three-fifths of the Marx Brothers' domestic lives continued to be turbulent. Zeppo had divorced his first wife, Marian, and would soon marry Barbara. Chico and Betty were now divorced, and their daughter, Maxine, grown. Groucho's marital fortunes seemed to wane as his professional fortunes waxed. This had been true with Ruth, and now it was true with Kay. They were divorced in 1951 just as *You Bet Your Life* was establishing itself as one of the top-rated programs on television. Recidivous by nature, at least as far as marriage was concerned, Groucho married for a third time in 1954, this time, Eden Hartford. They had met during the filming of *A Girl in Every Port*, where she had come to visit her sister, Dee, who was appearing in the film with Groucho. Eden fainted and Groucho came to her rescue.

You Bet Your Life ran on NBC until 1961, and was followed by a short-lived sequel, *Tell It to Groucho*, on CBS. "It [*You Bet Your Life*] was some of the best stuff I ever did," Groucho told me once just after we had watched a rerun. "I really had to think. I never worked so hard." I asked him if there was any significance to the duck which appears at the magic word. "No. It's just easier to crack a joke about a duck than an elephant."

Talking with me about *You Bet Your Life*, Groucho said, "The audience is the straight man. It's what they say that makes what you say funny. You can't make up people like that." When people would come up to us to tell Groucho that they watched the seventies reruns of his show, he always responded, "I do too."

The great success of *You Bet Your Life* left Groucho with little time for other professional activities. He did, however, find time to make two brief movie appearances after *A Girl in Every Port*. One of them, Irwin Allen's *The Story of Mankind* (1957), featured his brothers, too, but not together. They appeared together for the last time in *The Incredible Jewel Robbery* on the *General Electric Theatre* television show in 1959. From 1957 through 1960, he toured *Time for Elizabeth* in summer stock, his first non-Groucho acting part since he had done *Twentieth Century* in Maine twenty-three years earlier. For Groucho, who so greatly appreciated Gilbert and Sullivan, one of the highlights of his career was appearing as the Lord High Executioner in a telecast of *The Mikado*, produced by Goddard Lieberson in 1960.

After *You Bet Your Life*, Groucho didn't bother to announce his "retirement" as the team had done twenty years before. Instead he became a kind of comedian emeritus, appearing as guest on many television programs. He played his last film role in Otto Preminger's film *Skidoo* in 1968. Preminger summed up for me his impression of Groucho the actor: "He was a complete professional. He came on time, he knew his lines, and he was totally prepared. He was a star, but he didn't overact."

Groucho had told me of working with Otto Preminger:

GROUCHO
He's a good director. And he's a gambler.
I
A gambler?
GROUCHO
Not like Chico. I mean he's not afraid to take chances.

One of Groucho's most memorable guest appearances was on *The Hollywood Palace* in 1965, when he and Margaret Dumont re-created Captain Spaulding's arrival from *Animal Crackers*. Two weeks later, she died.

The decade of the sixties was also the final act for Chico and Harpo.

Chico died in 1961, and Harpo in 1964. No matter how old they had grown, as long as the Marx Brothers were alive, there was always the hope that they might be reunited in front of an audience again. Groucho was left to carry on the act alone.

A lot of erudite, not very funny books have been written about why we laugh, but nobody has ever really been able to explain it satisfactorily. Perhaps Groucho came closest when he said that all great comedy grows out of believable characters. Lee Strasberg agreed, commenting to me about the comedy of the Marx Brothers:

"Groucho and Harpo were the great ones. Chico and even Zeppo were important because they all worked well together, but it was Groucho and Harpo who really established characters."

Toward the end of the sixties, Groucho's third marriage started to founder. He and Eden were finally divorced in 1969. Their parting was amicable, and they continued to see each other from time to time.

Minnie's Boys, a musical comedy based on the family life of the young Marx Brothers, opened in New York at the Imperial Theatre in 1970. The show was not as great a success as it might have been, but as producer Arthur Whitelaw mentioned to Groucho and me, *Minnie's Boys* has continued to play in one amateur production after another ever since. Arthur, Groucho, and I went together to one such performance in Los Angeles. Some of the music was written by Marvin Hamlisch, who had not yet met Groucho.

From the mid-sixties on, Groucho was making fewer public appearances, while the fame of the Marx Brothers was soaring with a new generation. In 1971, Erin Fleming catapulted into Groucho's life to become his secretary. Because Groucho didn't want to disappoint Erin, and because what she wanted him to do was what he wanted to do anyway, he returned to show business. "I hit the road and it didn't hit back," Groucho told me. The show at Ames, Iowa, the Carnegie Hall concert, the re-premiere of *Animal Crackers*, all followed.

Groucho told me, "I wish you could've met Harpo and Chico. We played every town in America and I think we were the only group that never fought. No act in vaudeville got along better than we did. There never was anyone like my brothers and me."

I first met Zeppo and Gummo in the bar of the Tamarisk Country Club in Palm Springs, shortly after I had interviewed Groucho for *Playboy*. Though in his seventies, Zeppo looked much younger, and he still had the voice of the fourth Marx Brother in the Paramount films. He sat politely through our meeting, but he was visibly impatient. There was still that empty chair waiting in a card game somewhere.

Gummo was the least known of the Marx Brothers, but in Palm Springs, where he lived, he was a celebrity. When we arrived, the adjoining club-restaurant had not yet started filling up for lunch. By the time Zeppo left, people had started coming in, and most of them greeted Gummo. He was asked for his autograph, and some people asked him if he could get Groucho's autograph for their son. He said he would.

When I arrived, Zeppo was waiting for me in front of the club. We went inside where Gummo was sitting at a table.

ZEPPO

I thought your interview was just excellent, and probably one of the best I've seen on the Marxes, because you handled it *so* well—and you handled *him* so well. But I was surprised when I saw you. I thought you were probably an eighteen-year-old girl with very big busts and the usual beautiful face, and everything—that's why you got this great interview from Groucho, because usually he isn't this tolerant. But you're still a very attractive lady—I don't mean to bring you down in any way. It was done very well, and I must compliment you on that. It's one of the reasons why I am subjecting myself to this interview.

I

What are you doing now?

ZEPPO

I'm a commercial fisherman. Strange, isn't it? But I've been in a few businesses in my lifetime. I was in the horse-racing business, raising horses with Barbara Stanwyck. We had a breeding farm, and we boarded horses. We boarded horses for Alfred Vanderbilt, Liz Whitney, and L. B. Mayer on our ranch in the Valley, which we owned jointly. Before that, I had been with the Marx Brothers, which I hated. I was very unhappy doing what I had to with the Marx Brothers, and I was so confined with them, because I couldn't do what I wanted to do. I had to be a straight man, which I didn't want to be. I wanted to be a comedian. But there were three comedians already, and there was no room for another comedian, especially a younger brother that came in later. So I had to content myself with being a straight man and being subjected to, well, a small part in the group, which I resented. I not only resented it, but I felt inferior. So, eventually, it got to the point where I couldn't take it anymore, because I wasn't doing what I wanted to do and what I thought I was capable of doing. You know, at one time I took Groucho's place. He was ill, in Chicago. And coming on the train into Chicago . . . did you know this?

I

Yes, but you tell me, then I'll tell you what Groucho said.

ZEPPO

Oh, I know what he said, because he said it to me the other night on the phone. Well, anyway, I felt this was something I could do, but I had no opportunity with the Marx Brothers. I had to be the straight man.

I

Tell me about the night you took his place.

ZEPPO

Well, the day we arrived in Chicago, he was rushed right to the hospital, and I didn't understudy him or anything, because who expected it? He had an operation for appendicitis, and I had to jump in and do five shows a day. I had to do Groucho five times a day at the Chicago Theatre, which I did. Actually, some of his friends didn't even realize it was me. They thought it was Groucho. They came backstage, and they wanted to see Groucho. But, anyway, it got pretty bad after a few days, because I never smoked cigars, and I'd smoke those goddamn cigars every day. I used to vomit every day after the last show—four or five shows a day, you know, and it was very difficult. But, anyway, I knew I could do it. And this frustrated me more, because I knew I could get laughs, but I wasn't allowed to with the Marx Brothers. So when we got out here, I didn't have any money, and I didn't know what the hell to do. I had no education. I went to about the fifth grade in public school. Or sixth. Then I got a job as a mechanic in Chicago at the Ford Motor Company.

When Gummo joined the Army, they were playing in Rockford, Illinois, and my mother called me down at this garage where I was working, and said, "Come home immediately." I came home immediately, and she said, "Get packed and go to Rockford and join your brothers." So, I had to take his place. I had to dance, and I had to be the juvenile and the straight man, which I did. 'Course, I don't think either one of us were too great (*Laughs*) as actors. But I stayed with them through the vaudeville days, and through the shows, and then the pictures. Finally, I did about four or five pictures, I can't remember how many. Then I just said, "Boys, I'm leaving."

I didn't have any money. I didn't know what I was gonna do, had no education, but I had to go because I would have collapsed mentally. I didn't want to do that. So I said to myself, "What is the best thing for me to do that I don't need a fine education, but that has something to do with show business?" So I figured out the agency business.

I opened an agency, I got a little office, had no clients, (*Laughing*) not even the Marx Brothers. I had started to go around looking for clients, and finally joined some people I was friendly with in the agency business. They had an agency called Orsatti and Brent. Now, Orsatti was a very close friend of L. B. Mayer, so he had all that stuff. And Brent was a pretty sharp guy. So I talked to them, and they thought I'd be a pretty good agent. I bought a third interest in their company. I borrowed the money, and after I was in that company about a month, I could see Brent and Orsatti were not exactly speaking to each other.

Brent would say, "Well, Zep, what did you do today?" And I said, "I went to Paramount, and I went to Warner Brothers, and I picked up a couple of clients." He said that was good, and I said, "What about Frank?" He said, "Well, go in and see him." Now, I'd go in to Orsatti, and he said, "What's Brent doing?" Finally, I found out these guys were not speaking with each other. I knew I was in a trap. So I said, "I want out," and I got my money back, and I opened a little office on the Sunset Strip, and had no clients.

I'd been with Orsatti and Brent about two months, and I had developed some very good friendships and rapport with some of these clients. Now I started to concentrate on the people I had known in that agency, and finally I started to get a few. And I started to get a few more clients. I started to build, and I worked. I worked my ass off, eighteen hours a day, going to every studio, every actor or actress or director or producer. I would just go up to them and say, "Who's representing you?" In those days the contracts weren't too strong, and I picked up a lot of guys who couldn't get jobs with the agents they were with. And I got them jobs. They would say, "Jeez, go to Zeppo Marx. He'll get you a job." Finally, I built up a very, very good business.

Now Gummo was in New York, and he was in the dress business or something and he wanted to go into the agency business. So my brothers came in and said, "Jeez, what about Gummo?" So I said, "All right. We'll open a New York office and let Gummo take over the New York office. So he opened an office and he did very well. He got New York actors signed up to our agency, sending them out here, and I'd sell them if I could. Eventually, he closed the New York office, took the clients, and he moved out here.

As I've told you before, I was a mechanic. I love mechanical things, and every place that I've had, I've always had a shop in back of my house, because I love it. I have one right here now. So, the agency business kept flourishing. Gummo kept bringing in clients, and my partner kept bringing in clients, and I brought in clients, and I'm selling them. Now we've got about 250 clients in this agency business doing fabulously. We were the third largest agency in the business. But in the meantime, I didn't like it because they drove me crazy, these actors and directors and everything. They came in and they said, "Why didn't I get that job? Gable got it!" Well, this little punk who was getting a hundred dollars a week with Goldwyn or something, he wanted Gable's part that was out at Metro. So you had to contend with those things in the agency business. You had to be their manager, you had to be their analyst. You had to do everything for some of those people. And it got to me. So I just sold out.

In the meantime I had started a mechanical business. I had a little shop in back of my house. And I had that horse ranch with Barbara Stanwyck which didn't work out too good. The expenses were too high for what we could make. Eventually, we sold the ranch. Anyway, while we were in this horse ranch, I let Gummo and my partner, Miller, run the agency business mostly. I didn't spend too much time there. I was out at Santa Anita one day, and we had a box right next to the vice president of Douglas Aircraft, who had some of his horses on our ranch. He said to me, "You know, we're very shy of machine shops and machinists." The war had come along. Well, I had met a fella at RKO when I was going around to the different studios selling clients and getting jobs for my clients. I always used to hang around the machine shop at RKO. Every studio had a machine shop. And I got very friendly and close with a fantastic machinist there. So I said, Charlie, I've got a little machine shop in back of my house in the Valley. I'd love to play around with it with you. I have different ideas and inventions. And he said, "That's wonderful. I'd love to play around with it and work with you." Incidentally, I invented the stoplight on cars, which I never followed through with. It was an idea of mine as well as several other things that are now being used.

So this vice president of Douglas Aircraft said, "I hear that you have a machine shop. Well, we need some machine work very badly. We're very short of machine shops." I said, "All right. Send some stuff and the prints over, and we'll machine it for you." Now, a box comes over, about half the size of this table, with parts to be machined. And I've got a little shop in the back of my house in the Valley! So after I worked in the agency business going around to all the studios, I'd go now and we'd work until one or two o'clock in the morning machining these parts and getting them ready, because the war was important.

We got them all set, sent the box back, and about four days later a box comes twice the size. They liked the work so much they wanted these parts done, machining castings. So I said, "Jeez, Charlie . . . it looks like I've got myself into something here. If they're gonna do this, I'll have to rent a little place." So we machined those parts, and I rented a little place in the Valley, because now they sent back three boxes. I hired some mechanics, and we had this little place in the San Fernando Valley about the size of this place here. And I bought some machinery, and I kept getting bigger places and hiring more people. Finally, I built two factories and had five hundred people working for me.

I couldn't devote too much time to the agency business now. I had this tremendous thing going. So Gummo handled it. Then I made a deal with MCA, and Gummo went with MCA, and I got out of that agency business, which was driving me crazy anyway. So now I'm in the machinist business. I've got five hundred people working, and we're working twenty-four hours a day, three shifts. We're working like mad turning out these parts for all the aircraft companies.

Finally, one day I started to take stock of myself. I said, "Look, I've got a machine shop here, and I'm machining things. If the war gets over very quickly, I've got a million dollars' worth of machinery here, and who's gonna use it? And what am I gonna do with it? We've got to get a proprietary item—something we can split the government work with something of our own."

Well, one day a fella came into the shop and to the office, and the girl came in and said, "There's a Mr. King out here who would like to talk to you." I said, "I don't know a Mr. King." She said, "Well, he's got an invention, and he wants to show it to you." I said, "Bring him in." 'Course, I would see anybody. I brought him in, and he sat down. He had holes in the bottoms of his shoes. Terrible-looking man. He had a little clamp, a coupling device, and it appealed to me. He had his patents, and he said he'd been all over, but he couldn't get in to see anybody because on account of the war, they were so busy, and they didn't want to take on anything like that.

I said, "I'll make a deal with you. I'll take it on, and I'll give you the regular inventor's royalties." So, we made a contract, and I took this thing on. It was really a very good coupling or clamping device. As a matter of fact, right now, most everything that moves and some stuff that doesn't move has this item on it. We had it all over airplanes, we had it on boats, we had it in oil fields, we had it every place. This man finally became a millionaire. He rode around in a Cadillac with a chauffeur, and had a yacht and everything due to his royalties from this thing, because it turned out to be so big.

I stayed with that for a while, then eventually I sold out. I was getting divorced, and I wanted to make a clean break of everything, so I gave my wife what she was entitled to, and I sold out. Now I had nothing going for me, but I had some money. I was a bachelor now, and played the field. Incidentally, I did all right that way. Eventually, I met this girl—oh, Christ, do I have to go through all this? Anyway, I don't know if I should bring this into it or not. She was a very attractive gal, and we went together for a year, then we broke up. We broke up for a year, and we went back together. The reason we broke up, we couldn't get along too well. But when we went back together, we got along very well. So I married her, and it lasted through about thirteen or fourteen years, and of course now I'm single again.

In the meantime I had invented a watch, a wristwatch this size that would warn a person of a heart attack. I have all the patents for it, and now it's being pursued. If a person is getting a heart attack or they have their blood pressure going down so low or up so high where they're in big trouble, this thing will give a warning, a sound, a beep-beep-beep. And it's also a watch, no bigger than this. We have it working, and I think it's a very revolutionary item. I have the controlling interests, I own most of the stock, and other people are working on it.

Right now I am a commercial fisherman. I have a commercial license, and I have a boat. I was gonna have a fleet of commercial boats to fish when all of this came on with fuel and the economy, and I didn't think it was too good an idea for me to go out and spend a lot of money on more boats. So I'm now just running the one boat as a charter boat and also as a commercial fisherman. This is the only business I have right at the moment.

I

What do you call your company?

ZEPPO

The Marx Brothers. That's the name of the boat, and that's the name of the company. The other company, the watch, is called Lifeguard. Which it is. I think it could be very big, it could be very helpful. The idea for it started with my family. My father died, his heart went, my mother had a stroke, and then Harpo had a bad heart, and Gummo's heart isn't too good, and neither is mine. I had two operations recently, open heart surgery. But I didn't know about that then. So I thought this would be a great thing to help people out that have problems. This will tell them. I've had many doctors, heart specialists tell me that they think it's a very wonderful idea. I patented it in Japan and Germany and France and England and the United States and in the Iron Curtain countries, so that's it, and that's where we stand right now, and I'm very happy to have met you . . .

I

Before you go away, do you want to talk anymore about your early days, about how you feel about the Marx Brothers, about the Marx Brothers' movies . . . ?

ZEPPO

I told you all about that. I told you that I was very unhappy.

I

Didn't you get *any* fun out of it?

ZEPPO

No. Well, the only fun I got out of it was the chorus girls. And laying all of them, or as many as I could. That was the fun I got out of it. I am not a ham, and I don't care about publicity or anything like that. (*To Gummo*) Now you take over.

I

(*To Zeppo*) Groucho told me a story last night about you. He told me about how when you wanted Norman Krasna . . .

ZEPPO

Oh, I knocked out a couple of guys who were bothering him. That's when I was in the agency business. Well, there were a lot of those things, but I can't go through all that. It would take two or three days. Okay? Nice meeting you, honey, and I hope everything turns out all right for you. I hope you make a lot of money on it.

GUMMO

Well, thanks for the drinks.

ZEPPO

You're welcome. (*Laughs*) Okay. 'Bye! (*He leaves*)

I

(*To Gummo*) Groucho said he thought you were a natural agent, and he told me you discovered quite a few actors.

GUMMO

Dennis Morgan, Glenn Ford, Rhonda Fleming, Evelyn Keyes. It was only last week when Glenn Ford said, "If it hadn't been for Gummo, I would not be where I am today." Because he was passed up by every studio in town. But I found a method for building him, and I made a star out of him. I had a special feeling when I saw someone like him.

I

What were the early days with the Marx Brothers like?

GUMMO

I'll tell you just one thing: I knew I was not a good actor, and I didn't want to stay in show business. Zeppo took my place, and I had to teach his dancing partner how to dance. She, incidentally, married Groucho.

I

Groucho said you were a good dancer.

GUMMO

I was not a very good dancer. I was known, perhaps, as America's slowest whirlwind dancer. I attribute the success of the Marx Brothers largely to me. I quit the act.

I

Zeppo complained about being the youngest brother. He said it was kind of hard being the youngest brother because he could only follow . . .

GUMMO

I was the youngest brother outside of Zeppo. Now, when I left the act, they put Zeppo in my place. Zeppo was not a great dancer and neither was I, for that matter. But I wasn't too bad. I read that interview you did with Groucho, and I thought it was good. The reason Zeppo liked it so well is because Groucho said that Zeppo was the funniest of the Marx Brothers. Well, my friends think *I'm* the funniest.

I

Last night Groucho said that you were very funny too, though he still says that he thought Zeppo was the funniest of the Marx Brothers in real life.

GUMMO

Could be. Chico was a very funny man. But Chico was irresponsible. There's been stuff written about Groucho, but there's been none written about Chico. His life was so fantastic that it's a shame that there hasn't been a book written about him. There is a book being written about Chico, by his daughter, Maxine. The things that happened in Chico's life are so fantastic that it should be written. I'm not qualified to write it, and I don't think there are enough people alive who know all the things that happened to him while he was alive. His daughter has no knowledge of the things that I'm talking about.

I

Such as . . .

GUMMO

I can remember one time when his wife Betty used to watch him to catch him cheating. Why, that's like trying to catch a gnat in a net! It's just impossible. Well, anyway, they were playing in New York in one of their plays, and she sneaked up into the flies to catch him. And there he was, kissing one of the girls on the mouth. A real mouth kiss. So she said, "I caught you that time!" He said, "Caught me what?" She says, "Kissing that girl in the mouth!" He says, "I wasn't kissing that girl in the mouth. I was whispering in her mouth."

He would find ways of fighting with her. That was when he was still in the money. But he was never in the money because he never kept it. They lived in a two-story house on Rexford or something. And her room was here and his room was there. So they had a hell of a fight, which he wanted, because if he could get a fight, he could go out and play bridge. This went on for about six weeks. Do you know after six weeks, she just couldn't stand this separation. She loved him very much. So, she thought of an idea. She took a deck of cards, and she spread them all the way up the stairs. In front of her door, she put the queen of hearts. And on her nightgown, she pinned the ace of hearts. Now, to get to his room, he had to pass her room. He must have seen these cards all the way up, but he went right into his room and went to bed. She heard him, and she got up and said, "You no-good son of a bitch! After I thought of such a wonderful idea to make up, you walk right into your room!" "Honey, when I saw the queen of hearts in front of your door, I knew you had the ace of hearts on your nightgown, and I just couldn't help but finesse." He finessed right past her room into his own room.

I know a thousand stories about Chico. But that belongs in a separate book, because he was a character that doesn't live very often. He was the best-hearted man, unless he was cornered like a rat. Then he got tough. I know that I made a deal for him, with the help of Groucho, that he got $50,000 a year from NBC to do three shows a year. Well, we knew it wouldn't be enough for Chico. So some of the money came from Groucho and me. I had ten percent of Groucho's income. I paid ten, Grouch paid the other forty. Well, it didn't mean much to Groucho, because he was earning a lot of money. And it didn't mean much to me either, 'cause

I was doing pretty well. So, I had put $10,000 in cash into my vault for one purpose: I knew that no matter what Chico got from NBC, it was not gonna be enough.

So, every week I got a call from Chico. He said, "Gummy . . ." and I knew what was coming. I says, "How much do you need?" He said, "I need $300. I had a bad time last night." So I'd give him $300 from the money I'd put away. Every week—and mind you, he's getting $50,000 a year from NBC—I'd get a call. "Gummy, it was very bad last night. Can you let me have $500." Well, he went through the whole $10,000.

I

And what happened when the $10,000 was gone?

GUMMO

I don't recall what happened. He was reaching the end of his string by that time. He was close to dying.

I

Do you think that Chico was a happy person?

GUMMO

Yes, and one of the most selfish persons I've ever met in my life. It's a strange thing that a person can be selfish and still be generous. And he was. You know, there's a man who's still alive who was Chico's closest friend. They both made out their wills leaving whatever they had left to each other. Neither one had five cents.

I

How would you describe Harpo?

GUMMO

Harpo played the right instrument. He was an angel. There was nobody like him, there never will be anybody like him. He was just simply wonderful. He never had a bad word for anybody . . . not like me. I at least occasionally say something. But Harpo . . . they don't make that kind anymore.

I

How about Groucho? How would you describe Groucho?

GUMMO

Groucho is very stern, or was, but very just, and in his way, very good-hearted. If it wasn't for Groucho, I would never be in the position I'm in today, which is fairly affluent, though I'm not rich. My wife's been very sick. And there isn't really any more that I can tell you.

I

Do you like the Marx Brothers pictures?

GUMMO

I love them.

I

Do you have a favorite?

GUMMO

Yes. *A Night at the Opera.* Then *Day at the Races.*

I

Last night Groucho talked about one special deal you made as his agent, and he said that you did a good job.

GUMMO

Well, I had always felt that I alone couldn't give Groucho enough service. I shouldn't say that—I could, but if I could get assistance, it was to Groucho's benefit, even if it took half the commission away. So, I called in the Morris office, and we represented Groucho together. I made a deal for him for radio, and then for television. It was *You Bet Your Life.* The Morris office went to New York with me and my lawyer, and NBC and CBS were bidding for the show. Groucho was on CBS, and I called up CBS and said, "We want to buy our contract from Allen Gelman." He had the show on radio. He's died since then. He had the Elgin-American Company that made cigarette cases, compacts, and so forth. And we wanted to get the contract from him so that we could make a deal. We had a deal ready. Gelman wanted $50,000 for the contract. We wanted to go on television, but Gelman couldn't go on television under any conditions, because he couldn't afford it.

So I called CBS and said, "Listen, we have a deal, but Allen Gelman wants $50,000 for his contract. Now he can't pick it up, but if we wait until his contract runs out, we will lose the deal that we have. I'll tell you what we'll do: you pay the $50,000, and I will agree to stay with CBS for fifty weeks, which is practically two years." They tell me, "That's a one-way deal." So I says, "Forget about it." I went to the Morris office, and I says, "Let's you and I buy the contract. Then we can go ahead with the deal," which we did. So CBS came out and said they wanted the show. I said, "Well, you had your chance for $50,000, which would guarantee you having the show for two years." I said, "You made a costly mistake, because NBC is bidding, and so is ABC." In the meantime, the Morris office is ready to sell the show for a quarter of a million dollars. I said, "Not a chance." Well, to go through the thing that we had at my house, NBC, CBS, and ABC's men started bidding until it got to be a million and seven hundred and fifty thousand dollars. And I said, "Gentlemen, we'll have to put a stop to this bidding. You're each gonna have one more bid, and whoever has the best bid, we're going."

Well, NBC offered two million dollars. Now, this was just for the rights of the show. Groucho still had to be paid for the show. The deal was set. We wanted to stay with CBS, but we took the NBC deal. And that's how it happened. That's the deal that he was talking about.

I

Did you ever have any regrets about not remaining with the Marx Brothers as a performer?

GUMMO

No. I didn't have enough talent to ever be great, and I wasn't happy just being what I could be. It didn't come easy to me the way it did to the others, like for Chico and Groucho. When I had to get up on the stage, I was always afraid. I couldn't live the rest of my life with a thing like that. I could never ad-lib my lines like Groucho. I was always afraid of forgetting my lines and being stuck up there. My friends think I'm a funny man, but you can't go by your friends. I was goddamn lucky to get out and be something on my own by my own ability and my own work. I've never regretted leaving the act.

"Is it sad or high kickin'?"

"We were playing a small town in Ohio, and a man came to the box office and said, 'Before I buy the ticket, I want to know one thing: is it sad or high kickin'?'

"That's the best line I ever heard about show business. That's all of show business."

For Groucho the phrase "sad or high kickin' " said all there is to say not only about show business but about life as well. Groucho's own life was mostly "high kickin'," especially when he was before an audience.

"Groucho is really most on when he's performing," Morrie Ryskind observed. "And if it's an appreciative audience . . ."

"There's no business like show business," Groucho interjected soberly. "I believe that."

He never officially retired from show business, once telling me "I'd like to die right onstage." After his second TV quiz program, *Tell It to Groucho*, ended in 1962, the number of Groucho's professional appearances diminished. At the same time, paradoxically, the Marx Brothers were becoming more popular than ever before with a whole new generation of fans.

Seeing the Marx Brothers movies for the first time, college-age audiences began to feel about Groucho the same way they did about Humphrey Bogart, many of them not realizing that Groucho Marx was a *living* legend. Because he made so few personal appearances, many fans were unaware that he was still around. "I'm a square, but I'm still around." There was a great demand for him as soon as it became known that "the kingpin of the Marx Brothers act," as Woody Allen called him, was very much alive. Clearly the time was right for Groucho Marx Superstar, although Groucho, who had turned eighty in 1970, was not aware of it.

He was sitting there contemplating his navel when Erin came along, and his interest in show business and life was tremendously buoyed just by the thought of contemplating hers instead.

During those years, he was in the hospital more than once, and Erin shared credit with his doctors for the recovery of his spirit, if not for the recovery of his body. "When I met him," Erin said, "sometimes he didn't care if he even got up or not. Now he's filled with plans." Groucho frequently acknowledged his debt to Erin, repeating, "If she ever left me, I'd quit show business." And for Groucho show business was life.

When Erin arrived on the scene as Groucho's part-time secretary, among the thousands of unanswered letters that had piled up at his house was one inviting him to appear at Iowa State University. Erin urged him to accept and try out the one-man show they had been getting together. Ames, Iowa, where Iowa State University is located, was one of the few towns in America that the Marx Brothers hadn't played, and Groucho, who placed a tremendous value on learning and formal education, was always sympathetic to schools.

He and Erin, with Marvin Hamlisch as Groucho's accompanist, arrived in Des Moines in April 1972, and were met by a limousine from a funeral home. "Is this Death Moines?" asked Groucho. In Ames there was a sign on the marquee of the motel where they stayed that proudly proclaimed on one side, "Welcome to Ames, Groucho Marx!" The other side proclaimed with equal pride, "Midnight Buffet Friday and Saturday $1.75." "Midnight Buffet, who's he, a rock star?" Groucho asked. "Look, it says, 'All You Can Eat for $1.75.' Hey, this is the big time!"

Eric Lax, writing for *Life*, was part of the entourage. He remembered riding with Groucho past the theatre where he would be performing. Asked if he wanted to go inside and see it, Groucho declined. "No, that's like asking Lincoln to go back to the box."

Before the performance, Groucho was a little glum as he applied his makeup. "This is an old face," he told Eric. "You wake up in the morning and look in the mirror, and there's no help. It makes you want to go back to bed and stay there."

But he didn't go back to bed. Instead, he regaled an audience of about 2,500 with stories and songs. Before the show even started, Groucho received a standing ovation for all the memories of his films evoked by his presence onstage. After the show he received a standing ovation for his performance.

Groucho reminisced about Iowa with Marvin Hamlisch, Mike Nichols, and Erin just after the 1974 Academy Award ceremonies:

GROUCHO
Remember that place in Iowa?

MARVIN HAMLISCH
Oh, Iowa's the greatest place. We had so much fun there. Ames, Iowa.

GROUCHO
Catching girls.

MIKE NICHOLS
When was this?

GROUCHO
We did a show in Iowa.

MARVIN HAMLISCH
It was Groucho's first concert. We broke the act in. Actually, it was this guy at Iowa State who had the whole idea for the concert anyway.

GROUCHO
(*To Erin*) What was the name of that guy that you were kind of stuck on?

ERIN
Oh, Tom Wilhite. You know the play *The Butter and Egg Man*? This guy was that part. It's incredible. We got these letters from Iowa on letterhead stationery from Thomas L. Wilhite Productions, making this tremendous offer for Groucho and everything. We needed a place to try out, and we thought, "Well, we can go there, and if we're terrible, we'll just sneak away, and no one will know the difference." He arranged for limousines and all this—talk about Thalberg, we thought he was the impresario of the Midwest! We arrived with *Life* magazine, a record company, and a couple of bigwigs—and here's this child! I think he was about sixteen.

MARVIN HAMLISCH
And what an operator. He was sharp. There was this sign, "Ames Welcomes Groucho." He had everything worked out. And they had a Groucho dinner for $3.99 at the Holiday Inn.

ERIN
The limousine was a hearse.

MARVIN HAMLISCH
Tell all about the kissing.

GROUCHO
Every time the bell rang, we kissed all the girls.

MARVIN HAMLISCH

You were allowed to kiss a girl—any girl—when the steeple bell rang. And there was this one girl, and her last name was—this is true— Kissinger. She hung around outside our room at the Holiday Inn waiting for a kiss. She was from Iowa State, and they had this thing where every time the bell would ring, you were allowed to kiss the girl you were near . . .

GROUCHO

You were allowed to kiss a girl, any girl. But Marvin—I didn't want to have to say this—I really only wanted to kiss you.

MARVIN HAMLISCH

. . . Every time the bell would go off, you would say, "Where's Kissinger?" 'cause you adored this girl. She was a cute little blonde, and she drove us crazy, so I had to corral Kissinger. I would look at my watch, and if it was fifteen minutes after the hour, I knew it was coming. I would say, "Kissinger, get over here quick, because it's gonna happen," and the bell would ring. I only scored on the rebound. I only got what was left over. Whoever couldn't get to Groucho came to me.

GROUCHO

I didn't miss any bells or belles.

MARVIN HAMLISCH

Groucho heard bells ringing even when no one else did.

Tom Wilhite, the youthful producer of the Ames show, was later brought to California to work for Rogers, Cowan & Brenner, the agency that represented Groucho. At dinner with Groucho and me, Tom recalled some of the circumstances that surrounded the Ames concert:

TOM WILHITE

Groucho, I wrote you so many letters that I started to sort of give up. I thought you weren't ever going to answer. Then it happened so fast, and you and Erin were there. I'm going back soon, and I thought I might see what happened to Kissinger. Do you remember her?

GROUCHO

She was a pretty girl. I was a devil in those days. The bells rang, and I kissed all the pretty girls. Whoopeeee! So now you're the assistant to the president at Rogers, Cowan and Brenner. What do you do?

TOM WILHITE

It's a smorgasbord. I work with clients and do things for Mr. Cowan.

GROUCHO

You take his wife out? She's a good-lookin' dame.

TOM WILHITE

No, I don't get to do that. I'm going back to Iowa for a visit. Do you want me to bring you back anything?

GROUCHO

Kissinger.

In May 1972 at New York's sedate Carnegie Hall, the frenetic turnout proved Groucho to be an all-time "hot ticket," according to Ron Delsener, the young producer of *An Evening with Groucho*, who was more accustomed to producing Elton John, Mick Jagger, David Bowie, and Bette Midler. Groucho said of the evening, "It was so hard to get in, *I* almost didn't." The program featured Marvin Hamlisch as all-time piano player and sometime straight man, and Erin, who sang a few of the songs with Groucho.

The record of the show has since become a collector's item. Groucho said his nurse Donna would be able to auction off the records he gave her, "along with my teeth she's been saving."

Ron Delsener told me how the Carnegie Hall performance came about:

"We wanted to do something with Groucho, but we didn't know how to reach him. So we just wrote to Groucho Marx, Beverly Hills, and got a response.

"We'd said something about how we'd supply dancing girls and we wanted to do a show with him at Carnegie Hall. The response said, 'Forget about the dancing girls, but how much money you gonna pay me?' The next thing I knew, his agent called me and said, 'Groucho Marx wants $10,000.' I said, 'That's a lot of money, but we'll pay it—we'll just charge more for the seats.' Not that it was really a lot of money; it's just that Carnegie Hall only holds 2,800 people.

"We made arrangements on the phone, and the dickering went back and forth as to who would provide what. I spoke to Erin Fleming about the program itself, and I suggested they send some pictures to use for the ad. I still hadn't met the man himself.

"The agent said it was Reel 4 we should show from *A Night at the Opera*, the stateroom scene. We were told whom to contact for it in New Jersey, and everything was prepared for the Carnegie Hall engagement. Then it came time for my moment to meet the man, and I was told to go to the Regency Hotel.

"Erin opened the door, and right behind her was this man who looked a little different from the way I'd pictured him from the movies. The smile was there, and he was older than I expected, but he had that little twinkle in the eye. It was Groucho Marx. He said, 'Who are you?' and Erin said, 'This is your producer, Ron Delsener.' So he said, 'Hello, how are you? You look kinda young to be a producer,' and some other remark like that, and I hit him back with a one-liner, and right away we got along. We hit it off. He was my type of person.

"There were a lot of one-liners, and everything was a joke. Then he put on his beret, and he had a turtleneck and a blazer, and we went to lunch at the French restaurant on Sixty-third Street, Perigord Park. He ordered either eggs or chicken, something light, and we talked about the show. As we walked to the hotel, he said hello to everybody in the street.

"That afternoon, we decided to have a run-through. This was before Groucho came to do a sound check, and I decided to show the film scene. I thought it was Reel 4 of *Night at the Opera*, the stateroom scene. We're showing the film and waiting and waiting for the stateroom scene, only it doesn't happen. We watched the entire reel, and it's not there. I panicked. I called up Erin and I said, 'Wait a minute—this can't be the right reel!' Actually it *was* the right reel. We'd rented exactly what the agent had told us, but somebody had given us the wrong number, and it was a Saturday.

"I got my car and raced over the George Washington Bridge to Jersey, where we had picked up the reel. I pounded on the windows, tried to break in, but nobody was in there. I called the place up. Maybe they had an after-hours number. No answer. So I went back and said, 'Look, we're gonna have to do that concert without that scene,' and Erin said, 'No! No! No! I'll find that reel somewhere in town.'

"As it turned out, we should have used that scene we had. It actually made no difference, because it was a funny reel. Erin found a film buff who had the reel we were looking for, only instead of being in 35 mm, it was a 16 mm, which meant that the 35 mm projector that I had rented was no good. We called up the head of the projectionists' union at home and pleaded with him to come in with a 16 mm sound projector. He brought it in, the film arrived in time, and even though we hadn't tested the film, the show was about to begin. The projectionist was still frantically trying to thread the 16 mm reel as the show went on.

"Then Groucho came out. It was really an extraordinary evening. People came dressed as Groucho Marx—young fans who had never seen the man before, only the films. He had a cult following. At the time, Lindsay was mayor, and he came, and so did Woody Allen, Simon and Garfunkel, Elliott Gould, and a lot of other celebrities. Dick Cavett was emcee that evening. Everybody in town was there. It was a hot ticket. The show had sold out, ten dollars top.

"Groucho came out to a standing ovation, brought on by Dick Cavett. And it started: he went from the year one, the day he was born, right up to the present time. Came time for the film clip, the screen was brought down, and Groucho went backstage as it started.

"You could see it was a very old film. It was on a very rickety reel, and it kept falling off the reel. The film had to be stopped repeatedly, and the audience was laughing, but it didn't seem so funny to me. We decided to do away with it, just stop it and pull up the screen. As we pulled up the screen, there was Groucho looking almost half asleep sitting there, and that brought the house down. From then on it was complete hysteria, and he was sensational. Marvin Hamlisch backed him up on the piano, and Erin Fleming came out and did a few numbers with him.

"Afterwards he was stormed. Groucho just couldn't get out of Carnegie Hall. He tried to get out one door, and we had to run him around to the front door. He was almost mauled in the ensuing chase. They lost me, but he insisted on circling around the block and finding me. Well, I finally caught up with them, and we dashed off to a place called Raffles in the basement of the Sherry Netherland to have something to eat. They stuck us in a little private room, and we just continued the concert. We were very happy.

"The show had been recorded, and the next day we heard the tapes. I was with Groucho at the hotel, and he was telling stories about Swayne's Rats and Cats, about Coney Island, about the Marx family, and I was so impressed with this man's memory. I can't remember what I had for lunch later the same afternoon, but this man had a very, very vivid memory. His sentences seemed to flow so easily about what people wore, what they said, names, streets—the instant recall amazed me. And the punch lines! For the life of me, I can't tell a joke. And here's this man who was eighty at the time telling these fantastic stories.

"It was a very emotional evening and afternoon for me, and I think it was for Groucho, too. He was impressed at now being a recording artist. Something new was added to his career, and he was very excited about Carnegie Hall.

"I had presented him with the lighter that day. I bought the lighter at

Dunhill—a gold lighter. It said 'SRO Carnegie Hall' and the date of the concert. I could see he was quite moved by it. He asked me if anybody else sold out the hall, and I said, 'Well, I don't think anybody else could.' "

Max Hamlisch, Marvin's father, who was himself a professional musician, talked about the Carnegie Hall show:

"In his act, Groucho says he isn't going to play the violin like Jack Benny, and to prove it he breaks a violin on the stage. On the day of the show, my son remembered he needed two violins to break: one for rehearsal and one for the show. So I went looking at a Carnegie Hall shop. I couldn't get dummies, so I had to get two comparatively expensive violins. Groucho didn't break one at rehearsal, and at the performance he *couldn't* break the violin. Finally he had to step on it, which got a big laugh. Groucho gave the other violin to Marvin with a silver plaque on it."

Marvin and his parents were with Groucho, Erin, and Ron and Ellie Delsener after the concert at Raffles, and Mr. Hamlisch told about it:

"We all went to the Sherry Netherland for dinner. But first, we went with the limousine around the block to see all of the crowd waiting at the stage door. When we got to the restaurant, the service was slower than usual, so all we had was some cold lox."

In the overture to the Carnegie Hall concert Marvin opened with Beethoven's "Waldstein" sonata, which then evolved into *Captain Spaulding,* followed by a medley of tunes from the Marx Brothers films, interspersed with quotations from Mozart and Gershwin. Everything was played in the appropriate style for its period, especially difficult with popular music.

Marvin told me how he became Groucho's pianist and friend:

"Erin was looking for a pianist for Groucho, and I went over to his house and I started to play these tunes and songs. I always remember Groucho saying, 'You're the second George Gershwin.' He really liked the way I played.

"He was very encouraging, very nice. It's funny, I think, when you put two Jewish boys in a room together, a lot of Jewish jokes fall where they may, and I used to always want to try to make him very happy.

"When we would play a song which Irving Berlin wrote, he would go into this Irving Berlin story. It didn't matter if I'd heard it. I always loved the way he tells it. Then he met my sister and my nephew, and he had my mother over. It was *fan*-tastic! He was kind of a grandfather for me.

"Groucho gives you love. He talks with you a lot, and offstage he's a lot like he is on. He puts out all the time. He really cares about music.

"When we started, he was the one who wanted me to do ten or fifteen minutes with him in the concert, and for me to personally go out and entertain. He'd say, 'You do some stuff, you play this, you play that.' So when we went out to Iowa I did ten minutes, not really alone, because he was onstage, but still I entertained while he was out there. It wasn't the easiest job in the world, though I'd try to make it look like the easiest job in the world.

"At a certain time, he would want to throw me a line, and we'd rehearse it, the exact timing of the line and stuff like that, and he'd coach me. It would look spontaneous. We worked hard, but we had such a good time.

"It was always changing a lot, and I had to keep up with him. It was a lot of following things, but it was a very enjoyable time, you know, sitting with him in the Cadillac limousine, always going somewhere.

"I think it made him extremely happy when the New York reception was so spectacular. They really did a thing in New York. They just went mad for him, just absolutely crazy about him. The kids in the audience dressed up like him. All of a sudden, you saw a kid who looked like Groucho Marx, or some other kid who looked like Harpo.

"What a night! There was an overture that I did, and in the overture I played 'Hooray for Captain Spaulding' as if Beethoven were playing it. It was very quiet, then, all of a sudden, the place went nuts. I mean, the overture got a hand already! 'My God!' I thought. It was that kind of a crowd. They were ready to love. To be a part of that kind of event is probably one of the things I'll always remember.

"It's funny about my life. Certain events in my life are standouts. The first time I met Judy Garland, and I actually played the piano and she sang—you'll never take that away from me. Recording with Barbra Streisand—you'll never take that away from me. These are great moments, and so was being on the stage with Groucho in Carnegie Hall. If I had died then, I would have died with a smile on my face. It would have been the most."

Betty Comden and Adolph Green described their reactions to the Carnegie Hall concert for me:

BETTY COMDEN

It was something he'd been planning on a long time, and he had a lot of anecdotal material to talk about. It was kind of a stream-of-consciousness thing that happened to him. And Marvin Hamlisch helped pull things together, because he was at the piano, and he played connective stuff and participated.

ADOLPH GREEN

Hamlisch was brilliant. He had a great feeling for Groucho's style.

Morgan Ames took away these onstage impressions of him:

"It was an opportunity to get a glimpse of a world that's almost gone; the world, maybe, of vaudeville and burlesque. Strong lines. Good broad lines. Playing the piano for him, I noticed that right away, with his thin reedy little voice, you can't get him off the track. He knows what's right on an instinctive basis—not a musician's basis, but on a performer's basis. He can communicate with a musician. When he told me, 'Play it in waltz time,' instead of saying to play it in three-quarter time, I knew immediately the kind of sound and tempo that he needed.

"When I get off when I play for him, he just keeps going. He doesn't try to fix it. He knows how to lead and go right down the line. Then I fix it, which is the balance which should take place. Any performer may know that, but Groucho knows it in a very special way.

"His concentration is still just wonderful. Sometimes he drifts off—just sort of floats in and out of stuff. It's like there's this stream running along beside him, and every once in a while he gets in and floats along. Then he gets back, and he's in this other place. He does that when we sing and play together. He's that way in everything. I guess that's how he got to be who he is. Probably nobody could get him off the track, because he doesn't even know he's on it. He's just never felt good being anyplace else. He's got that kind of drive and knows where to put it."

In May 1972, shortly after the Carnegie Hall concert, Groucho went to Cannes to be decorated by the French government. At eighty-one he was made a *Commandeur dans l'Ordre des Arts et des Lettres*, an award that had also been presented to Charlie Chaplin and Alfred Hitchcock. In honor of the occasion there was a gala, and *A Night at the Opera* was shown to an overwhelmingly enthusiastic crowd. He was greeted with cheers and cries of "Grooocho! Grooocho!"

He and Erin attended the Cannes Film Festival, and Groucho quickly exhausted his French, which consisted of "*Ooo-la-la*," "*Vive la Beaujolais*," and "*Voulez vous couchez avec moi?*" With pride he told everyone, "My father was a Frenchman."

Louis Malle, the French film director, accompanied Groucho and

Erin. "I was sort of an official host for Groucho," Malle told me, "but he was always ahead of me. He was so sharp, and he was always ready to sing. I've never known anyone who loved to sing like that. He is indescribable. How would I sum him up? Well, I would say he is impeccable."

Groucho was indeed "impeccable" in his respect for his Legion of Honor. Having lunch at Burkes in London with Michael Caine, he mentioned a party given for him in Beverly Hills several months earlier at the home of Sidney Sheldon. Michael was intrigued by Groucho's formal attire. "You came with him. Tell me, why did he wear tails to an informal party?"

I explained that he was wearing his Legion of Honor decoration as a way of paying tribute to the party, the host, and the guest of honor, and tails were *de rigueur* with the wearing of this decoration. (At Groucho's house before the Michael Caine party, Groucho had said, "I'll wear the medal." Erin said, "Not with your turtleneck. You know the rules. And don't wear your pants so high.")

In 1974, Oscar came to Groucho. When he received word that he was to be the recipient of that year's special Oscar, his less than sentimental response was, "It's about time."

Actually, he was much more moved than his response would have indicated, but he would have gone to any extreme to avoid revealing his true feelings. He considered emotional responses unamusing, out of character, and intensely personal. On the other hand, the only thing he minded more than *not* being taken seriously was being taken seriously. His considered reaction to this moment was more truly reflected in his total rejection of the usual flippancies and "ir-references." The occasion of receiving the Oscar was one of those rare times when he didn't want his audience to laugh.

Groucho was the embodiment of the American Dream, the child of immigrant parents whose children actually found the streets paved with gold—the streets being Broadway and Hollywood Boulevard. A self-made millionaire, he built his success on doing what came naturally, which by happy coincidence also brought pleasure to millions all over the world.

GROUCHO
I'm gonna say on the show, "I'm taking this bow not only for me, but for Chico and Harpo." They're gonna run about eight minutes of our old movies.

I
How your mother would have loved this night!

GROUCHO

With all her struggles, she finally saw us become stars. She was a great woman.

During the week preceding the event, Groucho waited anxiously for congratulatory telegrams from his friends. Then, when the telegrams arrived, he would make light of them, as he did in *The Cocoanuts*. "This one's from my Aunt Fanny. She's just had an eight-pound baby boy, and we're invited to the wedding next week." But each telegram was carefully preserved. Bill Cosby's was the first. "He's a real friend," Groucho noted.

On April 2, 1974, the evening of the awards, Erin and I ate an early dinner with Groucho. She was more nervous and excited than he was:

ERIN

Oh, I didn't get a chance to wash my hair!

GROUCHO

I'd wash my hair if I could find it.

We ate dinner earlier than usual because Groucho preferred to eat his own food. If he had waited until after the awards to eat the catered supper, he couldn't have depended on it being salt-free. During dinner he tried out his acceptance speech for us. As he spoke, acceptance speeches that would never be delivered were being rehearsed all over Beverly Hills. Only the recipients of special Oscars know in advance that they are winners. Groucho had waited a long, long time to get his Oscar, but at least he was certain before the ceremonies that he was really getting one. In the car on the way to Dorothy Chandler Pavilion, he rehearsed with Erin.

For the Academy Award ceremonies, Erin wore a silver lamé dress. The dress itself lived up to the occasion by falling down. Erin, with Groucho's interspersed comments, told Nunnally Johnson the story during tea at the Johnsons' house just after the awards. Groucho had brought Oscar with him, which was appropriate since it was Nunnally Johnson who had written the letter to the Academy of Motion Picture Arts and Sciences nominating Groucho.

ERIN

They lent us a $50,000 Stutz Black Hawk in order that we would drive up and be seen in the car and advertise it. So we had the press agent in the front seat with the chauffeur, and we're in the backseat, and I'm all dressed up, and I'm wearing $60,000 worth of borrowed diamonds, also for advertising. You know the way they do that. So, on Sixth Street, about four blocks from the Pavilion, the car breaks down. The chauffeur's going crazy, and he can't fix it. And we're in the middle of the street, everyone's going by.

Bill Feeder, the press agent, jumped out and flagged the first car that came along. It belonged to two young men who hadn't expected in the least bit that they would be driving us to that. I was wearing a gown, so I sat in the front seat. It was a convertible, and I guess the seat was dirty. I didn't know it until we got there. So you have the shot of us getting out of this old, broken-down convertible. We didn't even know we were on television, but you can imagine the Stutz Black Hawk people waiting to see their car, and here comes the old red convertible, and we jump out.

GROUCHO

But you still didn't tell 'em about your knockers. One was peeping out.

ERIN

That's *your* favorite part.

GROUCHO

She had a very low-cut dress . . .

ERIN

I was supposed to pick up some double-stick tape to put on the inside of my dress, and I forgot. So when we finally got inside I noticed that I'd gotten dirt on the back of my dress from the car. So the wardrobe lady was rushing around to get something to clean my dress, and the next thing you know, without the double-stick tape, one of my boobs popped out. Burt Reynolds came over and said, "Nice going."

At the Dorothy Chandler Pavilion, when I got out of the car I was greeted by one tremendous cheer from the bleacher crowd awaiting the celebrities. Later that evening at the party, we talked about my cheer:

ERIN

When you arrive you feel like you're a lion in a cage or something. They're all going, "Oooooooo!" And all of the people are cheering for everybody, anything. I mean, *anybody* could come along and they'd get a big cheer.

I

I got a very big cheer.

GROUCHO

You got what?

I
I got one cheer.

ERIN
She got one of the biggest cheers.

GROUCHO
Just one?

I
Well . . . it was a good one.

From then on Groucho often called me "One-Cheer."

At the Academy Awards ceremonies, the dress is formal, but the elegance far surpasses any formal requirements. The theatre sparkles with jewels, shimmers with metallic trim, and yards of flowing chiffon waft about breezily. The men look neatly chic in tuxedos, but it's really the night of the resplendent supercoiffed ladies.

One supremely endowed European starlet rushed toward Groucho and embraced him, kissing the air on both sides of his cheeks. Groucho always considered this kind of European kiss a great waste. He didn't recognize either the face or the décolletage, but she said warmly, "Groucho, won't you join me?" Eying her cleavage and the overtaxed bodice of her dress, he responded, "Why? Are you coming apart?"

For awards night temporary grandstands are erected on either side of the entrance, facing the street. The way leading to the Pavilion itself is covered with a long red carpet, along which guests walk from their cars to the entrance. Uniformed young men, some of them aspiring performers hoping to be discovered, scurry back and forth helping people out of cars, then parking them if there is no chauffeur to drive them away to garages. Many arrive in their own chauffeured limousines, or ones that have been rented or lent out by the studios, or provided by *Playboy*. A few, like Marvin Hamlisch, drive themselves.

Walking along the red carpet, the stars stop at Army Archerd's interview platform, where they are interviewed on national television. The crowd reaction on arrival is the barometer of stardom. The photographers' flashing strobe lights are almost blinding. There is a potpourri of foreign languages, for this is where members of the foreign press are stationed.

Inside the Pavilion the scene is not unlike an opening gala at a major opera house, except that in Southern California few furs are to be seen, nor is the checkroom as busy as it might be in another part of the country. Many people actually wear light wraps, but they tend to leave them in the trunks of their cars. Champagne is served in the lobby, and opera glasses are available to those whom the pecking order has relegated to the outermost regions of the auditorium.

Groucho gave me his ticket. "I won't need it," he explained. "If they don't let me in, I'll go home and watch it on television." My seat was next to Cher, who was one of the Oscar presenters. Like all the presenters, she was cued well in advance of her appearance in order to allow her to go backstage and adjust her hair and makeup. Many of the participants in the Academy Award ceremonies rehearsed beforehand in the auditorium, as had Groucho.

Owing to the importance of television coverage, the best seats are considered to be those which the cameras can pick up. It's important to the networks that the stars, nominees, and sometimes their escorts can easily be located in the audience for reaction shots. Some very good seats are out of camera range, and these are occupied by important but less-known people—studio heads, producers, and behind-the-scenes people. Winners don't return to their seats. They disappear backstage, where they spend the rest of the ceremonies being interviewed and photographed. The losers usually remain in their seats to grin-and-bear-it as "good sports"—a grueling ordeal, especially for those who have been assured by all their friends that they were "certain" to win.

Marvin Hamlisch told me what it was like for him as a three-time winner:

"I don't remember anything from the time I got the first one. After that I was numb. It was *fan*-tastic! The next thing I remember, we were all [Marvin, Terry, and their parents] having the chocolate cake my mother brought from New York before we went to the Academy dinner."

Terry Hamlisch added:

"When Marvin went to the Academy Awards, nobody asked for his autograph, and only Army Archerd even knew who he was. When he came out, they were tearing and screaming at him for autographs."

Groucho remained backstage most of the evening having his makeup done and talking with the press. Just before he went on, a scene from *Minnie's Boys* entitled "The Act" was presented live with Danny Fortus playing Groucho. Jack Lemmon, who himself later in the evening was to win the Best Actor award, presented Oscar to Groucho. When Groucho appeared onstage, he received a long standing ovation. Before he went up onstage, he told me:

"This is one occasion I can only be serious about. I don't think any jokes are appropriate. I've always had a joke for every moment, but not for this one."

True to his word, his acceptance speech was serious. He singled out the three important women in his life—his mother, Margaret Dumont, and Erin—for special praise, and he also said that he wished Harpo and Chico could have been there that night.

Nevertheless, he did get a laugh in spite of his serious intentions and restrained demeanor when he told about Margaret Dumont's consistent reaction to his jokes. "She never did understand the jokes. She would ask me, 'What are they laughing at, Julie?' " But the Academy audience understood.

Though apparently less excited than Marvin, Groucho, who was so accustomed to deference, reverence, and the adulation of crowd and peers, was far from blasé. His own Oscar stood on his dining-room table for all of our meals during the next several days. When finally retired, Oscar was placed in a stage-center position of prominence on the table in the hallway leading to Groucho's bedroom. Erin expressed a desire to have a spotlight on it, but he demurred, saying the idea was "too flashy." After the Awards, we started out for the Hilton Hotel, where the Governors' Ball was to be held, "Governors" referring to the Board of Governors of the Academy of Motion Picture Arts and Sciences. Groucho called it "The Governor's Balls."

First, however, we had to wait for his car. As Groucho observed, the real leveler is waiting for your car after the Academy Awards. "Winning an Oscar doesn't get you your car any faster." You still have to wait through the crowd of limousines and Rolls-Royces.

While waiting, we met William Wyler, who recalled, "Do you remember, Groucho, the year we were waiting for our cars, and the loudspeaker called out, 'Simone Simon'? You said, 'I know both of them.' "

The Governors' Ball is a dinner party held afterward. Not everyone invited to the Oscar ceremonies is invited to the ball, but all of the nominees are invited. Losers, though invited, sometimes don't attend the party. "You lose a few along the way," Groucho remarked, indicating some empty chairs nearby. "It's not any fun to go to the Governors' Ball for sympathy." For this event, the ballroom of the Hilton Hotel is set up with tables, except for the area that is reserved for dancing to the music of a live orchestra. The places at the tables are preassigned.

After dinner, there is dancing. The conversation is shoptalk about films and the people who make them and about the Academy Awards. This particular year, a nude male "streaker" ran across the stage while David Niven was speaking, so this, naturally, figured in many conversations.

Seated at Groucho's table was the late Henri Langlois, who had received an Oscar for saving and preserving sixty thousand films in the Cinémathèque Française. Many great films would have been lost had he not saved a print, even at the risk of his life during the Nazi occupation. Greeting Langlois with "Crepe Suzette," Groucho asked him if he had a copy of *Humorisk*, the Marx Brothers silent film. He didn't but wished he had.

GROUCHO
Which of our pictures do you like the best?
HENRI LANGLOIS
I like very much *Duck Soup, Night at the Opera, At the Circus, The Cocoanuts, Animal Crackers*, and *Horse Feathers*.
GROUCHO
Night at the Opera is my favorite.
HENRI LANGLOIS
But any Marx Brothers film we see is fantastic. I see *Duck Soup* many times in my life. But in 1940, just after the end of the French war and the invasion, I go to the South of France and I see *Duck Soup*. Fantastic! It was exactly like a documentary of the time I was a soldier in France. It was absolutely mad. So, if you want to know what happened in France between May to June 1940, you must see *Duck Soup*. It's the only film to explain what happened in France at this time.
GROUCHO
Do you think the Maginot Line is very safe?
HENRI LANGLOIS
Do you know what they make with the Maginot Line now? They sold the fragments of the Maginot Line, and nobody wants. They sold in public auction, and nobody wants buy the Maginot Line.
GROUCHO
It's very simple. Instead of attacking the Maginot Line, they went around it.
HENRI LANGLOIS
It's just like *Duck Soup* exactly.
GROUCHO
He was a great director, Leo McCarey. And a funny man. We had a lot of fun with him.
HENRI LANGLOIS
But I think the most great directors of the Marx Brothers films are the Marx Brothers.

GROUCHO

You know we're more popular now than we were thirty years ago? The kids have taken us up.

HENRI LANGLOIS

Every year new ones come to the Cinémathèque to laugh. The books write why, but not important. They laugh because the Marx Brothers make laugh everyone. There was a chair, and a philosopher and a scientist and others discuss the chair, in their way. Then a man came in who doesn't know better. He sat in the chair. And the chair she was so very happy, because that's what she was made for. Today I have discovered how much all these films are shown on television. I see Mae West today. She showed me the letters she receives now, letters of children of eight, twelve, and sixteen who said, "Madam, I have seen your films on television. You are wonderful. I love you." It's fantastic.

GROUCHO

Two eleven-year-old kids came to the front door today and brought me a box of cigars. Do you smoke cigars?

HENRI LANGLOIS

Cigarettes always. I smoke five *paquets* a day.

GROUCHO

How do you like America?

HENRI LANGLOIS

It's wonderful! I'm very happy because I've found a place in the world where when you say, "Please give me water," they don't think you are mad. Everywhere I go I say I want water, and they give me water. In all restaurants, they bring the glass of water without your asking.

GROUCHO

First thing they do in Paris is they slap a bottle of champagne on you whether you want it or not.

During dinner, Groucho turned to me and said, "I should have got this Oscar years ago." He was quite serious, as he had been all evening.

The next day, Erin received her own Oscar—a tiny gold charm. It was, in fact, Erin who decided where Groucho's Oscar would be displayed in his house:

ERIN

The Academy Award is going in the back of the hall in front of the picture of the four Marx Brothers, with a spotlight on it. I want you to round that corner on the way to your room and be absolutely thunder-

struck. I've got a little thing for the front hall, a little French settee . . .
GROUCHO
I've got a little thing, period.
ERIN
When you take people on a tour of your photographic collection, they're gonna be thunderstruck when they see that painting with the Academy Award in front of it. That's very dramatic.

One of Groucho's guests was Billy Wilder, himself the recipient of six Oscars of his own. Another guest, Bill Cosby, picked up Groucho's Oscar and examined it, observing, "He looks like one of my people as opposed to one of yours."

At the Governors' Ball, Henri Langlois had invited Groucho to a screening of some rare turn-of-the-century French films which he had brought from the Cinémathèque Française in Paris especially for the Los Angeles Film Exhibition. Several days later Groucho's grandson Andy and I accompanied him to the Paramount Theatre, where we were greeted by Gary Abrahams and Gary Essert, directors of Filmex, and led up to the balcony, which had been closed off. Although the rest of the theatre was full, we were there alone in the balcony.

Groucho was quite impressed with the films. His enthusiasm was articulated loudly and carried through the theatre, since the films were silent. "I'm glad I'm here." His voice was immediately recognized, and below us we could hear people saying, "It's Groucho Marx!" He continued to make comments throughout the films. The audience enjoyed not only the rare program but Groucho's occasional commentary. He got a big laugh when he said, "These films are as old as I am."

The program, which lasted two hours, began with films made before 1900 and continued with later films by such pioneers as Lumière, Mèliés, and Zecca. There was also a Sarah Bernhardt *Hamlet*, which reminded Groucho that he had once played on the same bill with her. Groucho's favorite was Zecca's *Victims of Alcohol*. He especially admired the performance of the drunkard, and he also liked Little Tich, a comedian in French silent films. Afterward Groucho stopped to talk with Henry Langlois and Dan Price. "I liked the drunk best," he told them.

Four weeks later Groucho gave a memorable party at Hillcrest Country Club for his Oscar. All of his friends were invited, and there were no insults—not even friendly ones. The party took place on April 30, 1974.

The afternoon of the party, Groucho, Erin, and I went over the guest list. Groucho wanted it checked meticulously to be certain that none of his friends were left out.

ERIN
Liza Minnelli is coming. Why don't we ask her to sing?
GROUCHO
She's a guest. I invited her. She's not coming to work.

On the evening of the party, I had dinner alone with Groucho while Erin went on ahead to make certain that all was in order at Hillcrest. She put the finishing touches on Groucho's apparel as his wardrobe mistress. She laid out his blue denim suit and white turtleneck sweater, then fastidiously brushed and fluffed up the blue beret. Demonstrating just how it should look, she explained to me that I was to make certain that he wore it exactly the right way. Erin's parting admonition as she went out the door was, "Groucho, don't wear your pants too high."

We finished a small meal. Even knowing what a feast he had arranged for his guests at Hillcrest, Groucho still preferred the regularity of his own dinnertime and the privacy of his own dining room, with limited partaking later on at the party. He also recognized that there wouldn't be much time for eating at Hillcrest, since this was not only a personal party but a command performance. "I never get a chance to eat at these things," he confided to me.

When Groucho and I arrived, Hillcrest Country Club was already filled with people. Making his grand entrance, he was greeted warmly by friends and acquaintances like Morrie Ryskind, Bill Cosby, Jack Nicholson, Marvin Hamlisch, Nat and Helen Perrin, Milton Berle, George Burns, George Seaton, Eden Marx, Steve Allen, Liza Minnelli, Jack Haley, Jr., George Segal, June Banker, Tony Navarro, Bud Yorkin, Robert Altman, S. M. Estridge, Alice Cooper, John Guedel, Terry and Lilly Hamlisch, Joe Hyams, Elke Sommer, Irving Wallace, Walter Mirisch, Carl Reiner, Cass Elliott, Freddie Fields, George Peppard, Lee Bowman, William Wyler, Hugh Hefner, Barbi Benton, French Consul General Jacques Roux and his wife, Gunvar, Warren and Josette Cowan, William Peter Blatty, Bill Feeder, and Marvin and Nan Meyer. Zeppo was there too, accompanied by his former wife Barbara, but Gummo hadn't been able to come. Groucho's cook, Martha, and his maid, Agnes, were invited, and Groucho posed for pictures with them.

Groucho ordered the best of everything in virtually unlimited quantities. It was accompanied by an endless stream of Mouton Cadet. As soon as any of the wine in the guests' glasses was even slightly diminished, it was replenished. There was a profusion of oysters, lobster, shrimp, and salads in such an elaborate cold buffet that most of the guests had already eaten well past their capacities when it was announced that dinner was served. Then followed prime beef, chateaubriand, chicken, veal, fresh salmon steaks, and all the accompaniments. The elaborate flower centerpieces at each table were festooned with ribbons to which were attached animal crackers. Desserts were festive bombes, tortes, pastries, ices, and petits fours.

Erin, wearing a clinging long white dress with ropes of pearls, sat on one side of Groucho, and I on the other, as each guest approached the table to greet and be greeted by the host, who was also the guest of honor. At the table with us were Keenan Wynn and his daughter, and Bill Cosby. George Burns came by to greet Groucho, and told us this story:

"Years ago there used to be a song that went, 'If you don't see your mama every night, you don't see your mama at all.' Well, I like sea bass. But every time I ordered sea bass for forty years, Groucho would hit me with 'If you don't sea bass every night, you don't sea bass at all.'

"It was a funny line forty years ago. Today after forty years, it's not that funny. So, the other day I'm hungry for sea bass. But I'm not going to order it in front of Groucho and hear that lousy joke again, so I whisper in the waiter's ear. The waiter comes back to me and says, 'If you don't sea bass every night, you don't sea bass at all.' "

Hugh Hefner and Barbi Benton came over and he told Groucho how much he admired the interview Groucho had given *Playboy*—and Groucho told Hefner how much he admired Barbi.

Tony Navarro verbalized one of Groucho's most striking qualities:

"When I first met him, what impressed me then and what still impresses me is that the character from the films and the real person coincide so perfectly. Look at him now. It's as if he just stepped off the screen."

Before the entertainment began, an orchestra provided music for dancing, an opportunity not missed by Groucho to dance with Erin.

Bill Cosby acted as the master of ceremonies for the evening's entertainment. Most of the famous guests performed, and so did a few of the less famous. Groucho's maid, Agnes, sang "Summertime," as she had often done at Groucho's parties at home. George Segal played the banjo and sang "Darktown Strutters' Ball" while Bill Cosby backed him up on the drums, Steve Allen and George Burns told stories, and Robert Altman lumbered up to the microphone to announce, "This is the best party I've ever been to." Alice Cooper presented Groucho with the second annual Alice Cooper Living Legend Award—a coiled snake on a plaque. "Do I have to keep this?" Groucho asked, then reciprocated with a stuffed gorilla wearing a "Tell 'em Groucho sent you" T-shirt.

Morrie Ryskind, one of Hollywood's and Broadway's best writers, got up and spoke. Although an interesting speaker, he didn't have the delivery of a professional performer, and he got few laughs. "I'm not a showman," he told me afterward. "If Groucho had said any of it, they'd still be laughing. Nobody ever asks for *my* autograph."

Near the end of the evening, after almost everyone had left, Erin got up on the dance floor. She looked at Groucho, then the music started again, and she began to do her solo dance for him. Starting at a modest frenzy, it accelerated to the point of wild abandon as the musicians tried valiantly to follow her gyrations. Erin was bending, spinning, and dipping, with her skirt often swirling above her head. (Afterward she asked me, "You couldn't see anything, could you?") Her agility and fervor merged with an intensity that left the small remaining audience almost more spent than the performer. No one left; in fact, scarcely anyone even moved until she had finished, and Groucho never once took his eyes off her. Tremendously pleased, for days he proudly told everyone how great she was.

The party ended, as so many of Groucho's parties do, with *da capo* choruses of the ubiquitous "Peasie Weasie." People left Hillcrest that night in a mood of poignant euphoria. The next morning *The Hollywood Reporter* called the affair "the most beautiful blast of this year or any year."

After the Academy Awards, Groucho continued to make professional and public appearances. He was on the *Bob Hope Comedy Special*, and the Emmy Awards, and he participated in numerous charity fund-raising events. He made front-page news with the New York opening of *Animal Crackers*.

For legal reasons, *Animal Crackers* had not been shown commercially for more than twenty years. Meanwhile, a whole new generation of Marx Brothers fans had come along. Through revivals and television they had become familiar with all of the pictures except *Animal Crackers*, and a huge demand was building up for this film, which, by the 1970s, had become something of a *cause célèbre*. But Universal Pictures, which had acquired *Animal Crackers* from Paramount, couldn't reissue the film until negotiations were completed with the George S. Kaufman estate, which owned the dialogue rights. On top of all this, Universal was not entirely certain that a big enough demand existed to warrant the expense of new prints, and of distributing and promoting a 1930 New York–made film of a dated 1920s Broadway musical comedy, even if the Marx Brothers *were* in it.

A group of students at UCLA who were also Marx Brothers fans decided to do something to convince Universal that *Animal Crackers* was worth rereleasing for theatrical distribution. They formed a group dedicated to bringing *Animal Crackers* back, and called it CRAC, the acronym for the Committee to Re-release Animal Crackers. CRAC quickly became a national group, and petitions with thousands of signatures from campuses all over the country were collected and presented to Universal.

Groucho himself was deeply concerned with and involved in getting *Animal Crackers* "out of the can," even though he no longer had any financial interest in the film. Universal was intrigued, even impressed, but less than totally convinced as to the potential drawing power of their acquisition from Paramount. Groucho's personal campaign for *Animal Crackers* included "bending the ear" ("which is a pretty funny expression if you ever saw a bent ear," Groucho told me, folding over his own ear) of Universal's Sid Sheinberg at the Jack Benny March of Dimes tribute dinner. At the Oscar ceremonies, Groucho buttonholed ("And he didn't even have a buttonhole") Universal's Lew Wasserman with his plaint. Wasserman visited with Groucho and Henri Langlois at the Governors' Ball after the Oscars, and Groucho talked with him about *Animal Crackers* openings in California and New York, and the planned Cinémathèque Française benefit. Perhaps Groucho's Oscar standing on the table next to the one Henri Langlois had received also exerted some silent ethosenhancing persuasion. Jennings Lang of Universal was virtually tackled as he walked in the streets of Beverly Hills by Erin, who was never timid in her role as Groucho's personal manager.

A special screening was held for an invited group so that audience response could be judged. This took place shortly after the Academy Awards. Many of the jubilant members of UCLA's CRAC group were in the crammed theatre that night, as were Groucho, Erin, and I. It was, therefore, the exact opposite of a scientifically controlled situation. The air of elation and mirth, however, proved an accurate precursor of things to come. The very young audience was thrilled afterward as we exited through an almost blinding glare of popping flashbulbs. Bill Feeder shepherded us through the crowd lining the way to the parking lot.

Perhaps the most sentimental showing of *Animal Crackers* for me was the first time I saw it. Groucho had it screened at his house for Jack Nicholson, Mike Nichols, Marvin Hamlisch, Erin, and me. Groucho shrugged off our enthusiasm, saying, "It's a silly picture." But clearly there was pride in his tone when he said "silly," and he did add, "It's a funny picture." Groucho, who considered false modesty a form of hypocrisy, was definitely a Marx Brothers fan.

On May 23, 1974, *Animal Crackers* had its official new premiere at the United Artists Theatre in Westwood. I joined Groucho and Erin for the occasion, as did many members of CRAC.

Groucho had arranged that the East Coast opening of *Animal Crackers* would be a benefit for the Cinémathèque, and he had agreed to fly to New York City to make a personal appearance on opening night. On his arrival in New York, one of the first things he did was to try to call Lou Soren, his old friend from Broadway days. His good mood turned to extreme sadness when he hung up after talking with Mrs. Soren.

"She told me he died a few months ago. He was wonderful in *Animal Crackers*. He was a wonderful man."

There was a phone call from Maxine Marx, Chico's daughter. She said that she would be coming to *Animal Crackers* with Toby (Harry Ruby's daughter) and that they would need only one seat. Maxine explained to me that, as little girls, whenever they were taken to see the Marx Brothers, "We were always expected to share one seat."

The new premiere took place on June 23, 1974. That evening, before going to the theatre, Groucho had dinner in his suite at the Regency with Adolph Green, Goddard Lieberson, Erin, and me. Groucho and I divided his favorite hotel dinner, a steak tartare. He liked to eat only half and couldn't bear to leave the other half. After dinner, Betty Comden arrived with her husband to have some coffee. Then we all proceeded to the Sutton Theatre on Fifty-seventh Street.

Betty and her husband went in their car, and Groucho, Goddard, Adolph, Erin, and I went in the chauffeur-driven limousine provided by Universal. As we approached within a few blocks of our destination, we were caught in a monumental traffic jam and literally inched along. We were prevented from reaching the theatre not only because of the cars that were blocking our way, but also because of the people filling the street. It took us more than twenty minutes to go one block. Finally, we reached the theatre, and it became evident to us that the traffic jam had been caused by Groucho's imminent arrival. All around us the street was filled with young people in a festive mood.

Our car was surrounded and people jumped on the roof, covering the top of the car with bodies. The most startling impression was the sound of coins being tapped on the roof of the car. It made an incredibly loud and extremely painful din, and intensified our confined, trapped feelings. We couldn't look out and see anything because the windows were totally obscured by flattened faces peering in at us. We heard a policeman's voice speaking through a bullhorn, saying "Don't tip the car, don't tip the car." At just that moment Adolph remembered an unreassuring story:

"I was in a bus once with Frank Sinatra, and we were surrounded by a crowd of fans. The bus was leaning way over to one side, and we thought we were finished, that they were going to turn us over for sure."

We were no more reassured when a policeman finally got through to open the car door, and flinging it wide open, he shouted, "Quick, run!"

We looked out at the aisle through which we were supposed to run. It was so narrow that Groucho, who was very slim, might have slipped through sidewise had he been quick enough. He wasn't. As we reached the middle of the aisle, it vanished. Adolph Green, who had gone first to clear the way for Groucho, was suddenly cut off from the rest of us. Goddard wielded a British-style umbrella in swashbuckling style, but he was also swept off into the crowd.

Groucho, Erin, and I were left encircled. Taking a stiff stance, Groucho bore a stoic expression. Erin screamed at the crowd, the police, and the heavens, but to little avail. She was drowned out by a gleeful chorus of exuberant fans who were on the verge of crushing us.

As the crowds on both sides of the aisle met in an effort to be closer to Groucho, we were caught between them. Fortunately, the strongest young male fans had made it to the front, and once they got the idea that their ideal might be injured by love, they reversed course. The front row linked arms to hold back the other surging fans. A narrow aisle suddenly reappeared, and we were able to make our way into the theatre.

Ron Delsener, who as a producer of rock stars had been through traumatic scenes like this before, witnessed the episode from a knowing vantage:

"When we showed up, there was a mob of kids outside the movie, and there was no real passageway to get in. Right away I said, 'There's going to be trouble here,' because the theatre hadn't anticipated this size crowd. The management hadn't any real setup, and it looked like they belatedly called the police, and some policemen showed up—some of them on horseback—but there was still no passageway to get in. When I waved my invitation up in the air, one of the ushers said, 'They're okay. Clear the way in.' The kids were in a jolly mood outside. They weren't in a violent mood, so a few cleared the way and we got in.

"I waited out front a little bit, then I kept getting up from my seat to see if Groucho was going to get through the mob. Finally he showed up in a limousine, and naturally everybody crowded around the car. You were in the limousine with him. Then he got out, and he was just buried in a sea of people. I thought he was going to be trampled to death. I said, 'This is it. Right here.' Miraculously, they pulled him through it, and he was white, he was like almost in a coma. He was almost like a robot.

"Inside there were flashbulbs popping in front of his face, and two people telling them in a lackadaisical manner not to do that. Groucho got up and sauntered down to the mike with Goddard helping him. He said a few words about his being lucky to be alive because he almost got killed coming in. Then they showed *Animal Crackers*.

"Getting out was a big chore. I saw what was going to happen. I knew the end of the movie was coming, so we got out of our seats, my wife and myself, and went out the door. The mob was still there, and it had swelled, and now the police were much greater in number. As I got out, the people outside started to close the exit aisle up.

"All of a sudden, my wife pulled me out of the way because a policeman's horse was coming down on me. This horse almost got me. Limousines were backing up, and we were caught in a cross fire, but somehow we got out. I didn't stay around too long, but I did see Groucho make it to a car and get pushed in. Then there were people jumping on top of the car, people screaming, horses neighing, and horns beeping.

"They should have treated it like I do with a pop concert. You check all the exits beforehand—how to get out afterwards, and how to get in, too. Maybe you have to arrive in an ambulance. Anyway, it's got to be different every time. You don't go in through the backstage door. You use a different entrance. You arrive long before the crowd."

The need for pop-star security conditions at the revival of a 1930 movie, even if Groucho Marx *was* going to make a personal appearance, was underestimated, as was his charisma, especially with his younger fans. When he was finally led up onstage to accept his award he commented, "I'm delighted to be here, although I was almost murdered."

We had all been seated in the last row, which had been reserved so as to enable us to get in and out easily. Adolph Green was on one end and Betty Comden and her husband on the other, with Groucho in the middle and Goddard and me on either side of him. Erin was so nervous she couldn't sit down, preferring to stand throughout the whole film. Before the showing of *Animal Crackers*, some fans came back with their cameras, getting so close with their flashbulbs that we were almost blinded. The audience inside the theatre was just as excited by the presence of Groucho as the young fans outside.

After Adolph Green and Betty Comden had introduced Groucho, he was led to the stage by Goddard Lieberson and presented with a plaque from the Friends of the Cinémathèque Française. In his acceptance speech, Groucho said, "It's all a lie. I have to give it back, but I'm gonna sell it back instead. Three cheers for the red, white, and blue, and thank you all."

During the showing of *Animal Crackers* Groucho made comments, and members of the audience close enough to hear him at all strained to catch every word:

• When the name Captain Jeffrey T. Spaulding first appeared on the screen, Groucho said, "That's me!"

• When Captain Spaulding appeared in his sedan chair, Groucho said, "Who's that young guy?"

• When he told Margaret Dumont, "You're one of the most beautiful women I've ever met, and that's not saying much for you," he was reminded that she never seemed to understand his jokes.

• When he said to Margaret Dumont, "Would you wash out a pair of socks for me?" he told me, "I had plenty of sox appeal."

• During the Hungerdunger, Hungerdunger, Hungerdunger, Hungerdunger, and McCormick sequence with Zeppo, Groucho told me, "I wrote the whole scene and added to it each day. That's a good scene. The original part was just, 'Take a letter.'" Later during this same scene he said, "I like where I took a swing at Zep, and I almost knocked myself out."

• When Chico said, "I see you just want a telephone booth," and Groucho said, "I'd get in touch with Chic Sale," Groucho explained to me what this meant. "You don't remember Chic Sale. That was before your time. He used to tell outhouse jokes."

We left early in order to escape before the exiting audience. That was all right with Groucho. "I know how it ends," he told us. Outside the mounted police had arrived, and the horses had entered into the spirit of pandemonium and were having a good time, creating as many problems as they were solving. Long after the occasion, Groucho reminisced with me about that night:

GROUCHO
Remember the night of *Animal Crackers* with all of the mounted police? Did I ever tell you that one of the horses asked me for my autograph?
I
Did he get it?
GROUCHO
Yes.
I
Was he pleased?
GROUCHO
I think so. He gave me quite a horselaugh.

That night, after the film, Groucho had a party in honor of the event, with Comden and Green entertaining. One of their songs was "La Marseillaise," sung to the tune of "Take Me Out to the Ball Game," and vice versa. Groucho added, "I was Napoleon in *I'll Say She Is* and I said, 'Ah, the Mayonnaise! The troops must be dressing.'" Groucho's party was in his suite at the Regency, and besides those of us who had accompanied him to *Animal Crackers*, he also invited Ahmet Ertegun.

The plaque presented to Groucho read:

To Groucho Marx,
Whose comedy is timeless; a gentleman and a gentle man; the
master of the illogical, of the deflated platitude, of funny truths,
of reductio ad absurdum,
Gratefully,
With all our laughs,
THE FRIENDS OF THE CINÉMATHÈQUE FRANÇAISE

In appreciation, Groucho wrote the following letter to S. M. Estridge, chairman of the board of the Friends of the Cinémathèque Française:

Dear S.M.,
I was honored to receive the plaque, and I'll wear it on my shoulder to eternity.
Groucho

Sometime later I talked with Betty and Adolph about that evening:

ADOLPH GREEN

I suddenly became aware of what a legend to young Americans he had become. I really got the picture instantly. I'd never thought of it before.

BETTY COMDEN

He's worshiped. But it was quite scary when Groucho tried to get into the theatre. I think even he was surprised that there was such a mob. I remember being deeply concerned for him, because there was a mob that just wanted to touch him and be near him, which is lovely, except that it was just a little bit frightening. You had to force your way in, and there were a zillion photographers . . .

ADOLPH GREEN

Obviously they were gentle . . .

BETTY COMDEN

Oh yeah, just ecstatic. They were so excited.

ADOLPH GREEN

That was the nearest thing to "I carved my way through a wall of human flesh, dragging my canoe behind me," because of Groucho.

I

They were tapping on the top of the car with coins, with us inside. It made a terrible noise.

BETTY COMDEN

That's kind of frightening.

ADOLPH GREEN

It *is* frightening.

BETTY COMDEN

Seeing the picture was great fun, of course, and then we both got up and presented Groucho with the award. Then, after the event, going back to the hotel, Groucho was very lively. The evening hadn't tired him in the least.

ADOLPH GREEN

I think after being scared he was sort of exuberant.

BETTY COMDEN

We sang for a while, doing numbers.

I

Groucho loves those performances you give when you come to his parties.

ADOLPH GREEN

Well, we *have* to! We have to come through. It's not even a command. It's "Or else!" We'd *better* come through.

During Groucho's stay in New York, two very special moments were the visits he made after many years to the East Ninety-third Street apartment where the Marx Brothers all spent their early years, and to the house in Great Neck where Groucho lived with Ruth and his young family after "making it." The Yorkville neighborhood where he grew up had changed less than might have been expected, but Groucho was disappointed when he couldn't find the corner grocery where he used to be sent to fetch the beer for dinner.

The trip to Great Neck was "produced" by Ron Delsener, who took time out from his summer concerts in Central Park and the Madison Square Garden rock shows to whisk us on a picaresque journey. Ron described it:

"One day at the Regency Hotel I said to Groucho, 'Let's go back to your neighborhood, your old neighborhood.' Of course, Manhattan was really his old neighborhood, the East Side in the Nineties, but he had told me that he'd lived in Great Neck. I said, 'I'll take the afternoon off, and we'll drive out there.' Well, it was a real rainy day, and I had to really convince him, but he'd told me he always wanted to go back and see his house in Great Neck.

"I said, 'Listen, we'll have fun,' so just before we got to the Fifty-ninth Street bridge, I stopped at a store and bought two cheap wigs, one for Groucho and one for me. I bought a blond wig and a brunette wig, and we tried them on. We were laughing, singing, and making jokes, and he was acting very effeminate. He told one of my favorite stories about this vaudeville team called Swayne's Rats and Cats. The rats sat on the backs of the cats like jockeys on horseback. He said he figured I had heard it before, but I enjoyed hearing it anyway.

"As we got into Great Neck, he recognized the street where he had lived, but there were a lot of changes since he'd been there. He said the street looked a little smaller to him. As he approached the house, you could see the memories start to come back, and as we went up the stairs, he was really excited.

"An elderly gentleman came to the door, obviously a robust sort of individual and in good health, but not much younger than Groucho. The minute he saw Groucho, he knew who it was. He said, 'Groucho Marx! Groucho Marx!' He was all excited, and he called the children in the house. There were two children. This was the children's grandfather, and he was just so delighted to see Groucho. He said 'You've come home. This is your house.' Groucho was delighted too.

"We went upstairs to the bedroom, and Groucho said, 'It's laid out a lit-

tle differently now. They must have taken down the wall.' The man veri-
fied this. Then the little girl came into the room, and the old man said,
'This is Groucho Marx, and once he lived in this house.' They had a big
poster of Groucho in the room, and giant blowups of scenes from Marx
Brothers films. The girl looked at Groucho, kind of shyly, smiling a little.

"The grandfather was very upset that his daughter wasn't home, and he
tried to contact her. He said, 'Won't you stay a few more minutes for
something to eat?' But we had to go back. The weather was quite bad. It
was still raining. But it was a great moment, and he's remembered it every
time I see him. He had a hell of a time that day!"

By the kind of rare coincidence that was always happening to Groucho,
the man who had shown us around Groucho's old Great Neck house was
E. Bruell, who had for years been a projectionist at the Sutton Theatre,
where *Animal Crackers* had just been newly premiered. As we left, Groucho said to Mr. Bruell, "When I was born, there were no movies, and now
there aren't any either."

We left 21 Lincoln Road, where Groucho had spent years of his life,
and headed into downtown Great Neck. He wanted to visit a bakery he remembered. "I used to buy a roll there that was full of nuts—just like me,"
he told us as we drove up and down the main street looking futilely in
every bakery. Groucho took a quick look in each but was disappointed.
"It's only been fifty years," he said in mock dismay. "Things change so
fast." We drove back to Manhattan in the pouring rain.

Back at the Regency, we rode up in the elevator with a bridal party of
bridesmaids and ushers. "Where's the bride?" Groucho asked. He was informed that the party was on the twelfth floor, and was invited to attend
by the giggling bridesmaids. We stopped at his suite for Erin, who was
waiting with Salwyn Shufro, Groucho's friend and financial adviser since
the twenties. Then we all went upstairs to visit the party, where Groucho
kissed the bride and all of the bridesmaids. As we left he told us about another bridal party that he and Harpo had inadvertently attended:

"When we were playing *I'll Say She Is*, we were invited to a bachelor
party for a friend of ours who was getting married. So Harpo and I got into
the elevator and took off all our clothes. We were stark naked. But we got
off at the wrong floor, where the bride was having a party for *her* friends.
We ran around naked until a waiter finally came around with a couple of
dish towels."

Just after Groucho's eighty-fifth birthday he was honored at the University of Southern California. On learning of the coming event, he pondered the gravity of it. Then, after a moment, he asked:

"What are they serving for lunch?"

"Groucho, it's really big!" Erin exclaimed.

"Well, I guess I'll stand up and say a few insincere words, then."

He was honored at USC on October 16, 1975. Reading excerpts from his plays, letters, and books were Jack Lemmon, Roddy McDowall, Lynn Redgrave, and George Fenneman. Afterward Groucho sang as Billy Marx accompanied him on the piano; then he answered questions from the audience. One of the questions was, "Who is the best comedian?" Without hesitation he answered, "Woody Allen."

Groucho was proud to have been in demand and working in show business in his eighties. He enjoyed earning money not only because he remembered the 1929 Depression and remained permanently insecure about lasting financial security, but because he felt that getting paid for what you do grades you. He said frankly, "I'm not available cheap. Free, maybe. Cheap, never."

One morning while we were having breakfast, the mail arrived. Groucho produced a check from one of the envelopes, payment for a recent guest appearance, and waved it at me: "Look, I got a check. I'm still alive."

Not very many people are fortunate enough in life to be able to enjoy some of the best times of their lives after the age of eighty. Groucho was the first to admit, "I've been lucky," despite his occasionally saying to Erin, "Just remember: I've given you the worst years of my life."

"I've got the key to my front door"

On a day late in May of 1975, the air was unusually clear in New York City, and it was slightly windy. Several times Groucho's blue beret was nearly airborne. He had been thinking about a walk down Fifth Avenue to buy gifts at Gucci to take back to California. But it took us half an hour to go only part of a block because so many people stopped to talk with us. We never did get to Gucci but decided, instead, to walk uptown on Fifth Avenue, where there was less pedestrian traffic.

During the walk up Fifth Avenue from Fifty-ninth Street, almost everyone we passed looked at Groucho with an expression of pleasant recognition. Faces lit up, and New York is not a place where faces light up lightly. Taxi drivers shouted out, "Hi, Groucho!" "Be well, Groucho." He autographed some *Wall Street Journals* and a few copies of the *New York Times*, some assorted business cards, and a few used envelopes, as well as one leather briefcase, which didn't take the ink very well.

One fan, who had seen Groucho as we started our walk up Fifth Avenue, raced to Rizzoli Bookstore and then caught up with us with a paperback copy of *The Groucho Letters*, which he breathlessly held out for Groucho's signature. He took the book and signed it, and the boy thanked him. "Nothing at all," Groucho responded. "It makes the book worth less."

Just past the Knickerbocker Club and almost back at the Sherry Netherland Hotel, which was temporarily home, something happened to Groucho. For a moment, he was almost unable to walk, almost unable to stand. Barbara, the petite nurse he had brought with him from California, fought to assist him and tried to hold her ground. But, resenting infirmity, he was in no mood to be helped, and somehow he made a supreme effort, fighting to maintain his equilibrium and his independence. With what was clearly a Herculean exertion, he managed to return to the hotel. As we literally inched our way back and finally reached the shelter of the lobby, passersby continued to greet him and to request autographs, totally oblivious to the strain he was undergoing.

In the seclusion of the elevator, Groucho held on for dear life, while two tweedy ladies, a French couple, and a stout matron chatted and chattered frivolously with him about *You Bet Your Life*. Even while suffering, he maintained a stoic composure and his stage presence, never one to let down even such a small audience. Surveying the intricately detailed painting and paneling inside the elegant old elevator, Groucho said, "This elevator's an antique. It's even older than I am." On this note, he exited stylishly, and only when he had reached the privacy of his apartment collapsed.

"I'm calling the house doctor," Barbara said.

Groucho, who was now lying in bed, said weakly, "Why? My house isn't sick."

The doctor arrived and said, "Mr. Marx, I'm going to take your temperature."

"Where are you going to take it?" he asked.

Fortunately, a long nap and the arrival of a friend resuscitated Groucho, who bounced back with restored vigor. The friend was a spinet. He had missed having a piano in his hotel suite, so he had rented one, which in due time appeared on the scene, carried in by four monumentally muscled movers. Knowing the piano was for Groucho, they took a preposterously long time to position it. The sound of Groucho's voice from the bedroom slowed them down immeasurably as they expectantly eyed the bedroom door from which the voice had emanated. Persistence had to be its own reward, though, because there wasn't any other. Finally, the movers retired from the apartment, clearly crestfallen and perhaps disbelieving the excuse that Groucho wasn't well. Living legends are only grudgingly permitted infirmities.

As soon as Groucho knew the piano was there, he experienced a resurgence of vitality. Pajama-attired, he took his place at the keyboard, ignoring nurse Barbara's remonstrances and Erin's pyrotechnics. He seemed almost to receive a transfusion from the keys as he began his repertory with "Father's Day." "That's what Groucho would have liked to have been," Erin commented, "a composer." Groucho was playing "Take Me

Out to the Ball Game" when Jack Nicholson, who also happened to be staying at the Sherry Netherland, dropped in. Jack, who sang while Groucho played the piano, admitted that his own repertory of songs was pretty limited. "But my mother used to harmonize," he said. Groucho nodded. "Mine too." Jack suggested that they try "Easter Parade," and they did.

GROUCHO
I just had a letter from Irving Berlin. He said we're a couple of *"alte cockers."* He said, "Keep on holding on. There are only a few of us *alte cockers* left."

JACK NICHOLSON
He was pretty smart. He published all his own music.

Later I asked Groucho what Irving Berlin meant. He hesitated. "I can't tell you." Then he thought for a moment and said, "An *alte cocker* is what I am, that's what it is. It's a very old man who isn't what he used to be."

Groucho had come to New York some days earlier to see *A Chorus Line,* for which Marvin Hamlisch had written the music. Marvin, since accompanying Groucho at Carnegie Hall, had acquired four Grammy Awards as well as his three Oscars. Groucho had been invited for the opening but resisted the temptation, feeling that he preferred not to be an attraction or distraction on opening night. He was well aware that the last thing he could be was anonymous. This visit was also planned to coincide with Marvin's thirty-first birthday.

Groucho's merry band had arrived from California on the Saturday night before the Sunday evening performance of *A Chorus Line.* With him were Erin, cook Robin, and nurses "Happy" Cooper and Barbara Odum. It was late when the plane got in and I met them, but Groucho was still wide awake. "I'll take you girls out on the town," he offered, but Erin said she was too tired.

"But what did you have in mind?" she asked.

"How about the Club Foot?" he responded slyly.

He settled for a late supper in his suite. The supper was served at 10 P.M. New York time, but with the three-hour difference, it was exactly 7 P.M. in California—just the time he always ate dinner.

As our entourage had passed, the young policeman on night duty by the elevator told me, "I go to see everything he does, over and over. I know all the lines. I laugh at the wrong places. I laugh too soon because I know what's coming."

Groucho had taken a luxury apartment on the tenth floor. "I remember," he told me, looking out the window at Central Park, "when I was traveling in vaudeville, and I was afraid I would jump out the hotel window at night in my sleep. I put theatrical trunks against the windows."

Sunday was planned as a quiet day. Goodman Ace was coming for lunch. I arrived early in the morning, but Groucho had already been up for hours. "I'm up at six every morning." He was reading Woody Allen's *Without Feathers* and Eric Lax's book about Woody, *On Being Funny*. He greeted me with, "Wax lips. Did you read about Woody's wax lips? He's a funny man."

Robin served the regular breakfast that Groucho had every day at home. We had orange juice, soft-boiled eggs, and toast, and Groucho had the decaffeinated coffee he always drank then. After breakfast, he read the *New York Times*. He read it all morning, quite carefully, making occasional comments. "Look at this name: Ratskin. You couldn't make up a name like that." He tried out "Groucho Ratskin" and "Julius H. Ratskin." Later he read the entire Russell Baker column to Robin and me, commenting, "Great."

"Do you believe in guilt by association?" I asked Groucho. "When I came in here this morning, two boys held out autograph books for me to sign."

He smiled. "Well, you got one cheer when they gave me the Oscar."

I admired his jaunty sport shirt, and he said, "I'm sending you some of these shirts as soon as I get back. It's about time I gave you something."

Groucho called Lilly Hamlisch, who was going with us to see *A Chorus Line*. "I'm sending a car for you tonight," he informed her. Marvin's mother protested that it wasn't necessary, but Groucho had the last word. "The car will be there. I'm very rich."

Then Goody Ace arrived for lunch:

GROUCHO
What do you hear from Kansas City?
GOODMAN ACE
I used to buy my shirts from Truman in Kansas City.
GROUCHO
I had lunch with Truman in Kansas City. He was a good president and an honest man.
GOODMAN ACE
Groucho, you're lookin' great. I wish I felt like you look.

GROUCHO

You're a young man compared to me. If you live long enough, you get old.

GOODMAN ACE

It's too bad about Jack Benny.

GROUCHO

I was at the funeral.

GOODMAN ACE

You know, I told him a joke, and in the story, someone called a spade a spade. The point of the story was it was against intolerance. And Jack said, "I could never tell a joke like that because I'm not mad at anybody." And I said, "What does it take to make you angry? When one door says 'White' and the other says 'Comedians'?"

GROUCHO

He was never angry at anyone.

ERIN

Where did you meet Groucho?

GOODMAN ACE

I met him in Kansas City. I was on a paper. It must have been about '28 or '29. I went to work on a paper when I was eighteen or nineteen. I know I left town in '33, and I'd already met him. He was in a show at the Shubert, either *Animal Crackers* or *The Cocoanuts*. I remember his leaving. I'd been with him for a whole week or two, and he threw a book at me, and he said, "If you're gonna stay in the humor racket, you better read this." It was a book written about fifty years ago by E. B. White and James Thurber called *Is Sex Necessary?*

GROUCHO

I like that piece you wrote about the milk situation. Everyone should have a cow. And I like that joke you told me when I called you. Tell it to her. (*Indicating me*)

GOODMAN ACE

Which one?

GROUCHO

"The Star-Spangled Banner."

GOODMAN ACE

Oh, you mean the Italian who learned to sing "The Star-Spangled Banner" at the ballpark, so he thought it ended, "Oh, say does that star-spangled banner yet wave o'er the land of the free and the home of the brave? Play ball!" And did you hear about the Pole and the Italian who were going to commit suicide by jumping off a ship, but the Pole couldn't find his way?

GROUCHO

A good joke doesn't depend on ethnic humor. I don't use ethnic stories anymore. I just say "the stupid one."

GOODMAN ACE

But you used to . . .

GROUCHO

I used to do a lot of things.

GOODMAN ACE

The things you got by with! Kaufman once said, "I'd only let the Marx Brothers ad-lib."

GROUCHO

The Marx Brothers were undisciplined, but they were funny.

GOODMAN ACE

One of them was a burglar. I always loved Harpo's routine, stealing all that silver.

GROUCHO

When are you gonna come out and stay at my house?

GOODMAN ACE

Never. Remember the last time? I had a suitcase and a garment bag, and you said, "How long you gonna stay?" And you gave me some orange juice and said, "Remember, oranges don't grow on trees."

After lunch, Goodman Ace departed, and Bud Cort came by with his two sisters. Bud was wearing a wide-brimmed Borsalino hat and a red T-shirt that said "Drink Coca-Cola." Groucho was wearing his Eric Ross Marx Brothers shirt with the titles of all the Marx Brothers films, which Bud admired.

GROUCHO

I'll get you one. I want you to have it at full retail price.

BUD CORT

I'll bet we're the three best-dressed men in the world.

ERIN

But you're only two . . .

BUD CORT

Groucho is number one, and I'm number two. The third one we don't know, but we assume there's someone somewhere.

GROUCHO

That was Ronald Colman. He always looked great. And he was a nice guy. He was in a picture with us: *The Story of Mankind.*

BUD CORT

How's your house, Groucho?

GROUCHO

(*Producing a key*) I've got the key to my front door.

BUD CORT

And your cats?

GROUCHO

They haven't written much, faithless creatures. You know, someone sent me a letter last week, and said he had seen *Duck Soup* twenty times, and that he has a racehorse he's naming after me. He's calling his horse "Groucho." Now I have a horse named after me.

BUD CORT

Wow! Have a vitamin C tablet, Groucho?

GROUCHO

No, thanks. I'm trying to quit. Are you working?

BUD CORT

There are a couple of movies going where I probably have to go out to California to meet the people. Guess what! I got my salary from my movie in Italy finally. Whew! What a relief. You don't know! I made the movie in January, right? And I just got paid yesterday. I got the check.

GROUCHO

Did you try to cash it yet?

BUD CORT

Not yet.

GROUCHO

My brother Chico gave a man a check once, and asked him to cash it at twelve noon the next Monday. The man waits until after twelve noon Monday, and the check still bounces. The man goes back to Chico and says, "I waited until twelve-fifteen on Monday, and it bounced." Chico says, "But I told you to cash it at *exactly* twelve noon!"

Groucho, Bud, his sisters, and I trooped out for a walk. As we got out of the elevator, Groucho was greeted by a lady he recognized. "That was Harriet Deutsch," he told us afterward. "Her husband was the one Loeb and Leopold were going to kill, only he didn't show up. You've gotta be lucky in life."

We walked for almost an hour, up Fifth Avenue and back along Park Avenue, with Groucho indicating places he remembered. He pointed out where George S. Kaufman had lived, saying, "You never get over one like that being gone."

That Sunday night, Groucho, Erin, and I went downtown to the New York Shakespeare Festival Public Theater to see *A Chorus Line*. Along the way, Groucho reminisced about where to turn off for Dinty Moore's. We passed the Flatiron Building, and he observed, "We used to stand there and watch the girls go by. We used to look at their legs."

As we drove, he continued. "People are pretty interesting. You never know what the next one is going to do or say. That was the basis of the quiz show. You can't manufacture people like that."

When we arrived at the theatre, there was a crowd standing outside waiting to enter. They saw Groucho and began to applaud, giving him a tremendous ovation which lasted until he had disappeared from their view. We were joined by Lilly Hamlisch and Elisa Pickholz, a friend of hers from Buenos Aires. They had been delivered by the limousine that was Groucho's grand gesture. Mrs. Hamlisch's friend spoke no English, only German and Spanish. They had been friends as girls in Vienna and hadn't seen each other for many years. Indicating me, Groucho said, "She met Perón, and she speaks Argentinian."

During the intermission Groucho announced, "I'm going to the can." He never did anything that something eventful didn't happen. Returning, he reported:

"At the urinal they asked for my autograph. I told them, 'Could you wait till I finish?' "

Afterward we went backstage to visit the cast. They already knew Groucho was in the audience, and his visit was eagerly awaited. When he arrived backstage, he was regarded with reverence and respect. For the opening night, he had sent one of Maurice Bonté's cakes decorated with a life-size female leg wearing a sexy black stocking with a hammer, implying the old theatrical opening night admonition "Break a leg."

The five of us rode back together to the Sherry Netherland, where Groucho was having a small party for Marvin's thirty-first birthday. On the way, Groucho, Lilly Hamlisch, and her friend sang old German songs. I translated the friend's comments in Spanish about the Marx Brothers' tremendous popularity in Argentina, and he said, "Just call me Gaucho Marx."

Back in Groucho's hotel suite, we found Marvin's father, who had finally managed to get past the tough security. Shortly afterward, Bud Cort and Marvin arrived. Robin carried out the cheese platter, and Erin brought in the huge chocolate cake with thirty-one candles. "Now we're a couple of old strudels," Groucho confided to Marvin. Groucho told stories which he asked me to translate into "Argentinian."

I

Keith Terpe, of the Seafarer's International Union, told me that your television program was the only one English-speaking people living in Spanish-speaking countries could count on getting in English. Desi and Lucy spoke Spanish, Ed Sullivan was believed to be Spanish because he was always dubbed, but you couldn't be translated, so you always came on in English.

MARVIN HAMLISCH

Fan-tastic! I believe it. There's nobody who could talk like Groucho.

GROUCHO

They even show our pictures in China, but I don't know if we talk Chinese.

Marvin was working on the music for the television version of *The Entertainer*, which would star Jack Lemmon in the role made so famous by Laurence Olivier. Groucho's gift to Marvin was his own copy of the book of *The Entertainer*, which had been given to Groucho by Olivier, who had written on the inside of the book:

> From The Entertainer to The Entertainer.
> Laurence Olivier

Marvin asked Groucho to tell his favorite story "about Annie Berger when she didn't give you any of her sauerkraut candy."

The next day, on a less festive note, Groucho met with his lawyers, Peter Fleming and John Sprizzo, "to press my lawsuit," as Groucho put it. He wore pajamas for the meeting, and, as Erin told it, he never lost his poise even though he lost his pants when the drawstring came open. He was doing a performance of "Peasie Weasie" at the time.

Although this lawsuit was a matter taken seriously, Groucho could still say, "I'll consult my lawyer, and if he takes the case, I'll get another lawyer."

Despite his having told me that "you never win" when you get involved in a lawsuit, he was suing the author and publishers of *The Marx Brothers Scrapbook*, a book which he had agreed to coauthor. He later regretted it, feeling that the book did not represent him, but he was unable to enjoin the sale of the book. The affair caused him continuing consternation, despite his usually successful efforts to maintain perspective and equilibrium.

Before going to lunch at CBS with Goddard Lieberson, Groucho and I were sitting in the living room of his hotel suite when Erin made a singing-and-dancing entrance from one of the bedrooms. She was wearing only flesh-colored, lace-lined panties and bra, though the outfit was, in fact, no more revealing than a conventional two-piece bathing suit. The song she sang, accompanied by high kicks, was improvised:

"We've got clothes,
We've got class.
Come on, gang,
Kiss our ass!"

Groucho looked disgusted. Her attention-getting attempts to shock him sometimes only displeased him. He put the look on his face into words:

"I'm a puritan. I'm an old-fashioned man. I was brought up on Horatio Alger and *Mrs. Wiggs of the Cabbage Patch.*"

While Groucho was in New York City, there were many requests for interviews. He didn't accept any, but he did see *New York Times* writer Israel Shenker because, "I have a book by him on my coffee table at home." He also invited Doubleday editor Ken McCormick over for tea.

KEN McCORMICK
The last time we talked about Somerset Maugham . . .
GROUCHO
He was a great writer.
KEN McCORMICK
Maugham is way down these days, and Conan Doyle is selling better than ever. And Edgar Wallace is hardly remembered.
GROUCHO
That's how it is. That's show business. That's life. You never know.
KEN McCORMICK
Are you having any riots this time? Last time you were here there was that incredible opening for *Animal Crackers* . . .
GROUCHO
I was nearly killed.
KEN McCORMICK
Goddard told me about being in the car with you. They had to get the mounted police to come and rescue you.
GROUCHO
One of the horses asked for my autograph.

KEN McCORMICK
Did you give it to him?
GROUCHO
Yes. Then I asked him for his autograph.
KEN McCORMICK
Did he give it to you?
GROUCHO
Neigh!

During this visit to New York, Groucho had a minor accident. As he was chewing candy, some of his teeth appeared to fall out, though it turned out to be only a bridge. He noted that they weren't really his teeth, and thus wouldn't join the collection of one of his nurses, Donna, who saved his teeth whenever he lost one. "She has three now, and when I die, she's going to auction them off. She keeps them in her purse."

He posed for us, flaunting the empty space in his mouth, while nurse Barbara tried to reassure him. "It's very becoming, Groucho." He came back with, "You mean begoing."

"Tomorrow I'll call a dentist," Barbara said.

"Call three, and we'll play bridge," he responded.

He tried plugging up the empty space with some chewing gum, proclaiming, "The whole tooth and nothing but the tooth." Then he summed up the situation with his characteristic lack of self-pity:

"Cavity emptor: Biter beware!"

The last event of Groucho's visit to New York in 1975 was a quick lunch with Betty Comden, Adolph Green, and Penelope Gilliatt, as Groucho was preparing to return home to California.

ADOLPH GREEN
(*Referring to Groucho's pending lawsuit*) How about the case, Groucho?
GROUCHO
It's cheaper by the case, only ten dollars a case.
ADOLPH GREEN
No, I mean the lawsuit.
GROUCHO
I'm having it pressed.
PENELOPE GILLIATT
Did you have a good time in New York, Groucho?
GROUCHO
I liked *A Chorus Line*, but I didn't get to visit any of my old houses.

Groucho liked to know who was living in his former houses. He never really moved away from his old homes. Reputedly unsentimental, he liked to visit his former homes and their current occupants, just casually dropping in, whether in Beverly Hills or New York.

Once he asked me if I liked living in a hotel.

"Yes," I said. "It's like living as a guest in my own house. Do *you* like living in a hotel?"

"It's only for a few days," he answered, "and I always know I've got the key to my front door."

To Groucho this key represented home. For him that was always of the utmost importance, starting with his first home, the East Ninety-third Street apartment, then the house in Chicago, followed by the grander house in Great Neck, to the houses in Beverly Hills, where he lived for almost half a century. Groucho's house represented security and privacy, two of his primary values. Home was where Groucho could indulge his whims. "It's not just a place to hang your head."

Groucho was born with a wooden spoon in his mouth, rather than the proverbial silver one. Then, just as he had achieved what seemed to him the pinnacle of economic security, the crash of 1929 took away everything. When your life is show business, economic security can be ephemeral.

There is not much room at the top, and once you have arrived there, you can't be certain how long you'll stay. Not totally without foreboding, Groucho watched for years the countless "for sale" signs that dotted the Beverly Hills landscape. Some houses are abandoned on the way up, others on the way down. Long at the top himself, he waited most of his life for that possible rainy day. The unsettling experience of vaudeville and boardinghouses never quite left him. "We stayed in those cheap boardinghouses so we could save money, then in 1929 we lost it all."

Groucho no longer cared much about traveling. His days of vaudeville travel seemed to have provided him with a lifetime supply, although he was proud to have visited almost every town in the United States and Canada. In 1930, when he wrote *Beds*, he described a person who liked to be in one bed as a "monobedder." I asked him if that still described him, and without hesitation he answered, "Yes."

His living room was far from being Grand Central Station, but his bedroom was his private sanctuary, a no-man's and no-woman's-land when the door was closed. To some extent he carried this over in a hotel. At the Sherry Netherland he announced, as he did at home in Beverly Hills, "I'm master of my house." Then he added with a faint twinkle, "I'm an old master."

When Betty, Adolph, and Penelope left Groucho, just before his return to California, Betty kissed him and said, "Goodbye, Groucho." "No," said Groucho firmly. "Not goodbye. Au revoir." Checking out of the Sherry Netherland, Groucho saw Jack Nicholson and Dick Cavett in the lobby:

GROUCHO
(*To Jack*) Are you working?
JACK NICHOLSON
Hiya, sport. Yeah. Too much.
DICK CAVETT
You know, Groucho, people are still writing to me and saying I should have defended Capote. Or I should have defended you. (*Noticing a long, thin box Groucho was clutching*) Hey, what's that?
GROUCHO
It's a yard of chocolate. She (*Indicating me*) gave it to me.
DICK CAVETT
Is that a front yard or a back yard? (*Groucho didn't laugh or even smile, so Dick Cavett went on to explain*) You used that one once on *You Bet Your Life*.

Before Groucho got into the limousine that would take him to the airport, he kissed me goodbye. He also kissed two pretty girls he'd never seen before who happened to be passing by. The doorman asked Groucho, "Aren't you going to kiss me?"

And he did.

"I wouldn't be 78 again for anything in the world"

Just before October 2, 1975, one of the radio news reports wished Groucho a happy "eightieth" birthday. He was quite perturbed. He was actually celebrating his eighty-fifth birthday, and, having paid full price, he thought he ought to get full credit.

The year before, when a reporter called up on Groucho's "seventy-eighth" birthday, Groucho said, "I wouldn't be seventy-eight again for anything in the world, I'm crazy about eighty-four."

Groucho had called me long distance saying, "I want you here for my birthday. Please come. I hope Melinda comes. Miles will be five, and I'll be eighty-five. I always give Miles a gift every time I give Jade something, and I give him the bigger thing. He wouldn't understand if she got a gift and he didn't."

On the morning of his eighty-fifth birthday, the doorbell rang, and Groucho was told that there were some young fans who had come to wish him a happy birthday. He went to the door and greeted them, saying, "You probably think I've always been this old." For the teenage boys at the door, however, the Groucho of the twenties, thirties, forties, and fifties still lived side by side with the Groucho of the 1970s. And they weren't disappointed.

During the first week of October, and especially on October 1, the telephone at Groucho's was virtually one continuous ring as friends called to congratulate him. He took it in stride, commenting, "Getting old isn't all that great. Now, getting younger . . . that would be something."

Television, radio, and newspaper interviews filled up much of the time preceding the birthday. The media sent more people with more paraphernalia than Groucho remembered being used to shoot *The Cocoanuts*. Their questions were frequently the same, but his answers were usually different. "Each one of them only listens to me once," he explained to me between interviews, "but I have to listen every time. So I have to entertain myself."

Groucho gave some advice to one young man who had come to interview him and who was smoking a cigarette.

"When you're eighty-five, you should quit smoking and you should quit sex. It was fun at the time," Groucho said fondly. Then he snapped, "When you're eighty-five, see what *you* can do!"

The mayor of Los Angeles proclaimed October 2 "Groucho Marx Day." On October 1 a large envelope arrived. "It's from the mayor," Erin announced. "I wonder if I'll also get something from Metro and Goldwyn," Groucho said as he opened the envelope. Then he read his version of the mayor's proclamation:

" 'Whereas and whereas and whereas and whereas the party of the eleventh part . . .' Sounds like a line from *Animal Crackers*, doesn't it?"

There was a thick piece of cardboard in the envelope to keep the proclamation from being bent. "This is the important part," he said, brandishing the piece of cardboard.

On the eve of Groucho's birthday, Erin, nurse Linda, and I joined him in his bedroom, where we all watched the NBC and ABC evening newscasts, which showed the films they had made for his eighty-fifth birthday. "Look at that yellow face," Groucho exclaimed when his image appeared on the screen. "It's the TV set," Erin reassured him, then nurse Linda adjusted the set so that Groucho's skin took on more natural tones.

The ABC newscast opened on a chocolate cake made by New York *pâtisserie* chef Maurice Bonté. He had decorated the cake with a yellow marzipan duck and an inscription which read, "The Secret Word Is Groucho." Later the cameras moved in on another yellow duck, a large papier-mâché piñata wearing a beret, smoking a cigar, and hanging from the chandelier in the dining room.

Groucho was in top form for his interview with ABC's Steve Lenz:

STEVE LENZ
Were you ever . . .
GROUCHO
No, not that I can remember.

When the programs ended, Groucho went over to a large picture of his mother and stood by it. For a long time he didn't say a word.

The Marx Brothers woo Lotta Miles during the Napoleon scene in *I'll Say She Is*. (The Theatre Collection of the New York Public Library at Lincoln Center)

The chorus never knew when they might find Groucho as part of the line. *The Cocoanuts*. (The Theatre Collection of the New York Public Library at Lincoln Center)

Lying down on the job Marx Brothers style on the stage set of *The Cocoanuts:*
(The Theatre Collection of the New York Public Library at Lincoln Center)

Four reasons why even Irving Berlin couldn't provide a hit tune for *The
Cocoanuts.* (The Theatre Collection of the New York Public Library at Lincoln
Center)

Reversing the more generally accepted custom, Groucho puts himself on a
pedestal while wooing Margaret Dumont in *The Cocoanuts*.
(The Theatre Collection of the New York Public Library at Lincoln Center)

Hattie Darling as she appeared in *On the Mezzanine Floor*. (Courtesy of Hattie Darling Weinstein)

(*Opposite, bottom*) Ruth and Groucho visit director Robert Florey at Lake Arrowhead in the early 1930s. The other guests are Gary Cooper and his wife on their honeymoon. The photo appears to be a composite because it was bent over two pages in an album. (Collection of Herman G. Weinberg)

Sam Marx poses with his sons at Paramount. This is the last time the Marx Brothers and "Frenchie" were photographed together.

Bert Granet took this photo of Harpo disguised as Groucho during a party at the Granets'. (Courtesy of Bert Granet)

King Vidor took this photo of tennis champions Ellsworth Vines and Fred Perry with Groucho and Charlie Chaplin, at the Beverly Hills Tennis Club in 1937.

I took this photo of Groucho and George Burns when we had lunch together at Groucho's in December 1974.

Melinda and Groucho in the early 1950s in a photo taken by friend Bert Granet. (Courtesy of Bert Granet)

Groucho asked me if I remembered when we talked with Adolph Zukor at Hillcrest Country Club. I said I did. "He's more than a hundred," he said. "I don't want to get to be that old."

Early on the morning of October 2, just before breakfast, Groucho and I looked out a window and saw the first of his "replicas" across the street. Sitting on the curb was a young man wearing the Groucho costume and mustache. We learned that he was Stephen Torrico, president of the Anaheim Groucho Marx Fan Club, which boasted 422 members. This was their birthday gift to Groucho. "We thought he would like it for his birthday to see us out here." Later that morning Andy and I left the house in search of some candleholders. By this time, the number of replica Grouchos had increased, and as we rode by, they called out:

"Do you know him? Do you know Groucho?"

"No, I don't," Andy responded, "but she does."

Reverently, one of them said, "It must be really great to be in there."

Groucho's parting words to us were, "I'll need eighty-five candles. On second thought, I'll use three. One for each of my ex-wives."

It had been decided to have two parties. The big party was to be held on the Sunday following Groucho's actual birthday. Another, more intimate party was held on Groucho's real birthday. This was a birthday dinner to which he invited Arthur Whitelaw, Dr. Morley Kert (Groucho's doctor) and his wife Bernice, Erin, and me. Also invited was actress Phyllis Newman, Adolph Green's wife, who arrived late, having been delayed by a TV talk show appearance.

Dr. Kert told how when Groucho came to his office he always advised everyone in the waiting room, "You've still got time to get out of here."

Groucho and Arthur Whitelaw reminisced about the opening of *Minnie's Boys* on Broadway. For the occasion, Arthur had wanted to present Groucho with an appropriate gift, but he couldn't think of what to get. Hearing that the old Ruppert brewery, near where Groucho grew up, was being torn down, Arthur rushed uptown to get one of the bricks. He took the brick to Tiffany's, where a silver plaque was made for it, and he gave it to Groucho on the opening night of *Minnie's Boys*.

Arthur had a joke for Groucho:

ARTHUR WHITELAW

Did you hear that they closed the Warsaw zoo? Their clam died.

GROUCHO

I don't understand.

ARTHUR WHITELAW

It wasn't much of a zoo.

GROUCHO

That wasn't much of a joke.

After Groucho blew out the candles (considerably fewer than eighty-five) on his cake, I asked him what he had wished, then added, "But perhaps you don't believe a wish should be told."

"I wished that my health remains good. Telling or not telling won't do it."

He helped cut the cake, then, in a moment of macabre inspiration, grinning fiendishly, he posed for a picture holding the knife to his throat.

In honor of the occasion, he discarded his normal regimen, and with reckless abandon devoured a heaping portion of the cake I had brought from New York.

"Thirty years ago I would have eaten the whole cake," he said. "I'm gonna eat this much if it kills me."

Finishing the last crumb, he added wistfully, "Nothing lasts forever."

After dinner Groucho opened the presents. Bud Cort gave him a T-shirt with the message "Bullshit" emblazoned across the chest.

"This'll be great to wear at Chasen's," Groucho said.

The Kerts gave him a cashmere sweater from Eric Ross.

"This'll come in handy when we get some hot weather," he said admiringly.

He seized the next box eagerly. "It's from Carroll and Company. That's where my son shops." In his excitement, he tore off the gift wrapping and ribbons, not heeding Erin's admonition to save them.

"We'd better have a lot of hot weather," he said on viewing yet another cashmere sweater. "This must be from my son, Arthur." He almost tore the card in half in his enthusiasm to read the greeting.

"Oh . . . It's from Irene, my son's first wife. It's made in Scotland." He paused. "Did you know my son was a great tennis player?"

Opening the Hermès box, Groucho took out the French silver duck dish I had given him. "I'll put nuts in this," he said. "Did you ever hear Bob Hope's line? 'California's full of fruits and nuts.' A great line."

I also brought Groucho a large chocolate bar from Krön that was decorated with a shapely female leg in a lace stocking. It read, "Have a high kickin' birthday!"

"I'm gonna put this under glass," he said appreciatively.

Nurse Linda gave him a plant with a card which read, "Let's come together to celebrate the day of your birth." Nurse Barbara's card said simply, "From the Barbara of Seville."

Goddard Lieberson couldn't think what to get for Groucho, so he composed some birthday music, inspired by his good friend the late Igor Stravinsky, who had written a *Greeting Prelude* for conductor Pierre Monteux on his eighty-fifth birthday. Goddard's song was called "Groucho's Day."

Disney Studios had sent a Walt Disney book with a picture of Mickey Mouse drawn on the inside front cover, wearing a greasepaint mustache and doing a Groucho imitation.

The gift that pleased Groucho most was Erin's. It was a hand-knitted Bordeaux sweater that she had ordered from Eric Ross. Knitted on the front of it was a portrait of Groucho.

Gifts had been pouring in all week, especially countless boxes of cigars sent by people who didn't know that Groucho had given up smoking. He donated these to charitable institutions. Many of the gifts were sent by people he had never met. The gifts that had preceded their givers by a few days had been mostly opened. Erin had neatly folded all the fancy gift wrapping paper and saved the ribbons.

After the gifts of birthday party number one had been unwrapped, inspected, and commented upon, Groucho felt the urge to sing. Arthur Whitelaw accompanied him on the piano while he sang "Peasie Weasie," "Show Me a Rose," and other Groucho specialties.

Phyllis Newman arrived, bringing with her a cassette greeting from Betty Comden and Adolph Green. "My mission was to get it to Groucho," she said breathlessly.

When Phyllis mentioned that she would like to have a picture of Groucho, he reminded her that Adolph already had one. She said that was exactly what she meant: "I want a picture of my own! I don't just want to be a messenger bearing the tape."

Groucho drank in her words, meditated briefly, then went to his bedroom. He returned with a photograph on which he had written, "This picture is for Phyllis, not for Adolph, not for Betty."

The tape that Phyllis had brought Groucho contained a comedy sketch about two screenwriters trying to get an idea for a screenplay. It was prefaced by some reminiscences about Groucho:

"We're thinking of years ago, when you used to come to parties, and you'd find out when we were going to be on. Then, when we finished, you'd say good night and leave. You had come to watch *us!* We were embarrassed, but pleased. We worshiped you from afar, and now from anear."

After listening to the tape, Groucho exclaimed, "Send them a telegram! Collect."

Dear Betty and Rudolph:

Long time no see. A good thing too. The record is uproarious. In spots it's even funny. You'll make a lot of money with this record. Especially if you don't release it. I love you both as if you were my own. More. Someday we'll meet in Heaven. New York. Or Philadelphia.

Sincerely yours,

H. Hackenbush

Groucho told us his favorite Betty Comden story:

"Betty said when she was seventeen, she stuffed a pillow under her dress so everyone thought she was going to have a baby. She got a seat on the subway every time."

Groucho returned to his singing with a song by Harry Ruby, "Omaha, Nebraska, in the Foothills of Tennessee." Afterward he commented soberly, "A part of my life went when Harry Ruby died, a very important part."

For another song, "Oh, How That Woman Could Cook!" he sang in a German accent, and asked Arthur Whitelaw to "play it in German."

"I can't play it in German," Arthur said in mock exasperation.

"You can't play it in German? Then what kind of pianist are you? Mozart could have played it in German. Marvin Hamlisch can play it in German."

Coincidentally, at this moment, Marvin's parents called from New York to wish Groucho a happy birthday. Mrs. Hamlisch sang "Happy Birthday" in German while Mr. Hamlisch accompanied her on the piano.

Numerous telegrams arrived. One was from Woody Allen, who said, "Happy Birthday. Now you owe me a telegram on my birthday." George Burns, who was out of town doing a show, wired Groucho, "Happy birthday. Don't stop. Keep busy." This emphasis on working—wanting to work and wanting to be able to work—was a value shared by George Burns and Groucho. King Vidor sent Groucho a card which read: "Happy birthday Groucho Segovia Marx from King Tildon Vidor." They both liked to play the guitar and tennis.

As he looked through all the telegrams and cards, Groucho commented, "I sent Johnny Carson a telegram for his thirteenth anniversary with NBC. I said, 'Better luck next time.' "

After the guests had gone home, Groucho squeezed my hand and said, "It's a night to remember." This was his *real* eighty-fifth birthday party. The one that was written about by the press and attended by celebrities took place on the afternoon of Sunday, October 5, 1975.

Groucho played a big part in the planning of birthday party number two. He always took his frivolity seriously. Besides Erin, Tom Wilhite assisted, arriving several hours ahead of time to help put up the decorations. These consisted mainly of balloons with "Groucho" written across them. There were so many that the décor that day could be described as "Early Balloon."

Shortly before four o'clock, when the party was scheduled to start, Groucho took the seat of honor in his living room, where he would receive the guests as they arrived. "This can't be much of a party if I'm the guest of honor," he said. "I may leave early."

The first to arrive were brothers Gummo and Zeppo, who had come from Palm Springs. They were forty minutes late. No one wants to arrive unfashionably first at a Hollywood party, so most parties usually start much later than the time announced on invitations.

Zeppo brought some tuna which he had personally caught and canned. Groucho accepted the token with his customary grace. "You needn't have bothered coming. You could've just sent the tuna." Zeppo understood and would, in fact, have been worried by any sign of greater sentiment from older brother Julius.

Whatever Zeppo does he does well—canning tuna, playing cards, inventing complex mechanical devices, or creating businesses. Uninhibited, and relatively unexhibited, Zeppo had the talent and energy to have been a pioneer, an inventor, a businessman, an agent—even a Marx Brother.

After Gummo's and Zeppo's arrival the guests began arriving until they started to overflow into other rooms and the patio. Eventually there was a long line of celebrities waiting to greet Groucho and wish him a happy birthday. He was asked again and again, "How does it feel to be eighty-five?" To amuse himself, he varied the answers:

"I'm crazy about eighty-five." Or, "It's better than eighty-four. I think I'll be eighty-six next year." Or, "I don't know why everyone's making such a fuss. I didn't get older in one day." He added more soberly, "They think you get a year older in a day, and all of you gets old at once. It's a part at a time."

Milton Berle asked him how he felt. "Clever," Groucho answered.

Elliott Gould greeted him with, "How are you, Grouch?"

"Compared to what?" Groucho asked.

Among those who gathered around him were Bob Hope, Peter Sellers, Jack Lemmon, Walter Mirisch, Sally Kellerman, Red Buttons, Carroll O'Connor, Liza Minnelli, Carl Reiner, David Steinberg, Edie Adams, S. M. Estridge, Irwin Allen, Stefanie Powers, Jacque Jones, Jerry Davis, Nat Perrin, Carol Burnett, and a few hundred others. After the general mixing, Bob Hope emceed and Groucho sang. The age range at the party was from eighteen to ninety. "Same as the IQs," quipped Groucho.

As he sat down to cut his giant strawberry birthday cake, he announced:

"Eighty-five and I'm still in perfect health—except mentally."

He was helped in blowing out the eighty-five candles by Edie Adams, the actress he would most have liked to play his mother in *Minnie's Boys*.

When Groucho started to sing, the guests all gathered about and listened intently. Far from being inhibited by the audience of celebrities, he relished it and was most at home performing for a gathering of discerning show people. Actually, those who have to stand up there alone on stage center themselves may be more generous in their approval than a "civilian" audience. There was nothing Groucho enjoyed more than singing, and as soon as he took his place beside the piano, the din of conversation ceased instantly. The refugees to the patio returned to the living room. The attention of all, whether they were sitting in chairs, standing, or sitting on the floor, was fixed on the star. Groucho called for a chord: "I'd like a chord, but a rope will do."

A mistake in the lyrics of one of the old songs made the empathetic audience feel more like insiders, and Groucho's own performance soared to greater heights as he felt the reverent enthusiasm of his audience. Liza Minnelli, in black pants and a shimmering silver sweater, sat on the floor at Groucho's feet working harder as a member of the audience than most people work as performers. She whispered to Jack Haley, Jr., who also nodded appreciatively. Between numbers, she rushed up and embraced Groucho.

When he sang "Oh, How That Woman Could Cook!" with Billy Marx accompanying him on the piano, Groucho nodded to Grace Kahn. She was at the party with her daughter, Irene, and Andy, one of the grandsons she and Groucho had in common. Grace Kahn had written this song with her husband Gus in 1916. While he was singing, Groucho looked at her several times.

"Are you cutting an album or something?" Bob Hope called out. Groucho said softly to the assemblage, "This guy has made me laugh."

"You don't *have* to say that," Hope rejoined.

"If you weren't here I wouldn't say it," snapped Groucho.

For the grand finale, Erin and Robin joined Groucho in some choruses of "Peasie Weasie." Robin had sung this song many times with Erin for Groucho privately. Afterward Groucho announced that he had paid only twenty-five dollars for this medley of doggerel. "I guess you got your money's worth," Erin commented dryly.

When Groucho sang, Elliott Gould stopped blowing up and tossing about balloons. After the song, Elliott commented, "That was very good."

"I used to be in show business," Groucho responded.

Following Groucho, Morgan Ames played and sang one of her own songs, and Bud Cort sang a song which he concluded with a perfect ragdoll backward flop on the floor.

Groucho was always the center of attention. Whenever he would say something, there were reverent echoes around the room of "Did you hear what he said?" Groucho, hearing this, editorialized, ironically, "Yeah, great line."

After the entertainment had ended, he said, "I'm not sleepy. I guess I'll go to bed," adding, "The pâté is over," as he adjourned to his bedroom.

"Always leave 'em laughing when you say goodbye," Groucho added. He slipped away relatively unnoticed, as he liked to do.

Repairing to his bedroom, he donned pajamas and received *en pantoufles*, then later in bare feet. Groucho could appear formidable even in his pajamas. With his bare feet sticking out from under the covers of his push-button bed, he informed guests who entered the sanctum sanctorum, "I've got the cleanest feet in town. It's one of my few distinctions." Welcome guests were some of Hollywood's prettiest girls, who he invited to get under the covers with him; he also invited favored male friends. That's how *People* magazine got the picture of Sally Struthers and Carroll O'Connor sitting in bed with him. *People* covered the event, if not the bed, calling it "You Bed Your Life." (Jon Nordheimer of the *New York Times* was also invited.) The picture turned out to be prophetic, for shortly afterward, Groucho's first book, *Beds*, was reissued after being out of print for more than forty years.

Beds were always important to Groucho. This one had a control panel which allowed him to tilt it in any direction he wished. Woody Allen had been intrigued by it, but said he wasn't asking any specific questions. The backboard consisted of the massive doors of a nineteenth-century circus wagon, rescued from an ignominious fate to serve again in a less peripatetic role. Over the bed was a picture of two little houses that reminded Groucho of the Marx family's Chicago home on Grand Avenue. "It isn't really the house we lived in, but it looks like it," he told guests who "dropped into bed."

After Groucho left the main party, the remaining guests made themselves at home, ate the food, visited with each other, gossiped about those who had left, and had the run of the house, except for the master's bedroom. The party ended about eight-thirty, which is not unusual for Hollywood parties. The successful Hollywood people have to get up early.

After the party, Groucho summed up his eighty-five years:

"I've been lucky. That's the most important thing to be—lucky."

"I look like George Washington with a mustache"

For many years Groucho shunned interviews because of how he felt about interviewers. "They don't listen to you," he told me. For a time he was so reluctant to do any interviews at all that it was difficult for even his grandson, Andy, to manage one with him.

"I was in college," Andy told me, "and I was taking a class called Art of Comedy, and I thought I'd do an interview with Groucho. I had a tape recorder with me and he said, 'Nobody interviews me with a tape recorder.' He said, 'Even for ten thousand dollars, I wouldn't let *Life* magazine use a tape recorder. You'll have to write everything down on cards,' which I did. About halfway through he told me I was a lousy interviewer, that I had no questions, I didn't know how to interview anybody, and all that stuff."

Eric Lax accompanied Groucho to Ames, Iowa, for Groucho's opening "concert," and he covered the event for *Life*. He told me that in interviewing Groucho, "I was more nervous than I'd ever been interviewing anyone before. I wanted to get every word, but he told me I couldn't use a recorder. I listened as hard as I could, drove away a short distance, and scribbled frantically."

After that, Groucho changed his mind, and we did the interview out of which grew the friendship out of which grew this book.

I
How do you see yourself?
GROUCHO
In a mirror.

I
What sort of person looks back at you?

GROUCHO

A backward person.

I

How would you describe that person?

GROUCHO

Well over four feet tall. (*Raising his eyebrows*) Did you ever see Lincoln without a beard?

I

No.

GROUCHO

Well, I look like George Washington with a mustache. That's from *On the Mezzanine*. Where do you want to begin, in the middle?

I

We might try the beginning. What was your childhood like?

GROUCHO

A knock came on the front door and everyone in the house hid in the closet or someplace. Because we didn't have the rent. My mother would go to the door and talk the landlord out of the twenty-seven dollars a month we owed.

Harpo used to skate in Central Park on the reservoir with one skate. And he used to have to tie it on with a rope. I was poor and thrifty. I saved up for four jawbreakers. I was sucking on one with three under my hat. There were some big bullies approaching. I said, "I don't have anymore." One of them hit me. I was thirty minutes lying in the snow. Then I took one of the jawbreakers out from under my hat and sucked on it.

We slept four in a bed. Two at each end. There were ten of us and one toilet. That I call pretty poor, but we didn't know it. We were happy. We loved our mother and father.

I

Then you didn't mind being poor?

GROUCHO

I always wanted to be rich. I still want to be rich.

I

But I've often heard you say, "I'm a very rich man."

GROUCHO

I'm a lucky man.

I

What did you feel being rich meant?

GROUCHO

You can support poor relatives if you have some. You can buy decent clothes, you can afford to have a decent automobile, you can afford to live in a nice house—I think I'm very lucky to have all those things.

I

When did you begin feeling rich?

GROUCHO

When I could stop and pick up something off the street without looking first to see if anyone was watching me. Of course, you can do that when you're really poor, too. And when you're rich you don't have to eat everything on your plate. You don't have to look at the prices first when they give you a menu in a restaurant. You walk because you feel like walking. And they can't come and take away the piano.

I

Tell me about your adopted sister, Polly.

GROUCHO

Polly was my mother's sister's baby, and when the baby was born, her husband ran away. She was left alone with the baby. And my mother adopted Polly and raised her. She had a big behind, but she was kinda pretty. She wore glasses. So, there was a tailor named Sam Müller, with two dots over the *u*. He was a good tailor. My father was a lousy tailor. My father could never make a suit properly 'cause Chico always stole the scissors and then hocked 'em. But Sam Müller, with two dots over the *u*, was a good tailor. He used to make suits for fifty dollars. That was a lot of money in those days, when bread was a nickel a loaf. And four cents for the day-old bread. My mother was determined to hook Sam Müller into marrying Polly. Now, my mother had my father cook a good meal, because he was a good cook and invited Sam over a few times, and said that Polly had cooked the dinner. My mother finally persuaded Sam to marry Polly. The wedding was in the Bronx at the Royal Casino. Harpo and I went in the lavatory, and there were two urinals there. We jumped up and down on these, and they sheared off. The water started running where the marriage was taking place. And the landlord of the casino came rushing out, and he said, "That'll be two hundred dollars." Now, we didn't have ten dollars, so Sam Müller had to put up the money, the two hundred dollars to get the urinals repaired. Then the wedding went on. And they lived happily ever after. They had four children.

I

After that did he ever notice Polly's cooking?

GROUCHO

Probably, but they were happy. Anyway, it was too late. He was hooked. I told you it was through my father's cooking that my mother got plenty of jobs for us.

I

What were his specialties?

GROUCHO

Oh, he could make anything, including my mother. Which he frequently did. Funny thing—my father was a Frenchman and my brother was an Italian. That's why I always wear a beret. My father was born in Alsace-Lorraine. He thought Ed Sullivan was a Jew. He used to call him "Ed Solomon." My father never hit us. He would take a whiskbroom when he was angry, and he would bring it up here, right by your nose, and he'd keep telling you what was wrong with you. But he never hit us. And he'd put the whisk broom down. He'd say, "*Junger, junger junger . . .*" He spoke *Plattdeutsch*. He was a lousy tailor. He would make a suit, and one sleeve would be down to here, and the other one would be up to here. But he always got new customers because he could speak *Plattdeutsch*.

I

And your mother?

GROUCHO

She was busy. She was always busy trying to get us jobs. She gathered us all together. She was a great woman. My father was always faithful to her, until she died. Then he got himself another girl. But not at the funeral! He liked girls—we all liked girls. There were no fags in the Marx family.

I

Did your father enjoy being an extra in your films?

GROUCHO

No, but he got ten dollars, and he was trying to make one of the girls. He finally wound up with a dame.

I

Did you mind? You cared so much about your mother . . .

GROUCHO

No. She was dead, and he was lonely. He died at the Garden of Allah.

I

And your grandparents?

GROUCHO

My grandmother played the harp and yodeled. This was in Germany. My grandfather was a ventriloquist and a magician.

I

Did you learn any magic tricks?

GROUCHO

No. I don't have any tricks. I have no talent at all. I can barely open a window.

I

Your grandfather lived to be a healthy 101.

GROUCHO

That I'm not worrying about. I won't make that. But he did live a long, long time, and there was never anything wrong with him. Except he ate everything in the house. He was a big eater.

I

What was your boyhood in New York City like?

GROUCHO

I think I told you about Weatherall, didn't I? I was an office boy on Pine Street. Offices were about the size of my bed. And I had to get to work at nine o'clock every morning. My job was, if Weatherall had any letters, to shove them into this thing there and turn the wheel and press them in a book. It pressed the letters. And I was getting three dollars a week.

I

What was the purpose of pressing the letters?

GROUCHO

I haven't the faintest idea. He didn't get many letters. I was supposed to be there at nine o'clock every morning. So I was there. And I had a bag of grapes. That was my lunch. And the next day I was there at nine o'clock, but Weatherall didn't come in. So the next day, I came in at ten o'clock. Then I started getting in at eleven o'clock, and he still didn't get in. So I was walking down Park Row. It was windy, and somebody's hat blew off. I ran out in the middle of the street to grab the hat to bring it back. And it was Weatherall. I got fired. I was going to the ballpark that day. (*Pause*) Did I tell you about how we used to stand in front of the theatre three-sheeting after the show and pick up girls?

I

I don't understand three-sheeting . . .

GROUCHO

We'd stand in front of the posters. It took three sheets to make a poster. So I picked up a girl one day, and she was pushing a baby carriage. I spoke to her, and I says, "You're a very pretty girl. Are you married?" She says, "No, this is my sister's baby." She was lying; it was her baby. She took me to her apartment, and I was smoking a cigar. Suddenly, I hear the sound of footsteps. So I run to the closet, but I left the cigar laying there, on the couch. And the guy comes in. He's about eight feet tall. He says, "There's a man in here." She says, "There is not." "What is that cigar doing here?" He looks in the closet. "If I find the son of a bitch," he said, "I'll kill him." And he felt in the closet, but there was a lot of clothes in there, and he didn't feel me. The minute he went in the kitchen, I jumped out the window.

I

What floor were you on?

GROUCHO

The first. In Chicago, Gummo and I had a car together. It was $300. We each put in $150. And we didn't know anything about automobiles. I knew one thing: the car had no brakes. And it had no horn. And it had no top to it. We had a couple of girls on the North Side of Chicago that we wanted to go to see. Every time that we wanted to go and see 'em, Zeppo would take the ignition out of the car. He knew a lot about a car. He could take the whole car apart and take all the different parts of the engine and put the whole thing together again. And we didn't know anything about a car at all. So whenever we wanted to go to the North Side to meet these girls, Zeppo would take the ignition out. We'd have to go on the elevated every time we wanted to meet 'em, 'cause he was using the car. I had a Scripps-Booth at one time. Scripps-Booth, hyphenated. It was an automobile you never heard of. I paid $200 for it. And I had a thing on the door—if you pressed that, the door would open. I took a girl out one night, and accidentally she pressed that thing and she flew out of the car. Then I took another girl out. She was all dressed up. She had on a pink dress and lovely hat, and we went to the Majestic Theatre. When we came out it was raining. And when we got to her house, she was soaking wet. Her hat was ruined, her dress was ruined, and everything else was ruined. When I took her home, her father came to the door. He says, "If you ever come to this house again, I'll kill ya!" So I never went back there. She was a beautiful girl. Now I don't even remember her name. I was so scared, I was glad to get out of there. We played in a colored theatre in Chicago. I never told you this. It was called the Pekin. And Jack Johnson came to visit the theatre one night. He was gonna fight Jim Jeffries for the world's championship, in which, incidentally, he knocked out Jeffries. And we used to do a song there. (*Singing*) " 'I'd like to be a friend of yours, and a little bit more. I'd like to see ya, and a little bit more.' " And we saw Johnson sitting in the box, and we had the parody arranged so Jeffries would knock out Johnson. But with Johnson in the box that night, we changed the lyric, making it Johnson knocking out Jeffries, which he actually did. All black audience. On State Street, Thirty-first and State. And he came backstage after the show, and we met him in the saloon. He had on a silk shirt—a handsome man. I told you about the three shirts, didn't I?

I
Yes. But tell me again.

GROUCHO
Chico had picked up a girl. Chico was always picking up girls, picking up girls for all of us. And we were living in a boardinghouse in Brooklyn. It was gaslit; it didn't have electricity. We could turn the gas very low so you couldn't see who you were screwing, if you wanted to. So we had bought three silk shirts—silk shirts with a black stripe down each one. Harpo had one, and I had one, Chico had one. I was in bed sleeping when Chico comes into my room. He says, "You wanna get laid?" I says, "Yeah." "Well, put on your silk shirt and come into my room." Which I proceeded to do. And I laid her a couple of times. Then he went to Harpo's room. He said, "You wanna get laid?" Harpo said, "Yes." "Well, put on your silk shirt and go into my room. I have a girl in there." So he went in there and laid her a couple of times. And then Chico came back and laid her again. And she didn't know who we were, 'cause the gaslight was low, and we were all wearing the same silk shirts. And the next morning we were standing by the stage door of the Bushwick Theatre in Brooklyn when Chico introduced her to Harpo and me. (*Pause*) Did I ever tell you how I lost my virginity? It was in Montreal. You don't forget a thing like that. She didn't have a room, and she picked me up. I was sixteen years old. Before I left town I had gonorrhea. You know, they say that once you get gonorrhea you have it the rest of your life. It's partly true. I didn't know anything about girls. Chico lost his virginity to the first girl he met. Zeppo was big with the dames too. Harpo was the one that didn't fool around much. He had a few dames. But Harpo only had three girls in his life that he was really stuck on, and they were all named Fleming. The last one, he married. Susan Fleming.

I
And for you, there's Erin Fleming. Is that a coincidence?

GROUCHO
No. It's no coincidence.

I
How would you describe Harpo in real life?

GROUCHO
Harpo was a beautiful man. He was shorter than I was. Not much, a couple of inches. He was always sitting down, playing the goddamn harp. And I hated the harp. I always walked out of the theatre when the harp came on. I'd heard it for so many years, it drove me crazy. It's not my favorite instrument, but I didn't mind it because at least it was soft. Harpo used to work hard playing the harp. Because by this time he was very

proud. There weren't very many harp players in vaudeville, you know. Harpo worked hard and conscientiously, and Chico never did. Harpo's harp's in Israel now. I don't know where Harpo is.

I

Do you think that you and Harpo were the most alike?

GROUCHO

And Gummo. Gummo and Helen, that's a real love affair. They've been married over fifty years. Gummo was handsome when he was young.

I

What was Gummo's part with the Marx Brothers?

GROUCHO

He played a Jew comedian. Gummo and I always roomed together when we were on the road. Harpo and Chico didn't room together. Chico was always looking for dames and crap games, card games. Chico was a show-off when he played cards. If he was playing you, and he could beat you easily—let's say he was playing for a thousand points, pinochle, whatever it was—he would say to the other one, "Look, this is too easy. You only have to make eight on the points, and I have to make a thousand." On the other hand, Harpo was a very shrewd gambler. He was a very shrewd poker player. He used to play with Franklin P. Adams and Woollcott and George Kaufman, and people like that, and he always came home with the money. 'Cause he wasn't a gambler; he played to win, that's all. And Chico was a show-off. Zeppo was a good card player. Gin rummy, I think. He was a funny man, Zeppo. Very funny.

I

I think he's still funny.

GROUCHO

Yeah. He's a funny man. He went on once for me in Chicago, you know. When I had my appendix taken out. And he got great reviews.

I

You said it made you hurry and get well faster.

GROUCHO

I got out of the hospital as fast as I could.

I

It wasn't like the understudy in *Cocoanuts* who had a nervous breakdown when he had to go on for you.

GROUCHO

That's right. He went crazy. Not Zeppo. He could have been a very funny comedian. Zeppo likes you.

I

He was going to play cards when I saw him.

GROUCHO

That's what broke up their marriage, you know. Barbara was living in the house that I owned in Palm Springs, and now she's married to Sinatra. Beautiful girl. (*Pause*) Chico was a great pool player. We would go to some town, and he would play anybody in the town and beat him. He was a *great* pool player. But he got mixed up with gamblers. I know when we were playing in Detroit, he disappeared for a whole week. Harpo and I had to do the whole show without him.

I

You must have been very disturbed.

GROUCHO

You bet I was. He was gambling up in Windsor. Once Harpo and I decided we weren't gonna make any more movies with him. We said, "When you get your salary, we're gonna handle it for you." And we had $200,000 saved. One day he came and he said, "I have to have the money, 'cause the gamblers are after me." So we gave him the $200,000, 'cause they would have killed him. Chico was sick. He was a compulsive gambler, and you're sick when you do that. But he had a great time.

I

You and Harpo thought ahead.

GROUCHO

We were both sensible. Chico died broke, but he had a great time.

I

Maybe that's what's important.

GROUCHO

It was Harpo I admired. He was steady. He married and had a good marriage and adopted four children and raised them well. I respected him. For Chico, the next best thing to gambling and winning was gambling and losing. Even when he lost, Chico enjoyed it. He said he had the pleasure of thinking he was going to win. And then, when it was over and he'd lost, he had the pleasure of thinking he was going to win the next time. Chico's philosophy was, "It's better to have lost and lost than never to have lost at all." (*Pause*) Did I tell you about Harpo being locked in the room with the rats?

I

Not yet.

GROUCHO

I was very young. We used to go to the hookshops then. We were in a hookshop one night . . . as a matter of fact, we were always in hookshops. We were the hit of the hookshops. It was the only place you could get laid in a strange town. They didn't want any actors. In a lot of towns they used to hide their daughters. We were in Cincinnati. In those days, the hookers used to come to the shows, and if they liked your act, they would send you a note backstage that you could come up and visit 'em if you wanted to. So we were a big hit in those places. Harpo and Chico both played the piano, and I sang.

We went to one house where Harpo had apparently insulted one of the girls. So she invited him upstairs, and opened the door, and put him in a room there. There was nothing in it but a cot. He took off his clothes, and there came the squealing of rats from the other side of the room. So he started to throw his clothes at them to scare them away. And then one of the hookers opened the door and let him out, and he ran down a whole flight of stairs. When he got to the sidewalk, he looked upstairs, and there were these five hookers laughing at him.

I

How do you think Harpo insulted the girl?

GROUCHO

I don't remember. 'Cause we were always very nice to the girls. Faulkner once said the ideal place to live was in a whorehouse. So he bought a house, and he rented the upstairs to these hookers. And he slept downstairs. It was good because they worked all night, and he worked all day writing. He was a great writer too. Have you ever read *Beds*?

I

Yes, I read it in bed. I located a copy of the original edition.

GROUCHO

It's one of the funniest things I've written—that and a check for ten dollars. It's a funny book about beds, various things that go on in beds. How we make love with the girls, or how they reject you, which they frequently do.

I

How did you feel about being rejected?

GROUCHO

I felt much better about being injected. Beds are more important than you think. We spend a lot of our lives in bed. I've had women put me to sleep by talking. They talk more than men, I think. In a lot of cases they have nothing to say. I like a woman to be a good listener, because I never stop talking.

I

Why do you suppose some women talk so much?

GROUCHO

They want to attract attention. It's like putting perfume on, raising a big stink. Or getting all dressed up.

I

What kind of clothes do you like to see a woman wear?

GROUCHO

None, if possible. Well, it depends on the woman. If it's a girl I was crazy about, I'd like to see her naked.

I

You say that sex and passion are behind you these days. Do other things become important and take the place of passion and sex?

GROUCHO

I don't think of it at all now. I like to see a good-looking woman—that's about as far as it goes.

I

When you were younger, was it something you thought about a lot?

GROUCHO

Well, not every minute. I could get a dame now and have her go down on me, but what good is it? If you're not stuck on the girl, what good is it? Unless there's love, what's the point?

I

Some of the stories printed about you present a different picture.

GROUCHO

I guess I'd know better than they would what I'm interested in. They come and ask you questions, but they don't listen to the answer. I'll be glad when I can go into the store and buy a copy of your book about me.

I

I'll be glad too. But *you* won't have to buy it.

GROUCHO

I want to buy one for everyone I know. Are you gonna have it ready for Christmas?

I

Yes, but not this one.

GROUCHO

Why don't you sell it in January? Then it's the book you can get when you bring back the Christmas present you didn't want. I want to tell you a story, but I gotta go to the men's room first.

I

Should I record that comment for posterity?

GROUCHO

"No matter how rich you are, occasionally you have to go to the can." I said that once when I was talking to a women's club. (*Leaves and returns*) I was going to tell you a story. No, I was going to tell you two stories. If I can think of 'em. One was in Chicago. There was a fortune-teller, a big black woman who told fortunes. My wife Ruth wanted to go. You paid five dollars. They passed around a hat, and you put in five dollars. First there were two great big colored fellows that came out dressed in some kind of uniforms with epaulets and all that stuff. They said, "Now Madam Zaza is gonna go and do her dream. And when she comes out, she'll answer any question that you wanna ask her." And they were burning incense all around, and it stunk like hell. I felt like vomiting. Well, anyhow, she emerged finally from this trance and says, "Now, I'll answer any question that you wanna ask." And I said, "What's the capital of North Dakota?" And the two big colored fellows grabbed me and hustled me out of the place.

I

Do you remember the capital of North Dakota?

GROUCHO

Fargo, of course.

I

And what's the other story. You said you had two stories.

GROUCHO

Wait until I think about it. I'm ready. There used to be a prizefighter, before your time. His name was Jack Root and he had been a heavyweight prizefighter who owned this theatre in Iowa. He was a real tough guy. So I used to rehearse the music for the show while the boys were home sleeping. 'Cause I was the only singer in the act. And I came in smoking a cigar. So he said, "That'll cost you five dollars." I said, "For what?" "You know it's against the law to smoke a cigar in the theatre." There had just been a big fire in Chicago, and two hundred people burned up. So I went to the boys, and I said, "I'm not gonna pay that five dollars." It was Christmas. Chico was always the great conciliator, and he said to this guy, Jack Root, "We'll put up five dollars if you put up five dollars, and we'll throw it all in the Salvation Army pot." So we did that, and we were getting $900 for the act. We had about twenty people in the act. So, we were leaving on the train at eleven o'clock, and it was nine-thirty. He paid all the money in pennies. All the $900. We had to get on the floor and count them, to see that we got the whole $900. We got on the train finally without scenery. As the train started, we were on the observation car. And Harpo said, "I hope that son of a bitch's theatre burns to the ground." The next morning we picked up the paper in Waterloo, and it was burned to the ground the night before.

I

Sometimes the stories you tell conflict with some other stories you have told. Which version should I believe, the first version, or the latest?

GROUCHO

Both. I'm a liar.

I

Did you and your brothers share a common sense of humor?

GROUCHO

It wasn't common. We each had our own. We all had a good sense of humor.

I

Did you ever not agree on what was funny?

GROUCHO

No. We got along fine. We didn't quarrel.

I

What do you feel was the real turning point in your career?

GROUCHO

That was *I'll Say She Is,* which we did before I knew Kaufman or Ryskind. We took the play because Chico had talked a guy in Philadelphia who owned a couple of coal mines and a pretzel factory into putting up the money. Also the guy was stuck on one of the girls in the chorus, who Harpo was also laying, which he didn't know. Originally the play was called *The Thrill Girl,* but we got together a lot of old scenery and changed the name. *I'll Say She Is* was a big success in Philadelphia. It was a real stinker, but now we felt we were ready for the big time, so we took it to New York, where Woollcott liked it. It was really hot that summer in Philadelphia, but the hot weather only makes a difference when you're as old as I am now.

Harding died that summer, and they asked me to make a speech about it during the intermission. It was raining that day, and the theatre had a tin roof, and the rain beat down on the roof while I was talking. I remember that because it was so eerie. You remember when I went to do the Mike Douglas show in Philadelphia? You didn't come, but I went to the theatre, and it was changed. But it still had the tin roof.

I

Did you always know you were going to be successful?

GROUCHO

No. Chico did. And he did the least work in the act. But he said, "We won't always be playing these dumps." And Chico got the guy who owned the coal mine to put up the money for us to become big time.

I

You told me Chico also persuaded Irving Thalberg to hire you at M-G-M after your Paramount contract expired.

GROUCHO

Yes, he did. Chico was a smooth character. He would be talking long distance on the phone to one dame and having his hat blown by another at the same time. Or else he'd be off in a crap game somewhere. Chico was a lost soul.

I

Before you went with Thalberg, you considered making pictures with Samuel Goldwyn.

GROUCHO

We'd been negotiating between Sam Goldwyn and Thalberg, and he says, "Look, if Thalberg wants you, go to him, because he has more talent in one finger than I have in my whole body."

I

I know you have great respect for Irving Thalberg.

GROUCHO

I think he was a great producer. Sam Wood was the director, but Thalberg came every morning and looked at the rushes for every scene we shot. And if he didn't like them, he'd make Sam Wood shoot them over again. He was the Boss. I remember the first time we met him. I met him with Chico. This was one day Chico wasn't in a crap game or chasing some broad. Chico played bridge with Thalberg, and had gotten into a gambling debt with him. He talked Thalberg into hiring us to get him out of hock. That's how we got our contract.

I

What do you remember about *Humorisk,* the first movie you made?

GROUCHO

Never saw it. We only made two reels over at Fort Lee, and Jo Swerling worked on it. But we were playing at the Palace Theatre at the time, and we used to run over to Weehawken and do a scene. We did two reels, which didn't make any sense at all. It was just trying to be funny. And that's all. It disappeared. I don't know who has it. No film of that around.

I

There's a rumor that someone left it on the subway . . .

GROUCHO

Not true.

I

You told me no one directed it.

GROUCHO

No. Because there was nothing to direct.

I

Who paid for it?

GROUCHO

We did. We wanted to be movie actors. We wanted to be in the movies. And we thought this was a good way to get into the movies. So, we made two reels of this. And then we stopped.

I

Do you have a favorite Marx Brothers film?

GROUCHO

I liked the war picture [*Duck Soup*] and *Horse Feathers,* and I liked parts of *Animal Crackers.* But I guess my favorite is *A Night at the Opera.*

I

Why is it your favorite?

GROUCHO

The best made. It has great scenes in it—great funny scenes.

I

What are some of the scenes you particularly like?

GROUCHO

Well, certainly the scene in the stateroom where I'm meeting this lady, Mrs. Claypool, and when she arrives at the room, fourteen people come out. I'm having a rendezvous with her. You can't do that with fourteen people! I also liked the contract scene—that was a fine scene. Good Kaufman and Ryskind.

I

What other scenes from your movies did you particularly like?

GROUCHO

Well, there are those two scenes at the beginning of *Animal Crackers* where Chico's a musician. And the scene with Zeppo where I'm a lawyer dictating a letter to Hungerdunger, Hungerdunger, Hungerdunger, Hungerdunger, and McCormick. I take a swing at him. That was great. Not only that—we had an imitation of Lunt and Fontanne, and a show that they were doing at that particular time, while we were doing *Animal Crackers.*

I

Strange Interlude.

GROUCHO

Yes. They were playing it on the square across the street, while we were doing it on the stage as a kidding scene where I was making love to two women — Rittenhouse and another woman.

I

You knew Bert Kalmar and Harry Ruby before *Animal Crackers* . . .

GROUCHO

Yes, I knew Kalmar and Ruby when I was in vaudeville. Ruby was a song plugger at Waterson, Berlin, and Snyder. I had gone there to learn a song, and Ruby was a song plugger then. And Kalmar always wanted to be a magician. Later on, when we toured during the First World War, Ruby played the piano and I sang and Kalmar did magic. We played in one place that was a federal prison. There were a lot of people there who were deserters from the Army. And it was a great audience. They were in there and couldn't get out. They couldn't walk out on us. Kalmar originally was an acrobat, and then he got into show business. Ruby wrote the music and Kalmar wrote the lyrics. Kalmar died many years ago. I must tell you a story about Ruby.

We were doing *Animal Crackers,* and we decided, as each one's birthday arrived, we would give him a bathrobe. So, Kaufman got a bathrobe, the four boys each got bathrobes. When the time came to give Ruby a bathrobe, we had decided not to give any more bathrobes. So we said we're tired of giving bathrobes. We didn't see any reason why we should give Ruby a bathrobe, but he had always chipped in for our bathrobes. So when we did *Animal Crackers,* we had a scene with a trunk. It was as big as this couch. And one night the top of this thing opens up, and there's Ruby standing there and saying, "Where is my bathrobe?" It had nothing to do with the show.

I

What did you think about his doing that?

GROUCHO

I thought it was very funny. I laughed. To see a strange man come out of a piece of African furniture and ask, "Where is my bathrobe?"

I

Did he get his bathrobe?

GROUCHO

Yes. You're too young to remember Walter Huston, but he had this berth under me on the train when we we were traveling in vaudeville, and he was laying this girl. Well, I had a lot of coat hangers in the upper berth — which you had in those days to hang your clothes on — and I kept throwing the coat hangers down on him while he was laying her. I always remind his son, John Huston, about it.

I

Life on trains apparently used to be more colorful.

GROUCHO

All sorts of things happened. Once there was this magic act, and there were six men in the act. All Chinese. And Chico had been up in the upper berth and had an affair with some hooker, or whatever she was, on the train. Then he invited all the Chinese to climb up this ladder to the upper berth, and they all laid her.

I

All together?

GROUCHO

No, one after the other. As the one came down, the next one went up the ladder.

I

All of this really happened on trains?

GROUCHO

Yeah! We were actors, and we used to pick out a lot of stuff. Our shows helped. We did a big act with W. C. Fields, and we had twenty girls in the act. It was a school act. And there was quite some humping went on there! And we used to ride motorcycles from town to town, too. With four girls on each one — two in the back and two in the front. The four of us had motorcycles.

I

How did you manage your luggage? There couldn't have been much room left on the motorcycle with you and two girls in front and two in back.

GROUCHO

We sent our luggage by train.

I

How long did you travel this way?

GROUCHO

Through the whole interstates tour. That was Montgomery, Alabama, and Birmingham, Alabama, and Fort Worth, Dallas, and San Antonio. And two other cities. At one time Harpo and I had a race. To see who could ride the motorcycle the fastest. I had an Indian motorcycle, and Harpo had a Henderson. And we're racing along this country road, and we hit a mule. And killed it. We got away from there as fast as we could. This was when we were playing small towns. I was about twenty. We had a cap tied right to your head so it wouldn't blow off. And goggles. We were crazy about motorcycles and later on became crazy about automobiles. A motorcycle cost about $150.

I

That was a lot of money then.

GROUCHO

But look at the money we saved in traveling. And we loved the motorcycles. It was exciting.

I

You didn't have your mustache in those days, or your famous walk, or the eyebrows . . .

GROUCHO

I had eyebrows. I didn't have a mustache. I hardly needed to shave. When I was the teacher I wore a white wig, I looked like I was a hundred years old. The act was called *Mr. Green's Reception*. When it started off, I was the teacher and there were the kids in the classroom. Then it was ten years later, and they had all come back to see me. It got to be very dramatic. We had a bowl on the stage with lemonade, and Harpo would stick his whole head in the bowl. Harpo liked lemonade. Harpo loved children. We were doing the football picture. There's a little girl, that high. She's five years old. And the cutest little girl I ever saw. Harpo was crazy about her. And he offered her parents $50,000 if they would let him take this little girl. Of course, they wouldn't do it. But it turns out to be Shirley Temple.

I

You were quoted once as saying, "We always played to ourselves rather than the audience."

GROUCHO

No, you've got it wrong. We always played *with* ourselves.

I

There must have been times when you had personal problems and had to go onstage when you didn't feel like it. What if you had a bad cold?

GROUCHO

When I was out there, I didn't feel it. When you're onstage, that's all you're thinking about.

I

Were you ever nervous before going on?

GROUCHO

I was never nervous, because I knew I was better than the audience. You have to feel that way or you can't get up there and do what you have to do. The first time Harpo went on, he shit in his pants. I missed a few shows, but not many. That one time, Zeppo had to go on for me, and he did well. Zeppo did all of us at one time or another. But of course he couldn't play the harp or piano.

I

Do you mind not being up there in the spotlight anymore?

GROUCHO

No, I had it long enough.

I

If you were younger, is there a particular part you'd like to play?

GROUCHO

Rip Van Winkle. I think it would make a great show.

I

If you were older, is there a particular part you'd like to play?

GROUCHO

Yes. Rip Van Winkle.

I

Betty [Comden] and Adolph [Green] told me that you found *Gypsy* for them, even though they didn't do it, and that you have a great eye for discovering potentially successful shows, as well as performers. For yourself, would you consider a small but interesting part in a dramatic film, not a comedy, if such an offer came along?

GROUCHO

I don't know. It would depend on the part and if the hours were short. I'm a better judge when it's comedy.

I

Was there ever a part that you would have liked to play that you didn't play?

GROUCHO

I would have liked to play in *My Fair Lady.*

I

The Rex Harrison part?

GROUCHO

I wouldn't have been a good Liza Doolittle. And I would have liked to play in *The Matchmaker.* I was asked to, but I sent the play back to them and told them it needed work. Ruth Gordon played it—took it to England. She wanted me to go along. It was a damned good play.

I
Are you happiest when you're working?

GROUCHO
It depends. I was happy working with Bill Cosby. It was all ad-libbed. We had a few signs there, but the guy kept mixing up the signs. I had a lot of fun with Cosby. He's a very funny man. Sure, I enjoy working and want to work. It gives me a chance to sing and to talk about many things, and it's great.

I
You wouldn't like to be retired completely?

GROUCHO
I could get along. I'd get a massage and take a walk and go see Nunnally and see *That's Entertainment* again with Erin. I've seen it three times. It's great. But I'm not gonna retire.

I
Would you say you enjoy performing more than anything else?

GROUCHO
No, I wouldn't say that. I like girls better.

I
What do you think makes things funny?

GROUCHO
That's an impossible question to answer. I do a show, and I talk, and some of the things are funny. It's easier to make people cry than it is to make them laugh.

I
Lina Wertmüller told me the same thing.

GROUCHO
It's true.

I
You have a funny inflection in your voice. Do you sound funny to yourself?

GROUCHO
Yes.

I
Did it surprise you when audiences laughed at something you didn't think was that funny?

GROUCHO
Yes. You try different things, and if one thing doesn't go, you take it out and try something else until you get something that the audience laughs at. If you keep talking long enough, you say something funny.

I
You do. That doesn't happen for everyone. Did you have the experience

of telling a joke that the audiences loved, and you didn't know why it was so funny?

GROUCHO

Yes. There's only one answer to an audience. If they like it, keep it. If they don't laugh, take it out and try another one. That's why we took *A Night at the Opera* and *A Day at the Races* on the road and tried them out before we made movies of them. There used to be an act in show business called the Klein Brothers. One was a comedian and one was a straight man. The comedian would say something that didn't make any sense at all, and the straight man would say, "What in the world are they laughing at?" And the comedian would say, "What do you care, as long as they're laughing?"

I

Do you ever feel badly when people don't laugh at your jokes?

GROUCHO

Everything you say can't be funny. I once did an interview with Sid Perelman for a London paper, and I think it was the dullest interview ever done with two men who were supposed to be funny.

I

Why?

GROUCHO

Because we were trying to outpunch each other. It's not funny to see people trying too hard. I don't like comedians who press. Did you ever hear of Robert Benchley?

I

Of course.

GROUCHO

Benchley was a wonderful man. He became a real big drinker. And I loved him, as I loved a lot of men. I like what Benchley used to say. He said to me once, "I realized I wasn't funny, but I'd been doing it for fifteen years, and I was so successful I couldn't stop." He went up to Harvard — this was after he'd graduated, many years later. He said he had a wonderful time there watching the football game except for an occasional heart attack. He was one of the few humorists I ever met that laughed at other comedians' jokes.

I

You always appreciate other comedians' jokes when they are funny.

GROUCHO

People have no respect for comedy. They think it's easy. But very few people have made a living doing comedy.

I

Do you think it's extremely difficult for even the very talented, or do you think being funny comes easily to some?

GROUCHO

It wasn't difficult for me to be funny.

I

Did you ever worry about being funny? Woody Allen said he worries about it.

GROUCHO

He doesn't need to. He's a genius. I worried when I got wiped out in the stock market in '29. People were jumping out of windows.

I

Are you ever sorry about any of your jokes that are taken the wrong way, when someone seems to be personally hurt by your style?

GROUCHO

No. I don't think so. They always remember what you said. That's what's important.

I

Does your name have anything to do with your disposition?

GROUCHO

What's a Marx disposition? No. I don't think so. Do you think I'm grouchy? I don't think I'm sarcastic or grouchy. I think I'm nothing.

I

I don't think you're grouchy at all. I know you don't believe in false modesty. I believe you tell the truth.

GROUCHO

Even when I'm kidding, I tell the truth, and that's no joke. I only kid with my friends. I don't walk up to strangers in the street and insult them!

I

Do people ever insult you?

GROUCHO

Not often, but sometimes people walk up to me on the street and stop me and say, "You know me, don't you, Groucho?" and I'll say, "Frankly, no!" They don't identify themselves. You know, I meet a lot of people, so it's stupid and it's annoying. People shouldn't do that to you.

I

But you rarely seem to take it badly when people stop you in the street or interrupt you while you're eating to ask for autographs.

GROUCHO

No. I always think what it would be like if they didn't want you anymore.

I

How would you describe your style of humor?

GROUCHO

Droll.

I

During the bad film we saw the other night, you told me once that character was the most important element in comedy, that the best comedy grew out of character.

GROUCHO

That's true. *I'm* a character.

I

Recently I heard that the Bugs Bunny character started out as a Groucho imitator. The carrot was originally supposed to be your cigar, and Bugs Bunny often used some of your lines, like, "Of course you know this means war!" What do you think about that?

GROUCHO

I'll sue him!

I

What about slapstick comedy?

GROUCHO

We used to do slapstick sometimes, but it was intelligent. The lowest form of humor is when a man stands on the stage and makes funny faces, like that movie we went to see. The best thing about it was the popcorn. That was the only thing that was fresh. And I don't eat in movies.

I

I don't either.

GROUCHO

You could've made an exception.

I

Not counting the Marx Brothers, who in your opinion was the greatest comedian?

GROUCHO

Oh, Chaplin, no question.

I

What did you think of Harold Lloyd?

GROUCHO

He used to get laughs by climbing up walls and stuff like that. He was a good comedian. Kind of an acrobat. Chaplin was great.

I

What did you think about W. C. Fields?

GROUCHO

A great comedian. He was also a writer. We were on the bill together in Toledo, at the Keith theatre. He walked off the show. He told the manager of the theatre that he had "humpers on the carumpers." It was just words he was making up. That's the way he was; he didn't want to follow us on the show. We did a big act with thirty people, and he was standing there alone on the stage with a cigar box, singing " 'Yankee Doodle went to town,' " and the audience was walking out of the theatre. It's five o'clock. In Toledo they didn't eat dinner at eight-thirty. So Fields decided to quit the show, and he took the next train for New York. I knew him years later when he worked in Hollywood. He used to hide in the bushes in front of his house and shoot at tourists who were passing by with his beebee gun. I liked the way he said, "To hell with the whole world," and *he meant it!* Did you ever hear of Moran and Mack?

I

No, I don't believe so.

GROUCHO

This was a comedy team, and they were great, one of the great ones that we ever had in vaudeville. And Mack was a great dice handler. He could throw dice and make 'em come up any way he wanted to. He took Harpo and Chico for $3,000. So the next night Harpo and Chico got him in a card game, and they had arranged signals. They won back the $3,000 and a couple thousand more.

I

What was their act like?

GROUCHO

They were blackface comedians. Mack says to Moran, who was the comedian, he says, "I hear you bought some pigs." He says, "Yes, I bought some pigs." "What'd you pay for 'em?" "I paid a dollar for each pig." "And what'd you do with 'em?" "Well, I kept 'em there, and in the autumn I sold them for a dollar apiece." "But you didn't make any money that way." "No, that's right, I didn't. But I had the company of the pigs all winter." Then one says, "Good morning," the other one says, "Good afternoon." And the other one says, "Good night." And the other one says, "Well, I'm glad *that* day is over."

I

You knew Will Rogers well.

GROUCHO

I used to visit him. And he used to sit in his dressing room punching out his jokes. On the typewriter. Then I taught him how to play the guitar. I got fifty dollars for a parody of the song "Oh, What a Pal Is Mary," and I bought a typewriter. It was so heavy I put it in my trunk. And the next town we went to, the typewriter dropped out of the bottom of the trunk. It smashed.

I

Do you remember your parody?

GROUCHO

(*Singing*) " 'Oh, what a bull was Mary, oh, what a bull was she. That she was born, on a September morn, and to prove it she kicked me in the knee. She tore a hole in my trousers, and she gave me a kick in the back. But though she is gone, the pain lingers on, for Mary's first name was Jack.' " This was when Mary Pickford was getting a divorce from Douglas Fairbanks.

I

The Marx Brothers were pretty bold and not easily daunted.

GROUCHO

We were young. When you're young, you're not afraid. You don't know any better.

I

As a celebrity, you are a visible target. Have you ever felt in danger?

GROUCHO

Well, I get threatening letters all the time.

I

What do you do about them?

GROUCHO

Nothing. You know, I once had a gun. And I had the bullets in one part of the house so the children couldn't get at them. One day someone tried to break into the house. I couldn't find the bullets. So I said, "If you stand there for a few minutes till I find them . . ."

I

Is that a true story?

GROUCHO

Yes, that's true. Did I ever tell you what happened on the Gus Sun Circuit? That was the man's name, Gus Sun, and he had about twenty theatres, small-time theatres. We were playing in Cincinnati, and there was a burly show in town, and we were dying to meet those girls. The manager of the show was stuck on the leading lady. I remember, she wore an American flag around here. And somebody said, "There's been many a battle fought beneath that old flag." Well, the manager gave a birth-day party for this chorus girl. And we were invited. There was a singer on the bill with us named Freddy Watson. He was a good singer, but a real fresh kid. So, when the manager gave this birthday party for the chorus girl, he says, "I love her. She's the idol of my ma. And she's only twenty-seven." And Freddy stood up and said, "I'd hate to hang for every year she's over thirty." The manager picked up a knife and started chasing us. He chased us right out of the building. He'd have killed us if he'd caught us. We played the Gus Sun's because it was very popular then, and they had about twenty theatres. The owner, Gus Sun, used to book in ten acts. And he'd try them all out, and he'd keep five of the acts, and let five go. We played on the bill with a fellow named Moe. I can't remember his last name. But he used a trick. He used to stick his chin way out like that. And the audience would laugh! And he sang in the school act. And he wanted thirty dollars or he was going to quit the act. We were each getting twenty-five dollars. So we says, "We can't give you thirty dollars." And he quit. So I started to sing instead of him. (*Pause*) You know what I liked?

I

Tell me.

GROUCHO

I think about that time we went with "Mr. Carnegie Hall" [Ron Delsener] to see my house. Every time I'm going to New York, I think about all the things I want to do, and never get to do them. I always have to do a lot of other things.

I

When we went with Ron to visit your former house in Great Neck, did you feel it was very much changed?

GROUCHO

It seemed different. I don't know anybody there now. Great Neck was a very fancy town in those days. I mean, Hammerstein and big names in show business used to live there.

I

You showed me the photograph of you in Great Neck, standing beside a big convertible.

GROUCHO

Yeah, I had a Packard. I never took it anywhere. I washed it every day. I also owned a couple of Cadillacs and a La Salle. I had big cars then be-cause I was making a lot of money. Then I got wiped out in '29—

$250,000—all the money I saved over the years just went like that. Now I keep my money in my sock. I've got sox appeal.

I

I know you've come to prefer living in California to living in New York. Do you think life in Hollywood has changed since you first came here?

GROUCHO

No. Just everybody's looking for a job, that's all. No jobs around.

I

What was Hollywood like when you came?

GROUCHO

Well, I was much younger. That's one thing. I arrived here in 1930 from New York and I immediately signed up with Paramount and did twelve pictures here. When I first came out here, I used to ride horseback on Sunset Boulevard, and there was no such thing as Beverly Hills. I dressed like a cowboy with a ten-gallon hat, only I wore a nine-gallon hat. They were cheaper. We had fun. We were young. Now there are fewer studios, fewer films, because of television, and a lot of people don't go to the movies anymore, unless it's a really unusual one, because it costs a lot to go to the movies now.

I

How would you describe Hollywood?

GROUCHO

How would I describe Hollywood? I love it! That'd be my only description of it. It's the only place that I'm happy in.

I

Do you like New York? Do you have a good time when you go back there?

GROUCHO

Yes, but it isn't my whole life.

I

Do you think the life of a star is different now than it used to be? Hearing about the way it used to be here, those days seem to me to have been more glamorous.

GROUCHO

I'll tell you what's changed—television has changed the movie industry, because this is where the average person gets their entertainment from. I think this is show business today.

I

Are you sorry television has taken over?

GROUCHO

No, because most of the movies are lousy. As people get older, they don't want to get in their car and go to a theatre and stand in line, even if it's a good picture. The average person turns on the television, and sometimes you see a good show. It's much easier to just take off your shoes and put on your bathrobe and look at a couple of lousy TV shows. That's about it.

I

Why do you suppose there are so few really funny movies made today?

GROUCHO

There's no comedians left. Now, you talk about funny pictures, let's start with Chaplin. He doesn't work anymore—he's too old. Buster Keaton is dead. W. C. Fields is dead. Mae West isn't dead, but she isn't working. Dean Martin and Jerry Lewis, when they were together, yes, it was a good team. All the others are dead. Laurel and Hardy are dead. One of the reasons why there are no comedians is there's no more vaudeville. There is no place to train a comedian today.

I

Do you think there is still as good an audience for comedy movies?

GROUCHO

You put on a funny picture today, and they'll go see it. That's all I can tell you. Give them entertainment, and they'll go see it. I saw *That's Entertainment* three times, and I'm going to see it again. (*Pause*) You should've come when Mae West was here to dinner. I said to her, "How's Bill Fields," and she said, "I only see him in my dreams."

I

I'm sorry I missed it. Who were the other comedians you admired?

GROUCHO

Fred Allen was great. A wonderful man. I miss him. He was a great writer. He had a rube comedian on his show, Titus Moody, who said he lived in a seashore town that was so small the tide went out one day and never came back. Then Fred said he was playing in a town so small that the assistant manager of the theatre was a bear. I think those are great jokes. That's Fred's writing. He wrote most of the show himself. He was like Woody. But he died young. He was in his fifties. Woody Allen's the genius now.

I

Which Woody Allen picture do you like best?

GROUCHO

Play It Again, Sam. He's a big talent—one of the few big talents around. I'm crazy about him.

I

I know how you feel about Bill Cosby.

GROUCHO

He's as great as any actor I've seen in show business. There's nobody can do what he can. The thing is, he doesn't tell any jokes. He tells what happened to people and how they behave. He talks about any subject. He could talk about you or a chair or anything. An extraordinary actor. I've never seen anything like him. Do you remember how he was at my party at Hillcrest, all ad-lib? Great, wasn't he?

I

Yes indeed.

GROUCHO

Phil Silvers was a good comedian too, and he was always a nice guy. You know, we go back a long ways together—back to when Melinda was a baby. He asked me not long ago, "Does Melinda still wear the cowboy suit I bought her?" I think she was three years old or something. Well, I'm so old now that they've just named a salami sandwich after me. Salami and provolone. It's a good sandwich! They call it a Groucho.

I

You don't have to be old to have a sandwich named after you.

GROUCHO

How many young guys do you know who've had sandwiches named after them?

I

Offhand I can't think of any. That was a lovely lunch with George Burns. I didn't realize you'd introduced him to Gracie Allen.

GROUCHO

I met him in Schenectady. I was having dinner with Gracie Allen. I liked her. She was a very cute little Irish tap dancer. I wasn't interested in her; I just liked her. But Burns married her. He came over. He was eating at another table. And he came over and saw Gracie, and he immediately fell in love with her.

I

Love at first sight . . .

GROUCHO

He'd seen her. But he'd never met her.

I

You were a friend of Humphrey Bogart.

GROUCHO

I was at Bogart's house all the time. He was a wonderful host. He had two or three shots of booze, and he had a yacht and he'd go on the yacht to get away from Lauren Bacall. Not that he didn't like her. He wanted to be around with men. I took a dame to his house one night. She had real big knockers. And he said, "Who's the broad you got there?" And I said she was my secretary.

I

And you knew Spencer Tracy . . .

GROUCHO

Katharine Hepburn came to my house with Spencer Tracy. I was walking one of Eden's dogs, and as I was getting close to the top of this hill, there was Katharine Hepburn with Spencer Tracy, and they had a big dog. Then they came to my house. I had a lot of peanuts—you know, I was a ball fan—and she said, "Oh, isn't that lovely! Peanuts!" I don't think she'd ever seen a peanut. In the shell, I mean. Like you get in the ballpark.

I

That sounds like Katharine Hepburn pulling your leg.

GROUCHO

I wish she would've. A wonderful actress.

I

Who is your favorite actress?

GROUCHO

Sarah Bernhardt. I only saw her once, when I played on the bill with her. She got $1,000 each night before she went on. She had one leg, and I had two legs, and I only got $200 a week.

I

What was her act like?

GROUCHO

She did a dramatic sketch where she was lying in a coffin.

I

Did the audience accept it well?

GROUCHO

Completely serious! She was one of the first acts that played the Palace Theatre because she was a big attraction.

I

Lee Strasberg told me that he thought Barbra Streisand is the actress who could play Sarah Bernhardt.

GROUCHO

I admire Streisand. She's a great singer.

I

When you were making *Room Service,* did you think that Lucille Ball would be such a big success?

GROUCHO

Not then, no.

I

Was she very noticeable?

GROUCHO

She was very attractive. I noticed that.

I

Whom do you consider to be the sexiest actress?

GROUCHO

Sexiest?! I'd have to go to bed with them to say. I'd have liked to have gone to bed with Jean Harlow. She was a beautiful broad. And the fellow who was stuck on her married her, and he was impotent. He killed himself. Did you know that?

I

No.

GROUCHO

Well, you know it now. Carole Lombard was a hell of an actress. She did a picture with Jack Benny which Lubitsch directed. A great picture. Benny was wonderful in it. It was called *To Be or Not to Be.* Lubitsch was one of the best directors, I guess, in this country. He wanted to do a movie with us.

I

Why didn't you make a movie with him?

GROUCHO

Well, we were tied up with Paramount then, making those five turkeys. He was a genius. I always wanted to do a picture with him.

I

René Clair told me he would have very much liked to make a film with you.

GROUCHO

Yes. There was nobody greater. We wanted him, but it never happened.

I

I know you like Jacques Tati.

GROUCHO

The tall guy. Funny man. The first couple he did I thought were very funny. Especially where he was going into a cemetery and putting a tire on somebody's grave. That was good.

I

Mr. Hulot's Holiday. You told me that some of the foreign comedy films lose a lot for you when you have to read the subtitles.

GROUCHO

I'd rather stay home and read.

I

Which Marx Brothers director did you like best?

GROUCHO

Leo McCarey. He was a great director. And a funny man. We had a lot of fun with him. He loved to shoot craps with Chico. Half the time you couldn't find either one of them. McCarey was the best director we ever had.

I

What do you think of audiences now?

GROUCHO

When they're laughing, I enjoy that.

I

But do you think that audiences are the same now or different than they were forty years ago?

GROUCHO

Different? Not the ones we get. At Carnegie Hall, half the audience was dressed like me and the other half was dressed like Harpo and Chico.

I

What was the average age?

GROUCHO

Fifteen or sixteen.

I

Why do you think people of that age enjoy you so much?

GROUCHO

Because there's nobody else around that can amuse them, except Woody Allen, and he's the only one I know.

I

What do you think about young people today?

GROUCHO

Well, I have a grandson five years old. You mean him? Miles is growing up. He's starting to ask questions I can answer.

I

I meant a little older than that. What do you think about the young people you meet who are your audience? Do you think they're just like young people always were?

GROUCHO

Well, I don't think they're different. Maybe they're brighter. Maybe the educational system is responsible for that. They're more worried. Maybe they have more to worry about these days.

I

Do you approve of film censorship?

GROUCHO

Yes, I approve of this. I don't think they should permit *any* old picture they make to be put on the screen. No. Because there are many children who go to the movies, too, and I think it's disgraceful, some of the stuff that they have. I don't like dirty pictures. I guess it's hard to make a good picture—and a successful picture—that's clean.

I

Did you go to the movies a lot when you were young?

GROUCHO

Yeah, all the time. I've seen all the Chaplin pictures at least ten times in my life. There wasn't anybody as good as he was. His pictures don't do good business today, though. They don't want to see him anymore.

I

Why not?

GROUCHO

He doesn't talk.

I

But Harpo doesn't talk, and he's very popular today.

GROUCHO

That's true, but there were other people in the act that did talk.

I

Does Chaplin still seem as good for you personally today as he once did?

GROUCHO

Some of his pictures are still really good. But some of 'em are just incredibly bad. He made good pictures and bad pictures. The last picture he made was so bad. *A Countess from Hong Kong.* He insisted on writing a good deal of it, and he even put himself in as a waiter. But I think he was the best, in his day. He once said to me, "I wish I could talk on the screen, like you can." That's when he was really big. He couldn't talk. Strange thing. He could talk pretty well in private homes. Then he had a lot of trouble and he went to Europe and stayed there.

I

Did you ever meet Howard Hughes when you were doing those two pictures for him?

GROUCHO

No. Hughes wasn't ever on the set. He was only interested in girls. He thought of the title *Double Dynamite*, which was supposed to refer to Jane Russell's knockers. It's a good thing the guy was a millionaire. Otherwise how would he have made a living?

I

As a big baseball fan, you met all the famous players.

GROUCHO

Yes, I knew Babe Ruth. He used to listen to our quiz show. He was old then and through with baseball. But not as old as I am now.

I

What other great ballplayers did you know?

GROUCHO

Christy Mathewson. You wouldn't know about him.

I

Pitcher, for the New York Giants.

GROUCHO

That's right. You're smarter than you look. Do you know about Tinker To Evers . . . ?

I

To Chance.

GROUCHO

Steinfeldt at third. Harry Steinfeldt played third base for the Cubs when they had Tinker To Evers To Chance. I also knew Joe DiMaggio.

I

That was a good game that we watched.

GROUCHO

Yeah. But I don't keep up with baseball the way I used to.

I

George Foreman seemed as happy to meet you as you were to meet him. He was impressed that you knew so much about boxing.

GROUCHO

Well, I worked for Benny Leonard, who was the lightweight champion of the world at one time. I told you he put up the money for one of our vaudeville acts.

I

On the Mezzanine.

GROUCHO

That's right. I was crazy about him, he was such a great fighter. He was stuck on Hattie Darling, the girl in our act. There wasn't a Jew in New York that wouldn't have married Benny Leonard. Really! Either sex. He was such a great fighter. Did I tell you about Jim Corbett?

I

No.

GROUCHO

He was heavyweight champion of the world. I used to play poker with him in New York. And I always lost. I wasn't a very good card player. I liked to go to the fights, even when I was married. My wives didn't go. None of them. I went with a group of boys, men. Men are very much interested in prizefighting, women aren't.

I

Do you understand why?

GROUCHO

Well, I guess it's the skill of one man fighting another to see who's the best of the two. People do it in the street. I had a fight with a fellow named Harry Applebaum. He was around twelve years older than I was. It was on the street, on Ninety-third Street.

I

What were you fighting about?

GROUCHO

Difference of opinion. I don't remember exactly. It wasn't about a girl.

I

Who won?

GROUCHO

I don't know. I hit him in the stomach, and he gave me a black eye. I had another fight on Fourteenth Street in New York. It was Christmas, and I was working at a department store there for two weeks. If somebody sold something to somebody, they gave me the slapper, the charge, and I would run over to the cashier. And then I had a fight with another cash boy. In the middle of the street, on Fourteenth Street, in the snow. It was a great way to have spent Christmas.

I

Who won this time?

GROUCHO

We came out pretty even.

I

Did you get hurt?

GROUCHO

Not much. The cops stopped us. But that was a hundred years ago.

I

Now you don't fight in the snow. You listen to music, Gilbert and Sullivan . . .

GROUCHO

And Mozart and Brahms and Tchaikovsky. I played so much Gilbert and Sullivan at one period in my life, that then I sort of stopped listening to it. It was just too much. I think there's only thirteen or fourteen plays of Gilbert and Sullivan, but they're great. You brought me the recording of their first operetta, *Thespis*. It was interesting to hear, but it wasn't as good as the others. I saw most of their plays. And I was so crazy about them that I finally did *The Mikado* for NBC. I played Ko-Ko. It's the way your life works out, you know. You have really no control over your life. Things happen. I don't think anybody has any control over what happens and the way he is. I was crazy about Gilbert and Sullivan, and I read everything I could. There are things that are important for a while, and then one day they aren't that important. You don't want the same things your whole life. My opinions change. I used to be against capital punishment.

I

What do you think about the trend toward actors and actresses becoming so politically active?

GROUCHO

I think they are entitled to their own opinions, same as anyone else. I have very strong political opinions myself.

I

You admired Truman . . .

GROUCHO

He was a great president. I knew him.

I

What was it that you particularly admired about him?

GROUCHO

He said, "The buck stops here." I feel that way. (*Groucho indicates himself*) The buck stops here.

I

Who would you like to see be president of the United States?

GROUCHO

Me. You know, I once had an offer to run for governor of California. And

I said, "What does the job pay?" And they said it paid $25,000 a year. And I said, "I'm making that every week on the quiz show." That was the end of my political career.

I

Do you think you would have made a good governor?

GROUCHO

I think so, yeah. I think I'm basically an honest man.

I

Do you think honesty is the most important basic qualification?

GROUCHO

Yes.

I

What would your platform have been?

GROUCHO

Democratic. Always a Democrat.

I

But what would your platform have been?

GROUCHO

I have no idea. It was a long time ago. Now it would be different. Now I'd worry about inflation and natural resources, like oil. Besides, I turned the job down!

I

You told me Henry Kissinger is one of the people you would most like to meet.

GROUCHO

Great man. I think he's an honest man. I'd like to see him president, but I guess he can't because he was born in Germany. That's where my mother was born, and she never made it to the presidency, either. I expect to see it someday in America, a woman president. No reason why it shouldn't be.

I

You showed me your invitation to the White House, when you met Eleanor Roosevelt.

GROUCHO

Yes. They had a Marine band playing in the courtyard of the White House, and I said to her, "Now I know why you keep traveling all the time." She was a great woman.

I

What did you talk about?

GROUCHO

About fifteen minutes. We talked about him, about FDR. It seems he'd gone on a hunting trip, to get away from Eleanor, I think. And when he came back, he had a long beard. She hardly knew him. He also had a girl, but she didn't talk about that. She talked about a lot of causes she was interested in.

I

What do you think about the preservation of landmarks?

GROUCHO

I think I should be preserved.

I

What about other landmarks?

GROUCHO

Things aren't good because they're old, but they aren't good just because they're new.

I

Can you believe there is some talk about tearing down Grand Central Station?

GROUCHO

It would be a crime.

I

How do you feel about pornography?

GROUCHO

That remains to be obscene.

I

What do you think about homosexuality?

GROUCHO

I don't think about it. It never appealed to me. I think they've got their rights.

I

What is the question you've been asked most often?

GROUCHO

People keep asking me if Harpo could talk. Of course he couldn't.

I

Is there any other question you're asked a great deal?

GROUCHO

Yes. They keep asking me, "How do you compare comedy today to comedy forty years ago?" This is the question I'm asked by college students.

I

Do you consider yourself an intellectual?

GROUCHO

I don't know. I don't think about it that way. I've read, and I've educated myself somewhat, but I don't consider myself an intellectual. Intelligent, but not an intellectual. George Bernard Shaw, I would say, was an intellectual.

I

Did you ever meet Shaw?

GROUCHO

No, Harpo did. Woollcott took him over there and introduced him to Shaw. Harpo went around with a different crowd than I did.

I

But you knew T. S. Eliot. Eden told me about your visit to his home.

GROUCHO

I met him and his wife in London. I wanted to talk about his works, and he wasn't interested. He wanted to talk about the Marx Brothers. He wrote me a letter once, and he said, "Since you've had dinner with me, all the tradesmen in the neighborhood bow their heads when I pass." He was crazy about our pictures. I wanted to talk about a couple of his plays and his poems, but he wasn't interested in that. He only talked about the Marx Brothers.

I

What do you do to relax?

GROUCHO

I don't. I can't relax.

I

Never?

GROUCHO

No. And I'm never sleepy. I don't sleep well.

I

Are you ever lonely?

GROUCHO

No.

I

Do you ever mind being alone?

GROUCHO

I'm never alone. I read. I always had a hunger to read. I used to sit in my dressing room and read. I left the door open so the other actors would think I was educated. I always wanted more education, but now my books are in the Library of Congress. I used to read people like Anatole France and Horatio Alger. I was brought up on Horatio Alger.

I

What other writers did you like?

GROUCHO

I was crazy about Somerset Maugham and still am.

I

You're a person who is able to go ahead and do something without worrying a lot in advance.

GROUCHO

Yes. Worrying doesn't change anything.

I

Do you consider yourself unusual?

GROUCHO

I'm unusual, all right. An unusual kind of man.

I

In what ways do you think you're unusual?

GROUCHO

I think the fact that I'm in my eighties is unusual. Most people die before they get to be my age. Do you know how I got to be this old?

I

How?

GROUCHO

Lucky. If a man is eighty-five, and he dies, nobody is gonna say, "Isn't that awful, a man dying, eighty-five years old." I've had a good life. Eighty-five years old is a long time. I hope I won't live to be a hundred. There's nothing you can do when you're a hundred. Getting old is a goddamn nuisance.

I

But in your eighties you still do a lot.

GROUCHO

I can go out and take a walk. I can have a little drink—of tomato juice— and I'm lucky. A lot of people my age don't have anything and they're ready for the boneyard. Did I ever tell you what my Uncle Al [Shean] has on his tombstone?

I

No.

GROUCHO

"I could have lived longer, but now it's too late. Absolutely, Mr. Gallagher, positively, Mr. Shean."

I

Do you ever find that you get bored?

GROUCHO

Not if I've got something good to read. I like to read the newspapers. I like to know what's going on in the world.

I

Do you believe what you read in the newspapers?

GROUCHO

Well, they can't make up *everything!* You know, I saw my obituary at the *Times*. It made me feel funny. I didn't think he should have shown it to me.

I

You consider yourself a disciplined person.

GROUCHO

Yes, I am. One day I said I would stop smoking, and I did. I said I would stop drinking, and I did. I said I would only eat two chocolates a day, and now I've eaten the two chocolates, and there's nothing to do but wait for tomorrow. I used to eat everything. Now I can't eat anything with salt in it. The only drink I used to like is bourbon. Now I can't drink, I can't smoke, I can't do anything anymore. I can't even go to Nate 'n' Al's, 'cause they have salt.

I

What kind of cigar did you smoke when you smoked your famous cigars?

GROUCHO

Famous wasn't their name. They came from Havana. They cost four dollars. *Real* Havana, not the Canary Islands, or any of those. Bill Cosby gave me my last box. Cosby is one of the most talented people in show business. Especially after he gave me the cigars.

I

You smoked a pipe, too.

GROUCHO

Yeah. But a pipe only tasted good after a cigar.

I

Do you ever get depressed?

GROUCHO

Not often, no.

I

I remember when there was the murder of the Israeli athletes at the Olympics in Munich. That's one of the few times I've ever known you to be terribly depressed.

GROUCHO

That was one of the most shocking things in my whole life.

I

When you get depressed, how do you get over it?

GROUCHO

Well, I don't get depressed that often, so I couldn't tell you.

I

What's your opinion of psychoanalysis?

GROUCHO

It won't get it up if you're eighty-five years old.

I

What do you think of psychiatrists?

GROUCHO

They're all right if they keep their nails clean.

I

Could you imagine yourself going to one?

GROUCHO

Yeah. I went to a psychologist a couple of times. Because I was troubled. I think they're very important. When you're in trouble, mentally, they can straighten you out.

I

Why do you sleep with your bedroom door locked?

GROUCHO

Well, if I think I'm all alone in the house, and there's nobody in, I'll do it.

I

I thought it might be because of all those years in vaudeville when you were staying in cheap hotels.

GROUCHO

Could be. I used to put the bureau up against the door. That was a phase during my vaudeville days. By this time we were living in good hotels. Big hotels, like the Statler in Cleveland or Detroit. I was always afraid of jumping out the window. So I used to put a big trunk up against the window. We had those big theatrical trunks. At that time I was living in hotels that were fifteen and eighteen floors high, and I was afraid that some night I might go to the window and open it and jump out. We didn't have the best rooms in the hotel, but each would have his own room, and I used to get scared at night. That's why I put the trunk up against the window.

I

But why would you be afraid of jumping out of the window?

GROUCHO

I don't know. I guess it was a kind of nervous point of my life, although we were pretty successful by this time. I'd seen some Boris Karloff movies. And I was scared. I was very young then. I saw one Boris Karloff picture, and I took sleeping pills for about a month after that, every night. It was the only way I could get to sleep.

I

But you knew they were just movies . . .

GROUCHO

I knew it, but they affected me. That sounds strange, I guess. I think a lot of people get scared when they go to a frightening movie. They frightened the hell out of me, those Boris Karloff movies. All I know is I couldn't sleep at night. So I took the trunk and put it up against the window. I finally got to know Karloff, and he was one of the sweetest men I ever knew in my whole life. I almost sold him a house that I had. A very well-educated man. English education—he was from England.

I

Which Karloff films terrified you most?

GROUCHO

Every one.

I

What did he do that scared you?

GROUCHO

He looked like a monster! I think those pictures scared a lot of people. I think all people have periods in their life when they are a little nutty or think they are.

I

Do you feel, as many people do, that life is more serious and problem-filled today?

GROUCHO

Not for me. I'm very lucky. I'm eating good. I went to a movie, and it was pretty good.

I

What was the movie?

GROUCHO

You know. The one we saw with Andy. Paris in the nineties. The movie was as old as I am.

I

Have you any regrets?

GROUCHO

Not now. I regretted that my last marriage broke up. I guess it was partly my fault.

I

Would you get married again?

GROUCHO

No. I wouldn't marry anybody. Too old. If I was gonna marry anybody, it would be Erin.

I

How did success and fame, and time and experience change you?

GROUCHO

I never did change.

I

What was the biggest change being famous and being a celebrity made in your life?

GROUCHO

I didn't have to wait. Before, we used to have to wait. Before we were known, we waited for jobs. Then, when we had jobs, but we weren't important yet, we had to wait around a lot. Then, we were a big hit. Then, other people wait for you. After that, we never had to wait.

I

What is the most valuable thing in life?

GROUCHO

This is very easy to answer. Screwing! You can't top *that!*

I

There's more than that . . .

GROUCHO

Well, there's also giving each other pictures, candy and chocolates, and entertaining them on the piano. How many hours a day can you spend humping?

I

Do you think you're different as a private person than as a public person?

GROUCHO

No. Not at all. But I do know this, that if I walk down Beverly tomorrow, there isn't hardly anybody who won't recognize me. And they'll stop me and ask how I feel. There's a lot of concern about me. A man came up and kissed me the other day. He was wearing a beard, and I don't like to kiss a man with a beard. He came up to me, and threw his arms around me, and kissed me on the cheek and says, "Groucho, you're the greatest!" Then, I was walking in the village, where the Bank of America building is going up. There were five men on the fifth floor of this building hollering down, "Groucho!"

I

I remember. I was there with you. Do you consider yourself a good judge of character?

GROUCHO

All I know is if I like somebody or I don't like them, that's all.

I

Do you have any favorite jokes or lines?

GROUCHO

The best lions are in the zoo. What's the difference between a man giving a woman a dog and a man running up a hill?

I

I don't know.

GROUCHO

I don't know either. One is taking a gal a pup, and the other is taking a gallop up. It's a small joke. There used to be a joke about crab legs. I said to a waitress in Dinty Moore's restaurant, "You have crab legs?" And she said, "No, rheumatism makes me walk like that."

I

I remember your telling that joke to one of the owners of "21" in New York. Only it was with frog legs. It was the night you took off your tie.

GROUCHO

I haven't worn a tie in years. I think it's silly to wear a tie. I'd like to go without pants.

I

Do you have any other favorite "small" jokes?

GROUCHO

(*Reciting*) "There was a little old lady who lived in a shoe. She didn't have any children, she knew what to do. There was a little old lady who lived in a shoe. She had a lot of children, and she didn't know what to do." "Old Mother Hubbard went to the cupboard to get her poor daughter a bone. When she got there, her cupboard was bare, and so was her daughter."

I

Do you ever feel that you're being used or exploited?

GROUCHO

I don't think about it.

I

You don't mind occasionally being used or exploited, almost like a beautiful girl?

GROUCHO

No. I wish I had one. One of the most beautiful things in the world is a pretty young girl.

I

In the time that I've known you, you have rarely used a four-letter word . . .

GROUCHO

I've used them, but not with you. I'm prudish in many ways, and chivalrous.

I

How would you describe yourself?

GROUCHO

As an old jerk.

I

And if you were telling the truth, how would you describe yourself?

GROUCHO

I just did.

"I keep the ones I want"

At lunch with Goodman Ace in Groucho's New York hotel suite, I referred to Groucho's sleight-of-tongue style of insulting people. I asked Groucho, "Do you find you lose a lot of friends along the way?"

"Yes, I do," he answered. "But I prefer it that way. It's good to lose a lot of people. I keep the ones I want."

"Do you agree with Oscar Wilde, who said, 'A gentleman is never unintentionally rude'?" I asked.

"Yes," Groucho said. "I get away with saying some pretty insulting things. People think I'm joking. I'm not. I'm just saying what I think. I don't tell jokes. I tell the truth. And that's sometimes a joke."

Groucho accentuated the negative to achieve a positive reaction—"Whatever it is, I'm against it." The classic iconoclast, Groucho uninhibitedly spoke what usually remains unspoken, articulating what others might only dare to think. For some, this meant he elevated the art of bad manners to new lows. A ranking member of the undiplomatic corps, he didn't hesitate to give pomposity its come-downance.

Once while walking with Groucho in Beverly Hills, I felt that his retort to a fan seemed excessively acerbic, so I asked him afterward if he didn't think he had gone rather far. "No. Because all her life she'll remember what I said to her," he explained. "That's what's important. If I'd said something ordinary, she would have gone away disappointed."

Max Gordon told me that he once commented to Groucho that he thought Groucho's telling of a joke at T. S. Eliot's funeral might have been a mistake. "I'm a comedian," Groucho had responded. He felt it was what Eliot would have wanted. Irene Atkins, who was married to Groucho's son, summed it up when she told me, "You accept things from Groucho that perhaps you wouldn't accept from other people."

His public image (and to a great extent his private image) was that of a man so clever that to engage in any sort of verbal duel with him would have been tantamount to committing social suicide. His close friend Norman Krasna refused to appear as a guest on the *You Bet Your Life* show, explaining to me, "He would've killed me if I'd gone on."

Seemingly, a license very much like the one possessed by James Bond was issued to Groucho, except that he was empowered to kill with words. Just as nobody walked up to Muhammad Ali, fists raised, and said, "I'm the greatest," few were daring enough to challenge Groucho's rapier tongue. He was in the enviable position of being not only a superior combatant, but the referee as well. In a world that plays by the rules, others were stopped by an inhibition barrier that he didn't observe.

Of course, he didn't *always* have the last word. Those who are exalted, and thus stand out, are also targets. No public figure escapes totally unscathed. A celebrity is someone people want to know things about that they wouldn't even want to know about themselves. Groucho enjoyed his pedestal and what was mostly a life of laurels, but he, too, came in for his share of attempted public put-downs. "My way of talking," he told me, "it's how I defend myself." Etched in his memory were some of the moments when his own verbal defenses were under siege:

• Some years ago when he was at Disneyland with daughter Melinda, a woman approached him and asked in a tone that was a virtual assault, "You're Groucho Marx, aren't you?" Groucho said that he made the mistake of telling her the truth. Her retort was "I wouldn't watch your show for a thousand dollars a night."

• Several years later, he was approached by another woman who wanted to put him down. Not giving him the chance to deny it, she said, "You're Groucho Marx. Well, you ain't funny."

• Writer Harry Tugend tells the story of a little boy who stared at Groucho in an elevator. When Groucho looked back, the boy said, "Don't worry. I know who you are."

But this is part of the price of being a celebrity, and Groucho paid it willingly.

"There are people who will knock you down if they can. It makes them feel good. But if someone says to me, 'You're a lousy comedian,' I say, 'You're no judge. You're no Alexander Woollcott.'

"When you get up before an audience, you've gotta go out there believing you're better than they are, or you can't do it. You make mistakes, but if you're not making mistakes, you aren't trying. You aren't doing anything.

"You can't expect that everyone is going to like you. If there aren't people who don't like you, you're nowhere. There are people you wouldn't want to like you."

Groucho's uses of abuse were meant to amuse. People didn't expect him to say anything ordinary, and his sensitivity to their expectations exerted a pressure on him not to disappoint his audience.

A man walked up to us on the street and asked Groucho for an autograph. "Would you please sign this for my son?"

Groucho started to write, then paused after writing only "Gro."

"Hold old is he?"

"Eleven months."

Groucho handed the piece of paper with half of his signature back to the man, saying, "He's too young to read."

With strangers and sometimes even with friends, he felt he was being tested, so he had to be "on." When he said something very commonplace, he was surprised at the extent to which his audience, even when it was made up of old friends, filled in, finding his comment hilarious beyond its due. The aura of the half century of mirth surrounding him carried with it a Pavlovian effect which frequently elicited anything from suppressed giggles to raucous laughter for what Groucho would call "a small joke." Raising his eyebrows, he summed up his style this way: "I always have a ready answer."

At times he was greeted so effusively by a stranger that he felt his privacy had been invaded. He had such an instantly perceived character and personality that people who met him for five minutes genuinely felt they knew him. Certainly, many more people knew Groucho than he himself knew. As we walked together, people not only loved to recognize him, but they loved to be recognized *by* him.

His friends were all in agreement that his public image grew out of his real self. Ethel Wise, who knew him as a boy, and Hattie Darling, who knew him in his late twenties, confirmed that the Groucho of movies and television was essentially the same person that they had known and that he did not change. If anything, the tremendous acceptance received by the Groucho character had the effect of making Groucho even *more* like Groucho. Lee Strasberg, a master of character study, told me:

"I remember meeting Groucho once a long time ago. I don't remember exactly what he said, but I remember that what he said was funny, and so perfectly in character. The actor was the expression of the person."

Genuinely loving to perform, Groucho was fortunate enough to be able to spend his life being paid to do what he would have been willing to do free. Of course he preferred being paid, and he lived in a world where your fee is considered to be the measure of your value. He was at his happiest when he was performing, especially when it was for his fellow performers.

When he was in New York for the re-premiere of *Animal Crackers*, Ron Delsener invited British satirists Peter Cook and Dudley Moore to visit Groucho in his suite at the Regency. They were funny, but Groucho was up to it all. "Nobody can upstage Groucho, even at eighty-three," Ron told me that evening. "Groucho got a bigger kick out of the evening than any of us. He had the chance to perform, and that's his life." The evening ended on this note:

GROUCHO
I'll see you at my house in California.
DUDLEY MOORE
That'll be terrific!
GROUCHO
I don't know about that.

It's possible that Groucho in his eighties was even more social than ever before. Irene Atkins remembered a sedate person, one not so inclined to romp and stomp. "When I was married to Arthur, we used to listen to records at Groucho's—Gilbert and Sullivan."

Groucho continued to be in demand as a guest, both socially and professionally. Frequently he had to ruffle a lot of feelings because he could not possibly accept all of the invitations that came his way. He had to be possessive about his time or he wouldn't have had any left for himself. He might accept an invitation to a party, saying, "I'll come at eight, and I'll leave at eight-thirty."

Although he was so much in demand as a guest, he was more often the host. He took great pride in not being a freeloader. Even at restaurants he preferred to and usually did pick up the check. "I used to like to go to Danny's Hideaway," he told me, referring to the New York restaurant. "But I had to stop going. He never let me pay."

Socially, one of the stresses for Groucho was that he brought out the desire in non–show business people to perform. They often told him jokes, mistakenly feeling that they had to entertain the entertainer. Plumbers, gardeners, and TV repairmen all had jokes for him. A typical reaction of his was, "Why did you have to tell me that terrible joke? It'll take me three months to get over that." They laughed.

Because "civilians" treated him as too special a person, he preferred the more relaxing companionship of his fellow performers and writers. When he had company for dinner, he liked to invite show business people or family—his concept of family extending beyond blood and legal relationships to include anyone he chose to include. Although he would say some funny things at the dinner table, he liked to relax while eating and not talk much while chewing, and he felt less pressure to perform with his peers.

He enjoyed some respite from being social, especially from professional sociability. Walking along Camden and Sunset with David Hixon and me, he was asked by David, "Groucho, why do you take this particular walk almost every day? Do you know a lot of people who live here?" Groucho answered, "No. It's because I don't."

Like all supercelebrities, he sometimes wearied of having to live up to the expectations of the general public, liking to be able to retreat into the protective cocoon of his own home, his private world peopled only by his intimates. One night I was riding to a public appearance with Groucho, who was terribly depressed by one of his regular visits to his sick friend Arthur Sheekman—visits which he continued to make even though they always depressed him.

GROUCHO
I told you how I met Sheekman . . .

I
He was writing for a Chicago newspaper . . .

GROUCHO
Chicago Times. And he had been to interview me, and I'm so tired of doing these interviews. I said, "I'll do one for you. I'll write it myself." So I wrote it. Then we came to the Coast. I sent for him to come out as one of the writers. His wife was in a number of pictures. She was a good-looking dame. Gloria Stuart. And now he's an old man and very sick. It's not like when you saw him here. I went today to see him. I brought him chocolate and cookies, but he just wanted to sleep. There's no more happiness. And Ruby's dead. A part of me went with him when he died. I cried when he died. Two of my brothers are dead. There's nothing you can do about it. Did I ever tell you what Kaufman told me? He said 'I'm supposed to seem happy and be entertaining when I feel down and sad.' I feel like that."

Groucho didn't just seek shelter in a coterie of cronies. Even in his eighties—perhaps *especially* in his eighties—he was constantly adding new people. His friends spanned the whole gamut in age and background. With friends like George Jessel and George Burns, Groucho could share a frame of reference that included Swayne's rats riding jockey-style on the backs of cats. With Groucho's young friends, there was a rapport born of their sense of historic importance when they were with him. Terry Hamlisch expressed it when she described what it was like to watch *Duck Soup* with Groucho:

"It's like you're living a moment in time that you couldn't possibly repeat because here's the person who did this, and he's sitting right there and commenting about it, and yet he watches it like it's the first time he's seen it as well as somebody who's lived with it for a long time. He's the person who did it, and now he's just a fan. It's like a historic moment, and then he puts his hand on your knee."

Judging his friends on merit, Groucho tended to be quite democratic, with a small *d* as well as a capital *D*. Though he didn't share the political opinions of Morrie Ryskind and George Jessel, they remained his friends over the decades. When he went out to fashionable restaurants, he frequently took along whichever of his nurses happened to be on duty. "Someone said to me," he told me, " 'How can a big star like you who is getting the Academy Award go to Chasen's with a girl who just works for you?' I don't understand that kind of thinking."

Groucho's favor, however, could sometimes be elusive. He had a low tolerance for boredom, and was more likely to be bored in the company of non–show business people. At Chasen's restaurant, after too many drinks, a fan came up to Groucho and started to praise him in wildly extravagant terms. Groucho squirmed for several minutes, then silenced the man's effusiveness with a peremptory "You're drunk!"

The desire to display our adult success to a grammar school teacher who gave us a low grade or told our parents we were unpromising, or to show adult acclaim to childhood peers who didn't find us likeliest to succeed, is a readily recognizable shared human trait. Young Julius Henry Marx, B.G. (Before Groucho), was generally considered by all who knew him as likely to make something of himself. The position he attained, however, far surpassed that which anyone, except possibly Minnie, could have envisioned. When just after his Broadway success, he met childhood friend Dave Geiger on the street, Groucho relished basking in the appreciation of one who had been among the most successful of Groucho's grammar school peer group.

GROUCHO

I told you about David Geiger, didn't I? He lived on Ninety-third Street where we lived.

I

You said that everyone thought he'd be a Supreme Court justice . . .

GROUCHO

That's what we figured, or something that good. He became a lawyer and he was getting $150 a week. I was getting $1,500 in *Animal Crackers*. He came backstage to my dressing room, and he didn't mention anything about the show—and it was a very funny show! I said, "How'd you like the show?" and he said, "Why don't you quit this thing? You're jumping around chairs out there, acting ridiculous. That's nothing for you to do, a man of your age. Why don't you settle down?" I says, "Well, I've been thinking of it, Dave. How much money do you make?" He said, "I make $150 a week. And next week I expect a raise to $200." I didn't tell him how much I was making. He left after that. Next time I saw him was on Fifth Avenue, and he had two kids, about six and seven years old. He says, "Groucho, do you remember what I told you?" I said, "What?" He said, "About your quitting this thing that you're doing. It's so silly. When are you going to settle down and do something with a future?" I was now getting $2,000 a week. I said, "How much are you making?" He said, "I'm making $200 a week now." I says, "Yeah. That's a lot of money. I'll think about it. I might take you up on that." I never could convince him that I was a success in show business.

Groucho's future proved to be a very secure one, and he survived his "failure" to impress his boyhood friend. But he told me the story with the admonition "You do better to have most of your friends in the business," the "business" being show business.

A subject occasionally discussed by Groucho's friends was success:

SIDNEY SHELDON

What about the letdown that you have after a big success, when you wonder if you'll ever be able to do it again?

GROUCHO

I never felt like that.

SIDNEY SHELDON

But what happens when you get there, and "there" isn't there?

MARTY ALLEN

Your psychiatrist gets richer.

GROUCHO

Bogart used to say, "The only point in making money is so you can tell some big shot where to go."

One day Groucho and I talked about friendship:

I

What do you expect from your friends?

GROUCHO

I don't. Expecting ruins friendships.

I

What qualities do your friends have in common?

GROUCHO

They like me.

I

What else?

GROUCHO

They have taste. Taste is one of the most important things. It makes the difference in whatever you do.

I

What do you value most in a friend?

GROUCHO

Honesty.

I

Are you always honest with your friends?

GROUCHO

Honestly, no.

I

Why not?

GROUCHO

Good manners are very important. I don't like rude people.

I

Besides good manners, what other qualities do your friends share?

GROUCHO

They're smart.

I

What do you think they like most about you?

GROUCHO

I'm seething with charm.

I

And what else do they have in common?

GROUCHO

My friends aren't common. But mostly they come from some part of show business. People in show business are different. They have their own language. A lot of my best friends have always been writers. Erin should marry someone in show business.

I

You?

GROUCHO

No. Someone who can give her what she needs—sexually.

I

Do you know Maugham's *Theatre*?

GROUCHO

Yeah. Maugham was right. Show business people *are* different.

I

Did you always know you wanted to be in show business?

GROUCHO

Yeah. No, for a little while I wanted to be a doctor. When I was a boy, I wanted to be a doctor, like Dr. Beltrofer. He was our doctor when we lived on Ninety-third Street. But I knew pretty early, and I never wanted anything else.

I

Is there anything your friends have in common besides being writers or in show business?

GROUCHO

They're all crazy.

I

Is that an essential prerequisite?

GROUCHO

Yeah.

I

Why?

GROUCHO

Because I'm half crazy.

I

Which half?

GROUCHO

Not the bottom half anymore.

Groucho admitted that he had often played cards and golf mainly as an excuse for engaging in entertaining conversation. Harry Tugend remembered that Groucho's propensity for talking could be a bit disconcerting on the golf course:

"We used to play golf with him. Very few people did because he kept talking on the backswing as we tried to get the balls off. But he never knew what his golf score was and never gave a damn. It was a reason for taking a little exercise, although he'd been playing for forty years. Getting a little exercise, and talking."

But Groucho also listened. Although his friends may not have been in perfect agreement on everything about him, they all agreed that he was a good listener. He didn't use the time while others were talking to plan his next remark. He placed a high value on being a good listener, and he frequently told me how annoyed he was by people who didn't listen:

"You're a good listener. Some people never listen. At Hillcrest a man who wasn't in show business sat at the roundtable where we'd eat lunch and tell funny stories. Somebody told a joke, and this fellow looked pretty sad. So someone says, 'It wasn't that bad a joke.' And this fellow says, 'I feel awful today. The doctor said my mother's dying.' And at the other end of the table a voice says, 'You think that's funny, wait till you hear this one.' "

Groucho had no difficulty in spanning the time from mah-jongg to backgammon by playing neither. Despite the interest of other members of his family in playing cards, Groucho never shared their enthusiasm for games. "I used to do some crossword puzzles," he told me. Harry Tugend noted, "Groucho was interested in conversation with cards, while his brothers and even Sam and Minnie really took their card games seriously."

At dinner at Groucho's, Arthur Sheekman and his wife, Gloria, told me how Groucho *almost* learned to play bridge. They had hired a very prim and proper little old lady to teach them the game. While Sheekman was away from the table, Groucho happened to mention with a lascivious leer, a furtive glance at Gloria in the kitchen, and a few suggestive raisings of his eyebrows that "Sheek lives with his sister, you know." The bridge teacher made a hurried excuse, disappeared out the front door, and never returned.

Many of his friends not only valued his friendship, but also felt that in ways big and small Groucho's encouragement helped them professionally. Bert Granet recalled the time Groucho gave his film a totally gratuitous plug on *You Bet Your Life*—something money couldn't have bought:

"I was sitting there drinking some coffee and right in the middle of *You Bet Your Life*, he stopped and said, 'You know Bert Granet. He's my friend. He just made a picture, a very good picture.' I'd spilled the coffee I was drinking. It was a completely unsolicited comment, and worth a lot. Now, if I'd turned around and asked him to plug that picture, he wouldn't have done it."

He did much the same thing when Dick Cavett's publisher asked for a book jacket endorsement for Cavett's book on television. Groucho wrote it with an enthusiasm that in his case could only be genuine. When Groucho asked Dick Cavett for a picture, Cavett sent one of himself at about four years of age. Groucho immediately put it up on his wall.

Generosity was conscious on Groucho's part, and he was well aware of the value of what he gave. But he counseled me, "Never expect gratitude."

He enjoyed being an unofficial talent scout, something like a freelance baseball scout and an unpaid agent, promoting new young performers who then frequently became his friends. A young Steve Allen was someone for whom Groucho went around giving unsolicited testimonials. His respect for talent was great, and this respect was the basis for many of his friendships, old and new, from Jack Benny to Woody Allen. As a talent scout, Groucho had talent, having very early recognized performers like Lucille Ball, Marilyn Monroe, and Marvin Hamlisch before they became major-leaguers. One he didn't recognize, at least on their first meeting, was Bud Cort, who described for me what happened the first time he walked up to knock on Groucho's front door:

"I put up my hand to knock, but before I could knock, Groucho opened the door. He was so startled to see someone standing there, especially someone who wasn't allowed to cut a single hair, and who had a beard and a ponytail. At that time I was with the Brotherhood of the Source, and I was working in their restaurant squeezing grapefruits. Groucho took one look at me, and he just slammed the door. I was almost as startled as Groucho when the door opened before I knocked.

"About thirty seconds later, while I was still standing there, the door opened again, and this time Goddard Lieberson was standing there. He said, 'Groucho, it's Bud Cort.' And Groucho said, 'I thought it was Manson.' That was how I met Groucho."

Groucho faithfully watched the performances of his friends on television. He believed that most of show business was now in "that box." Usually right after the program, he would call up the friend to let him know how much he enjoyed his performance, but *only* if he really did. With Groucho and Erin, I watched Elliott Gould's TV special, *Out for Lunch*. As soon as the film credits ended (Groucho always watched the closing credits), he reached for the phone. He was extremely conscientious in showing professional consideration and, without false modesty, recognized the value his friends gave to his opinion. Elliott Gould later told me how pleased he was when he received that phone call from Groucho.

Sometimes Groucho had to face a friend whose work he didn't like. This is a problem shared by everyone in show business. He was faithful to his friends, but he would endorse only what he really liked. His answer was often, "Well, I'm not crazy about it," then he would get off the subject as adroitly and as fast as he could. In a case like this, a typical Grouchoism might have been, "It'll be a big grosser. The biggest grocer I know is the A&P."

If he liked a film, he would stand up for it against a dissenting majority. Billy Wilder's *The Front Page* got a rather mixed reaction at its showing in the Motion Picture Academy Theatre, but Groucho loved it. Afterward, out in front of the theatre, he went around telling everyone how much he liked it, challenging negative reactions wherever he ran across them. "It's a pleasure to see two great actors in a well-written script. They're both great actors [Lemmon and Matthau]. The credits were wonderful." Jack Lemmon, Walter Matthau, and Billy Wilder were all Groucho's friends, but his staunch support of the film was professional rather than personal.

Even friends were known to flinch and tremble at Groucho's candor. All of them at one time or another had a preview of coming detractions. Harry Tugend told of the time, shortly after World War II, when they ate at a Japanese restaurant where Groucho made a Pearl Harbor reference that Tugend found more discomforting than amusing. Groucho sat there looking as innocent as only the guilty can.

Occasionally someone wasn't at all entertained by one of Groucho's unwise cracks. King Vidor told me, "A few weeks ago I went into the Polo Lounge with a friend, and I saw Groucho. I said, 'Hello, Groucho, I'd like you to meet a friend of mine,' and I introduced the fellow. And Groucho said, 'Should I be impressed?' I didn't like it."

Friends and acquaintances in the show business world sought out Groucho's opinion and sometimes regretted it. After the preview of *Samson and Delilah*, Cecil B. De Mille asked him what he thought of his latest epic. "I don't think the picture'll be a success," Groucho answered quite matter-of-factly. Astonished, De Mille asked him why. "The leading man [Victor Mature] has bigger tits than the leading lady [Hedy Lamarr]." De Mille never consulted Groucho again.

After Charlton Heston had just finished a film about Michelangelo, he met Groucho at a party. Heston commented on how expensive the film had been, and Groucho said, "You could have saved a lot of money if you'd painted the Sistine Chapel floor instead of the ceiling." Heston did not find the joke exactly uproarious.

Groucho had no regrets about those comments that were taken in the wrong spirit. "What's done is done, and you can't do anything about it," he told me. On occasion, however, he was known to admit that he was sorry and not make a joke out of it.

Bert and Charlotte Granet once received a note of apology, accompanied by a big basket of fruit, candy, and liquor, sent from the Hillcrest Country Club:

Dear Granets,
Sorry I blew my top.
    Groucho

Charlotte Granet explained to me what had happened:

"We had six tickets for a play, opening night seats in the eleventh row. We invited Groucho and Eden and another couple. It was quite a feat getting that many tickets and such good seats for a play everyone wanted to see. The theatre was packed with celebrities. James Garner, for example, was sitting five rows behind us. Everyone knew someone and still they had difficulty getting tickets.

"Groucho minded not having house seats, the first four rows. He kept complaining. Eden was upset because she thought other people could hear him. After the first act, he said he didn't like the play and that he was leaving. We said, 'You're our guests, we brought you here, and we'll drive you home.' But we weren't thrilled about it.

"The next time we were at a party with Groucho, there were bridge tables set up for dinner. I was sitting with Groucho, and when he's made a mistake and knows he is wrong, he goes over and over it. He kept talking about the play and how bad the seats were and he couldn't see or hear anything. He kept doing it and I just couldn't eat. I got up and said to him, 'You have bad manners,' and I moved my chair to another table.

"The next day the packages and the note arrived."

Although Groucho was a man of strong convictions and beliefs, he was willing to listen to new and different ideas, and even to change his mind if he thought he had been wrong. Fortunately, most people didn't take his jokes seriously, even when they should have. On the other hand, sometimes he was taken too seriously. Bert Granet told me about an evening when Groucho's humor failed:

"We were giving a catered dinner party, and the attractive black maid who was serving Groucho offered him the turkey platter, asking, 'White meat or dark?' He looks at her and says, 'I'll have the dark meat. I'll take *you*,' whereupon she got on her high horse and walked out right in the middle of serving dinner.

"Actually it was a joke that didn't come off, but it was a shame because nobody thinks less about color than Groucho."

Groucho expected people to make themselves at home when they visited him, as I learned when I was staying with him, and he expected to make himself equally at home when he was a guest in a friend's house. Bert Granet described what it was like to have him over for dinner:

"When we used to invite Groucho over around the time of *You Bet Your Life*, he'd always make himself really at home. He'd sit at the end of the table saying, 'I'll sit at the head because I'm the oldest.' "

"Dinner at Groucho's was like a Cracker Jack prize," Sidney Sheldon told me. "You could never be sure who you'd find there." Bert Granet confirmed this.

"At Groucho's you're likely to meet interesting people, and he mixes people in interesting ways. One night basketball star Wilt Chamberlain and Edward G. Robinson were invited to dinner. Eddie came up to Wilt's navel."

Norman Krasna was delighted to find Artur Rubinstein at Groucho's one evening when he arrived. Or, at various times, one might have found Spencer Tracy, Humphrey Bogart, Ring Lardner, George Gershwin, Joseph von Sternberg, Eddie Cantor, Robert Benchley, W. C. Fields, Fanny Brice, Mischa Dichter, Cary Grant, Dinah Shore, Gregory Peck, Mae West, S. J. Perelman, Mike Nichols, or Jack Nicholson. Not only did Groucho always invite the celebrated and the interesting to his house, but he did so with an eye for unusual juxtaposition, avoiding the "couples" party or the homogeneous group.

Celebrities are interested in and enjoy meeting other celebrities. Groucho's own position in the celebrity pantheon long enabled him to invite to his house individuals he didn't know but would have liked to know.

They were usually pleased and accepted his invitation. Frequently, they sought him out. Mutual friends brought Groucho together with celebrities he might not otherwise have known, like Alice Cooper, Elton John, and Dr. Jonas Salk.

Some of the people Groucho said he would have liked to know were Hank Aaron, Henry Kissinger, Golda Meir, and Lee Strasberg. He would have also liked to know Einstein. Another person he wanted to meet was fighter George Foreman. Just after the Foreman-Frazier championship fight, I was with Groucho in the lobby of the Beverly Hills Hotel when we saw George Foreman coming out of the Loggia restaurant. I walked up to him and said that I was there with Groucho Marx, who was a fan of his. Groucho and I had just watched him win over Frazier on closed-circuit television at Hugh Hefner's house. Foreman was a man of imposing physical stature, and he and Groucho, standing together, made a striking picture.

When I saw George Foreman again, in New York on Fifth Avenue as he was shopping at Gucci's, he remembered our momentary meeting, and said to me, "Hi, Beverly Hills! How's Groucho? That Groucho, he's my man!"

He told me that Groucho had kept in touch with him ever since we met in Beverly Hills:

"You know, after that day when I met him and you, he called me a lotta times, and wished me luck every time I had a fight. That meant a lot to me. Yeah, he's my man. Groucho, *he's real big!*"

Jennifer Bogart Gould, then Elliott's wife, told me about her first meeting with Groucho:

"It was a big party, and I didn't know anyone. As soon as I met Groucho he seemed to like me right away, and he offered to take me around and introduce me. It was a typical Hollywood party in Beverly Hills. Groucho took me over to the first couple, and he said, 'I want you to meet Mr. and Mrs. Smith.' Then we went over to another couple, and Groucho said, 'I want you to meet Mr. and Mrs. Smith.' And to the next people, he said, 'I'd like to introduce you to Mr. and Mrs. Smith,' and so on. To Groucho they were all 'Mr. and Mrs. Smith.' "

When he entertained, guests were encouraged to perform if they cared to. They often did, but no one was ever made to feel forced to do so, for it was recognized that when Liza Minnelli got up to sing, or Fred Astaire to dance, or George Jessel to tell stories, these were, in a way, professional appearances.

Many of Groucho's friends weren't geographically close to him. They lived all over the world and traveled a great deal professionally, but Groucho kept up a tremendous correspondence over the years. He was proud of his book *The Groucho Letters*, a collection of some of that correspondence. This included letters from George S. Kaufman, Fred Allen, T. S. Eliot, and grandson Andy as a child in summer camp.

Groucho derived much pleasure from the letters he continued to receive from E. B. White and Irving Berlin, as well as one from the niece of Ninety-third Street neighbor Marie Wagner. The Wagners had lived at 172 East Ninety-third, across the street from the Marx family. She wrote: "My grandmother Wagner was a wonderful cook, and the Marx Brothers had many *goodies* out of her kitchen." Her aunt, tennis champion Marie Wagner, who Groucho remembered well, was still alive at the time and in her nineties.

I suggested to Groucho that one could be judged not just by the letters he writes but by the letters he receives—perhaps even more by the letters he receives. "Or by the bills he receives," Groucho added.

"I don't write so many letters now because so many of the people I communicated with are dead," he told me sadly. As he grew older, his list of old friends kept getting shorter. It was the price of having lived so long. "I miss so many people," he told Nunnally Johnson.

Although Charlie Chaplin was one of Groucho's oldest friends, they saw each other only briefly after Chaplin left California to live in Europe. When I went to Switzerland, Groucho gave me a copy of *The Groucho Letters* to give to Chaplin in Vevey. In the book Groucho wrote, "Dear Charlie, I knew you when."

Groucho liked to talk about his friends, but he never gossiped. His emphasis was always on what they were doing professionally. For him, a really basic question was, "Are you working?" rather than, "How are you?" The "working" referred only to show business. Whenever he visited an old friend who was ill and it seemed the friend would never get better, Groucho would say with sad resignation, "He'll never work again."

Groucho was not a meddler. As his grandson Andy said, "He's pretty much live and let live." Living in his house, I noticed that he tended to avoid personal or intimate questions and to respect others' privacy. When there was trauma, Groucho didn't verbalize his grief or depression. When we heard the news that Jack Benny had died, Groucho spent the rest of the afternoon far more quietly than usual, sitting and reading in his bedroom. Andy recalled a Groucho who always reacted that way to sad news about friends. "He just goes to his room and closes the door."

The conversation at Groucho's wasn't always light, but when it did take a turn toward weightier subjects, he would usually end the conversation on a humorous note characteristically his:

ERIN
Don't you think a woman has a right to expect fidelity in marriage?
GROUCHO
Yes.
ERIN
What else do you think a woman ought to expect in marriage?
GROUCHO
Infidelity.

Because so many of his friends were show business personalities, it became essential to have alternating or rotating friends. Making Hollywood films requires people to be up at dawn, and after an exhausting day of performing and even more exhausting waiting, only the super-energetic are prepared to do anything but collapse at night. They are, therefore, often absent from any evening affairs while working. Or, many of his friends would be appearing on the New York stage or working abroad. Groucho deliberately tried to space invitations, so that his guests remained interesting to him and to each other. He liked to maintain some interval between their visits. Even about his favorite friends, he would say, "They've just been here."

The property value of Groucho Marx as a supercelebrity was well recognized by Groucho:

I
You are often used, even exploited by people. Your very appearance at a party can make it a success. People say, "We went to a party and Groucho Marx was there." The hosts will get acceptances from other celebrities who only come because you are going to be there. Being seen with you is a kind of status symbol, and you are sort of a celebrity-in-residence even for your good friends. Do you agree with all that?
GROUCHO
Yeah.

I

Do you mind being used like this by close friends, acquaintances, and even virtual strangers?

GROUCHO

No. I think what it would be like the other way.

Groucho shared all of his friends with me. In his long lifetime he enjoyed many cherished and enduring friendships, and through him some of these became mine.

Any interviewer, even an unobtrusive one, influences the interview. His or her personality affects what the subject says and how he says it, evoking responses that reveal only certain aspects of the person being interviewed. Having a range of people with whom to speak allows us to speak in a range of ways. Groucho, talking with his friends, displayed the multifaceted private person as well as the familiar public figure.

It was important not only to see him *with* his friends, but *through the eyes* of his friends, to share the images his friends had of him. We find out who we are through knowing other people. Each of us is someone different for every person we know.

GODDARD LIEBERSON

Goddard Lieberson was himself a witty man, specializing in recondite puns and esoteric non sequiturs. His friendship with Groucho went back about thirty years, during which time Groucho always considered Goddard his ideal intellectual. It was one of Groucho's most cherished relationships. Goddard's photograph hung on Groucho's wall, as did Groucho's on the wall in Goddard's office. The inscription on the photo Groucho gave Goddard read, "To the only man I ever loved." As he was for the late Igor Stravinsky, Goddard was Groucho's first choice to be the executor of his estate. But it did not happen that way; at the age of sixty-six in May 1977, Goddard Lieberson died.

Besides having distinguished himself as an executive in the recording and broadcasting fields, Goddard Lieberson was the author of *Three for Bedroom C.* He was a noted composer. Among his friends and professional colleagues were Bartók, Ives, Schoenberg, and Stravinsky. His catalogue of compositions includes works for symphony orchestra, chamber music, instrumental music, and works for the theatre, ranging from a symphony to *Piano Pieces for Advanced Children or Retarded Adults.* As senior vice president of CBS and president of Columbia Records, he was responsible for many historic firsts, including the production of Stravinsky's first American recordings, the first recordings of complete dramas on LP (he won a Grammy Award for the Columbia release of *Who's Afraid of Virginia Woolf?*), and numerous original cast recordings of hit Broadway musicals, such as *South Pacific, Kiss Me, Kate, My Fair Lady, West Side Story,* and *A Chorus Line.* He also signed a little-known singer named Bob Dylan to his first recording contract in 1961, and followed this by signing Simon and Garfunkel when, as he said, "Everybody thought it was the name of a Baltimore store." Just before his death he had prepared a television special celebrating the hundredth anniversary of recording, a tribute to American music.

When Groucho, Erin, and I joined Goddard for lunch in a private dining room at CBS, Groucho's greeting to Goddard was, "You look like my father." Reminiscing about mutual friend George S. Kaufman, Groucho told us this story:

"He took this woman to lunch, and he ordered tomato soup. The waiter brings the tomato soup and puts it down in front of him, and the woman reached over, picked up his spoon, and tasted his soup. Kaufman called the waiter and said, 'Waiter, bring me another spoon. No, bring me another bowl of soup.' Then, after lunch, in the taxi he had both arms and legs wrapped around her, and he was trying to kiss her. And she said, 'What do you mean trying to kiss me when you had to get a new bowl of soup because I tasted it?' And he said, 'Tomato soup is one thing, and this is another.'"

Goddard was one of the few people not inhibited by Groucho. On occasion, he would say to Groucho, "You already told me that one," a reaction which never seemed to disturb Groucho—when it came from Goddard.

Goddard was with us in New York when we searched in vain for Groucho's lost lighter, treasured souvenir of the SRO performance at Carnegie Hall, the loss of which had precipitated a mild stroke.

Goddard was in the car with us when we were trapped there by the riot that was occasioned by Groucho's personal appearance at the New York re-premiere of *Animal Crackers.* Just as I can, Goddard told me that he could still close his eyes and vividly see "those faces with noses squashed against the car windows, shutting out all else."

In his own office, filled with autographed photographs of the Sitwells, George Gershwin, Stravinsky, Albert Schweitzer, and the cultural and intellectual elite of the past few decades, Goddard talked with me about Groucho:

GODDARD LIEBERSON

We met just when Melinda was born. I knew Harpo before, but it was Oscar Levant who introduced us. Oscar was one of my oldest friends until his death. Groucho was married to Kay, a very sweet girl and a little frou-frou. Our common bond was always music, because, I must say, Groucho always loved music. And Harry Ruby, whom I loved, was always around. He was, I think, closer to Groucho than almost any other person. I think Groucho misses him more than anybody else, except perhaps Harpo. I asked Groucho one time, "Were you really closer to Harpo than anybody else?" He said, "I guess so." Harpo was a very sensitive person. Of course, you know the Gilbert and Sullivan side of Groucho. He could quote reams of it. He knew the music as well. He did *The Mikado* with Helen Traubel on television. He really loved Gilbert and Sullivan, and show music. He greatly admired composers like Irving Berlin. You know how he admires Irving. You remember that day when you came to CBS with Groucho, and we had lunch, when we talked with Irving?

I

Groucho was so pleased speaking with him again. After that day at lunch with you, they started corresponding again. Groucho told me that he always thought that the Berlin story would make a great play. He tells everyone that Irving and Ellin Berlin had one of the few great marriages he's ever known.

GODDARD LIEBERSON

Groucho always asks me to play "Stay Down Here Where You Belong." He says Irving offered to pay him for every time Groucho *didn't* sing it. I wonder why Groucho never learned to play the piano himself? He loved it. You know how much he likes to sing. Every time I go there, I have to play the piano for him. He always wanted me to play the piano for him, though, I must say, the repertoire is limited. I'd play some of the early songs, and then maybe some Jerome Kern. I'd play songs like "Love Walked In." Oscar Levant used to play for him. (*The telephone rings; coincidentally, it is a call from Irving Berlin*) Hello. Hello, Irving. (*Pause*) Thank you, dear fellow. I did indeed. I got the lyrics you sent me in California. And I also went to see Groucho, and I gave him your love. By the way, I just got back a letter today that I sent you. They didn't know you there. I'll tell you, you'd better start paying your bills! (*Pause*) You didn't tell me you wrote a song called "How Do You Do It, Mabel, on $20 a Week?" It's very funny. It's a marvelous song. (*Pause*) "Stay Down Here Where You Belong"? Groucho never sang that, did he? (*Pause*) He kids about it. (*Pause*) There was a funny song in the Yiddish theatre about a girl getting married, and her father sings to her, "Don't pay any attention to the family tree; look at the business plant." (*Pause*) Go ahead, sing it . . . (*Laughing*) "Cohen Owes Me $97." (*Pause*) Yes, I remember that. (*Pause*) Okay, Irving, I'll call you as soon as I get back from Barbados. Bye. (*Hangs up*) Irving's incredible. He sang the whole lyric for me to "Cohen Owes Me $97." Do you know that song?

I

No. I never heard it.

GODDARD LIEBERSON

An old Jewish man is dying, and before he dies he says to his son: "Cohen owes me $97; please collect—I don't give credit." Then he gets paid before he dies, and he says, "This is no time for a businessman to die." That other song, "How Do You Do It, Mabel, on $20 a Week?" This guy comes in, and he looks at her hats, her fur coats, her dresses, and he says to her, "How do you do it, Mabel, on $20 a week?" Obviously, she's a hooker. In the tribute to American music I'm producing, I'm doing it by professions, and this is one of the professions.

I

If asked to do so, how would you characterize Groucho?

GODDARD LIEBERSON

Groucho is actually a literary man who in his jokes shares his privacy with the abandon of a painfully truthful autobiographer. But he never reveals everything, for at a certain point, there is epistemic privacy. If I had a headache and tell you about it, you can't really feel it. Groucho is always reaching. He has always been a person of serious aspirations and intellectual searching.

EDEN MARX

Once when I was staying at Groucho's house during a visit to California, Eden dropped by with a festively wrapped Christmas gift for Groucho. Though divorced for a number of years, Groucho and Eden had remained friends. After dinner, we all sat in Groucho's bar/den, surrounded by Marxabilia, and I asked Eden to tell me about how she and Groucho met.

EDEN
Groucho was making a picture with my sister Dee at RKO . . . (*To Groucho*) Will you correct me if I'm wrong?
GROUCHO
Yeah. But who'll correct me?
EDEN
After we do this, we may marry again, right?
GROUCHO
Orville or Wilbur?
EDEN
You were doing a picture with my sister Dee at RKO, and Irwin Allen was the producer. It was *A Girl in Every Port* with Marie Wilson.
GROUCHO
We were sailors.
EDEN
Right. I remember 'cause that's where I met you. And I fainted. (*Laughs*)
GROUCHO
And the first I knew I was married.
EDEN
(*Laughs*) I hadn't had anything to eat, and it got to be three o'clock, and I said, "Hey, I feel faint!" So you took me to the dressing room. You were so adorable. You gave me cushions and everything, and I thought how marvelous a man you were.
GROUCHO
Did I give you food?
EDEN
No, that's all. And you said, "I'll call you in about six weeks when I'm through with the picture." I said, "Okay," never expecting to hear from you. But I did.

GROUCHO

It cost me a pretty penny. Tell her (*Indicating me*) about our trip to Europe.

EDEN

That's four years later. We went on many trips to Europe. Paris, London . . .

GROUCHO

We had a De Soto car. Dodge Risotta, that's an Italian De Soto.

EDEN

. . . Gee, Vienna, everything. We made commercials over there. Every time I see you now, you say, "Didn't we have fun in Holland!" You said it to me the other night when we were at some dinner party. We went to many countries. Why do you say Holland? I'm curious.

GROUCHO

Unusual country. Windmills.

EDEN

Where we lost Melinda.

GROUCHO

Yeah, but we found her again. That wasn't in Holland.

EDEN

One of the Scandinavian countries?

GROUCHO

In Denmark. That's where I bought that rug.

EDEN

Oh yeah. I love that hanging. It's supposed to be a rug, but I said it's too beautiful to be a rug, so I hung it. Someone said that it's the Marx Brothers, with the pointed hat like Chico. But you know what it is? It's the United Nations. Look . . . yellow, white, brown, black. It's all the races together. Do you know that?

GROUCHO

No, it never occurred to me.

EDEN

Oh, here's Gloria's [Gloria Stuart Sheekman] painting of the barn. And she's giving her new show.

GROUCHO

She's in show business now.

EDEN

She's giving her new painting show in February in Palm Springs. Can you come down for it?

GROUCHO

I doubt it. I went down to see Zeppo and Gummo.

EDEN

When?

GROUCHO

Two weeks ago, and she (*Indicating me*) came with me. Zeppo's stuck on her.

EDEN

Where did you stay?

GROUCHO

We didn't. We came back that night. It only took us two hours.

EDEN

Oh, for heaven's sake! What a drive! To go down and have dinner and come back. Oh, I wish you would have told me you were going. Remember our house in Palm Springs that I sold to Barbara Marx?

GROUCHO

She took care of Zeppo while he was sick.

EDEN

I wish you could have gone over to see our house.

GROUCHO

(*Motioning to some photos on the wall*) I had other pictures about this size on the walls there with different people who had been on the quiz show.

EDEN

I have those. Do you want them?

GROUCHO

Well, if you're not doing anything with them, I'd put them up in this hall here.

EDEN

They're in my mother's garage.

GROUCHO

How is your mother's garage?

EDEN

(*Laughing*) You know, they're such marvelous pictures. Would you really like them?

GROUCHO

Is there a picture of Hitler? Do you think he'll run again?

EDEN

In fact, those pictures would be kind of great here. They're almost antiques . . .

GROUCHO

So am I.

EDEN

. . . Almost collector's items. Would Erin want to put them up there?

GROUCHO

It's *my* house . . .

EDEN

They'd really be divine here.

GROUCHO

. . . Not Erin's house.

EDEN

They'd be divine here.

GROUCHO

I'll sell them.

EDEN

Hey! I'll trade you those for the hanging.

GROUCHO

No.

EDEN

Well, let's see what other deal we could make. (*Laughs*) Do you remember when we were over in France, at the George V. It was fun then.

GROUCHO

I was over there last year.

EDEN

I know, and you said you didn't like it very much.

GROUCHO

I didn't say that at all. I was a big sensation. I remember when we lived in the hotel in New York.

EDEN

Overlooking the park. Eloise's hotel, the Plaza.

GROUCHO

It was snowing, and you didn't have any overshoes. And I went out one morning while you were sleeping to get you a pair of overshoes. I went from Fifty-ninth to Sixty-second Street and I couldn't get a taxi. They were all going back to the barn, or something. A policeman stopped me and said, "I'll get you a cab if you'll answer one question." So he got me the cab, and I said, "What's the question you wanted to ask me?" He said, "Could Harpo really talk?"

EDEN

What did you say?

GROUCHO

I said no. You remember the couple that worked for us? At our house in . . .

EDEN

London. I sure do. They were delightful.

GROUCHO

She was the cook, and he cleaned the house. And you had the only good bedroom. Every Sunday they went off, and they bought a hundred condoms and went over to Ireland and sold them. He made more money selling the condoms than we were paying him.

EDEN

We rented a house for about three or four months, didn't we?

GROUCHO

The man who owned it had been in love with Margaret Sullavan.

EDEN

He was married to Margaret Sullavan, he was her last husband. And when you say I had the only good bedroom, I almost felt I was in a room with a ghost, because there was a big portrait of Margaret Sullavan.

GROUCHO

And all the linen in the house had her initials on them.

EDEN

Yes, it was sort of like living with a ghost. Groucho was working, doing the *You Bet Your Life* show over there.

GROUCHO

She was a fine actress. Gregory Peck lived next door.

EDEN

Oh, and Veronique and I used to shop all the time, and we became very good friends.

GROUCHO

Gregory had never smoked a pipe, and he was in a movie where he had to smoke a pipe. So he went to the famous pipe store in London, and he bought ten pipes. He never smoked them except in that movie. Somewhere there's ten valuable British pipes. That's where I met T. S. Eliot . . .

EDEN

Oh, wait a minute. We've got to finish this, just for fun. You took Gregory to a pipe store, and you're not supposed to try the pipes. But you said Gregory Peck was just like a little boy in the store. He said you're not supposed to try the pipes, but you said, "There's no one looking. Try them." So he went puff, puff, puff, puff, while no one was looking, because you told him to. You said, "Isn't that like a little boy?"

GROUCHO

You can't tell anything about a pipe until you smoke it.

EDEN

Right, right. That was fun. It was really fun in London, because some newsman from the *Observer* or some newspaper . . .

GROUCHO

That's where I met T. S. Eliot.

EDEN

Oh, didn't we have a lovely time there? But this was fun because the reporter knew I was an artist, so they took me out to the park, I guess Hyde Park, and had me sketching. And it was in the paper and all. I have the clippings. I drew one or two pictures, and we came back to our house, but couldn't get in because I'd forgotten my key. I knew you were home. We buzzed and we knocked, and I yelled Grouch—which he thought was funny, but that's what I called you, not Groucho, Grouch. And I said, "Let's see if we can get through the Pecks' place next door." I was frantic. We had something to do that night, and here we were at the park, me drawing and everything. The maid let us in, no one was home at the Pecks'. So, we went up to the backyard of their place, and the reporter had to climb over the Pecks' wall with his camera and everything, and break into our place, where he found you shaving. You couldn't hear because of the electric shaver. It was in the paper. Anyway, it was fun in London.

GROUCHO

I was in London at the Savoy . . .

EDEN

Isn't that a great hotel!

GROUCHO

. . . on New Year's Eve . . .

EDEN

I love that hotel.

GROUCHO

. . . and Noel Coward was at the Savoy.

EDEN

I wish we could go back there.

GROUCHO

He danced on the table . . .

EDEN

We had a great time there.

GROUCHO

. . . and I got up on the table and danced with him. I danced with Noel Coward on the table at the Savoy.

EDEN

I loved that, living there for four months.

GROUCHO

We were young.

EDEN

(*Laughing*) Right. Let's see, where else did we have fun? I think when we traveled we always had fun. We always took Melinda.

GROUCHO

On the *Queen Mary* she didn't talk to us.

EDEN

No, because . . .

GROUCHO

She had her own gang.

EDEN

We were in first class, and she wanted to go second class because that's where the fun was, and I didn't blame her. You know, all the young boys and everything were in second class. They couldn't afford to travel in first class, and she was bored to death. So she'd pick up boys and girls in the second class. Had her own gang. She was coming toward us on the first-class deck with them, and we said, "Hi!" and she'd go by. (*Laughs*) She didn't want to recognize us because she wanted to be one of the gang. She did that in Hawaii, too. That's growing up.

GROUCHO

That's normal.

EDEN

It is very normal in growing up. But we were hurt.

GROUCHO

I remember when I went to Hawaii on the boat. You were with me.

EDEN

Sure, and Melinda was fifteen.

GROUCHO

The boat was still at anchor in the harbor, the crowd at the shore waving. We went to the side of the boat. I vomited.

EDEN

(*Laughs*) You're not a very good sailor.

SIDNEY SHELDON

Sidney Sheldon and Groucho were longtime pun-pals. Novelist Sheldon, author of *The Naked Face*, *The Other Side of Midnight*, and *The Stranger in the Mirror*, at twenty-five had three hit plays running simultaneously on Broadway. In Hollywood, he wrote the Academy Award–winning screenplay for *The Bachelor and the Bobby-Soxer* and received Screen Writers Guild awards for the Best Musical of the Year for *Easter Parade* and *Annie Get Your Gun*. For the Broadway musical *Redhead*, he won a Tony. He has written scripts for twenty-five major motion pictures and over two hundred TV scripts. For the long-running TV series *I Dream of Jeannie*, he not only conceived the idea, but also wrote all the episodes himself.

Although *Jeannie* was an immediate popular success, not every critic took to it. Cleveland Amory, writing in *TV Guide*, said that the idea was terrible, the acting was terrible, the production was terrible, the directing was terrible, and the conception was terrible. Sidney Sheldon suffered in silence for a few days, then wrote to Cleveland Amory:

"I read your review, and if there's one thing I don't like, it's a wishy-washy review. Couldn't you just say whether you liked it or not?"

Sidney Sheldon waited in vain for a reply. At the end of the year, however, Amory devoted his entire article to the funniest letter of the year, Sidney Sheldon's.

Though he was never intimidated by Groucho's barbed wit, his wife, Jorja, admitted to having been. Sidney Sheldon told me how Jorja and Groucho established their détente:

"One of my earlier memories of Groucho, before I was married to Jorja, was when I would take her to Groucho's house. She was terrified of him! He was always very nice to her, but she was afraid he would turn his acidulous wit on her, and she couldn't cope with it. So she begged me never to leave her alone with him. He'd go up to her and say, 'When are you getting pregnant?' and it would just put her away because we weren't married. She didn't know how to respond to that.

"After Jorja and I were married, our first dinner guests were Groucho and Eden. It was a Saturday, and I was playing gin, and either because I was winning or losing, I was very late getting home. I got home after seven o'clock. I later learned that Jorja had heard the doorbell and thought that I'd forgotten my key. She opened the door and found herself face to face with Groucho and Eden. Jorja was panicky, because she felt I wasn't there to protect her.

"Now, Jorja had never *had* a drink, I don't think, let alone *mixed* a drink before we were married. She didn't know *how* to make a drink. So, when Groucho said he would have a scotch and water, she went to the bar, filled the glass with scotch, and then added a little bit of water to it. *That* broke the ice! When I came home, they were all having a great time."

Sidney Sheldon recognized that Jorja's initial wariness was not unreasonable:

"Groucho, like most comics, has two sides to him: he can be very cruel and he can be very sweet. I remember once we were walking down the street, and a man came up to him and said, 'Groucho, do you remember me?' Now, there are a lot of answers to that question. Groucho's answer was, 'What have you ever done in your life that I should remember you?' The man didn't think it was funny, and I told Groucho that I thought that that kind of behavior was unnecessary.

"Years ago we went to a place called Billy Grey's Bandbox, which used to be on Fairfax. That was Joel Grey's father. We went to see *My Fairfax Lady*. That was the name of the show the comic was doing. They gave us a front table because Groucho was there. We were right in front of the comedian. He started doing the show, doing it mainly for Grouch. Now, during the whole performance, I don't think Grouch even smiled once, let alone laughed. Jorja was so embarrassed by this that she was laughing uproariously trying to make up for Groucho not laughing; and she didn't even understand any of the jokes, because most of them were rather ethnic.

"Unlike most comics, however, he can be very generous toward other comics, and most comics are *not*. I remember Groucho told me about Jackie Gleason when he was doing *The Honeymooners*. Groucho thought it was a marvelous show, and I didn't like it very much. He said, 'Well, look at it again,' and I did, and I learned to enjoy it.

"The next time I remember him talking about someone was when he said Shecky Greene was a comedy talent. I'd never seen Shecky Greene. Because of Groucho's enthusiasm, the next time I went to Las Vegas, I made it a point to see Shecky.

"He was really enthusiastic about Woody Allen. Just a few days ago, he said that he was in love with Buddy Hackett, whom he had met recently. So, he is very generous about the talent of other comedians. In a comedian this is an unusual trait.

"I think that Groucho is probably prouder of being a writer than he is of being a comedian. Most comedians are not that literate; they're not that well read. Groucho is extremely well read. He's written perhaps half a dozen books. He's a member of the Screen Writers Guild of America. I produced a show for the Guild one year, and Groucho appeared on it, and he's appeared many times since. The last time he was there, he got a standing ovation.

"Most of his friends have died, and I think he feels rather close to me, as I feel close to him. Groucho has a loyalty to his old friends, those who are still alive. He frequently goes to visit Arthur Sheekman and Nunnally Johnson. He's really outlived most of his contemporaries. He was very badly hit by Jack Benny's death. Up until about a year ago, Groucho never talked about that. He said he never went to funerals. He went to Benny's funeral, and now he does talk about that. He doesn't seem to mind it so much.

"A couple of days ago, he said, 'When I'm helpless and really feeling lousy, then I don't want them to keep me alive. I want to go.' He'd never talked that way before.

"Another interesting facet of Groucho's character—which again is very unlike most comedians—he takes pleasure in his friends' successes. When I had a hit picture or a play, or when my book became successful, he would tell me how glad he was and he would talk to other people, and he really was genuinely pleased. That's a rare trait for a comedian to exhibit.

"Groucho is well aware of the fact that he is indeed a living legend. He talks about all the film festivals of the Marx Brothers that are going on around the world. He came to a party at our house one evening wearing his French Legion of Honor. Groucho was dressed in tails and the party wasn't formal, so I asked him about it. I don't know if he was being serious or not, but he said you were not allowed to wear the Legion of Honor unless you wore tails. So, he went to the trouble of putting tails on.

"Another story that involves Groucho's clothes happened on an evening when the four of us had a date for dinner. As it turned out Jorja and Eden were unable to make it. I called Groucho and said it was just the two of us for dinner tonight, and he said, 'Where are we going?' I said, 'I don't know. We'll go someplace nice.' He said, 'How should I dress?' and I said, 'Dress nicely, I don't want to be ashamed of you.'

"I arrived at his house to pick him up. He opened the door and he was wearing Eden's skirt and blouse, earrings, little cloche hat, high heel shoes, and smoking a cigar. He said, 'You want to come in for a drink?' and I said, 'Fine.' We went into the den and were having a drink when the doorbell rang, and Groucho went to answer it.

"What he had forgotten was that he had a date with some network executives who were coming over to talk to him about a new show. Well, Bill Dozier and two other men walked in, and I watched their faces. No one reacted to the way Groucho was dressed! Not a word was said. *He* didn't say anything. They talked business for about an hour and a half, and they left, Groucho ushered them out the door, and then he said to me, 'I'll change.' He got into his clothes and we went out to dinner. And nothing more was ever said about that episode.

"I ran into Bill Dozier a couple of years later, and I said, 'Bill, what did you think when you came to Groucho's house that night and found him dressed in women's clothes?' He said, 'Well, I didn't think anything of it. If it had been anyone but Groucho, I would have been very suspicious.'

"I think because of the financial insecurity of his earlier days, Groucho is very careful about his money. He was not known as a great spendthrift. Yet, when I was going to New York and I was staying at the Plaza, he called the manager, who was a friend of his, and I got a beautiful suite for half the price it ordinarily would have cost. I remember being surprised that Groucho had made that long-distance phone call for me.

"A number of years ago I talked to Grouch about doing a series, and he said he didn't want to do another series. I was producing at Screen Gems then, and I gave him an idea that he liked about a host who was a kind of irascible character, not lovable at all, who went around telling people off and screwing up their lives, and Groucho loved it. I talked to Screen Gems, and they were all for it. I wrote the pilot script, and it was approved. At that time one of Groucho's brothers died, and Screen Gems got nervous. Someone said, 'Wait a minute . . . Groucho may be too old to make this series.' I tried to talk them out of it, but I couldn't. So I had to tell Groucho the series was off, and he said, 'Why? Did they think I'm too old?' I said, 'No, of course not,' but he kept bringing it up, and he was very hurt that they didn't go ahead with the series. I think Screen Gems made a mistake, because if they had made it, I think it would have been a big hit. It would have been wonderful for them and wonderful for Groucho.

"An example of Groucho's never taking his own success for granted: One evening we were having dinner at my house, and someone suggested that Groucho take a vacation for three or four weeks, and let someone else take over *You Bet Your Life*. And Groucho said, 'No I'm not going to do it.' I said, 'It sounds like a great idea.' 'No, not really. What if the person who comes out and does the show instead of me is so good they don't want me back?'

"At the time, shows like *The $64,000 Question* were on, a lot of big-money giveaway shows; and at that time Groucho's top prize was sixty-four dollars. So it was obvious that people were not listening to that show just because they were trying to win those prizes. It was Groucho. Yet, he didn't want to be away for a few weeks lest they could replace him.

"As Groucho got older, and after he and Eden were divorced, I think he became very lonely. I introduced him to a girl who was attractive, a writer and an actress and very bright, and he responded to her. She came to me and said, 'I don't know what to do. Groucho wants me to move in with him, and travel with him.' And she said, 'You know, I really can't devote my life to doing that.' I don't think it was sex, but he felt very strongly the need for companionship. There was a series of girls around him all the time. Then, when Erin came along, she fulfilled his needs.

"I think most people have aggressions in one form or another, but society has taught us that when we don't like people or when people do something we disapprove of, we keep quiet about it. We don't speak out, and we're not honest about it. For whatever reasons, Groucho started out very early to say exactly what was on his mind. And out of that he built up a whole career. Because of that people thought he was not serious. They took insults from him that would have gotten anyone else a punch in the nose.

"He would say outrageous things to very important people. It takes a certain kind of mentality to do that. I was going to say a certain kind of security, but, all in all, I don't really think that's it. There's something in him that allows him to say these outrageous things to people, except that they think he is joking about it. But the truth is, he means every word he says, although he's mellowed over the years. He doesn't insult people he likes."

Jorja Sheldon added:

"Sometimes I look at him when he first comes in, dropping by our house in the late morning, and he smiles and I know exactly what he looked like when he was five years old, and his aunt came in and said, 'What beautiful eyes you have, Julius.' Anyway, when Groucho comes in the morning, and he smiles, I see that five-year-old boy, and I'm pleased to know him."

On Sunday when the Sheldons had Groucho, Erin, Marty Allen and his wife, "Frenchy," and me over for brunch, Sidney Sheldon and Groucho reminisced about the early days of their friendship:

GROUCHO

Where's the first place I met you? M-G-M?

SIDNEY SHELDON

No, it was Madam Kitty's. Actually, Grouch, we met at the Granets'.

ERIN

Did Groucho take to you immediately?

SIDNEY SHELDON

I don't know. I think we started bantering back and forth. I was at M-G-M under contract, producing and writing. I did *Easter Parade, Annie Get Your Gun,* and it was that period. I gave him a business card with my name on it.

GROUCHO

And I immediately destroyed it.

SIDNEY SHELDON

Yeah, I took to him immediately. Every Thanksgiving since, we've had Groucho to the house. We had a house that was quite a bit larger than this, and we would have eighty, a hundred people in for Thanksgiving dinner. It was traditional. Groucho would come over and he'd say, "I don't eat turkey." Talk about Mr. Gracious at a dinner party!

JORJA SHELDON

You know, Groucho always changed his drink request. One time it's a Bushmill he wants, so I say, "Okay, I've gotta have a bottle of Bushmill . . ."

GROUCHO

Now it's Irish whiskey.

JORJA SHELDON

". . . for Groucho." So, I have it there. Groucho comes in and I say, "Bushmill, is it?" "No. Don't you have any Campari? Everybody has Campari." Well, of course I didn't have Campari. So I'd get another bottle. We have in storage at least fifteen bottles with one drink missing.

SIDNEY SHELDON

He'd keep switching each time.

JORJA SHELDON

And then he'd berate me because I didn't have this strange thing he's drinking.

GROUCHO

Now I don't drink at all.

SIDNEY SHELDON

But you still berate her. How do you explain that?

GROUCHO

Well, I was entitled to.

SIDNEY SHELDON

We were driving from a restaurant one day, and a police car pulls me over. I'm at the wheel. Before I could say anything, Groucho leans out the window and says, "You're absolutely right, officer. He should be put in jail." All I did was have a bright light on, because it wasn't working properly. But by the time Groucho was through, I was almost arrested.

GROUCHO

I was picked up by a cop one day on a motorcycle. He came over to me and said, "Let me see your driver's card." I whipped out a cigar and gave it to him. He says, "You know, you took the wrong lane on Wilshire Boulevard." I said, "Well, I'm sorry, but those things happen." He says, "I want to ask you one question: Why aren't there more Laurel and Hardy movies on television?"

MARTY ALLEN

I met your brother Chico once. Chico was at the Sands Hotel, and I was there with Nat Cole. I did a pantomime. After the show, I was standing with Nat, and Chico walked by. I didn't know he was in the audience. He touched my hand and he says, "My brother Harpo would have loved your pantomime." When he said that to me, I went eight feet in the air. Nat Cole said, "What happened?" I told him what happened, and he said, "Well, you want to close the show?" I said, "I'd better, 'cause I'm flying!"

GROUCHO

You're a funny man under all that hair. (*To Marty Allen's wife*) My father's name was Frenchie too. But he wasn't as pretty as you. (*They get up to leave*) Can I take one of these eggs home for my cook?

SIDNEY SHELDON

It's hard-boiled. It's an Easter egg.

GROUCHO

I think I'll leave it here if you're gonna act that way. I don't need your eggs.

MAX GORDON

In his book *Max Gordon Presents*, Max Gordon wrote under a picture of a greasepaint-mustached Groucho, "This man needs no introduction. He was as mad then as he is now, and he has always been one of my dearest friends." On the photo Groucho had written, "To Max Salpeter, with affection, from Dr. Hackenbush."

Max Salpeter, later known as Max Gordon, was the producer who brought plays like *Three's a Crowd, The Band Wagon, The Cat and the Fiddle, Design for Living, Roberta, The Shining Hour, Dodszvorth, The Great Waltz, Ethan Frome, The Women, My Sister Eileen, Junior Miss, The Late George Apley, Born Yesterday,* and *The Sold Gold Cadillac* to Broadway. I talked with him in his New York apartment where he shared with me his recollections:

MAX GORDON

My first meeting with the boys was about 1920. Then, of course, they had just come in with a show that opened in Philadelphia and came into the Casino Theatre. As you probably know, they were a big hit, and we were very friendly. In fact, every time Harpo Marx came into New York, the first thing he did was to call me up, have dinner with us, and we would arrange for a show—take him to a show, or whatever he had in mind. When I was sick with a breakdown once, Harpo came up to see me, and when he went out the door, he threw a thousand dollars on my bed. Groucho called up the next day and said, "I want you to know that I have fifty percent of that." So, you see, it was a very warm relationship.

Then, I think, it was Groucho that said to me, "Why don't you come out and help us with *Duck Soup*? Go see Lasky. He can't give you any money, but go and see him, and see what." So I went to see Lasky. Of course, they were broke then—it was in 1932, 1933, when things were very bad—and Lasky made a deal with me for $250 a week plus that as soon as they got their money back with the picture, I was to get $10,000. Now, about fifteen years elapsed, and one day I got a call from Gummo Marx that reminded me about this thing. Of course, I'd forgotten all about it. So I got $10,000 more for that.

Then, every time Groucho came to New York, we would have dinner right away. Of course he was a great help for me in my first musical, *Three's a Crowd*. He wrote a sketch for it, too. He was really interested, and he was very helpful, and we were so close. I would go out of town with him, we were that close. I tell you, he was so wonderful with me for fifty years, until finally the last words I had with him.

I read a wonderful notice in *The New Yorker* about Groucho making a speech at T. S. Eliot's funeral. But this time Groucho had said something that I thought was in bad taste, trying to get a laugh. So I called him. I said, "Gee whiz, you shouldn't have said that. This man's dead; it's in bad taste." He says, "Well, I'm a comedian." And I says, "You don't have to be on *all* the time," which I regretted. I haven't heard from him since. I saw him in some audition film about three or four years ago, and I thought he was great. Then I saw that show about the Marx Brothers, what was it called?

I

Minnie's Boys. Did you know Minnie Marx?

MAX GORDON

His mother, no. I never knew his mother. I knew his father. Sam was wonderful. Of course, you're too young to have heard Harpo's imitation of his father. It was just great. Well, I don't remember a thing Sam Marx said, except that he was funny, and Harpo did this great imitation of him.

I

What do you remember about the older brothers?

MAX GORDON

Chico, of course, was the opposite of Groucho. He was a gambler, and he lived a wonderful life—for Chico. He was irresponsible. Gummo was the businessman, you know. He became the business manager. Have you seen Groucho recently?

I

I was there for his eighty-fifth birthday.

MAX GORDON

When I knew him he was so full of vigor. You know, he said that one thing I didn't like about T. S. Eliot. But, in general, he had taste. He would get off some remarks, though. Once I said something about my successes, and he said, "Oh, don't tell me about your successes." But, as I said, he was still wonderful with me. I would go up to places like New Haven, and I would go to their matinees. Then we would go places, and he'd stay over with me, or I'd stay over with him. What else can I tell you?

I

In the years that you had known Groucho, had you ever before criticized negatively anything he had done?

MAX GORDON

Oh no. Nobody dared; he'd let out that onslaught, and no one could answer him. But we never had any differences until this thing with T. S. Eliot happened. It was the first time in all those years. Before that, I used to call him all the time. He used to call me by my right name, Salpeter. And I got loads of lovable letters from him.

I

He always tells people about your calling him up when the stock market crashed in 1929.

MAX GORDON

I remember that very clearly. The market broke, and I called him up and said, "The jig is up."

I

I've heard Groucho tell that story to Jack Lemmon, and to Woody Allen.

MAX GORDON

Did you know I discovered Woody Allen? He was playing a café. I saw him, and I thought he was wonderful. I was going to do a play with him, but I had a complete nervous breakdown. I don't know what else I can tell you. Groucho's a great comedian, a genius. No question about it, he's an outstanding man. And Groucho was smart about his money. He was very conservative and took care of his money. Now he's a rich man, a very rich man. He has that young woman with him. When you look back on Groucho's life, he's had problems. But now I think he's a very happy man. That's about all.

HARRY TUGEND

Fred Allen combined the professional skills most respected by Groucho: that of the writer and that of the performer. Not surprisingly, he was a friend of Groucho's and they kept up a witty correspondence through the years. Allen's radio show producer and good friend was Harry Tugend, an ex-performer and writer himself from vaudeville days. Later Tugend became a Hollywood producer and screenwriter; more recently he produced television series and specials.

As well as being a friend of all the Marx Brothers, Harry Tugend was also associated with them professionally. It was he who produced the Marx Brothers' swan song (Groucho called it a "swan dive"), *The Incredible Jewel Robbery*, the last show business appearance of the three Marx Brothers together, on television. He also produced a TV version of *Time for Elizabeth*, starring Groucho and Eden. He recalled some of his memories of Groucho for me:

"He did *Time for Elizabeth* in summer stock over and over and over again, oh, I don't know how many times. And Eden had also done it. But Groucho insisted on having what we call 'idiot cards' all around so he could see the lines. He was afraid he'd muck the lines! Which was ridiculous. He'd been playing the thing besides having written it, but he's such a perfectionist.

"So I had to do it, and I did it until there was one speech that came along—a rather long monologue—which he delivered into a mirror speaking to himself. It was a sort of introspective thing in which he started analyzing himself, and so on. I saw no reason why he should have to have the teleprompter or idiot cards for it, because he had to look into the mirror all the time.

"So I said, 'Groucho, for heaven's sake, will you try it once without the damn idiot cards all over?' He used to make fun of idiot cards. Anyway, I said, 'I'm willing to waste film. Let's try it as you wrote it and as you've done it over and over again, looking into the mirror without the damn cards.' So he mumbled, swore, and did it in one take, without a single mistake. And yet, you never knew, they never knew, what they would do in a play onstage. Groucho would ad-lib anything at all, and it could throw everyone completely off their cues.

"He appeared at several of the Screen Writers Guild affairs. Up until a couple of years ago, they were the greatest shows in town, because you had the finest writers, the Billy Wilders, the Nunnally Johnsons, and everyone else contributing the material. We'd get a terrific show, and Groucho was in several of them.

"Very fine material. One was a satire on *You Bet Your Life* where he was interrogating Norman Krasna and Jerry Wald, who then supposedly were running RKO for Howard Hughes, but they had never seen him. They had been there almost seven months and had never made a picture. It was hilarious. At one time Groucho even agreed to be master of ceremonies for the evening. And his material, whether it was ad-libbed or prepared, always seemed ad-libbed. He was so wonderful he got the greatest standing ovation I have ever seen in any of the Screen Writers Guild shows. It was absolutely fantastic.

"He was always going for the laugh. If it wasn't funny and you didn't laugh, it didn't bother him. So every once in a while, he'd hit one and it was funny, and you'd laugh. He just took that as a matter of course. He was just letting it pour out, and when he hit a funny line and you laughed, he was gratified.

"We used to play golf with him. I remember one time my wife and I were playing with him in Palm Springs. You had to have a golf cart because there were no caddies. My wife was a hundred yards from the green and wondering what club to use. She turned and said, 'What club do you think I ought to use to get to the green?' And Groucho, without any hesitation, said, 'Use the golf cart!' Which was typical.

"I remember he took me to see Woody Allen, whom he admired very much, and Woody vice versa. He said, 'Come on, let's go to Vegas,' and we went there. Woody Allen was giving out with his routine, which was way over the head of most of the audience. Afterwards we went backstage to see him. He admired Woody as a writer because Woody wrote his own material.

"And his reading was along those lines. He'd get *The Atlantic Monthly*. I think his original ambition was to be a doctor. Somewhere early that got lost. Of course, his mother was the one who pushed him into show business.

"At the opening of *I'll Say She Is*, their first Broadway show, she had broken her hip, and it was in a cast. So before the box office was opened, they carried her and put her into a box seat, right next to the stage and facing the stage. And she said, 'No, no, no, no. Turn me around.' She'd been to rehearsals. 'I know what they're gonna say. I want to see how the audience reacts.' So she was facing the audience at the opening of that show.

"His father was in the audience, too. And two people behind him had been arguing about whether they were brothers or not. Really brothers. And Groucho's father was listening to their conversation. With an accent—he was quite a character—he turned around to this fellow who said they are not really brothers and said, 'You wanna bet?' And this fellow says, 'Yes.' And Groucho's father said, 'What are the odds?'

"Groucho is a man who hated publicity, who hated people rushing around for his autograph. He couldn't stand the sort of thing that stars are usually looking forward to. And yet there was another side of him, where at times he'd want to be known. I remember when we went to Vegas to see the Woody Allen show. We stayed at the hotel, and he said, 'Let's go down and take a walk.' So we went and walked through the lobby, and he had this funny hat with a feather in it on, and he was stopped mostly by young girls.

"Incidentally, I was the one who finally made him grow a mustache. You see, he never had a mustache because he didn't want to be spotted on the street. I said, 'Groucho, now that you're appearing on television, you've got to have a mustache.' The one that he used in the theatre was painted on, and it was phony as hell. You could see it was just some black greasepaint. So he finally grew a natural mustache, which he still has to this day. Now when you see Groucho, you recognize him, especially if he has those funny hats.

"Well, anyway, we were walking through the lobby of the hotel, and he's making a play for every young girl he met, which was part of his act. When you see him on television, you presume this is the great Lothario, a sex maniac, and he is everything but. But it is part of his routine. They recognized him, and he signed autographs, and he was having the time of his life."

With Erin at the Cannes Film Festival in 1972, when Groucho received the French Legion of Honor. (Courtesy of the Cinémathèque Française)

Gina Lollobrigida and Groucho making up at the Cannes Film Festival. (Courtesy of the Cinémathèque Française)

Groucho and Erin got into bed together but failed to shock photographer Charles William Bush. Just over Groucho's motorized adjustable bed is one of his favorite paintings, which he purchased because one of the houses in it "looks just like the one we all lived in in Chicago." (Photo by Charles William Bush)

Groucho, Erin, and a black gorilla doll in Groucho's living room. Groucho gave an identical gorilla to Alice Cooper. (Photo by Charles William Bush)

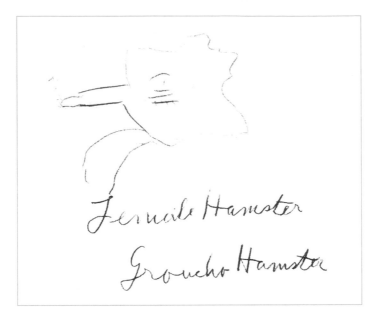

Groucho drew this sketch for me of the sole female member of the "Flying Hamsters—the only one who smoked a cigar." He signed it for me "Groucho Hamster."

Groucho cuts the birthday cake baked and decorated by Maurice Bonté that I brought him. The message attached to the yellow marzipan duck reads, "The secret words are Happy Birthday, Groucho." (Photo by Charlotte Chandler)

To Charlotte

Best from

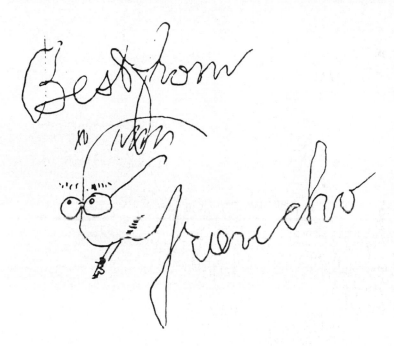

xo

Groucho

Groucho in the living room of his house on Hillcrest Drive with his piano, which was more than just a piece of furniture for him. (Photo by Charles William Bush)

Groucho in his den, where a pre-eminent position is given to the treasured Orpheum Theatre program, which proclaims the appearance of the four Marx Brothers in *Home Again,* as well as advertising shampoos for twenty-five cents and manicures for fifteen cents. (Photo by Charles William Bush)

Robin Heaney gave me this picture of her and Groucho vocalizing. At the time she was Groucho's cook, "The only cook I ever kissed." (Courtesy of Robin Heaney)

NEWS FLASH!

DATELINE: OCTOBER 2, 1890

BORN TO SAM AND MINNIE MARX, ANOTHER
SON, JULIUS HENRY MARX, HEALTHY AND
KICKING UPSTAIRS IN THE FRONT BEDROOM,
78th STREET, MANHATTAN. ★ ★

COME CELEBRATE MY 85th BIRTHDAY
★ ★ ★
AT MY HOME:

1083 HILLCREST ROAD
BEVERLY HILLS, CALIF.

SUNDAY, OCTOBER 5, 1975
FROM 4 'til 8 PM

Groucho

RSVP 271-7769

Groucho and the author, with the only picture he ever painted. (Photo by Charles William Bush)

BERT GRANET

When Bert Granet left George Pierce Baker's acclaimed drama workshop at Yale, he went to work at the Long Island studios of Paramount as Robert Florey's assistant director on *The Cocoanuts*. "It was quite an experience so early in sound films," he told me. "We used to pray every day the cameraman wouldn't suffocate," referring to the airtight camera booth that was necessary in early sound films. Working on *The Cocoanuts* was Bert Granet's first meeting with Groucho, whom he had earlier seen on the stage. "I admired him from vaudeville." The association began with the filming of *The Cocoanuts*, but the friendship really developed later when both were working in Hollywood.

Writer Granet became producer Granet, as well, and later was executive producer in charge of all production for Desilu Studios. He and his wife, Charlotte, remained among Groucho's closest friends, with Groucho sometimes spending Thanksgiving and Christmas at their home, where they gave large parties on those holidays.

The cabdriver who took me up the steep, winding road to the Granets' house refused to go all the way, saying, "I'm not driving back down that for anything!" I had to get out and walk up the rest of the hill.

I visited the Granets in their panoramic-view living room, high in the hills of Beverly Hills. The walls were lined with photographs taken over the years in Mexico and France by Bert Granet. Ironically, one of the most famous pictures of Groucho was taken not by Bert Granet, but by Charlotte. The photo, which appeared in *Life*, showed a group of Groucho's friends dressed and made up to look like Groucho. They included Arthur Sheekman, Nat Perrin, Norman Panama, Harpo, and Bert Granet, among others. Groucho often asked guests at his home to guess which was the real Groucho. The real Groucho was the one at the top of the stairs who was dressed and made up as Harpo. Billy Wilder and I shared the distinction of having correctly identified the real Groucho.

Charlotte explained how it happened that she, and not Bert, took the *Life* photograph:

"It was practically the only picture I ever took. Bert's the photographer, but he was going to be in the picture. Bert really set up everything for me—set the camera, arranged the lighting, told me where to stand. When *Life* sent me the check, I didn't want to cash it. I kept it for years."

Asked to sum up Groucho, Bert Granet answered:

"It's hard to sum up someone you've known as long and as well as I've known Groucho. The character that Groucho seems to have created is one of a kind. You asked me what I'd call a book about him, and that's what I'd call it—*One of a Kind*. He grew into the personality.

"He was a great iconoclast. The kids in every generation recognized his ability to disrupt society. That's why he's more popular than ever today. Groucho liked the idea of upsetting things. In his own lifestyle, he was the most hilarious type of guy in the whole world.

"A producer he didn't like very much used to say, 'What kind of show are we going to do?' and Groucho would say, 'I don't know. We'll stick four Jews up against the wall and see what happens.'

"Someone Groucho really liked and respected was Thalberg. For Groucho, Irving was kind of a saint. Groucho loved Thalberg and Kaufman. When I first went backstage to see Groucho, I had a letter from Kaufman to introduce me to Groucho. I was young, and an eager beaver.

"A lot of comics are really a pain because they are always trying so hard. They believe the world revolves around them. Bert Lahr would tear the buttons off your coat. Groucho is a very different type. He doesn't appreciate the kind who press. He never had an identity problem. He always knew who he was and what he wanted to do. One thing he never did was play Las Vegas—not his thing.

"Actors have to be pretty compulsive people. And stars have to be different from people who aren't. It's a strange thing to always see your name up there. So much publicity has to have its effect. It's a strange feeling to always be reading about yourself.

"Now, Bogart was a shy, sensitive man, but like Groucho, he would sometimes become the victim of the dialogue that had been written for him. Groucho would have to be grouchy and Bogart would superimpose toughness. On a one-to-one basis, the real person lets down his defenses. But when you're a star, you're expected not to let down your public.

"There was practically no one who ever could take stage center away from Groucho, and Groucho didn't have to try. The only person I ever knew who could come to a party and hold court even if Groucho was there was Leo Durocher, because it seems just about every actor wanted to be a ballplayer.

"What's unique about this community [Hollywood] is that there are very few people who are fortunate enough to come here with families. You come here, you migrate here, it's lonely. The first thing that touches your life is the fact that your friends become your family, so you have roots.

"Groucho preferred the company of men. For the most part, his attitude was that women were there as decoration. Women were for making passes at. They [the Marx Brothers] were real chasers. You remember Margaret Dumont, who played the dowager. It probably wasn't beyond them to make a pass at her. On the set for *Cocoanuts*, they were Peck's Bad Boy. They were real wolves with the chorus girls, though not Groucho, who was married. There were always mad antics. There was a story that they dropped their pants on the set, but I never saw that.

"Each time, Groucho would pick a younger wife, such as Kay. Kay was a vivacious, very young, happy child. Groucho adored her. He was a father with a child. She was pretty, she was sexy, she was charming. But Kay was hurt when Groucho told people he was old enough to be her father.

"We came over one night, and Groucho and I went to the ball game. My wife told me later how Kay was steaming. She said, 'All he does is he goes to Hillcrest, and they sit around that round table—Jack Benny, Jessel, Cantor—and he tells a story, then Benny tells a story, Jessel tells a story, Groucho tells a story. Then he comes home!'

"After having some affair with his wives, he threw understanding over the fence. Eden once said, 'If he had only come home to me and said, "I love you," I think I would still be married to him.' But with Eden he opened up, he became more extravagant. Before, if you weren't careful, he was up by an escalator buying a suit with two pair of pants.

"At Groucho's 1972 Los Angeles concert, we met Zeppo after the performance, and he said, 'Tell him I was here.' Then we met his former wife, Kay, and she said, 'Take me backstage.' As we arrived with Kay, Groucho was mobbed and being rushed out. Kay waved to him, but she didn't know if he saw her wave.

"At Hillcrest Country Club, people would walk up to him and say, 'Hi, Groucho,' whereupon his responses would be hard to determine in advance. Sometimes he would be very pleasant or sometimes very difficult. When you were with Groucho and someone walked up to him, you never knew what they were going to get. We were sitting there one night having dinner, when two boys walked up and they said, 'Hello, Groucho.'

"And he said, 'Hello, who are you?'

"They said, 'We're your grandchildren.'

"They *were* his grandsons—Steve and Andy."

I told Bert Granet the denouement of that story:

Groucho and I were walking on Beverly Drive in downtown Beverly Hills, and we met Andy.

ANDY
(*To Groucho*) Hello, who are you?

GROUCHO
I'm fine. Who are you?

Bert Granet continued:

"I remember once when a couple of teenagers came to his door and told him they wanted to see him and the inside of his house. With that, he very politely took them in and introduced them as guests. The boys were there all evening.

"The maids in Hollywood are proud of who they work for. Groucho told me this story:

"He saw these two colored maids talking over the fence, and the other maid said to his maid:

" 'Who do you work for?'

" 'I work for the Marx Brothers.'

" 'The Marx Brothers?'

"The other one didn't seem to know who they were. So Groucho's maid said, 'You know—they hit each other.' Groucho figured she didn't know the difference between them and the Ritz Brothers.

"Groucho was doing *Time for Elizabeth* in San Francisco with Norman Krasna, and he asked us to go there with him, and Krasna asked Eddie Buzzell. Groucho brought Miriam. We thought we would see the show once, maybe twice, but we found out Groucho expected us to see every performance, the whole performance. We missed one matinee, and he was really hostile about it. Then we would stay up till 4 A.M. every night, going back and forth between us, about what should go out and what should stay in.

"Groucho's friends pick up his mannerisms. I think I sound a little bit like Groucho sometimes. This happens to people who have been associated with him without their consciously realizing it. They take on his coloration. You find yourself making puns or jokes like his.

"It's hard to put Groucho into specific categories. He grew into his personality. I try to think about his motivations. There's a conflict between being a very sensitive human being and an actor's role, especially that of a comedian. It's a terrible thing to get up and be a star. But he's very three-dimensional. I don't think anybody has ever touched on his character in depth because everybody has tried to make a funny story out of it. Unpredictable—I would say he's *that*.

"To me, he is a public image, as well as a very private, complex man. I can't really put it into some simplified statement."

TERRY HAMLISCH

At Marvin's house in Beverly Hills, Terry Hamlisch reminisced with me about Groucho:

"I always think of the twinkle in Groucho's eyes when he sings those songs as he stands there in his shorts with the Mickey Mouse hat on, and he knows he's being a bit of an exhibitionist. It's this combination of the child who's learned a couple of songs and wants to sing them for the company and the performer, the polished performer, who's done this and knows how to get an audience.

"It's like what Marvin said about thinking of him as a grandfather figure: he sits at the head of the table and he starts promptly at seven o'clock. If you're a few minutes late, 'You're late' and you try to get out of it, and you can't get out of it; you're definitely late. Then when he has Robin the cook come in after dinner: 'Okay, Robin, let down your hair.' I mean, it's Rapunzel time, and he gets carried away in conversations.

"One night he got into a conversation about going on a safari so he could get an elephant which he would then present to Richard Nixon as a gift he couldn't refuse. But then, what would he do with it? It was his way of weaving a story, and once he got there he enjoyed it. He liked the whole idea of having this elephant brought up to the White House and being there . . . what would Nixon do with it? He didn't like Nixon.

"And I always remember the night of the American Film Institute dinner honoring Orson Welles, with Zeppo and Erin and Groucho. I went to the dinner with them, and after dinner while speeches were being made, Groucho got up from the table and walked to the closest exit on his way to the men's room, and Zeppo followed him. While they were gone, the master of ceremonies introduced Orson Welles to a standing ovation, and everyone in the room rose to their feet to applaud Orson Welles.

"The climax of the evening, and in walks Groucho back from the men's room. His eyes lit up as he faced the room of applauding people!"

GEORGE SEATON

When I asked George Seaton if he had ever contemplated writing a book about his experiences in Hollywood, he replied that he had not, but that if he did he would call it *George Who?* His impressive record as writer-director-producer notwithstanding, George Seaton has remained a remarkably private celebrity during a conspicuously successful Hollywood career that has spanned more than four decades. Even just after the tremendous success of *Airport,* which he wrote and directed, he said that people still confused him with the late George Stevens. As George Seaton left George Stevens's funeral, the minister said to him, "Thank you for coming, Mr. Stevens." Seaton merely pointed to the casket. Whereupon the minister quickly added, "I mean Mr. Seaton." "I suppose," Seaton said ruefully, "that's what I'll have on my gravestone: 'Here lies George Stev . . . I mean George Seaton.' "

Besides *Airport,* his films include *Miracle on 34th Street,* for which he won an Oscar, *Bridges at Toko-Ri, The Country Girl,* for which he won another Oscar, and *The Counterfeit Traitor* among many others. He has also directed for the stage, and has served as a president of the Academy of Motion Picture Arts and Sciences.

He is perhaps the only major Hollywood figure who not only doesn't change his telephone number, but whose home number is listed in the directory, and his office is located in a motel across the street from Universal City. He chose this in preference to an office in a glittering new structure because he would have to conform to the total decorating plan and give up the well-worn furniture that has served him since his arrival in Hollywood.

Seaton's friendship with Groucho went back to the mid-thirties, when he and Robert Pirosh, who were junior writers at M-G-M, were called in to work on a section of Kaufman's and Ryskind's *A Night at the Opera* script that had dissatisfied producer Irving Thalberg. They had already met Groucho and impressed him with an original story that Thalberg later rejected.

"Strangely enough, we had an idea of a producer, Groucho, who oversold a show, knowing it was going to be a failure, and then it turned out to be a big success. Years later a picture was made called *The Producers* with the same basic story. Thalberg didn't care for that idea, but Groucho did."

After *A Night at the Opera,* Seaton and Pirosh were assigned the next Marx Brothers M-G-M vehicle, *A Day at the Races.*

"Groucho had confidence in us, and Thalberg, I guess, did too. So he said, 'Go ahead and give us a story on *Day at the Races.*' Well, Bob and I did eighteen complete scripts! Now, I'm not talking about variations. These are complete scripts. I know, because later we had to testify in a plagiarism suit.

"I don't know if Groucho remembers this or not, but he received a postcard from some lady which said, 'Wouldn't it be funny if you crazy fellows ran a hospital.' And he threw it away. We never saw it. Well, of course, *Day at the Races* turned out to involve a sanitarium, and the woman sued.

"Now, it comes to trial. The judge is there, and Groucho is called. The judge said to Groucho, 'You know, you're one of the funniest men I've ever seen in my life. I admire you so much,' and so forth. And Groucho said, 'You're pretty funny, too, with that outfit on.' The woman got $25,000 from the studio."

Groucho, George Seaton, and I had brunch together on a Sunday at Hillcrest Country Club.

GEORGE SEATON

We showed Groucho the first script of A *Day at the Races.* He thought some of it was all right, some of it was not so all right. Thalberg said, "Keep this character, but start again." He was a very patient man, and we weren't getting much money, so it didn't cost him anything. We'd start all over again, add a scene or add a character, and he'd say, "That's fine, but throw the rest out." We just kept going over it and over it again. Then Groucho suggested we get together with George Kaufman, which was a very good idea.

GROUCHO

He was great. You never get over the loss of one like that.

GEORGE SEATON

I learned an awful lot from him, and so did Bob. Kaufman was out here, but he was doing a play in New York, so he didn't have much time. I'll never forget it. He just sat there with his deadpan expression and turned the pages over one by one. Not a smile, and we were just bleeding inside, because here was the great master of comedy, and this dour face he had. Finally he turned up the last page and said, "That's one of the funniest ideas I've ever read." Not a smile through the whole thing. Then we would take a scene to him, and he would give us very good advice. He said, "One thing you must remember with the Marx Brothers is that not only the answers have to be funny, the questions have to be funny. Because otherwise Chico gets very mad."

GROUCHO

He couldn't remember the right questions or lines anyway.

GEORGE SEATON

He couldn't even remember the horse he bet on. Speaking of horses, I remember once when we were stuck for a scene between Groucho and Chico, which was a block comedy scene. As Kaufman had it, the theory was that there were five block comedy scenes, and you would string the story in between these scenes. We were stuck for a block comedy scene, and Bob Pirosh's father, who was a doctor in Baltimore, played horses, too. He had sent Bob a telegram saying, "Bet on this horse," or whatever it was. I didn't bet and neither did Bob, but we showed the telegram to Chico, and Chico ran around saying, "I've got a hot tip!" Here was a doctor who had never won a race in his life, but Chico bet a lot of money on it, and called all his friends and said, "I've just had a tip from Baltimore." But, anyway, that gave us an idea. We went down to the corner of Cherokee and Hollywood Boulevard and bought every racing form we could find. A little bit of the tootsie-fruitsie scene came out of that. We tried to figure it out—you know, the code in the tip sheets. We had to buy a code book, and that became the genesis of that scene. Al Boasberg, who was a very, very funny man, added to it on the road.

GROUCHO

Very funny man. I was walking with him in Salt Lake City. He took off his coat and lay on the car tracks. In *Night at the Opera* he wanted me to take off my pants. And I said I never took off my pants on the stage. And I didn't. I once went to a farm with him about sixty miles from here. He took some books with him and the minute we got there, he went in the bathtub and filled it with water. And he had a thing across the tub so he could read books. He'd sit there for five, six hours reading books. Boasberg was a very bright man.

GEORGE SEATON

A very bitter man, too.

GROUCHO

I was crazy about him.

GEORGE SEATON

Oh, I was, too. I learned an awful lot from him. I don't know if you remember, Grouch, Al's line, "Either he's dead or my watch stopped." The first time it was a question: "Is he dead, or has my watch stopped?" and it didn't get anything. We were trying to figure it out, because it's a funny idea, certainly. Groucho said, "It's because it's a question, and they're expecting an answer. It should be a statement." The next performance he said, "Either he's dead or my watch has stopped," and the roof went off the place. I learned right then that you don't try to get a laugh on a question.

I

What were your impressions of the other Marx Brothers?

GEORGE SEATON

Harpo was a dear, dear, sweet man.

GROUCHO

A wonderful man.

GEORGE SEATON

Chico was very kind to us, to Bob Pirosh and myself. He was always trying to get us to do something on the side; write a script or he had an idea for something, and we would talk it over . . .

GROUCHO

Or borrow some money.

GEORGE SEATON

He knew he couldn't borrow money from us. We only made seventy-five dollars a week. Chico was very kind, too. But Chico, in my opinion, never had even a modicum of the talent that Groucho or even Harpo had.

I

Were Chico's ideas good?

GEORGE SEATON

Very bad. But I must say, and I don't know why, that when Chico got on that stage and started doing his thing, the audience loved him.

GROUCHO

He was an important part of the act.

GEORGE SEATON

Oh yes.

GROUCHO

Do you remember *Duck Soup*? That was a funny picture.

GEORGE SEATON

That only came into its own very recently, I think.

I

(*To George Seaton*) Did you look much at the earlier Marx Brothers pictures when you found that you were going to be writing for them?

GEORGE SEATON

Yes, but Thalberg cautioned us, and I think Groucho will bear me out on this . . .

GROUCHO

I'll be glad to.

GEORGE SEATON

. . . He said that his formula for the Marx Brothers was that they had to be helping somebody so you could really have sympathy for them. Groucho did these outrageous things with Dumont and whatever the boys did, but as long as they were trying to help the young lovers, let's call them, the audience would forgive them and be on their side. I think it was a good formula. In the early pictures, *Duck Soup* for instance, there were a lot of just wonderful gags, but as Thalberg said, there was no drive to help anybody. He said, "It's like a football game. You start here and you make ten yards, then they throw you back five, and you go twenty more, and they throw you back ten, and then you go thirty. But you have to keep going towards that goal line." He kept insisting on this all the time.

GROUCHO

The first time we met Thalberg he said he'd like to do pictures with us. "But not lousy pictures like *Duck Soup*," he said. I was annoyed by this. I thought *Duck Soup* was a very funny picture. "Yes," he said, "but the audience doesn't give a damn about you fellas. I can make a Marx Brothers picture that would have half as many laughs but will be more effective because the audience will be in sympathy with you." He was right.

GEORGE SEATON

Groucho, let me ask you a question, because it's been interesting for me working in the theatre again. Looking back, did you get more fun out of the theatre or out of the films? I'm not talking about money now.

GROUCHO

The stage.

GEORGE SEATON

Yeah. That's the amazing thing. Of course the boys feel the same way, Matthau and Lemmon.

GROUCHO

You get an immediate response.

GEORGE SEATON

Walter Matthau said to me, "Making films is like pulling hairs out of your nose with a pair of tweezers, one by one. You know, you do that little thing. Here you're on for the whole evening, and you've gotta be part of the ensemble, you've gotta carry the show. There's nobody who says, 'Cut! Let's do it over again.' And if you muff a line, if you forget a line, you better be smart enough to protect it and figure out how to get out of your spot."

GROUCHO

I'm getting a big kick out of *You Bet Your Life.* It's on every night.

GEORGE SEATON

Yes, I know. I see it.

GROUCHO

It's in New York and Philadelphia and Chicago. It's a big hit. It's killing the news. People don't want the news at eleven o'clock.

GEORGE SEATON

I don't want it at six o'clock, I don't want it at five o'clock. It's pretty depressing.

GROUCHO

The news is usually bad. Somebody once said, "Nobody should read a newspaper more than once a month." There used to be a show called *People Are Funny,* and that describes people. There's all kinds of people, but collectively they're the audience.

GEORGE SEATON

But the amazing thing, Grouch, is that the matinees downtown are the best audience. We were trying to figure out why, because usually the matinees are . . .

GROUCHO

I hated the matinee audiences. They were mostly women with hats eating candy.

GEORGE SEATON

But Walter and I were talking, and we finally came to one conclusion, and I think we're right. In the evening people run down there, and they have a big dinner . . .

GROUCHO

They're sleepy.

GEORGE SEATON

Now they have a bar—you know, they have a couple of drinks before dinner in the theatre bar. And between acts, too. They're just that much slower. They're a beat off all the time. At the matinee nobody has a drink; they just maybe had a sandwich for lunch. They're so sharp.

GROUCHO

You didn't know Sam Harris.

GEORGE SEATON

Yes. 'Cause he optioned a play of mine once. I was only nineteen or twenty.

GROUCHO

We worked with him.

GEORGE SEATON

What's your favorite Marx Brothers picture, Grouch?

GROUCHO

I don't know. I like *Night at the Opera* the best. The heavy [Sig Rumann] in that was wonderful.

GEORGE SEATON

Well, that's my favorite Marx Brothers picture.

GROUCHO

And I like *Duck Soup.*

GEORGE SEATON

But *Night at the Opera* had form. I think it had more discipline. *Duck Soup* was very wild, and tremendously funny.

GROUCHO

Didn't we have a horse in the *Day at the Races* tryouts?

GEORGE SEATON

Yeah, for about two performances, and then we sent him home.

GROUCHO

You weren't at the opening of *Animal Crackers* in New York. I went with her. (*Indicating me*) The opening of *Animal Crackers* in New York was so crowded, I was surrounded by policemen to keep the crowds away. And they were on horseback, some of them. One of the horses asked me for my autograph.

GEORGE SEATON

So you probably gave him your footprint?

GROUCHO

In the sands of time. Well, do you think we've had it?

GEORGE SEATON

I can't think of anything else we haven't covered, Grouch. Except, how are you?

GROUCHO

I'm in the pink.

GEORGE SEATON

I'm in the red. Doing a show downtown for love.

GROUCHO

Well, God'll thank you for that. But he won't pay the rent.

ROBERT PIROSH

Robert Pirosh is a screenwriter who numbers among his credits not only the Marx Brothers' *A Day at the Races* but also *I Married a Witch*, which was directed by his friend René Clair, and *Battleground*, for which he won an Oscar. He has also directed films and has written and produced for television.

Eating breakfast with me at the Beverly Hills Hotel, he talked about his days with Groucho and the Marx Brothers:

ROBERT PIROSH
Did George [Seaton] tell you about our first meeting with Groucho? I'm sure he did . . .

I
Yes. But I'd like to have you tell it, too.

ROBERT PIROSH
My memory won't be as good as George's, but I do remember one thing which he may or may not remember. We had been at M-G-M as junior writers, and we had an option coming up. I had started at thirty-five dollars a week at Metro-Goldwyn-Mayer at the height of their glory, as a junior writer. And I was very glad to get it, but that was after having worked and made much more in New York in the advertising business. At any rate, they didn't lift my option for twenty-five dollars, so George and I, we quit in a huff, then got more money elsewhere.

We were not what you would call a howling success, but we did start building up a little. We had no big pictures at all. We had done one or two little pictures at M-G-M, and our agent got us a job at Republic Studios, which was the absolute bargain basement. We didn't know what the hell we were doing there, because what we had known—the little bit we knew—had been working on great big M-G-M pictures, or great big compared to Republic. They were all shoestring things then. I'll go on to something else if this rambles . . .

I
It's fine.

ROBERT PIROSH
You're used to rambling people, aren't you? Well, we were working for a man named Nat Levine, who was, I guess, a big executive producer at Republic. Then we got a call to go over and see Irving Thalberg, who was

going to produce this Marx Brothers picture. We got the job and went back, and had the laugh on M-G-M, because we got much more money than when they had dropped us! The point is that Nat Levine was, as I said, not a quality producer, and Irving Thalberg was God. Our agent then said, "Isn't this fantastic? From Nat Levine to Irving Thalberg! From the sublime to the ridiculous!" This I loved, because it made Nat Levine the sublime.

At any rate, I don't know what our first contact at M-G-M was. I think it was probably Herman Mankiewicz, who was a very colorful, witty, wonderful man. He sort of sponsored us. I had gotten to know Herman, and I was trying very hard to get a job, writing originals with nothing but rejections. And he helped. Anyway, we were given a script written by a team of writers which Thalberg and Groucho had decided they didn't like. We read the script, and then drove out to Groucho's house, very nervous, because we were going to meet Groucho. We had really terrible credits.

It was a drizzly day, and Groucho met us, then we went inside. He said, "Have you read the script?" And we said, "Yeah." He said, "Where is it?" and one of us said, "Oh, we left it out in the car!" He said, "Well, that's a good place for it, especially if it's an open car." George told you all these little things, didn't he?

I

Yes.

ROBERT PIROSH

Then what's the point of repeating it?

I

Because it's different when each person tells it.

ROBERT PIROSH

Okay. So, we not only had the script with us, but there had been an interval of time in which we had done an entirely new story for what eventually became A *Night at the Opera*. This was not the one that was used. Groucho loved it, though, and that's what really got us the assignment. And Thalberg liked it very much, too, but said, "I don't want to do it. But," he said, "I like those boys, and the work shows promise, so let them work on it." Then we wrote for about a year and a half.

Incidentally, though this has no bearing on Groucho, the idea was a story that eventually was done very effectively by Mel Brooks, as *The Producers*. This was the story of a man who oversold a show, expecting it to be a flop, and it turned out to be a success. So that was our original idea for A *Night at the Opera*. Groucho would get this great idea of producing the rottenest opera ever. He hires the good-looking guy, Allan Jones, and this pretty young girl, who's not too good a singer, expecting to have a big flop, and it turns out to be a huge success. So now he owes a hundred percent of the profits to about ten people.

At any rate, Thalberg turned it down. He liked the idea, but said, "You can't build insanity on insanity." He said, "I want a different kind of Marx Brothers film. That's why their pictures haven't been doing so well. Their stories are so nutty, that when they come on and do nutty things, it doesn't work."

So, we worked on A *Night at the Opera*, and then they brought in George Kaufman and Morrie Ryskind. They did a script, and that was the script that was used. But Thalberg kind of liked us, and we'd do a little scene here and there, and they'd use some of it. And then A *Night at the Opera* was a smash hit. When they did the next picture, A *Day at the Races*, that's the one we were working on for a year and a half.

I keep mentioning Groucho not just because you're writing about him, but because that's the way our relationship was. But we also had a relationship with Chico, and we liked him, but it was on a different basis. We saw quite a bit of him. He wanted to be a writer. He wanted us to write a story with him, and we'd have crazy conferences where he was on the phone with bookmakers and dames. I mean, it was impossible.

Harpo was a lovely, sweet person. But it was Groucho, for us anyway, who was fun to be with. It was our big experience, or at least mine. George has seen more of him in recent years, I suppose because of Hillcrest. Our big experience with him, the one that was the most exciting and that meant a lot to our careers, was when we went on the road, when we took A *Day at the Races* on tour. I guess it was Thalberg's idea. It may have been Groucho's, but Thalberg went along with it.

It was treated as if it were a Broadway show. We were going to make a comedy, and we were going to make a Marx Brothers picture. But they remembered very well that when they had their early plays, *The Cocoanuts* and all the others, they went on the road a couple of weeks, and finally when they got to Broadway, they knew where the laughs were. And they felt, whether it was Thalberg or it was the Marx Brothers, that comedy pictures were tough to time because they didn't know in advance where the laughs were, except with the pictures they had made from plays.

So, after months and months of work, we got a script, and they said, "Okay, let's go." And we had a regular rehearsal period at the Biltmore Theatre downtown. They rehearsed as if for a stage play for, I think, a couple of weeks. They rehearsed the comedy scenes, made changes, and so forth. This became an hour show. They called it a tab show, as in tabloid. Then, the great big movie palaces had stage shows. So this was taken out to be shown in various towns on the road in between the movies. They'd have the feature, and then they'd have an hour of this. It was three or four performances a day, in the Midwest mostly. We opened in Duluth, and then went to Minneapolis, Chicago, and various cities. Eventually, it kept changing and changing, with the comedy routines being concentrated on. We took a whole troupe. Margaret Dumont was along.

She was really quite a nice old lady with, I think, no sense of humor at all. And she was the butt of their jokes. They were always hiding her wig, which she desperately needed. That would be Groucho's idea of a joke. But I think it sounds more like Chico's idea of a joke. And then Harpo would be the only one who would think, "Poor old lady. That was a dirty trick. She was so embarrassed."

I remember in one of the towns on the road, we were changing and changing, and not succeeding in getting what everybody wanted: a scene in which there was a character particularly prominent in the newspapers then, some kind of gangster's girl or something, called a "Cokey Flo." So this was the scene that everybody called the "Cokey Flo scene." This was the scene that eventually became in A Day at the Races, where Esther Muir came in and Groucho went on the make for her, and it winds up with Chico and Harpo coming in and putting up wallpaper. A crazy scene. But it was called the Cokey Flo scene, and we were stuck on it.

After having worked for an hour or two at a restaurant where we went to have something to eat after the show, we went to the hotel, where the lobby was deserted. There was a poor old cleaning woman down on her hands and knees scrubbing the floor, and Groucho went up to her and said, "You don't happen to have a Cokey Flo scene in your pocket, do you?" And she just looked. She knew they were celebrities, and what could she do? She was so confused. And I saw, quite unostentatiously— the others had gone on up ahead—I saw Harpo slip her a bill, say a dollar or five dollars, because he felt bad and embarrassed. He didn't have the sadistic streak that I guess most comics have—or comedy writers. Harpo was different.

So the trip went on, and, like any show or picture, we became a family group. Everybody knew everybody, and it's great fun, and we're gonna be pals for the rest of our life. Then you go back and on to the next project, and you see each other once in a while. For a year and a half—it might even have been longer—we saw a great deal of Groucho. And then after that, I really didn't see Groucho an awful lot.

I

George Seaton told me you wrote *Day at the Races* eighteen times.

ROBERT PIROSH

Yeah. But you wouldn't have recognized it. It wouldn't have been called *Day at the Races* in many of the versions, because it didn't start out about racing at all. As I remember, we had a number of ideas that Thalberg or Groucho or somebody always tossed out. But probably the first eight were about the Marx Brothers in a sanitarium.

The first idea that we latched onto, they said, "Hey, let's explore that." If Thalberg would get tired of us, Groucho was our champion. So we had all these versions of the sanitarium. Somehow or other in one of them, there was a sequence that had to do with horse racing. And Thalberg said, "That's it. We combine the two. It gives us the excitement of horse racing, and the sanitarium gives us the stuffy atmosphere that their wild antics will seem funny in."

I

Did Groucho contribute many lines?

ROBERT PIROSH

Yeah, but nobody says gems all the time. But for this kind of comedy—I don't say it's unique, but it's certainly different—his style is recognizable, and every once in a while at a gathering, somebody says something, and you say, "That's a good Groucho line." Everybody knows what a Groucho line is. And he was simply wonderful with that. And the next best, in my experience, by far, was Kaufman, who also had different kinds of lines that weren't Groucho lines, a different kind of humor. Of course, many lines in his pictures that were wonderful Groucho lines, some gagman had dropped in, and they became Groucho lines. And he changed them around.

He was really a perfectionist in his work. On this road tour, on the *Night at the Opera* road tour, we'd have a scene down pat, and he would know, everybody would know where the laugh comes and about how long it's going to last, how long a pause to take. But he would try. He would switch them around. He'd try every possible thing, and sometimes by switching one word around or by using another word, he would get a laugh. He mispronounced a word once, and he got the laugh on it and he never would pronounce it right. It was an unpleasant word, like paraplegic or paralysis. It's a good example of what he would do when a thing was set. Then, with all his delight in improvising and changing, he'd cling to it, because that laugh meant more to him than he knew.

I remember one line. Harpo was playing a harp, and Groucho kept heckling him. S. A. Schearer was a well-known name then. They were pawnbrokers and they advertised a lot. So, one of his lines when he's heckling Harpo was, "There's a man outside. He's from S. A. Schearer. He's here to get the harp." It got a laugh. Then, the next time he came in, it would be different. "S. A. Schearer is here for the harp." And then the next time, it would be, "S. A. Schearer sent a man here for the harp." You know, he'd keep trying everything, and one of them would get a bigger laugh than the others. Nobody knows why, but he'd stick to that.

I

How did you feel about his changing your lines? Did you enjoy it? Or did you mind it?

ROBERT PIROSH

No. I didn't mind at all on the road tour, because then everybody could hear. They laughed more, they laughed less. He never argued with that. We had a director who was a very well-known, a very famous director, Sam Wood. If Thalberg had two on a scale of ten in sense of humor, Sam Wood had minus seven. He had no sense of humor whatever. Why he should have directed a Marx Brothers picture, I'll never know. And yet, the Marx Brothers liked him, respected him, and it worked. He didn't know if the joke was funny or not, but it had been broken in on the road, and he had nothing to do with that. He wasn't with us there.

That's interesting to me, how a man who has no sense of humor can direct a comedy. I don't know if that's possible on the stage, but it's possible in pictures, and I've seen it. Not very often. In my experience with comedy, like with René Clair, it's a separate kind of comedy. I know it's impossible for Sam Wood to have directed some of René's pictures from exactly the same script.

I

That is rather an extreme comparison, though.

ROBERT PIROSH

The Marx Brothers begged René to direct a Marx Brothers picture. Did you know that?

I

He told me that.

ROBERT PIROSH

You know everything! Actually, René was probably right not to do it. He wanted to do a different kind of thing.

I

But you don't think a René Clair picture could have been a Marx Brothers picture?

ROBERT PIROSH

Yeah, a René Clair picture could have been a Marx Brothers picture, but he could not have directed it if they said, "Here is our script." They'd say, "This got a six-second laugh in Minneapolis," and he'd say, "I don't care about Minneapolis. I do not like zee line." But Harpo would have been superb with René. Groucho would have, too. But René wouldn't have been interested in the block comedy routines. It would have been a question of control. It would have started out nicely, and they would have accepted his authority, and then one or more would have questioned it. There would have been chaos, because René doesn't like to have his authority challenged.

I

Do you think they would have challenged it? Because I know Groucho has tremendous respect for him.

ROBERT PIROSH

Yeah, I guess he would have accepted it. I honestly don't know. I think in the end their approach to humor is such a different kind of humor . . . I don't know. I don't think it would have worked out.

I

Did you ever go to see the early films before you wrote A *Night at the Opera* and A *Day at the Races*?

ROBERT PIROSH

Oh yeah. I had seen two or three, and loved them. But forgetting the story, I don't think their comedy changed an awful lot. I said Kaufman had an effect on it; I think that's very early in the game. I seem to remember that Kaufman wrote *Cocoanuts*. I think their first play was *I'll Say She Is*. Do you know the name of the man who wrote that?

I

Will Johnstone.

ROBERT PIROSH

He was a newspaperman. When we were stuck for a while, they brought him out. He was not a Hollywood man, and he stayed here three or four weeks. He worked in one corner and we worked in another. He did a treatment, and he left. Al Boasberg was on *Day at the Races*, too. Everybody was on *Day at the Races*!

I

It's extraordinary!

ROBERT PIROSH

They probably kept us on because we were cheap. They'd bring in the high-priced ones, and it didn't work out somehow, so they'd drop them. Looking back, it's pretty ridiculous to spend that much time on one picture, but that's the way it worked out. It was at a time in their career when it was very, very important, because the industry thought they were about washed up in pictures. Thalberg took the gamble, and they were tense, because they had had some commercial flops, and they were worried.

I

You didn't mention Zeppo.

ROBERT PIROSH

No. Well, I didn't know Zeppo very well, because he wasn't in any of those I worked on. When I knew them, I knew the other brother, Gummo, better. He was nice. I very much liked him—sort of a combination of all three of them. He was sweet, like Harpo. He had a better sense of humor than Chico, and not as nearly as good a one as Groucho's.

Zeppo I knew as an aggressive, successful agent who I would see whizzing past in the lot, or I had lunch with him in a group, so I didn't know him. In the older pictures, though, he didn't add anything to them, in my opinion, because it really was ludicrous with him playing the romantic leads. Probably he could have done Chico's part. Chico wasn't that much of an actor. He just happened to be there, and he could play the piano funny, he could do his odd little Italian accent. But he wasn't creative. Harpo was.

His own pantomimic stuff was very hard to get material for. Really, the only thing that I can remember that George and I wrote for him—and I believe this was in A *Night at the Opera*—was when he played a piano. He sat down and started playing a piano, banging on it, hitting it, and it was a breakaway piano—a grand piano. It started coming apart, and fell all apart, and he reached in and took the strings out. They were shaped something like a harp, and then he started playing the harp. That was ours. Outside of that, almost all the little pantomimic things that he did were his. He was very good at that. He was wonderful at that!

I

What about Chico? Did he add anything?

ROBERT PIROSH

Once in a while. He wasn't that interested. He was more interested in girls, in races, and cards. Chico and Harpo were great card players, as you no doubt know. Real whizzes, and they played for big stakes. They would play with all of the movie money men, but for huge stakes. Chico would win at that and lose at the races. He just threw his money away. He was a very undisciplined man. Very kind, very nice. But completely undisciplined.

They were very, very different, and not really close. Except for cards and things like that, their social lives were different. Harpo had his friends, Groucho had his; Chico loved the racy crowd, the sporting crowd. Groucho had, you know, cultural aspirations. He was bound and determined to write, and he did. He listened to music. At one period in his life, I remember, he became very interested in good music. I think he felt very much, as I'm sure you got from him, that he wished that he'd had more education. I think he very much regretted that he hadn't had more education.

They were all very loyal people. Groucho, as I'm sure you know, had a sentimental streak, and a loyalty to people who he felt had helped him. I remember that he wrote to me, "Dear Bob, thanks for *A Day at the Races.*" Well, I didn't give him *A Day at the Races.* I was just one of the people who worked on it, but it was nice. He didn't say, "with fond memories of the fun we shared," or anything like that. It was just a nice thing. I think if I'd ever gone to him for any help, I'm sure he would have given it to me. If I'd said, "Look, if you talk with So-and-So, that could help me," I'm sure that he would have made a big effort.

He had great warmth for those he liked, and I think, in my experience, except for Thalberg and one or two others, it always had something to do with their sense of humor. Except with some of the girls he's got attached to. I don't think he could value a person highly unless they could give him a laugh. Because he loved it. If he made one of his withering cracks to one of us, if we could top it, which didn't happen often, he would laugh uproariously. He would love it. Then, while he was laughing, he'd be thinking of a way to top us. But he didn't seem to have the petty jealousy that most comics have. If eight of us were in a room trying to think of a line that didn't get a laugh, he would try very hard to be the one that got it. And very often he would. But if somebody else got it, he wasn't eating his heart out because he didn't get it, as many people would.

MORRIE RYSKIND

Morrie Ryskind was a young newspaperman with an interest in writing theatrical comedy when George S. Kaufman invited him to collaborate on *The Cocoanuts* in 1925. That was the beginning of a long and successful association with both Kaufman and the Marx Brothers, especially Groucho. With Kaufman, and Ira and George Gershwin, he won a Pulitzer prize for *Of Thee I Sing* in 1931. For the Marx Brothers, he co-authored *Animal Crackers* and *A Night at the Opera* with Kaufman, and adapted *Room Service* for the screen. Other credits include *Louisiana Purchase*, and the screenplays for *My Man Godfrey*, *Penny Serenade*, and *Claudia*.

Shortly after Groucho received his Oscar, Morrie Ryskind and his wife, Mary, joined Groucho, Erin, and me for dinner at Groucho's home. "When Morrie and Mary got married," Groucho told me, "I was best man, including him."

GROUCHO

I'll bet I'm the oldest guy who's ever gotten an Academy Award. When we went to the Academy Awards, the crowd went wild when they saw me—I was wearing a frock coat like I used to wear, except that this was a good one . . .

MORRIE RYSKIND

The comedy frock coat like you used to wear?

GROUCHO

Oh no. This one was expensive. It cost $300. But that's got nothing to do with it.

MORRIE RYSKIND

Grouch, I don't remember you in the old days caring about a frock coat or even thinking of spending $300 for one.

GROUCHO

No. But I became a rich man. My pants cost $150!

MORRIE RYSKIND

I'll never forget George S. Kaufman . . .

GROUCHO

I'll never forget him either. I went to his funeral when he died.

MORRIE RYSKIND

The last time I saw George, we were in New York, and I called George up and said to come on down and have lunch with us. He said, "Morrie, I can't go anyplace. Do me a favor: come up here, will you?" Now, it's impossible to tell you of the respect, and the admiration and the awe that he had. Here Kaufman was so happy *we'd* come up to see *him!*

MARY RYSKIND

He called me up the next day to thank us for coming up.

MORRIE RYSKIND

He had trouble with his eyes and all the other problems of old age, and nobody knew who he was. Toward the end, some people wouldn't talk to him. As I get older, I wish to God people had a little respect for old age. I was brought up to have it, but now there isn't any.

The other night I went to see *The Cocoanuts* at a college. They asked me to talk, so I went over there. You would have thought it was the funniest picture in the world. Never in my life have I heard such laughter. I wrote the dialogue, but nobody heard it. First Groucho came on the screen, and they got up and cheered for fifteen minutes. Then Harpo came on, and they got up and cheered for fifteen minutes. At the end they applauded. Then they hailed me as the great God. I was very lucky that day.

So, Groucho, you've been pretty good. You had that tremendous success on Broadway. And, you know, you fellows were very lucky in that first show, *I'll Say She Is.* You would have never been seen by Percy Hammond, Woollcott, and all that bunch that first night, except that a dramatic show that was supposed to come in didn't come in. If you had received raves from the second critics, it obviously wouldn't have had the same prestige. But the big critics raved the next day. And, boy, they never got over it. Harpo—I'll never forget Harpo . . .

GROUCHO

That's the one that didn't talk.

MORRIE RYSKIND

You remember him, don't you?

GROUCHO

Yeah. He was a nice fellow.

MORRIE RYSKIND

They were so amazed one night when Harpo finally spoke. People genuinely believed that this was a poor deaf-mute. My recollection of Harpo was one thing: one cold night in winter, we'd had dinner together and were going over to the theatre. There was a guy with one of those big hats . . .

MARY RYSKIND

A professional beggar.

MORRIE RYSKIND

. . . and he was playing a violin on Forty-second Street. We passed, and Harpo went back. He said, "Would you lend me that a minute?" And he played the guy's violin.

GROUCHO

I thought he played the harp.

MORRIE RYSKIND

He would have, but this guy didn't have a harp. He did mighty good.

ERIN

How long have you and Mary been married?

MORRIE RYSKIND

Since 1929.

GROUCHO

That's the year I was born.

MORRIE RYSKIND

Yeah. We did it to celebrate Groucho's birth.

GROUCHO

Remember when I spoke at that school of journalism? And you were almost kicked out of Columbia.

MORRIE RYSKIND

I was asked to give a series of lectures at Columbia—a course. They wanted an excuse to give me a degree. So what I did was I got all the people I knew—I got Groucho, I got George Jessel, I got Lindsay and Crouse to come down and talk about all that stuff.

GROUCHO

They were pretty good, Lindsay and Crouse.

MORRIE RYSKIND

Yes, they were, and they're both gone now.

GROUCHO

Everybody's gone!

MORRIE RYSKIND

Not everybody has gone, Grouch. You and I are still here. Say, I saw a show the other night, and I loved it. *The Sunshine Boys.* I loved it because I think that's what the theatre is all about. Everybody came out happy and gay. Nobody was stuck on drugs, and there were no lesbians in it.

GROUCHO

Don't knock lesbians. Some of my favorite girls are lesbians. I wish you'd tell them about the ball game we played in Philadelphia. We played the whole game in one hotel room. And we tried to drop the piano out the window.

MORRIE RYSKIND

You *did* drop the piano out the window. Only it stopped on a ledge.

GROUCHO

Well, we *wanted* it to fall all the way down.

MORRIE RYSKIND

Well, this was to celebrate. We were all feeling good because we all realized that we had a hit on our hands—*Animal Crackers.* Ruby said, "Let's have a little to-do," so we all came up, and of course the girls, and you've never seen anything like it. Chico and I were having a catch, which Harry Ruby loved, and the waiters were passing around among us. I've never seen such a riot. Hollywood has never seen such an orgy, except that it wasn't quite sexual. Then, of all things, Harpo and Herbert . . .

GROUCHO

Herbert?

MORRIE RYSKIND

Your brother.

GROUCHO

Oh, you mean Zeppo.

MORRIE RYSKIND

Yeah. Harpo and Zeppo lifted the piano, and they put it on the ledge outside the window. Finally, about three detectives—house men—came in, and here's the room, all empty. All the chairs and furniture are gone, and they said, "Is there any furniture?" We said, "Never heard of any." When this thing was over, poor Ruby and Kalmar were sick. Groucho and I were going back to our hotel, and Groucho said to the clerk, "What kind of hotel is this? I've got Room 802, and there's a bunch up there yelling and screaming and carrying on all night long. It's impossible for a man to sleep. Get 'em out of there or I'm calling the police." With that, we walked off. I don't know if the police came, or what. And here were Kalmar and Ruby, the two most innocent people in the world, left to face the hotel executives.

GROUCHO

What about Harpo? Tell 'em about Harpo knocking on every door, and then rushing down to complain that he can't sleep because people are knocking on his door.

MORRIE RYSKIND

Well, Harpo did something else. He was playing the piano and stuck his head out the window. He also stuck out the lower part of his anatomy—right out the window.

GROUCHO

He was a wild man.

MORRIE RYSKIND

Harpo could get away with anything.

GROUCHO

I had his son here last week.

MORRIE RYSKIND

All of Harpo's kids were adopted, weren't they?

GROUCHO

Yes.

MORRIE RYSKIND

Harpo played with those kids—he was wonderful.

GROUCHO

You know, Harpo swore he'd never get married. Yeah, he was the one guy who would never get married. He went with three girls in his life, and they were all named Fleming. Well, there's no business like show business. Do you believe that?

MORRIE RYSKIND

Yes, I do. Grouch was at his best when he felt that the audience responded. When he felt they were dull, he wanted to get the whole thing over with. It's like anything else. Who was it who said that to have great artists you must have great audiences? If they don't respond, they don't get anything.

GROUCHO

When the market crashed, we were doing *Animal Crackers*, and that night I didn't think or say anything that wasn't about the stock market.

MORRIE RYSKIND

I don't know what you said, but I was having dinner at your house the night the market crashed, with you and Max Gordon.

GROUCHO

At Great Neck?

MORRIE RYSKIND

At Great Neck, yes. (*To me*) For years Groucho had been trying to get me into the stock market. I didn't know anything about it, but he was so sold on it, he finally got me to buy a hundred shares of something. We were out in Great Neck, and were playing golf one afternoon. About the third hole, Chico came up. And he could hardly breathe. He said, "Grouch, you gotta buy Canadian Marconi."

GROUCHO

That's what you bought, Canadian Macaroni.

MORRIE RYSKIND

Yeah. You did, too.

GROUCHO

I bought Goldman, Sachs. I lost my money in the best.

MORRIE RYSKIND

Wait a minute. I know what you did on this day: you bought Canadian Marconi. Back to the story, Grouch says, "Well, all right. I may pick up some tomorrow." "Tomorrow!" Chico says. "By tomorrow that thing will have gone up twelve points and you won't be able to buy." Well, Chico walks around—and three holes with Chico and oh, boy! That guy! Groucho says, "Come on, Morrie. We've gotta get that stuff now."

So we got into this cab—I think we've still got our golf shoes on—and Groucho says, "Hurry up, because the market closes at three o'clock." We go to beat the band, and a cop stops us. We're doing about eighty-two. He says, "Where do you think you're going?" And this guy here (*Indicating Groucho*) says, "Look, Officer, I'm Groucho Marx and my wife is having a baby, and if I don't get her to a hospital, she's likely to have it right in the middle of the street." And the cop says, "Do you want me to lead you—to escort you?" Now Groucho's scared because the cop is gonna eventually know he's going to the broker, and he's not going home to his wife. So he says, "No, no," and made up some excuse. We finally get to the broker, and it's five minutes of three. Groucho can't even talk by now, but he says, "Get me a thousand shares of . . ."

GROUCHO

Goldman, Sachs.

MORRIE RYSKIND

No, no. You said, "Get me a thousand shares of Canadian Marconi." It was only about ten then. Then he turns to me and says, "Morrie, why don't you get some, too?" I said, "But I don't know anything about the market." I used to wonder what those pages in the back of the paper meant. Groucho says to me, "Come on, Morrie—you're beginning to make a little money." So I said, "All right. Buy me a hundred shares." That's investing a thousand dollars. At that time, a thousand dollars . . . my God! So the next morning I am now an investor in the stock market, and I have now seen the insides of brokerage houses.

GROUCHO

Do you remember Gordon's famous line when he called me up?

MORRIE RYSKIND

Oh, I don't know. But I was with him in your house.

GROUCHO

"This is Salpeter," he said. "The jig is up."

MORRIE RYSKIND

He said it that day at your house, Groucho. That was the day of the crash. He was looking through the paper, and he had this punch line: "Well, I don't have anything, but I don't owe anything." He was very happy, and Groucho thought they'd lost the house in Great Neck. Do you remember that night?

GROUCHO

I lost everything I had in the crash: $250,000.

MORRIE RYSKIND

I lost every penny I had: $2,800. I lost a little more than that. I had bought by that time some Peruvian bonds at the bank . . .

GROUCHO

I always used to like those.

MORRIE RYSKIND

The bank advised me. You know, I didn't know anything. And then, when the crash came, I went down and said to them, "Can I sell these?" And they said, "Sell *what?*" It got to be in those days that the disaster was so overwhelming that everybody had it. It wasn't like you were alone. We'd sit there, and we'd gag about stuff.

MARY RYSKIND

You should tell the story about the line you wrote for Groucho and what he did to you.

MORRIE RYSKIND

We had several moments in the show when Groucho would just have to sit on the stage and listen to Harpo and Chico. He'd go crazy. For Groucho to sit alone on the stage for two minutes and listen to somebody else and not say anything—you know what that is.

GROUCHO

Who's talking?

MORRIE RYSKIND

Anyway, one night we had dinner, and he said, "Morrie, give me a line here, will you?" So I gave him a line the next night, and he fell off the chair laughing and roaring about it. He said, "That's it! That's one of the greatest lines I've ever heard." I had a lot of respect for his judgment when he said things like that. So that night he tried it, and he advanced upon it the way Maggie Dumont would advance upon things: Groucho would explain to her that something was funny, and she would walk out to the audience and ask them what was going on. So here was Groucho. He walks downstage to front center and says this line. *Not a snicker!* Not a sound. Nobody laughed. Then he says, "Well, that'll teach you one thing: don't have dinner with Morrie Ryskind!" The audience roared. They loved it.

I

Do you remember the line?

MORRIE RYSKIND

No. I don't. But a lesson I learned early was that if you wrote something and the audience didn't get it, you tried something else that they would get.

GROUCHO

I remember a lot of lines. I saw them in the zoo a couple weeks ago.

MORRIE RYSKIND

And you're the guy who sits around and sneers at puns! There is nothing like a good pun. They're the greatest thing in the world.

GROUCHO

I wrote a few good ones. Want to hear one?

MORRIE RYSKIND

If you can do it while we're eating, and it won't interfere with our appetite, go ahead.

MARY RYSKIND

It'll go with carrot cake.

GROUCHO

In *Animal Crackers* I said I shot an elephant in my pajamas. How he got into my pajamas, I don't know. Then I had trouble getting the tusks out . . .

MORRIE RYSKIND

Tuscaloosa.

GROUCHO

Yes. That was *my* joke.

MORRIE RYSKIND

Let me tell you something that is very true, Grouch, Tuscaloosa may or may not be great, but when you say it, it becomes terrific. You had that aggressiveness when you came on.

GROUCHO

Hey! Do you want to watch my show tonight? At eleven o'clock?

MORRIE RYSKIND

Yes, sure. The great verve he had—that was the thing that made Grouch. He'd come in and attack.

You know, I got a call from somebody the other day. They wanted the rights to *Animal Crackers* on the stage. Can you imagine *Animal Crackers* without Groucho, Harpo, and Chico? You just can't do it. You can write a show and then you cast it, as we did for *Of Thee I Sing*; but to write a show for the Marx Brothers, you must tailor it. Otherwise you haven't got a show. Nobody gives a damn if the boy loves the girl or not. Berlin wrote some excellent music for our show, but nobody paid any attention, because these guys could ruin anything.

One day Chico came to Joe Santley and said, "Joe, are you gonna use me? If not, is it all right if I go out for about an hour? I've got a headache." Joe said, "Sure, but be back." So the hour came and passed. Joe Santley came in and said, "Morrie, where the hell is Chico?" I said, "I don't know what the hell you let him go for." He said, "Where could he be?"

So I had an idea. This was in Astoria, and I called up the New York Bridge Club, and I said, "Is Chico Marx there?" They said, "Yes," and I said, "Tell him I want to talk to him." They said, "He can't talk now. He's got a six-no-trump hand." I said, "I don't give a damn what he's got. Get him over here, will you?" Chico had to grab a cab from there and come over for the scene.

GROUCHO

You know, somebody asked Chico how much money he lost gambling, and he said, "Find out how much Harpo has. That's how much I lost."

MORRIE RYSKIND

That's so true. You fellows had to bail him out of Chicago . . .

GROUCHO

A couple times.

MORRIE RYSKIND

. . . or they would've killed him.

GROUCHO

When we were playing in Detroit, he disappeared for a week over in Canada, in Windsor, and Harpo and I had to do the show alone.

I

(*To Morrie*) What did you like best of the things you wrote for the Marx Brothers?

MORRIE RYSKIND

I think the general feeling is that *A Night at the Opera* was the best thing.

GROUCHO

Kalmar and Ruby had written an original script for *A Night at the Opera*, and we said it was no good. Thalberg said, "What do you want?" We said, "Get Kaufman and Ryskind."

MORRIE RYSKIND

That's when Thalberg called us up.

I

What were your impressions of Thalberg?

MORRIE RYSKIND

I'd known Thalberg vaguely before. He was a young giant around here, you know. At the age of sixteen or something, he was running Universal. Well, anyway, I knew Thalberg was a big name, and of course he'd done some big stuff. But when we came out here, I said, "I'm gonna work at the hotel, if you don't mind." He said, "I don't care. Fine."

So I'd work at the hotel, and when I finished about ten pages of script, I thought I'd come over, so I called him up, and I said, "I've got some stuff that I think you ought to see." So when I got there, he sat there and read it, and he didn't even smile. Never a crack. Now, by this time I'm dying, you know. Then he turned to me and said, "Morrie, that's some of the funniest stuff I've ever read."

GROUCHO

We asked George [Kaufman] what he thought of Thalberg, and he said, "He's another Sam Harris."

MORRIE RYSKIND

That's as great a compliment I think you could ever pay anybody. Sam Harris was a great guy. I've never forgotten. Do you remember how we got Margaret Dumont?

GROUCHO

Through Sam Harris.

MORRIE RYSKIND

I wrote a line for this guy when we were trying out *A Night at the Opera* in Salt Lake. He tried it, and nothing happened. He says, "Morrie, let me do it again." I'm the kind of guy who says, "I won't argue with you," so we did it again that night and for two days. In spite of everything, he kept trying it. Finally I said, "You've tried it four times. What the hell, if they don't laugh at it now, they're not ever going to laugh at it." He said, "Just once more." And he came out and he got one of the biggest laughs in the show. You know why? He'd put one of the accents in the wrong place, and what they were laughing at wasn't the joke, but the wrong accent.

ERIN

There's so much left out of the movie version of *Animal Crackers*.

MORRIE RYSKIND

Yes. But I think that these versions are all cut. Even when I see *A Night at the Opera*, I know there's a scene missing.

GROUCHO

I remember one part that was cut. It was in a speech I gave. One line was "This would be a better world for children if the parents had to eat the spinach."

MORRIE RYSKIND

I think my favorite scene for the boys was in *Animal Crackers* where they're looking for the stolen painting, and they've gone all through the house, and no painting. So they decide to search the house next door. But there *is* no house next door, so they decide to build one! That, I think, is the best nonsense I've ever seen.

GROUCHO

The nonsense I liked best was when I dictated a letter to Zeppo. Hunger-dunger.

MORRIE RYSKIND

You know, we never really gave a break to Zeppo because we couldn't. But offstage Zeppo was a very funny guy.

I

Do you remember any examples of Zeppo's humor?

MORRIE RYSKIND

I'll tell you one story which I think is slightly risqué. Zeppo was, after all, my agent. There was a period of about a month once when I was trying to get ahold of Zeppo and couldn't. I was getting bloody mad, and I was thinking, "Why can't I get this guy?" So I raised a little hell, and finally he came up to me and I said, "Zep, I've been trying to get you for a month." He said, "Well, I'm going to tell you something. I'm being psychoana-lyzed." I just looked at him. If you knew Zeppo the way I did, for Zeppo to ever sit down and say that . . . even if he actually *was* being psychoana-lyzed! So I said, "For God's sake, why?" He says, "I was masturbating." Of course, that wasn't true. He was giving an alibi. I said, "What happened? Are you cured now?" And he said, "No, but I know *why.*"

GROUCHO

You know who I'd have liked to have met? Somerset Maugham. He went to the opening night of *Cocoanuts*—he had to pay a hundred dollars for his seat because he couldn't get a ticket for the damn thing. I always wanted to meet him.

MORRIE RYSKIND

He was one of my favorite authors, I think—one of the greatest guys of that period. I was stunned when I learned that he was . . . (*Long pause*)

ERIN

Bisexual.

MORRIE RYSKIND

I don't know if he was *bi*sexual or not. I thought he could picture men and women together so marvelously.

GROUCHO

He wrote *Rain,* and Sam Harris produced that. I want to tell a story. Am I permitted?

MORRIE RYSKIND

Yeah, but keep it dirty.

GROUCHO

After the Lindbergh baby was killed, there was terrible anxiety throughout the country. Nobody knew whose children were next to be grabbed. I was living out in a house on Sunset Boulevard, and I went to bed that night, and I heard a car in the driveway. So I looked out the window, and there was an empty car there—a Ford, an old Ford with nobody in it. So first I took Arthur and Miriam, and put them in my wife's room and locked the door. I'm meeting Arthur for lunch tomorrow. He's fifty years old now. Anyhow, the police came and took the car away. About half an hour later, I looked out the front door, and there was another car there. This was the maid from next door and her boyfriend making love in the car. That's all there is to the story, except that ten years later I was at the Mayfair Club in New York, and I was dancing with Ginger Rogers, and Larry Hart came up to me and said, "Did you ever find out about that car in your driveway? It was me." That's the whole story. It's not very interesting, so I think I'll shut up again.

MORRIE RYSKIND

I loved Ginger Rogers for one reason especially, and I've never forgotten her. I'd done a picture—I've forgotten which one—and I was over at RKO, and I'm walking along right in front of a newsstand. I saw Ginger. I hadn't seen her since the theatre, so we embraced each other. On the stand was a picture of the cover of *Photoplay* or one of those things, and there was Ginger, the most glorious thing you've ever seen. And she said, "Morrie, tell me something: do you think I'll ever look like that?" I think we'd better be going now.

GROUCHO

Aren't you going to watch my show?

MORRIE RYSKIND

We'll watch it at home. Of course we're gonna watch it.

GROUCHO

Afterward I'm going to get a massage.

MORRIE RYSKIND

By whom?

GROUCHO

By a pretty girl. Maybe I'll give *her* a massage.

MORRIE RYSKIND

May I have a copy of this *Playboy*? The one with your interview?

GROUCHO

Sure, go ahead. I haven't read it yet.

MORRIE RYSKIND

Fat chance. I'll bet you could recite it word by word.

MARY RYSKIND

Did you at least look at the centerfold?

GROUCHO

No, I'm not interested in naked broads.

MORRIE RYSKIND

When Harpo was going abroad, he bought a French book.

GROUCHO

Harpo was *with* a broad.

MORRIE RYSKIND

So am I. And I said to him, "What is this thing?" He said, "I'm going abroad, after all." Harpo didn't quite make the eighth grade, but he studied French. So I said, "What are you up to?" And he said, "I'll tell you. Every day I start at the first page. That gets me sleepy, and I go to sleep. Then the next day I wake up and start at the first page again." Here was Harpo, who was probably the least read of the brothers, and yet those guys loved him — Somerset Maugham, George Bernard Shaw . . .

ERIN

Did he read their books?

MORRIE RYSKIND

I don't know if he read their books, but they loved him. Harp, as I said, was a simple, outgoing person . . .

ERIN

But he had all these intellectual friends . . .

MORRIE RYSKIND

I'm sure Shaw didn't go into a discussion of Fabian socialism with Harpo.

ERIN

When Groucho went to see T. S. Eliot, he tried to read *The Waste Land*.

MORRIE RYSKIND

Groucho always made fun of me and said I was the guy who went to college. He always had this inferiority complex — and this to me is the stupidest thing in the world. I know many people who didn't go to college, and who have an inferiority complex about it . . .

GROUCHO

I have.

MORRIE RYSKIND

I know you have. This is stupid because an awful lot of guys who have a degree are the biggest bores in the world and don't know a helluva lot. Groucho was always better read than half the guys I knew.

ERIN

I wish some university would give Groucho a degree.

MORRIE RYSKIND

How about two degrees?

GROUCHO

I'll take the third degree.

MORRIE RYSKIND

Didn't Dartmouth want to give you a degree?

ERIN

They wanted him to come there and speak.

GROUCHO

I just had a letter from Notre Dame, and they wanted me to come there and talk. And a letter from Harvard for the same thing.

MORRIE RYSKIND

But no degree?

GROUCHO

Suppose I got a degree. What good is it?

ERIN

But Groucho, then you'd be a college graduate.

GROUCHO

So what?

ERIN

Then you wouldn't have an inferiority complex anymore.

GROUCHO

I don't have it now.

MORRIE RYSKIND

You do to some extent. I was just thinking today: I remember you in some of the old stuff you did, somebody would say, "Wittier," and you'd say, "The poet?" I'll bet if you said Whittier today, half the kids wouldn't know what you were talking about.

GROUCHO

Some eleven-year-old kids were at the door today to get my autograph.

MORRIE RYSKIND

Well, why not? They're only eleven—let 'em have it, Grouch.

GROUCHO
I did, but I kicked them out.

MORRIE RYSKIND
With this permissiveness, I don't know what you're going to do. Nobody haunts me or comes around to my house asking for my autograph. All they ever want is a check.

GROUCHO
(*Starts singing "God Bless America"*)

MARY RYSKIND
You know, it's so strange; people stand up for that as though it were the National Anthem.

GROUCHO
It should be the National Anthem.

MORRIE RYSKIND
When Pearl Bailey sang "The Star-Spangled Banner"—oh boy, you really got a thrill out of that!

GROUCHO
It's a lousy song.

MORRIE RYSKIND
No, it isn't.

GROUCHO
It's a song about war. "The bombs bursting in air . . ." That's a lousy song.

ERIN
He likes "God Bless America" better.

MORRIE RYSKIND
If you remember, Grouch . . . Do you know the circumstances under which that was written?

GROUCHO
Yes. When Washington was crossing the Delaware.

MORRIE RYSKIND
No. When Baltimore was being burned. And this guy is out on a British ship and wondering will our place survive. It's a hell of a song.

GROUCHO
It's a lousy song. "God Bless America" is a great song.

MORRIE RYSKIND
All right! I like Berlin, too!

GROUCHO
I don't like Berlin. I prefer Frankfurt.

MORRIE RYSKIND
To have written that . . .

GROUCHO

And so many other cities . . .

MORRIE RYSKIND

. . . and the bombs going off, and wondering . . .

GROUCHO

. . . all of them better than Berlin.

MORRIE RYSKIND

. . . if America was going to survive, and . . .

GROUCHO

You don't sell me on that.

MORRIE RYSKIND

So all right. You can Passover it.

GROUCHO

I will.

MARY RYSKIND

We should let Groucho have his massage now.

GROUCHO

I'm gonna put on my pajamas and watch my show.

MORRIE RYSKIND

Is it all right if I watch your show from my house?

GROUCHO

No. It's not the same. Tempus fugit. Or rather, tempus fidgets. Did you know him?

MORRIE RYSKIND

Yes!

GROUCHO

I knew him well. For the last forty years I knew him well.

BILLY WILDER

Writer-director-producer Billy Wilder was born in Austria and grew up in Vienna, where he often watched Trotsky play chess in the Café Central. As a young reporter, he met Richard Strauss, Arthur Schnitzler, and Freud. In pre-Hitler Berlin he worked as a full-time crime reporter and part-time *thé dansant* partner for unescorted ladies at the Hotel Eden. He had begun writing film scripts, including the classic *People on Sunday*, but with the ascension of the Nazis, he fled Germany.

For a while he was an expatriate in Paris, then he left for Hollywood. In 1938 he and Charles Brackett wrote *Bluebeard's Eighth Wife*, followed by *Ninotchka*, both directed by Ernst Lubitsch. Billy Wilder's first directorial credit was *The Major and the Minor*. Some of his other important films include *The Lost Weekend, Double Indemnity, Sunset Boulevard, Sabrina,* and *Some Like It Hot*. He has been nominated for twenty-one Academy Awards, winning six.

Just before Christmas of 1974, Billy Wilder came to have tea with Groucho, Erin, and me. A few days earlier Groucho and I had gone with Sidney Sheldon to see *The Front Page*, Billy Wilder's latest film, at the Academy of Motion Picture Arts and Sciences' theatre.

Billy Wilder arrived exactly on time. His attire was conservative-casual, combining the European emphasis on quality material with the emphasis on comfort characteristic of Southern California. He wore an open sports shirt, a cashmere pullover, peccary moccasins, and trousers with a perfect crease. Groucho commented on this after Billy Wilder had departed. "And he had two of them, two creases. They didn't look like the pants my father used to make. His tailor must've used a tape measure."

When Billy Wilder arrived, Groucho inquired about his wife, former actress Audrey Young:

GROUCHO
Where's Audrey?
BILLY WILDER
I hope she's out buying a Christmas gift for me.
GROUCHO
Where's I. A. L. Diamond?
BILLY WILDER
I don't take Izzy *everywhere* with me. I hear that you liked my picture.

GROUCHO

She (*Indicating me*) went with me. It's great! But it got some bad reviews.

BILLY WILDER

That doesn't paralyze me. I just get more anxious and determined. In Europe they think you're as good as the best you've ever been. In Hollywood it's "What have you done lately?" I don't look back. That would be like looking up a girl you slept with thirty years ago. The bad reviews hurt for a week, and then you get over it. You have to. If you think about it, and feel they're going to kick you in the stomach again, you can't do the next thing. I remember talking to Mary Benny the day after she was robbed of all her jewelry at the Pierre. She said she was on her way to Harry Winston. You have to get right back on the horse. (*Looking at the cake Erin has just carried in from the kitchen*) Aaaah! It's a *Streuselkuchen*. Do you have a coffee klatsch like this every day?

ERIN

(*Lightly*) Of course.

GROUCHO

(*Truthfully*) No, we're just doing it to impress you. (*To Erin, who is cutting the Streuselkuchen*) Don't I get some of the *kuchen*? I'm master of the house. (*Groucho bursts into song in German, and Billy Wilder joins him*)

BILLY WILDER

I think it's words by Heine and music by Schubert.

GROUCHO

(*Indicating Erin*) She doesn't speak German. She's from Canada. The last time we played there it was ten below zero, and the audience was forty below zero.

BILLY WILDER

(*Observing the painting on the wall of Groucho's dining room*) That's *The Peaceable Kingdom*. And what is that? (*Indicating a smaller painting on the opposite wall, depicting three women*)

GROUCHO

Those are my three hookers. It's my three ex-wives.

BILLY WILDER

It should be in the bedroom.

ERIN

It's just a picture he picked up somewhere. It's not of anyone.

GROUCHO

(*To Erin*) All right, girlie. (*To Billy Wilder*) Have you read the book about Kaufman?

BILLY WILDER

That was a long time ago.

GROUCHO

No. There's a new one. It's great. Eight hundred pages.

ERIN

Groucho reads about six books at a time.

BILLY WILDER

So do I. Maybe I'm in the mood for one. Maybe another. Sometimes a paperback mystery or something in German. You were in Europe, I understand, Groucho.

GROUCHO

Yeah. That's where they gave me this. (*Indicating his Legion of Honor*) You know Gregory Peck? (*Billy Wilder nods*) When I was living in London, we lived in Mayfair, next door to Gregory Peck and his wife, and we had a couple keeping our house, and every weekend, they used to buy one hundred condoms and go over to Ireland and sell them. They made a lot of money.

BILLY WILDER

The Pecks?

GROUCHO

(*Over laughter*) No.

BILLY WILDER

When I was making a film in London, we had the Greek king and queen on the set, the parents of the deposed king, and one of the electricians hollered down, "Hey, Queenie, where were you when I needed you for my inside straight?" The queen didn't understand at first, but someone translated for her. Then she laughed and applauded. What do you hear from Krasna these days?

GROUCHO

He's doing a play on Broadway. When he lived in Beverly Hills, he had a Japanese butler he used to play tennis with every day, and Krasna beat him every day. Until Krasna fired him. He gave him two weeks' notice, and in those two weeks the Japanese beat him 6-0, 6-0, 6-0.

BILLY WILDER

Is he still living in Switzerland?

GROUCHO

Yeah. I wrote him a letter the other day, and I signed it Al Ritz. When he got married, he married someone named Erle, so I sent him a telegram: "You finally struck Erle."

BILLY WILDER

You can be funny.

GROUCHO

I was in show business for quite a while.

BILLY WILDER

You were funnier on purpose than anybody else.

ERIN

Groucho, why don't you show Billy the rest of the house. (*We go to the back part of the house, where Groucho shows the photographs and treasured souvenirs to Billy Wilder; Groucho pats his Oscar, which has stage center on the back hall table*)

BILLY WILDER

I got six, but that's the past. (*Billy Wilder looks at the photographs that line the wall to Groucho's bedroom*)

GROUCHO

Look at this one. (*It is the photograph taken by Charlotte Cranet which appeared in* Life *magazine, showing a group of Groucho's friends dressed up as Groucho; at the top of the stairway is Harpo*) Do you know which one I am? (*Billy Wilder points to Harpo*) Yeah.

ARTHUR WHITELAW

Arthur Whitelaw, who produced *Minnie's Boys* on Broadway, took Groucho and me to the Westside Jewish Community Center in Los Angeles to see an amateur benefit production of this play.

Following dinner at Chasen's before the show, we had to wait longer than usual for Groucho's car. He checked his Groucho watch. "It's twenty-five past Groucho," he said with some consternation. He never liked to enter late for a show, still remembering the days when the Marx Brothers were the opening act on a vaudeville bill.

GROUCHO
(*To parking attendant*) Get that lousy car out here, will you? (*To Arthur and me*) I wonder if we can get the car without giving him a dollar. (*When the car arrives, he hands the very tall parking attendant a dollar*) Here you are, Shorty!
ARTHUR WHITELAW
He's taller than we are, Groucho.
GROUCHO
Only in inches.

When we arrived at the Henry Weinberger Auditorium, Groucho was the object of much covert attention as we were whisked inside. The play had begun, and our seats were in the front row. As we came down the aisle, the performers stopped speaking and watched as we groped our way to our seats. Recovering, they went on, amid whispers throughout the audience which virtually drowned out the words being spoken onstage. "It's Groucho." "Groucho came." "Groucho Marx is here."

Had the role he was to play in that night's performance been contemplated, he undoubtedly would have received credit in the program as one of the players. He uttered frequent asides which met with enthusiastic laughter from the audience. He filled in details from his own memories, calling out corrections like, "Not All-bee, Albee!" when the producer's name was mispronounced. The young actor playing Groucho went back and corrected his mistake, but it was drowned out by the laughter that continued after Groucho's comment.

Minnie's Boys ended, and the audience gathered respectfully around Groucho, orderly but eager. As the actors finished removing their makeup, they also came out to meet Groucho. They were all very happy. So was the audience.

MAN
What did you think of it, Groucho?
GROUCHO
Fine. They're much better than we were.
WOMAN
May I shake your hand, Mr. Marx?
ANOTHER WOMAN
Groucho, may I kiss you?
GROUCHO
I've never been kissed before. This is wonderful. The biggest thrill of my life. (*But he moves away, avoiding the kiss*)
FRIEDA (THE USHER)
My name is Frieda, F-R-I-E-D-A.
GROUCHO
Like fried potatoes? I can spell *that*.
ANOTHER WOMAN
(*As Groucho signs autographs*) Are you reliving all the memories?
GROUCHO
Yeah. I wish I was dead.
ANOTHER WOMAN
I finally get to meet the man I adore.
GROUCHO
So do I.
SAME WOMAN
I still watch your show every time it's on.
GROUCHO
So do I.
ANOTHER MAN
(*With a beard*) I just want to thank you.
GROUCHO
I don't blame you. Get a shave. (*Indicating Arthur*) This is my brother. (*After signing a great many autographs*) Write your name, and I'll sign it.
ANOTHER WOMAN
I already wrote my name.
GROUCHO
Write another one. I don't like that one.

ANOTHER MAN

Is there anything you want, Mr. Marx?

GROUCHO

Yeah. To get out of here.

ANOTHER MAN

Groucho, I've been watching your program for many years.

GROUCHO

No kidding? Well, there's a fellow in Philadelphia who watches it too. (*Indicating Arthur*) This is my uncle. I'd like you to meet my uncle.

ANOTHER WOMAN

(*To me*) Are you Melinda?

I

No. A friend.

ANOTHER WOMAN

I have nine grandchildren. Would you write their names for me and sign yours for each of them.

GROUCHO

No. *You* write their names, and I'll sign it. *Once* for all of them.

DAVID WEITZ (the actor who played Groucho)

I'm very happy to meet you, Groucho.

GROUCHO

You were much better than I was. I knew you right away.

DAVID WEITZ

Only by the glasses.

GROUCHO

I didn't wear those kind of glasses.

DAVID WEITZ

We'll have to do it all over again.

GROUCHO

I enjoyed it, and I had a very good time. Now I'll go home and whip the bishop.

TODD TATUM (the actor who played Harpo)

Thank you for coming, Mr. Marx.

GROUCHO

You were all very good. You were better than we were. Especially the jokes.

PRETTY GIRL

Thank you so much for coming.

GROUCHO

You were the best one in the show. (*To Arthur and me*) She *was* the best one. (*Starting to leave*) Happy Chanukah! A peaceful harmonica to all our friends. (*We leave. Outside, to Arthur*) *You* were the best.

Groucho commented to me the next day at breakfast, "They were amateurs, but for amateurs, they were very good. I told them they were better than we were. It's when they try to do comedy, that's when they fall down."

Arthur Whitelaw, who was one of Groucho's friends and favorite piano players, met Groucho in 1958.

"I first met Groucho when I was about eighteen years old. Groucho was touring in *Time for Elizabeth*, and I went up to Westport to see the play. That wasn't the first time, however, that I fell in love with the Marx Brothers. That goes way back to my early childhood when I was about three years old.

"I was taken to see A *Night at the Opera*. That was in 1943. I remember coming out of the theatre and not being able to breathe because I was laughing so hard. That was my first introduction to them.

"I'd always wanted to meet Groucho, and my first opportunity was when he came to Westport, because I lived on Long Island, and it was just an hour and a half away. I went backstage after the show and met Groucho and his daughter, Melinda, and Eden, whom he was married to at the time.

"We sort of corresponded for a little while after that. Then I got to be a producer two or three years later. Seven years later we were discussing the Rolling Stones and the Monkeys and the Beatles, and I noticed that they were all doing what the Marx Brothers were doing years ago—that same irreverent kind of putting down the establishment and individuals. So I thought, 'What a good idea to do a musical about the Marx Brothers.'

"I came out to California in 1968 and met with Groucho, and explained exactly what it was that I wanted to do. He thought it was a super idea. I said the thing that I thought was really interesting was to show their lives off the stage—at home with Minnie and Frenchie and Hannah, and all the people that surrounded Groucho on Ninety-third Street, the people who really affected their careers. The characters onstage were drawn from their real experience.

"We used scenes from Groucho's book for a lot of source material, including what Groucho had to say, as well. It described the period and what a lot of people never knew about the Marx Brothers: in many respects, as kids, they were exactly the same offstage as they were on.

"A lot of hard work went into it, and finally in 1970 we opened. It was moderately successful. But it wasn't the show any of us really wanted to put on the stage. The emphasis was really on Minnie, and it shouldn't have been. It should have been on the boys, even though Minnie was a fabulous figure. Minnie died playing pinochle, you know.

"The real success of the show is it never stops being done somewhere by all kinds of groups.

"Zeppo came to the opening of *Minnie's Boys* in New York. I'll never forget. I said to Zep, 'At the curtain I'd love for you to get up on the stage and just make an appearance.' And he said, 'No, no. I leave all that to Groucho.' And Groucho got up at the end of the show, and he said to the audience, who was then standing and applauding him, 'I only wish Harpo and Chico could have been here tonight to witness this.' "

One night at dinner Arthur talked with us about one of Groucho's unrealized ambitions:

"Grouch, do you remember how you wanted to play Snoopy? (*To the rest of us*) We had the *Peanuts* opening party at Arthur's, the Arthur's that opened in Los Angeles. It was so noisy, and Groucho said, 'Do we have to stay here?' and I said 'No' because I knew they didn't have ice cream and saltines, which was what Groucho really liked. We wound up here at the house and Groucho said, 'I'm serious. I'd like to play Snoopy.' I said, 'I wish I'd known sooner, Grouch. It would have been great. Sometime we'll do a celebrity show, and you can do it.' "

MIKE NICHOLS, JACK NICHOLSON,
AND MARVIN HAMLISCH

Shortly after the Oscar ceremonies at which Groucho received his special Oscar and from which Marvin Hamlisch took home three, Groucho, Erin, and I ate dinner with Marvin, Mike Nichols, Jack Nicholson, and Andy Marx.

GROUCHO
(*To Mike, Erin, and me—Marvin and Jack had not arrived yet*) I've gotta tell you about my son, whom I had lunch with today. You know it's strange to see your child get middle-aged. He's fifty years old, and he's the youngest bootlegger in America. We were playing in Canada, and Arthur had on a dress . . .

MIKE NICHOLS
How did you justify this dress? I thought you said he was fifty?

GROUCHO
No! He was six months old, and we carried him. It was Prohibition then, and you couldn't bring liquor into this country. So we got two quarts of whiskey, and we hid it in the folds of Arthur's dress. And we brought it in.

MIKE NICHOLS
They wouldn't have arrested him.

GROUCHO
The kid? No. They would've arrested me . . . You were talking about Greta Garbo before. I remember once I was in the Thalberg building, and this woman backed into me on the elevator. And I took her hat and lifted up the brim, and part of it almost fell in her face. She turned around, and it was Greta Garbo. I said, "I'm terribly sorry, but I thought you were a fellow I knew from Kansas City."

MIKE NICHOLS
How did she respond?

GROUCHO
She walked out of the elevator. I met her ten years later, and she remembered. She was the biggest star of M-G-M.

MIKE NICHOLS
You didn't know it was Garbo until afterward?

GROUCHO
Oh no. I didn't know her until she turned around and looked at me, and I saw it was Garbo.

MIKE NICHOLS

Do you remember how you couldn't get on the elevator with Winchell?

GROUCHO

Walter Winchell?

MIKE NICHOLS

Yeah. Anytime he got on the elevator, nobody else could get on.

GROUCHO

I don't blame him.

MIKE NICHOLS

He'd earned that. He just preferred to be alone. The elevator guy at the Pierre or the Plaza or wherever he lived would hold people back when Winchell was in, and they wouldn't stop for anybody else, because he preferred it that way.

GROUCHO

I was in the elevator at the Plaza, and a priest came in and said, "You're Groucho Marx, aren't you? My mother's crazy about you." And I said, "I didn't know you guys had mothers. I thought it was done by immaculate conception."

MIKE NICHOLS

Did he laugh?

GROUCHO

No. I *quickly* got out of the elevator.

MIKE NICHOLS

Did you hear about Woody Allen interviewing Billy Graham on television, and he asked him, "What's your favorite commandment?" (*Jack Nicholson enters*)

ERIN

(*To Jack*) I was speaking to your answering service, and they were answering, "Nichols residence," you'll be glad to know.

JACK NICHOLSON

That's not surprising.

GROUCHO

Well, you crook. Coming here at eight.

JACK NICHOLSON

I'm certainly sorry I'm late.

GROUCHO

An abject apology is the only thing. Where's your girlfriend?

JACK NICHOLSON

She hasn't come home yet.

GROUCHO

Has she got another fellow?

JACK NICHOLSON

That's a very good possibility, judging from my behavior.

GROUCHO

Maybe she has another appointment.

JACK NICHOLSON

Don't rub it in, Grouch. Don't rub it in. (*Marvin Hamlisch enters*)

GROUCHO

(*To Marvin*) It's wonderful what you got there. Three awards. I'm surprised you talk to me anymore.

MARVIN HAMLISCH

You know, Groucho, the best thing that came of those Oscars . . . (*Turns to the other guests to explain*) See, I'm really a native New Yorker. My heart's in New York . . .

JACK NICHOLSON

Whoever would've guessed it?

MARVIN HAMLISCH

Right. Well, I was going back to New York, and a cop said to me, "Terrific!" He'd recognized me. And I thought, "Well, it's Hollywood." But I stepped into my town, New York City, and a cabdriver—you know how they are in New York—said, "Hey, that's really terrific, kid." Then it finally dawned on me what had happened. I was so nervous the day of the Academy Awards, I threw up twice. You keep getting nominated, and all these well-meaning people say to you, "I know you did a good job, so if you don't get it, don't let it bother you."

GROUCHO

You threw up twice? Well, tonight you'll have another chance.

MIKE NICHOLS

I think it's terrific.

GROUCHO

That he threw up?

MIKE NICHOLS

That he was able to feel anything. I never feel anything when I'm in that situation.

GROUCHO

Did you know it's twenty-five minutes of Groucho?

MARVIN HAMLISCH

(*Examining Groucho's Groucho watch*) That looks to me like it's two hours behind the times.

GROUCHO

I don't wind it anymore. I get tired of things after a while—a watch, a wife . . . (*They go into the dining room to eat*) It's every man for himself once you sit down.

MIKE NICHOLS

The year I lost, we were sitting there, and Haskell Wexler, the cameraman for the picture, won. And he got up and said, "Let us use our art for peace and love." I went, "Yuck!" and the TV cameras catch me. Did you see that?

JACK NICHOLSON

It's one of my all-time favorite moments.

MIKE NICHOLS

The next year, and I thought, at least Haskell isn't up for anything. Hal Ashby was up for something, as a cutter. And he got up and said—and I swear to you this is true—"As my friend Haskell Wexler said, 'Let us use our art for peace and love.' " And once again . . .

MARVIN HAMLISCH

If I ever win another one, I'll know what to say: "As two of my best friends have said . . ."

MIKE NICHOLS

You had to compete against *Jesus Christ Superstar* . . .

GROUCHO

Please! I'm a Jew.

MARVIN HAMLISCH

You are?

GROUCHO

For the last eighty-three years. Do you think Fatty Arbuckle is washed up?

MIKE NICHOLS

I don't think anyone is ever washed up, do you?

GROUCHO

They're still talking about that. And that hotel in Frisco. He was a great fat man in his day. I saw the most wonderful picture last week. The fat man who won the Oscar brought it from France. Did you see those pictures? They're eighty years old. Fascinating.

I

Groucho and I went to Filmex to see the turn-of-the-century French films that Henri Langlois brought over from the Cinémathèque Française in Paris.

MIKE NICHOLS

Listen to this: when I made *The Graduate*, my cameraman was about sixty-five at the time. When I was in high school, he went on a tour of M-G-M, and they took him to see Garbo's first silent picture, and he met the focus puller. And that focus puller was *our* focus puller on *The Graduate*. He didn't seem very old. He was a Sicilian, and his working life covers all movies, from the beginning to now.

GROUCHO
Focus puller sounds like chicken plucker.

MARVIN HAMLISCH
(*To Jack Nicholson*) Do you ever get back to New Jersey?

JACK NICHOLSON
I spent the first half of my life there, and I try to get back for a few days every year.

GROUCHO
I did a play there with Norman Krasna. It was called *Time for Elizabeth*. It was all about Elizabeth, New Jersey. What do you hear from Trenton?

JACK NICHOLSON
Alvin Kinney's still at the bar. "Trenton makes, the world takes." That's the motto of Trenton.

ERIN
What would you like for dessert—apple or strawberry pie?

GROUCHO
Apple pie for me. Because I'm an American. Strawberry is for fags.

MARVIN HAMLISCH
I'm going for both of them.

GROUCHO
Does that make you an American fag?

MARVIN HAMLISCH
(*To Mike Nichols*) Weren't you in Chicago?

MIKE NICHOLS
Yes. Northwestern.

GROUCHO
I spoke there about three years ago. They gave me $7,000, and I gave it back to the school because they had a deficit.

JACK NICHOLSON
I went there too.

MARVIN HAMLISCH
A terrific school.

After dinner they all returned to the living room, where each guest had a chance to perform. Groucho sang Harry Ruby's "Show Me a Rose."

GROUCHO

(*After singing*) What'll people think of me, standing here singing for nothing?

ERIN

You want to do "Lydia"?

GROUCHO

I don't want to do it, but I'll do it if I'm forced to. (*He sings "Lydia"*)

ERIN

Is there any chance Marvin could play my favorite song, Groucho?

GROUCHO

Perhaps later when I go to bed.

MARVIN HAMLISCH

How's your cat?

GROUCHO

The cat is sick today. He has crabs.

JACK NICHOLSON

What's your cat's name?

GROUCHO

(*Proudly*) Blackie.

JACK NICHOLSON

That must be a white cat.

GROUCHO

No, a black cat.

ERIN

Whose turn is it now? Jack?

JACK NICHOLSON

I'm ready to do my act.

ERIN

Jack is ready, Groucho.

JACK NICHOLSON

I'm in a perfect position to do my mind-reading act.

GROUCHO

May I watch it?

JACK NICHOLSON

You can even hold my hand.

GROUCHO

What's that supposed to mean?

JACK NICHOLSON

(*To Mike Nichols*) Tell me a number from one to ten.

MIKE NICHOLS

Say it out loud?

JACK NICHOLSON

Yeah.

MIKE NICHOLS

Seven.

JACK NICHOLSON

Right.

GROUCHO

That's pretty good.

MIKE NICHOLS

I can do a magic trick.

GROUCHO

It's a pretty hot party. Jack, sing a song.

JACK NICHOLSON

I don't think I know an actual song. Except maybe "Happy Birthday."

MARVIN HAMLISCH

(*From the piano*) I know that.

JACK NICHOLSON

Is this what goes on here every night?

ERIN

Every night!

MARVIN HAMLISCH

Well, what do you do when you have company?

GROUCHO

Then I sing. I may sing right now. Come on, tear it off, Mozart.

MARVIN HAMLISCH

I wonder if Mrs. Mozart said that to her little son?

BETTY COMDEN AND ADOLPH GREEN

Betty Comden and Adolph Green met in their teens and began their collaboration as performers and as writers of sketches, lyrics, plays, and films. In their early days together, they appeared, along with Judy Holliday, at the Vanguard in Greenwich Village. Their Broadway credits include *On the Town, Bells Are Ringing, Wonderful Town,* and *Applause.* Among their film credits are *Singin' in the Rain, The Band Wagon, On the Town,* and *It's Always Fair Weather.* Recently they appeared in *A Party with Betty Comden and Adolph Green,* a musical comedy retrospective of their work.

   Whenever Groucho visited New York, one of the highlights for him was seeing Betty and Adolph. He was an appreciative audience for their talents, and if there was a piano anywhere around, Groucho expected and got a command performance ranging from "The Party's Over" to "Take Me Out to the Ball Game," done to the tune of "La Marseillaise." They talked with me at Betty Comden's house about what Groucho's friendship meant to them:

ADOLPH GREEN

We met Groucho in the very early fifties. Or it could have been the late forties.

BETTY COMDEN

We were out there writing some movie, I don't know which one. But from then on we were delighted to be counted as friends of his. We were kind of stunned and staggered. I mean, there are some people you meet in a lifetime where the whole experience seems so unreal—someone you have literally worshiped and adored from childhood, who's so much a part of your growing up.

ADOLPH GREEN

Over the years we've gotten to meet almost all of the people we worshiped as kids, and I guess two of the most important ones were Chaplin and Groucho. We got to meet both of them out there. And we've stayed friends over the years. Groucho became a constant friend, and he would turn up at parties where he knew we would be appearing, or we would be his guests. He would call up ahead of time and ask, "Are they there?" Then he'd drop over, watch us perform, and leave! Sometimes we were pretty embarrassed, but we loved it. We started going to his house when he was married to Kay.

BETTY COMDEN

We used to have dinner with him, and he used to come down to whatever strange rented houses we had and have dinner with us. When we came to New York, he used to call us, and we used to exchange letters from time to time. He did one marvelous thing for us the year after Judy Holliday died. Adolph and I put together a benefit evening for a hospital in Denver which had a wing dedicated to her. And Groucho came all the way there with Melinda and appeared in the show. We did Dr. Hackenbush, and he did a couple of other things, and he was enchanting, marvelous. He used to invite us to dinner when he had someone special he wanted us to meet. He was crazy about Martyn Green, one of the leading players of the D'Oyly Carte. He invited us to dinner when Martyn Green was out there. Groucho was so thrilled and impressed with him—he admired him so.

ADOLPH GREEN

I'm afraid he was more impressed with the *idea* of him than the actuality.

BETTY COMDEN

The dinner *was* tough going, wasn't it? Martyn Green was personally a lovely man, but his humor was mostly stories about the vicar. Not what Groucho was expecting.

ADOLPH GREEN

I think that was a very important evening for Groucho. He had both Harpo and Chico over.

BETTY COMDEN

I remember Groucho telling me once that he always kept a Gilbert and Sullivan book in the front seat of his car. When he stopped for a light he'd open it somewhere and read a few lines.

ADOLPH GREEN

He likes the old vaudeville songs now.

BETTY COMDEN

A lot of people wonder whether comedians themselves are really fun to be with, or are funny. We've always found Groucho enormously quick. I mean, just as fast as he will deliver a line in one of the old Marx Brothers pictures, he'll do the same in a public event. One we loved was at a party at "21." There was a man there who very much wanted to meet Groucho. It was Frederic Morton, who wrote a book called *The Rothschilds.* So I said I would introduce him. I took Freddie Morton up to Groucho to introduce him, and I said, "Groucho, this is Frederic Morton. He wrote *The Rothschilds.*" And he said, "Did they answer him?"

ADOLPH GREEN

I was impressed by that one, because there was no instant of thoughts grinding. Just the answer was out, RUP!

BETTY COMDEN

Like breathing.

ADOLPH GREEN

Spontaneously and like a hatchet at the same time.

BETTY COMDEN

We used to see him all the time in New York. Lüchow's was one of his favorite things. I remember having dinner once with him in Lüchow's when he excused himself from the table. It was sort of their May wine celebration. The restaurant was festooned with flowers, and the German band would get up and parade around, in and out of the tables as part of the celebration. Groucho didn't come back to the table, and we looked for him. Suddenly, there he was—following the band, walking through the restaurant doing his bent-knee walk with his cigar, the last one in the band.

ADOLPH GREEN

I'll never forget, it must be almost ten years ago, we went to some event with Groucho, after which there was a large gathering at a restaurant. It had something to do with a big Off-Broadway theatre group. It was a restaurant in the East Eighties. Maybe this is a pointless story, since I remember no names. The only thing I remember is that I was so bowled over by the fact that when we came in with Groucho, the place went mad! They were just shaking with excitement.

BETTY COMDEN

But it wasn't like just walking into a restaurant, because there were people like Mike Nichols and George Segal there. We have shared many, many things together with Groucho. In fact, I remember we even invited Groucho to the first run-through of *Bells Are Ringing* . . .

ADOLPH GREEN

It wasn't even a run-through. It was a rehearsal.

BETTY COMDEN

That's right. He was in New York, and he was so interested in what we were doing. He felt kind of concerned always, and we asked him to come by. He was the first person to see *Bells Are Ringing* outside of the people in the cast.

ADOLPH GREEN

There was about an hour cut out of *Bells Are Ringing* after Groucho saw it.

BETTY COMDEN

Steve, my husband, says when Groucho went backstage to see Judy Holliday, after the performance when the show was running, Steve and he were waiting in the little anteroom outside the dressing room. Judy said, "Just a minute, I'll be out soon." There was an ironing board there where her dresser had been ironing, so Groucho said to Steve, "Quick, take your trousers off right away!" So Steve took his trousers off right away. Groucho put them on the ironing board and was pressing as Judy came out. A sight to behold.

ADOLPH GREEN

Truth to tell, to repeat myself, Groucho is one of those things that makes it a pleasure to have had some degree of success. It's been a dream come true knowing him. As a kid I saw him in vaudeville. I saw them at the Palace. I saw *Animal Crackers* about a dozen times when it came out. The Marx Brothers, especially Groucho, became embedded in my mind, a part of my thinking day and night, my approach to life and humor. It's so astonishing these days to hear kids, my kids or other kids, who know all the old Marx Brothers lines, and can zip them off.

BETTY COMDEN

I must say that, as a girl, a female, to have his admiration is very lovely for me. I just love the fact that he likes me, that he likes to see me, and that we get along so well. I enjoy that relationship so much.

I

I saw your picture from Groucho over there. He's written "To my secret love" on it.

BETTY COMDEN

I keep it on the mantel.

ADOLPH GREEN

He still sees a lot of people.

BETTY COMDEN

A lot of young people.

I

There's a very wide age range.

BETTY COMDEN

He's kept active, always doing new things. I remember when he came east to do *Time for Elizabeth*. Then he came here to do his evening at Carnegie Hall. We saw that. Adolph and I did a series of pictures for *Esquire* once about the movies. We posed as all the stars. We did a Garbo and Gilbert thing, a Scarlett O'Hara and Rhett Butler, and a whole bunch of them. And we did Groucho and Margaret Dumont. But I played Groucho, and Adolph played Margaret Dumont.

I

Did you ever think about writing anything for Groucho?

ADOLPH GREEN

We wouldn't dream of it! We wouldn't dare. I remember one time when Groucho came to our apartment for dinner. Our son Adam, who was about four, used to do Chaplin imitations. And he came down with a derby, mustache, and cane. Groucho turned to him and, half angry, said, "At least you could have done *me* when I came here!"

I

Has Groucho changed much over the years?

BETTY COMDEN

I think his basic qualities are immutable, unchanged. He's funny and endearing and warm.

ADOLPH GREEN

I think in general he's less inclined to anger. Maybe he can't waste his emotion and strength on being angry as much. But I never knew him to shout.

BETTY COMDEN

He would get incensed about things, but I can't remember what. Do you remember anything that could get him mad?

ADOLPH GREEN

Politics, both political and studio, and people he thought were idiots.

BETTY COMDEN

He always speaks of Harpo with such affection and love.

ADOLPH GREEN

I wish I'd known Harpo better. I met him a few times. He seemed to be a man of lovely qualities, a real gentleman.

BETTY COMDEN

Groucho used to think about us quite a lot, I know, because I remember he recommended something to us for a show. He was the first to mention *Gypsy* to us. He had read an excerpt from it somewhere, and he said, "There's a show in this."

ADOLPH GREEN

He said, "It's a terrific show."

BETTY COMDEN

"You ought to go and get after this," he said. On the basis of it, we did get hold of the book. We didn't do *Gypsy*, but I wish he'd do this more often!

ADOLPH GREEN

Right. I wish we'd followed through then. We did have the rights to it, then we got involved in some other work and relinquished them.

I

Groucho really loves those performances you give when you come to his house or to his parties.

ADOLPH GREEN

Well, we *have* to! We have to come through. It's not even a command. It's "Or else!" We'd *better* come through!

I

(*To Betty*) One of Groucho's favorite stories, which he often tells when your name occurs, is how you used to get a seat on the subway by stuffing books under your clothes.

BETTY COMDEN

I used to stand in the subway and try to look pregnant. It's the way to get a seat in a crowded subway car.

ADOLPH GREEN

He really likes that. He tells it all the time.

BETTY COMDEN

I'm famous for that. It's a very attractive story for me because he tells it.

GRACE KAHN

"I thought I might be going to work at Sears Roebuck. I didn't know I could play piano well enough," Grace Kahn told me when I visited her at her Beverly Hills home.

Born in Brooklyn, when she was one her family moved to Elgin, Illinois. At fifteen, she went to Chicago, looking for work. "I was trying to sell something I had written, a piece of ragtime which was really terrible. But the man I played it for liked the way I played the piano and offered me a job. I accompanied the musicians who came in and was a song plugger."

When she met Gus Kahn, they became collaborators, though she is modest about her part of the collaboration. They wrote songs like, "Oh, How That Woman Could Cook!" one of Groucho's favorites.

Grace Kahn had known Groucho since her teens, even before she met Gus Kahn. They remained friends from that time on, and "family" since her daughter Irene married Groucho's son, Arthur. Grace remembered Groucho always saying to her and Gus, "When are you two kids gonna get married?"

"He really believed in marriage," she told me.

Grace Kahn recalled "Arthur at seven and Miriam at four when we lived back to back. We lived on Arden, and they lived on Hillcrest. They were in our house practically all of the time and were darling little children. I was very fond of Arthur." After Arthur grew up and married young Irene Kahn, Groucho and Grace Kahn had grandchildren Steve and Andy in common. The marriage ended when Arthur fell in love with his sister-in-law, Lois, who was married to Irene's brother. Arthur married Lois, and Irene later married someone else.

A few weeks older than Groucho, Grace Kahn was still pretty, petite, her face framed by soft white hair when I saw her. We met in her house filled with musical memorabilia. Gus Kahn's sheet music was on the piano.

On the walls were the charcoals and paintings that she had done over the years. She pointed out a painting of a bouquet of flowers. "Someone gave me that beautiful bouquet of flowers, and I knew it would wilt, so I painted it to preserve it."

When not playing golf, she could still be found at her piano, collaborating with her grandson, Andy Marx.

On Groucho's eighty-fifth birthday, she called to wish him a happy birthday:

"He was very pleased. Then I said to him, 'You know, Groucho, I always thought you didn't think I was pretty. You didn't talk to me like you did to girls you thought were pretty.' And Groucho said, 'You're pretty now.' "

I

When did you first meet Groucho?

GRACE KAHN

When I was about twenty years old, I worked for a music publisher in Chicago, a firm called Jerome H. Remick. I was what you called a song plugger. I was, I think, the only song plugger that they ever had. Evidently, I must have been a pretty good one, because I could get people to sing songs, and it wasn't too hard. Now, at this point Groucho was doing an act in Grand Rapids, something in vaudeville, so my boss sent me to Grand Rapids to get Groucho to sing a song when he arrived in Chicago. Groucho liked the song, and when he got to Chicago he sang it.

Now, this was my introduction to Groucho: I was only twenty, and I didn't even know Gus then. I rapped at the door, Groucho said, "Come in," so I came in. When he saw it was a girl, I think he was rather surprised. He said, "Sit down," so I sat down. He said, "Have a cigar," and I said, "No, thank you." I told him who I was and that I had this song I wanted him to hear, and he said, "Well, fine. Go ahead and play it." I played it, and he said, "I like it. Very nice. How would you like to take a bath?" He had to take a shower. I said, "No, thank you." Well, anyway, we became very friendly, and when he got to Chicago I came to see him, and he was doing this song.

Now this was, as I said, before Gus. In later years, when Groucho's son was about seven, we met again, and this time we met with Gus. Gus and Groucho really became very good friends. We were friends through all those years, except when Groucho was on the road and then we didn't see him. Sometimes we didn't see him for almost a year. But we did become very, very good friends and remained so. My daughter, Irene, was married to Groucho's son, Arthur. Gus and I and Groucho and Ruth lived back to back, our gardens almost came together. I've known Arthur since he was seven years old. He and my daughter went to school together. But they were divorced. So, this broke up the family a little, but Groucho and I always remained friends. Unfortunately, Gus died in 1941, which is a long time ago.

I

Do you remember the song you were plugging when you met Groucho?

GRACE KAHN

Yes, I certainly do. "Sailin' Away on the Henry Clay," that was the name of the song. They'd travel around the country for about a year in those days, and Groucho kept the song on for all that time. Then after Gus, he, and I became good friends, Gus and I wrote a song for him, a funny song which he sang last night. You heard him sing "Oh, How That Woman Could Cook!" Well, Gus and I wrote that before we were even married, so you know how long ago *that* was.

> I

Groucho always sings that song.

> GRACE KAHN

He sings it wherever he is. He's so funny, you know. On his birthday I called him, and I said, "I want to wish you a happy birthday on your *real* birthday. But you never wished me a happy birthday, and my birthday was a week ago." He said, "Oh, if I had only known that, I'd have come over and sung your song to you!" He loves to perform.

> I

Did Groucho always like to perform that much?

> GRACE KAHN

Oh, he could perform every five seconds, no matter where he was. If there was a piano, there he was singing, and the songs were funny, too. Now, the song I got him to sing was not a funny song, so that was quite a feather in my cap. It was just a straight song, but he did it for a long time.

> I

Was Groucho very different when he was young?

> GRACE KAHN

He's different now. You know how old he is. But his mind is still funny; he still says funny things. I wish I knew more stories, but I really can't think of stories, only a nice association with him all these years.

> I

Did you ever meet his mother, Minnie?

> GRACE KAHN

Of course. As I recall, Minnie really was the backbone of the whole thing. She kept the act together. Now, he had a father, too. He always used to kid about his father, but I never met him. When I met Groucho, he wasn't married yet. I think we got married almost at the same time he did. His wife was in the chorus. She was a beautiful, beautiful girl, and a nice one. We were very friendly for a long time. My daughter Irene and Ruth became good friends until Ruth died. I met Ruth at the same time I met Groucho. She was also in the show in Grand Rapids.

> I

Was Groucho always the Groucho character? Is it his real self?

GRACE KAHN

Yes, he'd always been himself. I think that's why he was named Groucho. He used to come to our house all the time, and he was always funny, on- or offstage. He was just as funny off as he was on. As I say, he and I, we get along just great, and I'm really very fond of Groucho. I was also very fond of his brother Harpo. Harpo was such a gentleman. Harpo could have traveled in the most gentlemanly circles. The other brothers were . . . what shall I say? Characters. Chico was a character. He was an extreme in every way. He was the opposite of any of them. He did everything; he liked to gamble, he liked everything, but was very lovable.

I

What do you think was the secret of his great charm? Groucho still ponders it.

GRACE KAHN

I think it was his love for people. He really had great warmth.

I

Groucho always wondered what was Chico's great secret with women — why women loved him so much. Groucho said I would have to ask a woman.

GRACE KAHN

Because he was a warm, warm person. I mean Harpo was warm, but in a gentlemanly way. But Chico, the moment you met him, you had to like him. Now, Groucho was always caustic, even if he didn't mean it. I don't know what made him that way, but he had to say something sharp. I don't mean derogatory, really, but now what would you call it? Repartee? He could be caustic. Half the time he may not have meant it. But not everyone understood. Then he'd turn around and do some of the sweetest things.

I

Did any of the sharp things Groucho said ever bother you?

GRACE KAHN

No, it never bothered me because I used to tell him off.

I

You could because of the respect Groucho has for you.

GRACE KAHN

And I have respect for him too. But when I thought he said things that were out of line, especially in front of my friends who don't understand those things, then I had to stop him a little bit. Now, I never heard Harpo say one word that would ever hurt anybody. I don't even remember hearing Chico — who was funny, very funny — I never heard him say anything to hurt anybody. Sometimes, I think Groucho's almost ashamed to say anything sweet.

ANDY MARX

Before lunch at Groucho's, June Banker, of the Academy of Motion Picture Arts and Sciences, was introduced by Groucho to his grandson Andy:

"Have you met my grandson Steve?"

For years this was a private joke of Groucho's. Steve is Andy's older brother, although Groucho said that Andy's older brother is "Amos."

Andy, who is a composer, is also a grandson of Gus and Grace Kahn, and his father is writer Arthur Marx. An excellent pianist, Andy often accompanied Groucho at parties.

Groucho and I had lunch with Andy and June shortly after he had received his Oscar. Nurse Julie was also there. As he regularly did, Groucho counseled Andy against a man getting married too young:

GROUCHO
I was thirty when I got married. You don't want to get married now.

ANDY
Yeah, but there are people who've gotten married in their twenties who did all right. You've been married three times. What went wrong?

GROUCHO
To marry beauty isn't enough. I married three of them. And each one was a disaster.

ANDY
When did you find that out?

GROUCHO
After I divorced them.

ANDY
What should you have looked for?

GROUCHO
I should have looked for a girl who is very smart.

JUNE BANKER
Weren't any of your wives very intelligent?

GROUCHO
No. That wasn't what I looked for. And beauty fades.

ANDY
But how do you know when to do it? How long should you wait?

GROUCHO
You certainly shouldn't get married until you can support a girl.

ANDY

I can. I've supported two girls. I had one on each shoulder.

GROUCHO

(*Not amused*) That's a good joke, but it doesn't make any sense. So, I'm gonna look at TV for a while. (*But he doesn't leave*) I remember when I first met Andy Marx. He was a big clout then.

ANDY

Know how much I weighed when Groucho met me? Twelve pounds when I was born. I even had glasses on.

GROUCHO

You were born with glasses on? Well, you could scc through life, I think. (*To June and me*) I remember him when he was about ten years old. He used to come for Christmas, but I didn't give him anything.

I

I don't think that's true.

ANDY

No, he always gave me something.

GROUCHO

I remember one Christmas what I got. I hung up my stocking, and I got a half orange and half a banana.

I

Were you disappointed?

GROUCHO

No, I was very happy with them. I was very simple. And I got a watch for my bar mitzvah. A gold watch. Which turned green the third week.

ANDY

I never had a bar mitzvah. I'm thinking about going back and having it done now.

GROUCHO

Why not? I'll give you a Groucho watch.

ANDY

And it'll turn green in three hours.

GROUCHO

Well, I got the gold watch. Chico immediately hocked it.

ANDY

No wonder it turned green! You think Chico would have hocked his Oscar?

GROUCHO

Yeah. He could have hocked it. Or he would have lost it in a card game. Or he would have given it to some dame.

ANDY

While we're on that subject. I would like to say a word about oral contraception.

GROUCHO

As long as you keep it to just one word.

ANDY

I had an extremely good case of oral contraception about two weeks ago. I
asked a girl to go to bed with me and she said no.

I

Maybe it wasn't her bedtime.

ANDY

It's really a Woody Allen joke.

GROUCHO

Remember when you used to come here, Steve?

ANDY

I'm Andy, Groucho. He always calls me that, "Steve." Steve's my older
brother.

GROUCHO

His older brother is Amos.

ANDY

Groucho gave me one of his books, and he wrote in it "To Andy, from
Amos." Anyway, I used to come over and throw water on the French poodles. De Soto and Rainbow. Those were the names. But Groucho didn't
mind. As a matter of fact, in a letter he *told* me to. He said, "Come over
and throw water on the French poodles. Hoping this reaches you by pony
express."

GROUCHO

I remember when I was in Atlantic City . . .

ANDY

I was there, wasn't I? Wasn't I with you that time?

GROUCHO

Were you with me?

ANDY

I was with you in Atlantic City.

GROUCHO

Not this time.

ANDY

I was with you, though, in the Santa Clausland Parade.

GROUCHO

You were?

ANDY

Yeah. In my mom's stomach. Steve was there with Melinda, and my mom was pregnant with me. I was on my way. Then I popped out. She's been sorry ever since.

GROUCHO

You don't want to hear about Atlantic City?

ANDY

I don't know if I do. I think I know what story this is. I think half of it's myth.

GROUCHO

When I was in Atlantic City, I was living in a very crummy boarding-house. And all we had to eat was fish. We had fish for breakfast, lunch, and dinner. By Thursday we couldn't eat any more fish. We were sick of fish, and I don't like fish anyhow. So there was this fellow selling roast beef sandwiches on the boardwalk. It was ten cents a slice, but we didn't have any money. So I swapped my watch for eight sandwiches of roast beef. When I gave him the watch, it slipped and fell into the ocean. But we had already eaten the sandwiches. Anyhow, we were gonna get paid Saturday. But we were two more days without money and we had to go back to eating fish.

ANDY

Do you remember, Groucho, when you ordered the bowl of noodles at Trader Vic's? We used to go there for birthdays, like mine on June 26.

GROUCHO

Your father's is July 21.

ANDY

Groucho would always complain but, for some reason, the next time, it would be Trader Vic's. Well, this one time we went there and Groucho just ordered a bowl of noodles, "a bowl of noodles and a glass of water." The waiter comes and serves the bowl of noodles to Groucho, who says, "Take these and dump them on the chef's head." Do you remember that, Groucho?

GROUCHO

No.

ANDY

Once I took Groucho to the doctor and we were stuck in traffic, and there was a hippyish guy on a bike stuck next to us. Grouch rolls down the window and says, "You need a shave." Another time, I was with a guy I knew who had fairly long hair, and I was with him and these two girls when we ran into Groucho. Groucho said to me, in front of them, "Oh, I see you're with three girlfriends." Do you remember that, Groucho?

GROUCHO

No.

ANDY

Groucho used to try to break me up when we'd be someplace somber where you were supposed to be quiet and respectful. He'd make faces and look at me till I laughed. He still can do it. (*To Groucho*) I saw Nanny the other day.

GROUCHO

I knew your grandmother before you did. I knew her before your grandfather did. She was eighteen years old then. (*Explaining to June*) She's Grace Kahn. She was married to Gus Kahn. They had the same name. He was great. (*Groucho sings a few lines of* "Oh, How That Woman Could Cook!")

ANDY

My grandmother, Grace, I've always been real close with. I went to Europe with her when I was fifteen, and I've been on a lot of trips with her. I remember when I told Groucho we were going on that trip to Europe. Maybe I was fourteen. He said, "Be careful. Take plenty of condoms."

JUNE BANKER

How old is your grandmother now?

ANDY

About as old as Groucho, I guess. But she doesn't seem old. You know, we all went out last night for my mom's birthday, and we went to Shelly's Manhole to hear the jazz thing. It was kind of boring, but my grandmother puts up with it. I know she didn't really enjoy it, but it was kind of funny to see her there. I usually take her my songs; if she likes it, I know it's good, because she's usually right. She just happened to like those two that the publisher took. They let me record them.

GROUCHO

He's more advanced than his father for his age.

ANDY

You know, I guess my grandmother doesn't understand a lot of the lyrics. I've shown her not just my stuff, but lyrics of just anybody's. I showed her some of the Elton John stuff. She thought that was a little weird. You know, coming from Tin Pan Alley.

GROUCHO

I met John Elton.

I

Groucho had lunch with Elton John, only he called him "John Elton."

ANDY

You know, for a while, Elton John and Woody Allen were my two idols.

GROUCHO

Which is not exactly the same thing.

ANDY

I've found that you have to sort of discard your idols.

I

Even Groucho?

ANDY

That's a whole different thing. I think everybody sort of identifies with their parents or grandparents. I don't care what business they're in. Everybody tells me I sort of identify with my dad, or try to, which is probably true.

I

(*To Andy*) What about your childhood as "Groucho's grandson"?

ANDY

You mean with Lois [Arthur's second wife] and all that? I was young—about ten—but I was around for all that. But you're too young to really realize it. You're at that age where you'd like to cash in on all the goings-on. You know, you try to get as many toys out of each set of parents as possible. And that's about it. It's funny, when I read *Son of Groucho* it sort of brought some of that back.

I

Do you remember your grandmother, Groucho's first wife, Ruth?

ANDY

I remember Ruth. I liked her a lot. I used to always go over to her house. We would have Christmas, and we'd go over there with Dad and the presents and everything. I don't really remember Kay at all. I saw Eden the other night at the Academy. She came up to Groucho at the Governor's dinner, just as we came in.

GROUCHO

You mean the Governor's balls. She said to me, "Congratulations."

I

And what did you say?

GROUCHO

I said, "I deserved it."

ANDY

Once I was in Nate 'n' Al's delicatessen when Groucho was there, and I went up to him and said, "Hi!" He said something like, "I'm real ashamed

to see you here." And I said, "Well, that's exactly how I feel about you."
He seemed to think that was hilarious or something and he laughed.

GROUCHO

I must have been pickled. Dill-pickled.

ANDY

You never laugh at any of my jokes.

GROUCHO

You never tell any.

ANDY

Once I did some Woody Allen jokes, and you liked them. I just kind of
ad-libbed it. That's what you usually have to do. You know, Groucho tells
these jokes, but he doesn't seem to get any of them when *you* tell them.
Or he doesn't seem to laugh. Well, I can understand him not laughing.

GROUCHO

I don't know any jokes.

ANDY

(*To June*) It's too bad you didn't get to see those turn-of-the-century
French films. They were really great. The three of us went. It was all
silent, except when Groucho said something like "I've gotta take a leak."

GROUCHO

No matter how rich you are . . .

ANDY

Groucho, what was that one you liked so much?

GROUCHO

The drunkard. That was funny.

I

(*To Andy*) Henri Langlois thought it was very funny when he came here
for tea and you introduced yourself to him as "Groucho's grandson."

ANDY

Nobody introduced us, so I said, "I'm Groucho Marx's grandson. I might
as well say it. Everybody else does." Sometimes it seems that the most interesting thing about me is that I'm Groucho Marx's grandson. It took me
a while to get used to that.

I

Did you?

ANDY

No.

JUNE BANKER

Does it ever bother you being the grandson of such a famous man?

ANDY

Well, I used to try to compare myself, like, with Groucho or even with my dad. Then I sort of realized that I'm kind of young. But you can't, like, put yourself in their perspective when *they* were twenty years old. You know, even Marvin Hamlisch is, like, eight years older than I am, and I'd be embarrassed to play the piano for him. I have a lot to learn, I know. When I was younger, I used to wonder if I could measure up to the Marx Brothers. Then, I realized maybe I wasn't ever going to have that kind of success, but I didn't have to. I said to myself, "So I'm not going to be that great. I can live with it. I'll be myself and do the best I can do."

I

Who are some of the people you remember meeting over the years at Groucho's?

ANDY

Let me think . . . well, I wasn't here much when anybody was here, mostly family. I guess Irwin Allen was one guy who really impressed me. The first words I ever said were "Iry's car." Now whenever he sees me, he yells, "Iry's car!" He had a big convertible, and the top went down. I thought it was a monster. I can still remember lying on our driveway—I didn't start talking until I was four—and that was the first thing I said: "Iry's car." So he must have really impressed me. Groucho, I saw Billy Marx today, and he had a bumper sticker on his car, and it said, "The right to arm bears." And there was a picture of a bear holding a gun.

NURSE JULIE

Why do you always say Billy Marx instead of just Billy? Groucho and everyone here always says Billy Marx or Andy Marx instead of Billy or Andy.

ANDY

Well, there are so many Bills in the world. And there are lots of Andys—Raggedy Andy and me—but there's only one Groucho.

GROUCHO

(*Looking at his Groucho watch*) It's twenty-five minutes to Groucho. I've gotta go brush my fangs. (*He gets up from the table*)

ANDY

I've gotta be leaving too.

GROUCHO

(*To Andy*) Goodbye, Steve.

ANDY

(*To Groucho*) Goodbye, Bob.

NORMAN KRASNA

Besides being a famous playwright, Norman Krasna is a producer, writer, and director of films, as well. Among his stage successes are *Dear Ruth*, which is based on the Groucho Marx family, and *John Loves Mary*. His record as a screen playwright is just as distinguished:

He wrote *Fury*, Fritz Lang's first American film, the screenplay for Alfred Hitchcock's *Mr. and Mrs. Smith*, and the original screenplay for René Clair's first Hollywood film, *The Flame of New Orleans*. For *Princess O'Rourke*, Krasna won an Oscar for the best original screenplay.

I had the opportunity to talk with him in New York when he arrived for the opening of his play *We Interrupt This Program*. He and his wife, Erle, met with me in their hotel apartment and at the Oyster Bar of the Plaza Hotel. I also went with him to a preview of his play at the Ambassador Theatre on Forty-ninth Street, and on the way there and back, we talked about Groucho. We also spoke later in Switzerland, where he has been living for a number of years.

As well as being one of Groucho's best friends, Norman Krasna collaborated with Groucho on the screenplay of *The King and the Chorus Girl* and the play *Time for Elizabeth*.

I

What was it like collaborating with Groucho?

NORMAN KRASNA

I did the work at the typewriter while Groucho paced around and talked. The only way I can concentrate is by facing a blank wall. So I would sit facing the wall, twisting paper clips into Jimmy Durante's profile. Groucho kept talking all the time, usually about other things.

Groucho had an incredible repertory of jokes to draw on, but he didn't just use old jokes. We were working on *The King and the Chorus Girl*, and talking about a scene in which there's a fellow in the royal box, and a comedian comes out and tells a lot of jokes. The king is someone who has heard everything, and so is jaded. He can sleep with his eyes open!

I said to Groucho, "We need some used jokes. Can you tell me some jokes?" Groucho said, "About what? Tell me the subject." I didn't have anything in mind, but we'd just been talking about how I'd been losing my hair, and Groucho had recommended I have some scalp massages, so I said, "The subject is hair," and he started. He said six or seven jokes in a row about hair, like "Hair today, gone tomorrow," "My hair is getting thin, so who needs fat hair," "How do you save your hair? In a box," "How do you avoid falling hair? You step aside." And he went on and reeled off just about any joke anyone ever thought of about hair. He wouldn't use any of these, of course, but I realized that he had a wonderful memory, and he went on to make up his own.

Time for Elizabeth was written over a number of years. Neither Groucho nor I was in any special hurry. Originally the part was for Groucho, but we did it with Otto Kruger. The lines were written to have been Groucho's, and I think the play would have been a success on Broadway if Groucho had done it. Groucho got an entirely different reaction when he finally did *Time For Elizabeth*. Nobody else could get that reaction with the same lines.

I

Wyatt Cooper, who played with Groucho in *Time for Elizabeth,* told me that Groucho ad-libbed a great deal.

NORMAN KRASNA

Yes, he did. But *Time for Elizabeth* was quite strictly written. Groucho always thinks of himself as a writer, and likes writers as his friends, especially if they're good. But I think he's even more of a performer than a writer.

I

He's always told me he's proudest of being a writer.

NORMAN KRASNA

Yes, true. I'll never forget after the preview of *The King and the Chorus Girl* when we were walking out of the theatre. Standing there was Mervyn LeRoy, the director, who said, "Did you like it?" Groucho just said, "Coney Island," in a disgusted tone and walked off. He was referring to a line in the film, which meant that he hated it. Groucho wasn't afraid of anyone. He never was easily inhibited. I remember being in an elevator with him, and there was a man in the elevator with us who kept staring at Groucho and who was engrossed in listening to every word we said. I was going to the theatre, and Groucho asked me what play I was going to see, and I told him. He said, "That's not much of a play unless *this* guy wrote it," meaning the man who was hanging on our every word. The man got out at the next floor. Do you know about the time Shufro took Groucho to Wall Street?

I

I met him once with Groucho. Salwyn Shufro.

NORMAN KRASNA

Right. They're still friends, and Shufro's been his broker all these years. Well, this story happened back in the thirties. Shufro took Groucho into the stock exchange, and Groucho started singing "When Irish Eyes Are Smiling." Nobody laughed. They were just shocked and perfectly still. Then Groucho made a short speech explaining. "In one day here, I lost $250,000. And now I'm going to sing 'When Irish Eyes Are Smiling.' " He did, and they loved it.

I

Has Groucho changed much over the years?

NORMAN KRASNA

He used to be more irreverent about himself.

I

He still is very much so.

NORMAN KRASNA

Not as much as he used to be. Now he might get upset if he didn't get the right table in a restaurant. Before, he wouldn't ever have taken himself that seriously. But Groucho never did complain much. Not then, not now. He's not a complainer.

I

It's the same thing now. He has health problems. But you don't think about them because *he* doesn't. Or I should say he doesn't *appear* to.

NORMAN KRASNA

Did you know *Dear Ruth* was about the Marx family? Groucho is the judge, Groucho's wife Ruth is the Ruth in the play, and the children are Arthur and Miriam. Poor Miriam and her liberal causes! That family really meant a lot to me. I practically lived with them for a while as part of their family. They made me feel so much at home until I was going there for dinner several nights a week.

I

When did you first meet Groucho?

NORMAN KRASNA

I don't remember exactly *when* I first met him, but what was important was the first time he took an interest in me. It was at the Garden of Allah. I had been a journalist, and I was working in publicity at Warners. Arthur Caesar was there holding court. He was a wit of his time, sort of challenging people verbally and insulting them.

Well, I was a nobody and you couldn't crush me. I guess this was before *Louder, Please!* So he said, "You wanna have a duel of wits?" and I said, "All right, but if we're gonna have a duel of wits, we've gotta set up some rules." There were about four stock phrases he'd been using over and over, and I said, "You can't use any of these," and named them, the four things he'd been repeatedly using.

Well, he'd been drinking, so it wasn't quite fair, but Groucho noticed me, and I guess he thought I was a witty kid. He invited me to his home for dinner. After that I was there all the time. I was a bachelor, and I was free, and they had me there to dinner several times a week. It was like my home.

In *Dear Ruth,* they were the characters. A lot of the jokes were little family jokes that were real. A lot of it is just echoes of the dinner-table talk at Groucho's house. I was crazy about Ruth. She was the kind of girl men were crazy about. They all liked her. She was so lively.

Groucho liked to listen to Gilbert and Sullivan. He really loved Gilbert and Sullivan, and it was my real introduction to it. In those days he liked to stay home more and listen to the radio. He just wasn't a lively enough companion for her, and she had so much energy and zest. She started going to the Beverly Hills Tennis Club, and she kept coming home later and later.

Groucho's always cared tremendously about women. But he's a sap about women. What a romantic! He always expects so much, the women can't live up to it. Kay and Eden were the kind of girls who attracted him. He wanted noncompetitive girls; he didn't want a modern girl with a man's mind. That kind was all right, but only as a friend.

When he married Eden, she saw the round bathtub in Zeppo's house and wanted one herself. So Groucho built his house around her round bathtub. She was like a four-year-old, so enthusiastic and pleased. Groucho isn't cheap. He never wanted to give the twenty-five cents for checking his coat, but he was prepared to lose $20,000 on *Time for Elizabeth.* He always measured everything by the price of pumpernickel. He said, "I remember when you could hardly carry sixteen cents' worth of pumpernickel."

I

That was probably at the turn of the century!

NORMAN KRASNA

Yes, Groucho is older than I am, and the age difference seemed great when we first met. Now it isn't anything. But then it meant a lot to me that he was willing to accept me.

I

What were your impressions of the other Marx Brothers?

NORMAN KRASNA

All the Marx Brothers were completely different from each other. Each of them had a different philosophy of life. Harpo was a pixie-like person—a giant pixie. He was completely kind. Chico loved gambling and women, and he threw away every cent he ever earned. But he was a good person in spite of it. Zeppo was just the younger brother. He was a gambler, something like Chico. But he was the funniest one offstage.

I

Groucho told me that, too.

NORMAN KRASNA

Really? Well, he should know. People used to say, "You must really be laughing all the time, rolling in the aisles, because you're fortunate enough to spend all those hours with Groucho." It wasn't like that. Groucho is pretty serious. He could be quite dour, though of course he would say some really clever, funny things. But Zeppo used to have me rolling on the floor. I once actually got so hysterical that I rolled around on a car floor and out the door.

I

Groucho has told me that Zeppo was one of the funniest people he's ever known. Billy Marx said he remembered Groucho rolling around on the floor laughing at something Zeppo had said. What was Zeppo's humor like?

NORMAN KRASNA

He just told about his own personal experiences. It was his way of seeing it and saying it that made it funny. Groucho's standard of wit was very high. He didn't just have people around to laugh at what he said. You couldn't deal in platitudes, and he wasn't interested in just hearing jokes. He'd heard them all anyway. He expected a lot, and you had to measure up. It was very flattering when he accepted you. It was very flattering to be his friend. If you dropped by, you'd find someone like Artur Rubinstein there. He was not just a comedian, not just an actor. He was somebody to admire, by golly!

I

People don't seem to mind his insults.

NORMAN KRASNA

Groucho could say anything, and people just laughed. Very few people got insulted. I was with him once when he'd just insulted someone, and I said, "Groucho, you can't say something like that to a person." He said, "They like it. They go home and tell their friends." But once he said something to Lee Shubert that wasn't funny at all. It just came out all wrong. He wrote a letter to him the next day explaining that he was sorry. He would do things like pushing up Greta Garbo's hat in an elevator, but I'll never know if he knew who it was before he did it. Everyone was afraid to follow Groucho onstage. Eddie Cantor told him once before going onstage, "Don't be too hard on me, Groucho!"

I asked Groucho once if there was anyone he was afraid to follow onstage, and he said, "Frank Fay. He was wonderful."

NORMAN KRASNA

Groucho wanted me to appear on *You Bet Your Life,* but I was afraid. "You go easy on me," I said. He told me, "I'll kill you!" so I didn't go on the show. I knew I couldn't compete on my feet with Groucho. He had a Congressional Medal of Honor winner on the show once, and the fellow went for the top and lost it all. I told Groucho he should have let him win, but Groucho said he couldn't help it. It was a matter of integrity. The show wasn't rigged. He was very proud of that when the scandals broke about shows like *The $64,000 Question.* I thought he should have been honest and have integrity, but *not* for a Congressional Medal of Honor winner. It's so rare that there's a live one. Usually the medal goes to a widow or relative. But Groucho believed he did the right thing.

Once he makes up his mind about something, he doesn't often waver.

NORMAN KRASNA

Groucho's a very strong man. I think it's impossible for someone of your generation to appreciate Groucho in his moment. Looking back isn't the same thing. When I first knew Groucho, for a while, maybe, that was the best credit I had.

JACK LEMMON AND WALTER MATTHAU

An unshaven Jack Lemmon came for lunch one Saturday while I was staying at Groucho's. Apologizing for being less than his normally fastidious self, he explained that he had a stage matinee that afternoon and his part necessitated the unkempt appearance. The play was *Juno and the Paycock,* a production at the Mark Taper Forum.

"I hope you won't mind my dirty fingernails," he added, displaying them for us as he sat down at the table with Groucho and me. "It's for my part. So I can be in character for the people in the first few rows, I always go into my garden and make my fingernails dirty."

This part was important to him in that special way that film actors feel about their stage appearances, especially in Los Angeles, where the audiences are so often made up of their peers. He told me that he wouldn't ordinarily eat before a matinee, but for lunch at Groucho's he had made an exception.

There was also a place set for Jack Benny, whom Groucho expected. We waited a long time, but Jack Benny did not arrive, and there was no phone call. I have never known Groucho to wait so long for anyone, but finally in deference to Jack Lemmon's matinee, Groucho asked Robin to serve, and we began without Jack Benny.

Jack Lemmon talked about all of the physical ills that had plagued Walter Matthau during the run of the play and described the one tiny dressing room they were sharing. He also told us how exciting the visit was of Sean O'Casey's widow, who came to Los Angeles to attend the opening. "They served wine, and she could really put it away."

The conversation got around to the Depression, and Groucho recalled how he had lost everything in the stock market crash of 1929. Jack Lemmon also remembered that time:

"I was four or five. I remember my father coming home and putting all of his things on the dresser: his change, his keys, his cigar cutter. I could hear him whispering with my mother. I didn't hear what they said, but there was something in the atmosphere. And I knew that something terrible had happened."

As soon as we finished lunch, Jack rushed to the theatre. Groucho cracked nuts and with hurt feelings pondered why Jack Benny hadn't come to lunch or even called. Several days later we learned why.

On December 26, 1974, during Groucho's morning walk, we met Milton Berle, who told him that Jack Benny was dying and perhaps had only a week to live. Milton Berle finished by saying, "Nobody could ever say a bad thing about him."

A shaken Groucho returned home, not saying anything at all. Then he sat quietly by his record player listening to Ruth Etting sing "It All Depends on You."

Before going to see *Juno and the Paycock*, Groucho invited Billy Marx to have dinner with us. Billy came prepared to interview Groucho for me, but Groucho wasn't in the mood. He was too involved with thinking about the play, almost as if he himself were going to be in it. *Juno and the Paycock* was the theatrical event of the moment, and tickets were much sought after.

At dinner Billy reminded Groucho about a story Arthur, Groucho's son, had told him:

"You told Arthur he was to be in by ten o'clock, and he was late. So he came in as quietly and carefully as he could, tiptoeing through the house, trying not to make a sound, getting undressed in the dark. And just as he was about to get into bed, he heard your voice saying, 'I hear you.'"

In the car Billy and Groucho talked about writers and musicians.

GROUCHO
Franklin P. Adams was very good. But he wasn't Kaufman.
BILLY
You and my father both loved music. Harpo liked Gershwin and Ravel.
GROUCHO
I liked Brahms. I liked Gilbert and Sullivan. I liked Irving Berlin. Irving Berlin was in love with Ellin. Her father was very rich and wouldn't let them get married, but they got married. Then the stock market crashed, and after that Irving was the rich one. It's like the kind of plot he would have set to music. They had one of the few good marriages. It would make a good play. (*They sing some Irving Berlin songs*)

At the Mark Taper Forum, Groucho attracted the usual amount of attention. This was as true when the audience was made up of celebrities as when it was a noncelebrity audience. A cute young usherette greeted him with a delighted squeal of glee, and Groucho rose to the occasion by kissing her.

As we were about to be seated, Groucho, who usually liked an aisle seat, reversed his usual course, trading seats with Billy. The reason was immediately obvious—a Grace Kelly–looking blonde. Groucho sat down next to her, raising his eyebrows and giving the lady a lecherous ogle worthy of his "mangy lover" days. She remained coolly oblivious. Not one to be put off by an icy rebuff or a house falling on him, Groucho tried again.

"Kiss me, babe." The blonde grew even cooler. Then, with a haughtily scathing glance, she changed seats with her escort.

"I guess she didn't recognize you," Billy unassured Groucho.

"I guess she *did*," Groucho responded, undaunted.

During the first act, Groucho whispered to me, "That's a part I could've played," referring to the part of Joxer Daly being played by Jack Lemmon. Throughout the play, Groucho studied Jack Lemmon's performance with professional interest. "He's a fine broth of a lad," he commented to me in a heavy Irish brogue as the curtain fell at intermission. Groucho continued to speak with an Irish brogue as members of the audience of all ages approached and asked him to autograph their programs. The ensuing melee was more orderly than usual.

One young man respectfully said to Groucho, "You're really neat!" In a mildly perplexed tone, Groucho asked, "You mean I'm meticulous?"

The intermission was spent signing autographs until Groucho announced, "I'm going to take a leak."

"You're trying to escape from signing all these autographs," I said.

"No," Groucho said, "I've gotta sign them there, too."

After the final curtain, we all went backstage. Whenever friends of his were performing and Groucho was in the audience, his visit backstage was *de rigueur*. Climbing up the narrow stairway, Groucho apologized for holding on to the banister: "I'll just hold on to the third rail."

As we walked toward the star dressing room, several of the actors approached Groucho and asked him for his autograph—a special compliment. Before we reached the dressing room Groucho confided to me, "Lemmon's performance was fresh-squeezed." Then he editorialized, "Bad joke."

Billy noticed the actor who had played Harpo in *Minnie's Boys* and said, "There's my dad!"

In the tiny dressing room, which scarcely contained them, not to mention us, we found Jack Lemmon, who was stripped to the waist, and Walter Matthau, who still had on the special padding for his part. "John Wayne wore this in pictures," he told us. "Can you believe that?!" He was gray-haired for his part. "I'm the only person whose hair gets black when I come out of the shower."

Walter Matthau opened a small portable refrigerator and asked Groucho if he would like to join him in some buttermilk. "It'll be too crowded," Groucho said, then he added one of his favorite "small" jokes: "What's a cow good for but-her-milk? That's an old vaudeville joke."

A pretty young actress passed by the open door, and Groucho, who rarely failed to notice feminine beauty, nodded approvingly. Walter Matthau, observing Groucho's wandering gaze and noting the object of his attentions, commented, "But she's boring."

GROUCHO
All young girls are boring. You shouldn't expect any more.
JACK LEMMON
I do.
GROUCHO
I'm in love with your wife.
JACK LEMMON
I'll tell her you said so.
GROUCHO
I already told her.

Groucho had been trying to call Walter Matthau and his wife, Carol, to invite them for lunch, but had been frustrated because their number had been changed. Many of the stars constantly change their telephone numbers to guard their privacy, even though it creates an obstacle course for the friends they really want to be able to reach them. They are also highly peripatetic, both from choice and necessity, and keeping an up-to-date address book is exceedingly difficult. As we left, Groucho took Walter Matthau's new number, saying, "I have your new phone number now in case I don't want to call you."

NUNNALLY JOHNSON

Among Groucho's oldest and best friends was the late Nunnally Johnson, who, although basically a writer, also wrote, directed, and produced numerous films, including *Night People, Black Widow, Oh, Men, Oh, Women,* and *The Three Faces of Eve.* He wrote the screenplay for and directed *The Man in the Gray Flannel Suit.* His most recent screenplay was *The Dirty Dozen,* but he was perhaps best known for *The Grapes of Wrath, The Gunfighter, The Mudlark, The Desert Fox,* and *How to Marry a Millionaire.*

Groucho, who was a regular visitor to Nunnally Johnson's house, talked about him with Erin and me as we rode back from afternoon tea with the Johnsons:

ERIN

He must have been a terrific guy, huh?

GROUCHO

Nunnally was a wild man when he was young. He did great things.

ERIN

In what way?

GROUCHO

With the girls.

ERIN

Oh yeah. I figured. They liked him.

GROUCHO

He had everything. He was tall, intelligent, and capable.

On several occasions I went with Groucho and Erin to visit Nunnally Johnson. His wry, understated sense of humor contrasted with Groucho's ironic iconoclasms. His wife, Dorris Bowdon, had starred in *The Grapes of Wrath.*

On one visit, Lauren Bacall was there when Groucho and I arrived. Tall, slender "Betty" (as all her friends know her) was in California to promote *Murder on the Orient Express.* They talked about mutual friends, like Comden and Green, and she told how she was going to visit Ira Gershwin, whom neither Groucho nor Nunnally had seen for some time. Groucho showed her a picture of Melinda and grandson Miles:

NUNNALLY JOHNSON
Why don't you show him yours, Betty?
LAUREN BACALL
Show him my *what?* I don't have pictures . . . but I have *other* things.

As she left, she spoke to Nunnally in her famous sulky tone:

LAUREN BACALL
Take care of yourself, you silly man. Next time we'll go upstairs.
NUNNALLY JOHNSON
There is no upstairs.
LAUREN BACALL
Well, now . . . we don't need an upstairs! (*She exits singing "Baby It's Cold Outside"*)

Groucho and Nunnally reminisced about the old days and old friends. Nunnally talked about Herman Mankiewicz, author of *Citizen Kane.* He told how, when Mankiewicz was assigned to write a Rin-Tin-Tin picture, he turned in a script which had Rin-Tin-Tin carrying the baby *into* the burning building instead of rescuing him. Mankiewicz was never assigned to a Rin-Tin-Tin picture again.

Excusing himself for a moment, Groucho returned from the bathroom beaming:

GROUCHO
You must come in and look at the picture in that room I was just in. Come on. It's very interesting.
NUNNALLY JOHNSON
It's a very foolishly religious picture, and it must date back eighty years, because one of the sins depicted is Sunday railroads.
GROUCHO
It said, "There is one road to damnation and one road to . . ."
NUNNALLY JOHNSON
One is the straight and narrow path. Dorris got it in one of those thieves' marketplaces in London. It's got an automobile in there, but the automobile wasn't invented at the time this was dated, so it's been reproduced and altered.
GROUCHO
It's a great picture. I'd like to own it.

NUNNALLY JOHNSON

Well, it'd help you, Grouch. Because when you don't know if something's right or wrong, you go in there and check on it.

GROUCHO

But you've *got* to go to the toilet.

NUNNALLY JOHNSON

Yeah, you go to the toilet to check on morals. In our other house, she had framed three cathouse cards from Paris in the twenties.

GROUCHO

You lived in Great Neck when I lived there . . .

NUNNALLY JOHNSON

Yeah.

GROUCHO

There were some wild parties there. Sam Harris, Ring Lardner, and Hammerstein and all those people lived there.

NUNNALLY JOHNSON

Hammerstein wasn't any wild party fellow. *You* were the wildest party— you folks.

GROUCHO

There was a guy there named Quinn Martin. He used to write the reviews for *The Morning World.* Anyhow, he came over to my house one day, and it was Rosh Hashanah. He stuck his hand out and he said, "Groucho, Rosh Hashanah."

NUNNALLY JOHNSON

He was a critic. That's the way a critic talks. Once the Marx Brothers got hold of Sam Helman, who used to write stories for *The Saturday Evening Post.* Sam was a big fellow, looked a little like George Kaufman, and was probably the most unvain man anybody could discover. But they played some childish games.

GROUCHO

Pinchie Winchie.

NUNNALLY JOHNSON

Yeah, and got black all over Sam's face. And this whole thing was a buildup to get Sam to go to the mirror and see what a jackass he looked like.

GROUCHO

Pinchie Winchie.

NUNNALLY JOHNSON

Pinchie Winchie was a game originated by Zeppo in which the participants all sat around in a circle. The rules were simple. The man to the left of the "dealer" pinched the dealer on the cheek or the nose or the ear, and said, "Pinchie Winchie." Then the dealer pinched the man to his right and said, "Pinchie Winchie," and so on until it returned to the first pincher. Then he made a new pinch, and it went around the circle as fast as the players could pinch until someone made a mistake. Then he was out, and the game continued until there was only one player, who was the winner.

Simple as this game seems, it had a novel twist: one of the players was unaware that the player to his left had a piece of burnt cork concealed in his hand, and he was being smudged each time he was pinched. This, of course, was the whole point of the game. Well, Sam was loaded, and they took him in front of the mirrors in the bedrooms, in the bathrooms, and Sam never even looked in a mirror. He kept talking to you. So they took him down to the ice-cream parlor near the theatre in Great Neck, and that place's walls were *all* mirrors. And they walked Sam around, and Sam never saw himself. Damnedest thing you ever saw. Finally, in desperation they *had* to have him find out what he looked like, so they all drove over and woke me up. My wife and I got up, 'cause on the roof there rose such a clatter, we got out of bed to see what was the matter, and it was the Marx Brothers and Sam Helman. And they just forced Sam to look at himself. He was very astonished.

GROUCHO

Zeppo was responsible for that. It was just a game of Pinchie Winchie. You had some black on your fingers, and you turn to the guy next to you, and you say, "Pinchie Winchie!" and pinch his cheeks.

NUNNALLY JOHNSON

A rather intellectual game. One guy was the fall guy.

GROUCHO

Yeah. That was Sam Helman.

NUNNALLY JOHNSON

The others didn't have black. He thought it was just people pinching each other's cheeks.

GROUCHO

Some game. I didn't tell you about Lardner in my house.

ERIN

Do I have to survive through this one again?

GROUCHO

Don't pout. We have to go soon. (*Looking at his Groucho watch*) It's a quarter to Groucho.

ERIN

I still want to hear about Pinchie Winchie and Sam Helman. Did you have to get him drunk to do this?

GROUCHO

No, you didn't *have* to get Sam drunk.

NUNNALLY JOHNSON

You'd just show Sam some liquor and he'd drink it. The other day I pulled a book out on Fred Allen.

GROUCHO

So did I. I sent one to Gummo the other day.

NUNNALLY JOHNSON

Well, he was telling about the routines they had. And I must tell you, there was some pretty dull stuff then.

GROUCHO

He had one great line. He was talking about how they played a town, a very small town on the New England coast. "The town was so small, the tide went out and never came back." Now, that's a great joke.

NUNNALLY JOHNSON

He was a brilliant man. You know, he lived in a hotel called the Windsor about Fifty-eighth and Sixth Avenue in New York City. I brought him out here for a movie.

GROUCHO

I remember that movie. What was the name of it?

NUNNALLY JOHNSON

Thanks a Million.

GROUCHO

That was when he was having the feud with Benny.

NUNNALLY JOHNSON

Harry Tugend came with him. He used to work for Fred Allen. Well, he and Portland [Fred Allen's wife] . . .

GROUCHO

I met Portland last year in the Beverly Hills Hotel.

NUNNALLY JOHNSON

Well, they had two rooms in this Windsor Hotel—a nice enough hotel. They lived there all the time they were in New York, and they never bought one thing to make it look like a home or their place. The pictures on the wall were hotel pictures, you know. Two straight chairs and that kind of thing. I don't think he owned anything.

GROUCHO

Ring Lardner used to write in a hotel in New York. He had four boys at home and couldn't get any writing done, so he used to go to the Pennsylvania Hotel and take a room and pull all the shades down, because there might have been somebody in another room across the alley from where his room was. That's the only way he could write. He would stay a week or two, then he'd go back to Great Neck. He used to come to my house and get drunk.

NUNNALLY JOHNSON

I know someone who tapes your shows, Grouch, and plays them all day long.

GROUCHO

He's crazy. Well, I have to go stand on my head now.

NUNNALLY JOHNSON

Thank you for coming over.

GROUCHO

It's always a pleasure to see you. You're a funny man and you amuse me. I think you'll like that book I brought.

NUNNALLY JOHNSON

That's all I do these days—sit around and read.

GROUCHO

That's all I do too.

NUNNALLY JOHNSON

You're leaving your Oscar?

GROUCHO

I'll sell it to you. I was offered a thousand dollars for it the other day, but I wanted eleven hundred.

BRONISLAW KAPER

Composer Bronislaw Kaper got his start with the Marx Brothers: He wrote "Cosi Cosa" for A *Night at the Opera*, "As If I Didn't Know" for *Go West*, and music for A *Day at the Races*. Although he knew Chico and Harpo better than Groucho, "because they were musical," he came to know Groucho quite well over the years.

"In the last three or four years, I have visited Groucho at his house or come to one of his parties. He would call and invite me. I knew why he really wanted me, but I pretended I didn't. He wanted me at the piano. After lunch we would go into the living room, and he would sing his songs while I played. Groucho has all of the music there at the piano, and we played early songs of Irving Berlin's.

"He gave a concert in Los Angeles, and Marvin Hamlisch played for him. Marvin looked at him with tenderness and affection. Even when he forgot his lines, the audience was with him. They were in love with him.

"Today Groucho is not as biting and aggressive as he used to be. He's more mellow, but there's still that spark.

"Once I brought Mischa Dichter, the pianist, and his beautiful young Brazilian wife to see Groucho. They are very gifted young people. They wanted to meet Groucho. I called Groucho and told him about my friend and his wife, and he asked:

" 'Can he play "Cosi Cosa"?'

"I said, 'He can play more than *that*.'

"They were terribly shy and very reverent in Groucho's presence. Groucho went to the bar and offered her a drink. He asked her what she wanted.

"She said, 'May I have some gin.'

"Groucho said, 'Only *schwartzers* drink gin,' and of course that rather finished the party.

"Groucho's ideas come from nowhere. His humor is from nowhere; it's pure nonsense. I've always liked their song, 'We are four of the three musketeers. One for all, two for five . . .'

"This was absolutely typical of their nonsense. The team was beautifully balanced. They were great together: Groucho, Chico, and Harpo. Even Zeppo was important when they were together.

"Harpo was unique. I used to go to his house. I remember his oldest son [Billy], who was adopted. His parents had been killed in an automobile accident. He played several musical instruments.

"Chico was the sweetest of all the Marx Brothers. He was naïve. Chico would be playing his stuff, and I would sit down and imitate what he did with his fingers. Chico payed me a great compliment. He said I was the best imitator of his piano style.

"Harry Ruby was one of the kindest and most beautiful people in the world. He didn't drive a car. In Beverly Hills, you would always see him walking, and everyone would say, 'Harry, do you need a ride?' If you were lucky, he did.

"One thing I like about Groucho that I find special is that he laughs at other people's jokes. He has an open mind. Other comedians, you feel, can hardly wait to come in with their own joke.

"Many people seem to think that stars are their property. People talk to a star on a familiar level. Strangers come up and always say, 'Hello, Groucho,' not, 'Hello, Mr. Marx.'

"I was walking with Groucho on Santa Monica, and a man came up and said to Groucho, 'Everyone tells me I look like you when you were young.'

"Groucho looked at the man and said, 'If I'd looked like you, I would have killed myself.'

"The man was struck dumb and retreated.

"Once in a while now, someone comes up to Groucho and insults him very rudely. I suppose it is the revenge of humanity!

"Groucho seems to care more about his clothes now. When I go to his house, he is always so beautifully dressed. Very chic, with elaborate suspenders.

"Working with the Marx Brothers was a very young part of my life. It was beyond my imagination to get to do a picture."

WYATT COOPER

When writer Wyatt Cooper was an actor, one of the parts he played was the young romantic lead in *Time for Elizabeth*. He told me what it was like to work onstage with Groucho:

"*Time for Elizabeth* is a serious play. It's about a man who retires in California and is bored. Groucho started off at rehearsals quite serious, but an audience inspires him. Audience reaction and laughter is for Groucho a whiff of oxygen to the brain which lifts him to heights of madness. The script grew and grew.

"In the play I played his son-in-law. We've just discovered that his money has been lost in washing machines and oranges, or something like that. Groucho tells me about the loss of the money, and then he quotes his father about something, and I'm supposed to follow with, 'I'll get a job.' But instead Groucho started to ad-lib, and as each ad-lib got a big laugh, he kept adding to it:

" 'I don't know why I keep quoting him. He didn't have a penny when he died.' Audience laughs. 'As a matter of fact, I was stuck for the funeral.' Audience laughs. 'It cost me $49.58.' Audience laughs. 'I tried to write it off on my income tax, but they wouldn't let me.' Audience laughs. 'I tried to write it off under "amusements." ' Audience laughs."

"I think Groucho was sorry about that last joke."

"I was really broken up. And when I would break up, he would make some kind of personal remark about me such as, 'My daughter married a sex fiend,' which didn't help me much."

"He responds very well to women. He is very different with women. He made them feel wanted. The women adored him."

"Groucho's sense of humor was not the analytical type; it was a certain kind of inspired madness. He tries to be funny all the time, thus he says a great many things that aren't funny. Groucho liked to think of himself as an intellectual, but he wasn't really; he was an intellectual's pet, which is not quite the same thing. Groucho really admired George S. Kaufman and identified with him.

"Groucho's feeling about what other people feel is practically nonexistent. Groucho's wife, Eden, was an object. She had the patience and detachment of a person who has become accustomed to being an object. She was young and very beautiful. Groucho would always tell people, 'I married her for her money.'

"Melinda was on the tour. He really adored her. Anything she did was funny, divine. A few years ago, I met Groucho, and I asked about Melinda, and he just mumbled something. To his dismay, Melinda grew up. To adore someone doesn't mean you have any idea about her."

IRWIN ALLEN

Groucho's friendship with producer Irwin Allen, whom Groucho for some long-forgotten reason sometimes referred to as "The Falcon," went back to the late forties when Groucho was making pictures apart from his brothers. Later Allen produced *The Story of Mankind*, which featured, among other stars, all three Marx Brothers, but not together. Films like *Voyage to the Bottom of the Sea*, *The Poseidon Adventure*, and *The Towering Inferno* brought Allen increasing fame and success.

I went with Groucho and Erin to the premiere of *The Towering Inferno*, where I sat next to William Holden, one of the stars of the film, who fidgeted all through the screening. Groucho had been cautioned by Erin not to be obstreperous, as he had been at the opening of *The Poseidon Adventure*, where he made some comments that got laughs during one of the film's most dramatic moments.

The next time I saw Irwin Allen was just after Groucho's eighty-fifth birthday. He and his wife, Sheila, Groucho, Erin, and I headed for Matteo's, a restaurant in Westwood. It was a Saturday night, the night before Groucho's big "second" birthday party. We drove to the restaurant in the Allens' brand-new silver Rolls-Royce:

IRWIN ALLEN
What do you think of my car, Groucho?
GROUCHO
It's a lousy car.
IRWIN ALLEN
(*Turning up the car radio very loud so that the rear speakers almost blasted us from our seats*) I'm going to do that every time Groucho insults me.
SHEILA ALLEN
He didn't insult you. He insulted the car.

Arriving at the restaurant, Groucho got out of the car, saying, "Thank God I made it!" (The night before, Groucho had tripped getting out of the car at temple.) We were joined by Steve Allen, who was already there waiting at the table for us. He explained why his wife, Jayne Meadows, couldn't make it for dinner.

STEVE ALLEN

Jayne's been working, and when she's working she really puts everything into it. She's exhausted.

GROUCHO

(*Wistfully*) Yeah, when you're working, that's the way it is.

Steve Allen proposed a toast "to exhaustion," and Groucho raised his glass of tomato juice. Anxious to please his guests, Irwin Allen turned to Groucho and asked him if there was anything special he wanted:

IRWIN ALLEN

Do you want them to use your salt substitute in the kitchen?

GROUCHO

(*Proffering the container of salt substitute that had been brought along*) Everything I have is a substitute.

ERIN

Not me.

The maître d' presented the menu and explained some of the house specialties.

GROUCHO

I'd like what I had when you took me here last year.

IRWIN ALLEN

What did you have?

GROUCHO

I don't remember, but I'll know it when I see it. It was something like chicken.

IRWIN ALLEN

Was it chicken?

GROUCHO

No.

IRWIN ALLEN

Did it come with gnocchi? You know, those wobbly noodles.

GROUCHO

That's what I am: a wobbly noodle.

Groucho decided to have the hot seafood appetizer, but Erin asked the maître d' if it had salt. Groucho then decided to try one of the pastas, but Erin's questioning confirmed that salt had already been added.

STEVE ALLEN
Give him a graham cracker.
GROUCHO
Make that an animal cracker.

The order was finally given, and the conversation went on to shoptalk and Irwin Allen's next film:

ERIN
Guess what, Groucho: He wants to do a sequel to *The Poseidon Adventure*. (*To Irwin*) But how are you going to use Gene Hackman after the way you finished him off in all that oil and water?
GROUCHO
Oil is very expensive.
IRWIN ALLEN
In the first scene, Gene is standing there, and he says, "I'm going to find out what happened to my twin brother . . ." But, seriously, Groucho, what's this I was reading about how you told some reporter that Gummo is buried in Israel? I bet Gummo wasn't at all pleased to read that.
GROUCHO
They don't listen. I don't know why. I told him that Harpo's harp is in a museum in Israel, and it came out Gummo's buried in Israel. They don't listen.

As we left the restaurant, Groucho stopped to say hello to his old friend Henry Fonda and his wife, Shirlee. Out in front of the restaurant, James Caan waited with us. His pickup truck arrived first, and he drove off while we were still waiting for Irwin Allen's Rolls.

Driving back to Groucho's, we passed a movie theatre with a long line of people waiting to go in and see *The Hiding Place*. Irwin Allen slowed down to enjoy the sight, commenting, "I love to see a line for a movie. I don't even care whose film it is."

Groucho said, "You can tell if a movie's a success when you walk by and smell fresh popcorn."

NAT PERRIN

Nat Perrin had just finished law school in New York and was studying for the bar in 1931 when he submitted a Marx Brothers skit to Groucho. He liked it and invited Perrin to come out to California to work on their next picture. Taking the bar exam on Monday and Tuesday, Perrin was on the train to California on Wednesday. The postcard arrived saying he had passed the New York bar after he had begun working on *Monkey Business*. He stayed on to write other Marx Brothers films, and never did practice law.

We had met briefly at Groucho's eighty-fifth birthday party. Shortly afterward I visited him (Groucho sometimes referred to Nat Perrin as "Deacon") at his Beverly Hills apartment, where he talked about his forty-five-year relationship with Groucho:

NAT PERRIN

Groucho's exterior belies a somewhat different interior. He's a much more sentimental man than people know. He has enormous loyalties, and, for me, that's the giveaway. He has many of the old friends he's always had. Even though he's famous for being one of the world's greatest insulters, making people the butt of his jokes, he doesn't seem to alienate many people because apparently he doesn't strike very deeply with anyone. I've known him forty-five years now.

He has a very high regard for talent. He's taken up a few people and always tried for them and pushed friends to listen to those he thought were good. He's a different kind of person from what his brand of humor would indicate. He's always had a lot of interest in family and family ties. He was always good company, and is. He doesn't just sit back, but he works hard to make things pleasant. But it's not that he's always "on." He doesn't use people as an audience.

In his eighties, he's become a cult figure, and I think he gets an enormous satisfaction out of that hint of immortality that's in store for him. He had that phase in his life when he was an enormous success but not recognized in the streets. He'd been using a charcoal mustache, and when he walked around without it, the world knew Groucho Marx was successful but didn't recognize the person.

I

How did you meet Groucho?

NAT PERRIN

I'd just finished law school, and I'd been studying very hard. I'd always fooled around writing for the Borscht Circuit, and I was in the law library writing a skit. Somebody looking over my shoulder said, "That's funny. I know the agent who sold Moss Hart's play, *Once in a Lifetime.* I'll get you that agent." It turned out that his friend was sort of a delivery boy in the woman's office. I didn't want to waste the trip downtown, so I dictated my own letter, signed it, and I took this forgery and my skit to Brooklyn, where the Marx Brothers were appearing at the Albee Theatre.

I gave the letter I'd done to the doorman, with the sketch. He came out about ten minutes later, and he said, "Mr. Marx will see you now." I was shown into Groucho's dressing room. He had read the material and liked it. He says, "We don't use sketches now. We're going to Hollywood to make a picture. We might be able to use a fellow like you. Why don't you come out?"

I

What was your sketch like?

NAT PERRIN

Chico comes to Groucho for a job, and they start discussing money. Chico wants fifty dollars and Groucho offers him ten. They finally settle on a salary, and Groucho says, "Now what about references?" Chico says, "You don't need any reference. I like-a your face and that-sa good enough for me." And Groucho says, "I want references from *you.*" Chico says, "Oh, reference," and he doesn't know what that means. Anyway, Groucho finally calls somebody, and he tells him Chico is applying for a job. "I'd like to know what you think of him." And we hear Groucho say, "What? Yes! What?" Chico says, "I'll take forty." Groucho keeps listening and making these shocked exclamations and Chico says, "Thirty." Then Chico says, "Twenty," and so on.

I

What was it like working with the Marx Brothers?

NAT PERRIN

Being around the Marx Brothers was always a bit chaotic, but it was fun. It was *always* fun. Through the years I've seen many people in difficult circumstances, and there's anger, frustration, and total disgust, and a wanting to run away from it all. *Nothing* could have been more chaotic than working on a Marx Brothers picture, but I never ran into that kind of feeling about it. I kind of took it in stride and had fun despite the fact that there was so much confusion.

I don't think Chico ever knew what the plot was about. I don't think Chico ever looked at any of the lines but his, and hardly those. Harpo brought in a lot of his own material; things, props, business, ideas, all typically Harpo, whether they related to the plot or not. Groucho always was an enormous contributor during the writing of the script; on the set, onstage, for himself, and for everyone. He never took any writing credit, unlike many who took credit who didn't deserve it. So there, too, is a difference between the hard-bitten, insulting Groucho Marx and many "lovable" comedians.

I

You knew their father. What was he like?

NAT PERRIN

He was like the man on the cologne bottle. He'd always make a little sign with his forefinger and his thumb holding his mustache—you know, "It's perfect!" It's a French sign. He was so dapper. All he ever wanted to do was to go fishing, which kind of surprised me. It's not a big-city pastime. I did go fishing with him once, and nothing happened. We didn't catch any fish. The thing that was interesting was the way the Marx Brothers always had this genuine affection for him. It was never just that we-must-respect-and-obey-him thing because he's our father. They found him amusing. I knew their uncle, Al Shean, who started them in show business. He was a likable rogue, and we went to the fights together. Zeppo worked with him in an act called *Quo Vadis, Upside Down*—don't ask me why. They had a fake horse in the act and Zeppo was either the front half or the back half.

I

You knew Harpo well too . . .

NAT PERRIN

An imp, on- and offstage. One night in Palm Springs we all had dinner and started to say good night. Well, we saw each other all the time, so we didn't shake hands, but this time Harpo did, and all the silverware started falling out of his sleeves. He'd taken it out of the restaurant. He took it back, I guess. Harpo used to love funny hats. Groucho, too. Harpo used to like to wear a French gendarme hat.

Harpo used to play golf at Tamarisk Country Club. He'd wear his swimming shorts. There were houses, lining the course, and everyone had a swimming pool. Harpo would play a little golf. Then, he'd jump in someone's pool, cool off, play some more golf, and then jump in someone else's pool. If you heard a splash, it was Harpo.

I

And Chico?

NAT PERRIN

I was enormously fond of Chico, too. He had some of the traits of my own brother. If Chico had three of a kind, he'd throw two away to see if he could buy two pairs. He was a really good card player, but he had to show kibitzers that he could do it the hard way. I had a brother like that. He never did anything the easy way, and Chico would do everything the hard way, too. Chico was a big spender, and I think that's why he wound up so broke. He was an enormous gambler, but he made an effort to be liked. Harpo wasn't really making an effort to be liked. Harpo was just genuinely likable, lovable, and pixieish.

Zep is the slugger of the outfit, you know. But Zep is fun to be around. He is a very humorous guy. I wouldn't want to get into any battles with him, though. He's the dead-end kid of the Marxes. I never really got to know Zeppo too well, but I've always been genuinely fond of Zeppo, as I've been fond of all the Marxes. Their wives, too.

I started with the Marxes at a very early age. I'd just finished school. A great deal of my feelings toward them are kind of bolstered and maybe have grown in retrospect because I realize I was a kid, and here they were, famous stars, and I was just the errand boy really. I'd throw in what I could, and they could not have been kinder to me. They couldn't possibly have included me more in what they were doing. I was invited to all their homes. I played tennis with them. They made me feel perfectly at home. They were mythical people to me, and I never for one minute dreamt that I would be in this kind of company. It all happened overnight. No one in my home believed I was going into professional show business.

I

You mentioned the Marx Brothers' wives. What were they like?

NAT PERRIN

Ruth wanted to dance, go to nightspots, and she was athletic. She was a good tennis player. She wanted to do a lot of things that she couldn't get Groucho to do. Groucho had his likes and dislikes, and his tastes. He liked to sit around with his cronies, his friends, and make jokes, talk about show business, listen to Gilbert and Sullivan. I'm sure Groucho was very fond of her, but they were pulling in different directions.

Kay was a high-strung woman. Our relationship was purely social. We'd meet at parties. A very pretty girl. She seemed a little tortured in her relationship with Groucho. She felt—and I'm only guessing—on the fringe of things. She felt she didn't belong with Groucho's friends, who were kind of cultivated literary people. He corresponded with world-famous people, which you well know. I'm sure many people who came to his home were very literate, articulate, and famous, and Kay was just a little girl. I think she couldn't quite cope with these people. Eden was up here just a week ago. She and Groucho seemed crazy about each other. Then, suddenly, they're divorced. She's friendly with Groucho now, actually. He never had any battles in the courts with his wives over money. That shows how generous he must have been with them in spite of the fact that he'd been poor and wasn't cavalier about money.

Chico's wife, Betty, was a good-hearted dame from a low- or middle-class background. She seemed the most pleasant kind of woman, and suddenly they're divorced. I can't tell you why. She seemed the perfect wife for Chico. Well, Chico was a hard guy to harness. She turned the other cheek, and after a while Betty ran out of cheeks, so a divorce was inevitable. I still see Zeppo's wife, Marian. She is a very good-hearted dame, and she turned a good phrase, too. An extremely attractive woman, with a lot of style. She was crazy about Zeppo, and he was crazy about her, too But I wasn't there and I'm not a house detective. I can't tell you what caused breakups, but I'm positive they still like each other—very much, as a matter of fact.

Zeppo was a gambler, and a very smart guy in business. Highly underrated, a success in most everything he did except the Marx Brothers. There, he was a part of their success. He broke away from that. Then he was an extremely successful agent. He sold that agency for a lot of dough. Then he got into some ammunitions thing, and again he did well. He did something with citrus groves, and I understand he's an expert on that. He had a most unusual home in Beverly Hills which I understand he built mostly with his own hands. A very stylish house right in the heart of Beverly Hills. He's a man of many varied abilities, but people just don't seem to realize it. He was kind of a curious guy, but he's a very likable guy. I really do respect his talents, and I know that he probably was the unhappiest with the Marx Brothers because he was the low man on the totem pole. I don't think he was happy to be in the romantic parts of the Marx Brothers pictures. He must have felt sappy.

I

What was it like writing a Marx Brothers picture?

NAT PERRIN

Arthur Sheekman and I would meet early in the morning, and it might be afternoon before we really got started. Sometimes we would talk, read the papers, play chess, anything to keep avoiding it. He was a very decent, honest man, but there was one thing I found difficult. It was in the step when we had to go and see the producer. I found that most producers are nervous and shaky enough about most material without his making them more uncertain by telling them he knows it's only a first draft. If you don't have absolute confidence in what you bring in, you immediately have two and a half strikes against you. But he was never the kind of person to use "I" instead of "we" about anything where we were collaborators. We sank or swam with the material submitted.

I remember Sheekman used to criticize Groucho for not letting contestants finish their sentences on *You Bet Your Life*, and Groucho never minded being criticized. Of course, he still didn't let the contestants finish their sentences, but he didn't mind being criticized. I think it wasn't that he didn't hear the criticism, nor that he didn't pay attention, but that his style was so ingrained that it was a part of him, and he was a part of it. He was Groucho, and he couldn't change, and he shouldn't have.

I

I saw you at Groucho's eighty-fifth birthday party, but we didn't have an opportunity to speak. There were so many people . . .

NAT PERRIN

It was awfully crowded, a lot of people I didn't know, and there were a lot of young people like you. It wasn't exactly a place for group discussion. It was more of a situation where somebody could rub up against somebody if the somebody was attractive. You know, some guy's standing there with some broad trying to get her to his pad, and somebody else in a corner is talking about TV today and ratings. The food and drink was plentiful and very palatable, and an enormous number of people turned out to pay their respects to him. It was sort of an open house.

I

But a closed open house.

NAT PERRIN

Yeah. A closed open house.

I

Groucho loved singing at his party. Did he always enjoy that so much?

NAT PERRIN

He used to like quartet singing a lot. He'd always grab a guitar and sing. He'd love to be around a good pianist with a group of five or six or seven fellows who could sing harmony. He seemed in my estimation to get greater pleasure from that than from doing one of his songs solo, like

"Captain Spaulding." He'd always do his share of the performing or talking, but in conversation he was always just as interested, or more interested, in hearing what the other person had to say.

I

You did the original script of *The Big Store*. Do you remember what that was like?

NAT PERRIN

Nothing like the film that was done. I had a legitimate mystery story. Good, bad, or indifferent, it was more of a story than any of the Marx Brothers films had except those with Thalberg at Metro. My plot went by the boards, sacrificed for comedy routines, but I always felt the comedy routines were funnier with a real plot to hang them on.

I

You saw Groucho just a few days ago at Julius Epstein's house for dinner.

NAT PERRIN

That's right.

I

Besides obviously being forty-five years older, do you think Groucho has changed basically since you've known him?

NAT PERRIN

No. Maybe he spends more now, as a concession to old age. What's *your* slant on writing about Groucho?

I

I'm emphasizing the later years during the time I've known him.

NAT PERRIN

That's interesting. I think that's the most interesting slant. The way people feel about him now is extraordinary. You go to a party and there are the rock groups, the country singers, Elton John, Alice Cooper, and all the new cats. You would think that the guest of honor would be twenty-seven or twenty-eight, but a man of eighty-five steps out, and it's all for him. All of them are important in their own ways, and yet they have this enormous respect for Groucho as an equal or more, not as just an old-timer. Age seems to be washed away.

In many ways, he's kind of an ageless man. He might be the oldest guy around but he doesn't think of himself that way. He could look at another eighty-five-year-old, and it would be another world he'd be looking at. He doesn't relate to a world of old age except that he's not physically able to spring up and do things the way he used to. I don't think he relates an iota to the aging process. He thinks like he's young, he doesn't hold back, then he just runs out of gas. But while he's got gas, he uses it, that's all.

JULIUS EPSTEIN

Writer Julius Epstein, who won an Academy Award for the *Casablanca* screenplay, was a friend of Groucho's dating back to the middle thirties when he first came to Hollywood. I talked with him at a party given by Sidney Sheldon. Just a few weeks earlier, Groucho had attended a dinner party at Epstein's house.

In order to talk, we went upstairs to one of the bedrooms in Sidney Sheldon's house, closing the door behind us. During the interview, Sidney Sheldon's daughter, Mary, and a group of her college friends opened the door and were startled to find us there. Jokingly, Julius Epstein called after them as they rushed away, "You know, it's impossible to have an affair in this town."

JULIUS EPSTEIN
What do you want to talk about, his later years?
I
No, not just the later years. Tell me about when you met Groucho.
JULIUS EPSTEIN
It must be forty years ago. Groucho's friends of forty years ago are still his friends today, and I'm talking about the friends he always had who weren't necessarily top echelon celebrities. He always had a great respect, a great love for writers, and you still see those who are alive at Groucho's today. I have two Groucho stories which reflect his attitude toward writers.

In the first one, we were at somebody's house. The man is here today — I won't mention his name. I was just married at the time, so I guess it was twenty-five, twenty-six years ago. It was summertime, and it was an outdoor barbecue. The host was a very skillful barbecuer. I can't do anything like that. I can't even drive a nail. It seemed that Groucho and I have two things in common: first of all, both of us are named Julius. That was a common bond. The other bond was that neither one of us could drive a nail or do anything a man is supposed to do around the house. The host was very skillful with the barbecue, so my wife, who kind of resents my being such a schlemiel around the house, said, "Watch him! See how he barbecues." Groucho flew into a fury and said, "Why should he watch him barbecue? Barbecuing is for people who have no talent." He was resenting what he considered an attack on a friend, me, when for me it wasn't anything.

The other story happened quite a few years after. It was again at a party, and I was talking with a very good friend of mine, a woman who was a story editor at a studio. We were all sitting around talking about my low cholesterol diet. My doctor was one of the pioneers of the low cholesterol diet, and I was one of the first guinea pigs. The woman said to me, "Do you follow the diet strictly?" and I made a very bad joke. I said, "I follow it strictly six days a week and religiously on Saturdays." She said, "That's a very bad joke," and I said, "Yeah . . ." but Groucho flew into an absolute fury.

He turned on this woman and said, "How dare you say that to this man! Have you ever made anybody laugh in your life? Have you ever entertained anybody? Have you ever done anything that's worthwhile? This man has made people laugh and entertained people over the years, and you're telling him that's a very bad joke." He drove her to tears, and I kept saying, "Groucho, I don't care. It's just a joke, she didn't mean it," but Groucho was absolutely livid. He does this all the time: he defends people in show business, especially writers, against what he considers the "civilians" or the outsiders.

Groucho has a tremendous quality of loyalty. He has had the same friends over forty years, always defending them. I'm sure you'll hear this from a lot of other people. He's very protective. And he's unique in another respect: He's the only comedian everybody knows who will speak highly of other comedians he thinks are talented. I remember being at a party with him in Malibu many, many years ago, and he kept saying, "I've got to meet this young man. I just heard him on the radio. He's a disc jockey and he's on at eleven o'clock at night. His name is Steve Allen." You go to Groucho's house now, and Steve Allen's there. Groucho discovered him and plugged him to everybody around. As soon as he heard Woody Allen, Groucho knew he was funny and told everyone. I never heard one comedian praise another. This was one of Groucho's best qualities.

I

Have you found Groucho to be the same person over the years?

JULIUS EPSTEIN

Well, compared to twenty years ago, everything is slower; it's like under water. But his mind is still there. He'll say clever things. I remember even on his brightest, chirpiest day, he was always difficult about one thing: when he came to dinner, if dinner wasn't served very quickly, he let you know about it.

I

At seven o'clock preferably.

JULIUS EPSTEIN

Well, as early as possible. And then Groucho's attitude about women. I did a screenplay many years ago of *Minnie's Boys*, which later became a musical. My screenplay wasn't done because the studio said, "Who are we going to get to play the Marx Brothers as kids?" It was mostly about the younger years, the growing up of the Marx Brothers.

I

I didn't know there was a screenplay. You did it before the play?

JULIUS EPSTEIN

Oh yes, many years before. It was '55 or '56. And when we got through with it, where were the actors who were gonna play the Marx Brothers? Who can make you believe it was the Marx Brothers and be as funny as the Marx Brothers? They couldn't cast it. I don't know what they did in the musical, but I imagine they ran into the same trouble. When I did the screenplay, Groucho always acted as consultant. He told me all the anecdotes of being in trouble, of having to climb out of windows and leave town. He was quite interested in seeing that those episodes were in the screenplay. All the Marx Brothers are very proud of their prowess with women. He always talked about Harpo — Harpo was the great he-man of all time.

I

And, of course, Chico.

JULIUS EPSTEIN

Well, I remember my first wife's uncle tried to beat up Chico. But Harpo everybody loved, and Harpo was evidently the great one. Groucho always would say, "Put this in the screenplay: We were in Punxsutawney, Pennsylvania, and we had to climb out the window when the husbands came," and things like that. He was quite proud of that. But I think Groucho should be proud that his friends for years are *still* his friends. Except for the ones who aren't alive anymore, you still see them when you go to his house.

I remember Bogart there one night — I'll never forget this: he was drinking from a little bottle with thick white liquid in it, and he would periodically give it a swash. He'd take a drink of this white liquid — medicine, someone said. We asked, "What's wrong with you?" and Bogart made a big joke, saying, "I have cancer." We didn't know he had it at the time, but he did have it. He was taking the medicine for the pain in his throat. But all those people, Groucho's old friends, were there. Some of them were writers at the bottom of the totem pole. I think the majority of Groucho's old-time friends, the ones he's known the longest, were there forty years ago. People like Nunnally Johnson, Nat Perrin, Harry Tugend, Sidney Sheldon, and Bert Granet are still his friends after all these years. To me, that's always been his outstanding characteristic — that and his absolute generosity toward other performers, which is very unusual with performers.

His hold on the young people is incredible. It's something like Bogart. Groucho and Bogart had quite a lot in common. It's strange to think that if Bogart were alive today, he'd be past seventy. I remember about two years ago we had a small dinner party, and Groucho was there. My son, who was then nineteen, came with a friend who said to Groucho, "You can't imagine what a thrill this is for me to meet you, Groucho," then he went into a long spiel. Of course Groucho was embarrassed and made a typical Groucho remark like, "What the hell do you know?" Irving Brecher was there, and he got up and said, "Groucho, this is also what we have thought about you throughout the years." Well, Groucho with all his aplomb and everything couldn't really take it, but he had to. It was a quiet moment.

I

And what was your son's friend's reaction to Groucho's reaction?

JULIUS EPSTEIN

It's what he expected from Groucho. It's my own personal opinion, though, that Groucho feels he has to live up to the legend. He *has* to be insulting to everybody; he feels they expect him to treat them like he treated Margaret Dumont.

I

Were you ever insulted by Groucho?

JULIUS EPSTEIN

No, I can't remember being insulted, and I can't remember any of Groucho's friends being insulted by him. I think he saved it for the civilians.

I

Do you find Groucho the same in real life as he was in the films?

JULIUS EPSTEIN

Yes, yes. I also have a slight feeling that he has to sort of play the character. But Groucho's also a very liberal man, and he's always been interested in politics and everything that's going on in the world, an omnivorous reader. I know a lot about his background, not from Groucho, but from doing research on the screenplay.

I
You knew his wives.

JULIUS EPSTEIN

Yes. I think Groucho's always married the same woman. I knew all of them. Ruth was the first wife; like all of them, she was gentile, attractive, pretty. She was a good tennis player. I guess she was the only athlete among his wives. That's where Groucho's son, Arthur, gets it. He was a really good tennis player. Have you talked with Nunnally Johnson?

I
Several times.

JULIUS EPSTEIN

Nunnally made one of the greatest remarks at Groucho's house, one of the greatest squelches of all times. It was a sitdown dinner party right after the big success of *Guys and Dolls*. Frank Loesser was there, and Nunnally Johnson was there. There were twelve or fourteen of us, and the topic of conversation was about a lawyer in town, a theatrical lawyer. He was a big ladies' man, always married to a star or going with them, and the conversation turned to whether or not he had false teeth.

Frank Loesser, who considered himself very New Yorkish, said, "Is this all you people have to talk about?" Silence. Of course, he insulted practically the whole table, and Nunnally put his knife and fork down, folded his arms, and said, "All right, Frankie . . . let's hear some New York talk." There wasn't another word from Frankie the entire evening. It was something Groucho could have said. Sometimes Groucho's friends talk like he does. It rubs off. Groucho's friends say things in his style. Oh, the evenings with Groucho were always fun. He always had very entertaining people—no dead weights.

I
Who are some of the friends you can remember being with Groucho?

JULIUS EPSTEIN

A lot of them Earl Wilson would call celebrities. Bogart. Steve Allen was there a lot because I think Groucho kind of considers he discovered him. Irwin Allen is a great friend of his. Were you there for his birthday party?

I
Yes.

JULIUS EPSTEIN

Well, we were in Europe, so we didn't get there. But that would give you a pretty good idea of the kind of people Groucho always had over.

I
Basically, then, you find Groucho the same person he always was?

JULIUS EPSTEIN

The old delivery isn't there, but he'll occasionally come out with something. I guess Groucho will become a word in the language. A lot of people liked Harpo better than Groucho, but I thought Groucho was the important character. Without Groucho the veritable characteristics of the Marx Brothers wouldn't have existed. He was the lead character. The lines they always quote are about Groucho. What could you quote about Harpo? Punching on a horn or something like that? Harpo was, I think, one of the nicest men I've known. Very quiet, very soft. The most intellectual. I don't think any of them had any education at all. You know, Groucho's fairly well-read. If they had had any education at all, no telling what they would have done.

I

Maybe not as well.

JULIUS EPSTEIN

Maybe not as well! What's that Somerset Maugham story about the sexton?

I

"The Verger."

JULIUS EPSTEIN

Yeah. Well, he took it from an old Jewish folk tale. It was about a shammes, and he made him into a sexton who got fired because he couldn't write his name. Then he got into business and became a multimillionaire. At the bank they found out he couldn't even write his own signature, and somebody said, "Just think what you could have been if you'd been able to read and write!" And he said, "Yeah, a church sexton." It's an old Jewish folk tale, and it probably applies to Groucho. He's a self-educated man. He reads everything, or he did.

I

He still does.

JULIUS EPSTEIN

He's well-read. Knows everything that's going on politically, intellectually—everything. You know, civilians are afraid of him. Always have been. He never had much respect for anyone who wasn't professional. And most of his friends, I think, were writers. I remember when he wrote his book, he kept saying, "My God, my respect has increased so much! Now I know how difficult it is to put some words on paper."

I

He told me he didn't find writing books difficult.

JULIUS EPSTEIN

Well, he didn't say it at the time.

I

Do you have any idea what you'd call a book about Groucho?

JULIUS EPSTEIN

I don't know. Actually, I'm terrible about titles, even for my own pictures.
How about *No Relation to Karl*? As a matter of fact, Groucho was very
proud of his German background. His parents didn't speak Yiddish, they
spoke German. And he married three gentile girls, Ruth, Kay, and Eden.
I think the most vivacious of the group was Kay. Eden is a very good artist.
She's quite good. I don't think there was anything particularly outstanding
about any of his wives—no one really forceful character. You couldn't be
married to Groucho and be a very forceful character. Erin is different
from any of the wives. Quite a demarcation line, Erin. Groucho's still a
strong character.

I remember the concert appearance in Columbus, Ohio. I've never
heard such laughter from an audience in my life. Every time he came onstage there was another standing ovation. You know, I've heard a lot of
laughter in my time—on the stage, in the theatre, everywhere—but I've
never heard such laughter as Groucho got at that concert. I know the
title's already been used, but it really applies to Groucho's style: *Nothing
Sacred*.

WOODY ALLEN

Woody Allen interviewed Groucho for me on a cold February afternoon in New York City during 1973. Groucho was staying at the Pierre Hotel, noted for the protective shelter it provides its guests. Informally attired in jeans, an old sweater, saddle shoes, a pull-down "disguise" hat, and his Play-It-Again-Sam coat when he arrived in the lobby, Woody was delayed by a wary reception clerk until it could be determined for certain that Mr. Marx really *was* expecting him.

Informed that Woody was on his way up, Groucho exclaimed, "I'm crazy about him!" When Woody entered the suite, Groucho's first words were, "Here's a funny man." Paradoxically, Woody Allen was one of the few people seeing Groucho who never tried to be funny. On this particular occasion, Woody's demeanor was further sobered by the task of interviewing Groucho, which he approached with the utmost seriousness.

To Groucho, Woody Allen was "a very funny man"—no faint praise from one given to cosmic understatement. To this, a totally serious Groucho would add, "He's a genius."

Groucho best summed up the relationship between him and Woody: "I think he's great, and he thinks I'm great. So we get along fine."

GROUCHO
It must be hot out today. Nobody's wearing a hat.
WOODY ALLEN
Yeah, it's freezing. It is seventeen degrees or something.
GROUCHO
But if you're not wearing a hat, it isn't cold.
WOODY ALLEN
That's how you judge?
GROUCHO
You can wear a little something else. I'm wearing heavy underwear. (*Groucho reveals his undershirt, which reads, "Tell 'Em Groucho Sent You"*) If you were my age you'd wear it too. And you'd wear a hat.
WOODY ALLEN
You're supposed to get colder as you get older.
GROUCHO
You're damn right. Last time I saw Chaplin, all he said was, "Stay warm. Stay warm."

WOODY ALLEN

What year did he tell you this?

GROUCHO

When he got the Academy Award. He came to California. We were having lunch, and as he started to leave, he put his arm around my shoulder and said, "Groucho, stay warm." Then I didn't know what he meant, but I do now. So, when you get older, you should wear warmer clothes. And a hat.

WOODY ALLEN

I see.

GROUCHO

He told me once, "I wish I could talk on the screen the way you do." Chaplin was great but he doesn't work anymore. He did one turkey that was really something. *Countess from Hong Kong*. That was one of the worst pictures I ever saw. Marlon Brando was in it. I want to see the new Brando picture [*Last Tango in Paris*] because they say you can pick up a lot of stuff from it.

WOODY ALLEN

Have you ever seen any pornographic movies?

GROUCHO

No, I'm not interested. I've seen naked girls.

WOODY ALLEN

Did you do a concert after Carnegie Hall?

GROUCHO

Yes. I played in Los Angeles, and I played in San Francisco for Bill Graham. Frisco is an exciting city, you know.

WOODY ALLEN

Yeah. And it's so small, but it's more exciting than Los Angeles.

GROUCHO

I remember when we first came to Los Angeles from New York. There was no such thing as Beverly Hills then.

WOODY ALLEN

Did you like it better?

GROUCHO

Much better. All you could smell in those days was orange blossoms and lemon blossoms. Chico said that in California the flowers don't smell, but the women do. Well, he should have known.

WOODY ALLEN

What's the name of the studio near the airport?

GROUCHO

M-G-M. We shot five pictures at M-G-M—two of them with Thalberg. He was the best.

WOODY ALLEN

I know, I've heard you say that. I always hear very conflicting stories about Thalberg. I know you were crazy about him.

GROUCHO

He was the master. The first picture he did with us was A *Night at the Opera.* We started another one, A *Day at the Races,* and he died in the middle of it. He was younger than I was when he died. That was in 1936. Now it's 1974 and I'm still alive.

WOODY ALLEN

How do we know that?

GROUCHO

I can tell when I get up in the morning. If I don't get up, that means I'm dead.

WOODY ALLEN

Do you still have that bed that . . .

GROUCHO

Yes! And if you ever want to spend the night with me, well, don't be reluctant about it.

WOODY ALLEN

It was the first time I ever saw a bed that could buzz up your feet, your back, whatever you wanted. It was that switch under the mattress.

GROUCHO

I've got everything on remote control—the television, the lights, everything—so I can sit in bed for days without ever having to get up.

WOODY ALLEN

So who are your friends?

GROUCHO

I have no friends.

WOODY ALLEN

Well, who have you been seeing lately?

GROUCHO

I see Nunnally Johnson, who I think is one of the great writers in Hollywood. And I see George Seaton. I don't know if you know who he is.

WOODY ALLEN

I do. I don't know him personally but I know who he is.

GROUCHO

Nice guy. And talented. And I see Arthur Sheekman.

WOODY ALLEN

Harry Ruby?

GROUCHO

Yes. I have eight or ten friends.

WOODY ALLEN

So you just kind of relax during the daytime, and you see them and play cards . . .

GROUCHO

I don't play cards.

WOODY ALLEN

You don't play cards. What do you do?

GROUCHO

I read a lot. Junk.

WOODY ALLEN

Un-huh. You don't get bored reading after two hours?

GROUCHO

No. I just look at some more junk.

WOODY ALLEN

Do you see any movies or watch TV?

GROUCHO

I watch *Sanford and Son, All in the Family, Maude,* and a couple more programs. Do you like the two *schwartzers*?

WOODY ALLEN

I've only seen *Sanford and Son* very, very briefly.

GROUCHO

What about *Maude*?

WOODY ALLEN

Well, she's a funny actress.

GROUCHO

You bet she is.

WOODY ALLEN

All in the Family would be a very typical play on Broadway.

GROUCHO

The wife bothers me. She's just too stupid.

WOODY ALLEN

She's funny. Like Art Carney on the Jackie Gleason show. Do you know Art Carney?

GROUCHO

Of course.

WOODY ALLEN

He was hilarious when he played stupid with Gleason.

GROUCHO

But Carney is a good actor.

WOODY ALLEN

Sure. He and Jackie Gleason did some fabulous things on television.

GROUCHO

I did some unfunny things with Gleason—a couple of shows. One was good, and one was lousy. He used to drink half a gallon of booze before he went on.

WOODY ALLEN

Do you ever see S. J. Perelman?

GROUCHO

Not so much.

WOODY ALLEN

Do you ever see Max Gordon?

GROUCHO

No. You know, he came home one night, and his wife, Mary, was painting an apple. He came home around midnight, and he was hungry. So he looked around for something to eat, and couldn't find anything. He opened the icebox, and his wife had a half an apple in there that she was painting. So he ate the other half. Do you know him?

WOODY ALLEN

Oh, sure. I've known him for years. He's a wonderful old-fashioned character. So who *do* you see in New York?

GROUCHO

I see Comden and Green and Goddard Lieberson, Dick Cavett, and Goody Ace. I see a few people like that. They're people I'm fond of. I'm never here very long, anyhow. I remember when the market crashed in 1929. Did you know Max Gordon's real name is Salpeter?

WOODY ALLEN

Yes, I read it in his book.

GROUCHO

He wrote a book?

WOODY ALLEN

Oh, sure, Max has a book—*Max Gordon Presents*, it's called.

GROUCHO

I didn't know Max Gordon could write.

WOODY ALLEN

He's got a book, though. It's a book of his experiences.

GROUCHO

I used to go around with him in Great Neck. We used to play golf together. The market was so high then, everybody was making a million dollars. Then one day the crash came in '29, and he was living in New York, and I was living in Great Neck. I was doing *Animal Crackers*, I think. And he calls me up and says, "Marx"—that's the way he talks—"this is Salpeter. The jig is up." And hung up. I lost $250,000 that week.

WOODY ALLEN

How were you in the market? Were you really badly hurt?

GROUCHO

I was wiped out. But I was getting a thousand dollars a week for *Animal Crackers*, so I recovered very quickly.

WOODY ALLEN

Over the years, have you observed any sort of diet?

GROUCHO

I eat anything I want. Even an occasional girl.

WOODY ALLEN

I want to get back to Charlie Chaplin. Were you friends years ago?

GROUCHO

Yes. I met him over sixty years ago in Canada. I tried to look at one of his movies a couple of weeks ago, but Chaplin's not very funny anymore.

WOODY ALLEN

I think he had three great films. They had a revival of all of his films here, and three of them I think are still funny, but the others are not. Well, three and a half, I guess. There's certain of them I find are too mawkish. I like *Modern Times, City Lights,* and *The Gold Rush.* The others just seem so tedious to me. I don't like *The Great Dictator* or *Monsieur Verdoux* or *Limelight.* Did you know Keaton?

GROUCHO

Yeah.

WOODY ALLEN

Did you find him funny?

GROUCHO

Yeah. He used to work for Harpo when we were at M-G-M. He put in gags.

WOODY ALLEN

Did you think he was funny in his movies? *The Navigator* or *The General*?

GROUCHO

Yes. I thought *The Navigator* was great. But, you know, with the exception of you, there are no more comedians around.

WOODY ALLEN

For some reason, nobody's making comedy films now. I don't know why. People ask me that question all the time, but I don't know why they're not.

GROUCHO

They're hard to make.

WOODY ALLEN

Yeah. Physically hard, you mean. There's just nobody trying to make comedy films. For a few years there was Jerry Lewis.

GROUCHO

They asked me in France when I was over there last summer what I thought of Lewis, and I said he was very good when he was with Dino Martin.

WOODY ALLEN

What I don't understand is this: why is it that at one time there were six, eight, or ten comedians of your stature—Keaton, Chaplin, you, Fields—and why there should be a group of them in one period of time, and then all of a sudden, nothing?

GROUCHO

Don't you think that when vaudeville disappeared that that had something to do with it? There was no place to be funny anymore when vaudeville died.

WOODY ALLEN

Those were all vaudeville comedians, all music hall comedians. I guess it's just an incredible thing to me. I'm just amazed by the fact that it was like a renaissance, or the impressionist painters—you know, they all came at once. Did you ever see any Bob Hope movies you've liked?

GROUCHO

He's just made one—*Cancel My Reservation*. I didn't see it yet.

WOODY ALLEN

What about twenty years ago, in the forties or fifties?

GROUCHO

I think years ago when he worked with Crosby, they worked well together. The audience liked them. Hope's a funny man and Bing's a good singer.

WOODY ALLEN

Now, I never found Harold Lloyd funny. Or Laurel and Hardy.

GROUCHO

All Harold Lloyd ever did was climb up buildings.

WOODY ALLEN

So what was the difference between Chaplin and Keaton? Why was Chaplin more popular than Keaton?

GROUCHO

I think Keaton had a couple of good, funny pictures, and I think Chaplin had many of them.

WOODY ALLEN

You think so? You think all those two-reelers and shorts were funny?

GROUCHO

No, but I remember when Chaplin did one called *Easy Street*, when he's a policeman.

WOODY ALLEN

Right. That's a great one.

GROUCHO

It's a funny picture. Really funny.

WOODY ALLEN

It's very short. I think Keaton was a better filmmaker but Chaplin was a funnier man.

GROUCHO

Maybe the day of the comedian is over, except for you.

WOODY ALLEN

Maybe, I don't know. What about Tati? Jacques Tati?

GROUCHO

The tall guy? He's made one funny picture, or maybe two, I don't know. I liked *Hulot's Holiday*. But he did one not long ago, and I hear it's not good.

I

Traffic.

GROUCHO

That's right. You did that interview with him in Paris.

WOODY ALLEN

Now I want to hear how you met Chaplin in Canada.

GROUCHO

It's not much of a story. This is way before your time. There were two circuits out there, the Pantages and the Sullivan-Considine. You've never heard of either of these because you're too young.

WOODY ALLEN

I've heard of the Pantages.

GROUCHO

Anyway, we were playing in Canada and Chaplin was playing in Canada. He was doing an act called *A Night at the Club*. It was a very funny act. I remember they had a lady dowager in the act and she used to sing. While she was singing, Chaplin was chewing on an apple and spitting this stuff in her face. This was the kind of comedy that he was doing sixty years ago.

Well, all my brothers were pool players. Not professional, but good. When we got to Winnipeg, the boys all disappeared looking for a poolroom. We had about a three-hour wait there before we started toward the coast. Since I don't play pool, and I don't gamble, and I don't play cards—I smoke occasionally, just enough to cough—I passed this dump theatre, this Sullivan-Considine theatre. I'm walking past there, and I hear the most tremendous roars of laughter. So I paid ten cents and I went in. It was the greatest thing I'd ever seen.

WOODY ALLEN

Why was it the greatest thing you'd ever seen?

GROUCHO

He was so funny.

WOODY ALLEN

What was he doing?

GROUCHO

Crazy things. He was walking around kind of funny. Like this. (*Groucho demonstrates*)

WOODY ALLEN

What did the others do?

GROUCHO

Well, I don't remember after so many years. But I do know that we opened in Winnipeg with Chaplin. He was on the Sullivan-Considine Circuit and we were on the Pantages Circuit. He had a shirt that he wore for the whole six weeks 'cause he was only getting twenty-five dollars a week, and he didn't want to spend any money on getting a clean shirt. We got acquainted with him. I went backstage the following week to visit him and tell him how wonderful he was. Then, each week we would be in the same towns in Canada. I can't remember all the towns 'cause this is a hell of a long time ago, but we used to go to the whorehouses together.

WOODY ALLEN

Um-hmm.

GROUCHO

Because there was no place for an actor to go in those towns except, if you were lucky maybe, you'd pick up a girl. But as a rule, it wasn't a girl. You'd have to go to a hookshop, and then we got very well acquainted. Not together. I mean, I wasn't with him. I was *with* him, but not . . .

WOODY ALLEN

I understand. Now at that point he had never made a movie.

GROUCHO

No. He'd never made anything.

WOODY ALLEN

Did he speak about movies at all? Did he say that he wanted to make them?

GROUCHO

No. It never occurred to him. He was a big hit in his act. Then, when we got to Seattle, Mack Sennett saw Chaplin in A *Night at the Club*, and he offered to sign him up. I was talking to Chaplin one day and I said, "I understand you were offered a job with Mack Sennett and he offered you $200 a week." And he said, "I turned it down." I said, "You must be crazy! You turned down $200 a week for this lousy vaudeville act you're only getting twenty-five dollars a week for?" He said, "I figured it out. Nobody could be worth $200 a week. And if I don't make good, where will I be? So I turned him down. I wouldn't take the job." He was afraid, and he went back to England after that. Now, six years passed, and I'm playing the Orpheum Circuit . . .

WOODY ALLEN

I have to stop you for a second. Would you have felt happy if Sennett had made you an offer to appear in films at that time?

GROUCHO

No. I was working with my brothers, but they were busy shooting pool.

WOODY ALLEN

Right. But suppose Sennett had wanted all of you to work in pictures. What would you have thought at the time? Would you have accepted Sennett's offer and worked in silent pictures?

GROUCHO

Probably not.

WOODY ALLEN

Why not?

GROUCHO

Because we didn't think we were good enough for $200 a week.

WOODY ALLEN

But that's the same reason Chaplin had!

GROUCHO

Yes!

WOODY ALLEN

But what I want to get at here is, do you think that the Marx Brothers could have played in silent movies? Chaplin played in silent films, obviously. You didn't get into films until there were talking pictures. Do you think you guys could have been funny—could you have played in silent pictures?

GROUCHO

In the first place, Harpo didn't talk at all in the act.

WOODY ALLEN

That's a good point.

GROUCHO

And Chico didn't talk if he could find a dame.

WOODY ALLEN

Um-hmm.

GROUCHO

So the only one who really talked was me.

WOODY ALLEN

Well, you're the kingpin of the act. So do you think that if Mack Sennett had wanted you to be in pictures that the Marx Brothers could have been funny in silent pictures?

GROUCHO

We *did* make a silent picture. And it was the worst turkey of all time.

WOODY ALLEN

When?

GROUCHO

Around 1921. We each put up a thousand dollars and made it in New Jersey. We shot most of it on a vacant lot next to the theatre where we were playing.

WOODY ALLEN

What was it called?

GROUCHO

Humorisk. I don't remember much about it except that I was the villain, and it only played once at a kids' matinee in the Bronx. I wish I could find a copy of it. Anyway, we were more interested in Broadway than movies.

WOODY ALLEN

Broadway was definitely bigger then. But, as you were going to say, six years later Chaplin comes back . . .

GROUCHO

Chaplin comes back, and we're playing the Orpheum Circuit. I'm talking, and Chico's talking, and Harpo had nothing to say. He did pantomime mostly. And it was funny. So in Los Angeles we get an invitation from Chaplin, who by now is a movie star. He was so rich by this time, he had bought the Mary Pickford home. She was a big star at the studio you're going to go to in Hollywood soon. So, he invited us to this house, and there was a butler in back of each chair and solid gold plates. We had the most magnificent meal! But when he first said to me, "Nobody can make good for $200," I knew he was crazy or something. Or had no confidence in appearing in pictures. Well, he became the greatest thing in pictures, and we were still playing small-time vaudeville.

I

Did Chaplin seem different after his great success?

GROUCHO

He seemed richer.

WOODY ALLEN

You have no interest in writing anything anymore?

GROUCHO

I wrote five books. That was enough.

WOODY ALLEN

How many of them have I seen? I saw *Memoirs of a Mangy Lover* and . . .

GROUCHO

That was a lousy one; I mean a mangy one.

WOODY ALLEN

I've read *The Groucho Letters*, but I wasn't thinking of that so much as a book. What was the earlier one?

I

Beds, Many Happy Returns, and *Groucho and Me.*

WOODY ALLEN

Beds is the one I meant. It's out of print, but somebody I know has a copy of *Beds* . . .

GROUCHO

I don't even have a copy of it. I can't find it. It's a thin book.

WOODY ALLEN

Are you planning to do any more movies?

GROUCHO

Erin's busy putting together a documentary about me. In the meantime I plan on dying.

WOODY ALLEN

Well, that's laying it on the line! Do you have a copy of *Animal Crackers*?

GROUCHO

Nobody has.

WOODY ALLEN

Why hasn't *Animal Crackers* been seen?

GROUCHO

It's very simple. George Kaufman willed this picture to his adopted daughter, a very nice woman who sounds just like him when she talks. But it belongs to the Kaufman estate, and they can't get together with Universal.

WOODY ALLEN

All these years? But I saw it at a movie house, I'd say twenty-five years ago, and I haven't seen it since.

GROUCHO

We get mail all the time saying, "Why can't we see *Animal Crackers*?"

WOODY ALLEN

I have a script of it—I assume you do too. Didn't you do something from *Animal Crackers* on a Hollywood Palace program about ten years ago? You did a funny monologue on the show, too. You had just gone to Paris, and you had met Bardot, or you were going to meet Bardot.

GROUCHO

I have no recollection of that. My memory's lousy.

WOODY ALLEN

Well, you seem to be full of stories of thirty-five or forty years ago, and that amazes me. Do you still practice the guitar?

GROUCHO

No. I don't do anything.

WOODY ALLEN

Nothing at all? You don't watch baseball?

GROUCHO

No. I have no interest in baseball. I don't know the teams. You know, if they say Memphis beat Dallas, I don't know any of these teams. So how can you root for something when you don't know who's playing?

WOODY ALLEN

I remember being at your home a few years ago, and you were talking about the Dodgers. You were a big fan at that time—a big fan of Sandy Koufax.

GROUCHO

I'm still a fan of Sandy Koufax, but he's been out of baseball for years!

WOODY ALLEN

I know, but when you're a baseball fan your whole life, it's hard to turn it off. So, what have you been doing?

GROUCHO

Nothing. And I'm crazy about it.

WOODY ALLEN

Do you get up every day and read the *Times*?

GROUCHO

The *New York Times*? No. I only get it on Sunday. I can't take reading the news all week. It's just too much. Do you read it every day?

WOODY ALLEN

I read it every day, yeah. I don't like the news too much, either. But I read it every day.

GROUCHO

Did I show you my Carnegie Hall lighter?

WOODY ALLEN

Dunhill, right? I must tell you that when they announced your concert at Carnegie Hall, I was so surprised at the speed the thing sold out. I suspected that you would have a following that would want to see it, but what sells out at Carnegie Hall are music and folk acts, you know, and those kinds of things—rock acts. But yours was a quick, sudden sellout, and I was so surprised that it would go that quickly. It was just amazing.

GROUCHO

They turned away three thousand people that night.

WOODY ALLEN

I know. People were offering a lot of money for tickets.

GROUCHO

That's right. And also for my life.

WOODY ALLEN

I think it's important that you work now. I think that your public at this point is as big as it ever was, if not bigger. It's conceivable that your public is bigger now, because all the young people, all the college people, have been brought up to date on it, and all the middle Americans have seen the quiz program. They showed film clips during your concert, didn't they?

GROUCHO

Of the stateroom scene from A *Night at the Opera*. And the projector broke down. Or maybe it was the projectionist.

WOODY ALLEN

I always get the idea in this kind of concert that if you see clips of the person first it's better. I saw this with Gloria Swanson. First they showed film clips of her, then by the time she came out . . .

GROUCHO

Who's this?

WOODY ALLEN

Gloria Swanson. And they showed these clips . . .

GROUCHO

She was a good actress. Is she still alive?

WOODY ALLEN

Yeah. She looks good. And they showed these clips . . .

GROUCHO

She must be sixty, anyway.

WOODY ALLEN

Easily. Easily. Anyway, they showed a film clip of her in a very funny movie, a silent movie. She was on a subway train acting wonderfully funny, really good. But Chaplin said that she would never be a comedian, that she wasn't funny, and didn't like the idea of using her. But she was very funny.

GROUCHO

When will you be coming to California?

WOODY ALLEN

Soon. I'm looking to rent a house while I film *Sleeper.*

GROUCHO

A small house?

WOODY ALLEN

Yeah. It's gotta be right near Martindale's bookstore.

I

Do you . . .

WOODY ALLEN

You know, right near where those stores are. I'd never move out there. (*To me*) I'm sorry—did I interrupt you?

GROUCHO

She doesn't do anything. She just brings cake. I've never seen her without cake. Have I?

I

Well, on occasion. A few times.

GROUCHO

When?

I

Today.

WOODY ALLEN

That's a time!

GROUCHO

Today? But I still have your cake from last night.

I

That's true.

WOODY ALLEN

That's good. You can't get the same cake in California that you can in New York, you know.

GROUCHO

No.

WOODY ALLEN

In fact, I don't know how you live in California. For a man of your piercing intellect to be able to live on the West Coast is incredible to me.

GROUCHO

Well, we have a good bakery out there. What's the name of it?

I

Pupi's.

GROUCHO

Could you want a greater name for a bakery?

WOODY ALLEN

Listen—I don't know how to break this to you, but I have to go.

GROUCHO

What about the cake?

WOODY ALLEN

I'm not going to have any cake because I have to be someplace.

GROUCHO

Hadn't you ever heard the story before about how I met Chaplin?

WOODY ALLEN

No, I've never heard that story before.

GROUCHO

Then why won't you eat the cake?

WOODY ALLEN

Oh well—it's not *that* good a story. I have to go, and I'll see you in California next week, because I'm going there tomorrow.

GROUCHO

Well, we'll save the cake for you. You're going tomorrow, huh?

WOODY ALLEN

Yeah.

GROUCHO

I've got a dame on that plane that I'd like you to meet. She's a wonderful girl. Wonderful pair of knockers this girl has. You've never picked up a girl on a plane, huh?

WOODY ALLEN

Not me. I just read.

GROUCHO

You know, I tell these old stories so often I'm forgetting them. I think I'll take a nap. If I sleep, I won't smoke, and if I don't smoke, I won't cough. And if I don't cough, I might get to sleep. "It isn't the cough that carries you off, it's the coffin they carry you off in."

BILL COSBY

Groucho shared with me his appraisal of friend Bill Cosby's talent:

"Have you ever seen Cosby in a nightclub? He's fantastic. He doesn't tell any jokes. He does impressions of people. Like how a mother will talk to her child, and how a father will talk to the same child. Things like that. And he'll show you people who take dope. He's brilliant, this man."

After dinner at Groucho's one evening, Groucho, Bill Cosby, Erin, and I went to see Jean Anouilh's *Waltz of the Toreadors*, with Anne Jackson and Eli Wallach. After the play, we went backstage to congratulate them in their dressing rooms.

Wearing the Wagnerian horned helmet from the play, Groucho told me when Bill Cosby left:

"I was watching Cosby one day with George Burns. George turned to me and said, 'I wish he was a Jew.'"

What follows is the conversation that took place during dinner at Groucho's house before we went to the play.

BILL COSBY
You say there was once a song called "Under the Matzo Tree"? Now, did you make that up?
GROUCHO
No. "Under the Matzo Tree" was a tribute to Israel.
BILL COSBY
Am I going to have to put up with this all night?
GROUCHO
That was a song somebody really wrote.
BILL COSBY
And it was a tribute to Israel?
GROUCHO
It was a tribute to trees.
BILL COSBY
But you just said it was a tribute to Israel. You're pulling my leg.
GROUCHO
No I'm not. My hands are right here.
BILL COSBY
Well, then, who's touching my leg?

GROUCHO

It must have been one of the girls.

BILL COSBY

Isn't that awful? But last night at the Academy Awards you were really handsome. You had that tuxedo on . . .

ERIN

Tailcoat.

GROUCHO

Frock coat. Sounds dirty, doesn't it? I used to wear a frock coat for the girls.

BILL COSBY

Did they enjoy it?

GROUCHO

I don't think so. I wasn't very good in the sack.

BILL COSBY

But how about in the coat?

GROUCHO

I was much better in the coat than in the sack.

ERIN

How about in Dallas, Groucho?

GROUCHO

I once had a girl in the Adolphus Hotel in Dallas, and I laid her eight times that night. I was eighteen years old.

BILL COSBY

Good. Good. I was beginning to get worried. I thought it was last week.

GROUCHO

No, that's all over now.

BILL COSBY

Is it?

GROUCHO

(*Singing*) "I used to love you, but it's all over now. It's all over town."

BILL COSBY

So what do you do now? I mean, you just . . .

GROUCHO

I just whip the bishop.

BILL COSBY

But getting back to my point . . .

GROUCHO

What is your point? Seven?

BILL COSBY

No, it was six, and we sevened out.

GROUCHO

Your baby's all right now, isn't she?

BILL COSBY

Yeah. We put her in the hospital, but it turned out she just had a little cold.

GROUCHO

But your wife was crying.

BILL COSBY

You know how mothers are about the children.

GROUCHO

I remember my mother had five boys. She really had six, but one died when he was three years old. She told me, "Sam can cough all night, and I'll never hear it. But if one of the children coughs once, I'm wide awake."

BILL COSBY

Poor Sam.

GROUCHO

(*Singing*) "Sam, you made the pants too short."

BILL COSBY

What did you think of the tribute they did to you on the Academy Awards show, with the four fellows singing and . . .

ERIN

We just went by the monitor on the way to the stage when they were doing it.

BILL COSBY

So you didn't see the film clips?

GROUCHO

I had the clip once.

BILL COSBY

You did?

GROUCHO

I was fifteen years old, and I had the clip up in Canada. That's the best place to get it.

BILL COSBY

To get the clip . . .

GROUCHO

We used to use Argyrol.

ERIN

Oh, my God, Groucho! We're gonna eat now . . .

BILL COSBY
What's the Argyrol for?
ERIN
It's for the clap.
BILL COSBY
Oh, for the *clap!*
GROUCHO
That's what they used to shoot in your penis to cure it.
BILL COSBY
You're kidding!
GROUCHO
Sure. You take a syringe and shoot it in there.
BILL COSBY
And it cleans it right up?
GROUCHO
Not *right* up. It takes about four weeks.
BILL COSBY
Four weeks? Oh my goodness!
GROUCHO
They didn't have penicillin when I was a kid. They didn't have automobiles. And they didn't have airplanes.
BILL COSBY
But they had the clap.
GROUCHO
That you could always get.
BILL COSBY
I was always interested about those days and times, even before you were born . . . about having VD and walking around with it.
ERIN
Winston Churchill's father died from it.
GROUCHO
Well, I didn't die.
BILL COSBY
I guess so.
GROUCHO
You're not sure of it?
BILL COSBY
Where's the Oscar?
GROUCHO
It's in the dining room.

BILL COSBY

Well, leave it there. We'll see it when we go in to eat. Does it have a wick on the end? Can we light it?

GROUCHO

No.

BILL COSBY

Well, what's the fun of it, then?

GROUCHO

A guy offered me a thousand dollars for it last night.

BILL COSBY

A guy? Did you hit him in the face with it?

GROUCHO

No. It was too heavy to lift.

BILL COSBY

Oh yeah? Well, maybe they were trying to give you a hernia while they were giving you a present. But you looked good last night. You had the Legion of Honor medal hanging and everything.

GROUCHO

I don't have anything hanging anymore.

ERIN

Did you tell Bill about your lawsuit against the book?

GROUCHO

It's full of dirty words . . .

BILL COSBY

Ah-ha!

GROUCHO

. . . and vulgarities. We're suing for ten million dollars.

ERIN

It was fifteen, but we'll settle . . .

GROUCHO

We'll settle for four.

BILL COSBY

I'd settle for a free lunch at Nate 'n' Al's.

GROUCHO

I can't eat there anymore.

BILL COSBY

Why?

GROUCHO

Because I can't eat salt.

BILL COSBY

Well, haven't they got stuff there without salt in it?

GROUCHO

Yeah, a few things.

BILL COSBY

Cottage cheese?

GROUCHO

That's a fine meal!

BILL COSBY

Well, I was just thinking of things you could eat. Let's see . . . there's cottage cheese and . . . and parsley . . .

GROUCHO

I could make a whole meal of parsley.

BILL COSBY

Yeah. Fried parsley. And you could have Jell-O and skim milk.

GROUCHO

What else?

BILL COSBY

And, uh . . . a matzo.

GROUCHO

I used to sit under the matzo tree.

BILL COSBY

Yes, I know. Now, that alone should fill you up.

GROUCHO

I would think so. Just the parsley.

BILL COSBY

By the way, how's that dinner coming? Are we having cottage cheese?

GROUCHO

You ever been to Atlantic City?

BILL COSBY

I used to push people in the chairs.

GROUCHO

No kidding? You may have pushed me sometime.

BILL COSBY

I might have pushed you and not known it.

GROUCHO

Yeah.

BILL COSBY

If I'd'a known it, I'd have pushed you in the water. If I'd'a known it was you.

GROUCHO

That's where I did the first play, *Cocoanuts*. Irving Berlin used to go home every night and start writing songs. (*They start eating*) "Groucho Marx, strong and able, get your elbows off the table." That's what they used to say at camp up in the Catskills when I was young.

BILL COSBY

I would think that at the time that you were a kid, it wasn't even necessary to have a camp. Nothing had been explored . . .

GROUCHO

My son Arthur went to that camp too.

BILL COSBY

Oh. I went to Camp Green Lane in Pennsylvania.

GROUCHO

I played all over in Pennsylvania. Who's hiding the gravy?

BILL COSBY

Where's the salt substitute? And don't ever try to keep it from me again.

GROUCHO

Are you on a low-salt diet too?

BILL COSBY

I am . . . after looking at you!

GROUCHO

Well, I have to be.

BILL COSBY

But I figure I better start now. Then when it comes time for me to be on one, I won't miss it. What do you think of that?

GROUCHO

I don't think much of that.

BILL COSBY

Then pass the salt. I guess I better have some.

GROUCHO

When I was in the Navy, I was an old salt.

BILL COSBY

Well, then, you *can* swim!

GROUCHO

I can swim, yeah.

BILL COSBY

Well, then, what happened when you almost drowned in the pool the other day?

GROUCHO

Well, I haven't swum in a long time.

BILL COSBY

But you never forget how to swim.

GROUCHO

No. You go like this.

BILL COSBY

Right. Well, why didn't you come to the top?

GROUCHO

I did. I went to one end of the pool and started back, then I got tired. Erin grabbed me and pulled me out of the pool. Otherwise I'd be dead at the bottom of the pool.

BILL COSBY

And I wouldn't be here at dinner.

GROUCHO

That's right.

BILL COSBY

But I could have all of your salt substitute.

GROUCHO

I'm not sure of that.

BILL COSBY

And I could have gotten all of your old cigar collection and a couple of berets.

GROUCHO

I had lunch with an English author named Richard Adams today. He's written a whole book about bunnies. I don't mean bunnies with big knockers, I mean real bunnies.

BILL COSBY

How many pages is it? Five?

GROUCHO

No, it's a big book. She (*Indicating me*) bought a copy of the book.

ERIN

Charlotte could have gotten a copy free if she'd only known.

BILL COSBY

Yeah, but she writes, you see. So out of respect, she buys. Therefore, the other authors must buy hers. I do the same thing when I go someplace and I want to pay for the ticket, you know.

GROUCHO

He was so excited about meeting me, this English author. He wrote me a letter and said there's only one man in the United States that he wants to meet.

BILL COSBY

Other than Bugs Bunny.

ERIN

How about Bugs Siegel?

GROUCHO

Hey, I met another Siegel this morning.

BILL COSBY

Where? By the seashore?

GROUCHO

You remember Sol Siegel? He used to be the head of M-G-M. Well, the other day I met one of his sons, and today I met another one. He's got three sons. I better stop walking on the street. He has no daughters.

BILL COSBY

Sometimes if you put food out on the windowsill, they come right up and eat it.

GROUCHO

That's a different kind of seagull. These are young Jewish boys. And they don't go on your windowsill.

BILL COSBY

Say, this is something! (*He examines Groucho's Oscar*) Brilliant! It's got the word brilliant on it.

GROUCHO

That's a lie.

BILL COSBY

(*Lifting the Oscar*) Oh, God, this is heavy! Why do they make them so heavy?

GROUCHO

It must be worth at least ten dollars on the actual market.

ERIN

That's not true, Groucho.

GROUCHO

Why do you say that, girlie?

ERIN

Because, big Julie, if we put that on the market, somebody would pay thousands for it. It's actually priceless.

GROUCHO

This isn't for sale.

ERIN
Of course it isn't. My point is that it's worth thousands.

GROUCHO
My point is on the top of my head.

BILL COSBY
(*Reading from the Oscar*) "Manufactured under world rights guaranteed by the Academy of Motion Picture Arts and Sciences . . ."

GROUCHO
You ought to get an award.

ERIN
We heard your picture's terrific.

BILL COSBY
Who told you that?

ERIN
Our press agents.

BILL COSBY
Oh, those people tell you everything's terrific. I've never heard them say a bad thing about anybody yet.

ERIN
Really?

BILL COSBY
They can go to your funeral and find nice things to say.

GROUCHO
You should get an award.

BILL COSBY
I'm gonna give myself one.

GROUCHO
I'm not kidding.

BILL COSBY
I'm not kidding either.

GROUCHO
That act I saw you do that night . . . that's as great an act as I've ever seen in my life.

BILL COSBY
Well, thank you. I just got my award.

ERIN
What was it?

BILL COSBY
He just gave it to me. I got the Groucho Marx Sitting-at-Dinner-Telling-

You-How-Great-You-Are award. You know what I'm going to do?

GROUCHO

No. What are you going to do?

BILL COSBY

(*Singing*) "What can I do, when you are far away, and I am blue, what can I do?" (*Groucho joins in*) But now I'm going to go to the trophy store . . .

GROUCHO

You're gonna go down in a taxi, honey . . . (*He starts to sing "The Dark-town Strutters' Ball"*) "Gotta be ready about quarter past four . . ."

BILL COSBY

Oh no, not quarter past four! What're you gonna rhyme with four? You gotta say "eight" so you can say, "Don't be late."

GROUCHO

(*Singing*) "I'm gonna be there when the darkies start playing . . ."

BILL COSBY

Not the "darkies"! "Band" not "darkies." You mess up everything. You just embarrassed me so many times!

GROUCHO

Now, the guy who wrote that song was playing on the bill with me in Canton, Ohio. And they wouldn't let him go in the lake there because he was a black man.

BILL COSBY

That's right. He was colored at that time. That was before he was black.

GROUCHO

He was like you. And he was a great songwriter. But they wouldn't let him go in the water.

BILL COSBY

And so he said, "But I wrote this song . . ."

GROUCHO

He wrote a number of songs.

BILL COSBY

And they said, "We don't care what you wrote, you're not going in the water because you'll disfigure it."

GROUCHO

That's right. He'll get it dirty.

BILL COSBY

"You'll leave a ring around our lake."

GROUCHO

He had one song he sang about. He'd gone to the circus, and a lion had broken loose. The song went, "While the lion was marching through Tennessee, I was marching through Georgia." He was a great songwriter.

BILL COSBY

You know who I recommend to have dinner with you, Grouch? You know Bobby Short?

GROUCHO

No, but I knew him when he was long.

BILL COSBY

Well, he's short now.

GROUCHO

He was short about fifty dollars when I saw him.

BILL COSBY

And a haircut, because he was the party of the first part.

GROUCHO

Yeah, and who's the party of the second part?

BILL COSBY

I have no idea. I'm confused. Whose party is it?

GROUCHO

I did that scene in one of my pictures.

BILL COSBY

I know you did. And you kept tearing the paper.

GROUCHO

That's right.

BILL COSBY

And you said, "Well, if you got it, then you tear it off."

GROUCHO

Then he says, "What about the final clause? There ain't no Sanity Clause."

BILL COSBY

But Bobby Short knows great, great songs.

ERIN

Is he around?

BILL COSBY

Sure. He sings in the lounge of the Carlyle Hotel. I'll have him give you a ring.

GROUCHO

On the finger? Is he long again?

BILL COSBY

He was, but now he's having trouble paying the rent. Anyhow, he knows all the songs you know, and he can run 'em at the piano. One night we were sitting there . . .

GROUCHO

Sitting where?

BILL COSBY

In the Carlyle Hotel . . .

GROUCHO

Oh.

BILL COSBY

. . . in the lounge, and Bobby had finished singing.

GROUCHO

What happened?

BILL COSBY

He came over and sat down with us. He congratulated me on this book I had written the introduction for, called *The Black Book,* which is about . . .

GROUCHO

Couldn't you write a White Book?

BILL COSBY

Well, I tried to, but they told me somebody already had. So he said he looked up all the old songs that this book had, and that in his collection of songs he has hundreds of songs written in the olden days that were anti-Negro and anti-black. But really like hit tunes. And he started singing this one song. It was so funny. It was called "You May Look Like a Hawaiian, But You're Just Another Nigger to Me."

ERIN

Really!

BILL COSBY

But it was funny. Listen to this: (*Singing*) "You may straighten your hair, and you may have a certain color in your skin, but you're just another nigger to me. Oh, you may look like a Hawaiian, but you're just another nigger to me." Bobby was really getting into it, you know, like he was playin' it, man! He went on this black program, and the guy was talking black, and he said, "Have you ever heard of any of these songs?" Bobby started to run down some of the songs, and this guy, militant as he was, couldn't take it. He couldn't listen.

GROUCHO

I was reading Truman's book . . .

BILL COSBY

I love it! I love it!

GROUCHO

He was telling about how his grandfather had slaves. Once he told me when a couple got married in those days, they would give them four slaves. They would give them a cook, and somebody working the garden, and a nursemaid, and another maid. They'd *give* them to you!

BILL COSBY

I never got anything when I got married.

ERIN

You got a very pretty wife.

GROUCHO

Did you get a dose?

BILL COSBY

I got a wife, I didn't get a dose! Lord, man, I wasn't in Toronto.

ERIN

You didn't even touch your salad.

BILL COSBY

Who, me?

ERIN

No, Groucho.

GROUCHO

I didn't see it. Has it been there all the time?

ERIN

Yes, it has.

GROUCHO

Well, shucks!

BILL COSBY

And hush your mouth!

ERIN

We're going to leave in about fifteen minutes.

BILL COSBY

This restaurant sure does close early. I'd rather take it easy, you know. Relax a little. But now the owner's telling me to get out.

GROUCHO

She's not telling you to get out. She said, "Go out!"

BILL COSBY

Oh. Well, we get to catch *The Waltz of the Toreadors.* You know what this play is about?

GROUCHO

No.

BILL COSBY

It's about *you!* It's about this man, and he's going around trying to hump everybody.

ERIN

That's true!

BILL COSBY

And his wife is upstairs, sick, and an invalid. And he's downstairs . . .

GROUCHO

Humping.

BILL COSBY

No, *trying* to. He never gets any. He just loves to go around trying to hump anything that moves.

ERIN

Oh, you must tell Bill Chico's joke. Remember it?

GROUCHO

Which joke?

ERIN

Chico's favorite joke. I'll tell it if you like.

GROUCHO

You tell it.

BILL COSBY

She wants to be rude tonight.

ERIN

He's not allowed to talk while he's chewing. Dr. Kert's rule.

BILL COSBY

Why? What's that got to do with it? You know these stories coming out about you? I don't believe any of 'em.

GROUCHO

It's "The Secret Life of Groucho Marx."

BILL COSBY

Say the secret word and gag on yourself. (*Martha the cook enters*)

MARTHA

Want some more coffee?

BILL COSBY

I don't care what it is as long as it's dark and hot.

GROUCHO

Better be careful, Martha. (*Martha exits giggling*)

BILL COSBY

(*Inspecting Oscar*) Now, you take this gold streaker . . .

ERIN

He's rather tight in the rear, isn't he?

BILL COSBY

He looks like one of my people as opposed to one of yours. Got some nice buns. And a great profile. I could see a woman at home getting quite horny over that, and going out in search of it.

GROUCHO

It's rather phallic, isn't it?

ERIN

Yeah, and there's a picture today in the *Herald* of Groucho kissing it. Can I please tell Chico's favorite story?

BILL COSBY

(*Singing "Taps"*) Ta-ta-taaa, ta-ta-taaa . . .

ERIN

Okay, here's Chico's favorite story. Ahem!

GROUCHO

Clear your throat. Don't cut it, just clear it.

ERIN

This old prospector has been out in the woods for a year, and he hasn't seen a woman during this whole time. He's absolutely desperate and just plain horny. All of a sudden this one nice spring day he comes into a clearing and there's a log cabin. At just the right height there's a knothole. He can't believe it. He tears over there, he rips off his clothes, and he starts goin' to it! Suddenly the door of the cabin opens, and a man comes out He taps the prospector on the shoulder and says, "Excuse me, sir. Would you mind coming in and doing it from the inside out? The family's at dinner."

BILL COSBY

Ain't that awful?

GROUCHO

You're a nice guy. A little dark, but a nice guy. Do you want some pumpernickel?

BILL COSBY

You know, I have trouble with pumpernickel bread.

GROUCHO

How come?

BILL COSBY

If the restaurant's very dark, sometimes I butter my hand.

ERIN

Did you know I've been starring in a play down at the Music Center?

GROUCHO

Why wasn't I told about this?

ERIN

I had quite a part. I took off my blouse and showed my bare boobs!

GROUCHO

That's why you didn't tell me.

BILL COSBY

I heard Groucho bought up all the tickets for every night. And he wouldn't let anybody go see 'em.

GROUCHO

One of 'em almost snapped out last night at the Academy Awards.

BILL COSBY

What, one of her boobs?

GROUCHO

She had a very low-cut dress, almost a gownless evening strap . . .

ERIN

I was supposed to pick up some double-stick tape to put on the inside of my dress, and I forgot. What a night! Our car broke down on the way to the Academy Awards, so we flagged down an old crummy car. We didn't care what the car was but it was dirty, and I got dirt on the back of my dress.

BILL COSBY

Oh, shucks!

ERIN

So the wardrobe lady was rushing around trying to get something, even though I wasn't going on or anything. So, I'm looking off toward Groucho, and the next thing you know . . .

BILL COSBY

One of 'em came out?

ERIN

Yes! And Burt Reynolds came over and said, "Nice going!"

BILL COSBY

It's a wonder he didn't do that "Lady, you lost your baby" joke. You remember that joke? About the lady whose breast popped out, and she's sitting there when this drunk comes along and says, "Miss, I don't want to be rude or anything, but you lost your baby." You don't get it?

GROUCHO

I don't want it.

BILL COSBY

What was it that guy said last night on television? That "small" joke?

There's this emcee on television who reminds me so much of you, Grouch, and he's talking to a guy named Cushion. The emcee asks, "What do your friends call you?" And the guy says, "Pin." The audience laughs, and the guy continues, "Since my name is Cushion, my friends call me Pin Cushion." So the emcee says, "That was the *smallest* joke I've ever heard." Then the guy told another one, and the emcee says, "I beg your pardon. *That* was the smallest joke I've ever heard!" You ought to watch that show sometime. That guy reminds me of you. It's called *The Best of Groucho.* And they have this emcee who really looks like you, but he's not so smooth, you know. He keeps being funny, but he's not as debonair as you are.

GROUCHO

You say that awfully well. You're so sweet.

ERIN

Are you ready for your pie, Groucho, because we've got to hurry now.

BILL COSBY

Why don't you just mash it against your chest? This sounds like a rush job. In some restaurants, you know, if you don't eat all your food, they mash it on your clothes. Then you can go to wherever you're going *with* your meal. Just put your salad in your hip pocket and your steak in your back pocket. Then put your toast in your wallet and mash your pie on your shoulders, and say, "That was a wonderful meal we had! *And* we made it out on time!"

ERIN

We've only got six minutes, Groucho, and you're only on your salad.

BILL COSBY

Now, here's a lady here, our authoress, Charlotte. If she didn't want her food, all she'd have to say is, "I don't want it." Why mush it up and make it look like you ate some of it?

GROUCHO

Yeah, now I'm going to tell you a story about two old Jews.

BILL COSBY

We're getting the bum's rush, you know it? What I suggest is that we don't leave a tip.

GROUCHO

Then I'll leave the tip. I take it you don't want to hear my story about two old Jews?

BILL COSBY

Yeah.

GROUCHO

Well, they're in Israel, in adjoining urinals, and the one looks over to the other one and says, "Are you a Jew?" The other man answers. "Yes, of course I'm a Jew." "Well, then how is it that you're not circumcized?" And he says, "I'm not sure I'm going to stay." (*Laughter*)

BILL COSBY

They'll laugh at anything.

GROUCHO

That's fairly evident.

BILL COSBY

Yes, it is. They laughed at "Pin Cushion" last night. (*Martha re-enters with a coffeepot*)

MARTHA

More coffee? (*She starts to pour, but the pot is empty*)

BILL COSBY

No, thank you, because we have to go and I'm afraid mine'll be poured down my sweater. "Wait," she says, "how'd you like more coffee?" And there isn't any. Now, what kind of a household are we running? Why go around trying to show off? (*Martha exits*)

GROUCHO

We have to cut down on some things.

BILL COSBY

But she was trying to show off. It's like the cooks in the back are saying, "Oh, I hope nobody wants any more coffee, but we'll go out and ask them anyway." So they come out and say, "Who'll have more coffee?" And I say, "I will." Then they pour it out, but there's no coffee. It's embarrassing.

GROUCHO

It sure is.

BILL COSBY

Would you like some mangled pie? By our authoress? You know I talk to her on the telephone. She told me I have a sexy voice.

GROUCHO

You do, but not on the telephone. Only in the sack.

BILL COSBY

Oh! My mother's very upset. I told her what you said, about not wanting to meet her.

GROUCHO

You don't blame me, do you?

BILL COSBY

No, I don't. I told him my mother was 48-48-48, and you know what he said? "Oh." And I said, "She'd like to meet you." And he said, "Oh." And I said, "Well?" And he said, "Oh." Then he said, "You know, I'm very sick." So I said, "When did you become sick?" And he said, "On the third 48."

ERIN

We've got to leave *right now* if we're going to get to the theatre on time.

BILL COSBY

I think we're being put out of this joint. Copy down the address so we don't come here anymore.

ERIN

Groucho's got to brush his teeth yet.

BILL COSBY

He does? Well, take him out and let the maid work on him. Let her brush them for you with some Bab-O. We can still eat the pie.

GROUCHO

Eight girls invited me to a party the other night, and I was the only man. She (*Indicating me*) was there too.

BILL COSBY

Charlotte's real quiet, and she blinks a lot. I love it.

I

I didn't realize it.

BILL COSBY

But you have to be careful. When you blink a lot, people think you're taking their picture.

ERIN

Okay, are you ready to brush your teeth?

GROUCHO

Yes, babe.

BILL COSBY

Weeelll, now! Sounds like perky uptown.

GROUCHO

You don't mind if I take this small piece of pie with me?

BILL COSBY

It's so seldom he gets a good meal like this—only when company shows. I've heard about you.

GROUCHO

No, we have a good meal every night. We have a good cook.

BILL COSBY

I heard you were told to say that. I've come to rescue you. We're getting you out of here. We heard they keep you in that room with your fly down and your belt open and cue cards that say "Get it up!"

GROUCHO

With my fly open? (*Singing*) "With my fly wide open, I'm dreaming . . ." Did you ever hear that one?

BILL COSBY

Now I've heard it.

GROUCHO

Those weren't the precise lyrics.

BILL COSBY

Well, you cheat sometimes.

ERIN

Let's go.

GROUCHO

I'm not going anyplace until I brush my teeth.

BILL COSBY

That's right!

GROUCHO

What time is this turkey going to start?

BILL COSBY

Eight o'clock.

GROUCHO

We've got plenty of time. Why are we rushing like this?

ERIN

Because we've got to *be* there at eight o'clock.

GROUCHO

But it's only seven.

ERIN

It's seven-thirty!

BILL COSBY

Isn't she nagging us enough now? She going to get worse now? Going to nag, nag, nag more?

GROUCHO

Just call her Nagasaki.

GEORGE BURNS

George Burns was known to a small circle of intimates for "cracking up" Jack Benny. "Jack was George's best audience," Groucho told me. "He could always make Jack crack up. He could make him laugh so you could see tears in his eyes."

"Jack and I aren't leaving because we're both booked," George told Groucho and me at lunch one day. But shortly afterward, Jack Benny died, before he was able to make his return to films in *The Sunshine Boys*. Jack Benny's part went to the man he would have certainly chosen for it. In the part of the old vaudevillian, George Burns won his first Oscar.

On receiving the Oscar, George said, "If you stay around long enough, you become new." Groucho commented, "If you stay around long enough, you become you."

Though George Burns modestly appraised his place in the Burns and Allen team, with "I just had to stand there," his performance as a straight man was of inestimable importance to their success. And performance it was, for George Burns was always an actor. When they first started out, it was George who told the jokes, and "Gracie was the straight woman, but whatever she said, they laughed because her delivery was funny." George Burns gallantly relinquished the greater glory of getting the laughs throughout their career together, which spanned vaudeville, radio, movies, and television. They began as a vaudeville team in the early twenties and, after a few years together as an act, married in 1926. George characterized their start in vaudeville as a "disappointment act, which meant you sat home with your grips packed, and if some act got sick, you got called in."

Groucho and George had shared that experience of vaudeville with Jack Benny, George Jessel, and others no longer here. George told us, "I know more dead people than alive people. I'll sure know plenty of people there, if there *is* there." When Groucho and George were together the conversation usually turned to vaudeville, which George Burns contrasted with television:

"Then with seventeen good minutes, you could work for seventeen years."

A combination of restraint and enthusiasm, George was buoyant and even boyish when we had lunch, his vital appearance giving no hint of the open heart surgery he recently had undergone. Groucho's young nurse, Julie, was there too. In his dry, gravelly voice, George greeted Groucho with, "Hiya, kid."

After George Burns had left, nurse Julie commented, "I thought it was so wonderful, if we did it again for dinner, *I'd* probably have a heart attack!"

I

Tell me about your first meeting with the Marx Brothers.

GEORGE BURNS

Now, when I first met the Marx Brothers they were already stars. I didn't get to know them then. I met the Marx Brothers when I worked with Gracie, when I was already doing well. I wasn't doing as well as they were doing. We were just a little standard man-and-woman act. That's when I met Jack Benny, too. He was doing very well. He was a monologist.

GROUCHO

I met Benny before you did.

GEORGE BURNS

Yeah. He was getting about $450 a week. That's what he was getting. And Gracie and I were getting about $350—the two of us. And he got that alone.

I

Did you ever play on the same bill with Jack Benny?

GROUCHO

I played with Benny.

GEORGE BURNS

Yeah. I played with Benny twice.

GROUCHO

We played the whole Orpheum Circuit together.

GEORGE BURNS

I played with Benny once at the Palace Theatre. And he wanted to do a bit with me. So I went out on the stage, and I stood there. I was supposed to read the first line, and I didn't. I just stood there, and looked out. He's waiting for the first line, and I wouldn't read it. And he says, "Aren't you gonna say anything?" and I said no. He says, "Then what did you come out here for?" I said, "I wanted to see you work. I like the way you work." That was the end of Benny. He fell down, and I walked off the stage. But Groucho's known Jack Benny longer than he's known me. And he met Gracie before I met her. The Marx Brothers played on the bill with them. She did an Irish act.

GROUCHO

That's right. I was having dinner with her when you met her.

GEORGE BURNS

I don't think you had dinner with Gracie when I met you.

GROUCHO

She never ate?

GEORGE BURNS

No, you had dinner with Gracie, but you didn't meet me. I didn't know you then. When you had dinner with Gracie, she was with Larry Reilly. Isn't that right?

GROUCHO

That's right. She was a good dancer.

GEORGE BURNS

Gracie and her sisters might have been the greatest Irish dancers in the world. You know how they judge Irish dancing? Irish dancing is very, very tough. You dance on a platform with the judges sitting underneath, and it's the taps that count. Your personality has nothing to do with it.

GROUCHO

How lucky.

GEORGE BURNS

The old Irishmen sit under the platform, and you miss a tap, they say, "Out!" That's all, they just listen. It's only taps, because Irish dancing is from the hips down, that's all. Tough dancing. I don't think I'd come in first. I was always a right-legged dancer. I couldn't move my left foot

GROUCHO

Did you ever get the hook?

GEORGE BURNS

Yeah, I got mine at the Bowery. But did you ever get the hoop? You know what the hoop is? The kind you spin. They used to have them on sticks. The guys with the hoops would sit in the front row, and if they didn't like you, they'd catch you and pull you over the footlights. How 'bout that? Wasn't that nice? That was worse than the hook. With the hook, they just pulled you offstage.

GROUCHO

Once I went to the Dewey Theatre with Harpo. And we didn't have any act. And we didn't have any talent, but we put on funny makeup. The manager came back and says, "Wash your dirty faces and get the hell out of here."

I

Did you ever get on the stage?

GROUCHO

No. We stood in the wings, and I was wearing this funny makeup. But we never got on the stage.

GEORGE BURNS

I also played the Dewey Theatre. They tore it down to make the Jefferson Theatre out of it. On the other side of the street was the Academy of Music. Anyway, I'm playing the Dewey Theatre and I'm doing this skating act. And the other act is just about getting finished, and my partner, Sam Brown—it was Brown and Williams, my name was Williams—he had to go to the bathroom, and he couldn't go because the act was on their last number. That meant we had to go on the stage. So he wee-weed in the wings. In those days the orchestras were level and the stages were pitched. See, now the orchestras are raised and the stages are level, but in the other days everything was downhill. So, when he wee-weed, it went into the footlights. It started to smoke and stink. Needless to say, our act stunk a little worse than the others.

GROUCHO

I'm gonna tell about Harpo.

GEORGE BURNS

Go ahead.

GROUCHO

We played Henderson's in Coney Island . . .

GEORGE BURNS

I played it too.

GROUCHO

And that was the first time Harpo had ever been on the stage, and he shit in his pants. He was so nervous.

GEORGE BURNS

Well, I'll tell you something: you gotta be good to be nervous. That's number one. And you gotta be able to go to the bathroom, too. That's number two. But I never got nervous, because I was never good. I was lousy. I finally got to be somebody when Gracie retired, because when Gracie was alive and she worked, I didn't have to be good.

GROUCHO

You were the straight man.

GEORGE BURNS

I wasn't even a straight man. I was retired while I was with her. I'd go on the stage and say, "How is your brother?" She'd stand and talk, and talk and talk and get laughs. And I'd stand there and smoke my cigar. You know, we played Oklahoma City, and the papers came out and said Gracie Allen was a brilliant actress. And she's got a great future. She could be a great star if she ever worked alone. That was the review in the paper. That's how good I was.

Then after Gracie left, I didn't want to retire, see? So I learned a lot of songs, a lot of jokes, I always could dance a little bit. If you can dance, you get off the stage, and it's easy to get on. You just smoke and say, "Hello, folks." You've got an exit, you can work. So then I started to do something. But while I was with Gracie, I knew all the mechanics off the stage, 'cause I had four or five television shows that I owned. So I knew that backstage business, but I couldn't do it on the stage. I don't know why. I just stuttered, stammered, anticipated everything. And for instance, I used to go on the stage and say to Gracie, "I want to talk to you." I'd point my finger. Know what I would do when the music would start to play? I'd stand backstage with my finger pointed. And walk on and say, "I want to talk to you." That's how pathetic I was.

GROUCHO

Remember the Princeton Hotel in New York?

GEORGE BURNS

Yeah, Gracie stopped there. Gracie stayed at the Princeton when she went around with Benny Ryan. Gracie and Benny Ryan were supposed to get married. Bud Hanlon and the Marx Brothers stopped there.

GROUCHO

Berlin used to come in and play the piano.

GEORGE BURNS

I never would go into the Princeton, because Benny Ryan didn't like me.

GROUCHO

Well, he was going with Gracie.

GEORGE BURNS

He was going with Gracie, and Benny Ryan was a very big talent, as you know. He could sing, he was a great dancer, he wrote great songs. He wrote "When Frances Dances with Me." You know, he wrote some great songs. He wrote "M-I-S-S-I-S-S-I-P-P-I." So he was a big talent. He was a great talent in a big act—Ryan and Lee—and I was nothing! Like, I went around with the music under my arm to prove to people I was in show business. But I only got to be somebody in Gracie's eyes when we were in small towns. In Altoona I looked good. In Schenectady I looked good. But in New York City I looked lousy. 'Cause Benny Ryan was there. But in Altoona I looked like Benny Ryan. So I kept her on the small time for years.

GROUCHO

Where's lunch?

GEORGE BURNS

It'll be here. Maybe we already ate it.

GROUCHO

We did yesterday.

GEORGE BURNS

Funny thing about the lunch. I don't even know if I can have it. If there's a lot of salt in it, I'm not supposed to . . .

GROUCHO

We have a fake salt.

GEORGE BURNS

Salt substitute? Any good? (*Tastes it*) Are you kidding? That's for sand dancing. You put that on the floor when you run out of sand.

GROUCHO

I can't dance.

GEORGE BURNS

That's bad salt. No good. There's better salt than that. Better phony salt than that. This explodes in your mouth, like little crystals. Taste that. The worst. Here's a man who's worth millions of dollars, invites you to lunch with cheap salt.

GROUCHO

You know who's coming to dinner? Jessel.

GEORGE BURNS

Well, he's a lot of fun. Good sense of humor.

GROUCHO

I think so.

I

Groucho, you were going to ask about the name of that songwriter you and Bill Cosby were talking about.

GROUCHO

The one who wrote "Darktown Strutters' Ball"?

GEORGE BURNS

Shelton Brooks. And he wrote "Some of These Days," too.

GROUCHO

I played with him in Canton, Ohio.

GEORGE BURNS

Did you ever work with a fella called Joe Whitehead?

GROUCHO

The name sounds familiar.

GEORGE BURNS

He was a great dancer and monologist. And I worked with him. On the bill with him was an act called The Gascoynes, who were jugglers or something. And they were very big drinkers. Gascoyne was; he was a big drinker. And Joe Whitehead was also a big drinker. What made me think of it was you said Canton, Ohio, and this happened in Akron.

GROUCHO

That was a split week.

GEORGE BURNS

Yes, it was. Canton and Akron. So, Gascoyne got the DTs, and they sent for a doctor. Joe Whitehead was with them in the room. And when Joe Whitehead came out, I said, "How is Gascoyne feeling?" And he says, "Awful. Just the worst." And he says, "The doctor said to him, 'Do you see any pink elephants or green mice?' Gascoyne says, 'No.' " And he looked at me, and he says, "George, the room was full of 'em!"

GROUCHO

Imhof was a great act.

GEORGE BURNS

Roger Imhof. The greatest.

I

What was that act like?

GEORGE BURNS

There was a hotel, and this fella's horse dropped dead right in front of the hotel. So he came in and spent the night. They had one line that I thought was the greatest line I ever heard in my life in show business.

You see, after his horse died, he came into the hotel, and they only had two rooms in the hotel. But they were taken, so he had to sleep in the lobby. Where he slept, there was a big coal stove in the middle of the lobby; you know, one of those belly stoves they had that they used to put coal in. And the coal was under the bed, so every few minutes they had to wake him up to get the coal. The clerk of the hotel kept waking him up and saying, "How about a game of checkers?" And he said, "I don't feel like checkers. My horse died, and I loved that horse. I'd like to go to sleep." He'd go to sleep, and they'd have to get some more coal. And he'd come back again and wake him up and say, "Just one game, one game of checkers." He said, "I don't *want* to play checkers. I loved my horse. It was a fine horse, and he's dead. I don't feel like amusing myself with checkers." And he woke him up again, and he says, "Just one game." So he says, "Well, okay. We'll play just one game." And the guy looked at him and said, "Have you got a board?" (*They all laugh, including Burns*) That was the great line: "Have you got a checkerboard?" A great act. I followed them for about eighteen weeks on the Orpheum Circuit. How would you like to follow that act? That could be as bad as following the Marx Brothers or W. C. Fields.

GROUCHO

Baby LeRoy was six months old . . . in a movie with Fields. They had to have a nurse on the set in those days. So when the nurse went to the toilet, Fields took the milk bottle and half emptied it, and put gin in there. They had to stop shooting for three days. Fields said, "The kid's no trouper."

GEORGE BURNS

I'll tell you another story about W. C. Fields. I think it's an amazing story. You know, when Fields was a young man, he went to England. It was an opening act. He wasn't a comedian, he was a juggler. He worked with his wife. He was married to this beautiful young girl. Fields was then in his twenties and so was his wife—in her young twenties. His big finish was juggling the cigar boxes, which he kept all through the years after he became a great comedian. Anyway, on the bill was this great English comedian, an elderly man . . .

GROUCHO

Tate?

GEORGE BURNS

Maybe it was Tate. Tate's Motoring, or something. And he went for Fields's wife, and she went for him. She liked him, so she stayed in England. She never came back to America with Fields. But what Fields did, he stole Tate's delivery. As long as he took his wife, he took his delivery. Fields got the best of that bargain.

GROUCHO

Once Fields was playing on the Ziegfeld Follies. Ed Wynn was trying to be funny . . .

GEORGE BURNS

Oh yeah, with the pool thing. Hit him over the head with the pool cue. Ed Wynn was making faces under the pool table. They called it catching flies while you were on the stage. Well, you couldn't get a laugh if there was somebody in back of you looking around, 'cause the audience would start to look too. There's no flies there, but there's no laughs either. So that's what Wynn was doing—catching flies under the pool table.

W. C. Fields couldn't imagine why he didn't get those tremendous laughs, because that pool table did everything. Then they told him that Wynn was under the table. So the next time he went out there he looked under the table, and there was Wynn, and Fields hit him over the head with the back of a pool cue. Needless to say, that was the end of Wynn. From then on, W. C. Fields got his laughs again. And Wynn had a headache for, like, four weeks.

GROUCHO

Fields was a tough guy.

GEORGE BURNS

I used to invite him to my house for dinner, and he'd come, and his vest pocket had four little pockets. And in each pocket he had a drink of gin, in case you didn't have any gin in your house, because he only drank gin. He always took four big slugs of gin with him.

GROUCHO

He kept thousands of cases of gin in his attic, 'cause he was afraid Prohibition might come back.

GEORGE BURNS

I was doing a picture called *International House* with W. C. Fields, and Gracie was a guest in a restaurant. There were about six or seven people sitting at the table. Anyway, Fields said something to Gracie, and Gracie hit him with an off-center line, one of her dizzy lines, and she left. He felt he needed a line, and he said to Leo McCarey, who was the director, "Can you think of something that I can say right now after she goes, because I must say something. You know, she leaves me unconscious."

They were trying to think of a line, and they couldn't think of one. So I went over, and I said, "Mr. Fields, I think I can help you." He says, "How?" And I says, "Well, you've got a glass of water on the table, and you've got a glass of scotch, and you've got some black coffee. Why don't you take two pieces of sugar, put it in the water, mix the coffee, and drink the scotch." Then he says, "You're the nicest Jew I've ever met!"

GROUCHO

You don't remember what you said to me when we were watching Bill Cosby? When his act was over you said, "I wish he was a Jew."

GEORGE BURNS

That's right. A lot of talent.

GROUCHO

Great nightclub entertainer.

GEORGE BURNS

Look, if the whole world were Jews, we'd have no problems. (*Laughs*) Right now, I wish he'd marry my sister. (*Pause*) You've got tea? Any kind of tea, just so it's hot. I find if your food is hot, nobody knows it's bad. You can have a marvelous dinner at your house, and have marvelous food, but if it comes in cold, it's a spoiled dinner. Nobody knows the difference. But you can always put a little catsup on it. Anything with catsup on it isn't bad. I can't have any catsup anymore.

I

There is salt-free catsup, too.

GEORGE BURNS

Yeah. Well, I tried that. It's like this broken-down salt that he's got here. (*To Groucho*) Why you put salt in there I'll never know, because that soup doesn't need it.

GROUCHO

I put salt on apple pies.

GEORGE BURNS

You do? I put catsup in vanilla ice cream. I even put catsup on Trixie Hart.

I

Who's Trixie Hart?

GEORGE BURNS

She's dead now. Funny thing about Trixie, but you never know how old you are. When I was young, when I was in my early twenties, I went around with this Trixie Hart, and my idea of sex, that was it. Whenever I thought of Trixie Hart, for the next fifty years, I had to wear a double-breasted suit. If not, you could tell I was thinking about her. So, I'm coming out of the Brown Derby, a couple of years ago, and this little old woman met me—little gray-headed old woman. Little hat, little bow under her chin. "You don't remember me, do you?" And I said, "No." She said, "I'm Trixie Hart," and I knew how old I was. I looked at her, and says, "Well, kid, if I were you, I'd change my first name. It's time to go to St. Mary." (*Laughs*)

GROUCHO

Tell her about the fellow that used to write for you.

GEORGE BURNS

Oh, John P. Medbury. Well, a great Medbury story—I'll clean this up a little tiny bit—Medbury had offices at the Hollywood Plaza Hotel, and working for him was this young writer, Harvey Helm. He worked for him in the other room. In later years they both worked for me. Anyway, his wife came into the office, and she opened a drawer, and there was a pair of lace pink panties in his drawer. She picked the panties up gingerly, and she said to Medbury, she says, "What is this doing here?" And Medbury, without blinking an eyelid, hollered, "Harvey!" Harvey came in, and he says, "You're fired!"

GROUCHO

Well, there's more to it than that. The party.

GEORGE BURNS

Oh, the party's different. The party's the party he gave for Gracie and my-self, and Olsen and Johnson. That's the party you're talking about, aren't you? There was a tent and there was a guy . . .

GROUCHO

There was something about a toilet.

GEORGE BURNS

Yeah. A guy sitting on the can in the tent, and one guy taking a bath. And you had to go through the tent to go to the party. Oh, the first place you came to, there were four donkeys tied up outside. See, you parked your car, and you don't know what's going on. Then you go through the tent, and there's a man sitting on the toilet. One man taking a bath and the guy sitting on the toilet was reading a paper. You came through, and you're all dressed up, and he says "The party's that way."

You went to the party, and on the way in, there were about eight or ten guys sitting in trees. He had quite an approach to his house—they were sitting in trees fishing. Don't ask me what any of this meant, 'cause I don't know. I don't understand. And when we passed his garage, he had that made like a hookshop. He had the beads outside, you know, like they have in the whorehouse. And the bed inside, and the dame outside trying to hustle you in. Then when you came to the door, there was Medbury with this woman, dressed up great. He said, "I want you to meet my wife, Mrs. Gladys Medbury." And as you went in, she goosed you. He got her from the actors, the extras, or something.

When you got in the house, there was a Santa Claus. It was in July. A big tree, and a Santa Claus who was very mad if you got near the tree, and hit you with a stick. And every half hour, a bellboy went around to the guests—there were about 250 people—this kid kept saying, "It's now eight o'clock! It's now eight o'clock!" Then at eight-thirty he said, "It's now eight o'clock!" At nine . . . it was always eight o'clock. I have no idea why. Then a Russian came in. Sort of a Russian diplomat, with the breeches and with the sash, and a big gold medal, and got up and made a speech—absolute and honest—for about twenty minutes in Russian.

But the greatest gag was when someone came in. As soon as somebody came in the door, they'd say to you, "Have you got a match?" So, you'd put your hand in your pocket, and you've got a box of matches, and you give him a light. The first thing you know, he took your matches. Now, at the party, there's 250 people without matches. They took *everybody's* matches! But there were matches in little glass things, and you'd get those matches and they would light, but they'd go out right away. So, wherever you looked around the room, everybody was trying to light a match, but they couldn't. He did all kinds of things. A real wild party. And Olsen and Johnson came to the party in a hearse.

GROUCHO

Tell her about Venus.

GEORGE BURNS

Naw! I can't. It's too dirty. I'll tell another English story instead. They have a funny sense of humor, you know. For instance, when Gracie and I went there, there was an act called the Ward Brothers, a dancing act. The Ward Brothers were Englishmen, and they wore a yellow vest, you know, it came down with two points over your trousers. And they wore striped trousers, and black, short coats, with a yellow handkerchief in the pocket. And then they wore sort of felt hats . . . like in the gangster era here. They looked very sharp. I was very stupid when I first went into show business. I thought all English people dressed that way. Forgot it was just stage vaudeville.

So Gracie and I were booked in England, and I said to myself, "I'm not gonna be conspicuous. I'm gonna dress like the English dress." I got myself a yellow vest, the striped pants, the black coat, and the hat. I looked like an idiot, but I went down to see Henry Sharick—we were booked in the Victoria Palace. There was no Palladium at that time. The Palladium came the following year. Sharick took a look at me, and he couldn't believe his eyes. He said to me, "Look, kid, you can take that off. You don't open until Monday." He thought I was wearing my stage clothes.

GROUCHO

Tell her about Wienig's. Remember? It was right by the *Variety* office. Around Forty-fifth Street, between Third and Lexington Avenue. It was a kosher restaurant. And a full meal was thirty-five cents. Unless you had poultry, and then it was forty.

GEORGE BURNS

Yeah, right near the Princeton. Well, these were two Jewish fellas, and they owned a restaurant called Wienig's on Forty-fifth Street. They were characters. Like you would come in, and Swerber would never know that you were talking to him. He always remembered the last conversation, but not the one that's happening at this moment. So if you'd come in and say to Swerber, "Hello, Mr. Swerber. Is Manny Manashur in?" He'd say, "Look on the floor. Maybe it fell down." Or some silly line like that, you know? And everybody's eating there—all the big stars . . . and all the fighters . . . and all the prostitutes, late at night.

So Jolson is in there one night, having vegetables and sour cream. And Swerber passes Jolson, and he says to Jolson, "You know, Rockabye"—he used to call everybody by their billing, whatever they sang. Like, "Rockabye Your Baby" was a big hit then. He called Jolson "Rockabye." Eddie Cantor he called "Whoopee." You know, whatever. He never called you by your real name, by your billing. So he says, "You know, Rockabye, I love you, because I love the way you sing, and I love music." And Jolson looked at him and says, "You really like music?" Swerber says, "I come from Chicago." Now what the hell that means, I don't know. He says, "I come from Chicago, and I go to all the operas. Take *Carmen*. I have seen *Carmen* twenty times. I know it by heart." Jolson says, "How does it go?" He says, "Good."

And then, the phone would be on the wall. And to answer the phone, you'd have to turn your back on the restaurant, see? So as soon as the phone would ring, either Swerber or Wienig would pick up the phone. And when they'd pick up the phone, they wouldn't face the wall, they'd face the customers. 'Cause everybody picked up a piece of sugar. And Swerber—let's say he answered the phone—he'd say, "Hello!" and he'd duck, and everybody threw sugar. And these two Jews got sick of being hit with sugar, so they put in granulated sugar. So nobody came in to eat, until he put back the lump sugar. Spoiled their show. Crazy restaurant.

GROUCHO

The tips were something.

GEORGE BURNS

Well, the five-cent tip was the normal tip. But a ten-cent tip was a real big tip. Because the meal was thirty-five cents—seven-course dinner. Finally got to be forty cents. Finally got to eighty-five cents. That was the tops. But this time was thirty-five cents. So you'd tip a waiter five cents. So the waiters all watched the tippers. Let's say Groucho would come in. He'd tip ten cents when he'd leave. That was considered a big tip when your meal's thirty-five cents. He'd give ten cents. So the other waiter would come over from the other table, and he'd drop five cents and steal the ten cents. They'd steal from one another. He'd pick up your ten cents and drop a nickel. And then your waiter would say, "That Groucho's a cheapskate." They were really characters. I'm trying to think of some of the things they used to do. Oh, Damon Runyon was in there once. And next door was Abe and Jack's, a cigar store. So they raised the price of herring from five cents to six cents . . .

GROUCHO

Herring, six cents?

GEORGE BURNS

Sure, herring. A whole herring. Well, a meal was thirty-five cents. Anyhow, they got into a big fight with Abe of the cigar store. He says that Wienig and Swerber are both crooks to charge six cents for a piece of herring that they only paid five cents for yesterday. Got into this big fight. And Runyon, sitting there, was a great newspaperman, he went out, he bought a piece of herring, and he put a little note on it and attached it to a string. And he says, "Wienig and Swerber are crooks." Then he threw it into the restaurant. Swerber picked up the herring and went next door to the cigar store, and threw it in the cigar store. Well, all night long they were throwing herring at one another. It was a wild restaurant.

I

Groucho told me you were a good friend of Harpo's.

GEORGE BURNS

I knew him very, very well. Harpo I knew the best of all the Marx Brothers.

GROUCHO

Great man.

GEORGE BURNS

I thought so. Really great. One thing he said to me that was so, so nice . . . He adopted four children, you know. So I said to him, I said, "When are you gonna quit? How many children are you gonna adopt?" He says, "I'd like to adopt as many children as I have windows. So when I leave, I want a kid in every window, waving goodbye." Nice, huh?

GROUCHO

Wonderful man.

GEORGE BURNS

I thought so. And he did something. He told it in his book, but he didn't tell it right. Going into the Pantages Theatre, there's Gracie and Susan, and Harpo and myself. And he loved black jellybeans. He couldn't get any black jellybeans, and all of a sudden there's a little candy store next to the theatre. It's during the war. All of a sudden he sees this candy store, and in the window there's black jellybeans. He went in and he says, "How many black jellybeans have you got?" The guy says, "Well, I got an order today. I paid thirty dollars for the black jellybeans." Harpo says, "I'll give you thirty-five dollars for all the black jellybeans." Have you any idea how many jellybeans you can buy for thirty-five dollars?

Well, Gracie carried a bag of jellybeans, and Susan carried a bag, 'cause we're going into the theatre, and the little candy store would be closed when we left. And we couldn't walk down to where the car was or we'd have missed the beginning of the picture. So the four of us are carrying about twenty-five pounds of black jellybeans into the theatre. But . . . before we went out, he also bought some colored jellybeans—ten cents' worth of white, red, and pink jellybeans. That is, if *we* wanted a jellybean, he'd give us the colored ones because he didn't want anyone to touch the black ones!

GROUCHO

I don't blame him.

GEORGE BURNS

How 'bout that? (*Laughing*) He didn't tell the truth in his book. He told the story, but he forgot the finish.

GROUCHO

He forgot black jellybeans, too. He never ate them after that.

GEORGE BURNS

The funniest story that I know about show business, and I think the greatest, and it's a true story, they say, was when Wilton Lackaye played Cincinnati—I think I told you this story—but it's a great story. On the bill was a dancing act—Brown and Williams. And when they went into a bar at twelve o'clock to get a drink, there's Wilton Lackaye, and of course they were thrilled that they were on the bill with Wilton Lackaye. They never played a big-time theatre, and this was a big-time theatre, and Wilton Lackaye was the star.

They went over to him—he was standing at the bar—and they said, "Mr. Lackaye, we're the Brown and Williams dancing act that's working with you, and it's a thrill to be on the bill with such a big star." Lackaye says, "Thank you, boys." And Brown says, "We would deem it an honor if you would let us buy you a drink." And he said, "Boys, I'd just as soon drink alone 'cause I just got a telegram saying I lost my mother." And Brown turned around and said, "We know just the way you feel. Our trunk is missing." That's the greatest show business story that I know, because your trunk was your life savings. Your trunk came before your mother. Great story.

GROUCHO

You didn't know my mother!

GEORGE BURNS

No, I didn't. I didn't know the Marx Brothers then. You see, don't forget that I did nothing but play small-time theatres until I was twenty-seven years old. And they were a big-time act by that time. You know, they were Broadway stars.

I

Then, you were all under contract to Paramount?

GEORGE BURNS

Well, that came later. That's after I met Gracie. See, when I met Gracie, I got to be something. 'Cause she's the one that took me, you know? So, then I met them later in life and Groucho and I got to be pretty close friends. Susan was . . . I think that was about the greatest marriage that I know of, Susan Marx and Harpo. Anything Harpo wanted, she would do. Like she had these four children, and she'd have dinner on the stove. Let's say, seven o'clock at night, dinner is ready. And Harpo would come in and he'd say, "Susan, let's eat out." She'd say, "Okay." Bop! Turn out all the lights, and out they'd go. Isn't that marvelous? Great woman.

GROUCHO

Great man.

GEORGE BURNS

Yeah. And one day, one of his little boys, Alex, was playing hooky from school. Harpo got up in the morning, and there's Alex. It's nine o'clock in the morning. He says, "Alex, what are you doing here?" "Shhh! Not a word to anybody!" He says, "I'm playing hooky from school." And Harpo says, "You get your books right now, and go back to school!" So the kid got his books, and looked at his father, and says, "Harpo, I'll never tell you anything again!" I love the way they all called him "Harpo."

I

You knew Chico, too?

GEORGE BURNS

Yeah. I'm gonna taste that little salt-free cheese. I just want a little snip. Not bad! See, what I do sometimes, if I sit down and have a martini. I can't have any hors d'oeuvres—all the hors d'oeuvres are salted. So I have a little bit of cheese on a bagel.

GROUCHO

You can come again for lunch, because Erin wants to see you.

GEORGE BURNS

All right, I'll do it.

GROUCHO

She's doing a picture now. She's a great dame.

GEORGE BURNS

Well, you're lucky to have her.

GROUCHO

She's lucky to have me, too.

GEORGE BURNS

Of course! You're at the point now where you just want somebody to keep you warm. So am I, Groucho. That's why I can say that to you. The other thing is out the window.

GROUCHO

Would you like a box of good cigars.

GEORGE BURNS

No. Because I don't smoke good cigars. They're too strong for me. And I only smoke cigars that fit my holder. I smoke these domestic cigars. I love 'em, because they fit my holder. I think that when you smoke a Havana cigar, you should get paid for smoking it. They're very strong. Like Milton Berle's cigars. You know, two dollars. If I spent two dollars for a cigar, first I'd go to bed with it. It's ridiculous, two dollars for a cigar.

GROUCHO

When I was a young man there was a cigar called La Preferencia, and it said "30 minutes in Havana." It was a ten-cent cigar, so I bought one and went to my room, got in bed, and lit it. I set the clock. After twenty-five minutes the cigar was out. So I went back to the cigar store, and I said, "You advertise thirty minutes in Havana, and it only lasted twenty-five minutes. I want another cigar." So they gave me another cigar. The same thing happened. So I went back again, and they gave me another cigar. The third time I went in, they threw me out of the cigar store. It wasn't Havana; it was tobacco that was made in Connecticut. And when I was a boy, I used to smoke rolled-up newspaper.

GEORGE BURNS

I did something that was very sharp when I was young. My mind was just in show business. I was a cutter for ladies' dresses. Now, in a very cheap house they made these cheap dresses that you wear around the house cooking, you know. So what they would do is they would take the goods and put one the right side up and one down—one up and one down, one up and one down, one up and one down, so that way you'd only have to cut half a dress. When you cut one sleeve, there'd be another sleeve there. You'd cut a half a front, there'd be the other half front. The goods had a match.

Well, stupid me, my mind was on "Tiger Girl" and I'm thinking of some other songs. And I laid all these goods right side down. Now, when I tell you 250 piles—that's 250 pieces of goods on a table, maybe sixty or seventy feet long, a whole block—now, that's thousands and thousands and thousands of dozens, and here I am cutting. And you can't match these goods. You can match expensive material but not cheap material.

Well, the boss came over to me. I'm in the middle of the cutting and I'm singing "Tiger Girl" and he looks at the ruffles and stuff, and he notices it's all right side down. He said, "You know, you laid this material right side down." I said, "Oh, I didn't know that." He said, "Yeah. How long have you been working here?" I says, "About six weeks. My sister got me the job." "Your sister works here too?" "Two sisters—my sister Mamie and my sister Sarah." He said, "Go get your sisters and come up into my office." We went up and he fired the whole family.

Another thing I did once was I'm working for M. D. Mersky and the guy's stuck with all these middy blouses. You know what a middy blouse is? A white little thing with a navy blue collar with two stars in the corners.

GROUCHO

All it needs is a young girl.

GEORGE BURNS

Yeah, that's right. Well, he's got thousands of dozens of middy blouses. I go to Mersky and I said, "Mr. Mersky, I know how to get rid of those middy blouses." He said, "How do you do that?" I said, "Send everybody thirteen dozen middy blouses, and say ENCLOSED FIND TWELVE DOZEN MIDDY BLOUSES. They'll all get a dozen free." I went on to say, "You might lose a dollar or something, but you'll get rid of all your middy blouses." He says, "You're a very clever young man, and what d'ya make a week?" "Eleven dollars." He says, "From now on, you get thirteen dollars."

He sent everybody thirteen dozen middy blouses and said, "ENCLOSED FIND TWELVE DOZEN MIDDY BLOUSES." Two weeks later he came over to me and he says, "That idea of yours was a good idea but everybody kept the dozen and sent back twelve. But I'm a man of my word, and I said I'd give you a two-dollar raise. You're still making thirteen dollars a week, but you're not working for me anymore."

GROUCHO

We were playing a small town in Texas, a farming town. The farmers came in and tied their horses up beside the Pantages Theatre. We were doing a singing act, The Three Nightingales. None of us could sing. While we're doing the act, a mule runs away, and the whole audience caught the mule, and they came back. By this time we were so angry, we started making sarcastic remarks. This is the first time we ever did comedy.

GEORGE BURNS

You were forced to talk. And the audience laughed at your sarcastic remarks.

GROUCHO

Yes.

GEORGE BURNS

From then on you stopped singing, and kept in the sarcastic remarks. So you owe your success to a mule!

GROUCHO

Donkey schön.

GEORGE BURNS

I'll tell you a story about Chico and then I'll have to go. He came to the club and he liked to gamble. I'm not a gambling man. I play bridge every day, but not for much. I met Chico at the club one morning at about nine o'clock in the morning, and nobody was in the club but me. And as I said, Chico loved to gamble. He didn't care about winning or losing. The only thing that interested Chico was gambling—an inveterate gambler.

He said, "Let's play a little gin. Five cents across gin." That's a big gambling game. I said, "Not me, Chico. I don't play gin for money." He said, "Two and a half cents." I said, "I don't play for two and a half cents. That's too much money for me." Then I said, "Chico, I don't like gin." He said, "I'll tell you what. Let's play for a penny. Three games. We'll put ten points on each one of your scores. You can't be blitzed and I can. I'll start you with ten points." It's a hundred points a game, and he wanted to give me fifty points finally. Anything to lose his money!

GROUCHO

Which he did.

GEORGE BURNS

Yeah. Oh, sure.

GROUCHO

He died broke.

GEORGE BURNS

A funny story about Harpo . . . Harpo and myself and Mack Gordon—the guy who wrote "Did You Ever See a Dream Walking?" Mack Gordon and Georgie Raft were playing bridge at the bridge club. I'm Mack Gordon's partner and I've got seven spades to a queen. That's all I got as far as any points go in my hand. Queen, jack, ten, nine, eight, et cetera. But I got no king, I got no nothing. Just seven spades. And my partner opens the bid with a heart. I got no hearts. I said a spade.

Now, Mack Gordon was a . . . he thought he was a great bridge player. He was a good songwriter, but not a great bridge player. But neither am I, by the way. Anyway, so he says two hearts. I says two spades. Now he took his cards and he folded them and he laid them down on the table and folded his arms and looked at me for about ten or fifteen seconds, and without moving a muscle, just his mouth, he said, "THREE HEARTS." So I took my cards, I folded them up and put them down, I folded my arms, I looked at him, and I waited fifteen seconds, and then I said, "THREE SPADES." Now he looked out the window—we were sitting by a window—and he hollered out the window, *"FOUR HEARTS."* I said, "I didn't know we were playing with anybody across the street, but if we are I'd like for them to hear me, too, and I yelled, *"FOUR SPADES."* Well, anyway, he said six hearts. He's being silly, you see. And I said, "Look, Mack. I've got as much money as you have—seven no-trump." Which is impossible.

Now by this time Harpo and Georgie Raft knew there was a game going on between us, and they weren't even going to double, because they knew damn well we wouldn't even play the hand. But Mack Gordon called me downstairs for a fight, and I'd never had a fight in my life. Just because I said seven no-trump. And he was a big eater—double order of baloney—he kept eating these squares of baloney about an inch thick. So I said, "Yeah, let's go downstairs and fight, 'cause when I punch you in the stomach, I've gotta see that baloney again." And on the way down— Harpo was going downstairs with Georgie Raft, Mack Gordon, and myself—I said to Harpo, "Harpo, the greatest song I ever sang in my life is, 'Did You Ever See a Dream Walking?' " Then Mack Gordon says, "Let's go and finish the game." It was his song.

GROUCHO

Harry Ruby was great. Did you know Harry Ruby?

GEORGE BURNS

Of course! Who doesn't know Harry Ruby? But he's gone. Everybody's gone—but what can you do about it? There's nothing you can do about that. When they knock on your door, and give you back your pictures, you leave. If there was another exit, we'd find it. But when I go, I'm taking my music with me. (*Getting up*) I'm gonna leave ya, kid. I gotta go.

JACK BENNY

Groucho and Jack Benny first met in 1909 when The Four Nightingales played Jack's hometown, Waukegan, Illinois. Jack was a violinist in the Barrison Theatre pit orchestra, "the only one in knickerbockers," he recalled. Groucho described their meeting when he spoke at the 1974 March of Dimes tribute to Jack Benny:

"When we first met, Jack was sixteen and I was nineteen. Now he's eighty and I'm eighty-three. Time sure goes by fast."

A tremendous ovation followed Groucho's words. The large cardboard violin-shaped programs were enthusiastically waved in the air.

On our way to the tribute, Groucho told me how he had met Jack Benny:

"We got off the train, and there was this fellow who charges us fifty cents apiece to get to the hotel. He picked up the reins of the horse, and the horse walked across the street, and the hotel was there. The next day I went to the theatre. There was a young fellow playing the violin. So we asked his mother—my mother asked his mother—if he could go along with us. And she says no, he was too young. 'Cause he was only sixteen years old. I met him over the years on the Orpheum Circuit, and many circuits."

I went with Groucho and Erin to this dinner, which took place March 21, 1974, in the International Ballroom of the Beverly Hilton Hotel. Jack Benny was being honored as the March of Dimes Man of the Year, and was presented with their Humanitarian Award. On the dais with Jack Benny and Groucho were Dr. Jonas Salk, Rosalind Russell, Lucille Ball, Bob Hope, George Burns, and Johnny Carson, who was the toastmaster. Groucho was excited about the affair not only because his friend Jack Benny was being honored, but also because Dr. Jonas Salk was going to be there. "He's someone I've always wanted to know," he told me in the car on the way to the dinner.

As we entered the hotel, walking along the red carpet that had been laid for the occasion, many of the fans who had lined up on either side of the roped aisle reached out to touch Groucho. Someone grabbed one of my buttons, trying to tear it off. Groucho was distinctly unamused as he observed my newly acquired celebrity status. I asked him if he ever minded being handled by so many strangers, and he said, "No, the other way is worse—if nobody wants you." We entered to an almost musical accompaniment of "Hello, Groucho," "How are you, Groucho?" As always, he showed little emotion.

Before we met Jack, Groucho said to me, "Now I want you to talk with Jack Benny. He'd like you to do an interview with him." When he introduced me, he said to Jack, "She used to be in vaudeville with me," adding more seriously, "Remember she's mine." Jack had read the interview I did with Groucho, and he had written to *Playboy* about it.

When Jack left our table, Groucho said to me:

"He used to do whatever he could in vaudeville; take little bits in other people's acts, anything—and without getting paid. But he learned a lot. He made it here the same way we did: vaudeville, cheap rooming houses, lousy food.

"He's a very well-educated man, and tremendously talented. Great timing. Brilliant. And Jack Benny is one of the nicest men I ever knew. He's a credit to the Jews and show business. He's eighty, you know, and still working. He's a big star."

At the Beverly Hills Hotel a few days later, Jack talked with me about Groucho and the Marx Brothers:

"They were always doing crazy things. They didn't have to act in the films. Those films were *about* them. *Nobody* could follow them. And my style was especially impossible for following them. They created such pandemonium, no one was even listening to me because I worked quiet, like now, except I was even more quiet. It was pretty frustrating, but it was a big challenge. W. C. Fields said they were an impossible act to follow. But it really made me work, and I think, in the end, it helped me.

"They used to break me up watching them before I went on, but you know, if you asked me what exactly it was that they said or did, I don't know. Even then, I don't think I could have told you exactly. You couldn't exactly explain the Marx Brothers. Also, they never did it twice the same way. I always sort of envied the way they got up there and it seemed to come so easy, and they seemed to be having such a good time. In those days, I was working very hard trying to find the real Jack Benny. Now I guess I understand that they were working too, though it looked like they were playing.

"The worst was when the manager of one of the theatres suggested that they come out with me as part of an act together. It was my act, and I felt they would take over, but after a while, I got to love it. I had a great time with them.

"I roomed with Zeppo for a while, and there never was a funnier person in real life, so it was strange that he was the straight man in the act. I don't know if his brand of funniness could have been carried off onstage or not, but when you're here talking with me, you might be disappointed with me because I'm not like I am when I'm performing—just a quiet man. But Zeppo offstage didn't know how *not* to be funny.

"But Groucho was the genius. Groucho is a writer. That doesn't mean he wasn't great onstage, and he can be pretty funny off, too. He's always funny at Hillcrest. When Groucho was very young, he used to read a lot, whenever he had time. Other people would be going out with their friends, and he would be reading a book. When he found a good book he didn't know before, he'd be as excited as other people would be if they met a new person they really liked."

When Jack joined Groucho after lunch at Hillcrest Country Club, a longtime favorite place for both of them, the conversation was mostly about good health, a subject of inestimable importance to both of them:

JACK BENNY
You know, don't think I'm staying here because I'm so nuts about your company. I just don't want to go out and play golf . . .
GROUCHO
I'm not crazy about you, either.
JACK BENNY
And you don't want to play golf! You're stuck both ways!
GROUCHO
Yes. I have to stay and be told what I can eat and what I can't eat. Erin knows everything I'm not supposed to have.
JACK BENNY
Well, that's right. And there's certain things I can't eat. See, I've got something else. I have . . .
GROUCHO
Crabs?
JACK BENNY
No. *That* I've had longer. I have . . . You know, where you can't have sugar. Diabetes. I've had it seventeen years, but I've never had to take insulin. I had a blood sugar test this morning. I bet if I call up, they'll tell me, "You're fine." Isn't that amazing?
GROUCHO
It's not amusing. But it's amazing.
JACK BENNY
It *is* amazing. I've never had any problems. Now the only thing you have

to be is careful. Careful! But as far as my diabetes is concerned, I can eat practically anything. And my doctor says, "If you feel like having a malted milk, have it!" Isn't that amazing? I don't eat what I shouldn't eat, unless I just can't eat anything else. Unless I want it badly. Then I eat it.

ERIN

Isn't it difficult traveling?

JACK BENNY

No. Then I just don't have sugar. Sometimes I'll cheat a little bit with a little dessert. But then when I come back, I always go and get a blood sugar test. The damnedest thing happened: I went to Sinatra's once to spend a week, and for some reason or other, I didn't give a damn. I played golf every day, I had a lot of fun, ate everything, ate pie and ice cream and cake, and got drunk for only the third time in my life that I can remember getting drunk. Now, I come back and I'm afraid to have a sugar test. So I called the nurse and said, "Come to my house and give me a sugar test. But I want you to tell the doctor all the things I did." I expected the blood sugar to be very high. "I did cheat *all* week long. I drank and I ate pie and I ate cake." Sinatra loves Boston cream pie. And I would fill myself with Boston cream pie. You know how it is: full of sugar. Now, I come back, and I'll be a son of a bitch, my doctor calls me up, and I'm afraid to answer the phone. He says, "Jack, I gotta tell you something; you defy everything in medicine." Now, I didn't know which way he meant that. He says to me, "With all the things you did, your test is absolutely normal!" He says, "I can't get over it; everything you did!" Then he says to me, "You must have had a lot of fun and an awfully good time." I says, "I certainly did." He says, "Well, that has something to do with diabetes, with how bad or how good your condition can be. But that doesn't mean that every week you can go out and do what you did last week." Imagine doing everything wrong, every day! So he said, "You must have had a ball, 'cause your test is fine." Now, I just got back from a concert tour through Canada—Winnipeg, Calgary, Vancouver—and when I go away, I *do* cheat a lot on food. By the rule, he calls me immediately if there's anything wrong, which he didn't. So I'm gonna call him in a little while. He'll probably tell me I'm all right.

ERIN

And you still won't play golf.

JACK BENNY

I always have to force myself to play golf. It's so good for you, and the weather's so beautiful, and I'm always looking out, hoping it's gonna start to rain so I can't get out, hoping I can't play. Isn't that awful? Now I get mad when the change of season happens, and it gets dark too early. The reason I get mad is because then I say I don't have time to play golf. Now I've got all the time in the world. I have nothing to do today if I don't want to.

GROUCHO

I don't like to ask you, but what kind of score do you shoot?

JACK BENNY

Just awful. I don't even keep score. I just play.

GROUCHO

That's a coward's trick.

JACK BENNY

I know it is. But I just play. I play worse than I ever played, and I love it better.

GROUCHO

Thank God I don't play anymore. I was a lousy player.

JACK BENNY

When I used to play fairly well, I was a miserable man to play with, because I always wanted to play better. And everybody hated to play with me. Now that I can't play at all, I love every minute of it. I just go out and hit the ball, and that's it.

ERIN

Who do you play with now?

JACK BENNY

Anybody. I usually get the pro, or I take a caddie and a cart, and the caddie drives and I walk. All the caddies love me because they drive and I do all the walking. And if I get tired, I get in the cart, and that settles that.

GROUCHO

All those years of not tipping have paid off.

JACK BENNY

All these years of tipping them more than anybody else has paid off! May I tell you a story? You know, because of my stingy character, I'm always a very big tipper, particularly with waiters and taxi drivers. I usually take a taxi a short distance, and I'm afraid I take them away from a good corner, so I get embarrassed.

So once in Las Vegas I take a taxi from the Sahara Hotel. It's raining a little bit, and I want to go to the Riviera. The fare was, like, $1.10. So I gave him $3.00 and told him to keep the change. And these are his exact words. He looked at me and said, "Mr. Benny, I wish you hadn't done that." I said, "Why?" He said, "I wanted to be able to go home and tell my wife what a cheap son of a bitch you are," and that's just the way he worded it. I said, "You can still tell her. Give me back my tip! And then you can tell her. But do me a favor: I don't want the tip back. Tell her I *am* cheap. It's funnier if they think I'm cheap."

Some people actually got angry at me for giving big tips and being out of character. Do you know that if you played in pictures or anything, the people who actually know you, almost around the world, are taxi drivers. I can go someplace where nobody would recognize me, but for some reason or other all taxi drivers know who you are.

ERIN

Isn't that interesting! Marvin Hamlisch was over at Groucho's house the other night, and we said to him, "Was it a big thrill when you got the three awards?" And he said, "You know what was the biggest thrill? I got into New York City to record something, and I just got out of the baggage claim thing, and I was standing in line for a cab, and all of the cabbies said, 'Hamlisch! Hey!' "

JACK BENNY

I never heard of him before, you know.

ERIN

He played for Groucho.

GROUCHO

He played Carnegie when I played Carnegie.

JACK BENNY

I'm sitting here talking to you because I don't want to play golf.

GROUCHO

That's the most flattering remark I've ever heard.

JACK BENNY

I flattered you enough this morning.

ERIN

I heard about that. You called Groucho this morning and said you saw his quiz show last night . . .

JACK BENNY

And Groucho looked . . . he didn't look fifty years old last night.

ERIN

Isn't it amazing? He was sixty-five or something.

JACK BENNY

But he didn't look it.

GROUCHO

But I never had Boston cream pie.

JACK BENNY

No, but I tell you, that was a wonderful show. All those shows were great. But you see, you have it easy, Groucho, because you only have the announcer, and that's all you have to worry about. Now, if I want to do my show in reruns, which MCA can distribute, then they gotta go through everybody who's been on my show, all the actors. But they should be tickled to death to go on, just to be seen. That's the only reason I wanted my show to go on. But then my show's different. If it's Christmas, it's a Christmas show. But Groucho could have done his show any week.

ERIN

The argument that I got when I tried to sell it was that it was a quiz show, and who wants to see a quiz show? But now that it's on, they can see that it's funny.

JACK BENNY

Last night's show was just great, and it's on a half hour before Johnny Carson, which makes it great for the people . . .

GROUCHO

I gotta tell you about my golf game.

JACK BENNY

Jeez, there's a switch if I've ever heard one. Go on.

GROUCHO

I was playing golf with Frank Crumit. You remember Frank Crumit? Used to play the guitar and sing.

JACK BENNY

Yeah.

GROUCHO

We were playing golf in San Francisco, and he was a very good golfer. And I had never played, maybe three or four times. We were playing at the Municipal Golf Course. We came to the seventh hole then, and it's 155 yards. I hit the ball to the green, and it rolled to the carpet. I had a hole in one! The reporters heard about this, and the next day the *Chronicle* and the *Examiner* say, "Marx Joins the Immortals." There was a picture of Bobby Jones and Walter Hagen, and I was in the center. So we go out and play golf again, and there's a lot of reporters out there. I hit the green, and it rolled into the sand trap. I hit it out of the sand trap, and it rolled into another sand trap. To make it short, I shot 140 that day. And the newspapers came out the next morning and say, "Marx Leaves the Immortals." There was a picture of Bobby Jones and Walter Hagen, and my picture wasn't in there. But I've always been a lousy golfer.

JACK BENNY

I'll never forget, years and years ago I played with Harpo and George Burns. And when George Burns and I were playing fairly good, I used to shoot this course in the eighties. Now, that's good . . .

GROUCHO

Who could shoot in the eighties? You?

JACK BENNY

Yes. Now, I was a miserable man to play with, because then I wanted to shoot in the seventies, you see. And George Burns played not even as good as I did, but he played. One day he got so mad, he came in and he said, "Jack, you've seen me play my last game of golf." Now, you know, Groucho, millions of people say that, and it never happens. But he has never touched a golf club since then, and that's about twenty-six years ago. He just sits and plays bridge.

GROUCHO

I don't play anymore either.

ERIN

Was Harpo a good golfer?

GROUCHO

Fairly good.

JACK BENNY

Yeah, but Harpo and George used to play all the time. And George tells the funniest stories about playing with Harpo. He was afraid to breathe when Harpo was playing, 'cause Harpo blamed him for everything. I'll tell you one golf story, and then I'll leave you.

You know Norman Krasna so well, and I have to preface this, and I hate to preface it this way, but it's the only way it's funny. Norman Krasna's one of the greatest fans I have in the whole world. He thinks that everything I do in show business is perfect, whether it's a movie, whether it's radio, whether it's television, whether it's the stage—he thinks I can't make a mistake. Now, that's the kind of fan Norman Krasna is of mine. All right.

Now, we're playing golf one day, and I'm getting mad all through the game—mad as a son of a bitch. Now, Norman is getting mad at me, and he throws his clubs on the ground. He says, "For Christ's sake, Jack; everything you do in show business is perfect. You want to be that great in golf too?" Then I got mad. I says, "Listen, Norman: I would just as soon have a couple of television shows that *aren't* so good, and play a little better golf." He says, "All right, how good golf do you want to play?" I says, "Norman, that all depends. How lousy do you want my television shows to be?" And he started to laugh, and the whole thing was over. He had been mad as hell.

GROUCHO

I never shot an eighty. I used to shoot in the late nineties.

JACK BENNY

I wish that I could shoot *now* in the late nineties. I would be the happiest guy in the world. I shoot about 110. You know why I play golf? I either play golf or walk 'cause I want to exercise. Or a fella comes over and gives me a little exercise. Now, I had a little exercise today. If I didn't go out to play golf, I'd want to walk from here to my office. But I got my car here.

GROUCHO

I like to walk on the street 'cause you can pick up dames that way.

JACK BENNY

When I walk on the street, I don't just ramble along. I actually walk, and I get good exercise that way.

GROUCHO

I do it every day.

JACK BENNY

You get better exercise doing that, actually, than golf. I do what Dudley White, the doctor, used to say: walk everyplace you can walk, even if you have to climb stairs.

GROUCHO

I'll give you one of my Groucho watches when I get them.

JACK BENNY

I gave you one of my money clips, didn't I?

GROUCHO

I don't know. You didn't give me any money with it.

JACK BENNY

I know, but I gave you the clip.

GROUCHO

I'd rather have the money.

JACK BENNY

I know.

GROUCHO

It's easier to carry money in your pocket. You don't need a clip.

JACK BENNY

You know, once I sent my money clip to President John Kennedy. I had to be emcee for his birthday at Madison Square Garden, and I put his caricature on one side and my caricature on the other side. Now, I forget to bring it and give it to him, so the next day Pat Lawford was in having some drinks in the hotel with me, and I said to her, "Pat, I forgot to give the president (who is her brother) this. Now I don't know what to do.

Imagine going there and forgetting to give him this present." She said, "I'm going to see him pretty soon, 'cause he's going to be at the hospital visiting his father."

So she takes it, and I put a lousy dollar bill in the money clip, and I sent it to the president. I wrote, "Dear Mr. President . . ." We were very close friends, you know. If we were alone, I'd call him Jack. All right, "Dear Mr. President," I said, "here's a birthday gift for you. If you don't need it send it back. Not the clip—the dollar." So he sends me a long letter in longhand, and he said, "Dear Jack, I received your money card." I guess that's what they call them in Boston. "Now let me tell you what Pat Lawford did. I'll bet you must have put in $500 or $1,000 in that clip. And by God"—this is just the way he worded it—"when she gave it to me, there was only one lousy dollar in it." But he said, "I'm keeping the dollar because I'll use it on the next campaign, but I won't tell anyone where I got it." Isn't that wonderful?

GROUCHO

Do you sing at all when you go to parties?

JACK BENNY

No, and I don't play my violin. I let George [Burns] sing. But do you want to hear something? I was just so delighted with my last three concerts. I had been practicing up, and by God, I played pretty well. Acoustically the halls were just wonderful, you know. And by God, in seventeen years it's the first time that a critic said, "Jack Benny spoiled a myth. He *does* play pretty good violin." Oh, I couldn't get over that!

Morrie Ryskind, who was having dinner with Groucho and me one night, commented on the charisma that men like Jack Benny and Groucho have for audiences:

"I watched Jack Benny come on yesterday. He did *The Dinah Shore Show* and I saw it. I feel about Jack the same way I feel about Groucho. When he comes out, the audience is so grateful for his coming out. It's the same kind of affection they have for Bob Hope and Groucho—for all the things they've done. If you start with that in your favor, you can't go wrong."

A favorite film of Groucho's, and one that he had grandson Andy project at home over and over again for him and friends, is *The Jack Benny Show* on which he appeared. It was based on Groucho's own TV quiz program, *You Bet Your Life*. Curiously, Groucho had been somewhat reluctant to do this show after having been initially enthusiastic. He liked the idea but later objected to the script. Jack told me that it was one of his favorite shows, and that I should try to see it. He explained to me what happened:

"Groucho used to really like my show. He was always telling me how much he liked my writers. So I invited Groucho to do a show with me, and I practically lost the writers—these same writers Groucho had always raved about.

"Groucho was always a nervous perfectionist. I think he decided he didn't like the script before he read it. My feelings were sort of hurt by the whole thing, but when I saw Groucho at Hillcrest, he seemed surprised that I felt that way. I told him I believed it was going to be a good show. Well, he finally did it, and we were both really glad."

It was Groucho's tremendous respect and reverence for the written word that caused him anxiety when he read the *Jack Benny Show* script. Once something was printed, Groucho didn't see it as ephemeral at all. He saw the written word as permanent. Because of this, it became extremely important to him that every word was just right; thus he exacted a high standard from himself and from those who worked with him.

Groucho told me, "I've got something for you. There's something I want you to see." As soon as Groucho, Andy, and I had finished lunch, Andy was sent to the projector. "Wait till you see Benny," Groucho said in the tone of restrained elation that characterized his most enthusiastic moments.

The film of *The Jack Benny Show* began with four people dressed as Groucho doing a song and dance. Groucho watched with amusement. The highlight was the *You Bet Your Life* segment with Groucho. Jack appeared as contestant Rodney Forsythe, first violinist with the Los Angeles Symphony. He was disguised, but not very, wearing a wig, and he talked nonstop in an effort to "say the secret word." The secret word was "telephone," and Jack said, "You can tell a phony," thus happening upon the secret word in an indirect fashion.

Occasionally, when the phone would ring at Groucho's he would say to me, referring back to that program, "It's the telephony."

The segment ended with "Rodney" missing the jackpot when he answers "Thirty-nine" to Groucho's question, "How old is Jack Benny?" At the end of the program, Groucho recognizes Jack and asks him why he did it. Jack Benny explains, "I may not be a spendthrift, but, brother, I know a bargain when I see one. Where else can you buy twenty-two years for only three thousand dollars?"

"He's very good," Groucho commented as Andy finished running the film for us.

When Andy found the film of this show buried in a closet, Groucho was enthralled by it. He had Andy run it so many times that Andy memorized all the parts. Groucho usually had him screen it for him as a "double feature" with the excerpt from *You Bet Your Life* of twelve-year-old Melinda dancing with Gene Nelson. I expressed interest in talking some more with Jack Benny, so Groucho said, "*You* call him and invite him over here for lunch."

Jack was pleased when I called and told him about Groucho's enthusiasm for his show. "There's no praise for a comedian that equals the praise of another comedian," Jack pointed out, adding, however, that although he enjoyed doing the show immensely, it didn't happen as smoothly as it appeared on film. Comedians work hard to achieve their casual spontaneity. Jack was very excited and pleased about doing Neil Simon's *The Sunshine Boys*. He loved the idea of doing another film, and he was giving all of his time to learning his part when he died.

Groucho told me, "He was a very funny man, and a nice man—I hope they say that about me."

GEORGE JESSEL AND BILLY MARX

"That's something to conjure with," Groucho said on hearing that George Jessel was free to come to dinner. "That's what Jessel always says," he added.

George Jessel's career spans vaudeville, stage, films, radio, and television, going back to Gus Edwards' days and to *The Jazz Singer* on Broadway, in which Jessel played the lead. A noted raconteur, he is known for having a phenomenal memory for anecdotes and show business history.

Before dinner one night, George Jessel, Groucho, Billy Marx, and I sat in the den of Groucho's house, surrounded by the memorabilia of Groucho's own long show business career. The good feeling that Jessel felt for Harpo, whom he particularly liked and respected, carried over to Billy, Harpo's adopted son. Jessel always called Groucho "Julius."

GROUCHO
How old are you?
GEORGE JESSEL
Seventy-six, Julius.
GROUCHO
You're a kid! I'm eighty-three.
GEORGE JESSEL
I'm trying to think when I first met you.
GROUCHO
Gus Edwards' act.
GEORGE JESSEL
No.
GROUCHO
Earlier than that?
GEORGE JESSEL
Later. *On the Mezzanine.*
GROUCHO
With Hattie Darling. And Benny Leonard invested in the scenery.
GEORGE JESSEL
He was stuck on Hattie Darling.
GROUCHO
He was a great fighter. And there wasn't a Jew in New York who wouldn't have gone to bed with him.
BILLY
Do you remember what the Marx Brothers did in *On the Mezzanine*?

GEORGE JESSEL
I don't know. I've forgotten.

GROUCHO
I cracked jokes. And Chico said, "I'd like to say goodbye to your wife." I says, "Who wouldn't?"

GEORGE JESSEL
(*To Billy Marx*) Then your father played the harp, and Chico played the piano.

GROUCHO
And Harpo kept kicking Chico in the rear end.

GEORGE JESSEL
Was Gummo in the act then, or Zeppo?

GROUCHO
No, Zeppo.

I
About what year was that?

GROUCHO
About 1850.

GEORGE JESSEL
1921.

GROUCHO
And Benny Leonard was the champion of the world.

I
I expect to see Hattie Darling.

GROUCHO
I think she lives in . . .

GEORGE JESSEL
Chicago.

GROUCHO
She's married to a jeweler.

GEORGE JESSEL
He died.

BILLY
How old is she now?

GROUCHO
She's younger than me.

GEORGE JESSEL
She was only about eighteen or nineteen. She was in the Winter Garden with me in 1923.

GROUCHO

Did I tell you when I went to the Winter Garden one night? I wasn't wearing a mustache, and Houdini was doing a trick onstage. He took some needles and put them in his mouth, and put some thread in there, and he would thread the needles. So he asked for a volunteer from the audience, and I went up on the stage. He didn't know who I was. He says, "What do you see in there?" and I says, "Pyorrhea."

GEORGE JESSEL

I'll tell you the funniest story about Houdini. Do you remember Joe Cook?

GROUCHO

Sure, very well.

GEORGE JESSEL

Great comedian. We had a big benefit that Heywood Broun gave at the George Cohan Theatre. Every star was there, and Joe Cook came on very late. He said to the audience, "You've all heard of Houdini. And his famous trick is they lock him in a milk can and throw him in the ocean, and he gets out. But ladies and gentlemen, you'll always notice," he said, "that he used his own milk can. Now, if anybody in the audience has got a milk can, bring it up. I'll be very glad to get out of it." And he waited a second and said, "Well, if I can't get one . . . !"

GROUCHO

When I saw him, he wasn't in the ocean. He was in the Delaware River.

GEORGE JESSEL

Yeah. Wherever he was, he got out.

GROUCHO

He always broke free. He lived right across the street from me.

GEORGE JESSEL

He's one of the few men who believed in people coming back to life.

GROUCHO

Yes, I know. He gave $50,000 if anybody could prove that anybody could come back alive. The money is still there.

GEORGE JESSEL

I played with Houdini.

GROUCHO

Harpo and Chico said that after they died they'd send out a message if they could.

GEORGE JESSEL

Have you heard anything from them?

GROUCHO

Not a goddamn word.

GEORGE JESSEL

Fred Allen's been dead over twenty years now. Wasn't Allen good?

GROUCHO

Great.

GEORGE JESSEL

Now, let me tell you something that every great comedian must have: you must have a staying quality, and part of that staying quality is sex appeal. People go for a Fred Allen or a George Gobel, who is a funny man and a charming man, and a lot of guys. This is not saying that women in the audience will get up and say, "I want to go to bed with him." But you have to have a little tiny bit somewhere . . .

GROUCHO

Of sex.

GEORGE JESSEL

Of what attracts a woman. And I never heard anybody say, "I'd like to sleep with Fred Allen." Or George Gobel or Bob Hope or Don Rickles or me. The Marx Brothers—all of them had a feeling of sex. There's no question about it.

BILLY

Don Rickles has been too overexposed on television.

GEORGE JESSEL

My dear Billy: there is no question about overexposure. There's no question of anything else except the client. I worked for a woman called Mrs. Clark, who had a thing called Tums. And I had to sing at every performance, and people didn't want to hear that every night. Nobody knows why anyone is on or off television.

GROUCHO

I'm getting a big kick out of *You Bet Your Life*. It's on every night.

GEORGE JESSEL

Yes, I know.

GROUCHO

It's in New York and Philadelphia and Chicago. It's a big hit. It's killing the news. People don't want the news at eleven o'clock.

GEORGE JESSEL

I'm usually in bed by then anyway.

GROUCHO

The news is usually bad. Somebody once said, "Nobody should read a newspaper more than once a month." I read the Sunday *Times*.

GEORGE JESSEL

Did you know Amy Leslie? She was a newspaper dramatic critic. Remember her?

GROUCHO

Chicago Daily News.

GEORGE JESSEL

She had been the dramatic critic in Fort Wayne, Indiana, where Eddie Foy opened *Mr. Blue Beard.* It closed on Saturday night and opened Sunday at the Iroquois Theatre in Chicago. To show her new managing editor at the *Chicago Daily News,* she wrote the review that night because she knew the show, and brought it right in to the newspaper that morning. He said, "That was wonderful, Miss Leslie, wonderful how you wrote how Mr. Foy took all those encores. Except that the theatre burned to the ground last night and there *was* no show."

GROUCHO

When we played downtown here, we had an act called *Home Again.* The Los Angeles critic came out and said, "The Marx Brothers in *Home Again* should be."

GEORGE JESSEL

In Chicago there was a theatre on Halsted Street called the Grand. If the show was good, the manager would walk up and down the aisles with a cigarette in his mouth and a cap and say, "You see? These are the kind of acts that I'm booking here. See how good it is?" Otherwise, whatever you said to him, he said, "I'll kick the shit out of anybody!" If you said, "How are you this evening?" he said, "I'll kick the shit out of anybody!"

He got stuck on a big fat soprano. She came out and sang, and they hissed her and they booed her. He says, "Quiet! I'm hiring this woman from Italy, and she gets a lot of money. I don't want to hear any more insults. I don't want to hear any more hissing. Go ahead." Then he looks down at a guy, and he says, "On account of this son of of a bitch I've gotta insult every bastard in the audience." I was on the bill!

And when I played in London, they had a place called the London Shortage—tougher than the Bowery, the old Bowery of New York. Never was anything tougher. And you know, in England they say anything. Four-letter words don't mean anything. There were seventeen acts on the bill, and we were fourteenth—Jessel and Edwards, *Two Patches from the Crazy Quilt.* That was our billing. We were awful. I said, "Fourteenth? Christ, it'll be twelve o'clock!"

But the acts took about two minutes. The master of ceremonies would say, "And now, Sandy MacDonald from Glasgow," and he would come onstage and sing, "I'm a laddie . . ." and they hollered, "Piss off! Go on, piss off!" Then this cockney Englishman came out with the derby over his head and sang. He was lousy. Then he put a bandana around his neck and he sang, "My name is Woppo, I own the barber shoppo. Oh, I takes a stiletto, and eats my spaghetto." They hollered, "Piss off!" but he wouldn't get off. He said, "Ladies and gentlemen, I was sent here to entertain you, and I'll do the fuck what I was sent for with a bottle."

Then I came on with my partner. We did some chatter, which was lousy, and I went into a song called "Nathan, Nathan, Tell Me for Vy You Are Vaitin'," and they liked that. We started to talk again, and they yelled, "Never mind that, lad. Give us a bit more 'Nathan.' " I sang about six choruses, and we were held over.

BILLY

I traveled with Chico and my dad through the vaudeville circuit of the British Islands. London Palladium, 1948.

GROUCHO

I was only a boy then.

BILLY

A mere lad. And I remember Chico and Mary. You remember Mary.

GROUCHO

It's right near Christmas.

GEORGE JESSEL

She was Chico's second wife. My first wife, you knew. Not as well as your brother Chico knew her. But you knew her.

GROUCHO

Chico was laying her.

GEORGE JESSEL

Not while I was married to her!

GROUCHO

Chico even tried to lay me.

GEORGE JESSEL

Oh, sure! Chico didn't button his fly until he was over seventy.

GROUCHO

Chico had everybody's wife.

BILLY

Chico, I have to tell you, I didn't know anywhere as near as well as Groucho. He was "Uncle Chico." But I always had the feeling that nobody could say anything bad about Chico. Nobody could.

GROUCHO

Except his wife.

BILLY

Except his wife. Chico was a loner, really. That's the feeling I got. Was he a loner, Groucho?

GROUCHO

He always was. Even when we were kids. He never played with us. He went over to the next block, Ninety-fourth Street, and had a crap game.

BILLY

Did he have family ties? I mean, did he always come back to the family?

GROUCHO

Yes. In one show he was laying twelve chorus girls. There were twenty-four. He was very busy.

I

(*To Billy*) You made a trip with your father and Chico . . .

BILLY

Well, according to my dad, that's kind of how vaudeville really was. We traveled up and down the British Isles in 1948, and we had the juggler, we had the roller-skating duos who were man and wife that would do all kinds of feats of magic on roller skates. We had the animal act. We had a magician.

GROUCHO

Swayne's Rats and Cats was the best animal act I ever saw.

GEORGE JESSEL

I played with Swayne's Rats and Cats. They were a very hard act to get along with. They disliked Jews very much.

BILLY

We had one guy, which was not an animal act, who came out and sat in front of a set of drums and beat the hell out of the drums and would tell one-line jokes.

GROUCHO

Why? Was he angry?

BILLY

Apparently. He would tell one-line jokes, and that was his act. Dad would tell me that this was what vaudeville was all about, whether you got into Swayne's Rats and Cats or Max Bacon. He was three hundred pounds and he would sit in front of a set of drums, and he would beat the hell out of the drums, then tell a one-line joke and hit the drums. I had a chance to travel with Dad and Chico, and see how life probably really was in the twenties.

I

What was their act like?

BILLY

They did the cutting of the cards, which Groucho recalls. It's the card game from, I guess, *Go West*. They did an act where Dad paid Doc Rockwell royalties. Doc Rockwell was a comic . . .

GROUCHO

He was very funny.

GEORGE JESSEL

Doc Rockwell was the father of the fellow who was the head of the American Nazi party.

BILLY

Dad paid him for the rights to cut an opera singer's skirt off. He did that for years. I think you'll recall the act. He also dropped the knives. He did a whole bunch of stuff. And Chico played the piano and told some stories. They did about forty-five minutes of stuff that was pretty good. And my recollection was that I really knew something about vaudeville without having been in American vaudeville through that experience. I was really thrilled to be a part of that. I was fourteen years old. And, Groucho, I used to walk on the stage carrying Dad's harp in an angel's outfit. There was a sign on the back of my angel's outfit saying "Eat at Joe's" that lit up. That was my big fling with vaudeville.

GROUCHO

When Harpo died he willed his harp to Israel.

GEORGE JESSEL

Harpo was exactly what harp actually means: an angel.

GROUCHO

A nice man.

GEORGE JESSEL

I introduced him one time to someone, and I said, "You know, there's a church in Brussels, and on top are all little cherubs. And they all look like Harpo Marx." On the other hand, Al Jolson was not considered an angel. I buried him, without ever saying anything about him as a man—only about his accomplishments and his attack on audiences. A God-given thing, and something that he did unwittingly. He never realized that he changed the whole portrait of a Jew onstage. Before Jolson—you can ask Groucho—every guy who came on who looked like a Jew had a beard this long, an ill-fitting suit, and his opening line was something like, "We had a meeting of B'nai B'rith—three hundred of us—and one Irishman chased us out of the building." And Jolson came, like a Georgian prince, on the stage and changed it all. All the beards came off, most of us blacked up . . .

BILLY

That may be his greatest contribution.

GEORGE JESSEL

He didn't realize it. That reminds me of the funniest thing W. C. Fields ever said. We were in a saloon called the Seven Seas, and we had a group of guys who drank a great deal, including me — Spencer Tracy, Errol Flynn, Jack Barrymore, Bill Fields, and John Decker. We'd meet at about five-thirty every night. Fields was late, and when he came in growling, we asked, "Where you been?" "Ah, I was at Universal." "You gonna make a picture there?" "No. Goddamn Jew Cliff Work. I can't get along with him." We said, "Cliff Work's a Roman Catholic!" Fields said, "That's the worst kind of Jew."

GROUCHO

I was playing with W. C. Fields in Toledo, Ohio. He closed the show, and we were the added attraction. We had twenty-five people in our act, and he came out with boxes . . .

GEORGE JESSEL

Yeah, juggling.

GROUCHO

So, at the matinee, the audience was walking out of the theatre while he was on, because they had to get home to fix dinner for their husbands. He went to the manager and says, "I'm leaving. I've got rumpers on the carokers, and I can't juggle anymore. So he left, took the train, and went to New York. I met him ten years later at a party he had for Ed Sullivan. And I said, "How are the rumpers on the carokers?" He says, "There wasn't a goddamn thing wrong with me. I just didn't want to follow you fellows."

GEORGE JESSEL

Let me tell you about Fields. Fields was a complete phony. Fields was a juggler with cigar boxes. He juggled. Pool table business. And he played in Leeds, England, and his wife was with him. There were two English strong men acrobats on the bill, and one of them stole his wife.

GROUCHO

Did he bring her back?

GEORGE JESSEL

No, and after that he hated all Englishmen.

BILLY

I saw an act when I was working the London Palladium with Dad . . .

I

When you were an angel?

BILLY

When I was an angel, and the act was called Warren, Latona and Sparkes. It was the greatest acrobatic act I had ever seen in my life. I'd never seen anything like it. It was a comedy acrobatic act. Several years after, it played on Ed Sullivan's show once or twice. But it opened with a guy in the box seats where the Queen would sit. I mean, way up in the air. And he would act as a drunk. He would stand up, and he would teeter on the edge, and he would fall onto the stage into the arms of the two guys he was heckling. It was one of my dad's favorite acts.

I

How do you remember your father?

BILLY

Well, the best frame of reference I can give you is from Maxine Marx, who is Chico's daughter. She once said, "I've never seen a man change in his lifestyle like Uncle Harpo. For the first forty-eight years of his life, he was an absolute lunatic. A nice man, but one who had the gall of anyone who ever lived in Gaul. He would do anything. There wasn't anything he wouldn't do. He was a madman." But Dad did an about-face, as far as Maxine was concerned.

After my mother nailed him, he wound up in a world of his own, like a dream that he never thought would be fulfilled. From the East Side of New York to Beverly Hills, to a nice house that he built. He just advanced into a dream and lived there for the rest of his life—not in Beverly Hills or Palm Springs, but in that dream.

His life was fulfilled at the time he got married, and all he wanted to do was have a family and revolve around that family. It was like he was a child reborn into another family. He was not a father—he was going through his second childhood. As I knew him, I became *his* father, and I suppose I project a lot of feelings for Groucho because of that. I wound up being his father and looking after him, sweating bullets for every performance, and working with him. I wound up doing all of his harp arrangements.

We had a very interesting life together. We played golf together, we'd go to the ball games together. And I always felt that he was a fragile man at that time. He needed reassurance and confidence because he'd had a couple of heart attacks, and he just wanted to know that there was a family and caring. He was fifty years older than I am. I was about fourteen or fifteen years old when I really recognized the meaning of the relationship to a human being like him, and I started looking after him. Even before that, when I was twelve, I started to.

He had his own world, and we all revolved around it. We all loved him. There was nothing to not like about him. He was a genuinely lovely man who was able to take a situation like George Wallace, states' rights, and the federal government's position, and say, while he was sitting in his sickbed, "George Wallace is right. The federal government is right.

Which is more right for more of the people? The federal government!" He would strip everything of bullshit. That was his opinion, and it was based upon getting to the core of something, and not saying somebody's wrong or they're full of shit or any of that. He would recognize the right on everybody's side, and say, "What will subsequently be better for more people?" That was his great charm, his great feeling for humanity.

But he was a cynic, because he never really felt that anything would be accomplished by anything other than bloodshed, as he watched the Rochester riots from Mount Sinai Hospital. My dad did die a cynic. He did not really believe that mankind really had a bead on what was going on. But he was able to express himself and eliminate the clothes and get down to the naked body. That was the thing he kept. ‑

Once he told me, "You know, I'm the luckiest man in the world. If I didn't have four brothers to help me fight my way through what we all had to go through, I'd never have made it." He said, "I have the greatest empathy for the stand-up comic that gets out there in front of an audience, all by himself, and the first joke he tells, nobody laughs. That's tough." Even a burlesque comic he would root for. As far as saying anything about his particular career, he said, "I'm a lucky man. I got other people to play off of, to fight my battles for me." Chico fought his battles, and he fought Chico's battles. They looked very much alike.

I

To which of his brothers do you think he was closest?

BILLY

Well, I would have to say in his early years Chico, because they looked so much alike, and they complemented each other. I don't think he had any feeling that he was closer to any one of them, except maybe toward his later years I think he felt more empathy toward Gummo, only because of Gummo's approach toward family. But I think Dad was probably closer to Groucho intellectually. I wouldn't know exactly what to call it, maybe ego need. Dad did not appear on the surface to be an egoist. But in the final analysis, he loved performing. He would come out of retirement to play a benefit for the Riverside Symphony Orchestra.

I

What is your first memory of Groucho?

BILLY

My first memory of Groucho was where all five Marx Brothers were together at Dad's, and Zeppo was telling some vaudeville stories. And my first recollection of Groucho, truthfully, was of him almost on the floor with laughter. (*To Groucho*) You were laughing, and tears were coming down

your face. Zep was telling stories about how he was the other half of some
kind of horse that fell into the orchestra pit. I remember this very well . . .

GROUCHO

He was half a horse?

BILLY

Yeah. He was the back end of a horse.

GROUCHO

Which year?

BILLY

I don't remember, but this is my first recollection of you. And I remember
you just roaring with laughter. Zep was a great storyteller, apparently, and
he made you laugh. I'd only seen you make other people laugh, and he
was the one who made you just buckle over with laughter. And I remember your telling me three or four years ago that Zep was the one man you
thought was a terribly funny man and made you laugh.

GROUCHO

He was.

BILLY

I also remember you shooting pool at the Hillcrest house. And I remember you playing the guitar. I'm going way back.

GROUCHO

I played it today. Not pool, the guitar.

BILLY

There was a story that you told about one time . . .

GROUCHO

It's not true.

BILLY

(*Laughing*) I'm sorry. But you were going to a pool hall in Philadelphia
with Dad, and there were these pool sharks. They wanted to challenge
you to a game, and you said, "I'll be right back. I have a friend in town
who plays, and I'll come back and play with him." You were an adequate
pool player. You weren't a great pool player . . .

GROUCHO

Chico was a great pool player.

BILLY

But what happened was, you left, went back to the hotel, and I guess it
was Dad who came back with another guy. He broke and ran two
hundred balls. The guy was pool champion Willie Hoppe.

GROUCHO

(*To Jessel*) Tell 'em about the owl.

GEORGE JESSEL

Can you hear that again?

I

Groucho told me it was one of his favorite stories.

GEORGE JESSEL

I've told this story on several occasions. I told it at a dinner of The Lambs, which I resigned from years ago, to Alfred Lunt, a very sensitive guy. Particularly because of him, I gave the story a profundity it doesn't deserve. Well, years ago, alas and alack, there was a thing called vaudeville, long since practically forgotten—a great lost art. And particularly in Chicago, where there was a circuit called the Western Vaudeville Circuit. The actors that played on this toured throughout Dubuque and Joliet, and maybe Toledo . . .

GROUCHO

I was one of 'em.

GEORGE JESSEL

. . . had no ambition at that time to go to Broadway or anything like that. They just wanted to earn enough money to spend the summer, maybe, in Muskegon or some summer place. There was a restaurant called Henrici's on Randolph Street in Chicago where all the vaudeville actors either ate or stood outside. Most of them who weren't working would keep the collar on from when they were working that had greasepaint on it so they looked like they worked the night before.

Of this motley group there was an act called Pennavessi and Gilbow—a German comedian and his partner. They weren't too good, but Mrs. Pennavessi was a very attractive blond girl, very corpulent and young, who was an idea of particular beauty in Lillian Russell's day. The guy who booked the circuit was a man called Tink Humphreys. Every time Pennavessi and Gilbow needed any work, she'd go up and see Mr. Humphreys, and come down with at least a week's work. They would wait patiently, and as they stood there, she came running toward them. "You got a week?" "I got three weeks! We open in Dubuque, Iowa, on Sunday." "Jeez, how wonderful!"

There were no contracts or unions then, so every town you played, if the manager gave a bad report, you were canceled. So, anyway, Pennavessi went one way, Gilbow went the other to tell their other fellow performers of their good fortune. Pennavessi walked into Peppino, accordion player. Peppino said, "What's new, Penny?" "New? We got three weeks. We open in Dubuque on Sunday." And Peppino says, "Jeez, I'm sorry you're opening in Dubuque." "Why? Is the audience bad?" "Well, that ain't so bad. It's a very old theatre, and there's been an owl in the balcony for about thirty-five years. The manager's very eccentric. I don't care how big a hit you are with the audience, that manager looks at the owl, and if it hoots, he sends the act away." So Pennavessi says, "Oh, what the hell. We get along with animals. We played with ostriches, Cohn's crabs . . ."

Now, the other guy, Gilbow, meets some friends of his, and he tells them about his good fortune. And his friend says, "I'm sorry you're opening in Dubuque." "You mean on account of the owl?" "Well, that ain't so bad. But the stage manager is the best-looking man you ever saw in your life. Curly hair, open white shirt. Pennavessi will lose his wife sure as hell." "No! She loves him."

Anyhow, they come to Dubuque. They come in to rehearse their music, and the stage manager sees Mrs. Pennavessi, puts her in the star dressing room. She's not even in the act! He puts them down in the cellar with a pink stool.

The manager is there, the owl is watching the rehearsal, and the show goes on. They go on to a very sparse audience and they tell a few jokes. By this time, the stage manager has his arm around Mrs. Pennavessi in the wings. She's watching the show. The straight man sings a song, the comedian sings a parody. By this time, the stage manager is taking several physical liberties with Mrs. Pennavessi. And then they get to the big joke, and when the straight man says to the comedian, "Where did you move from Three Rivers, Michigan?" they look around, and the stage manager is doing it to Mrs. Pennavessi. And the straight man gives the cue again. "Where did you move from Three Rivers, Michigan?" Pennavessi says, "Jeez, look what that guy is doing to my wife!" And the straight man says, "Fuck him! Watch the owl!"

BILLY

Groucho, I always meant to ask you. Was it true that Dad had a couple of drinks one night and saw an adagio dance for the first time . . .

GROUCHO

A what?

BILLY

An adagio dance. You know, where the lady is thrown all over the place by the man. And Dad had a couple of drinks, and he never drank, and he'd never seen this kind of act before, and so he went out and started to attack the man?

GROUCHO

No. That's not true.

GEORGE JESSEL

The funniest thing that ever happened in a vaudeville act was an act called Duffy and Sweeney.

GROUCHO

Oh, what a great act!

GEORGE JESSEL

And they were both drunkards. At the Winter Garden in New York, they would come out in some tights, or whatever they had on, and suck a lollipop. Duffy would say, "My partner will show you where a half-pint bottle hit him." Sweeney had a cut in his head. Then he would say, "We'll make up a song. Most people make up a song as they're going along. We're going to do it as it's coming back. (*Singing*) See that gentleman over there? See that gentleman over there? You can tell he's over there, 'cause I can see he's over there." Then they'd both get under the piano and they'd say, "Let's phone the act over tomorrow."

Well, for New York, that was fine. But they played New Orleans, and the theatre had been a church, and the dressing room still had stained-glass windows. I was on the bill. They went on with their act, and they were hissed and booed. They wouldn't get off, and then one of 'em said, "My partner's just gone off the stage to get a baseball bat. He's gonna walk through the audience and beat the Jesus outa you."

When they got to the dressing room, the manager said, "You can't go on. You're drunk." Duffy said, "Would I do this if I was drunk?" And he pushed his hand through the stained-glass window and cut himself to pieces. Now, this is the finish.

I had a guy with me whom you knew well. (*To Billy*) He was a great pal of your father's—used to play pinochle with him. Sam Bennett. He was a very meticulous fellow, and he put the pants under the mattress at night to see that they were pressed. That kind of guy. He and Joseph L. Browning—remember him?—he and Browning were playing pinochle. It was an important hand. If you play the hand in spades, it's double. You lose double or you win double. A very important hand to Sam Bennett. He studied it quite a while. He needed 140 points, and he started to play the hand. Now Duffy—this is during Prohibition—had been drinking Ed Pinure's hair tonic.

GROUCHO

That's very good.

GEORGE JESSEL

He came in blind. And Bennett is counting his hand. In the meantime, Duffy's peeing on him. All over his pressed suit, all over everything. Bennett never said a word, and he never stopped counting until he got 140 points. Then he turned around and hit Duffy in the nose.

GROUCHO

My father went into business with a colored man, and the name of the act was Marx and Washington. The colored man's name was Washington. They weren't in show business. They were in pressing. They got a new kind of pressing machine to press trousers and they expected to press about 500 pair of pants a day, but they only pressed three pair of pants a day. They went bankrupt because they had paid about $500 for this machine. It was a new machine that pressed pants very rapidly. They had a lot of spare time. But isn't that a great name for a vaudeville act, "Marx and Washington"?

GEORGE JESSEL

In those days in vaudeville when you got to the stage door, there was a big sign: "Any act mentioning 'damn,' 'hell,' or 'God' will immediately be dismissed. Do not send your laundry out until we have seen your act."

GROUCHO

(*To Jessel*) I wanna ask you: Did you ever play the Gus Sun Circuit?

GEORGE JESSEL

Sure. East Liverpool, Ohio, Springfield, Hamilton . . .

GROUCHO

I know. He used to book in ten acts, and they'd all go on the first show. Then he'd pick five of 'em, and throw the rest out. There were no contracts in those days.

GEORGE JESSEL

Now there's one about George M. Cohan that you've gotta hear. Did you know John Golden?

GROUCHO

Of course. Very well.

GEORGE JESSEL

Cohan hated John Golden. When Cohan didn't like anybody, he used to tell me how he'd get rid of a guy. He had a signal. When Cohan and I would be sitting in the Plaza, if a guy he wanted to get rid of walked over, he'd say to me, "Do you know Jim?" And I'd say to the guy, "Would you please leave us alone. We're talking business." As soon as Cohan said "Jim," I knew that he thought the guy was a louse.

Now, Golden owned part of the Grand Opera House with Cohan in Chicago. He got hold of me and said, "I can't see George Cohan, and this is business. You're with him every night. Tell him I want to see him on business. No show business. This is to make money. I want to get rid of the theatre." I said, "I'll fix it. We see very few people, and when we don't like a guy, we call him 'Jim.' That means we get rid of him, but I'll arrange for you to meet him."

So I told George, "Look, Golden's got some business with the theatre. Meet him tomorrow in the bar in the Plaza, the Oak Room." He said, "Oh,

Christ, I'll meet him. But you come in ten minutes later. I don't want to sit with the guy." Ten minutes later, I came in, and Cohan was talking to Golden. As I came in, George said to me, "You know Jim Golden, don't you?" And Golden ran out of the building. Cohan said, "I told you that guy was crazy." I said, "No, I told him about the guy named Jim."

GROUCHO

I was a song plugger for Jerome Remick. I sang a song in Philadelphia standing in a theatre box, and I got twenty-five dollars every week for singing (*He starts to sing*) "In dear old Georgia, my southern home."

GEORGE JESSEL

(*To Billy and me*) That's how they used to get acts to sing a song. Then they sold sheet music, you see.

GROUCHO

We were called song pluggers. I was a song plugger, and so was Ruby.

GEORGE JESSEL

Then Ruby did a vaudeville act with Harry Cohn. Ruby played the piano, and Harry—he called himself Harry Edwards—sang songs. And Jack Benny was just a plain violinist, no jokes. Cantor used to do a funny thing. He'd say for several people in the audience to pick out cards, anywhere. He'd give out about ten cards, and then say, "All right, now look at them and remember what they are. Thank you. And now I will sing you a new song." You could do anything then. And if a guy had a writer, oh, my goodness! If you didn't do your own stuff, you were really a bum.

GROUCHO

I was crazy about writers.

GEORGE JESSEL

You didn't need them.

GROUCHO

Yes I did.

GEORGE JESSEL

You needed a premise.

GROUCHO

(*Singing*) "Oh, premise me . . ." (*To Billy*) You found out who your real mother and father were, didn't you?

BILLY

Yeah, I found out. One was a Jewish-Polish cantor.

GROUCHO

Like Eddie?

BILLY

No, not like Eddie. A real Jewish cantor. And one was a Polish-Catholic piano teacher. I found this out quite by accident. They were both very musical, and that's how I got some music in me.

GROUCHO

How did you learn to play the piano?

BILLY

By force.

I

When did you start playing?

BILLY

Alex Woolcott used to come over when I was about two or three years old, and put me on his knee and say, "I'm just a widdle wabbit wunning awound in da sunshine." That's what he would say to me and bounce me on his knee. And I would proceed to hum some theme from a Beethoven symphony—I don't know what it was. Then one day when I was five years old, Dad decided I should take piano. And that's when I started taking piano lessons. But I remember Woollcott bouncing me up and down. And I don't remember him at all. I just remember being bounced up and down. And I remember not seeing Woollcott ever again. He died not long after.

GEORGE JESSEL

He was in love with your father.

BILLY

I think he was. I really believe that.

I

Who were some of the other people you remember coming to your house?

BILLY

You know, the night I remember more than any other was when all five Marx Brothers showed up. Dad usually spent his time at the [Hillcrest] roundtable with famous people—(*To Jessel*) like you and the others. But there were rarely famous people at our table at night, because he wanted to spend it with the family. So it's hard for me to remember. The one night I remember at our house more than any other was when all five brothers were there, and Zeppo was telling these stories, and Groucho was falling literally on the floor with laughter. And I remember turning to my mother and saying, "I've seen Groucho laugh. I've seen him smile. But I've never seen him have tears in his eyes with laughter." That's one night I remember. I just don't remember famous people being over there, or any of that nonsense.

I

Was it rare that the five Marx Brothers were all there together?

BILLY

Very. In fact, that was the only time I saw them all together, except at Hill-crest.

I

Do you remember that night, Groucho?

GROUCHO

Not very.

I

(*To Billy*) Do you remember the first Marx Brothers picture you ever saw?

BILLY

The first movie I ever saw was *The Big Store*, at the Orpheum Theatre. My dad took me, and at the end of the picture . . .

GROUCHO

Harpo was on roller skates.

BILLY

So were you. Only there was somebody playing you who didn't look like you. It was another person.

GROUCHO

That was me. I was playing the stunt man.

BILLY

There was a double for you. And there was a double for Harpo. I couldn't stand the ending of it. That bothered me.

GROUCHO

Why didn't you leave?

BILLY

I couldn't. Dad was fascinated.

I

Did your father like to watch his films?

BILLY

I have no idea. That's the only film I ever watched with him. Other than *Night in Casablanca*. Most people don't like *Casablanca*, but I like that film. I thought it was a good film.

GROUCHO

It's one of the worst pictures we ever made.

BILLY

I know, but I liked it.

I

Which are your favorite Marx Brothers films?

BILLY

Horse Feathers. And then *Duck Soup* and *A Night in Casablanca*. If you ask me which is the best picture they ever made, it's *Night at the Opera*. But if you ask me what's my favorite picture, it's *Horse Feathers* and *Duck Soup*, and then *Night in Casablanca*. I think they're funnier. And then I like *Monkey Business*. I like the Paramount pictures better. I really do. They're funnier. I don't feel they're as good, but I like them more.

I

Which picture did your father like best?

BILLY

Duck Soup. That was his favorite film. I would say that of all the pictures, the really best comedy is in *Night at the Opera*. But as far as just sustaining my interest, it seems to me *Night at the Opera* took away from the Marx Brothers. Like there were production numbers and a lot of stuff, but what I really wanted to see was the Marx Brothers.

GROUCHO

(*To Jessel*) Tell 'em about Norma Talmadge.

GEORGE JESSEL

She was a wonderful woman. Until the third drink, she had the manners of a princess. Courted, she was like a queen. Third drink, she'd pee on the floor.

GROUCHO

Tell 'em about the diamond ring.

GEORGE JESSEL

I don't remember. She threw the ring in the toilet?

GROUCHO

You had a fight, and you gave her the ring, and she threw it back at you. She said, "I don't want anything at all to do with you." (*To Billy and me*) So she threw him out and slammed the door. He rang the bell, and she opened the door. He said, "I'm sorry I can't make up with you, but is it all right if I use the swimming pool?"

GEORGE JESSEL

Yeah, yeah. That's true.

GROUCHO

That was a very funny speech you made at Benny's tribute.

GEORGE JESSEL

It was all right, I guess.

GROUCHO

Well, they laughed at it.

GEORGE JESSEL

You played with Sarah Bernhardt, didn't you, Julius?

GROUCHO

Yeah. She got a thousand dollars for each performance, and she got paid before she went on. She had one leg, and I had two legs, and I only got $200 a week.

BILLY

Was she any good?

GROUCHO

She hardly had a leg to stand on.

GEORGE JESSEL

Well, in the first place, Billy, since there was no sound in those days, everybody projected and overacted. And she played plays by Racine and Dumas, like *Camille* and so on, and you could rant and cough and all. You had to project. Jolson never saw a microphone until he was age seventy. We had to talk to the audience. Mrs. Fiske was as close to the modern stage actress that I can remember. She and George M. Cohan could act in a theatre and play with their backs toward the audiences.

GROUCHO

It was safer that way.

GEORGE JESSEL

Ears were attuned to listening to the actor. I played the Majestic Theatre in Chicago with Bernhardt. And do you remember her leading man, Julius?

GROUCHO

No, who?

GEORGE JESSEL

A big handsome French fairy. Before Sarah Bernhardt there was another Jewess by the name of Rachel, who they say was the greatest actress in the world. She was a very religious girl, and she slept with Napoleon III, Dumas, father and son, Victor Hugo, and the Empire City Quartet. When she died, she had a funeral cortege of a quarter of a million people to her grave on a rainy day in Paris.

Now, I bought some books on her, and I wanted Lizzie Taylor to make a movie about her. But Miss Taylor had just married Dick Burton, and they stayed in bed for three years, didn't read the book, and played gin rummy during short sessions. I always see this picture—and now you could do it in a movie, 'cause now you can do anything—of Rachel lighting the Sabbath candles on Friday, and having two guys waiting in the hay for her.

GROUCHO

And one was Chico.

BILLY

(*To Jessel*) Do you remember an act called Clark and McCullough? My dad talked about them.

GEORGE JESSEL

Oh, my goodness, yes.

BILLY

What was their act like?

GEORGE JESSEL

Well, McCullough was to Clark as Zeppo was to Groucho. Bobby Clark was a very, very funny comedian, and beloved by the critics. There are certain comedians who are beloved by the critics, and can do no wrong. Ed Wynn, Bobby Clark . . .

GROUCHO

Jack Benny.

GEORGE JESSEL

. . . Jimmy Durante. And our host.

Groucho made friends and influenced people for a long time, but not in the manner of Dale Carnegie. Walking with me in New York, Groucho was gleefully approached by a woman:

"I'm very glad to see you, Groucho," she bubbled.

"You ought to be," he said.

Frequently when people he didn't know were introduced to him in response to an effusive "I'm happy to meet you," Groucho would say, "You ought to be."

On that day when he passed through the Pearly Gates, one could imagine St. Peter saying, "We're so happy to have you here, Mr. Marx," to which Groucho, halo askew, probably replied, "You ought to be."

Backward

When I told Groucho that I planned to have a Backward instead of a Foreword, and that I planned to have it near the end of the book, he said, "Why don't you have it in the front of the book?" I asked him why.

"Because I'm backward," he said. "I guess the Foreword should be in the back of the book, because by that time, you should know you don't like the book. Of course, you could have the Backward in the middle of the book, then you'd only have to read half."

The idea to write this book grew out of Groucho's pleasure over the interview he had done with me. He told me at that time that it was ". . . the only thing anybody ever did about me that came out right, where everything in it was the truth." After the interview appeared, Groucho wrote this letter to *Playboy*:

February 15, 1974
Mr. Murray Fisher
PLAYBOY
919 North Michigan Avenue
Chicago, Illinois 60611

Dear Mr. Fisher,
I went to Hefner's house the other night to see the Ali-Frazier fight on closed circuit TV and I accidentally came across an advance copy of the March issue in the Ladies Room. I want to congratulate you on the excellent interview which your magazine printed about me in that issue. If I'd have known it was going to be that good I'd have charged you a veritable fortune for it, at the least a dozen boxes of Havanas. Did you know that

Bill Cosby only gives me one at a time, and I have to supply my own Cuban?

Charlotte Chandler did a magnificent job of reporting. She's quite a dame. If I was twenty years younger I'd marry her and propose to you at the same time. She wrote everything I wanted to say without changing one word of my dialogue (for a change).

Anyway, it was quite an evening. Ali won. I ate a piece of Barbi's birthday cake and it wasn't even her birthday, and the girls were beautiful. Good interviewers are rare. So was my steak.

This has been quite a week and it's only Tuesday. At the moment I'm as punchy as Frazier. I was just informed that I'm getting the Academy Award on April 2nd. Heaven help Ali when he meets Foreman. He better have a pistol in his hand. I'm rooting for him, he's a fine boxer in the great tradition.

I tried to call Charlotte Chandler to thank her, but found she has gone to Spain, so I got Spanish fly instead. If you ever see her again, tell her I'm prepared to give her the most priceless gift any man can ever give a woman.

Hoping this finds you yours of the fifteenth—i.e., to wit in re the above; brevity is the sole of wit. Have you got one on you?

My best to you and that peculiar gang at *Playboy.**

Forever,
GROUCHO

When Groucho and Erin called me in Barcelona, they just missed me. Then, as I was arriving at my hotel in Madrid, the concierge rushed up to inform me that there was a call from the United States, from the same person who had been trying to reach me for hours. The transatlantic phone call was from Erin to tell me that Groucho was going to receive the special Oscar and that he wanted me to come for the ceremony, which I did.

At Groucho's house, after returning from the dinner party that followed the Oscars, Groucho and Erin and I indulged in an alcohol-free toast.

"To Oscar and Groucho, in reverse order," I suggested.

"No," Groucho said, abstaining. "I should have had it sooner when Chico and Harpo were here." He raised his glass. "To One Cheer—may she get a second one."

* Copyright (c) by *Playboy.*

In December 1974, I was staying at Groucho's house, where I shared his everyday-but-not-routine life from early morning until late at night, when we received word that Erin was returning from Paris and that Zeppo was arriving for a short visit. I started putting my things together to free his guest room. Groucho asked me where I was going and why. He was rather sharp.

"Don't you like it here?" he asked.

I assured him that I did.

"Then why are you going?"

"Zeppo is coming, and he might want to use my room," I suggested.

"Zeppo likes you, and both of you can share the room."

"I've been here quite a while."

"I'm not complaining," Groucho countered chivalrously.

I gave him an oversize chocolate bar that I had brought with me for that moment of departure. Written on it was "Hello, I must be going."

He read it, and then said rather tenderly, "I don't want you to leave."

"Groucho, I want to stay. But I feel there are only two times to go: too soon, or too late. I prefer to leave too soon."

He smiled and accepted my choice. I moved to the Beverly Hills Hotel, but stayed long enough to celebrate Christmas with Groucho.

Any human life observed for a given time will be interesting, and it will also be boring, for real life is not paced like a film. The amazing thing is that Groucho actually was the sort of person who would have been a hero to his own valet, if he had had one.

The mirror influences the reflection, and this portrait of Groucho has to have been influenced not just by what Groucho said and how he said it, but also by how I heard it. My intention was to be relatively objective; absolute objectivity is impossible, and perhaps not even desirable. One cannot really stand in anyone else's shoes, and only subjective objectivity is possible. Therefore, this represents an impressionistic verbal portrait of Groucho.

Groucho performed not only *for* audiences, but *on* audiences; just as Stokowski elicited different sounds from his players to suit the acoustics of different concert halls, Groucho adjusted his performance to suit the characteristics of his audience. I hope that he is presented here as seen and heard through many pairs of eyes and ears, as well as through my memories and impressions of his memories and impressions. He once suggested, long ago, that I call this book *Groucho and I,* but I preferred

Groucho and i. It was my hope that he would speak for himself in this book. He always did anyway.

A great deal of what Groucho says here has never been said before. Some of it has already been told or written about. But he was the sum of his eighty-plus years, and none of us really begins anew at any given moment. To edit out what he said just because he had said it before would distort any portrait of the man as he was. Also, for Groucho some of the old stories were the best, for they had stood the test of time. Nevertheless, in his middle eighties he came up with new material every day in Beverly Hills, smog or shine. He could still be the Groucho of the leering visage, but, being a humorist rather than a comic, he was sensitive to changing circumstances, so that his reactions changed too. He didn't just depend on unwise cracks or lapse into his anecdotage. He still excepted rather than accepted the "normal" rules of social conduct per se. Somewhat straitlaced, very straight-faced, always evenly paced, he still disgraced the social Graces.

Groucho had a strong style which is subject to analysis and to interpretation, to imitation, but not to duplication. He himself was not given to extensive analysis of his own style, or of anyone else's. His tendency was toward the intuitive belief that feelings and emotions, happiness and luck, as well as humor, would vanish if subjected to undue introspection. Whenever I asked him any question that touched on his style, he avoided any erudite attempts to explain his humor, responding simply, "I'm a funny-looking jerk," or, "I'm a character."

For Aristotle, the *ethos* of the speaker determined his credibility. *Ethos* represents the sum of overt and covert characteristics brought to the occasion from past and present situations by an individual. It determines his persuasiveness and success. Groucho's *ethos* always greatly enhanced the humor of whatever he said.

The monomial Groucho (whose first name alone was sufficient along with Bing, Liz, Elvis, and Jackie) was, even in his eighties, immediately recognizable. LeRoy Neiman, drawing him in New York, commented, "When you're drawing a person, sometimes you discover that he's already a drawing." Groucho was a charismatic figure who made people smile when they saw him, laugh when he spoke. The image that he brought with him made things funny or funnier. Morrie Ryskind pointed out that when he told the same funny story Groucho had told, no one laughed. Groucho shunned mellifluous tones, vivid metaphors, soaring similes, but as Dick Cavett told me:

"His voice has a magic ability to turn any straight line into hilarity. He says, 'You certainly could have fooled me,' or he says, 'That's the silliest remark I've ever heard,' and it's funny in Groucho's voice."

While considering modesty a form of hypocrisy, Groucho perhaps best summed up his own irreverent attitude toward even himself in the title he suggested to me for this book: *Groucho Marx and Other Short Stories.*

Groucho usually had the last word, and he ought to have it now.

"What should it be, Groucho?" I asked him.

"I trust you, One Cheer. You know me better than I know me."

I persevered. "I want it to be *your* word."

Groucho smiled approvingly, then spoke:

"Selah!"

Postlogue: "Never say goodbye, say *auf Wiedersehen*"

When I left Groucho after meeting him for the first time, I was admonished, "Never say goodbye." Groucho always expected me to remember this, even on the phone, and I did. "Until soon," I would say instead. As our relationship grew, he ended long-distance phone calls with "I love you," which replaced "Goodbye."

Groucho reminded close friends, "Say *auf Wiedersehen. Hasta la vista. Au revoir.* Say anything. But never say goodbye."

While Groucho never recommended old age as anything but the best of the available bad choices, he managed in many ways to live his late years quite fully, remaining active, productive, successful, and not lonely. The prayer he said every night before going to sleep best expressed for Groucho his philosophy of life:

"Unborn yesterday, dead tomorrow; why fret if life be sweet?"

GROUCHO
This is the last year I'm gonna be around. I'm not sorry, because I've had a good life. I've been around nearly a hundred years and I'm tired. You know what I'm sorry about?

I
What?

GROUCHO
I'm not gonna get to read that book you're writing about me.

I
Wait for me. If you could do that, I'd write slowly . . .

GROUCHO
I don't want you to sugarcoat me. I'm no saint. You know how I can tell

how old I am? Nobody ever says the word "death" to me anymore.

You'd think nobody's dying anymore. Death took a holiday. That's when I knew how old I was. It's like they keep saying, "You're looking good, Groucho," and I know what this old face looks like. I don't talk about death 'cause there's too much of it and nothing you can do about it.

There was some pain, along with the great pleasure, for Groucho's friends who knew him in his middle eighties. Saddened by the memory as he recalled the moment, Woody Allen told me, "I called him when he was in the hospital. He sounded very weak, but he seemed pleased I'd called. We talked, and he asked when I'd be in California, and we talked a little more, and then I realized he thought I was Cavett. It made me feel terrible."

In New York one afternoon LeRoy Neiman came by to see Groucho, who, in a rather expansive mood, talked more than usual. He told some favorite stories, some more than once. When LeRoy Neiman left, I walked to the elevator with him, and then returned to find Groucho looking depressed.

GROUCHO
Did I repeat myself a lot?

I
In the hall LeRoy told me, "He's awesome. Thank him for me. It was a gas!"

GROUCHO
Someone told me Nunnally said I was telling him the same stories all the time.

I
I was with you at their house several times, and it didn't seem that way to me. I'm certain Nunnally wouldn't have said that.

GROUCHO
Do I do it with you?

I
I hear you tell some of the same stories many times because you're telling them to a different person each time, and I happen to be with you. I think it would be difficult or impossible for anyone to know and see so many people and not ever repeat a story. Besides, you never tell it twice the same way.

GROUCHO

I'm not afraid of dying. The only thing I'm afraid of is senility. I don't want them keeping somebody alive, somebody who used to be me.

After Groucho's spectacular eighty-fifth birthday party, the pageantry came to an end, and the public Groucho virtually disappeared. Then, following a hip operation and another stroke, Groucho could no longer take those treasured walks through Beverly Hills. The little things in life became increasingly a struggle. Groucho told me, "Nothing can be taken for granted." The extraordinary life of Groucho Marx was in its waning phase.

I remember our last phone call:

GROUCHO

How's the book coming along?

I

When I started it, it was my hobby. Now I'm *its* hobby.

GROUCHO

We'll be on all the talk shows together, except I'll be dead.

The hostilities which had always existed between Erin Fleming and Groucho's only son, Arthur, accelerated. Erin, whose role in Groucho's life was considered by some to be detrimental to Groucho's well-being, was removed from her post as temporary conservator.

Longtime friend Nat Perrin accepted the post himself, although he expressed the sad realization, "It's not really Groucho Marx anymore. He seems in good spirits for a few hours, then tires rapidly and loses interest in staying awake."

Arthur and Erin faced each other in court, where the testimony was generally sensational. The sworn statements of witnesses depicted her as screaming, swearing, raging, threatening, slapping, physically shaking Groucho, generally tyrannizing him, and actually endangering his person. Erin denied these allegations.

Indeed, there was room for a mitigating interpretation of the testimony. A partially deaf Groucho couldn't hear her unless she screamed. A Groucho who was retreating from the rigors of life was sometimes jerked back from apathy into reality both verbally and physically by Erin in a manner regarded as cruel by some who knew and loved Groucho. Given the choice of Erin as she was or the loss of Erin, Groucho seemed willing to accept the

Sturm und Drang and its repercussions. To at least some extent, he seemed to relish her fervor and his position as an object of passion. "Anyway, I know I'm still alive," he told me once after one of Erin's rampages. In court Erin asserted that Groucho had wanted to marry her or adopt her.

Nat Perrin admitted that he found his appointment as conservator "too much of an emotional strain," and he asked to be removed from the post. Bert Granet, Sidney Sheldon, and George Seaton were asked to replace him, but each declined.

An accord was reached between Arthur and Erin and the court, in the person of Judge Edward Rafeedie, with bedside concurrence of Groucho. Andrew Marx, Groucho's grandson and Arthur's son, was appointed conservator.

Just before his appointment, Andy reminisced with me about better days with Groucho. "But now," he commented sadly, "it's like anybody else's family."

While the fame of the living legend grew stronger, Julius Henry Marx grew increasingly frail. But Groucho mustered all his forces to return to the house that meant so much to him. I could hear him saying, "I've got the key to my front door." But Groucho's return home didn't last, and he was rushed back for another "brief" hospital stay, which proved to be not brief at all.

Groucho's brother Gummo died on April 21, 1977, but Groucho was never told.

On August 19, 1977, at Cedar Sinai Medical Center, Groucho died.

Shortly before his death, Erin told the press, "Groucho's just having a nice little dream now. He's just going to have a nap and rest his eyes for the next several centuries."

Despite the full knowledge of Groucho's rapid decline in health, despite his age, none of Groucho's friends was really prepared for the finality of his death. You could think you were ready intellectually, but you could never really get ready for it emotionally.

His friends wondered with that feeling of guilt that accompanies the death of a loved person, "What more could I have done for him?" Dick Cavett summed up that feeling, questioning in retrospect, "Why was I ever busy?"

One evening, after dinner with Groucho and Goddard Lieberson, Groucho had talked with Goddard and me about a funeral he was expected to attend. He had referred to his own abhorrence of the ritual of the funeral and admonished us not to come to *his*:

"It doesn't do any good. When you're dead, you're dead. I don't want either of you coming to *my* funeral. I want you to go out and find a Marx Brothers film and laugh a lot."

A small memorial reception for family and a few friends was held at Arthur's house on Sunday, August 21, 1977. On the following Monday, there was a temple service for Groucho in Hollywood at Beth-El. Groucho had always said he didn't want a big funeral and had expressed his preference for cremation. "I don't want to take up space."

During the furious court battle between Arthur and Erin, Zeppo had defended Erin's role in Groucho's life, saying, "She kept Groucho alive." Zeppo, the last of the Marx Brothers, was not invited to either the Bel Air service at Arthur's house or the temple service. He learned of Groucho's death from press reports.

A separate small memorial reception was held by Erin at her house.

In a will dated September 24, 1974, Groucho left his estate, estimated at between two and six million dollars, in trust to his children, Arthur, Miriam, and Melinda. He left fifty thousand dollars each to Gummo and Zeppo, and five thousand dollars to each of his grandchildren. A twenty-five-thousand-dollar trust fund was established for his former wife, Kay, one hundred dollars a week for life, "or until the money runs out."

To Erin, he left his Legion of Honor boutonniere and one hundred fifty thousand dollars.

Anyone contesting the will would forfeit his share and, instead, receive one dollar, with the remainder of his or her share going to Jewish charities.

When I learned about Groucho's death, I had a sudden, strong sensory impression as my hand remembered the doorknob of the front door of his house. I had gone in and out countless times, but as I left for what indeed turned out to be that last time, I hesitated for a moment before closing the door. Milton Berle, who had gone out just ahead of me, asked, "Did you forget something?" "No, I didn't forget anything," I answered, as the door clicked shut behind me.

Chronology

Too Many Kisses, M-G-M film with Harpo	1925
The Cocoanuts	1925
Miriam born	1927
Animal Crackers	1928
The Cocoanuts filmed by Paramount	1929
Minnie Marx dies (age 64)	1929
Beds serialized in *College Humor*	1929
Beds published	1930
Animal Crackers filmed by Paramount	1930
Marx family moves to California	1931
1931 Varieties, in London	1931
Monkey Business	1931
Horse Feathers	1932
Duck Soup	1933
Zeppo quits the act, starts an agency	1933
Sam Marx dies (age 72)	1933
Flywheel, Shyster and Flywheel on radio	1934
Groucho appears in stage presentation of *Twentieth Century*	1934
A Night at the Opera	1935
A Day at the Races	1937
The King and the Chorus Girl	1937
Room Service	1938
The Kellogg Show, on radio	1939
At the Circus	1939
Go West	1940
The Big Store	1941
Marx Brothers announce "retirement"	1942
Groucho and Ruth divorce	1942
Many Happy Returns published	1942
Groucho meets Catherine Marvis Gorcey	1943
The Pabst Show, on radio	1943
Groucho marries Kay (Groucho is 55, Kay is 24)	1945
Melinda is born	1946
A Night in Casablanca	1946
You Bet Your Life, on radio	1947
Copacabana	1947
Time for Elizabeth	1948
Love Happy	1949
You Bet Your Life wins Peabody award	1949
Mr. Music	1950

"If it gets a laugh, leave it in"

"There's only one answer to an audience. If they don't laugh, take it out and try another one. If it gets a laugh, leave it in. If you keep talking long enough, you say something funny."

This is about as close to an analysis of his own comic style as Groucho ever ventured. The mystery of comedy is ephemeral, and he sensed that it could be dissipated by excessive scrutiny. In a darkened movie theater, watching a film he didn't find funny, Groucho leaned over and whispered to me above the sound of crunching popcorn around us, "Someone told me this was like the Marx Brothers, but it isn't. They're just punching. They don't have characters. All comedy is based on character."

Although the Marx Brothers' success grew out of their own characters and playing themselves ("with ourselves," Groucho always corrected me), their years in small-time vaudeville, trying out lines and routines and developing their stage personalities, were not wasted. As "Nightingales" and as "Mascots," they were mired in the mediocrity of the lower echelons of vaudeville, though it is unlikely that they would have languished there long.

As Groucho put it, "One day a mule inspired us to horse around. We started insulting the audience, and they laughed."

From then on, though there were peaks and dips, audiences never really stopped laughing. Groucho said, "If you have a lot of lucky breaks, it isn't just an accident," and lucky as it might have seemed, the school act was the most appropriate vehicle for the Marx Brothers' first comedy routines. What better place for disrupting vested authority than in a school? From *Fun in Hi Skule* to *Horse Feathers* and in virtually everything they did afterward, the Marx Brothers displayed the frenetic energy of boys from an apartment on East Ninety-third Street in the artificially restrained atmosphere of a classroom. Even *You Bet Your Life* is a classroom situation, but with the teacher instead of the students providing the disruptive influence.

Fortunately, records of what two of the Marx Brothers' stage successes were like survive in their films, *The Cocoanuts* and *Animal Crackers*. But the characters were already formed, and the lines and routines already tested, so there is relatively little change between the Groucho, Harpo, and Chico of *The Cocoanuts* and *The Incredible Jewel Robbery* more than three decades later. Some critics have attributed an important role in the formation of the film characters of the Marx Brothers to their writers. The one cinematic record of the Marx Brothers before *The Cocoanuts* has been lost. Groucho said there is no hope that a print still exists, and he reinforced his total conviction by saying, "I'd give fifty thousand dollars for a print." Even if *Humorisk* did miraculously emerge from a rusty film can in somebody's basement, it would give us only a limited view of what the Marx Brothers were like in 1921. Not only would it be silent, but it would also present the four Marx Brothers quite differently, since they didn't play their usual characters. The same is true of the silent film Harpo appeared in, *Too Many Kisses*, in 1925. So, without any sound or silent record of the pre-*Cocoanuts* Marx Brothers, it was only possible to speculate on what they were like based on what they themselves have told us and on other firsthand accounts.

A rare print displaying what the Marx Brothers were like as early as 1921 has recently been discovered. It became available to me through the late Henri Langlois of the Cinémathèque Française. In 1931, when the Marx Brothers arrived in Hollywood, Paramount had asked them to do a promotional trailer which could be distributed to exhibitors in advance of their next picture, *Monkey Business*. Because *Monkey Business* wasn't ready yet, they had to use one of their acts—one that would be simple to film yet hadn't been used before either in *The Cocoanuts* or *Animal Crackers*. They chose the opening scene from their first Broadway success, *I'll Say She Is*. Since this had also been the opening scene in *On the Mezzanine Floor*, it is possible to go back to 1921 and see what the Marx Brothers were like before George S. Kaufman and Morrie Ryskind appeared in their careers.

In this promotional trailer, the characters of the Marx Brothers are quite recognizable, except that Zeppo's part is bigger and more important than it ever was in the feature films. Instead of being "the fourth man through the door," he is the Marx Brothers' interpreter in the worlds they invade. He is neither totally a straight man nor totally a comedian, but combines elements of both, as did Margaret Dumont. Zeppo's importance to the Marx Brothers' initial success was as a Marx Brother who could "pass" as a normal person. None of the Zeppo replacements (Allan Jones, Kenny Baker, and others) could assume this character as convincingly as Zeppo because they were actors, and Zeppo was the real thing, cast to type. Significantly, when Zeppo left the act, Chico's straight-man status became more important. In the promotional trailer, Zeppo and the straight man (who plays a similar role in the *Monkey Business* version of this scene) maintain continuity by establishing a believable yet funny norm from which Groucho, Harpo, and Chico can deviate. The Marx Brothers are more or less as they always were, with a few minor differences. One of these is Chico's accent, which is thicker than usual when he enters, then inexplicably dropped during the remainder of the scene. Groucho has a smaller part than usual, but he gets a chance to use his coy smile and bobbing eyebrows on the bad joke that he so obviously likes. Although he seldom gets credit for it, Groucho was as graceful as a dancer, and as Lee Strasberg told me, "The way he moved greatly enhanced his character." Groucho's reactions can be as important as his actions, and he is expert in backing up his brothers when they are center stage. When Harpo enters, Groucho can usually be heard in the background making appropriate comments during Harpo's pantomime, or during any faint lull in the pandemonium.

The "plot" is simple: the four Marx Brothers enter a theatrical agency, one by one, and try out. All of them happen to have the same act—a bad imitation of Maurice Chevalier singing "You Brought a New Kind of Love to Me" from Paramount's *The Big Pond*. In *I'll Say She Is* they had imitated Joe Frisco, a popular dancer of that time, but Chevalier was substituted in the promotional trailer because he was then under contract to Paramount. Mr. Lee, owner of the agency, tells them, "Don't slam the door when you leave," almost as soon as they start singing, but since they are Marx Brothers, this is only an invitation to stay.

Lee's Theatrical Agency. Mr. Lee is sitting at his desk working when a knock is heard at the door.

MR. LEE
Come in. Come in. (*Zeppo enters*)
ZEPPO
My name is Sammy Brown, and I just came into town. Saw your ad, you're Mr. Lee. Say, you can make a mint on me.
MR. LEE
What do you do?

ZEPPO

Dance, sing.

MR. LEE

Play a role?

ZEPPO

Anything. Say, I'm a find for guys like you, 'cause there's nothing I can't do.

MR. LEE

Tell me, where did you work before?

ZEPPO

In a department store.

MR. LEE

Who told you you could dance and sing?

ZEPPO

Say, for money I'll do anything. Why don't you try me? You might as well.

MR. LEE

You might be great.

ZEPPO

Who can tell?

MR. LEE

What do you call your specialty?

ZEPPO

You mean my big sensation? I knock 'em cold when I pull off my Chevalier imitation. (*Singing*) "If a nightingale could sing like you, they'd sing much better than they do, 'cause you brought a new kind of love to me . . ." Well, what do you think?

MR. LEE

When you go out, don't slam the door. It's a wonderful imitation you gave of Ethel Barrymore. (*Knock on door, Chico enters, Zeppo sits down*)

CHICO

I'm glad you see me.

MR. LEE

Step right in.

CHICO

Are you Mr. Lee?

ZEPPO

My name is Sammy Brown . . .

MR. LEE

Come in. Do you want to talk to me?

CHICO

I wanta to talka to Mr. Lee.

MR. LEE

I'm Mr. Lee.

ZEPPO

That's him.

CHICO

I see. You wanta a good act?

MR. LEE

Yes.

CHICO

Well, I'm the guy you wanta get. I no speak very good English, but I'm full of the pep and got the ambish.

MR. LEE

What do you do?

CHICO

Acrobats.

MR. LEE

What's your name?

CHICO

Amalia. But the best thing I do is give imitations of Chevalier. (*Sings*) "When the nightingale, they look like you . . ."

MR. LEE

That's enough!

ZEPPO

When *you* go out don't slam the door.

CHICO

Well, what do you think?

MR. LEE

I need a drink.

CHICO

All right, I take-a the drink.

MR. LEE

You'll take the air.

ZEPPO

The air he cries!

CHICO

I no like-a the air. It's too cold outside.

MR. LEE

Will you please keep quiet.

CHICO

I no saya the word. (*Chico sits down*)

MR. LEE

Not an "and," a "but," or an "if." Not a word from you 'til you're spoken to.

CHICO

All right, you great big stiff. (*Mr. Lee starts to react, but another knock at the door distracts him, Groucho enters*)

GROUCHO

(*In a heavy Russian accent*) I vant to speak to Mr. Lee. I'm a dramatic actor.

MR. LEE

So I see. I'm Mr. Lee.

GROUCHO

Well, lend an ear to me.

MR. LEE

Can you play a role?

GROUCHO

(*Dropping accent*) Can I play a role? Do you know who you're looking at?

MR. LEE

No.

GROUCHO

Caesar's ghost. I play any kind of a role.

MR. LEE

You will?

GROUCHO

I eat it up like that. I played a part in *Ben-Hur* once.

MR. LEE

What part did you play, sir?

GROUCHO

A girl, she played the part of Ben.

MR. LEE

And you?

GROUCHO

I played her. (*Lifting his eyebrows and smiling coyly*)

CHICO

When you go out, take a slam at the door.

GROUCHO

You're kidding me, aren't you not?

MR. LEE

Kidding, you say? I've been here all day. Now show me what you've got.

GROUCHO

(*Resuming accent and chanting*) I vant to play a dramatic part, the kind that toucha a woman's heart, to make her cry for me to die . . .

CHICO

Did you ever get hit with a cocoanuts pie?

GROUCHO

(*Dropping accent*) There's my argument. Restrict immigration. I think I'll recite.

MR. LEE

Let it go. All right.

GROUCHO

I'll give you a recitation. Or would you prefer to see me give my Chevalier imitation? (*Singing*) "When a nightingale could sing like you, they sing much sweeter than they do, 'cause you brought a new kind of love to me . . ." Well, what do you think?

MR. LEE

Get me a brick!

GROUCHO

Here's a brick. I always carry one for this imitation.

MR. LEE

Say, I ought to lay this on your head!

GROUCHO

You can't do that. You don't belong to the bricklayer's union.

ALL

(*Knock on door, Harpo enters and the brothers are overjoyed to see him*) Ahhhhh!

GROUCHO

Poop-poop-a-doo! Poop-poop-a-doopie!

(*Harpo walks through the crowd with his hand extended, as if to shake hands, but his misses everyone's extended hand, except for Mr. Lee's, in whose outstretched hand he deposits his horn-cane. When he reaches Chico, they slap hands hard and do a "first-up" routine, treating each other as a baseball bat they're trying to get top grip on. Mr. Lee, outraged by such flagrant horseplay in his office, pulls Harpo away from Chico. As he does, Harpo takes a hot dog out of his pocket with a flourish and hands it to Mr. Lee.*)

MR. LEE

Hey, what do you think you are . . .

GROUCHO

Hey, wait a minute, wait a minute. You know who this is?

MR. LEE

No.

GROUCHO

He sells frankfurters. That's the Merchant of Wieners.

MR. LEE

Well, what do you want? (*With a flourish, Harpo whips a card out of his pocket and hands it to Mr. Lee, who reads it aloud*) "My name is What-Do-You-Care. My home is anywhere. People say I'm awful dumb, so I thought to you I'd come . . ." Say, listen . . . what *is* this?!

GROUCHO

Now just a moment. Wait a minute. He might be crazy. Wait, I'll find out. (*To Harpo*) You want to go on the stage? (*Harpo nods affirmatively*) Crazy.

MR. LEE

Say, listen, you tell me what you want or I'll throw you out . . . (*Harpo rests his leg on Mr. Lee's hand*) Never mind that or I'll give you a . . .

CHICO

Now wait, take your time. This fella's a good dancer. (*To Harpo*) Dance for him.

MR. LEE

Say, thank heaven there's no Chevalier imitation.

HARPO

(*Puts his hat on desk and takes Mr. Lee's straw hat off his head, putting it on his own head. He dances and whistles a few bars of the Chevalier song the others have been singing.*)

GROUCHO

What do you think of him?

MR. LEE

I wouldn't give him a dollar a week.

CHICO

Not so loud. He'll take it.

ZEPPO

Now listen, you're making a big mistake. These fellas are very clever. They're funny fellas, and I've got a play that I've written that I'd like to explain to you. (*Harpo, standing between Zeppo and Mr. Lee, continues his leg-in-hand routine, first with Mr. Lee, and then with Zeppo*) I'd like to read this manuscript for you. It's a wonderful play, and these fellas would fit in it. (*When Harpo gets tired of having his leg rejected, he climbs up on their shoulders*) Now if you'll sit down with me for a minute, I'll explain the whole thing to you. (*They push Harpo off their shoulders and move over to the desk, Mr. Lee sitting behind the desk, and Zeppo in a chair to the side; Chico and Groucho sit on the other side of the desk, pulling the desk over to them; Mr. Lee pulls it back*) Now this is not *Monkey Business* or is it *Pineapples. (By this time everyone is talking, and Zeppo has to shout to make himself heard)* I want to explain the whole thing to you. Now, the first scene takes place in a beautiful home. This is really a magnificent home. A mansion. When I say a mansion, I mean a mansion.

(The old-style pedestal phone rings. Harpo grabs a black rubber stamp and hands it to Mr. Lee, who thinks he has the receiver. Then Harpo himself grabs the receiver and listens, clicking the cradle in answer. After futilely listening to the rubber stamp, Mr. Lee retrieves the real receiver from Harpo. But now, there is so much noise, no lines of dialogue can be distinguished. Zeppo is still telling about his play, Mr. Lee is talking on the phone, and Groucho and Chico are chattering away about something that is unintelligible. Groucho pulls out a desk drawer and throws his cigar butt into it. Harpo also pulls out a drawer and spits his gum into it. From a pocket, Harpo pulls out a rubber glove and blows it up, so that it resembles a cow's udder. Putting his hat under it, he pretends to milk the glove into his hat, picks up the hat, and seems to drink the milk. Then he puts the hat back on his head. A telegraph boy enters with a telegram for Mr. Lee, but before he can accept it, Harpo has reached over and torn it up into little pieces, which he drops on the floor. A girl enters, and Harpo climbs onto the desk and sits on Mr. Lee's head and shakes hands with the girl. Mr. Lee, still on the phone, fails to notice Harpo sitting on his straw hat. As the scene fades out, Harpo is doing his arm-breaking routine on the girl, while the other brothers cluster around her.)

About the Author

CHARLOTTE CHANDLER is the author of biographies of Federico Fellini, Billy Wilder, Alfred Hitchcock, Bette Davis, and Ingrid Bergman. She has also written about Henry Moore, Mae West, Tennessee Williams, Henry Fonda, Pierce Brosnan, and Nicole Kidman. Her book *I, Fellini* was a *New York Times* Notable and has been translated into twenty-five foreign editions. Her first book, which was *Hello, I Must Be Going*, was a national bestseller.

She wrote a world-performed stage play, *Confessions of a Nightingale*, about Tennessee Williams. Her next book will be *Joan, a Personal Biography of Joan Crawford*.

Chandler lives in New York City and is active in film preservation. She is a member of the board of the Film Society of Lincoln Center.